I0819385

WE'RE HAVING MUCH MORE FUN

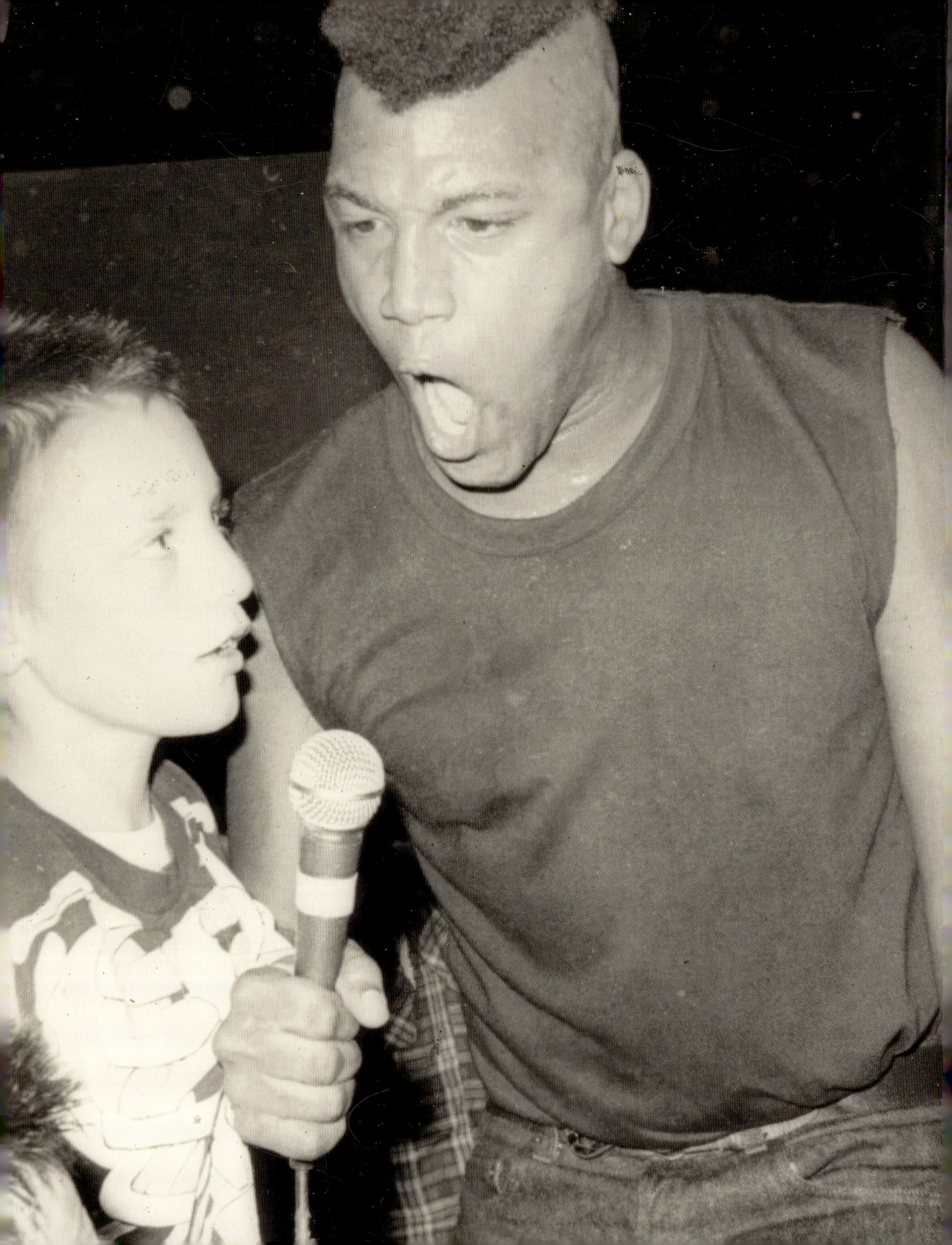

We're Having Much More Fun

PUNK ARCHIVES FOR THE PRESENT FROM CBGB TO GILMAN AND BEYOND

Judith A. Peraino
and Tom McEnaney

Cornell University Press | Ithaca and London

This publication has been made possible, in part, by funding provided by the General Fund of the American Musicological Society (AMS).

First published 2026 by Cornell University Press

Printed in South Korea

Librarians: A CIP catalog record for this book is available from the Library of Congress.

ISBN 9781501780325 (paperback)
ISBN 9781501780646 (pdf)

GPSR EU CONTACT: Sam Thornton, Mare Nostrum Group B.V., Mauritskade 21D, 1091 GC, Amsterdam, NL, gpsr@mare-nostrum.co.uk.

INTERIOR DESIGN AND TYPESETTING: Amanda Weiss
PRINTER: Pacom Korea

In memoriam

JAMES E. GIBSON

LANCE J. HEIDIG

FRANK MCENANEY

CONTENTS

PREFACE

A NOTE ON COLLECTIONS AND ARCHIVES

What's More Punk than the Public Library?
—T-shirt to support Mt. Pleasant Library, Washington, DC

"Archive" may seem too grandiose a word for a shoebox full of old cassette tapes and band stickers; and it may seem too institutional for *punk*—a word that conjures an outright refusal of nostalgia trips, let alone formal histories. This seeming conflict of punk versus history came to a head on November 26, 2016, when Joe Corré, the son of fashion designer Vivienne Westwood and producer and provocateur Malcom McLaren, set fire to his family's collection of punk history, including (allegedly) live and acetate recordings of the Sex Pistols and the bondage pants Westwood created for Johnny Rotten when McLaren managed the band.

Corré's controversial stunt gestured at the "no future" ethos of the Sex Pistols, but in the years since the torching on the Thames, punks across the United States have gone in a different direction. In October 2021, the 309 Punk Project officially opened the doors to an archive dedicated to documenting the scene in Pensacola, Florida. Two years later, in March 2023, Ian MacKaye, the cofounder of Dischord Records and a member of some of the most impactful punk bands from 1980 on—Minor Threat, Embrace, and Fugazi, among others—finished building his own punk archive. And that April, April Fools' Day to be exact, NOFX bassist and lead singer, and Fat WreckChords cofounder, Fat Mike (Mike Burkett) opened the Punk Rock Museum in Las Vegas.

Most every punk has a collection of some sort, whether it's the records we own, the flyers we've saved, the zines we hold on to, or the patches on our jackets. But we don't tend to think of them as archives because that word brings to mind imposing buildings and dusty shelves of administrative documents, or artwork and cultural objects behind glass, kept out of reach of the general public. Around the same time that Iggy Pop started jumping into crowds, historians and cultural theorists working in archives started to write about how institutional collections and record-keeping often led to selective histories that enshrine and justify "the victors": the people who won wars, enslaved and colonized others, stole cultural artifacts, and profited from plundering nature.[1] Museums and archives, the theories say, turn objects of action (meant to be listened to, read, or worn) into things to look at. They turn participants into observers. They threaten to turn something living into something dead. They memorialize like tombstones or preserve like canned fruit.

So why are so many punks making or contributing to archives? Not just Ian MacKaye or Fat Mike, but dozens of others, from Richard Hell to Kathleen Hanna, have built up their own collections over the years and sold or gifted them to universities (Cornell, NYU, UCLA, the University of Maryland, the University of Mississippi, among others) or similar institutions (the DC Public Library, the New York Public Library, the San Francisco Public Library, the Rock and Roll Hall of Fame Library and Archives) to preserve their materials for *future generations*. That's the principal aim of these punk archives: to safeguard and make accessible a counterculture's ephemera that might otherwise have ended up in a landfill, buried in a basement, or just remained in private hands.

That last issue goes to the heart of why, as that Mt. Pleasant Library shirt says, there's nothing more punk than your public library. Making resources accessible beyond an individual or a small group has driven many punks to contribute to archives and to continue a practice of refusal to leave control of the story in the hands of an elite few. There is another way to think about archives, one that stems from radical acts and approaches: eighteenth-century French revolutionaries insisting on public access to national (once royal) records;[2] Andy Warhol making art out of his personal archive by throwing the stuff lying around his studio into boxes that he called Time Capsules; and scholars and writers like Daphne Brooks, Ann Cvetkovich, and Saidiya Hartman breaking open what and who counts in the histories they trace, and reimagining archives to counter the marginalization, underrepresentation, or erasure of women, queer folks, and people of color.[3]

This way of thinking about archives sees them not only as tools for gatekeepers but also tools for gatecrashers. It draws attention to cultures that thrive underground, as alternatives to a mainstream yoked to capitalism, white supremacy, misogyny, and homo- and transphobia. Building and sustaining those alternative cultures involve the extraordinary labor of individuals and collectives, documented in objects that are artistic and personal. Punk materials are just that: the flyers, zines, photographs, ephemera, and of course the music and performances form something akin to what Cvetkovich calls "an archive of feelings"—repositories of emotions encoded in the resistant texts, objects, and practices of a subculture.[4]

CORNELL'S PUNK ARCHIVE AND ABOUT THIS BOOK

Cornell University's "punk archive" comprises more than fifty different collections housed in Cornell Library's Division of Rare and Manuscript Collections at the Ithaca campus in upstate New York. Ithaca might seem like an odd place to find some of punk's history (although the Ramones did play a show at Cornell in 1981, and the first owner of Max's Kansas City, Mickey Ruskin, was a Cornell alum). The archive came about from the visionary efforts of curator and archivist Katherine Reagan—no stranger to punk, having attended shows at Mabuhay Gardens in the early 1980s—who started in the early 2000s to seek out collections documenting subgenres of rock and R&B, which led to the establishment of the Cornell Hip Hop Collection in 2007. The punk component of that initiative took a large leap forward in 2012 with the arrival of the Los Crudos and Limp Wrist collections, and significant US and UK collections from the writer and music journalist Jon Savage, and from the curator and former Matador Records general manager Johan Kugelberg.

Archives sometimes grow like scenes—by word of mouth, reputation, accident, and knowing who else is there and what's going on. Aaron Cometbus's archive found its way to Cornell when a student—Isi Laborde-Edozien—told him she had read his work there in a class taught by Tom McEnaney. Cometbus's own massive collection of nearly fifty years of punk and underground materials from the Bay Area and across the country started to arrive at Cornell in 2015, and this news eventually led to Larry Livermore placing his Lookout Records archive at Cornell.

But these stories about the archive are only infrastructure for how the stories contained within the archive can come to light. And whenever we could locate an artist, photographer, or band member, they always had a good story to tell. That brings us to what this book tries to do and what you might try to do with what you'll find in these pages. From the thousands of objects housed at Cornell University, we selected over four hundred that focus on punk scenes in the United States, spanning the decades of the early 1970s to the early 2000s, and placed them in context with captions from the creators and longer interviews or essays by key participants. We also brought together celebrated bands, artists, and scene-makers with those who are less known but no less important to the diverse and intergenerational mix that has sustained punk collectives over nearly five decades. Our aim here is to highlight the strengths of this particular punk archive and make these materials available to the public as a sourcebook for research and inspiration. Their stories from the past are a trail map for the present.

ACKNOWLEDGMENTS

This book is an outgrowth of a long collaboration between Judith, Tom, and Katherine, starting with Judith and Tom developing and co-teaching an interdisciplinary course on punk in 2014, co-curating an exhibition with Jon Savage and Johan Kugelberg, and organizing a weeklong festival celebrating Cornell's punk archive in 2016. The project has been a labor of love that survived the terrifying 2016, 2020, and 2024 elections, a global pandemic, a cross-country relocation, deaths and births. Along the way, we have benefited from the tremendous generosity of many people. Thank you to X (D. J. Bonebrake, Xene Cervenka, John Doe, Billy Zoom) for permission to use their song title for the title of the book. Our deepest gratitude to all those who contributed an essay or an interview for this book; gave us a caption alongside permission to publish their materials; helped us connect with other artists, photographers, and flyer makers; and provided other important information:

KK Barrett
Aaron Cometbus
Jayne County
Bianca Daalder-van Iersel
Danny Fields
Elizabeth Fiend
Tommy Gear
Fayette Hauser
John Hawkes
Richard Hell
John Holmstrom
Jenny Lens
Ian MacKaye
Peter Montgomery
Suzanne Onodera
Gary Panter
Lisa Jane Persky
Gretchen Phillips
Sylvia Reed
Adee Roberson
Victoria Ruiz
Martín Sorrondeguy
James Spooner
Anna Joy Springer
Chris Stein
Jenny Lynn Stoever
M. Leslie Wimmer
Orlando Xavier

We want to give a shout-out to those who went above and beyond in their engagement with this project. There would be no punk archive at Cornell without the vision, wisdom, and dedication of Katherine Reagan, who worked with us every step of the way. Aaron Cometbus provided detailed feedback and suggestions as we assembled this book, generously giving his time to encourage us not to overlook people, bands, or scenes, or accept any narratives about punk without evidence to back it up (any errors are, of course, our own). He also kindly put us in touch with numerous people who added to the range and reach of this book. Across multiple conversations, Ian MacKaye shared his long history as a fan and creator, as well as his thoughts about punk archives. Lisa Jane Persky was an important connector and source of information, as was Sylvia Reed, who also brought the photography of Anya Phillips to our attention from James Chance's personal archive. Martín Sorrondeguy communicated with Los Crudos and Limp Wrist flyer creators on our behalf. And Tommy Gear spent an entire afternoon at Cornell looking through Screamers materials and telling stories, many of which ended up as captions.

This book has received financial support from the Division of Rare and Manuscript Collections, Cornell University Library; Cornell's College of Arts and Sciences; the Cornell Department of Music; the University of California, Berkeley Townsend Center for the Humanities; the UC Berkeley Department of Comparative Literature; the UC Berkeley Department of Spanish & Portuguese; and the UC Berkeley Office of the Vice Chancellor for Research. Cornell graduate student Sean Peters took on a heroic task of registering and tagging over four hundred items for digitization and preparing alternative texts for the ebook along with Cornell graduate student Michael Millenheft. And the Cornell Rare and Manuscript Collection and Library digital projects team, especially Tabitha Cary and Simon Ingall, graciously rolled with our many "this is the last one" requests to add images. We're indebted to Shane Greene, and to the second anonymous reader for their insightful suggestions. We would also like to thank Cornell University Press editor in chief Mahinder S. Kingra for his unwavering support and for shepherding this through to publication, and to the production and marketing team at Cornell University Press. We thank Jessica Schwartz for the invitation to present a keynote talk for UCLA's 2018 conference "Curating Resistance: Punk as Archival Method," portions of which became the introduction to this book.

Colleagues, friends, and family supported us throughout the years with enthusiasm, inspiration, and good company. We thank Jeremy Braddock, Paul Brennan, Jason Frank, Michael Holt, Javier Jiménez Westerman, Damien Keane, Ted Martin, Annie McClanahan, Pat McEnaney, Kate Morris, Tiffany Naiman, Jenn Naegele, Mike Oz, Carl and Nancy Peraino, Trevor Pinch (d. 2021), Alex Reed, Jon Savage, Selby Wynn Schwartz, Phil Strnad, Eric Sutter, Katy Zaugg, Mike Zaugg, our partners Carmen Enid Martínez (JP) and Amanda Jo Goldstein (TM), and Tom's children Finn Tamalpais and Vera Storm.

WE'RE HAVING MUCH MORE FUN

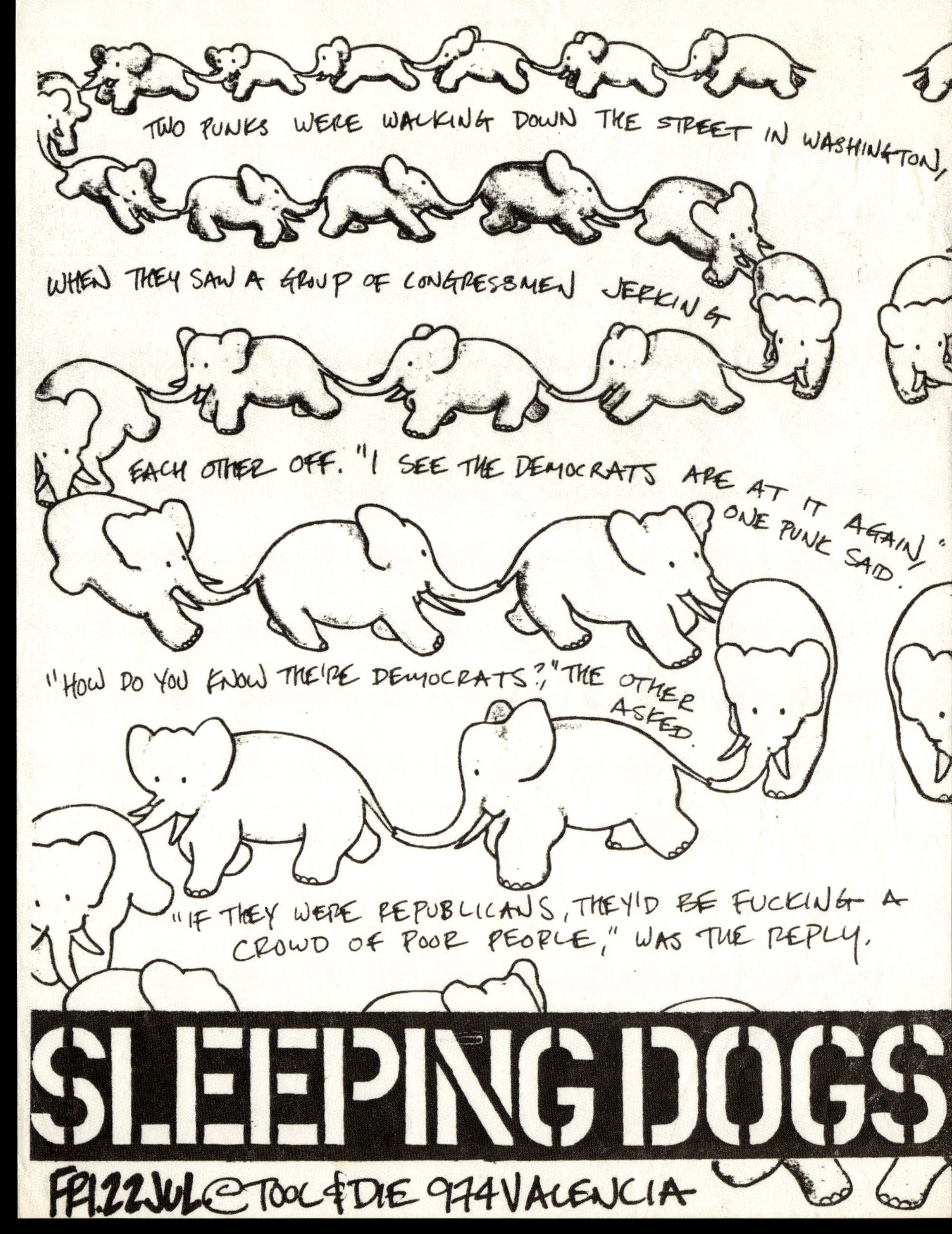

Flyer for Sleeping Dogs show, San Francisco, July 1983. Design: Dave King.

Introduction

THE FUTURES OF PUNK'S PAST, OR PUTTING THE ARCHIVE TO USE

> Well I don't care about history . . . /
> 'Cause that's not where I want to be.
> —The Ramones, "Rock 'n' Roll High School"

What did you leave behind crumpled in the sweaty haze after a show? That zine someone handed you between sets? Do you wish you'd saved at least one of those band stickers you plastered onto bathroom stalls and tollbooth stations? The shirts, the stencils, the silkscreens: are they stuffed into a lost corner of a closet, or do you wear or use them now? Maybe you still have a box of old flyers that you ripped off club doors or telephone poles, lying beneath a pile of patches, zines, and tapes. Maybe, without trying, you created your own collection, your own archive. It won't tell the whole story about you and the scenes you found and lived in. But looking back, this stuff might tell a story that you didn't notice before, or one that has a different meaning now than it did then.

This book owes its existence to the punks who held on to what others threw away without a second thought—punks who knew, in the words of the Minutemen, that every punk song is a "History Lesson." Even in the early years, as Johnny Rotten snarled about "no future," punks were repurposing nuggets from the past to invent a new language. The Sex Pistols' "no future" was adapted from the 1950s Situationists as revived by Jamie Reid, Malcolm McLaren, and Vivienne Westwood; Richard Hell's "Blank Generation" updated a 1959 novelty song "Beat Generation" by Bob McFadden; and the Ramones plucked the phrase "Gabba gabba we accept you, we accept you, one of us" from the 1932 cult movie *Freaks*.

The songs are only the beginning of punk's history lessons. Punks of all ages have been documenting the scene from day one by saving whatever seems important to them. Flip through the pages of this book and you'll see rarities from well-known figures (Jello Biafra's wedding announcement, a postcard from Anya Phillips to Diego Cortez, a photograph of one of Green

Day's first backyard shows, a letter from Kathleen Hanna to Aaron Cometbus, original art by Tomata du Plenty), but also countless flyers, posters, zine covers, and more designed by people unknown beyond a few friends or their local scene. All of it is the glue that holds community together. As Joey Ramone told Mike Watt, "Punk is like a big hay wagon. If you've got something to offer, c'mon, jump on."[1]

That's what the Minutemen called the "History Lesson Part 2": the invitations that you will see on every page of this book to make something, do something, and be part of something. For certain people, punk is mostly about starting bands and making music; for others, it's about community, identity and activism. If there is one through-line that connects all self-described punks over generations and across the country it's the reality behind the DIY cliché: throwing aside your inhibitions and *just getting on with it*.

The objects pictured in these pages were born in the thrill that self-described misfits have felt in a crowd, sharing for fleeting moments the experience of what Operation Ivy's Jesse Michaels once called "the reconciled world." That punk world has always been made by outsiders to mainstream America. To name just a few from punk's early days: Jayne County, assigned male at birth, escaped Georgia and found a home for her radically queer rock and roll at Max's Kansas City in New York; Tommy Ramone, born Tamás Erdélyi in Budapest, Hungary, was the son of Holocaust survivors and one of many Jewish innovators of New York punk (alongside Joey Ramone, Richard Hell, and Chris Stein);[2] Alice Bag (Alicia Armendariz) grew up in East LA and saw punk as a way of channeling her emotions into art and eventually education activism; fellow Angelino Karla "Maddog" DuPlantier, and New Yorker Elin Wilder were two of the few Black women in early punk scenes (Maddog became the drummer for the Controllers, and Wilder was a music reporter for *Punk* magazine); then there was that jazz fusion band called Mind Power in DC who changed their name to the Bad Brains after hearing the Ramones song in 1978.

Later, as punk subgenres appeared in the 1990s and early 2000s, they revealed that some Black, Latine, feminist, and queer punks didn't always feel like "punk" alone was capacious enough to recognize their difference from what Mimi Thi Nguyen called "whitestraightboy hegemony" in the pages of *Punk Planet*.[3] Not everyone felt included and the calls to renovate the scene are also part of the history unfolding in these pages. But that renovation has come from punks and for punks, across generations continually drawn to a scene that held out more hope than anywhere else.

Sifting through what these welcome misfits have made and saved to reveal the mad variety of punk communities is one purpose of this book. Showing how those materials tell the complicated history of punks representing themselves (often to themselves) is another.

PUTTING THE ARCHIVE TO USE: A DEEP DIVE INTO 1980S BAY AREA FLYERS

Flyers are punk's most public record: plastered along walls and stapled up and down telephone poles, their principal function is to catch the eyes of people on the street and lure them to the show. But flyers are also sites of symbolic attack, often encoded with whole histories of iconic struggle. What might at first look like a random collage instead emerges as part of a sustained series of stories about punk; the flyer filters the chaos of its times. "I'm a huge collector of flyers," Martín Sorrondeguy comments during his interview for this book. "I love this stuff. . . . You're looking at a time when a flyer became your space to advertise the show and maybe something else that you wanted. It's kind of like in South America where the graffiti becomes political and it's on the walls and that's *your* media."

Often that "something else you wanted" on the flyer pushed the information promoting band names, venues, and dates to the margins in favor of expressing a different message. In a 1983 flyer for Sleeping Dogs (IMAGE 0.1), whose members included Dave King, the designer of Crass's logo, the mainstream politics of Democrats and Republicans gets artfully upended if you read between the elephants. The parade line of elephants—the symbol of the Republican Party rendered in the style of Babar, a colonial cartoon—laughs at the mindless, trunk-to-tail conformity of political parties, while nodding to the chain of indoctrination, from childhood cartoons to Reagan, that kept the eighties propaganda machine churning. And in case we missed the point, the sexual politics of the writing sandwiched by the elephant parade literalizes the need to read between the lines.

The political messages aren't always so clear; and the jumbled juxtapositions of images and words in flyer collages can be seen in more than one way. For instance, how far are we supposed to read into the flyer for Verbal Abuse and 7 Seconds (0.2)?

What is that flyer saying about punk's relationship to racial identity? Like other punk iconography, this image rides the line between subversion or participation in racist caricature. Walking by the flyer on the streets of San Francisco could cause a double take in 1986, a couple of years after what *Maximumrocknroll* (*MMR*), punk's most influential zine in the 1980s, called "the summer of hate" amid the rising influence of neo-Nazi skinheads in the city.[4] Does "punk" in this flyer refer to this smiling older Black man, and therefore challenge some of the biases about who should represent the scene? Is he laughing at or shouting the word? Is this a vision of inclusivity or incongruity?

Thanks to the collections featured in this book, we can trace the source of the image to a picture of bluesman Willie Dixon, grabbed from the January 1986 issue of *Spin*, which included a short article about Dixon refusing a gift from then-president Ronald Reagan (0.3). What likely attracted the flyer maker to this *Spin* issue in the first place is a cover photo of Blondie's Debbie Harry and the headline proclaiming "The 10th Anniversary of Punk." In that context, Dixon doesn't look out of place next to the names of Christ on Parade and 7 Seconds, but instead appears like a forerunner of leftist punk politics. And as he was one of the most influential blues songwriters ("Spoonful," "Back Door Man," "Hoochie Coochie Man," among other hits), Dixon's image points to some of punk's roots in the blues, too. We can't know how many passersby on the street would have recognized the source material for the Dixon image, or if they bothered to think about what they saw. But we do know a little about the flyer maker's process of connecting the legendary bluesman to the place of punk at the time.

However, if Willie Dixon's smile makes it seem like punk was a happy extension of Black culture, other flyers complicate that picture (0.4).

How do we understand the meaning of the schoolyard fight between a Black boy and a white girl as an ad for a No Alternative show at UC Berkeley's Sproul Plaza? While we're left to guess at the inspiration for most of the flyers, in a few cases we know the name of the flyer designer and can ask about their intentions in the process. The designer here, Suzanne Onodera, was part of the East Bay and San Francisco scenes in the late 1970s and early 1980s, and began making flyers for shows when she was sixteen (0.5).

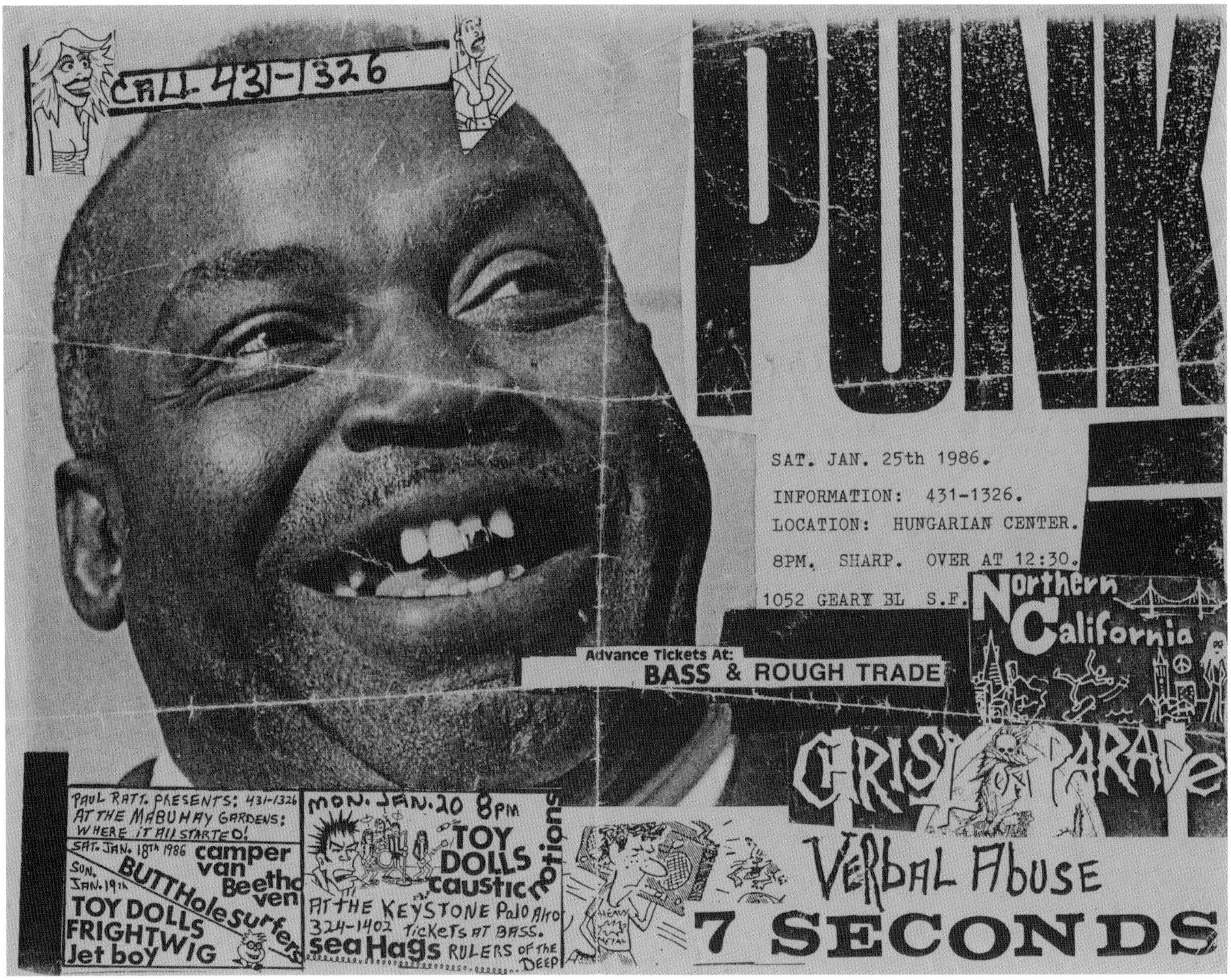

0.2. (*Above*) Flyer for Verbal Abuse and 7 Seconds show, San Francisco, January 1986.

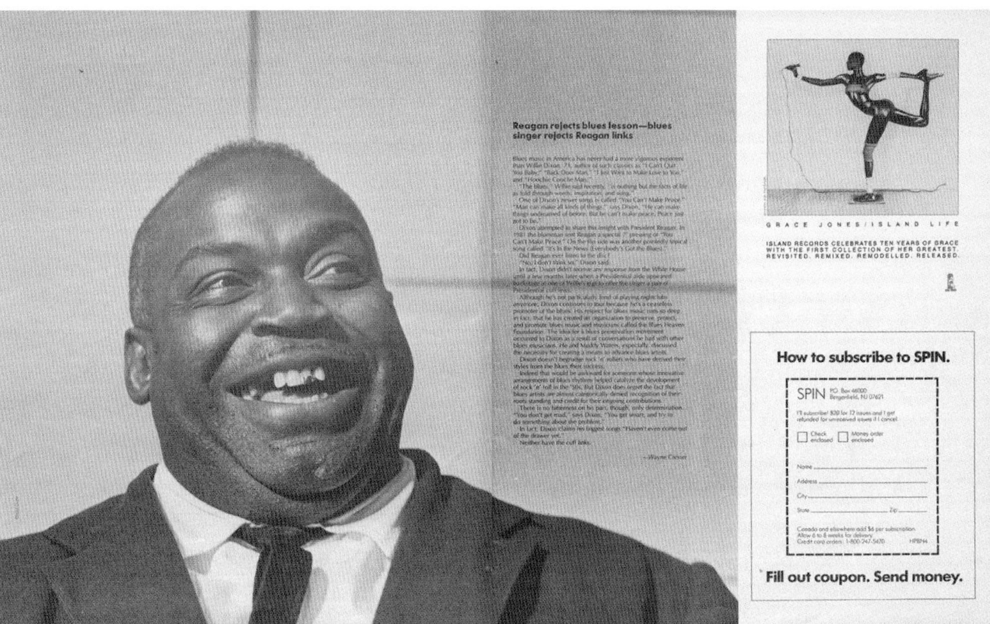

0.3-1 and 0.3-2. (*Right*) Pages 12 and 13 from *Spin* vol. 1, no. 9, January 1986.

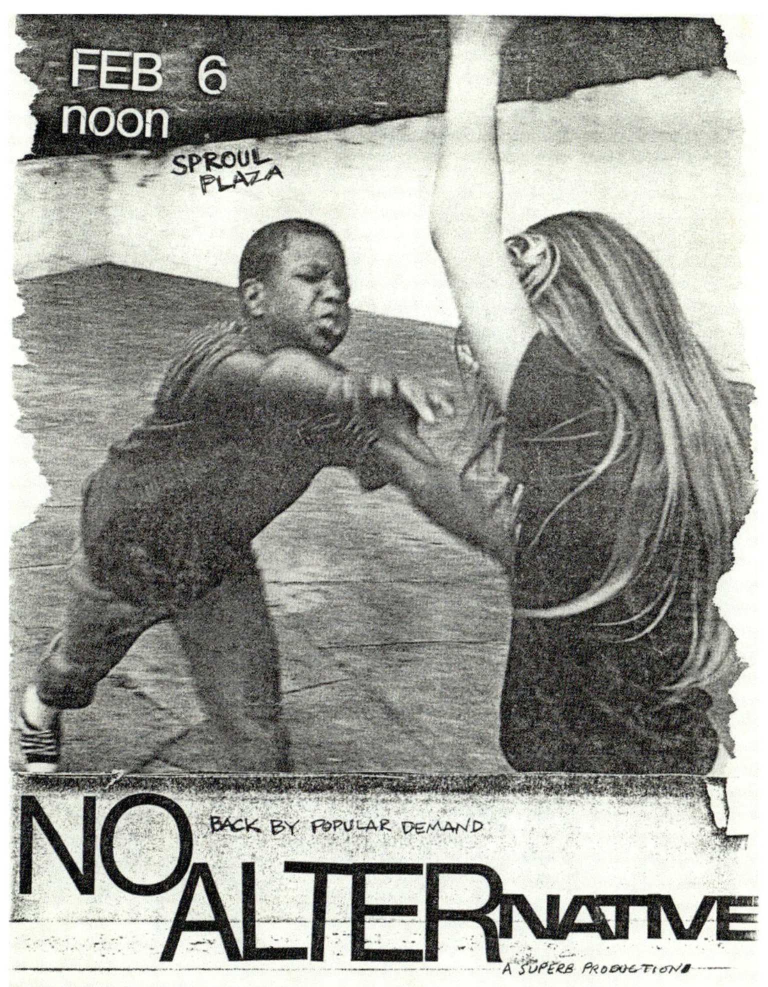

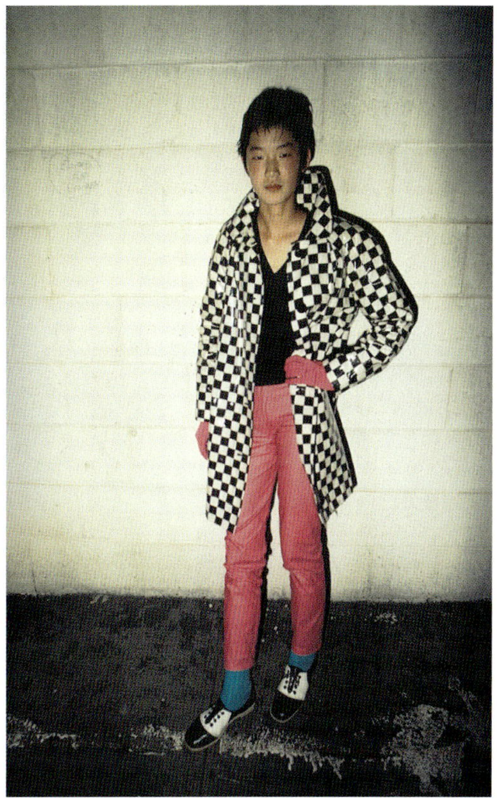

0.4. (*Left*) Flyer for No Alternative show, Berkeley, circa 1981. Design: Suzanne Onodera.

0.5. (*Above*) Suzanne Onodera, 1979. Photo © Jim Jocoy. From *We're Desperate* by Jim Jocoy, published by powerHouse Books.

Talking about the No Alternative flyer in 2020, Onodera said, "I was asked to design a flyer for the band, and I had a collection of images. I was always drawn to things that had some political edge to them. Not necessarily a picture of Reagan or Thatcher, but people fighting, people fighting for their rights, people pushing and pulling. That kind of angst. I liked to come up with connections between the band names and the images. Here a Black and a white kid are fighting in a schoolyard—it's violent in a way, but they're obviously kids. And then there's the name of the band: No Alternative. There's no alternative. So that's a statement about what's going on, fighting about race and sex. I did a word play where I switched the font, so 'no alter' is in the Helvetica and then 'native' is in a Microgramma Bold. 'Native' draws on some interesting suggestions there, and 'no alter' also suggests 'to alter.'" Onodera's description reveals the politics and care of design—even down to the font—found in so many punk flyers.

All of that care and thought comes from the intersection of personal and social histories. Considering herself a misfit within the Asian American community and strongly gendered identities that dominated her high school, Onodera recalled, "In my mind, punk wasn't about race. My perspective was: here I am, not part of any other thing. I saw punk as a very nonsexual, safe place for me to be." But she also commented, "I can count on my one hand how many people of color I interacted with [in the Bay Area scene of the late seventies and early eighties].

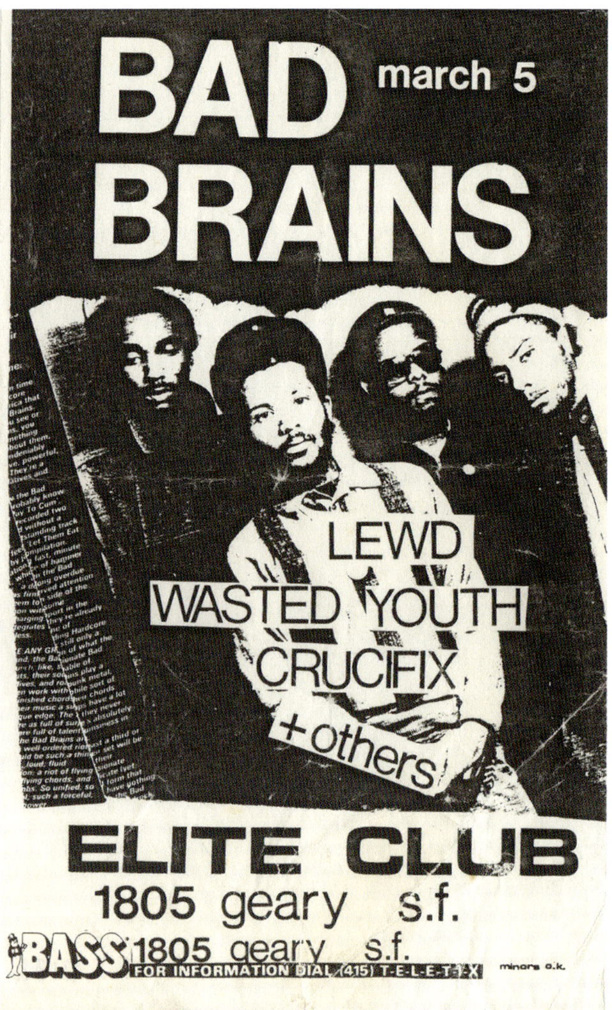

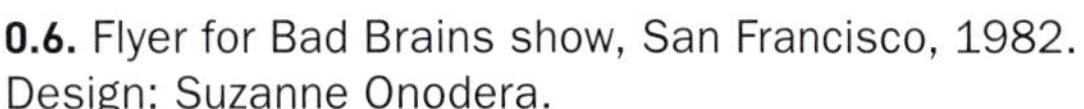

0.6. Flyer for Bad Brains show, San Francisco, 1982. Design: Suzanne Onodera.

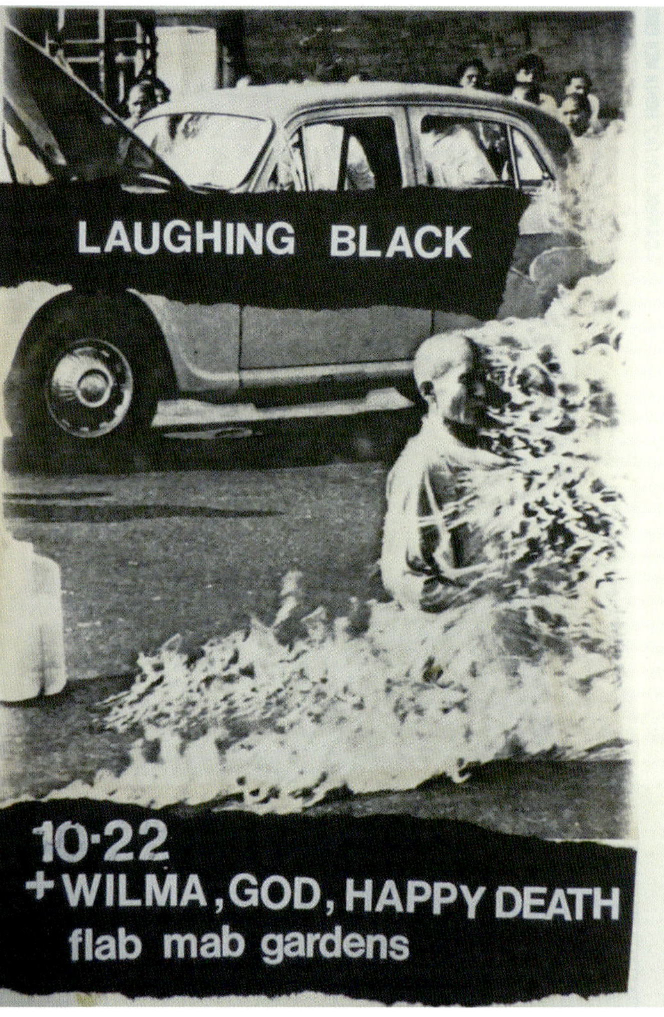

0.7. Flyer for Laughing Black show, San Francisco, circa 1982. Design: Suzanne Onodera.

I bonded with Sothira [Peng of Crucifix] immediately. And there was a really tall African American man named Orlando [Xavier] who was known for his dark sunglasses and his mohawk. You would get pushed into the mosh pit, and if you were getting beat up, Orlando was right there to save your ass. Everybody loved him."

For Onodera, and other punks in her scene like Orlando (interviewed in PART 3), punk's open door to everyone who didn't fit or who consciously rejected standardized categories of race, ethnicity, gender, and sexuality proved liberating. But this desire for a blank generation, a blank canvas to create your own identity, sometimes ran up against the overrepresentation of whiteness. For flyer makers like Onodera, a photocopied page could also be a space to push against the reality of a culture that continues to insist only certain bodies can be blank. Her flyer for the Bad Brains (0.6) is a case in point.

"I loved the Bad Brains, and they stayed with us [at the New Method warehouse in Emeryville, California] during that tour. I was so transfixed by this band. How can you be a punk reggae band? I don't remember where I found that image. Maybe HR gave it to me. I wanted to portray them as being proud as a band. How many all-Black bands were there back then?

I don't know any except for the Bad Brains. And so, let's speak truth, here. Let's put it out there. It's going to be all over every single poster. Every single telephone pole, for like a week, and then it'll be gone."

In another flyer by Onodera (0.7), the famous 1963 image of the serene Buddhist monk who set himself on fire in Saigon foregrounds the contradictions in the band names Happy Death and Laughing Black. Horrifying and stunning, it grabs your attention on the street and, as much as any image can, demands a kind of political action, or at least a recognition of how others have sacrificed their bodies in protest against government oppression and colonial occupation. It's hard to keep on walking by.

As Onodera explained, "So, Laughing Black, again, it's a powerful statement. Here's this monk who set himself on fire in protest. You talk about believing in yourself, in your spiritual self. But believing that your body can be action. And punk really is about asking, 'Is your body action?' Our bodies were action. People stage diving, throwing their whole body, their trust, into this crowd to catch them or not. Our bodies were making statements by walking down the street, by just being yourself, looking the way you did. You know, I have to say that I was driven more by vision and words than by their deeper philosophical or anthropological meaning. But I know that subconsciously, or maybe more consciously than I was willing to admit, that all those thoughts went through my head."

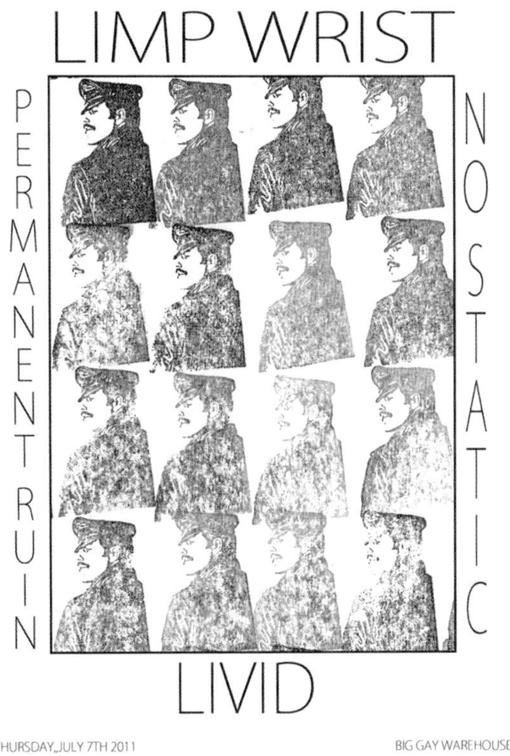

0.8. Flyer for Limp Wrist show San Francisco, July 2011. Design: Martín Sorrondeguy.

That subconscious or hidden side of meanings is familiar to other flyer designers, like Martín Sorrondeguy, who often made flyers for his bands Los Crudos and Limp Wrist (0.8).

Although he made the flyer in 2011, its design calls back to the 1980s in order to think differently about changes in its present moment. "This is from an amazing show at this queer squat space that was in South San Francisco. I made that flyer. I laid that out. I think it's a stamp made from a Tom of Finland image. I did this repetitive design. Not to be too heavy on it, I just love the fading because it almost seemed like there was a time when so many people were going away. And this made me feel that way, where it's super clear in one and just kind of gets lighter as it goes down." What at first looks like simple stamp art harbors a poignancy in the fading ink, linked to the fading away of people over the years, from AIDS in the 1980s, or from being priced out of housing in the 2000s and 2010s.

In contrast, the meaning of the Raymond Pettibon flyer from 1985 (0.9) seems more full-frontal, but then it surprises you with its subtext, and the sly questions it raises about symbols and bodies. At first we're confronted with the common punk caricature of 1960s counterculture: the naked, smiling, long-haired hippie, the peace sign, a quaint offer to share psychedelic

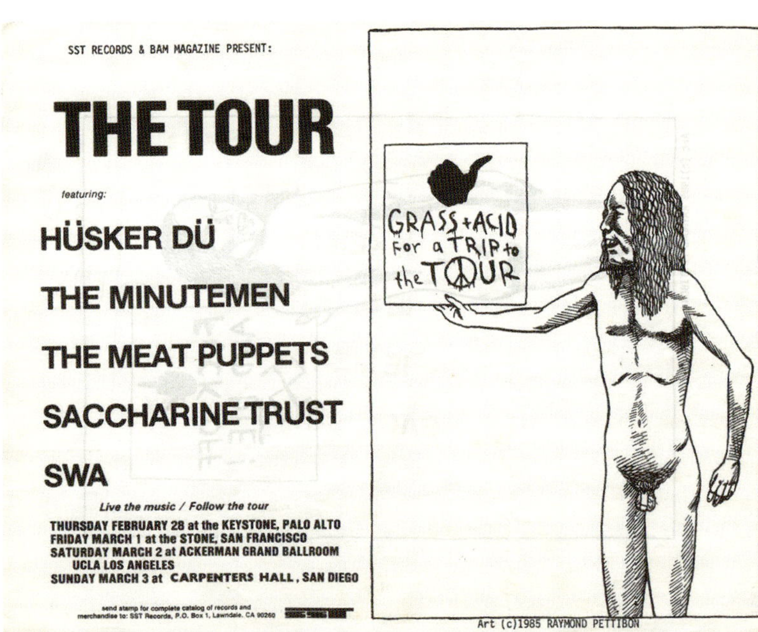

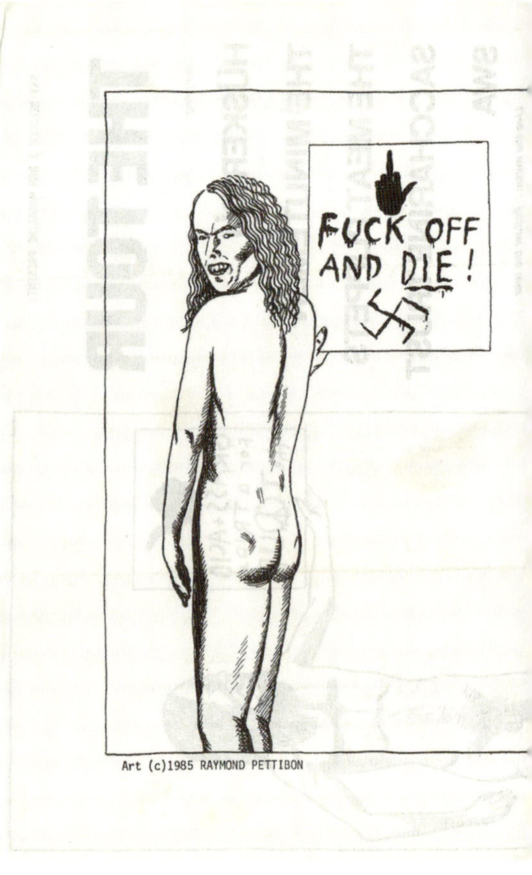

0.9. Front and back of flyer for tour by SST artists Hüsker Dü, the Minutemen, and others. Design: © Raymond Pettibon, 1985.

drugs for a free ride. But turn the flyer over and we see the image's symbolic flipside: a sinister laugh, a swastika, and a middle finger flanking a message of aggression. The flyer lays bare the central war of symbols and modes of resistance between hippies and punks. But it also laughs at how quickly expressions of resistance and change can become slogans and clichés—banners of conformity rather than rebellion.

Throughout the decades of creating iconography, punks can seem less like iconoclasts than obsessive collectors and inventors of icons and symbols. Similar to Pettibon's wink and nod to the possible conformity of punk, this 1983 Kover Band flyer (0.10) laughs at the contradiction, and shows us an image of icons run amok and fighting for space.

Anarchy sign, peace symbol, Iron Cross, pothead skull, and mushroom cloud all gather under the beer bong, the great uniter (at least for this designer) of surfers, skaters, and punks of all kinds. The alligator steps on the name of a wealthy town in the hills east of Oakland, and dances next to a grave from the same place. For this show at the Farm in San Francisco, the drawing points to class angst, but also a desire to reject, forget, or even destroy one's origins.

The Pettibon and Kover Band flyers illustrate the chaotic pileup of symbols that began with punk's earliest scenes

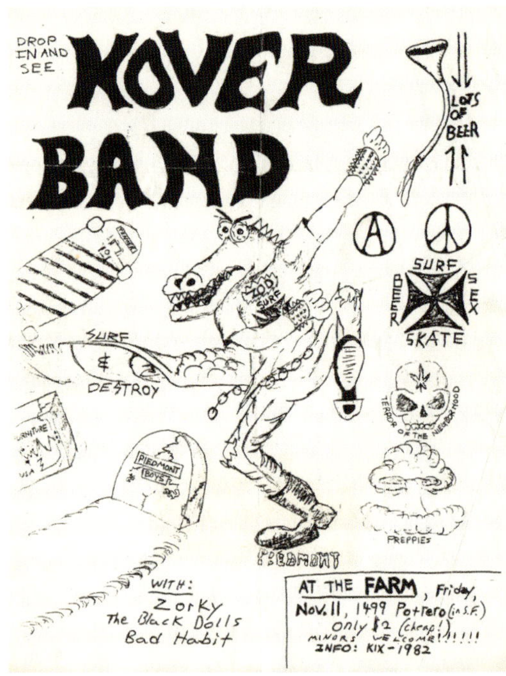

0.10. Flyer for Kover Band show, San Francisco, November 1983.

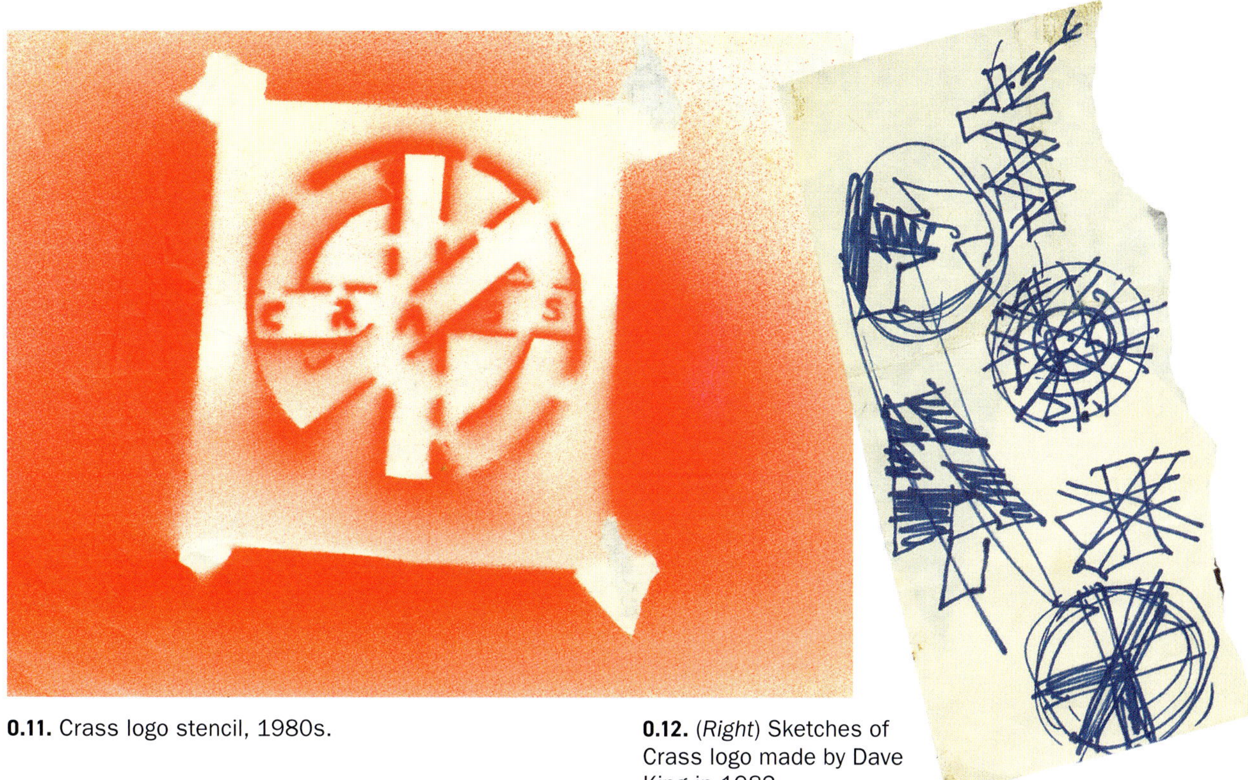

0.11. Crass logo stencil, 1980s.

0.12. (*Right*) Sketches of Crass logo made by Dave King in 1982.

when the anarchist circle *A* and the Nazi swastika circulated in proximity despite their contradictions. Some British punks used the swastika to shock and mock the nostalgic patriotism of their parents' generation, which clung to their victory over fascism in World War II but turned a blind eye to Britain's history of imperialist violence—ongoing in Northern Ireland and the Malvinas (Falkland) Islands—and the lavish spending on the Queen's Jubilee in the face of a domestic economic crisis. Meanwhile, Jewish punks in the US sang songs like "Master Race Rock" (Dictators) and "Blitzkrieg Bop" (Ramones), using morbid humor to grapple with how the Holocaust impacted their identity, and to laugh and shout about their own fragile place in the world.[5]

It is impossible, however, to dismiss the rationalized genocide attached to the swastika, whose display on clothing or flyers can also be read as sympathy with or allegiance to a white supremacist ideology, or at best an indifference. Clearly there was a need for a real alternative to the tired and fading shock of the swastika, and indeed, a new symbol of a competing ideology, or rather an anti-ideology, arrived with the logo of the anarchopunk British band and collective Crass (0.11).

The Crass symbol points in more directions, remains relevant for more situations, and, most importantly, doesn't rely on a single icon overburdened with hate and white power. Instead of ironizing a symbol, Crass strikes out against everything that can fit into the circle, combining nearly every possible permutation of rebellion in punk's visual archive. The symbol's designer, Dave King, untangled those icons in a series of sketches (0.12) made during a 1982 interview in Berkeley with his band Arsenal for the drummer and zine writer Aaron Cometbus. (See Cometbus's essay in PART 3). The sketch shows how the logo includes: the x'd-out Christian cross, the Union Jack, the ouroboros, the pharmakon (the snake wrapped around the cross), the anarchist circle *A*, and the international squatter's symbol. Moreover, according to Cometbus, King had recently discovered that a peace sign was also bound into the symbol. By joining these icons and their histories into Crass's new symbol, an image easily stenciled and made to travel, King's design became free to spread around by anyone with the simple means to copy it.

At the same time that King recognized a peace symbol inside a logo he'd designed five years earlier—showing how these designs can continue to reveal their secrets and their use as they move through history—Berkeley was experiencing the age of peace punk bands like Crucifix, Trial, and Atrocity. While Pettibon and other punks used the peace symbol as shorthand for what they saw as a burnout generation that failed in its political and cultural goals, these later punks recognized it as a historical emblem of protest and resistance against US imperialism. Crucifix generated material for their own political revision of punk by returning to a specific part of that 1960s archive: the media images of brutalized populations that had galvanized the Vietnam-era antiwar movement. Spotlighting this political legacy of the earlier counterculture, rather than the stereotype of the flower-wearing hippie, Crucifix envisioned a path to peace through a similar type of exposé in their flyers, which depicted the horrors that US supremacy had visited on colonized peoples all over the world (0.13, 0.14).

The band's logo combines the peace sign with a mushroom cloud, and together with photographs from the media spanning the Vietnam War to the Ethiopian famine, their flyers don't depend on subtext. The stark messages—"There is no solution for war but peace" and "Do you care?"—mean to spur direct action. You can hear this agitprop style in the opening track

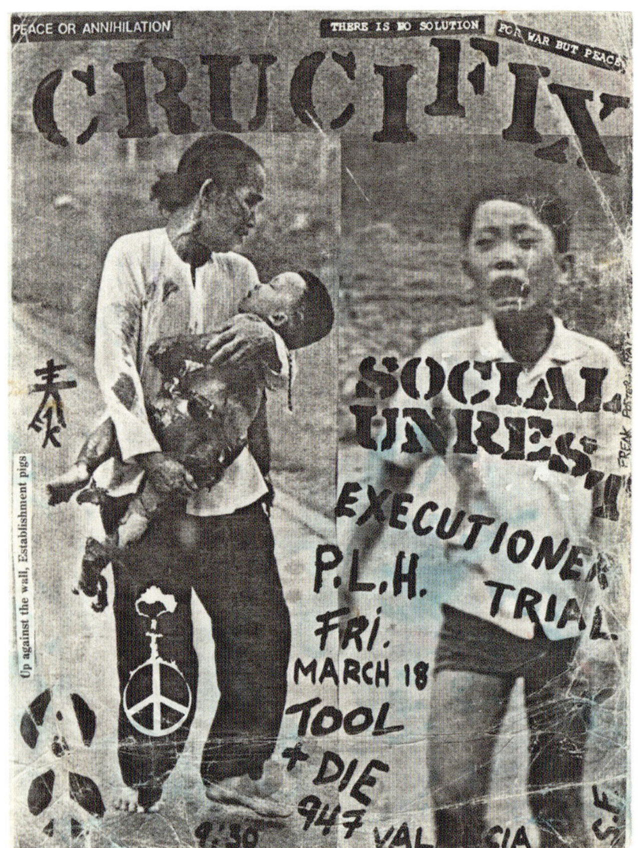

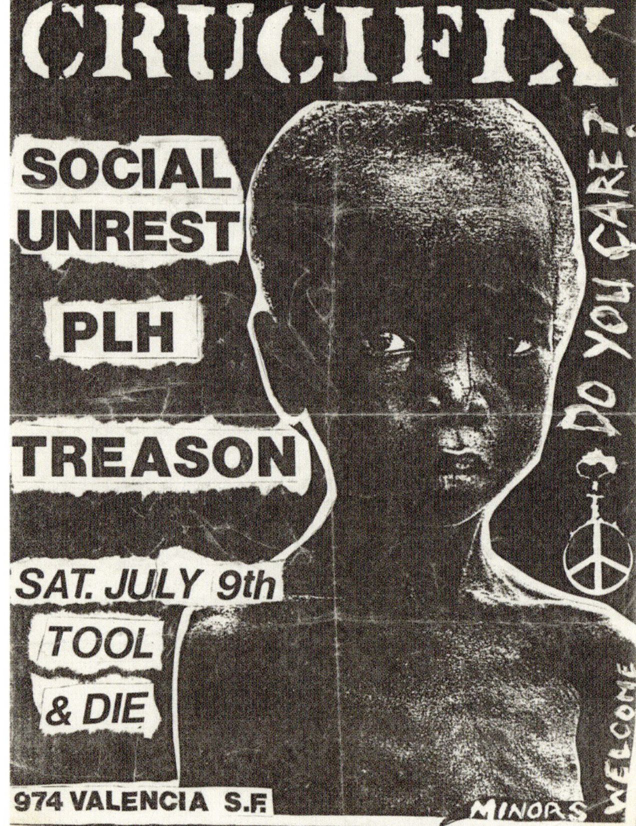

0.13 and 0.14. Crucifix flyers designed by members of Crucifix, San Francisco, 1983.

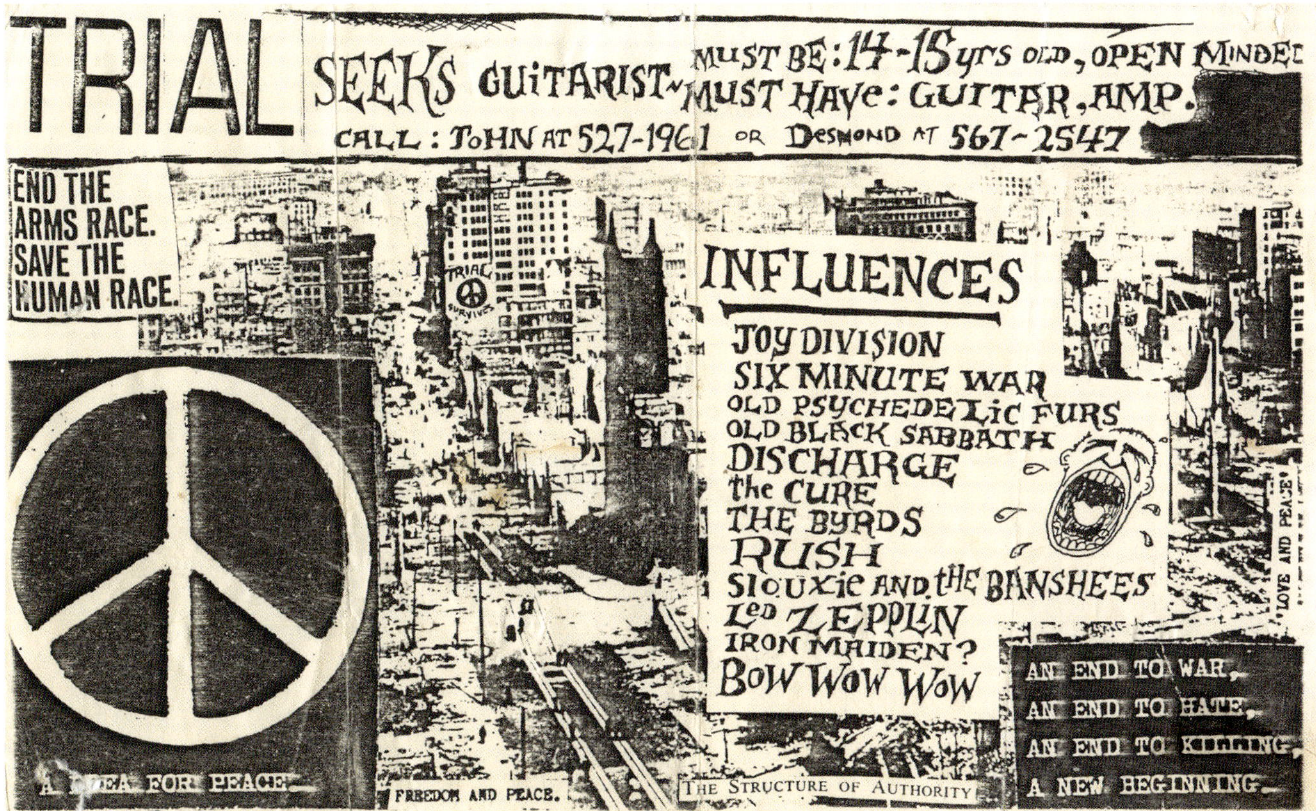

0.15. Trial seeks guitarist flyer, Berkeley, 1983.

to their full-length album *Dehumanization*. Its spoken-word intro lays out the life-and-death stakes of the political moment in the ominous year of 1984: “From dehumanization to arms production / For the benefit of a nation or its destruction / It’s your choice: peace or annihilation!”

Fellow peace punks Trial made the generational connection and divide clear in their own flyer for a guitarist (0.15). With their list of influences reaching from the Cure, Joy Division, Discharge, and Bow Wow Wow to 1960s mainstays the Byrds, they put themselves in a musical history but at the same time insisted any new member “must be 14–15 years old” and “open minded.”

These were some of the people making the most powerful claims to reimagine what punk could look and sound like in the mid-1980s, a sound you can hear in the 1984 song “Animal Fate” by Atrocity (3.31, 3.33) On that track, fifteen-year-old Katherine Harris and thirteen-year-old Sarah Borruso alternate and overlap their voices in a dissonant combination that entwines sung and spoken vocals over a wash of guitar fuzz with lyrics that interweave the lives of animal and human subjects. This multivocal denouncement of industrial farming and animal murder anticipates the sound of later Bay Area punk bands as different as Blatz, Spitboy, or Yaphet Kotto—groups who transformed fury about exploitation of all kinds into music. And while Atrocity’s message was as spiky and political as anyone’s, one of their set lists (0.16) reveals another side of peace punk. The humor and joy captured here—from a drawing of Limburger cheese (“pew”) to the whimsical lettering and the final declaration “This is art!”—show punks laughing again amid all the nation’s horrors.[6]

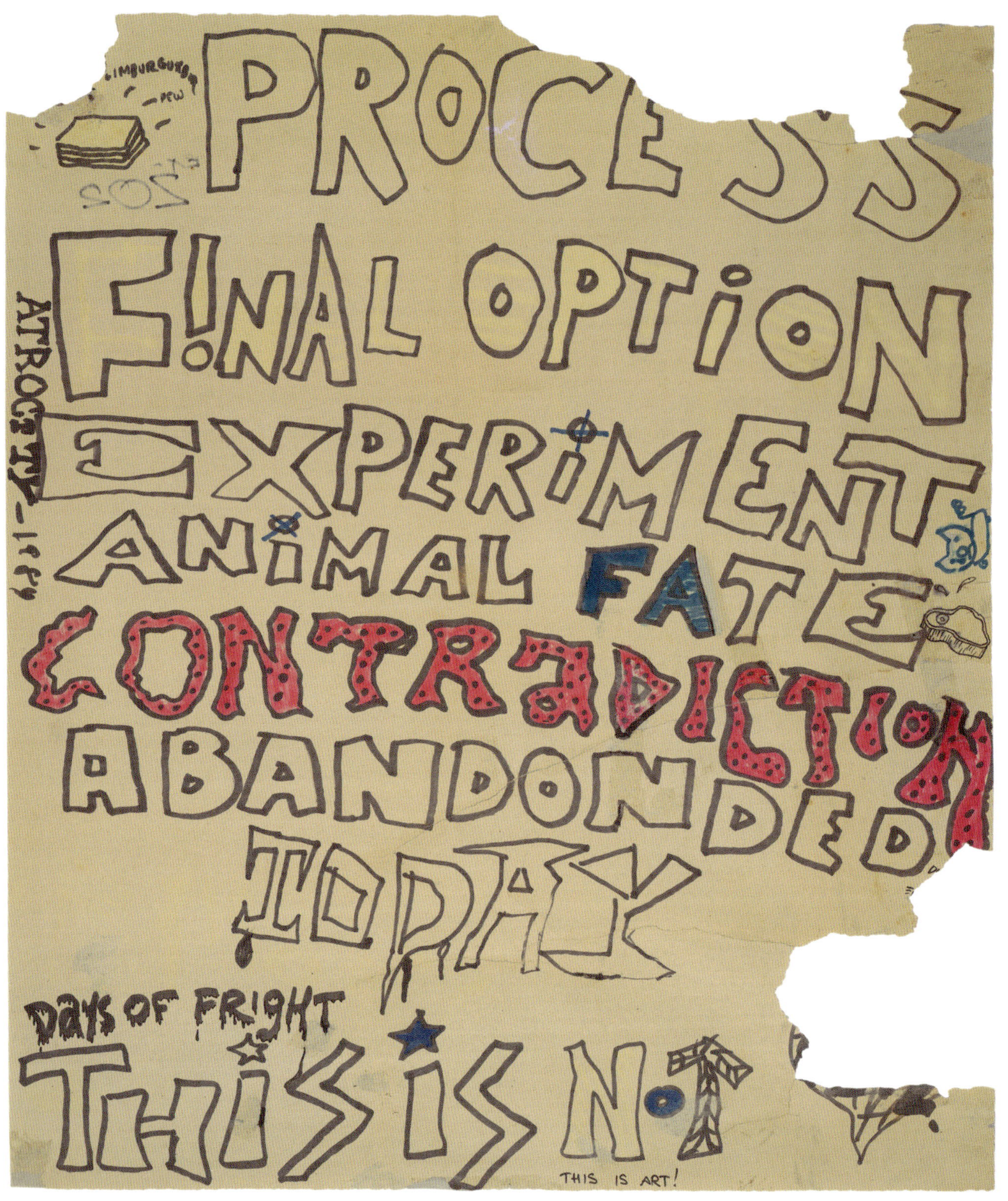

0.16. Atrocity set list, Berkeley, 1984. Design: Atrocity.

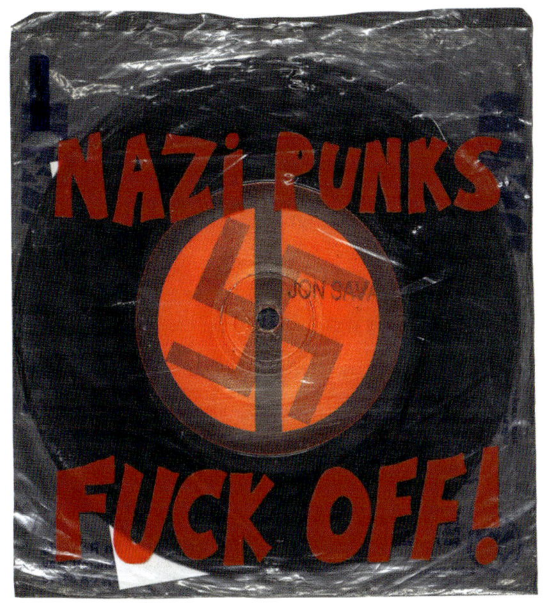

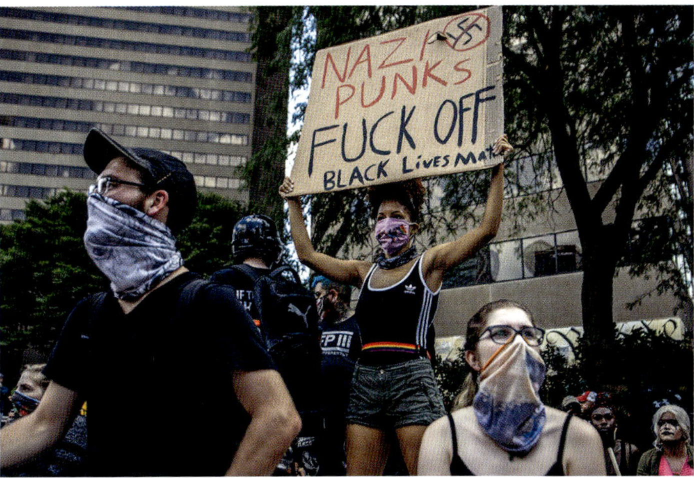

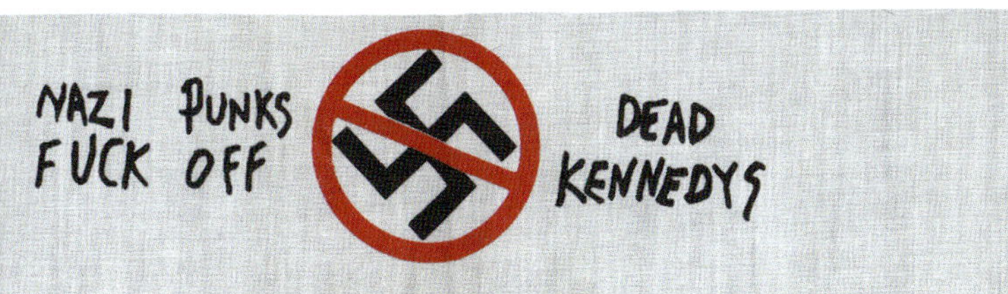

0.17. (*Left*) Dead Kennedys single "Nazi Punks Fuck Off" in original packaging, 1983.

0.18. (*Above*) Black Lives Matter demonstrator at Ohio Statehouse, Columbus, July 18, 2020. Photo Megan Jelinger / SOPA Images / Light-Rocket via Getty Images.

ARCHIVES ON THE STREETS

This brief tour of archived materials from just five years of one scene in punk's five-decade history offers a glimpse of the underground's sustaining energy. It shows punks committed to creating their own culture through sound, text, image, and action. The people and objects here show why punk matters so much for the present.

The fights that erupted on the streets between neo-Nazis and antifascist protesters during the regime of Donald Trump from 2016 to 2020 are the same fights punks have waged for years in the underground. And the ongoing battles over the meaning and transformation of the symbols associated with punk have been a central part of these struggles. For instance, the Dead Kennedys' "Nazi Punks Fuck Off" (0.17) has been taken up as a slogan on a Black Lives Matter sign (0.18), and Jello Biafra's record label Alternative Tentacles has been selling stickers and T-shirts with "Nazi Trumps Fuck Off" since Trump's election in 2016.

At the same time, protesters sustain the relevance of older antifascist and anticapitalist symbols (like the Crass symbol and what it contains) and the practices associated with them (squatting, protesting, resource sharing) in an unending challenge that continues to turn words into direct action on the street. When Milo Yiannopoulos brought his neofascist message to Berkeley in 2017, East Bay Punx put punk's image archive to use (0.19, 0.20).

The Clash's "bullshit detector" (from "Garageland") rings through the rallying cry "We call B.S." in the aftermath of the Parkland, Florida, school shooting; and we see and hear once again the voices of young women at the forefront of this crucial political movement against gun violence. Activists like X González, survivor of that school shooting, use punk's militant style in their own calls for disarmament (0.21).

These activists prove that punk's material archive continues to provide a vocabulary of symbols, catchphrases, and engagement that fuels action in the present.

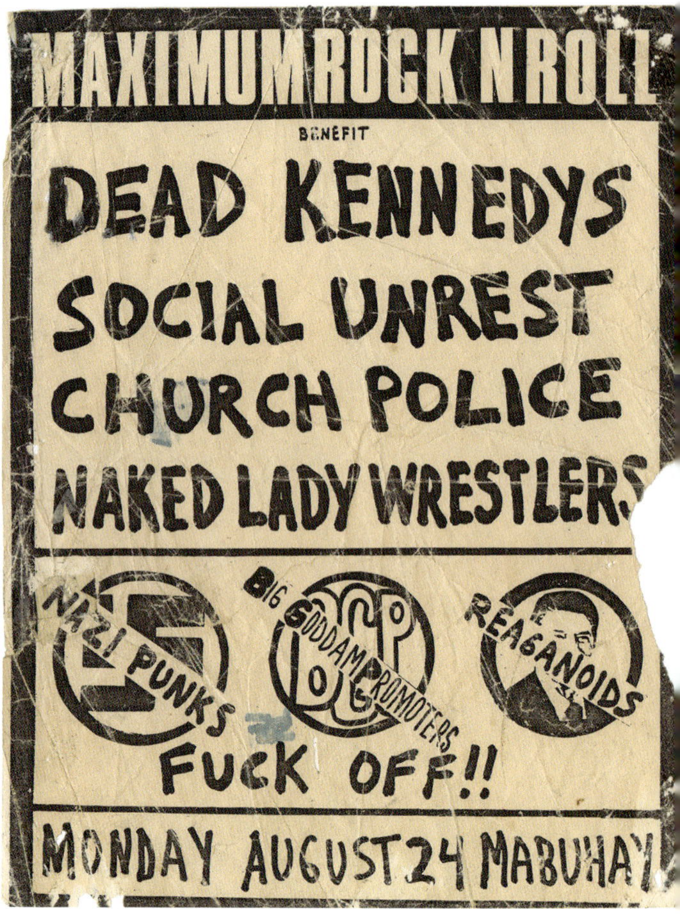

0.19. Flyer for *Maximumrocknroll* benefit show with protest symbols, August 1981.

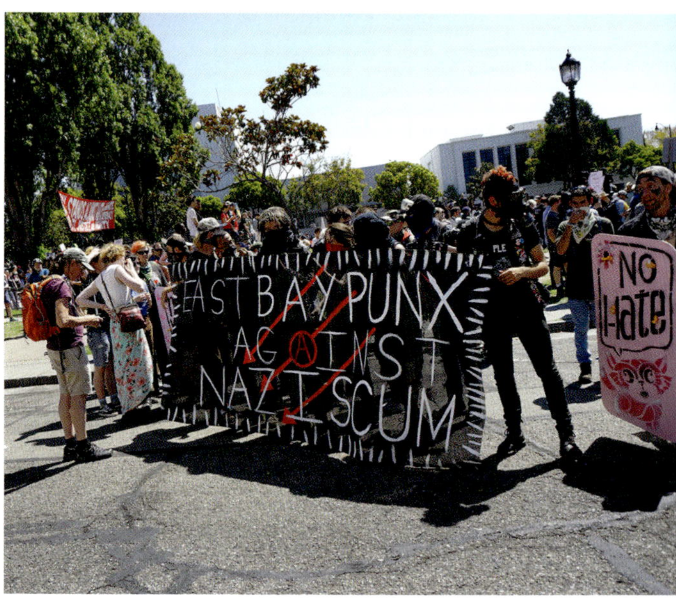

0.20. East Bay Punx protesting Milo Yiannopoulos in Berkeley, August 27, 2017. Photo: © Richard Nagler.

STORIES AND IMAGES FROM *WE'RE HAVING MUCH MORE FUN: PUNK ARCHIVES FOR THE PRESENT FROM CBGB TO GILMAN AND BEYOND*

We're Having Much More Fun breaks into four parts that document regional scenes and extraregional identities.

PART 1, "Being Different in New York: Punk Begins Underground," follows a trail of photographs, flyers, handwritten lyrics, cocktail menus, and zine pasteups to trace the formation of the first punk scene from its inspiration in the Velvet Underground, through key clubs (Max's Kansas City, Club 82, CBGB), magazines (*New York Rocker*, *Punk*), and people (too numerous to list). A wonderfully perverse mixture of New York School poetry, queer camp theatricality, and anarchic garage rock amateurism, early New York punks mocked the self-serious, corporate rock of the 1970s and a mainstream of corrupt conservatism. Rejecting mainstream rock also fit with a subculture that was refusing the norms of gender and sexual identities. The queer punk pioneer Jayne County, interviewed here, talks about how music showed her a life beyond her hometown and how she, in turn, introduced queer and trans strategies of "wrecking" into early New York punk. But Jayne County wasn't the only one wrecking gender norms. In the second interview for this section, Sylvia Reed offers a portrait of Anya Phillips, one of the few Asian American people in the scene, who cofounded the Mudd Club, managed the

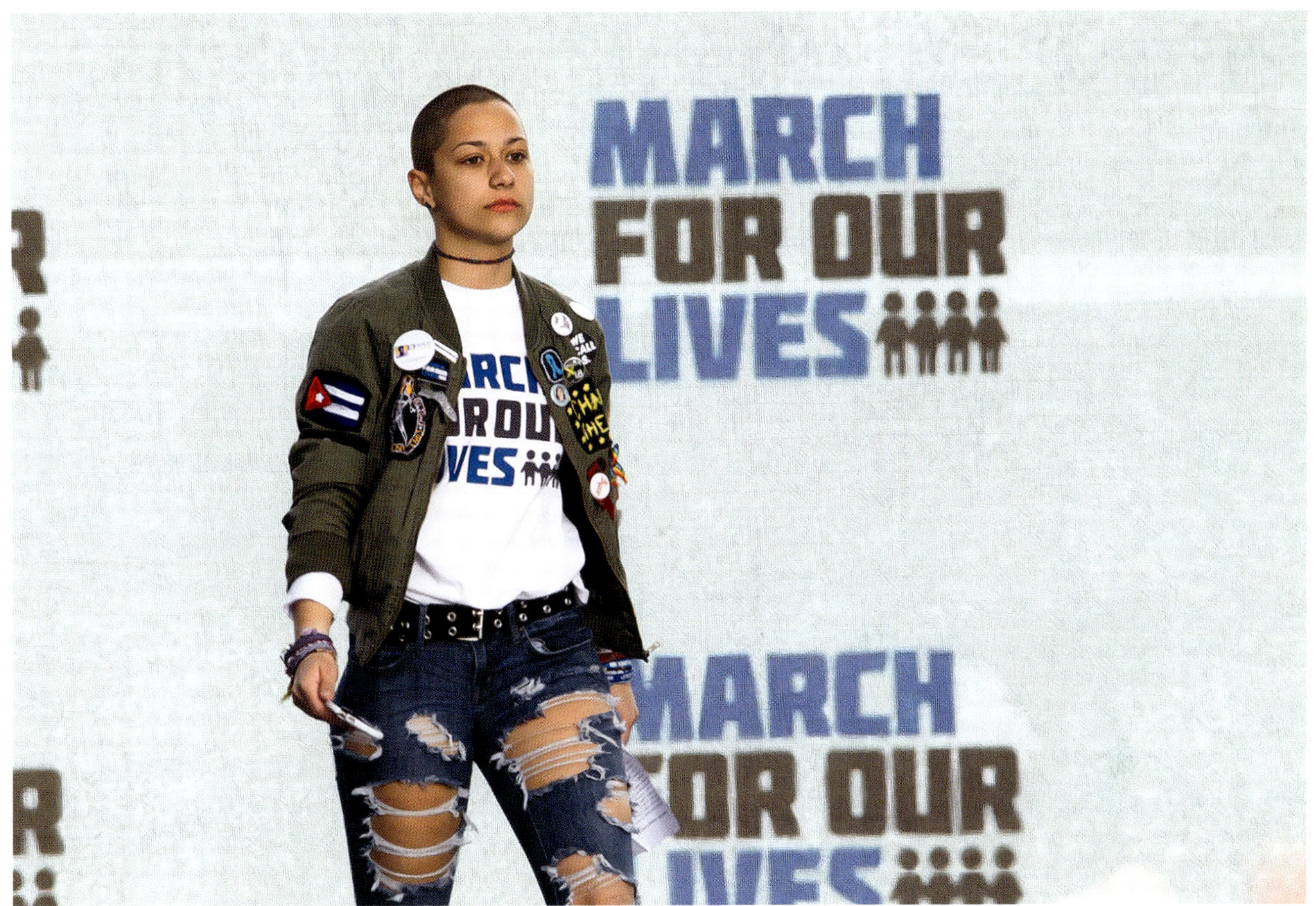

0.21. X González at the March for Our Lives Rally in Washington, DC, March 24, 2018. Photo: Noam Galai / WireImage via Getty Images.

Contortions, and designed iconic clothing for Debbie Harry, James Chance, herself, and others, transforming the look of punk in New York and beyond.

PART 2, "Doing the Future Yourself: The Screamers and Early Los Angeles Punk," looks at the magnetic draw and creative burst of the emergent LA punk scene in the late 1970s through the story of the Screamers. Jello Biafra claimed the Screamers as "one of the most important influences on the Dead Kennedys," and Masque owner Brendan Mullen called them "one of the biggest, disappeared, undocumented legends of all time."[7] Undocumented until now! The rare materials featured in this section—including handwritten budgets, a record label rejection letter, a scenario for a film project, and original art—illustrate a single band's entire career, and Tommy Gear's essay and detailed captions offer an insider view on the inner workings of a band pushing the edge of punk in musical, visual, and conceptual ways. Singer Tomata du Plenty's longtime friend Fayette Hauser and drummer KK Barrett give their firsthand accounts of the band's history and what it was like to be part of the underground community that helped power the punk scene around Hollywood. Additional flyers, photographs, and commentary set the Screamers in the context of their LA punk contemporaries and document the eruption of Black Flag and other SST bands onto the scene.

PART 3, "Peace or Annihilation: The Politics of Punk in the Bay Area," heads up the coast and covers nearly twenty years, featuring materials mostly drawn from the collection of Aaron

Cometbus that reveal the Bay Area punk scenes' intersection with leftist politics within the broader history and networks of collective action in the region. Cometbus, who has fomented punk scenes in several regions across the country, writes about the power of collecting itself, "the tiny germ or flame you carried home," and the culture of punk that exists off the stage and outside of clubs. Anna Joy Springer reflects on her participation as a singer in Blatz, Gr'ups, and Cypher in the Snow, and narrates a network of links between experimental literature, Gilman, homo- and queercore, and riot grrrl. In his interview, Orlando Xavier, singer for the Berkeley hardcore band Special Forces (1983 to 1987), among other bands, talks about growing up in the Bay Area and how he found a home in the punk scene.

PART 4, "Be a Crossroads! Punk Beyond Borders," turns to collections from scenes in Chicago, Texas, and the Pacific Northwest, as well as elsewhere across the country, to rethink punk's regionalism. These local scenes gave rise to movements and people that went far beyond their local borders, from the queer punk of the Dicks and Big Boys in Austin to the rise of riot grrrl in Olympia. Perhaps no other musician epitomizes this punk beyond borders more than Martín Sorrondeguy, the Chicago-based, queer Latine author, photographer, and singer for the hardcore bands Los Crudos and Limp Wrist. Sorrondeguy's interview and archival materials from Chicago and tours in Mexico, South America, and Japan, set alongside other flyers and zines from Alaska, Florida, and Kansas (to name a few), illustrate punk's expansive and continued relevance as a cultural movement across multiple regions and identities in the twenty-first century.

In the book's closing essay, Downtown Boys' lead singer Victoria Ruiz reflects on the histories and icons spread throughout this book as she puts her own stamp on punk in the present. Born and raised in San José, California, but finding her scene in Providence, Rhode Island, Ruiz taps into punk's network of communities in her own movement crisscrossing the country and the ways in which punk becomes a password to find a home wherever you go. Energized by almost half a century of examples, Ruiz looks forward to describe punks in a planetary, futurist metaphor, as "rogue planets, circulating collectively" in "the night that never ends."

We're Having Much More Fun borrows its title from an X lyric to remember that the people behind the materials here built their communities in *joyful* resistance to the mainstream. In the pages of this book, in the objects and voices you encounter here, we hope you will discover resources, strategies, and reminders of how much punks have done to cultivate a culture of resistance in underground scenes. When the worst of history repeats itself, the objects of the past aren't trivial. They hold lessons in how to spark a flame of creative action, or to keep the scene's pilot light burning for the future.

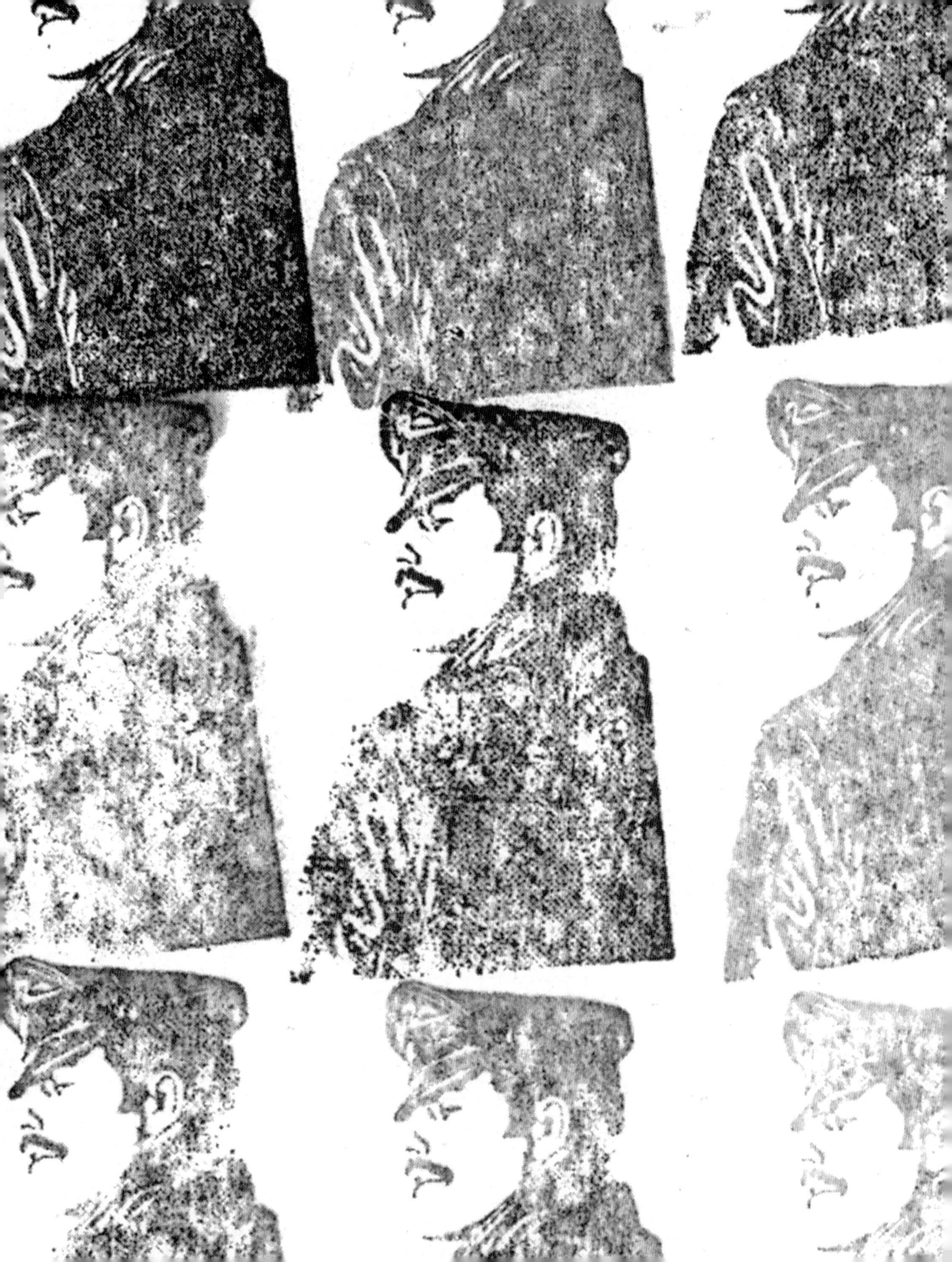

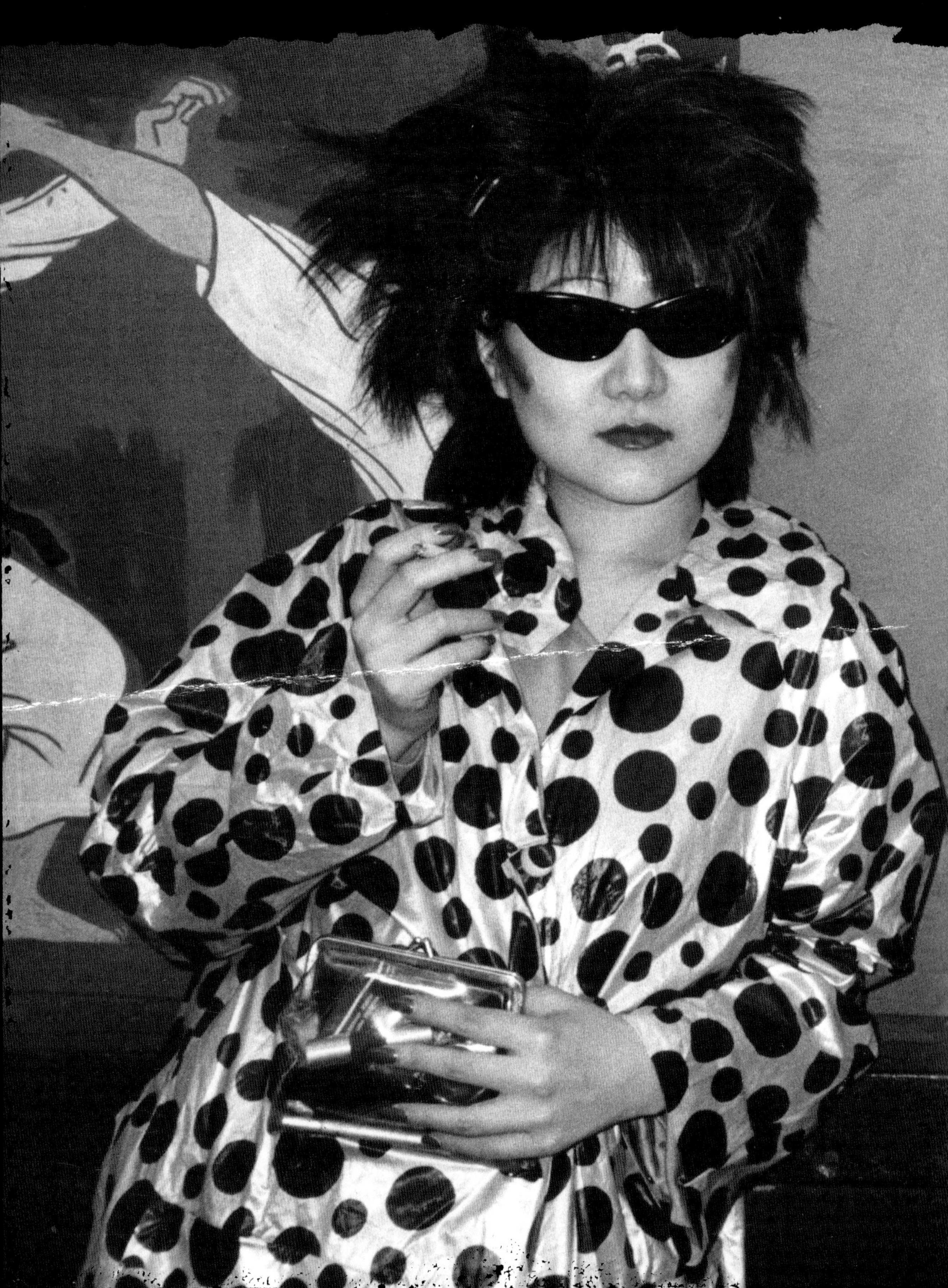

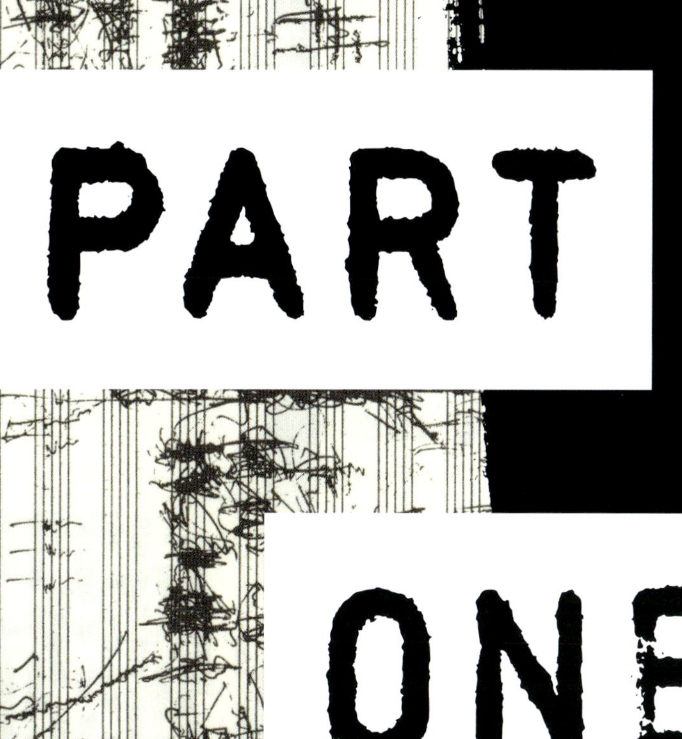

PART ONE

CH. 1 Being Different in New York

PUNK BEGINS UNDERGROUND

New York City in the mid-1970s was grimy, crime-ridden, and broke. Mary Harron, who interviewed the Ramones for the first issue of *Punk* magazine, described it like this: "Part of the feeling of New York at that time was this longing for oblivion, that you were about to disintegrate, go the way of this bankrupt, crumbling city. Yet that was something almost mystically wonderful."[1] The infamous urban planner Robert Moses had bulldozed entire neighborhoods to create white-flight freeways for suburban commuters. Slumlords in the South Bronx paid petty criminals to burn down residential buildings to collect on insurance. Downtown manufacturers cut costs and abandoned the city, moving their industries to cheaper locations and leaving behind vacant blocks. The climate of economic devastation fueled revolutionary writings and popular uprisings, but perhaps the most lasting revolutions were cultural and sonic. In the Bronx, hip hop was born in house and block parties where emcees rhymed over the ingenious mixing of breakbeats. The abandoned industrial buildings downtown became repurposed living spaces where both early disco and the loft jazz scene thrived. Salsa consolidated around the neighborhoods decimated by Moses's freeways. And in small clubs and performance spaces in Manhattan, scattered southward from Union Square to the Bowery, a new type of raw and experimental rock and roll was taking shape more from a shared attitude than a shared sound. This early New York punk, with its sheer variety, opened up "the sea of possibilities" (to quote Patti Smith's "Land: la mer(de)") for creative rebels of all kinds.

PART 1 plunges into punk history to follow a line of queer fomentation that starts with New York's harder-edge counterculture of the 1960s and its radical expressions of gender and sexuality. Famed Pop Art artist and underground filmmaker Andy Warhol provided an archetype for punk's irreverent attitude, and he remained an important, if somewhat spectral, figure in the early punk scene, as Bobby Grossman's photo captures (1.1). Punk's confrontational antics have a precursor in Warhol's early promotion of the Velvet Underground through the multimedia *Up-Tight* "happenings" codesigned by filmmakers Barbara Rubin and Jonas Mekas. A more perfect setting couldn't have been imagined for the inaugural *Up-Tight* event than the posh annual dinner of the New York Society for Clinical Psychiatry on January 13, 1966 (1.5–1.7). All the repression that the gathering enacted met its counterpart in the Velvets' performance. Gerard Malanga danced with a whip alongside Edie Sedgwick to the band's high-decibel low-fi haze of distorted riffs and drones against Moe Tucker's pulsing drumbeat. Nico's deadpan delivery and Lou Reed's quavering tenor conveyed stories about street life in the city—the grind of hard drugs, hustling, rough trade, and forgotten lives. "I'm ready to vomit," an attendee exclaimed on his way out the door.[2] Shocking and campy, the happening introduced the disruptive and seductive energy of a new type of urban music that jumbled together radio-friendly pop, Beat poetry, and avant-garde music to revitalize mid-1960s rock and roll as subversive outsider art. Similarly, Warhol's interactive banana cover design for *The Velvet Underground & Nico* (1967), with its instructions to "peel slowly and see," lured every consumer into a confrontation between desire and destruction (1.4).

Warhol's almost nightly presence at Max's Kansas City from 1966 to 1968 consecrated the venue as the public epicenter of the underground and a pilgrimage site for artists and musicians. Danny Fields, who circulated in the Warhol Factory crowd (1.8–1.9), became a key player there as well, bringing many musicians into the Warholian inner sanctum of the back room—including a young and shy Patti Smith and her friend Robert Mapplethorpe. Soon after, Smith and Warhol's former assistant Gerard Malanga shared a poetry-reading bill at St. Mark's Church (1.10); the event launched Smith into the New York City downtown scene. Meanwhile, Fields, publicist and talent scout for Elektra Records, helped get the anarcho-leftist "total assault" rockers the MC5 and their "little brother" band the Stooges signed to the label in 1968. Some years later Fields would become the first manager of the Ramones.

The MC5, the Stooges, and another leftist Detroit band, the Up, shared stages and communal houses and met force with force in hard-driving confrontational songs that voiced boredom with consumer capitalism and disgust with the government (1.11). But the Stooges' Iggy Pop became the breakout star. His physical provocations—diving into the audience, walking on top of them, or smothering himself in peanut butter—tore down the physical and social "fourth wall" dividing performers from their audience and inspired the next generation of punks to do the same (1.12). Iggy's wild behavior enacted the danger, violence, and lunacy that was the flipside of the peace-and-love era as antiwar and pro–civil rights demonstrations were routinely met with vicious police brutality.

The same was true for the clientele of clandestine gay bars and private clubs, where cops entrapped their victims, or raided the whole place, indiscriminately making arrests for disorderly conduct, indecency, or masquerading (1.13). During a raid at the Stonewall Inn on June 28, 1969, drag queens and trans women led the charge to fight back, unleashing a spontaneous revolt and several nights of street protests in Greenwich Village. Alongside and partly inspired by this foundational act in the modern "gay liberation" movement and its new visibility (1.14), musicians began to explore gender and sexual dissidence more overtly. You can see the force of this change in reviews by some rock critics, who, upset by glam rock's rebellion in style, started labeling it "fag rock."[3]

GETTING ALL DOLLED UP

Gender politics took center stage when the New York Dolls (1.15) stepped into the chasm opened by the demise of the Velvet Underground in 1970 and began their residency at the Mercer Arts Center in 1972, shifting the underground scene from midtown to downtown. Heavily influenced by the queer experimental Ridiculous Theatre of Charles Ludlam and Warhol's coterie of trans performance artists Jackie Curtis, Holly Woodlawn, and Candy Darling, the Dolls fashioned themselves as a street version of the Rolling Stones, exchanging the Stones' high-gloss glam for trashy drag, and playing the same Chuck Berry–inspired rock and roll with ferocious abandon.

When the Mercer Arts Center collapsed on August 3, 1973, the New York underground rock scene migrated to Club 82, a venue for drag shows since the 1950s. There, the New York Dolls inaugurated "live rock Wednesdays" on April 17, 1974 (1.16). Television opened for Leather Secrets on May 1, and throughout the rest of 1974 explicitly queer headliners such as Wayne County and the Backstreet Boys, and Harlots of 42nd Street shared bills with Patti Smith, the Fast, and the Stillettoes.

A perennial warm-up act, the Stillettoes (1.17–1.18) included a trio of women singers, Debbie Harry, Elda Gentile, and Amanda Jones, who updated the girl-group pop of the Shangri-Las for the hardscrabble 1970s. Debbie Harry and Chris Stein left that group to form Blondie and the Banzai Babies in early 1975 with Tish and Snooky Bellomo (founders of the punk boutique Manic Panic) (1.19), then later that year reconfigured the lineup into Blondie featuring a single female singer backed by an all-male band. Taking acting lessons from the experimental theater director Tony Ingrassia (whose credits include Warhol's play *Pork*, with Jayne County in the cast), Debbie Harry began to develop a stage persona for Blondie that resembled the artful performances of drag queens—exaggerated femininity laced with heavy doses of irony, toughness, and cool indifference.[4]

By January 1975, Club 82 switched to a DJ as the scene shifted to another Lower East Side club. Hilly Kristal opened his legendary bar on the Bowery in 1970, first calling it Hilly's (like his previous restaurant on 62 West 9th Street), then rechristening it CBGB-OMFUG (standing for "Country, Bluegrass, Blues, and Other Music for Uplifting Gourmandizers") in December 1973 (1.20). Initially intended as a venue for what he thought was an up-and-coming roots music scene, Hilly's club began to book some cabaret acts, including Hollywood Spit with Tomata du Plenty and Fayette Hauser (1.21; see Fayette's interview in PART 2) and neighborhood rock bands on Sundays, giving the headline slot to Club 82's warm-up bands such as Patti Smith and Television (1.22, 1.23).

Television formed around the teenage friendship of Tom Verlaine (Tom Miller) and Richard Hell (Richard Meyers), who drew their stage names from the French Symbolist poets and lovers Paul Verlaine and Arthur Rimbaud (author of *A Season in Hell*). Verlaine and Hell came to New York in search of the city's literary scene, but like Smith, they found a creative outlet within the downtown music scene. In addition to forming a band together (first the glam-styled Neon Boys), they also invented a poetic alter ego named Theresa Stern, creating a composite photograph of themselves in feminine wig and makeup (1.24, 1.25). As Hell writes in his memoir, "feminism and androgyny and transvestism were in the air (Andy Warhol, Mick Jagger, the National Organization for Women). We'd cash in!"[5]

When Hell split from Television in March 1975, he joined forces with Johnny Thunders and Jerry Nolan from the disbanded New York Dolls to form the Heartbreakers, revising some of his earlier songs, such as "High Heel Wheels" from the Neon Boys and Television sets, to fit the new band (1.26–1.29). Eventually Hell moved on to form Richard Hell and the Voidoids in 1976 with Ivan Julian (1.65), Robert Quine, and Marc Bell—his third iconic New York punk band—and to record the anthem "Blank Generation," joining in the edgy retro pop of Blondie and the Ramones.

PUNKING THE FAMILY

While Patti Smith, Television, the Ramones, Talking Heads, Dead Boys (1.30), and Blondie (1.33) attracted record contracts from major labels eager to fill in the blank and their bank accounts, too many bands that played regularly at CBGB and Max's Kansas City never caught a big break and have since faded in standard punk histories as stars of the scene: Suicide (1.31, 1.32), the Fast, the Miamis, the Shirts, Marbles (1.56), and the all-women band the Erasers (1.47). Another such band was the Mumps (1.34–1.37), whose story adds to the queer genealogy and cross-country networks of the early New York scene. The band took shape in 1974, formed by guitarist Rob Duprey, bass player Aaron Kiley, and three Santa Barbara transplants: keyboard player Kristian Hoffman, drummer Jay Dee Daugherty, and charismatic vocalist Lance Loud. Lance was already famous for being the first out gay person on television when his family had been the subject of a twelve-part PBS series *An American Family*, broadcast in 1973. The entire nation watched as Lance moved to New York City to find his hero Andy Warhol and join that underworld, exposing how the Louds struggled to cope with explicit queerness in the family (note the four-legged schoolgirl in the Mumps' 1977 flyer as a play on normalcy and monstrous aberration, 1.37).

The Mumps debuted in early February 1975 at the Greenwich Village cabaret club Trude Heller's but found a home at CBGB as an opening band for Television later that month. After some personnel shifts (Paul Rutner replaced Daughtry, who left to join the Patti Smith Band, and Kevin Kiely replaced Aaron Kiley) the Mumps eventually became headliners at CBGB and Max's. Their quirky and mannered power pop resembled Roxy Music and Sparks more than the Ramones, and they combined gay-themed lyrics ("Muscle Boys," "Dutch Boy," "Dance Tunes for the Underdogs") with an image that was decidedly not drag-inspired, anticipating later power pop queer bands Pansy Division and Imperial Teen. But, as Kristian Hoffman comments, "in what many have assumed was an only slightly veiled policy of homophobia on the part of contemporary record labels, Mumps remained the only unsigned act out of the original crop of CBGBs era headliners."[6]

If the Louds of *An American Family* betrayed the fault lines in the myth of "normal," then the Ramones, as a parody of an American family pop group like the Osmond Brothers, smashed "normal" into hundreds of punk pieces (1.38). With their uniform combed-down hair, ripped jeans, leather jackets, and adopted last name of Ramone (one of Paul McCartney's pseudonyms), they reimagined familial resemblance as conformity to a stereotype of tough masculinity. Their leather-clad look, at once a throwback to 1950s biker culture and a reflection of male hustlers on "53rd and 3rd" (to quote a Ramones song), paralleled Debbie Harry's feminine burlesque in Blondie. Both resembled the gender artifice of drag.

The Mexican-born performer and visual artist Arturo Vega joined the Ramones in 1974 as their "artistic director," designing their banners, T-shirts, and famous logo based on the US presidential seal, which first appeared on their second album *Leave Home* (January 1977). "I saw them as the ultimate all-American band," Vega recalled. "To me, they reflected the American character in general—an almost childish innocent aggression."[7] Tommy Ramone echoed this idea in interviews. As he told Lisa Jane Persky for the *New York Rocker*, "We think of ourselves basically as middle class American kids."[8]

Vega immigrated to the United States in 1971 at age twenty-four, fleeing Mexico's authoritarian government. As an artist, he explored emblems of power, nationalism, and capitalism—especially the eagle, which, in addition to the presidential seal, appears on the flag of Mexico, on US coins, and on oversize belt buckles as patriotic kitsch (1.40, 1.42). For Vega, the eagle also signified the Eagle's Nest—an infamous gay leather bar (1.41). Ramones posters and logos combine all these elements in a grand parody of American masculinist patriotism repurposed as a punk trademark. Like the density of meanings embedded in their logo, Ramones songs distilled bubble-gum pop and surf rock down to their simple musical essences and twisted their lyric innocence into sugarcoated menace. Inspired by the Bay City Rollers' chant in "Saturday Night" (S-A-T-U-R-D-A-Y Night!) the Ramones peppered their songs with infectious and deranged cheers—Lobotomy! Gabba Gabba Hey! Hey Ho Let's Go!—invoking and undermining the myths of US heroism and domestic bliss ("we're a happy family") with songs about pinheads, sniffing glue, and blitzkrieg hookups. Downplaying the Ramones' subversiveness, Sire Records' industry newsletter announcing their first album described them as "high energy rock and roll with simplistic lyrics and spit-fire enthusiasm" and suggested they could attract the same market share as mainstream rockers Kiss, Aerosmith, and Black Sabbath (1.39).

For its part, *Punk* magazine heavily promoted the Ramones and their "all American" parody as the core punk sound and image. The magazine, founded by Legs McNeil, Ged Dunn, and cartoonist John Holmstrom (1.43), was modeled in part on the irreverent *Mad Magazine*, and like *Mad*, *Punk* occasionally ran feature-length graphic novels in the style of *fumetti*, combining photographs and drawing. For the "Mutant Monster Beach Party" issue they enlisted none other than Andy Warhol as a mad scientist, coming full circle back to punk's queer father figure, and promptly killing him off (1.44–1.46).

Beyond satirizing the all-American family and mainstream pop music, punk in the mid-1970s, more than any other style of rock music at that time, created an alternative structure of kinship that provided an opportunity for cis- and trans women and people of color to reject the homogenized past and create a new clamorous and pluralistic present. Trans punk rocker Jayne County and Asian American punk fashion designer Anya Phillips personify that transformative force, and the interviews in PART 1 dive into their pioneering and central roles within the early New York punk community.

Of course, as much as things changed, there was always a pull backward to make even downtown life the same as it ever was. As Sylvia Reed cautions, "It's wishful thinking to say that there weren't issues. The music business has always been this cesspit of misogyny, and this was true then. What I did see were really strong women who were successfully surviving using their art."

That music industry machine quickly infiltrated the scene and tried to separate bands into ad-friendly genre labels they thought could attract a wider public. As a result, what was "punk" one month became "new wave" the next (1.47). And while the industry rechristened more pop-oriented bands like Blondie and the Talking Heads as "new wave," some noisier and more experimental groups rejected the consumer-friendly tag and archly called themselves "no wave." This splintering of energies ultimately meant that beyond Max's and CBGB, other venues, like the Mudd Club, Club 57, and Hurrah, became key performance and exhibition spaces for artists to explore a wide spectrum of gender and sexual difference in their image and music. Figures like Klaus Nomi (1.48, 1.49), a futuristic and ethereal German countertenor, mixed opera arias with quirky pop penned by former Mumps keyboard player Kristian Hoffman, and Tomata du Plenty returned from Los Angeles with the now legendary electropunk band the Screamers (2.62, 2.63).

CH. 2 IMAGE GALLERY

A month before meeting Warhol, an earlier incarnation of the Velvet Underground performed in Angus MacLise's "Rites of the Dreamweapon—I" on this program. Other participants included John Vaccaro, who had just formed the Play-House of the Ridiculous, and the drag performer and Warhol superstar Mario Montez.

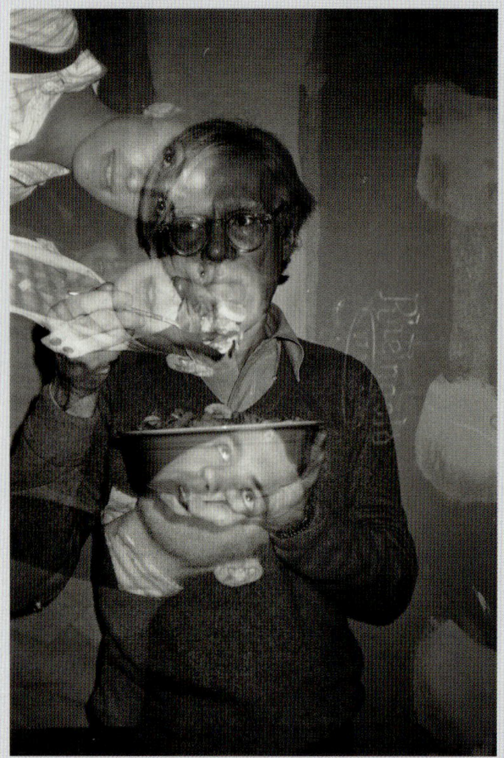

1.1. Double exposure photo with Andy Warhol, Diego Cortez (*bottom*) and two unidentified people, circa 1976. Photo: © Bobby Grossman.

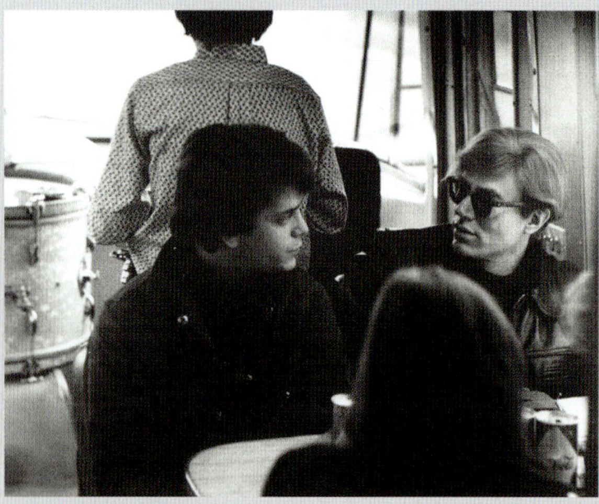

1.2. Lou Reed and Andy Warhol, circa 1966. Photo: Paul Morrissey.

FILM-MAKERS' CINEMATHEQUE
434 LAFAYETTE ST. AL4-4060

November 1, 1965

NEW CINEMA FESTIVAL I

OPENING NIGHT

RITES OF THE DREAMWEAPON - I

"THE TREMOR RITE"

Ritual - Manifesting of the Presence
Trance - Possession by the Presence

8:00 -- Pre-trance section
graudal buildup into movement

9:00 -- Trance section

10:00 -- Dream Confession

Coordination by Angus MacLise

Movers: John Vaccaro, Stan Alboun, Tony Conrad

Dreams: Elektrah & Gail, Mario Montez, John Cale

Trance Apparition: Frances Stillman

Music by: The Velvet Underground

John Cale
Lew Reed
Sterling Morrison
Angus MacLise

Other nights of the Dreamweapon listed on Cinematehque monthly bulletin

1.3. Film-Makers' New Cinema Festival opening night program, November 1965.

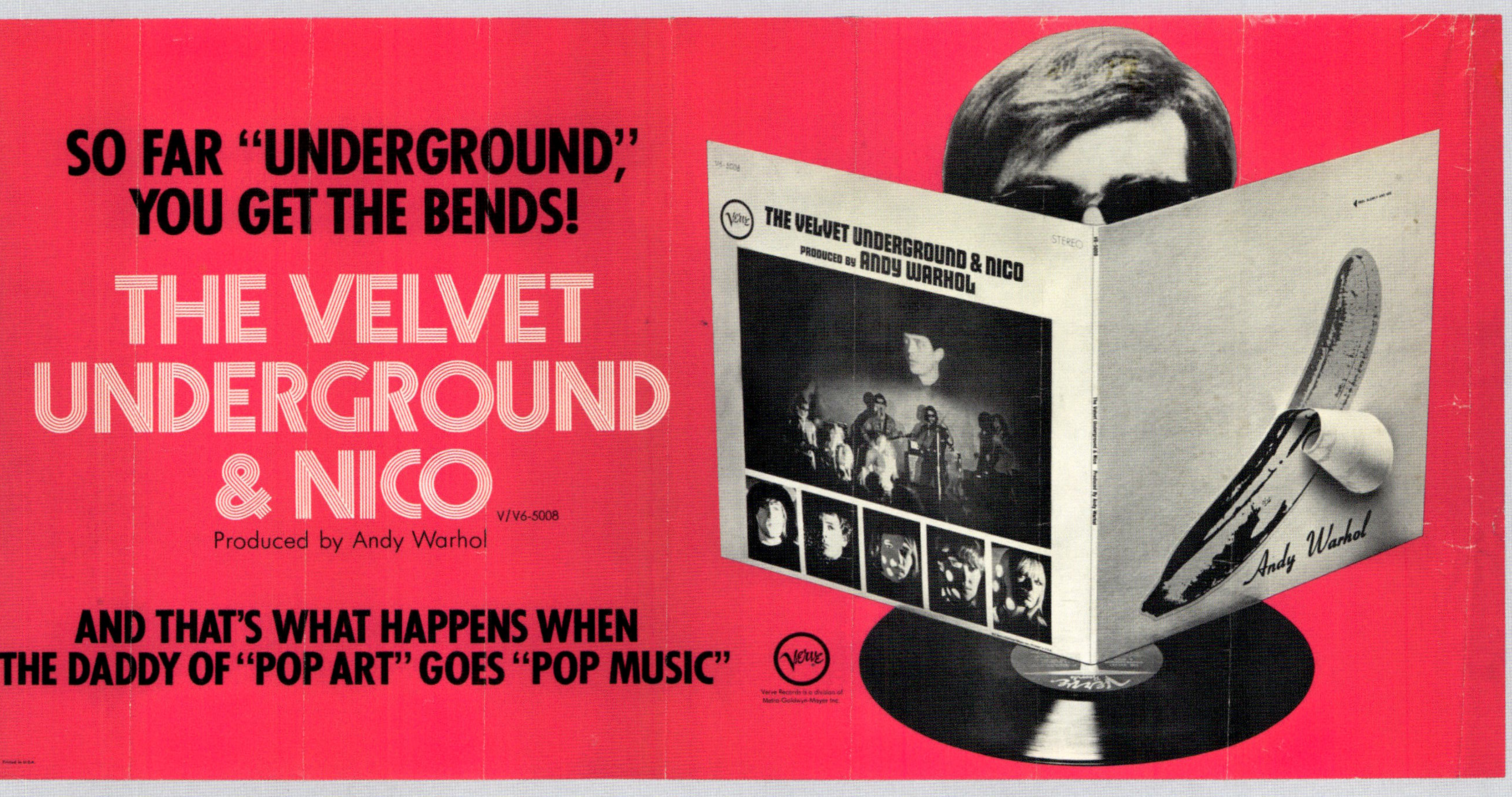

1.4. Promotional poster for the Velvet Underground & Nico, circa 1967.

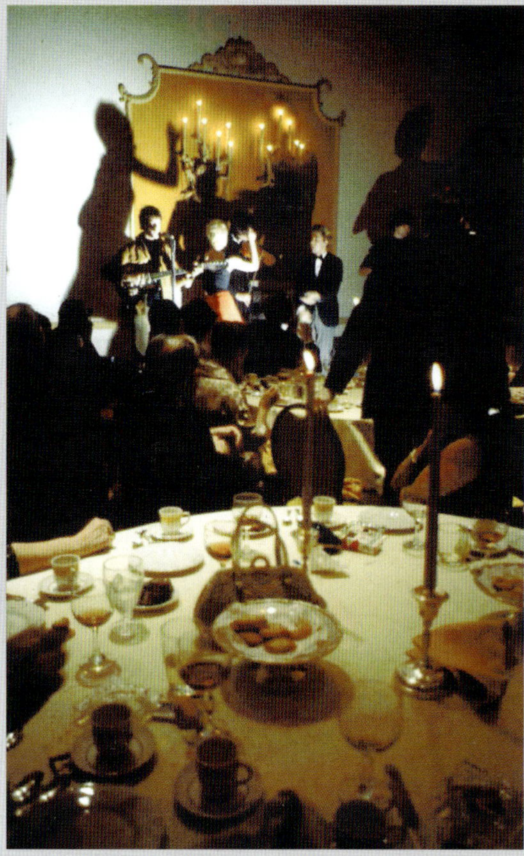

1.5. The Velvet Underground with Edie Sedgwick and Gerard Malanga dancing at the first *Up-Tight* event on January 13, 1966, at the Annual Dinner of the New York Society for Clinical Psychiatry. Photo: Adam Ritchie Photography.

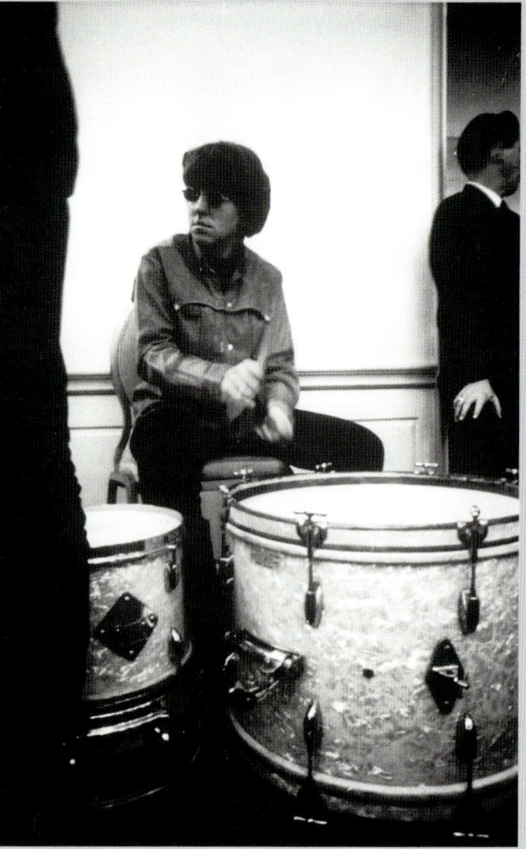

1.6. Moe Tucker performing at the Annual Dinner of the New York Society for Clinical Psychiatry. Photo: Adam Ritchie Photography.

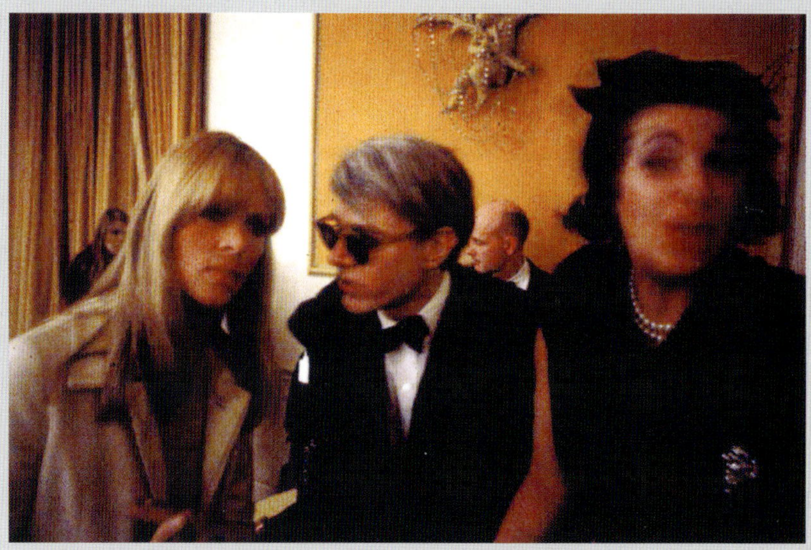

1.7. New York Clinical Psychiatrists' hostess (*right*) greeting Andy Warhol and Nico at Delmonico's. Photo: Adam Ritchie Photography.

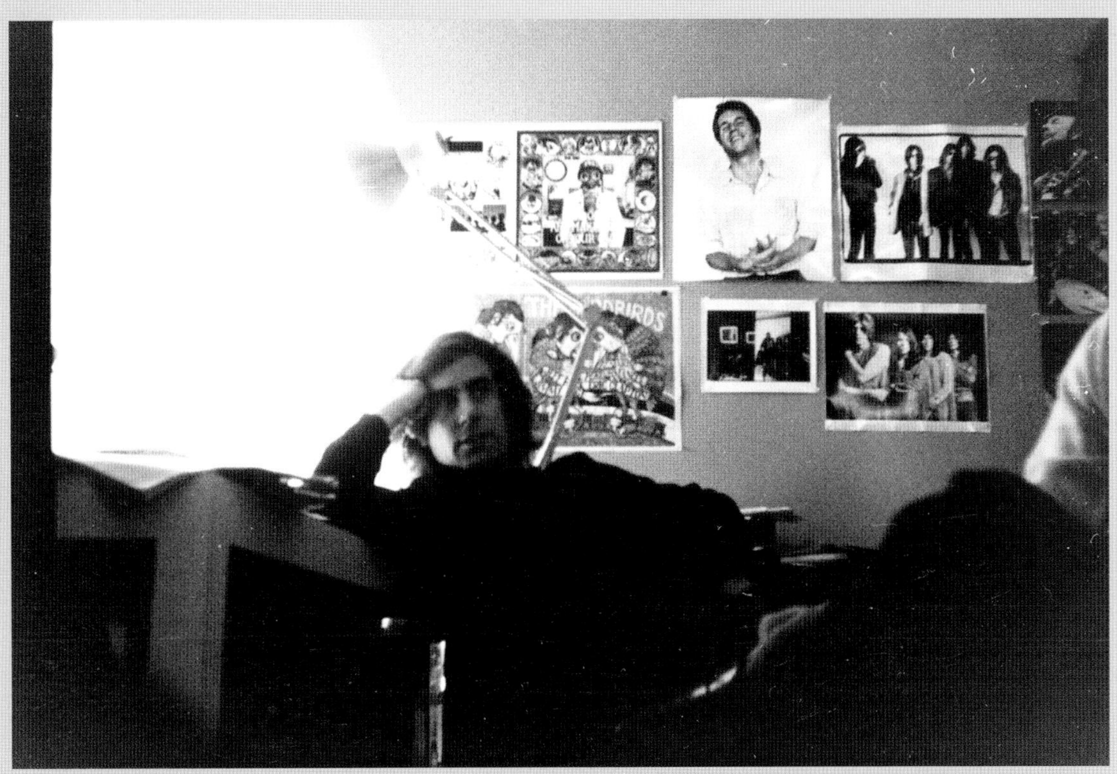

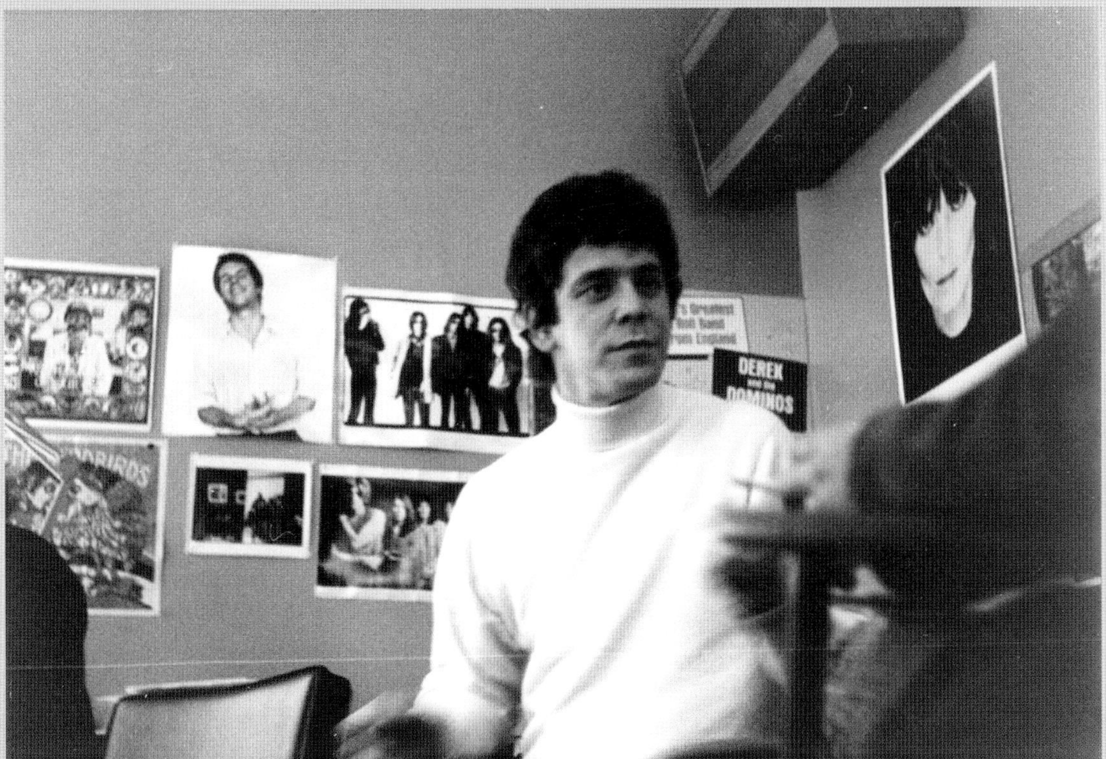

1.8 and 1.9. Elektra Records publicist and “company freak” Danny Fields with Lou Reed, December 1970. Photo: Connie Radulovitch.

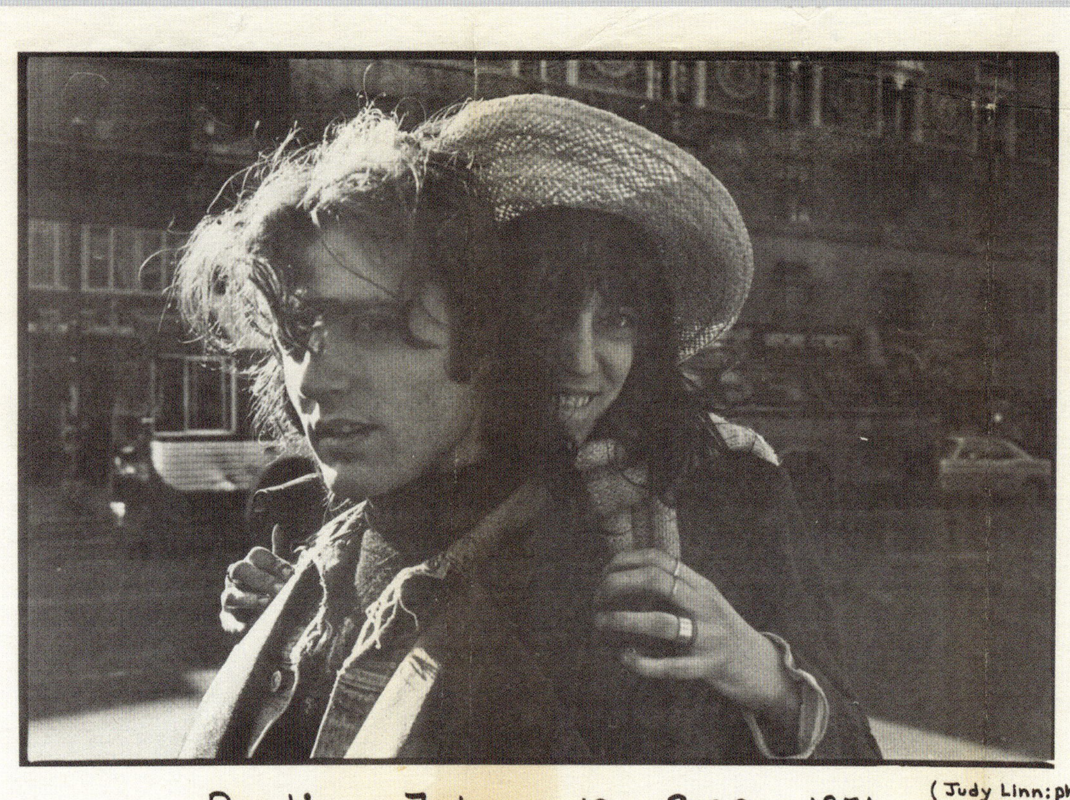

1.10. Flyer for Poetry Reading by Gerard Malanga and Patti Smith, with Smith's annotation, February 1971.

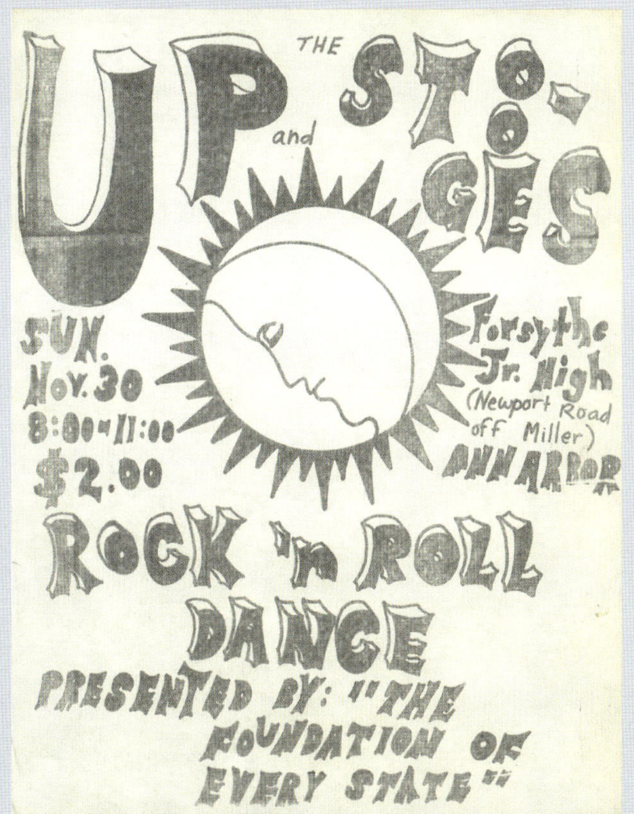

1.11. (*Left*) Flyer for the Up and the Stooges show, Ann Arbor, Michigan, 1969.

1.12. (*Below*) Iggy Pop publicity photo, circa 1979. Photo: London Express Service.

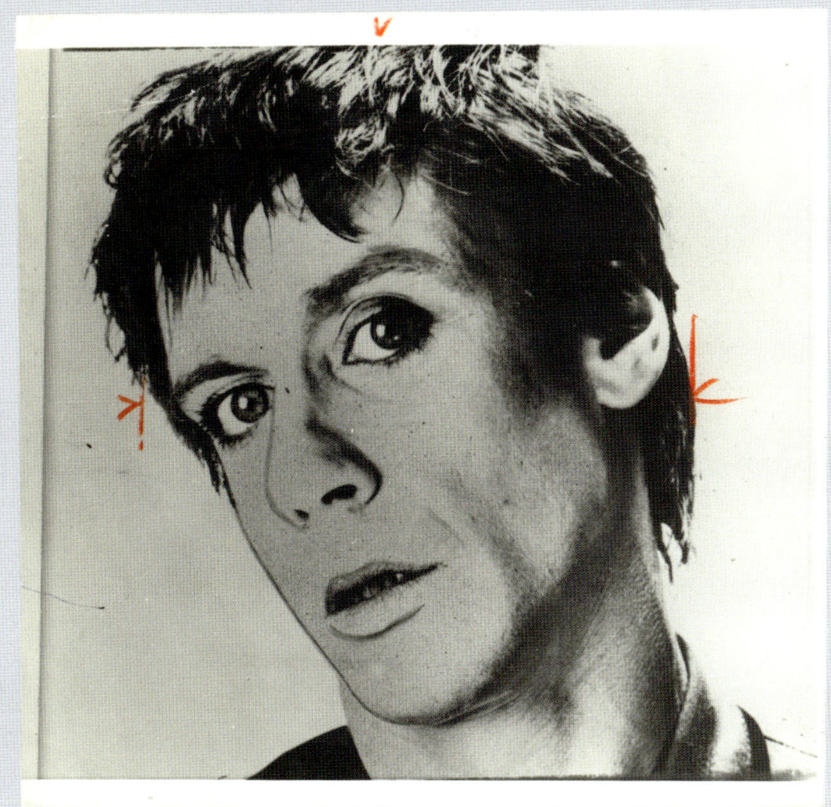

THE MATTACHINE SOCIETY INC. OF NEW YORK

The Voice
of the Homosexual Community

THE POLICE AND YOU

The police department recently announced a "clean-up" of Times Square and Greenwich Village. This usually means that they are harassing homosexuals for want of something better to do. If you are the victim of police entrapment or harassment, or if you are arrested--WE WANT TO KNOW ABOUT IT! As a result of a recent article in the New York Post on the Mattachine Society and cases involving police entrapment of homosexuals, the Police Department positively stated that entrapment was no longer to be employed. We admire this policy and hope it is completely enforced. WE WANT TO KNOW IF IT ISN'T!

Remember--if you are the victim of police entrapment or harassment, or if you are arrested--let us know so that we can take steps to protest innocent victims and end these unjust policies.

CALL: W A 4 - 7743
Monday-Friday 6-9 P.M. Saturday 2-5 P.M.

THE MATTACHINE SOCIETY INC. OF NEW YORK
1133 Broadway
New York, New York 10010
Suite 410-412

HELP US HELP YOU - JOIN MATTACHINE

1.13. Mattachine Society letter to the community about police entrapment, circa 1969.

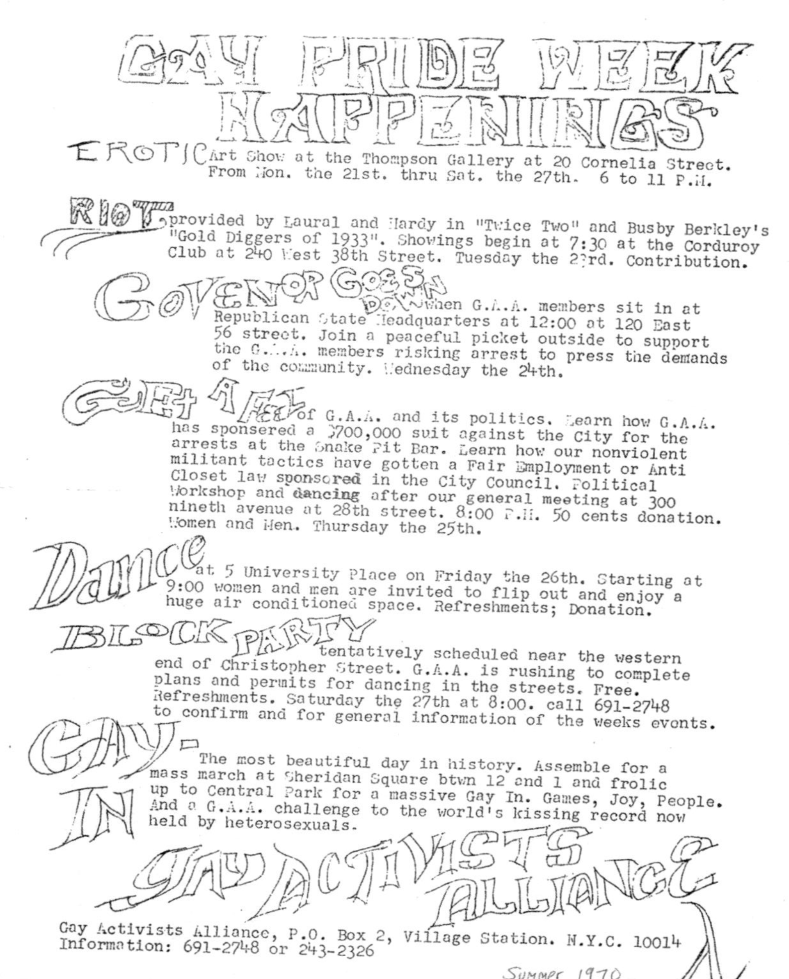

GAY PRIDE WEEK HAPPENINGS

EROTIC Art Show at the Thompson Gallery at 20 Cornelia Street. From Mon. the 21st. thru Sat. the 27th. 6 to 11 P.M.

RIOT provided by Laural and Hardy in "Twice Two" and Busby Berkley's "Gold Diggers of 1933". Showings begin at 7:30 at the Corduroy Club at 240 West 38th Street. Tuesday the 23rd. Contribution.

GOVENOR GOES DOWN when G.A.A. members sit in at Republican State Headquarters at 12:00 at 120 East 56 street. Join a peaceful picket outside to support the G.A.A. members risking arrest to press the demands of the community. Wednesday the 24th.

GET A FEEL of G.A.A. and its politics. Learn how G.A.A. has sponsered a $700,000 suit against the City for the arrests at the Snake Pit Bar. Learn how our nonviolent militant tactics have gotten a Fair Employment or Anti Closet law sponsored in the City Council. Political Workshop and dancing after our general meeting at 300 nineth avenue at 28th street. 8:00 P.M. 50 cents donation. Women and Men. Thursday the 25th.

Dance at 5 University Place on Friday the 26th. Starting at 9:00 women and men are invited to flip out and enjoy a huge air conditioned space. Refreshments; Donation.

BLOCK PARTY tentatively scheduled near the western end of Christopher Street. G.A.A. is rushing to complete plans and permits for dancing in the streets. Free. Refreshments. Saturday the 27th at 8:00. call 691-2748 to confirm and for general information of the weeks events.

GAY-IN The most beautiful day in history. Assemble for a mass march at Sheridan Square btwn 12 and 1 and frolic up to Central Park for a massive Gay In. Games, Joy, People. And a G.A.A. challenge to the world's kissing record now held by heterosexuals.

GAY ACTIVISTS ALLIANCE

Gay Activists Alliance, P.O. Box 2, Village Station. N.Y.C. 10014
Information: 691-2748 or 243-2326

Summer 1970

1.14. Flyer for the first Gay Pride celebration, June 1970.

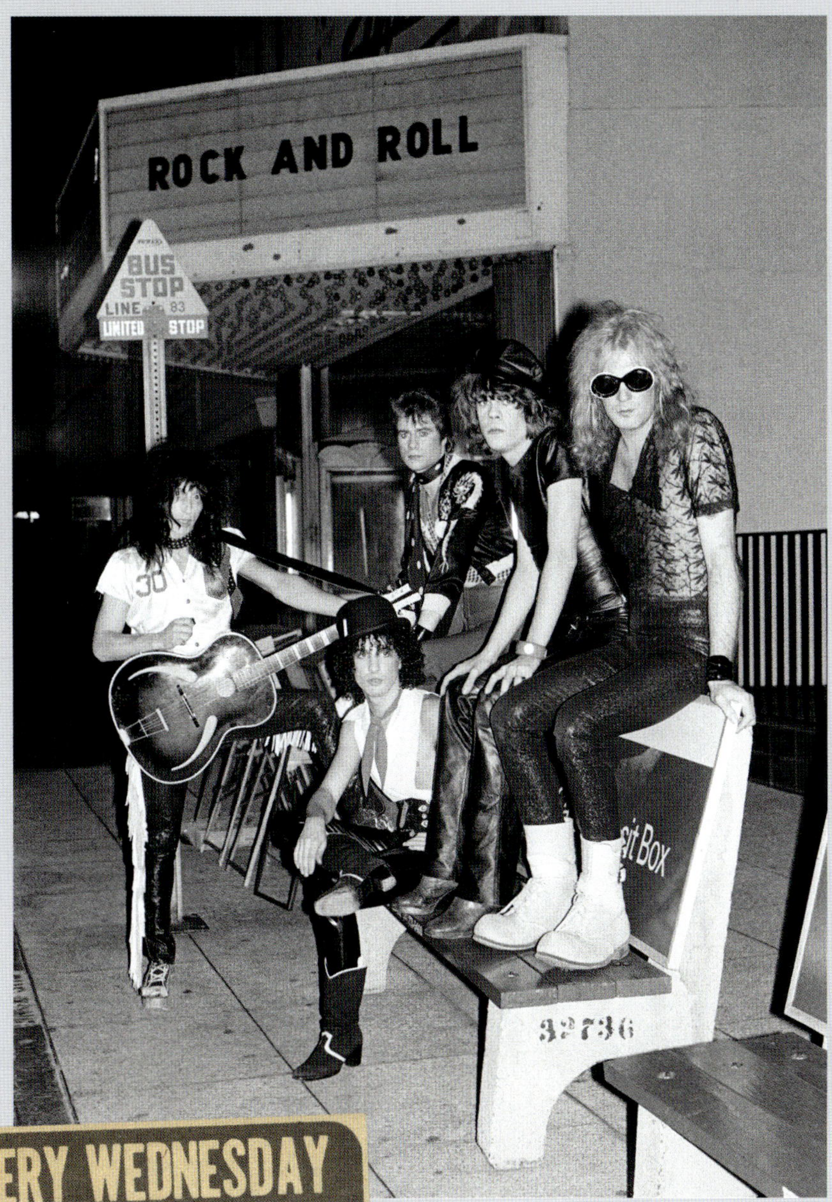

LIVE ROCK EVERY WEDNESDAY

this Wed. April 17 — NEW YORK DOLLS

next Wed. April 24 — TEENAGE LUST plus PALACE

Dancing***Drinking***Live D.J. 7-days-a-week

CLUB-82 — 82 East 4 Street (2 Avenue) (212) 677-3020

1.15. (*Above*) New York Dolls, 1974. Photo: © Bob Gruen.

1.16. (*Left*) Ad for Live Rock Wednesdays at Club 82, in the *Village Voice*, April 18, 1974.

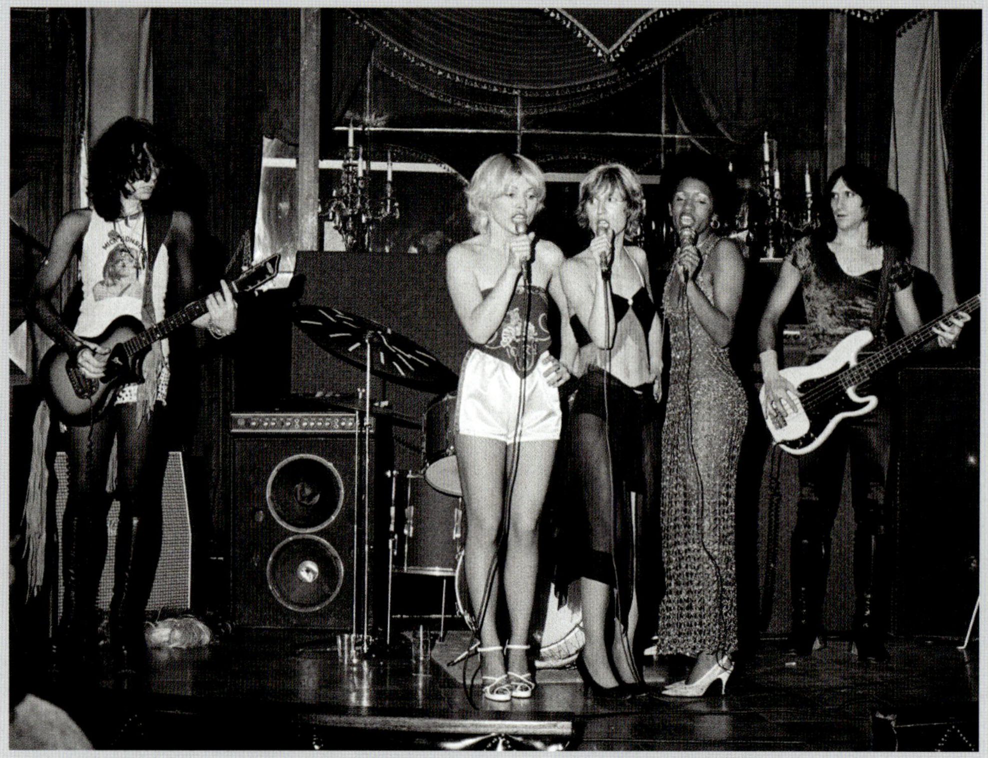

1.17. The Stillettoes in 1974. *Left to right*, Chris Stein, Debbie Harry, Elda Gentile, Amanda Jones, and Fred Smith; *not pictured*, Billy O'Connor on drums. Photo: © Bob Gruen.

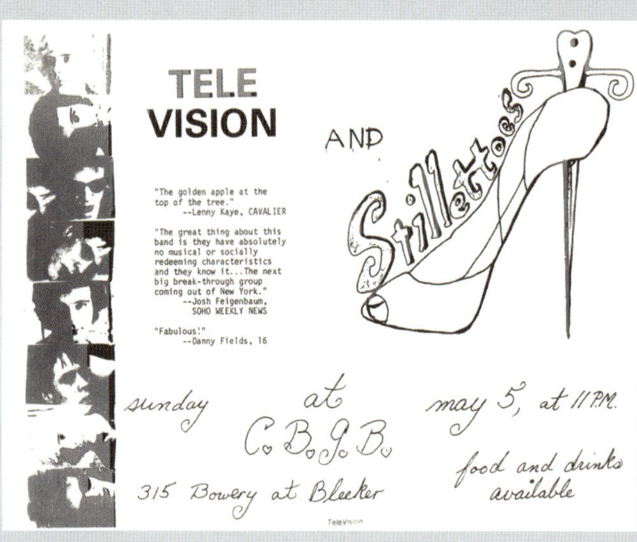

1.18. (*Above*) Flyer for Television and Stillettoes show at CBGB, May 1974.

1.19. (*Right*) Flyer for Blondie with the Banzai Babies (aka Blondie and the Bonzai Babies) at Hilly's (aka CBGB), circa 1975.

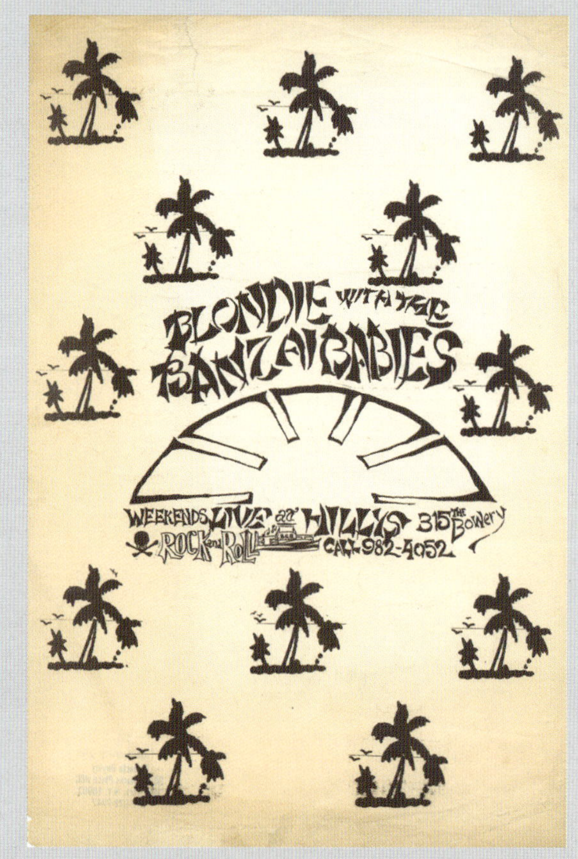

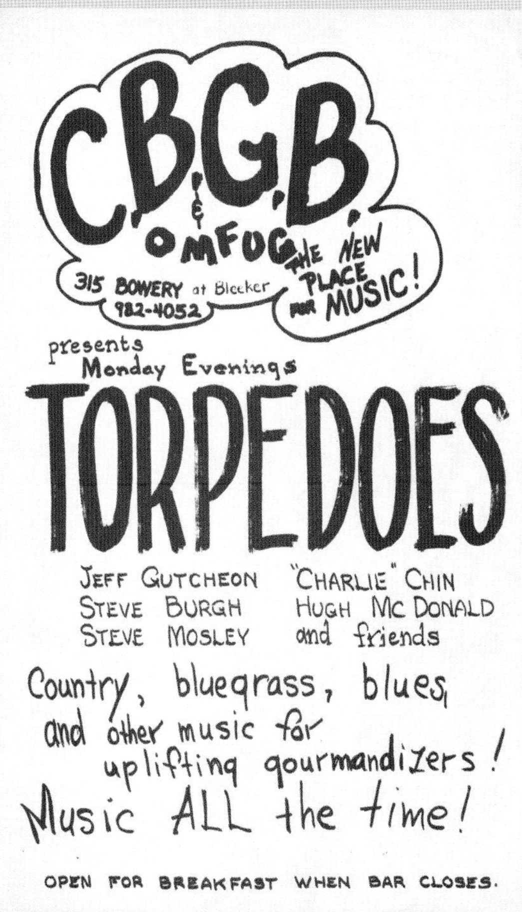

1.20. Early flyer announcing CBGB-OMFUG, December 1973.

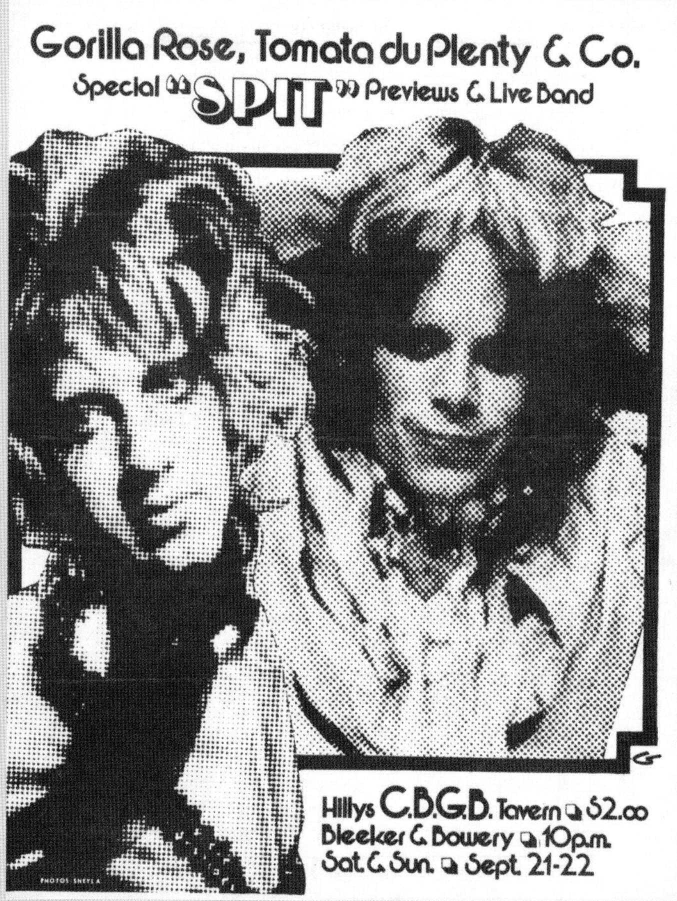

1.21. Flyer for Hollywood Spit show at CBGB, September 1974.

We had a bunch of people we used to work with frequently who were into gender bending. I don't know if they really had a name as a troupe. It was three guys and a girl, Fayette Hauser, one of the founders of the Cockettes in San Francisco. She worked with these three guys, Gorilla Rose and Tomata du Plenty, who later was in the Screamers, and another kid named Screaming Orchid. Those were their drag names. I did videos with them very early, in 1971, '72, I guess—before I met Debbie. Me and my buddy, Joey Freeman, who was an early Warhol person, we did a cable TV show [Hollywood Spit]. They'd do this weird drag comedy stuff. We did a few shows with them at CBGBs too. —Chris Stein

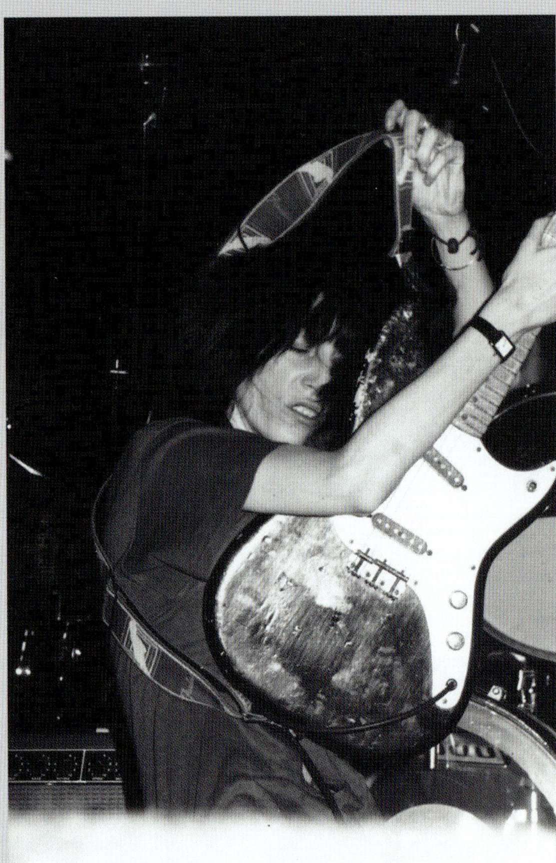

1.22. Patti Smith, circa 1978. Photo: Copyright Jimmy DeSana Trust. Courtesy of the Jimmy DeSana Trust and P·P·O·W, New York.

true life presents
TELEVISION

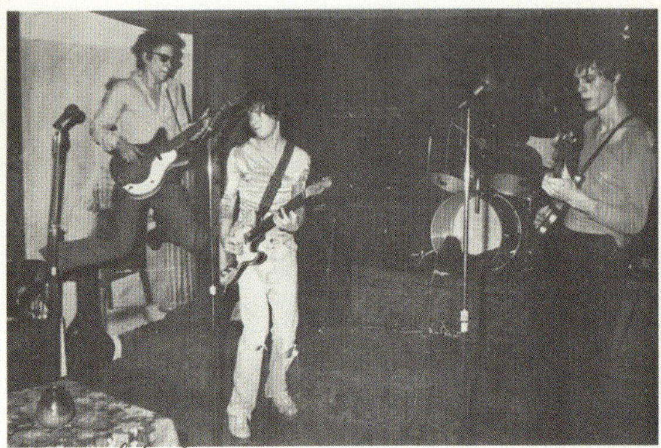

...PROVE IT
LOVE (COMES) IN SPURTS
(I LOOK AT YOU AND GET A) DOUBLE EXPOSURE
MARQUEE MOON
(THE ARMS OF) VENUS DE MILO
HARD ON LOVE
(I BELONG TO THE) BLANK GENERATION
FRICTION...

at C.B.G.B.'s
315 Bowery at Bleecker 982-4052
for four weekends
In January: Sunday 12th; Fri., Sat., Sun., the 17th, 18th & 19th; Fri., Sat., Sun., the 24th, 25th & 26th. Plus Sunday Febr. 2nd. At 10:00 & 12:00 with guest bands.

1.23. Flyer for eight-show residency in January and February 1975; designed and autographed by Richard Hell. Copyright © 1975 Richard Hell, used by permission.

"I guess I write in order to fulfill the primal need for artificial respiration.
Like myself, my poetry is so alive it stinks.
I don't have a birthday, I don't like movies,
I've dwindled my hopes down to a Puerto Rican deaf mute.
I do enjoy being dwindled. In fact I've just dwindled away the spic.
I think mysticism really sucks.
I'm the twentieth century --
I *am* interested in myself.
No I'm not"

I can think of no introduction to the work of Theresa Stern that would please her. She is the only person I have interviewed who didn't welcome the publicity. All I can say is that the outlook of her poetry is at once disgusted and impersonal, but she denies her sincerity with conviction.

I sought her out because she seemed to be the most alienated woman in America. Rumour held her to be a Puerto Rican hooker now living off welfare in a Hoboken tenement. I didn't believe this although I should have. Known only to a small cult following she didn't give interviews and she didn't want company. I was impressed by this uncompromising seclusion and I wanted to invade it. After all, curiosity is a basic human instinct. Ask Pandora.

I learned that five year years ago Theresa met publisher Richard Meyers in a New York bar. They became friends and he encouraged her to write. The result was '*Wanna Go Out?*', seventeen poems published by Dot Books in 1973.
Since then she has written an article on the Heartbreakers for New York Rocker and abandoned a novel Thin Skin. Some months ago I sent Theresa a copy of Punk and she was favourably impressed. As she has no phone, all my enquiries were directed through Richard Meyers: I would like to thank him for his tactful negotiations which led to an interview in early March.

I was nervous. What do you say to a woman who seems to be looking out at the world from behind six inches of plate glass?

THERESA STERN

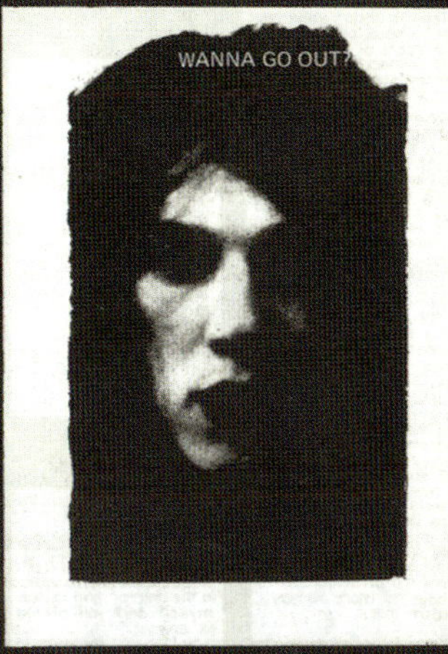

INTERVIEW BY MARY HARRON

LETTERIN LISA SHANOR

"The cars wish by my window.
They want the moon gleams on their chrome
to be gazed at more tenderly.
They are tired of divorce,
of drunken wrecks, they'd *rather*
not be driven at all
in the same way that souls in the astral plane
now.
would prefer not to enter bodies, and metaphors
don't want to be in language."

Anyway, in person most writers are a disappointment, and I cherish my illusions. In the dingy entranceway I checked the mailboxes for her name, as if the handwriting would give me some clue to her personality. The hallway was unlit, filled with muffled arguments and the sound of babies crying. Then a door opened and I saw a girl with heavy black hair. To my surprise, she shook my hand.

We settled down in her living room, lit by as much sun as can seep through two tenement buildings.

"Theresa, I know this is a very predictable question, but I'd like to start by asking you about your literary influences - and how and why you started writing."

"I started writing because it was so easy. I saw all this writing being praised and I knew I could do better with a splitting headache on the subway at rush hour. Most poets are such bullshitters -- they have so many vested interests, from keeping their associate professorships to keeping their self-respect, whereas I have hardly any interests at all (laughter). As for influences -- my favorite poet of the century is Breton. Infinitely passionate, profound and incorruptible, and whats more he's the smartest guy I ever came across and his poetry doesn't make any sense."

15

1.24. (*Above*) Punk no. 4, page 15 (first page of a two-page interview with Theresa Stern by Mary Harron. © 2023 by PUNK Magazine Inc.; and © 1976 Richard Hell, used by permission.

Theresa Stern

Finally I was born, the first poet
not removed from human life by even
the slightest trace of a personality.
The sensation of being read by one of my
poems has now completely supplanted
the banal nostalgia produced in the reader
by the best poetry created before me.

This is Theresa's newest poem. If you want to use some of her stuff please print this one and you can take a couple from the book as well if you want but let me know which ones you want before its' too late. Be sure to say that one is new and the others are from the book. Say that the book consists of 17 poems and that there are only a few left (at the same price and address as in issue #4). Thanks

Richard

1.25. (*Right*) Typescript poem of Theresa Stern on page also containing handwritten note from Richard Hell to the editors of Punk. Copyright © 1976 Richard Hell used by permission.

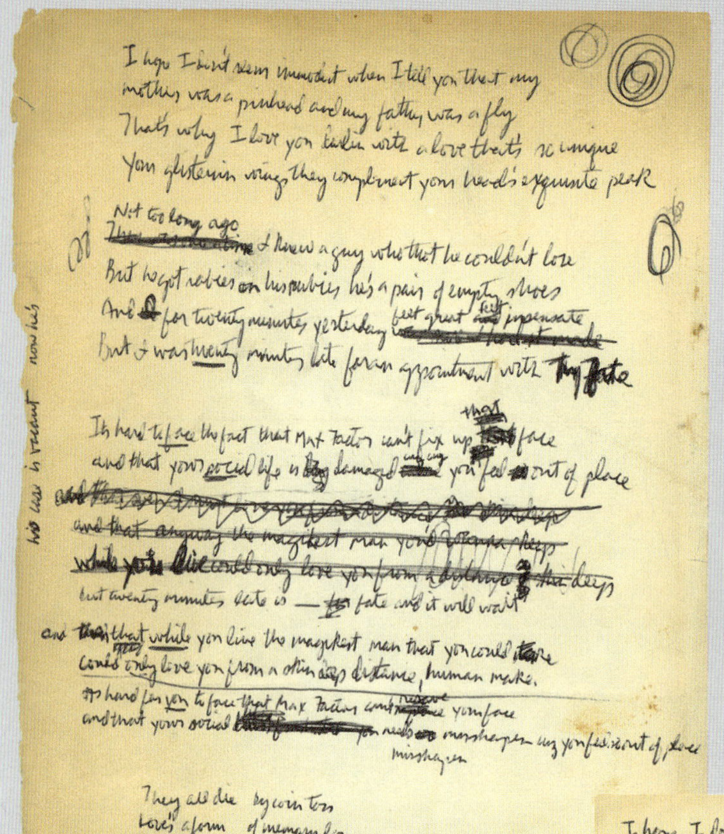

I hope I don't seem immodest when I tell you that my
mother was a pinhead and my father was a fly
That's why I love you darlin with a love that's so unique
Your glistenin wings they complement your head's exquisite peak

Not too long ago I knew a guy who thought he couldn't lose
But he got rabies on his rubies he's a pair of empty shoes
And I for twenty minutes yesterday felt great felt immensate
But I was twenty minutes late for an appointment with my fate

It's hard to face the fact that Max Factor can't fix up that face
and that your social life is damaged anyway you feel out of place
[illegible]
but twenty minutes late is — fate and it will wait
and that while you live the magikest man that you could [illegible]
could only love you from a distance, human make.
It's hard for you to face that Max Factor can't [illegible] your face
and that your social [illegible] needs misshapen anyway you feel out of place

They all die by coin toss
Love's a form of memory loss
I can't forget that triple cross
And I for twenty minutes yesterday felt great felt immensate
But that just means I'm twenty late to work and [illegible] my fate
But that just means I'm 20 minutes late to meet my fate

1.26–1.29. Four drafts of "You Gotta Lose" by Richard Hell, circa 1975. Copyright © 1975 Richard Hell, used by permission.

The "Gotta Lose" drafts are probably early 1975, just when I quit Television and signed on with the Heartbreakers. The music/backing tracks come from a song I wrote for Television ("High Heeled Wheels") but rewrote (different lyrics and melody) as "You Gotta Lose" for the Heartbreakers.
—Richard Hell

I hope I don't seem immodest when I tell you that my
mother was a pinhead and my father was a fly
that's why I love you darlin with a love that's so unique
Your glistenin wings they complement your head's exquisite peak

They all die by coin toss
Love's a form of memory loss
I can't forget that triple cross

You gotta lose
You gotta lose

Not too long ago I knew a guy who [illegible] he can't be beat
But he got rabies on his rubies [illegible]
And I for twenty minutes yesterday felt great felt immensate
But that just meant I'm twenty minutes late to meet my fate
(chorus) But when you're 20 minutes late your fate is and will wait

It's hard for you to face the fact that Max Factor [illegible] your face
And that your social needs misshapen anyway you feel out of place
And that the magikest man you'd make [illegible] to keep
Still could only love you from a distance (one man deep)

(chorus)
(first verse)
(chorus)

you gotta lose
you hafta lose
you always lose
You gotta lose
You gotta lose
You gotta lose
You gotta lose

I hope I don't seem immodest when I tell you that my
Mother was a pinhead and my father was a fly
That's why I love you darlin with a love that's so unique
Your glistenin wings they complement your head's exquisite peak

They all die — by coin toss
Love's a form — of memory loss
I can't forget — that triple cross

You gotta lose
You gotta lose

Not too long ago I knew this guy who sure he can't be beat water wings
But he got rabies on his rubies, unless [illegible]
And I for twenty minutes yesterday felt great, felt insensate
But when you're twenty minutes late your fate is patient, and will wait

(chorus)

It's hard for you to face the fact that Max Factor failed your face
And that your social need's misshapen cuz-cuz you feel out of place
And that the most magic man you'd take and ask your soul to keep
Still could only love you from a distance (one man deep)

(chorus)
(first verse)
(chorus –)
you gotta lose
you hafta lose
you always lose
you gotta lose
you gotta lose
you gotta lose
you gotta lose

I hope I don't seem immodest when I tell you that my
mother was a pinhead and my father was a fly
that's why I love you darlin with a love that's so unique
Your glistenin wings they complement your head's exquisite peak

They all die — by coin toss
Love's a form — of memory loss
I can't forget — that triple cross

you gotta lose
you gotta lose

Not too long ago I knew a guy who thot he couldn't lose
But he got rabies on his rubies he's a pair of empty shoes
And I for twenty minutes yesterday felt great felt insensate
But I was twenty minutes late for an appointment with my fate

It's hard for you to face [illegible] Max Factor can't [illegible] your face
and that your social life's damaged cuz-cuz you feel out of place
and that while you live the magikest man that you could pick
could still love you only from a distance human thick
[illegible]
still could only love you from a distance one man deep

(first verse)
(chorus)

you gotta lose
you hafta lose
you always lose
you gotta lose
you gotta lose
you gotta lose
you gotta lose

It's hard for you to face the fact that Max Factor lost your face
And that your social need's misshapen cuz you feel so out of place
and that the magikest man you'd make yours for keeps
still could only love you from a distance one man deep

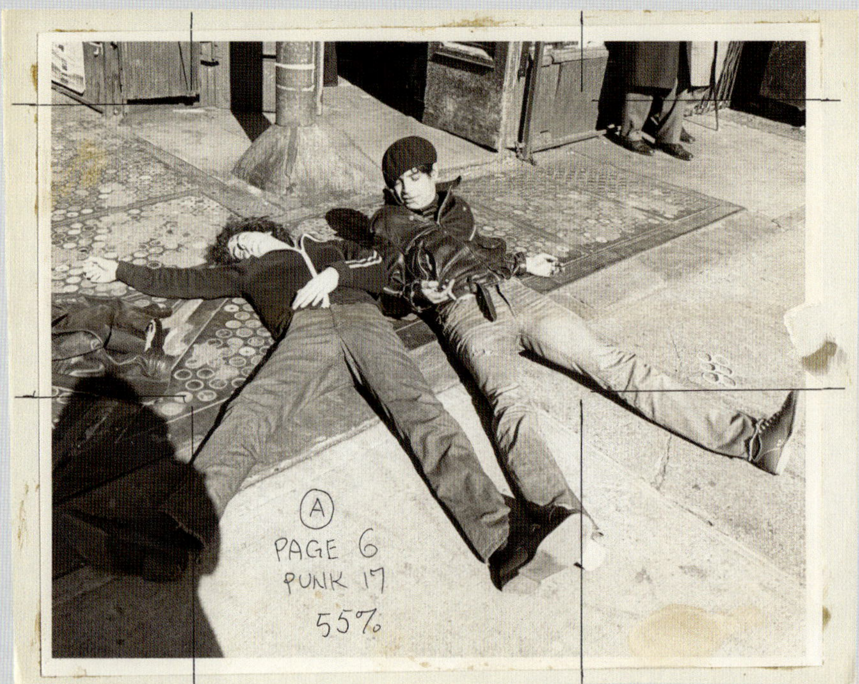

1.31. Original photo of Suicide (Alan Vega and Martin Rev) for a fumetti called "The Tang Connection" in Punk no. 10, Summer 1977. Photo: © Roberta Bayley.

1.30. Flyer for Dead Boys official fan club, circa 1977–78.

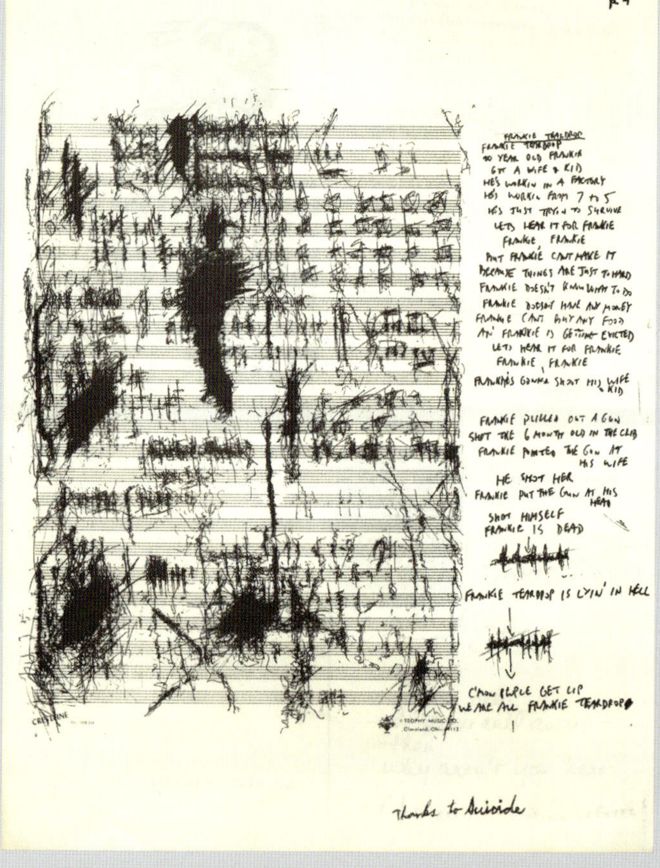

1.32. Fictional score for Suicide's "Frankie Teardrop" in Tuesday Night zine September 1977.

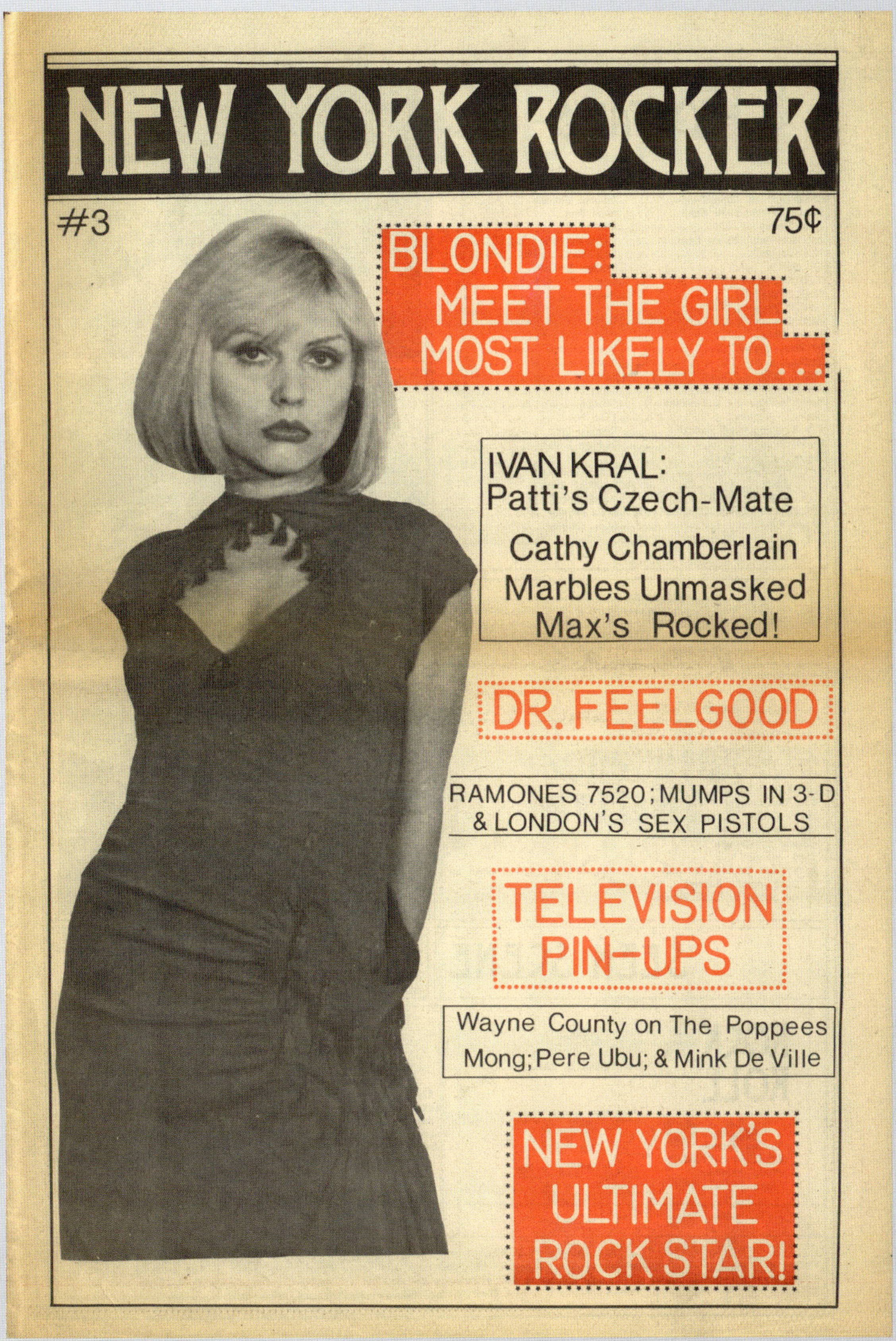

NEW YORK ROCKER

#3

75¢

BLONDIE: MEET THE GIRL MOST LIKELY TO...

IVAN KRAL: Patti's Czech-Mate

Cathy Chamberlain

Marbles Unmasked

Max's Rocked!

DR. FEELGOOD

RAMONES 7520; MUMPS IN 3-D & LONDON'S SEX PISTOLS

TELEVISION PIN-UPS

Wayne County on The Poppees

Mong; Pere Ubu; & Mink De Ville

NEW YORK'S ULTIMATE ROCK STAR!

1.33. *New York Rocker* no. 3, May 1976. Photo: Lisa Jane Persky.

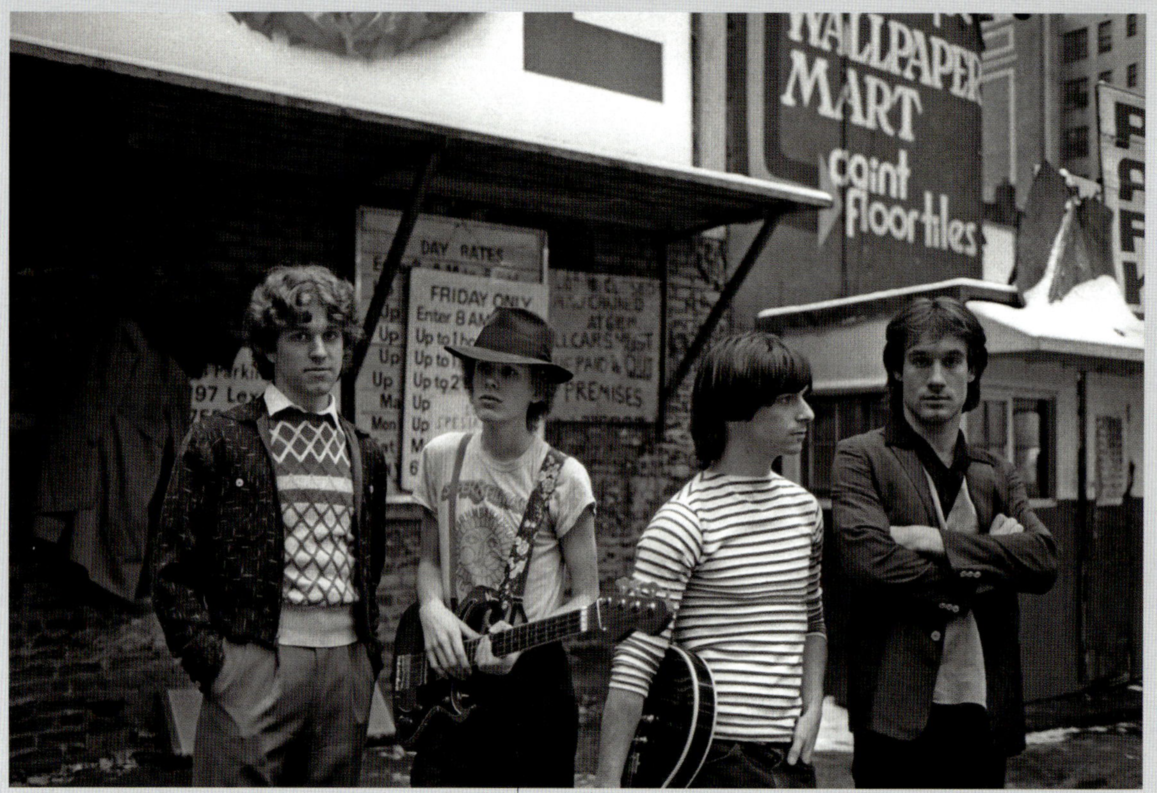

1.34. (*Above*) Photo of the Mumps in New York City, 1975. *Left to right*, Kristian Hoffman, Kevin Kiely, Rob Duprey, and Lance Loud. Photo: Lisa Jane Persky.

1.35. (*Right*) Mumps fanzine no. 3, circa 1977.

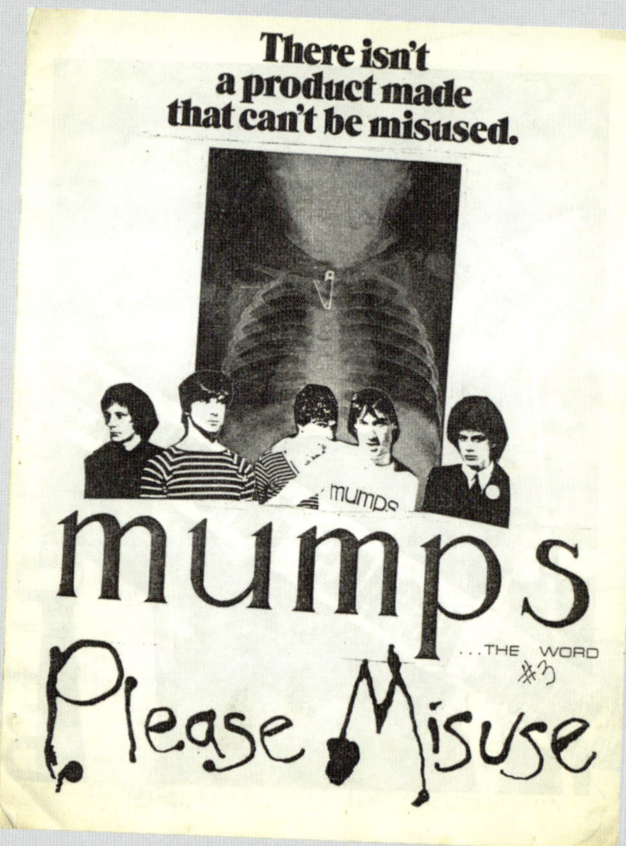

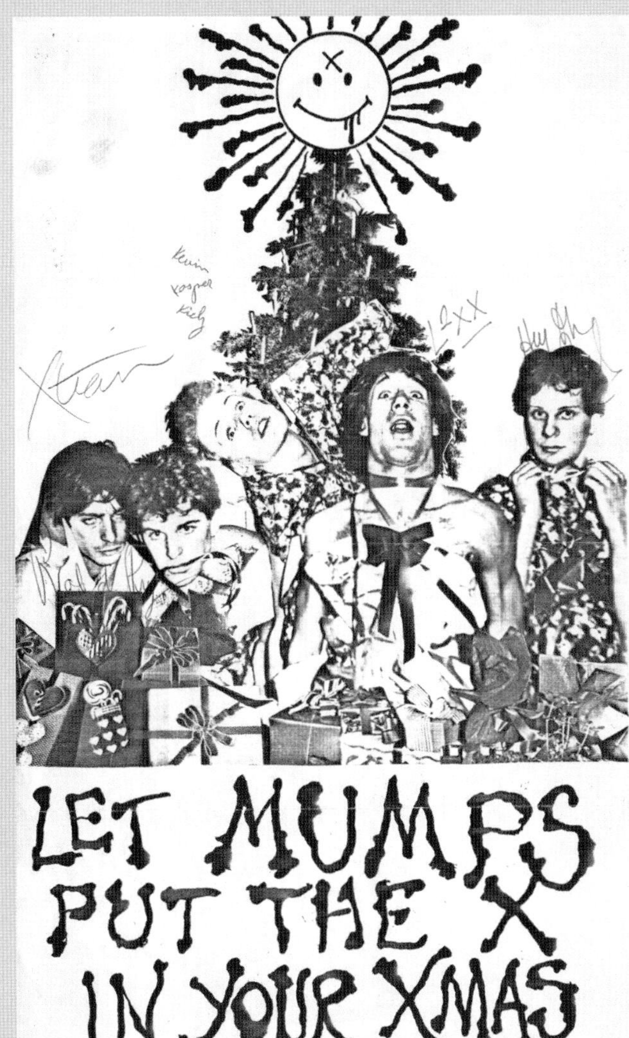

1.36. Mumps autographed flyer, circa 1977.

Mumps had such great songs. There really was an audience for them, but it wasn't that audience. And the Miamis were similar. And the Marbles, too. Clever, interesting, poppy.
—Lisa Jane Persky

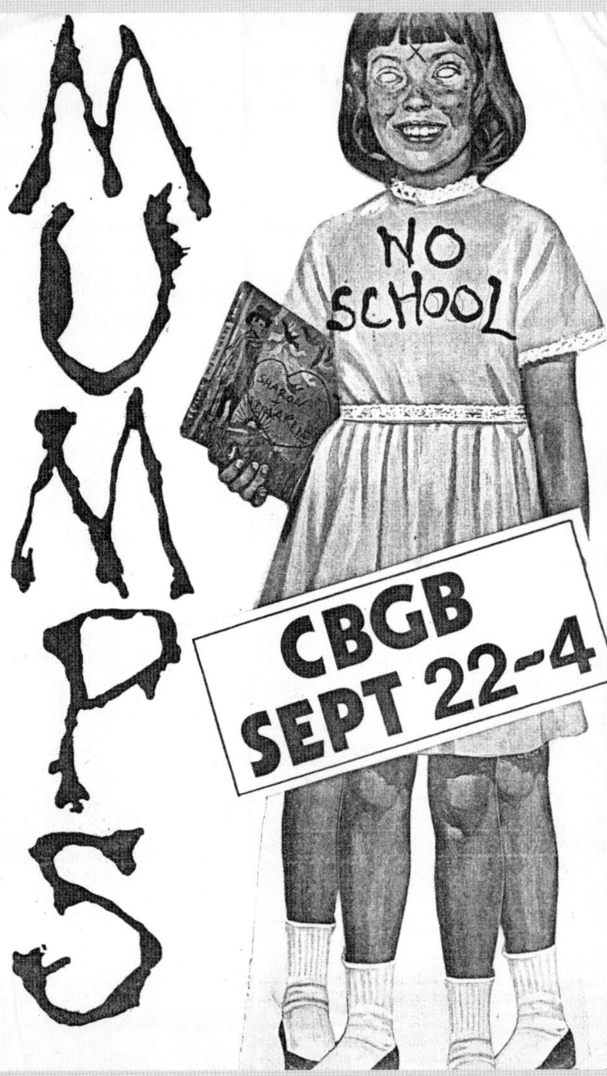

1.37. Flyer for Mumps shows at CBGB, September 1977.

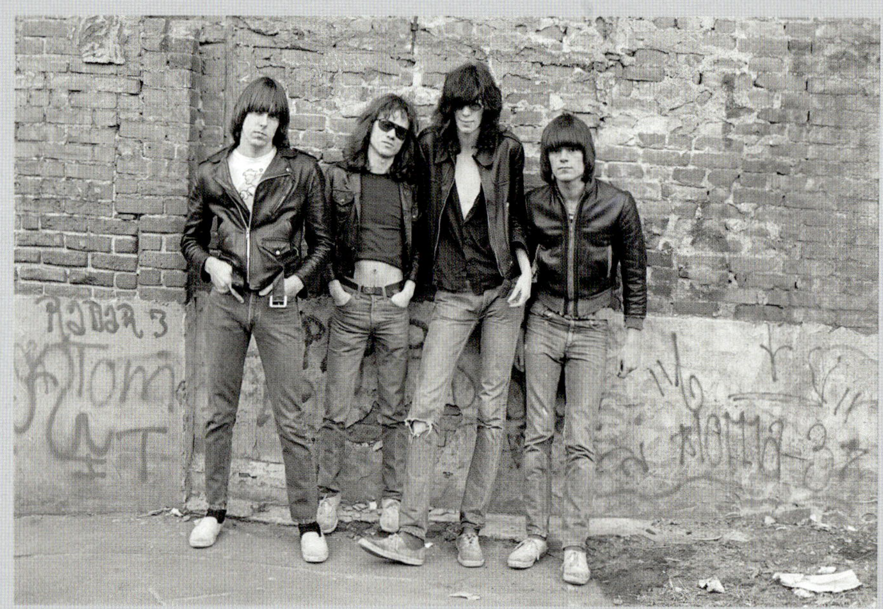

1.38. Photo of the Ramones used for their first album, 1976. Photo: © Roberta Bayley.

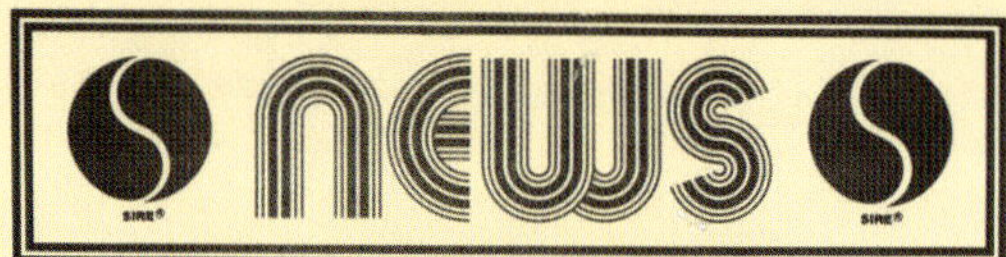

165 WEST 74 TH STREET · NEW YORK, N.Y. 10023 · (212) 595-5500

APRIL RELEASE

THE RAMONES SASD 7520

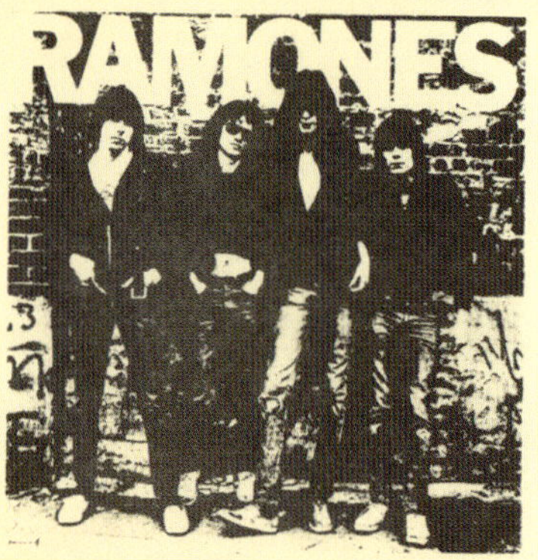

There have been many young groups who have tried, without much success, to translate the sound of "punk rock" on to disc. The Ramones, who have been a live phenomenon on the New York rock scene for over a year, succeed. Perhaps the best known of the bands that play the Max's Kansas City/CBGB's circuit, The Ramones combine high level energy rock and roll with simplistic lyrics and spit-fire enthusiasm. The pulsating beat of their music which never falters, even during their ballad "I Wanna Be Your Boyfriend" drives you from song to song. Though each tune on the album is a concise two minutes(some slightly more, some slightly less) the fourteen tracks take on the power of an approaching artillery fire. Containing some of the best material from their live act, the album boasts songs including: "Beat On The Brat," "Judy Is A Punk," "I Don't Wanna Go Down To The Basement," "53rd & 3rd", "Loudmouth," and their soon to be released single "Blitzkreig Bop." This band has already received an unorthodox amount of press for a previously unsigned band, including Rolling Stone, Creem, Circus, The Village Voice and the English papers New Musical Express and Melody Maker. The critics who have heard the album are already heralding it as one of the most important releases of 1976. With careful concentration in key markets including New York, Boston, Cleveland, Detroit and Memphis, The Ramones could equal or surpass the sales interest now garnered by Kiss, Aerosmith and Black Sabbath.

1.39. Sire News sheet from the press kit for the Ramones, April 1976.

**Arturo would go to the Eagle's Nest, and the Eagle's Nest T-shirt had this big eagle on it. He was thinking about that in terms of the Ramones, and the leather jacket. The Eagle's Nest was a leather club. Best fucking club. That's where the Ramones logo came from.
—Lisa Jane Persky**

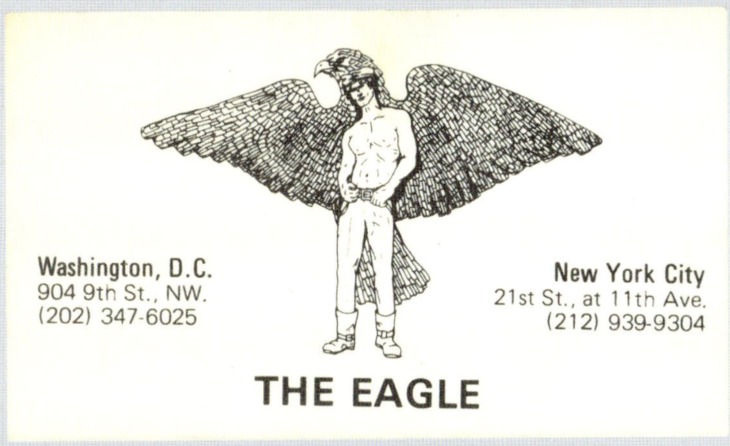

1.41. Business card for the Eagle (aka the Eagle's Nest), early 1970s.

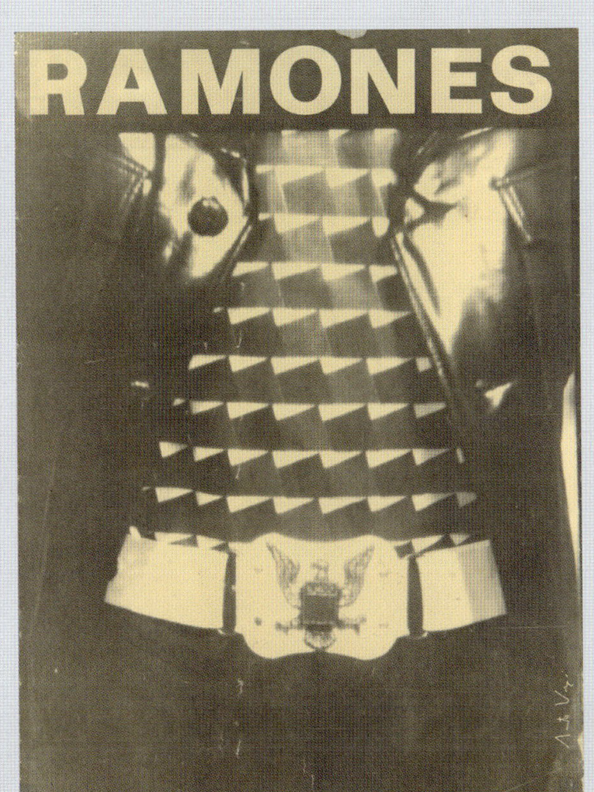

1.40. Ramones poster by Arturo Vega, circa 1975.

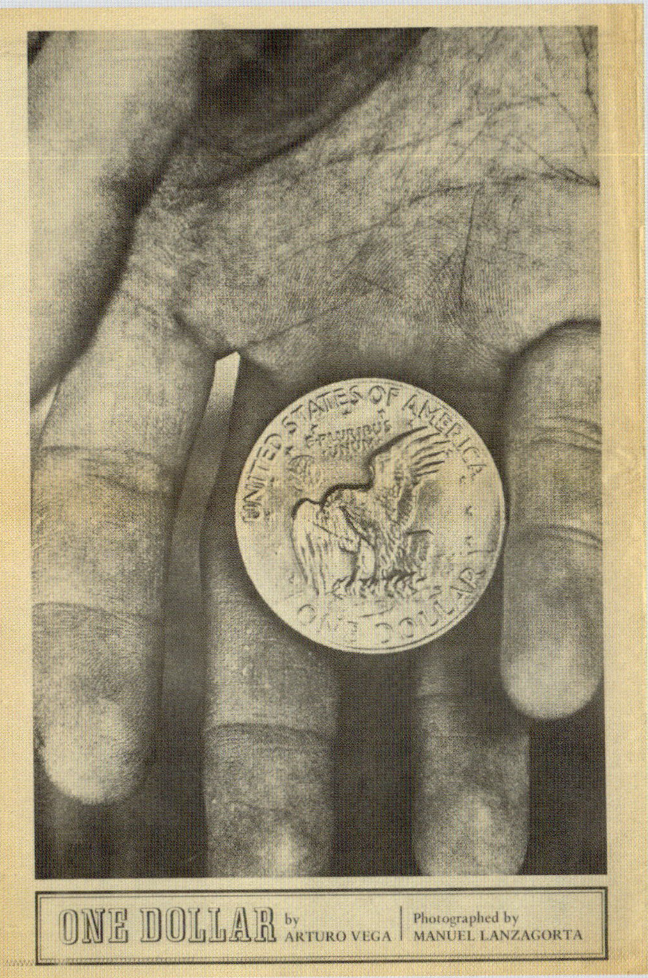

1.42. Back page of *New York Rocker* no. 3, May 1976.

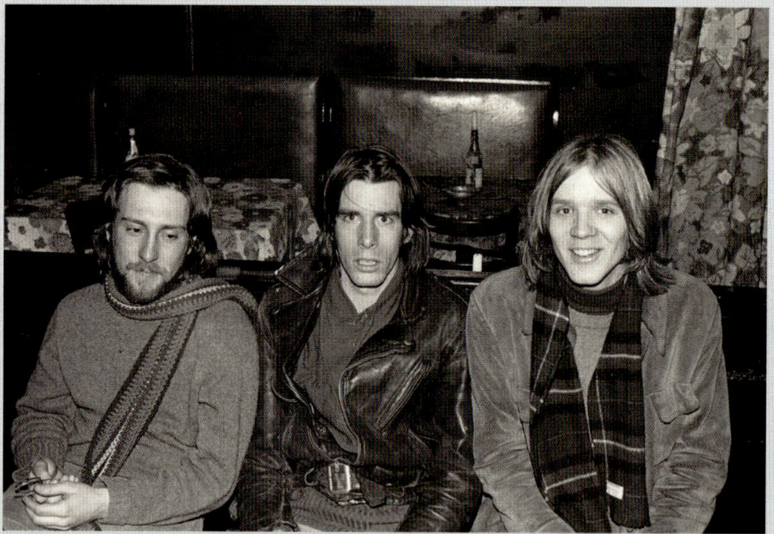

1.43. (*Above*) Founders of Punk at CBGB, 1976. *Left to right*, Ged Dunn, Legs McNeil, John Holmstrom. Photo: © Roberta Bayley.

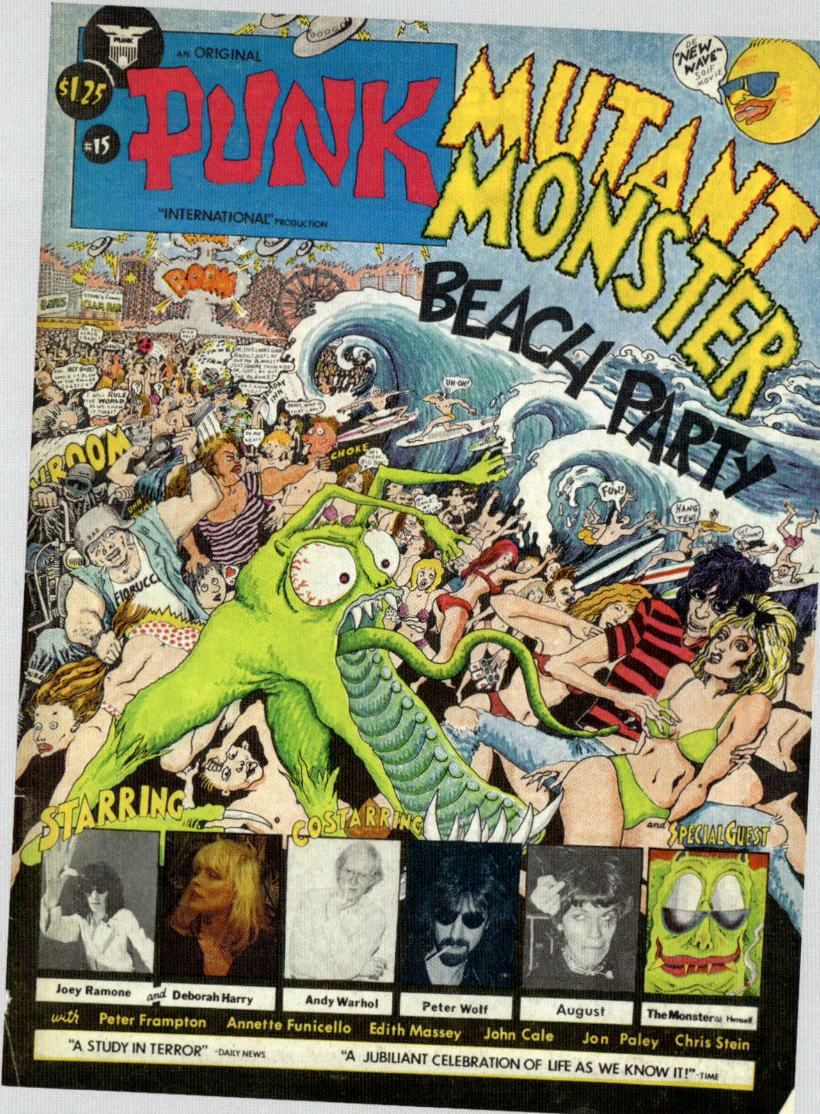

1.44. (*Right*) Mutant Monster Beach Party / Punk no. 15, cover. © 2023 by PUNK Magazine Inc.

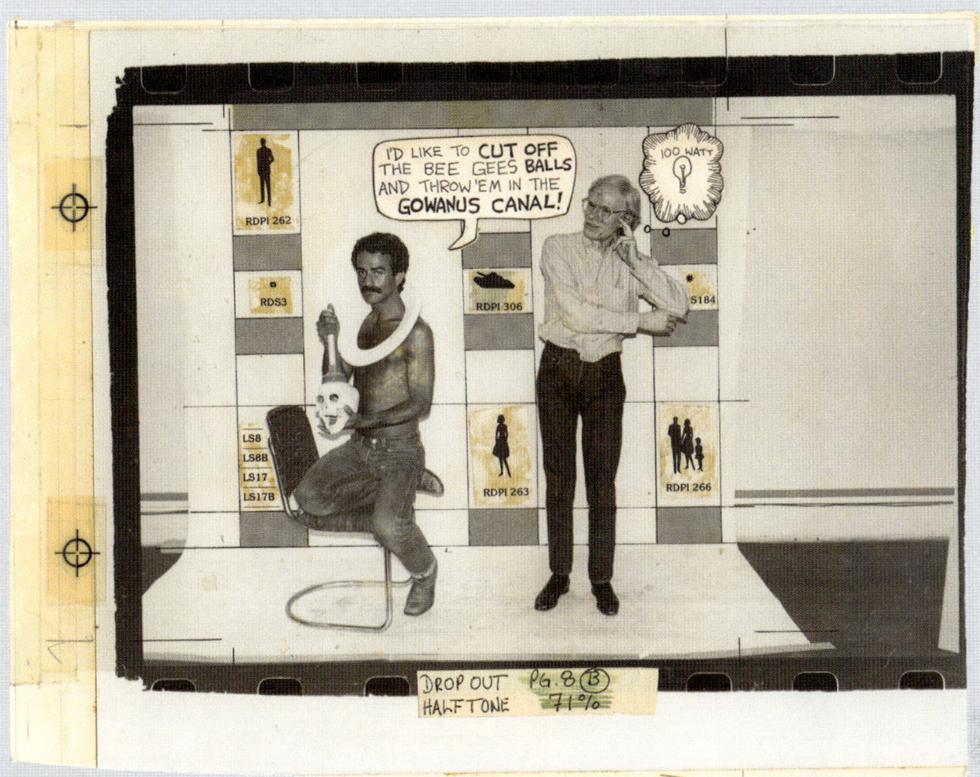

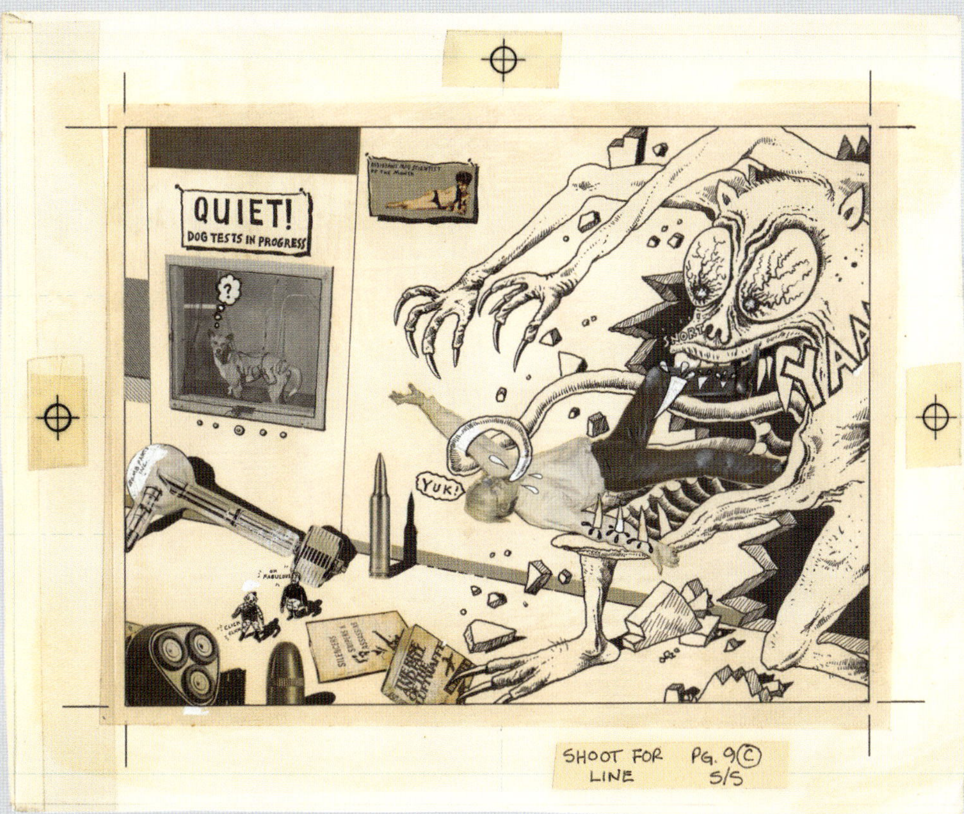

1.45 and 1.46. Pasteup pages for Mutant Monster Beach Party / Andy Warhol images.

THUR JULY 7 FRI JULY 8

TalkingHeads

with GUEST NEW WAVE BAND

ERASERS

VILLAGE GATE Bleeker at Thompson

1.47. Flyer for Talking Heads and Erasers show at Village Gate, July 1977.

This was not a safe space, let me put it that way. There were people getting damaged through either a lot of drug use or just pushed aside. My friend Susan Springfield, she had a band, the Erasers, and there's no reason why her band shouldn't have been signed. What I'm saying is, they're very strong women, a great band, and they're still in the place of being brushed aside. —Sylvia Reed

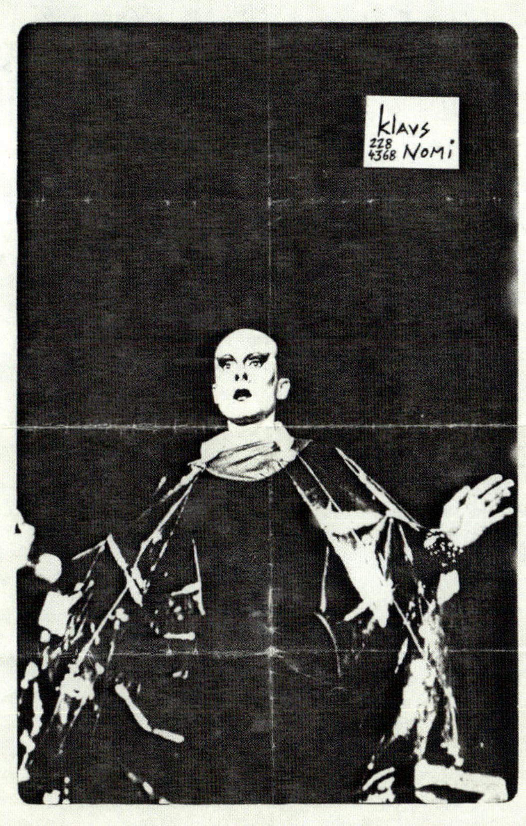

1.48 and 1.49. Klaus Nomi flyer with list of operas and arias on the back (handwriting unknown; possibly performance set list), circa 1978.

1 Turandot / Puccini aria "In questa Reggia"
transposed a third?

2 The Ring / Wagner Reinmaidens ~~turned~~ "warning" earthas Erda

3 Orfeo / Gluck O forro

4 Saint Saëns Samson + Delilah.

2 Rheinmaidens : opening: of beginning: water land fire gold maidens
extremely long echo.

5 organ Choral.

6 Air, If my complaints Could passions move.

John

7 Dido + Aeneas / Purcell

8 Don Giovanni opening

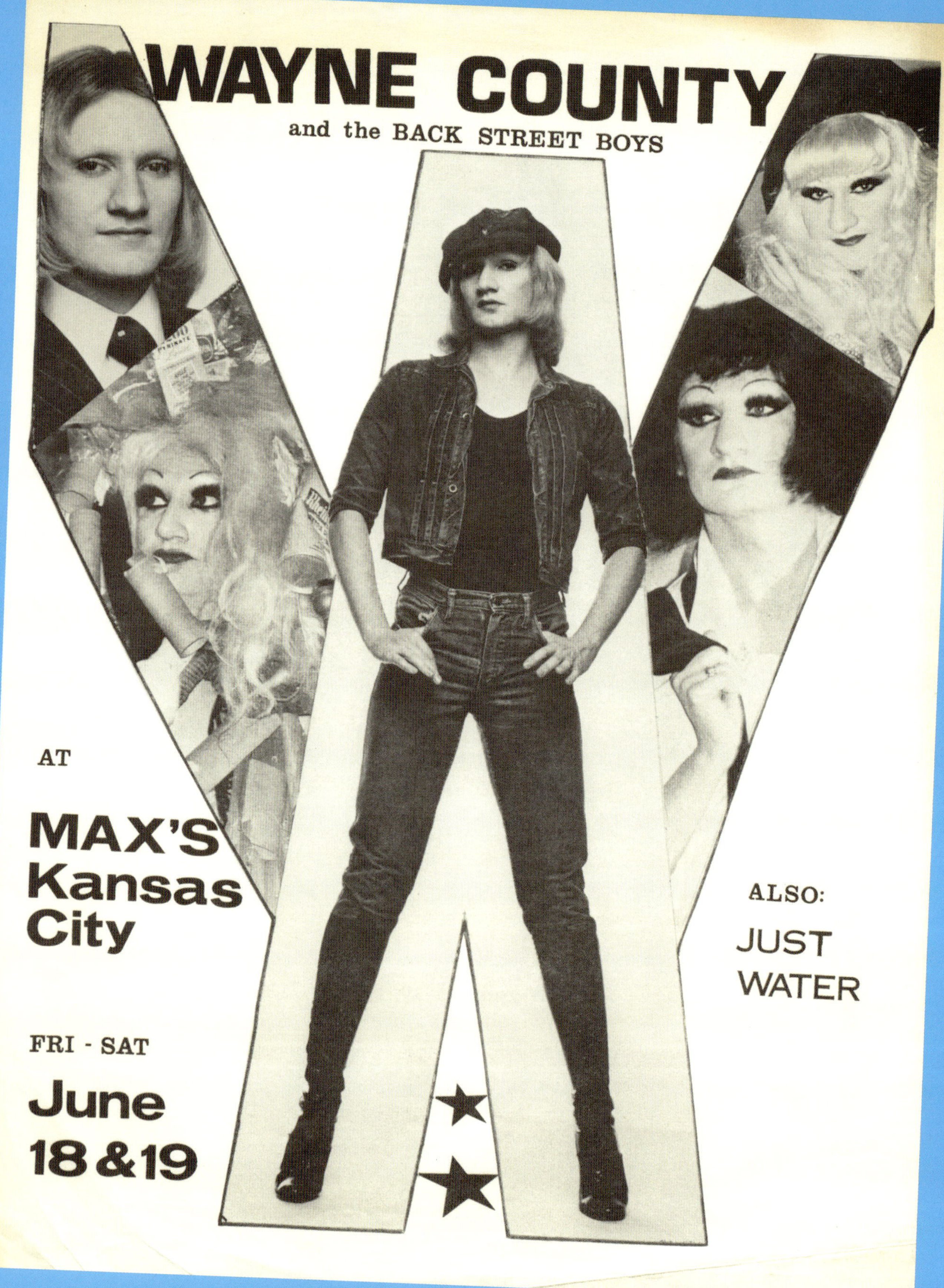

1.50. Wayne County and the Back Street Boys flyer, 1976.

CH. 3

"Punk was me onstage wrecking"

AN INTERVIEW WITH JAYNE COUNTY

Jayne County is a pioneer of the early punk era who brought an edgy, confrontational performance style from the queer community of Atlanta, Georgia, to the stages of New York, London, and Berlin. Moving to New York full-time in 1968, Jayne initially performed under the stage name Wayne County (a reference to the county of Detroit, home of Iggy Pop and the Stooges) and became active in the experimental Ridiculous Theatre movement alongside Warhol superstars Jackie Curtis and Holly Woodlawn and other proto and early punks like David Johansen, Patti Smith, and Debbie Harry. In 1972, Jayne formed her first band, Queen Elizabeth, fusing the queer camp of the Ridiculous plays with the raucous energy of a new gritty rock and roll that would become punk. In this interview, conducted on February 5, 2021, Jayne discusses the critical role music played in her youth, how to wreck on stage, and writing the first punk trans anthem.

JUDITH: Talk about the importance of music to your sense of self growing up, especially your interest in the Beatles and other British Invasion bands.

JAYNE: Music saved me, really. I was from a very small town and very conservative people. Things were rigid. Then the Beatles came along. They look so harmless today, but then when they came out, it was a big thing. In Atlanta, Georgia, they had laws on the books that if you were a boy and your hair touched the tip of your ears, you could be arrested for female impersonation. So when the Beatles happened, and all the boys started growing their hair, they couldn't enforce it anymore because people weren't trying to impersonate a female; they just had long hair, which was the fashion. But the police still used that law if they wanted to arrest someone for impersonating a female. Isn't that crazy?

JUDITH: That *is* crazy!

JAYNE: We've got some crazy laws. But music saved me really. It brought me out of my shell, more or less. And the Beatles and all the British Invasion bands, the Kinks particularly, they made me realize there's a whole other world out there and a whole other way of thinking. Another way of acting, another way of dressing: a whole new world. And it saved me from a life of staying in the South, or staying in the small town and slowly wasting away. Because I was creative, and if you're a creative person and you can't use your creativity, it wastes away. The Beatles, to me, were creative too, with the suits and the hairdos and the whole bit—all the other bands too. It brought me out of my shell. It really saved me from a mundane life. You know?

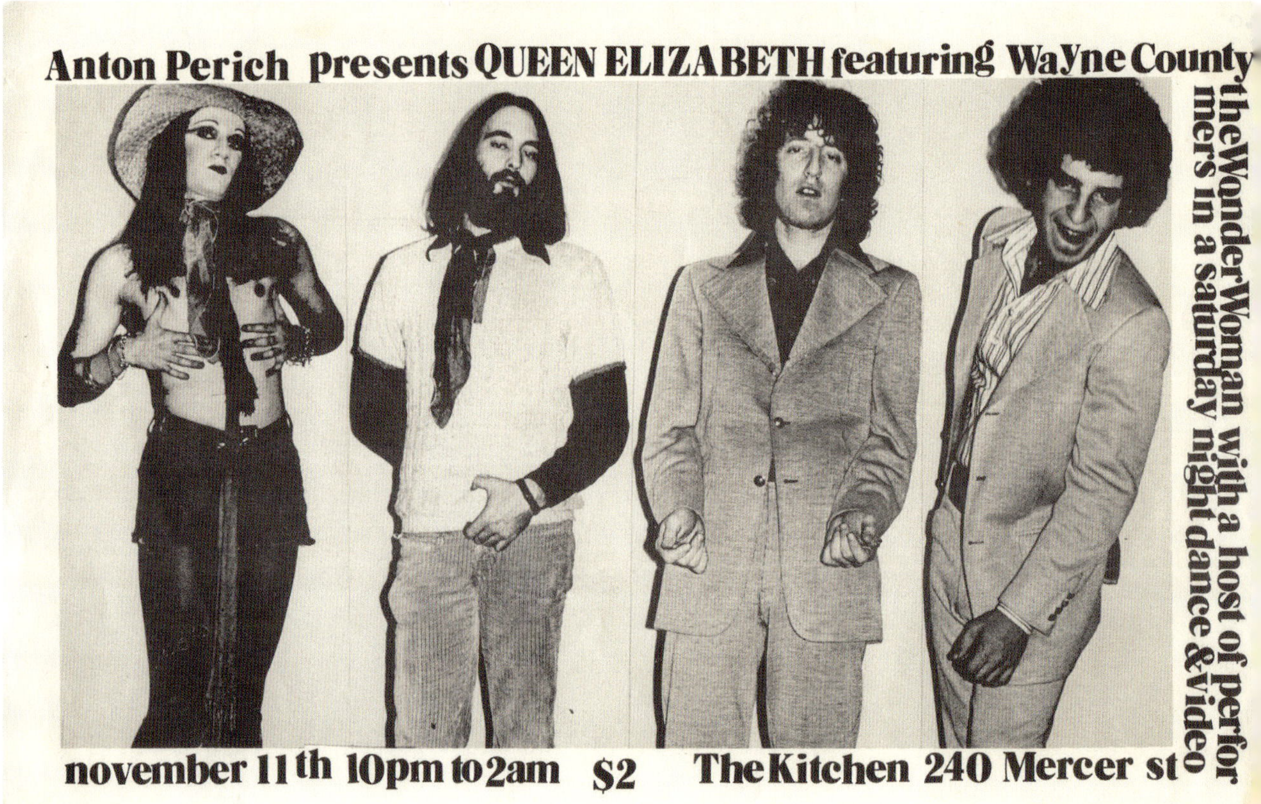

1.51. Flyer for Queen Elizabeth, circa 1973.

JUDITH: Yeah.

JAYNE: It really did. The Yardbirds, particularly, I *loved* the Yardbirds. My brother had an old guitar, and I'd try to make these psychedelic noises from his guitar, what I heard the Yardbirds doing. He thought I was crazy.

JUDITH: The Beatles were sometimes called queer in those days.

JAYNE: Yeah. In the South, people said, "Oh, those Beatles are queer. They've got long hair." Because up until that time, so-called queers or drag queens, or trans people and just gay people who are feminine, would grow their hair long because it was for certain reasons. So when the Beatles came along, a lot of people were like, "Oh, they're a bunch of queers" and stuff like that. "We're not going to let our children listen to them." When John Lennon said that the Beatles were more popular than Jesus, the Baptists got together and they burned all the Beatles records. They put a big pile of Beatles records up and set a big fire to them. Instead of book burning, Beatles burning. I remember that. But I had to break away from that place. I broke away from Georgia and everything, and left. I always look at the Beatles and the British Invasion for giving me the courage to do it. To take those steps to leave that whole life and start a new life for myself.

JUDITH: That's fascinating! I have a question about your early days and what you've described elsewhere as "wrecking." Can you explain what that is? Did wrecking relate to punk for you?

JAYNE: It did. Punk was me onstage wrecking, really. Wrecking was . . . I was young and all the screaming queens that I used to hang out with weren't old enough to go into the bars and drink, so we had to think of things to do, so we would wreck. We'd get together, walk down the streets wrecking people. Screaming at cars, yelling out crazy things at people, really awful things like, "Oh, honey. I had him yesterday." "Oh, look at your boyfriend. Oh, you didn't tell me you had a girlfriend." Stuff like that. We would just wreck people. And if we were at the department store, we'd ride up and down the escalator, and we would *scream*. Sometimes we'd go into the women's department and hold the lingerie up and say really loud so everyone can hear, "Aw, he's just lovely in this." Just wrecking people's nerves. Wrecking them out of their normalcy.

Another wreck was a bunch of us would get together and go into the men's room at the Greyhound bus station, and we'd walk in and just start screaming, saying things like, "Oh, I see his wee-wee," and "Oh, he was in here last night with me," and all this kind of stuff. The guys would be freaking out, trying to zip themselves up.

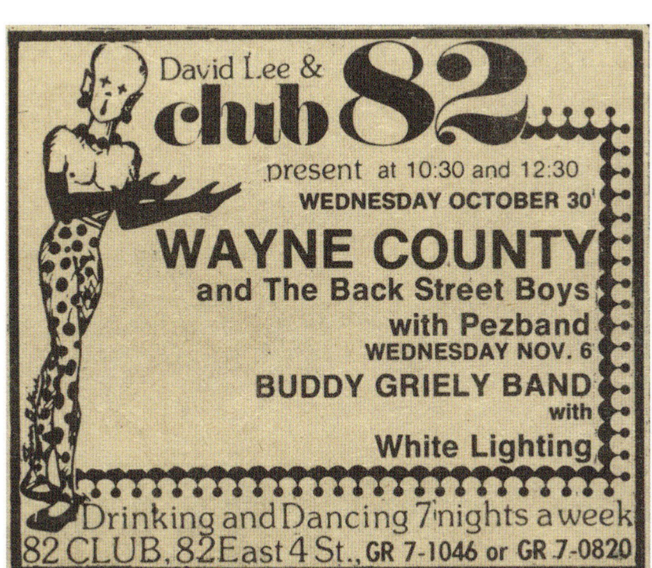

1.52. Ad for Club 82 in the *Village Voice*, 1974.

JUDITH: That's hilarious!

JAYNE: We just wanted to upset people. That was our way of saying, "Hey world, here we are! Take it or leave it!" That was our way of doing it.

JUDITH: That does sound like a punk attitude.

JAYNE: It was, I think. Then when I got to be onstage, I had a toilet, I had dildos. I had all sorts of things just to basically wreck people's nerves, and I purposely set out to upset people and shock them. I've always loved to shock people. I have fun doing it. It just tickles me pink. I did things like, sewed all my old wigs to a big, huge lampshade that I found at a thrift shop, and got under the lampshade, and sang a song called, "You Flip Your Wig," and after that my song "(If You Don't Want to Fuck Me, Baby) Fuck Off!" I used to do a lot of costume changes too. I used to come out as my twin sister Sharon County, and do a couple of country numbers. I used to have a makeshift dressing room on this corner of the stage at Max's. I'd go behind it and change costumes, come out and do something else.

It was nonstop wrecking people on the stage. People used to run out too. When we used to do the toilet thing, people got really upset and would leave and run out of the room. Couldn't take it. And I had Alpo dog food in the toilet. And I guess people were stupid enough to really think it was feces. I don't know. I took the dog food out. That used to wreck people like crazy.

JUDITH: [*laughing*] I bet.

JAYNE: People used to get really upset about that—*really* upset. People would say, "Don't listen to *her*." I'd say, "I'm a" whatever—I was Wayne then. I've had people go up to the stage and say, "Close your ears! Do not listen to this!"

JUDITH: Like you were the devil.

JAYNE: Yeah, like I'm the devil.

JUDITH: Do you think that the early punk scene in New York took some of that shock and confrontation from what was happening in the queer cabaret and theater scene and the drag queens?

JAYNE: Confrontation. That's a good word, confrontation. Yeah. A lot of it was. Drag queens in New York, they were very punky. I think that punk borrowed from a lot of sources, and I think it did borrow a lot from drag queens particularly. Particularly when those punk girls started doing their eyes, they used real thick eye makeup, like drag queens. Punk makeup was really very draggy, heavy makeup, heavy eyeliner like Siouxsie Sioux from the Banshees. I loved her eyes. It's kind of draggy.

JUDITH: You were in New York at the time of the Stonewall Riots in June 1969. Did they affect you?

JAYNE: Oh yeah. People just got fed up with the police hassling everyone. What they [the police] would do is they'd go into the clubs, the gay bars, and they would put the drag queens, or the trans people, behind the bar, and then a female police officer would lead the trans people, or the drag queens, lead them one by one into the women's room, and examine them and examine their genitals to see was you a male or female. The sex search. Somebody would come in and say, "I was at a raid and they did a sex search on me."

JUDITH: Wow. That's such a violation!

JAYNE: People were getting really fed up about the police coming in there. So we all started screaming and yelling, and marching up and down Christopher Street with our fists in the air yelling, "Gay power. Gay power." We'd go from Sixth Avenue to Fifth Avenue. We'd get to one end, turn around, and walk down it again. Just marching and yelling things, and some people set fire to trash cans and garbage, and got on top of some police cars and jumped up and down. I didn't, some queen did. I don't know which one. It might have been Miss Marsha [Marsha P. Johnson], I'm not sure.

But this was so long ago. It seems like another time, another world. It was 1969. I remember it, but it seems like it's some kind of film I saw or something. It's hard to believe I was a part of it, but I was. I have to step back sometimes and go, "Is that really me? Did I really do that?"

JUDITH: But that must have boosted the energy of the scene in some ways.

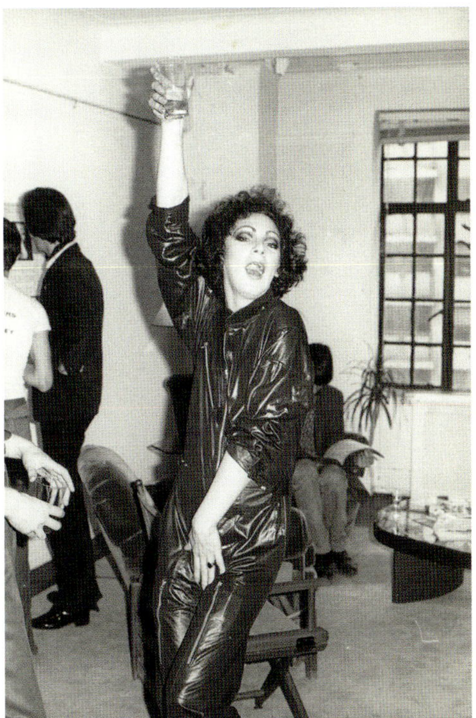

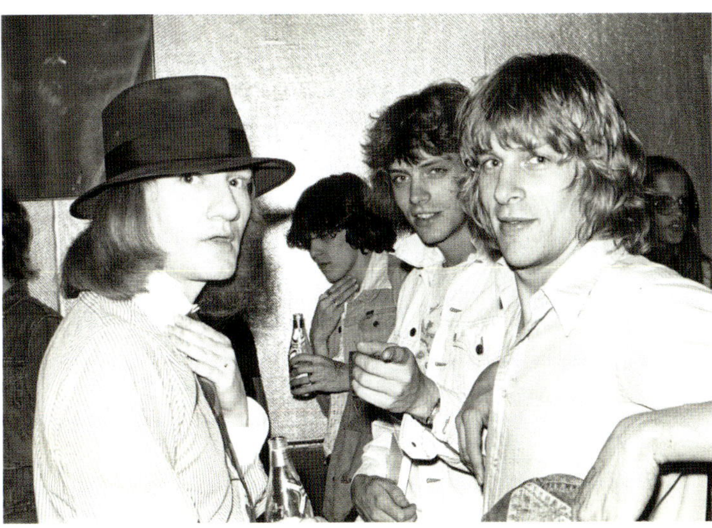

1.53. (*Left*) Holly Woodlawn, 1976. Photo: Copyright Jimmy DeSana Trust. Courtesy of the Jimmy DeSana Trust and P·P·O·W, New York.

1.54. (*Above*) Jayne County and the Paley Brothers (Jonathan and Andy), circa 1976. Photo: Leee Black Childers.

JAYNE: Oh, yeah. People had had enough, and they were rebelling.

JUDITH: You talk in your memoir *Man Enough to Be a Woman* about the influence of people like Jackie Curtis, Holly Woodlawn, and the Warhol crowd. Were they important to the different music scenes—glam and punk—that developed later?

JAYNE: Jackie was a big influence on me. She was the first drag queen that I ever saw who wore rips in their stockings. She'd get tears in her stockings and wouldn't care. She'd just wear them like they were, with holes in them. And she used to pin things together with safety pins. She didn't do it to be cool, she did it because her clothes were so ragged. She'd wear them until they'd just fall off her. She'd have to pin them to her, so that kind of filtered down to punk. But Jackie Curtis had been doing that for years. It was late sixties.

So when punk came along and people were wearing safety pins, we were all wearing safety pins. I'd wear my shirt with a thin tie, and I put a safety pin through the tie. Two safety pins through my shirt, which was really torn. If there were tears in our shirt or something, we would just make them worse. It just turned into a fad—ripped clothes and safety pins. It turned into a fashion. They weren't particularly doing it to be so cool. They were really doing it because they didn't have anything. We used to shop at thrift shops, and sometimes we would wear really old clothes that were falling apart. Then it became cool to do that, and then people started copying. But we were doing that in New York for years. The British bands, they Britishized everything. They took a lot of stuff from New York and they changed it and made it applicable to Britain. And then the British version of punk started to influence American punk. Influence just went back and forth across the ocean.

JUDITH: How did you feel about the straight performers taking on drag and androgyny? I'm thinking of David Bowie and the New York Dolls.

JAYNE: Oh, glam rock. Yeah, well, I like the Dolls. I like their music. I think it was fun. I thought it was breaking down barriers. There's two ways to look at that, I guess. You could say, "Oh, they're just copying gay people or transgendered people, and they're just ripping gay people off," or whatever. Or you could say, "Well, it's good to see straight guys in high heels and makeup and stuff." Bowie, of course, used to say he was bisexual, but I don't think he really was. I was around him quite a bit at one period of my life, and he basically liked girls and trans girls too. Bowie borrowed a lot from gay culture, I think. He didn't call it gay culture though. To him, he was just wearing makeup and stage outfits. It was just theater to him. It wasn't real.

Among the other artists and everything, I see how some people could get upset and say that people like Bowie were borrowing from gay culture, but I think they were just glamming it up for fun. As I said, it was good to see straight men doing that. Looking feminine and wearing makeup, and satin. Wearing the frilly shirts, the whole bit. The Kinks in the sixties wore the frilly shirts and the Edwardian outfits. I love the Kinks. The Stones appeared in drag on the picture sleeve, for that song, "Have You Seen Your Mother Baby, Standing in the Shadows." They were known for doing drag, and they fitted right into the androgyny category. Mick Jagger did. He was very androgynous, at one time.

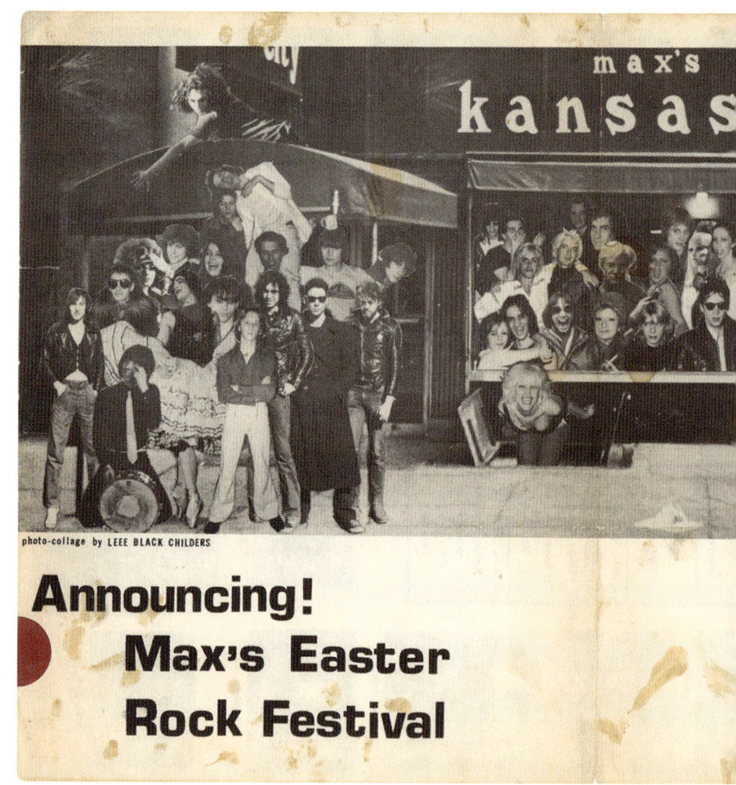

MAX'S KANSAS CITY *presents* NEW YORK ROCK

from the SOHO WEEKLY NEWS, March 25, 1976

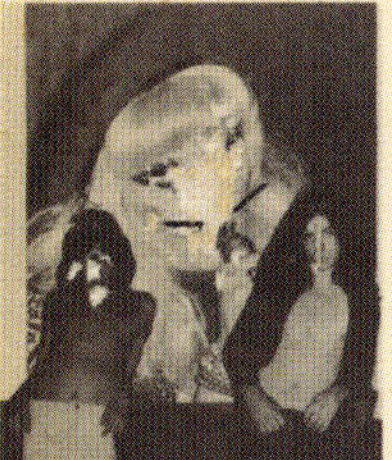

Wayne County & The Back Street Boys

If you missed swinging to the Mersey beat in Liverpool's hallowed Cavern in the early sixties—and if you failed to turn on to the San Francisco sound until everybody else's mind had already blown—all is not lost. Rumor has it, New York is currently the scene of the third great rock reformation—and it's about time, too. Rock and roll has been getting so straight and serious lately, what with a "rock crit establishment" and rock stars visiting the White House and all—it's imperative that rock gets back to its "roots," if you'll pardon the expression.

And that's just what's happening. Rock began as an exciting, spontaneous, raunchy, even slightly subversive type of music—and those qualities have been obliterated in a sea of MOR and, these days, disco sounds. The groups in New York's underground rock scene promise to bring back the "feel" of real rock music. What they lack in expertise they make up for in energy and enthusiasm. And taking into account the fact that the scene is for the most part underground, they can be as raunchy and as dirty as they please—at least for a while. For this rock scene isn't staying underground for long. The talent of the individual performers, composers and musicians and the support of the artists, writers and friends in the underground society insure emergence into the above ground rock scene.

PAT WADSLEY

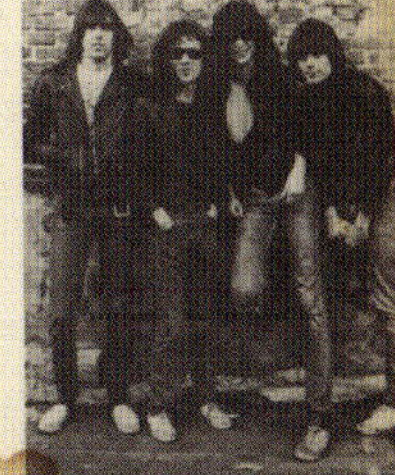

Ramones

Festival Schedule

All Shows Begin 9:30

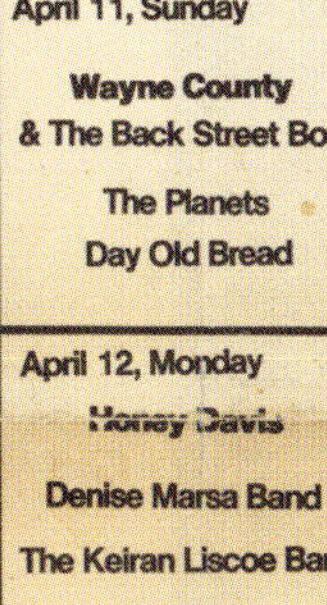

April 11, Sunday
Wayne County & The Back Street Boys
The Planets
Day Old Bread

April 12, Monday
Honey Davis
Denise Marsa Band
The Keiran Liscoe Band
Manster

April 13, Tuesday
Talking Heads
Suicide
Harry Toledo
Pere Ubu

April 14, Wednesday
Marbles
Just Water
Mumps
Dancer

April 15, Thursday
Heartbreakers
Tuff Darts
Mong

April 18, Sunday
Ramones
Blondie
Poppees

April 19, Monday
August
Dicey-Ross Blues Band
Rice Miller Band
Rags

April 20, Tuesday
Shirts
Uncle Son
Tricks

April 21, Wednesday
John Collins Band
Billy Falcon's Sunshine Thunder Band
Clear Cloud
Moonbeam

April 22, Thursday
Kid Blast
Best
Somebody Good
Startoon

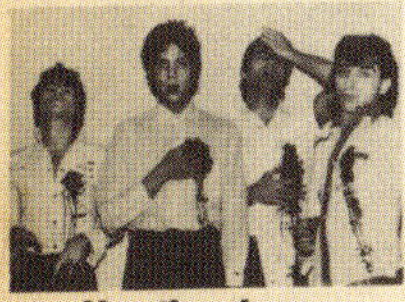

Heartbreakers

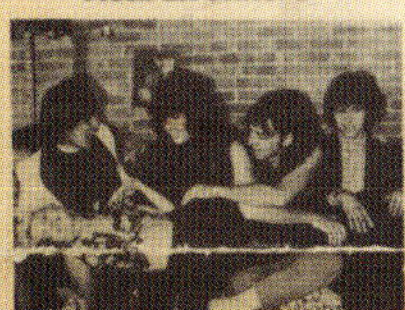

Blondie

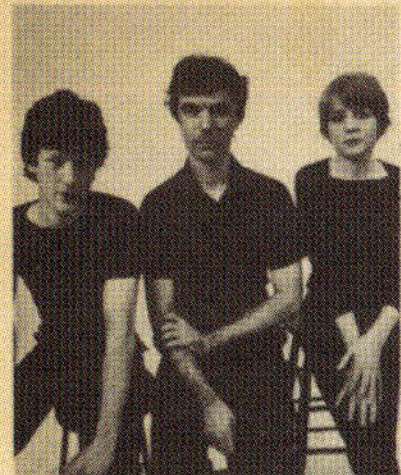

Talking Heads

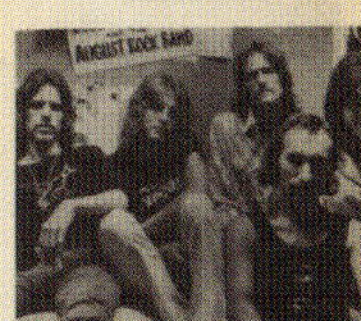

August

Tuff Darts

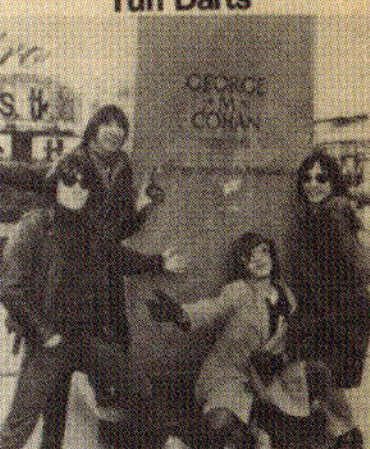

Marbles

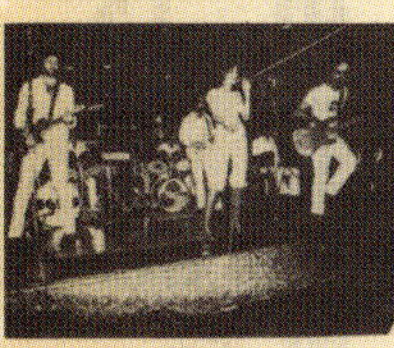

Shirts

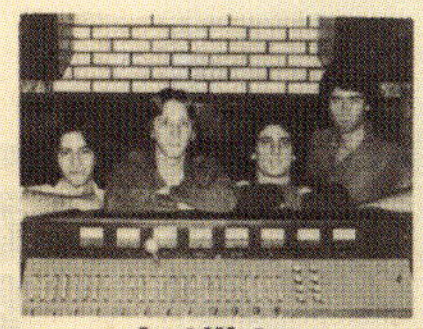

Just Water

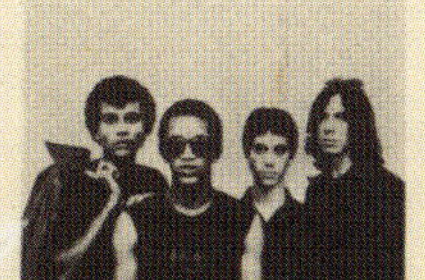

The Planets

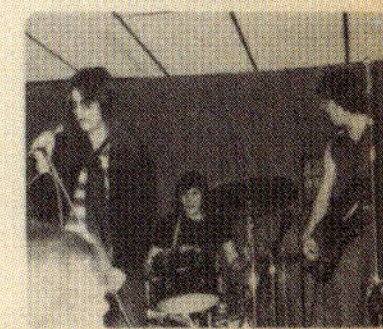

Honey Davis

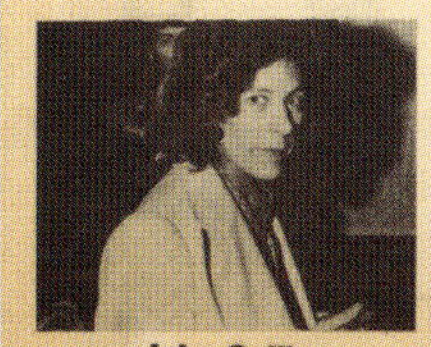

John Collins

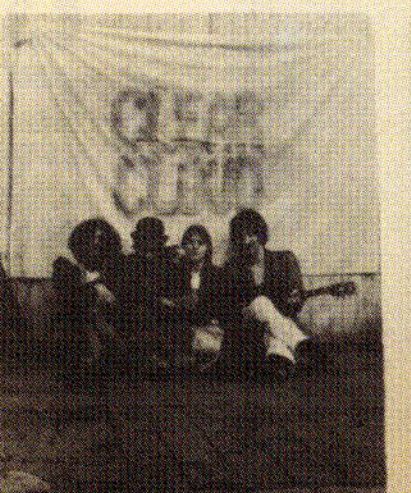

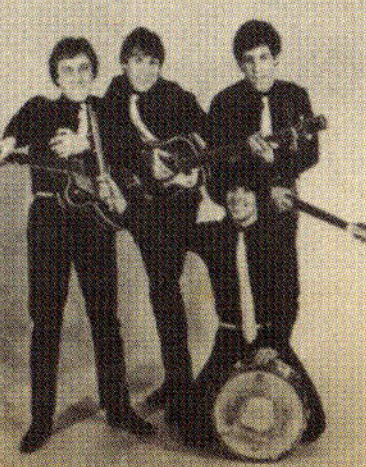

Dicey-Ross Blues Band

Poppees

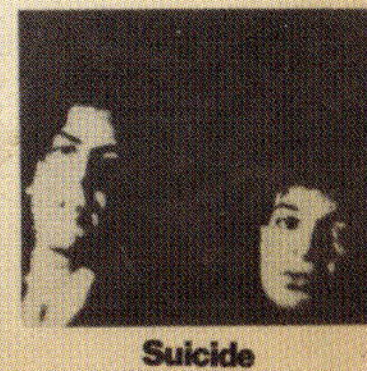

Suicide

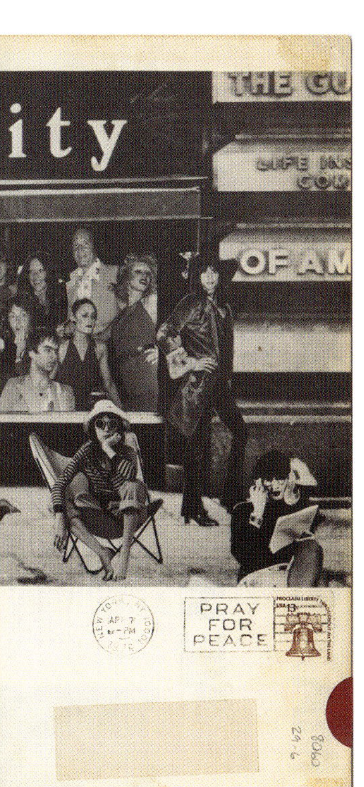

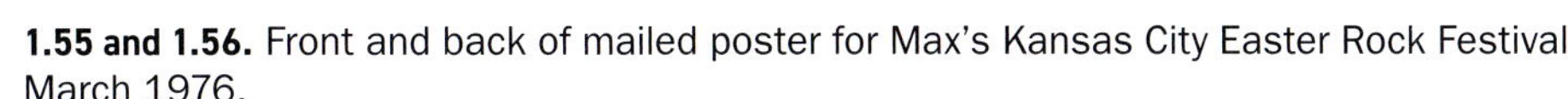

1.55 and 1.56. Front and back of mailed poster for Max's Kansas City Easter Rock Festival, March 1976.

EDITORIAL

IT WAS A LOT EASIER FOR US WHEN NOBODY READ THIS RAG. NOW THAT PEOPLE READ IT, WE GOT HASSLES. WE'VE RECEIVED A LOT OF COMPLAINTS FROM PEOPLE WHO HAVE RUN INTO WEIRDOS REPRESENTING THEMSELVES AS PUNK MAGAZINE. PLEASE DON'T FALL FOR THIS CRAP. IF SOMEONE SAYS THEY'RE FROM PUNK, MAKE THEM PROVE IT. ALL AUTHORIZED PERSONS ARE LISTED ON OUR MASTHEAD. SO ASK FOR SOME IDENTIFICATION, OR CALL THE PUNK BUSINESS OFFICE. DON'T TAKE ANYONE'S WORD FOR THE FACT THAT HE OR SHE IS A PUNK.

WE GOT ANOTHER LETTER.

FEB. 29, '76

DEAR ASSHOLES,

(NOTE: I KNOW THIS IS A CLASSIC CASE OF "PEARLS BEFORE SWINE" BUT FOR WHAT IT'S WORTH TRY TO LEARN SOMETHING ABOUT THE STREETS, SWEETIES, BEFORE TURNING OTHERS ONTO YOUR MISS-INFORMATION!)

FIRST, IT'S ABOUT THE WORD "PUNK" - EVEN COLLEGE BOYS LIKE YOURSELVES SHOULD KNOW THE LAMES WHO WRITE DICTIONARY DEFINITIONS OF STREET WORDS ARE BOUND TO FUCK UP THE MEANINGS. "PUNK" IS A PRISON WORD MEANING THE BOYS WHO GIVE UP THEIR ASS TO THE "WOLVES" (MACHO HOMOSEXUALS OR HORNY STRAIGHTS). MORE EXPERIENCED HOODS THEN USE(D) THE WORD "PUNK" AS AN INSULT TO YOUNG WOULD BE HOODS. THE KIND OF WIMPS WHO WRITE DICTIONARIES (AND PUBLISH MAGAZINES) OVERHEARD THESE KIDS BEING CALLED "PUNK" AND ASSUMED THAT "PUNK" WAS A WORD MEANING "A YOUNG RUFFIAN"

LESSON #2:

IT MIGHT HELP IF YOU GOT YOUR PREJUDICES STRAIT. FOR EXAMPLES, MOTHER'S, BEFORE ROCK, WAS A DYING QUEER BAR WHEN PETER CROWLEY (A NOTORIOUS FAGGOT) BROUGHT IN WAYNE COUNTY AND THE BACK STREET BOYS ALONG WITH NEON LEON'S RAINBOW EXPRESS FOR A WEEK OF R+R SHOWS IN AUG. '75. WE PACKED THE JOINT AND THE ROCK + ROLL CONTINUED UNTIL WE DROVE THE OLD QUEERS CRAZY, 'CAUSE THEY COULDN'T GET LAID FROM THE ROCK CROWD (WHICH CONTAINS LOTS OF FAGGOTS BUT NO QUEERS) SO THEY FOUND ANOTHER OLD QUEER WITH $ AND THREW US OUT.

FUCK ALL GOODY GOODY OUT OF TIME STRAIGHTS

Peter Crowley
MUSIC DIRECTOR
MAX'S KANSAS CITY

THIS IS A GOOD LETTER. IT DESERVES AN ANSWER, 'CAUSE IT BRINGS UP A LOT OF MOOT POINTS - LIKE WHAT A PUNK IS AND WHAT THIS MAGAZINE IS ALL ABOUT AND "WHERE THIS WHOLE THING IS GOING." (NO ONE SEEMS TO KNOW.)

1. FIRST, IT'S ABOUT THE WORD "PUNK." ANY IDIOT KNOWS THAT WORDS (LIKE MAGAZINES, ROCK ALBUMS, AND PEOPLE) TEND TO ASSUME SEVERAL IDENTITIES. YOUR OWN DEFINITION IS VALID BUT REVEALS MORE ABOUT YOURSELF THAN "PUNK".

2. COLLEGE BOYS. NOT EXACTLY. LEGS WAS THROWN OUT OF HIGH SCHOOL. I DROPPED OUT OF ART SCHOOL. NOW PUT ME DOWN BECAUSE I KNOW HOW TO READ. GO AHEAD.

3. PUNKS BEHIND BARS. (NO PUN INTENDED) THE FIRST MEANING FOR PUNK LAST ISSUE WAS "PROSTITUTE." WHAT I LEFT OUT- "APPEARS c. 1600." SHAKESPEARE USED THE WORD. PUNK IS NOT A TWENTIETH-CENTURY STREET WORD, DESPITE YOUR ROMANTIC FEELINGS ABOUT "PUNK" AND PUNKS.

4. I DON'T LIKE GLITTER ROCK. IT'S REALLY HAD IT, MISTER, YOU OF ALL PEOPLE SHOULD SEE THIS BY NOW! MY PREJUDICES ARE STRAIGHT, BUT MAINLY I DON'T LIKE ANY IDEALOGY SLIPPED INTO ROCK AND ROLL.

5. THE KEY WORD - TO ME, ANYWAY - IN THE PUNK DEFINITION WAS "A BEGINNER AN INEXPERIENCED HAND." PUNK ROCK- ANY KID CAN PICK UP A GUITAR AND BECOME A ROCK'N'ROLL STAR, DESPITE OR BECAUSE OF HIS LACK OF ABILITY, TALENT, INTELLIGENCE, LIMITATIONS AND/OR POTENTIAL, AND USUALLY DOES SO OUT OF FRUSTRATION, HOSTILITY, A LOT OF NERVE AND A NEED FOR EGO FULFILMENT. ROCK'N ROLL IS A VERY PRIMITIVE FORM OF EXPRESSION- LIKE CAVE PAINTINGS OR JUNGLE SCULPTURE. IT TAKES A LOT OF SOPHISTICATION - OR BETTER, NONE AT ALL- TO APPRECIATE PUNK ROCK AT ITS BEST- OR WORST (NOT MUCH DIFFERENCE). PUNK HAS BECOME A CATCHWORD FOR A LOT OF CRITICS TO DESCRIBE N.Y. UNDERGROUND ROCK, MOST OF WHICH IS NOT PUNK ROCK.

6. LEGS NAMED THIS MAGAZINE. I USED PUNK AT HIS SUGGESTION AS I FELT THE WORD WAS SO OVERUSED THAT IT WAS MEANINGLESS. I STILL FEEL THE SAME WAY.

— JOHN HOLMSTROM

1.57. Editorials by Peter Crowley and John Holmstrom debating the queer origins of punk in *Punk* magazine no. 3, March 1976. © 2023 by PUNK Magazine Inc.

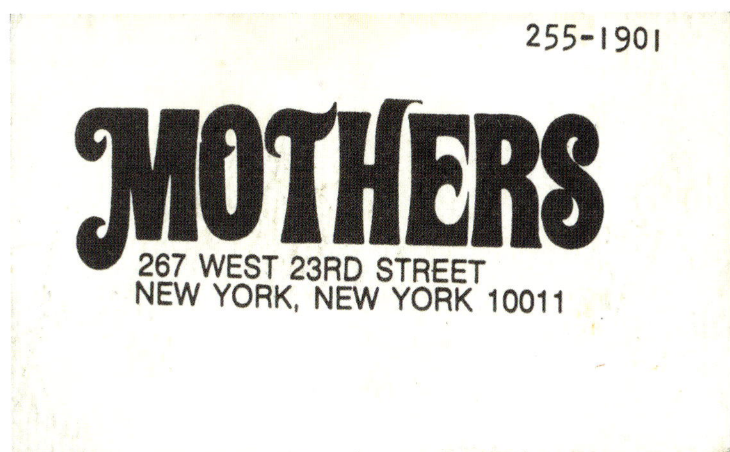

1.58. Business card for the gay bar Mothers referenced by Peter Crowley, early 1970s.

JUDITH: With so much circulation of androgyny and gender bending, it might be expected that gay, queer, and trans identified people would be welcome and celebrated in the punk scene.

JAYNE: That wasn't quite the case. Most people were OK with me though, but there was a lot of homophobia in the punk scene. Then I had that trouble with Dick Manitoba [of the Dictators], when he jumped up on my stage holding a beer mug. I thought he was going to clock me with it. I don't know if he actually was. I hit him with a microphone stand, and he fell into a table and hurt himself. That really caused a lot of homophobia. He had me arrested, and I had to go to court several times, but he would never show up. It started out as Wayne County defended himself against Dick Manitoba because he jumped up onstage. And all of a sudden, it went to poor little wrestler gets beat up by mean old drag queen.

That started a war between CBGB and Max's. You had the Max's people basically taking up for me, saying "Wayne County, not guilty." And you had a lot of the CBGB people saying, "Wayne County, guilty." Blah, blah, blah. It went back and forth. A lot of people took sides. It caused a division in the New York rock scene at this time. And it caused a lot of homophobia because Peter Crowley, who booked all the bands at Max's, he was gay. But this magazine called *Punk*, they published a lot of homophobic things. I think they tried to stir it up, make a bad situation worse.

JUDITH: It sounds like the crowd was different in CBGB and Max's. How would you describe that?

JAYNE: They were. You had people that went to both places though, but there was a definite difference between the majority of people that went to CBGB and Max's. A lot of people at Max's wouldn't be caught dead at CBGB and vice versa. A lot of people that went to CBGB I don't think they could get into Max's because they hung out at CBGB, which [was] just a run-down old bar. Hilly had these dogs, and these dogs would shit on the floor. And they served this chili that used to go right through you. You'd eat it and you'd go right to the bathroom.

The bathroom of course, it had no door on it. People could see you using the bathroom and everything. It was just trashy, but it became a cool place. Trashy became cool. But there was a big difference, I would say overall, between the Max's people and the CBGB's people. The Max's people were more diverse. There's a more diverse crowd; they were gay, straight, black, white, drag queens, gender bender artists, drug dealers, rich socialites, all mixed in together. The back room is outrageous. Anyone that was anyone would be seen sitting in the back room at Max's. I used to think it must have been like the Algonquin in the Dorothy Parker era. You know?[1]

I used to fantasize about that. The round table, because there was a round table in the back room of Max's, and the most important people were seated at the round table. I sat with Janis Joplin one night at the round table in Max's, and all these famous people kept coming up to the table to pay homage to Janis. They'd sit down awhile and pick at the food, and order drinks and everything. Then when the tab would come, they'd all get up from the table and run, and leave poor Janis with the bill.

JUDITH: I want to ask you about composing the song "Are You Man Enough to Be a Woman?" because that's such a powerful song. I teach it in my Punk Culture class at Cornell, and it really affects the students. What gave you the courage to write such an honest song?

JAYNE: It's just a song that comes from deep down. I write a lot of songs that are parodies, or that are funny or sarcastic songs. But that was one of my serious songs. That comes from my serious side, that song. I just had this tune in my head, and then I thought about the tune. Originally, me and Jobriath were supposed to record that song together. Jobriath was a singer and androgynous person who was very much like Bowie. I went off and wrote the song, and then I told him about the song. We turned titles around, you know, "It Takes a Man Like Me to Find a Woman Like Me." So we decided on "Man Enough to Be a Woman," but we never got around to recording it. That's a shame. I wish we had. But I recorded it, so at least I got it out.

JUDITH: Did you think of yourself as a pioneer?

JAYNE: Well, I kind of knew I was doing something that was different and other people would probably come along and do it, or their own version of it. I did think that I was kind of pioneering, but I wasn't really sure about how much.

JUDITH: Do you remember when you started to realize that you had been groundbreaking?

JAYNE: I guess around the 1980s. People began to tell me that, but I was just doing what I felt like doing. I would write my songs and then go onstage and perform them. I never gave a second thought about "Oh, this song's going to be considered pioneering or break ground, or whatever." I didn't think of it that way. I just thought, "Oh, it has a nice tune. Maybe this song will become popular or maybe these people will like it. Or maybe it will suck to some people." Different ways or different reasons I wrote songs.

The songs come to me, they just come inside my head from nowhere. I'll think of a tune and I can't get it out of my head, or I'll think of a lyric that won't go away. Then I will know: that's going to be a good song, because I can't forget it. So I'll write the lyrics right down, some words, and I'll hum the tune into my recorder on my phone. I'll go like, "Mmm, mmm, mmm, mmm, mmm. Mmm, mmm, mmm, mmm," like that. Then I'd get my guitar player on that, hum that to my guitar player. Before you know it, they're playing it on the guitar. Before you know it, we have a whole song. The songs come from just hums, little ideas that come into my brain.

JUDITH: You cover such a wide range of musical styles, from the garage rock of the Stooges in your early songs, to heavy metal on *Storm the Gates of Heaven* (1978), and then *Things Your Mother Never Told You* (1979).

JAYNE: That was experimental. One side was totally experimental. I get a lot of respect for it.

Some of the people, without whom there would have been no party:

Babette
Debbie Blondie
Richard Blum
Barbara Bothwell
Clem Burke
Bobby Butani
Jimmy Chicago
Leee Black Childers
Richie Colbert
Wayne County
Peter Crowley
Jackie Curtis
Laura Dean
Tommy Dean
John DeSalvo
Jimmy Destri
Willie DeVille
Divine
Elliot
Louie Erlanger
Chris Evans
Tom Eyen
Danny Fields
Paul Gellen
Robert Gordon
Richard Hell
David Johannsen
Anthony Jones
Alameda Manfred Jones
Peter Jordan
Ray Karl
Hilly Kristal
Steve Kroff
Murray Krugman
April Lawton
Ron Link
Walter Lure
Tony Machine
Max
Macs McAree
Tom Mooney
Tom Morongello
Jim Morrison
Jerry Nolan
Octavio
Brooks Ogden
Lisa Persky
Phillipe
Allen Rabinowitz
Dee Dee Ramone
Chris Robison
Mark Rockit
Tepi Rosen
Jeff Salen
Kenny Sanders
Herb Seupel
Reuben Siguenza
Sable Starr
Chris Stein
Joe Stepko
Michael Sticca
Sylvain Sylvain
Tally Taliaferrow
Johnny Thunders
Gary Valentine
Greg Van Cook
Cherry Vanilla
Buzzy John Vierno
Pat Wadsley
Michael Ward
Dore Weiner
Holly Woodlawn
Tony Zee

☆☆ A ☆☆

NEW YORK ROCK PARTY

☆☆☆☆☆☆☆☆☆

MAY 30

at

MANHATTAN CENTER

☆☆☆☆☆☆☆☆☆☆☆☆☆☆☆

1.59 and 1.60. Exterior and interior pages of the program for the Wayne County Legal Defense Fund benefit show, May 30, 1976.

A ROCK PARTY : NEW YORK STYLE

PROGRAM

The festivities should commence at 9:00 PM and proceed in more or less this order:

Your Hostess: Cherry Vanilla
Wayne County & Cherry Vanilla (historic duet)
August
The April Lawton Band
Cherry & Holly give a Door Prize
Holly Woodlawn
The Planets

Dee Dee Ramone
Tuff Darts
John Collins gives a Door Prize
Wayne County & the Back Street Boys
Jackie Curtis
Mink DeVille
Cherry & Wayne give a Door Prize

Lure, Nolan, Thunders, etc.
Neon Leon gives a Door Prize
Wayne County & the Back Street Boys
Divine & the cast of "Women Behind Bars"
Blondie
The Dolls
Cherry & Sable give a Door Prize
Sable Starr

Orchestra Luna
The Pez Band
Cherry Vanilla & her Staten Island Band
Wayne County & the Back Street Boys
Suicide

BROUGHT TO YOU BY :

Peter Crowley ....Producer

Barbara Bothwell ....Associate Producer

Leee Black Childers ....Associate Producer

Sound by Phaedra Sound

Lights by Hot Lights

Paul Zone...................... Disquaire

A special thank you to Max'sKansas City.

All proceeds go to:
The Wayne County Legal Defense Fund.

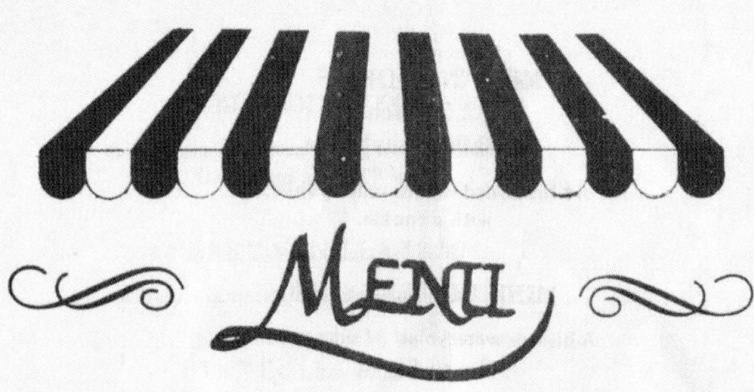

Maxi Burger With French Fries .... $ 2.70

Maxi Cheeseburger With French Fries...... 3.00

Hot Dogs With French Fries 2.70

French Fries.............................. 1.65

Potatoe Chips.............................. 1.65

Pretzels.................................... 1.65

Cheese & Crackers.......................... 2.00

Coffee or Tea.............................. 1.00

15% SERVICE CHARGE

Support Your Fave Band!

MILK 'N COOKIES
$2.50 each
$10.00 a pitcher
An old-fashioned brandy-milk punch, tall, with a cookie.

MINK DEVILLE $2.50
A high-powered blast of orange-rum flavored coke.

★ ★ ★ THE BRATS $2.50
A bit of the spoils.

THE RAMONES $2.50
Your favorite local beer, molested by a straight shot of whiskey.

SUICIDE $3.00
Green Chartruse and 151 proof rum...on fire. Only attempt it at the bar.

TUFF DARTS $2.50
A tall cool vodka-licorice combination, that will leave you seeing double...and in black & white.

WAYNE COUNTY PUNCH
$2.50 a glass
$10.00 a pitcher
A nice fruit punch, with a heavy dose of Southern Comfort.

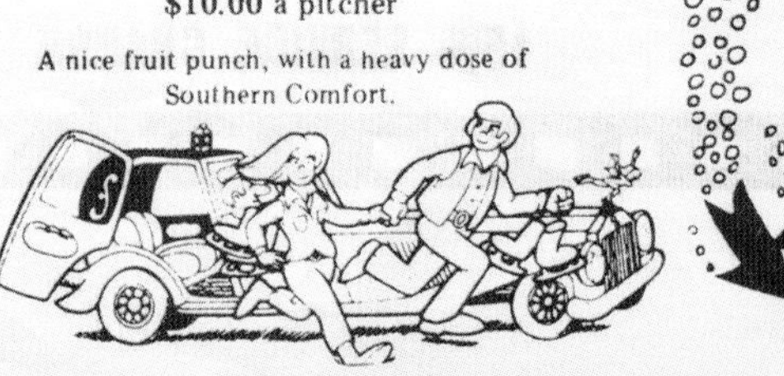

1.61 and 1.62. Front and interior pages for Max's Kansas City food and drink menu, with drinks named after local bands, circa 1976.

JUDITH: What do you think makes punk "punk"?

JAYNE: I don't know . . . the thought of being rebellious, I guess. Much like that book that was out years ago called *High on Rebellion*.[2] I really like that. But punk really was a label that was made up by *Punk* magazine. There was a New York thing going on, and it wasn't called punk, so they looked for a word. They didn't have a word to identify the music, so they came up with punk. Even the Ramones were going, "They're trying to call us punk. We're not punk, we're a rock and roll band." We just thought we were doing rock and roll, but the word "punk" stuck. Then people started using that word to describe the bands as being punk bands. But it started with people from *Punk* magazine. The original "punk" really means a guy in prison. It's a prison term. It's a guy that gets it. They call him a punk.

JUDITH: Do you relate to that term? Do you feel that that really describes what you did, or no?

JAYNE: No. I don't think it describes my music enough. My music's too much of a wide range, but I would say I'm punk to make it easier for people to identify where I'm coming from, but personally I wouldn't identify myself as a punk band, really. I just think of myself as a rock and roll band.

But still people are trying to figure out, what is punk? I don't think people really know. Punk, to me, was a special time and a special place. I don't know if any band could be described as punk today. Like a new band comes along and they're playing what they consider punk music, but I'm not sure that they could be considered punk because punk was a different time and a different place. I think of it as the history of a certain time.

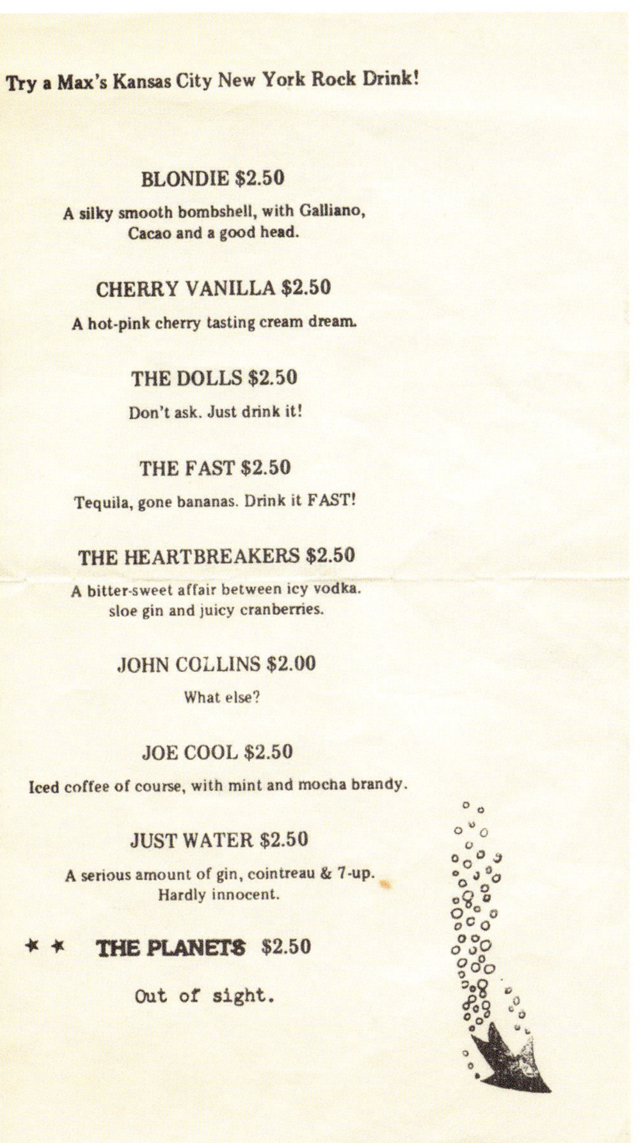
Try a Max's Kansas City New York Rock Drink!

BLONDIE $2.50
A silky smooth bombshell, with Galliano, Cacao and a good head.

CHERRY VANILLA $2.50
A hot-pink cherry tasting cream dream.

THE DOLLS $2.50
Don't ask. Just drink it!

THE FAST $2.50
Tequila, gone bananas. Drink it FAST!

THE HEARTBREAKERS $2.50
A bitter-sweet affair between icy vodka, sloe gin and juicy cranberries.

JOHN COLLINS $2.00
What else?

JOE COOL $2.50
Iced coffee of course, with mint and mocha brandy.

JUST WATER $2.50
A serious amount of gin, cointreau & 7-up. Hardly innocent.

★ ★ THE PLANETS $2.50
Out of sight.

JUDITH: Speaking of time and the different stages of your career, you had an early semi-drag phase when you were performing as Wayne County, and then eventually you fully inhabited your identity as Jayne County. How do you look back on the Wayne County years? Was it a phase in your life? Or a character for your performances?

JAYNE: A little of both. I definitely had to get in character before getting onstage. I would sit down in front of a mirror and start with the clothes and the wigs. You do become a character, and it's a stage character, but also, it's an extension of my personality. A theatrical version of my personality, where the wrecking comes into it and everything. That's what I think.

JUDITH: You have a moment in your memoir that I think is beautiful. You say that when you were presenting more fully as a woman, that you were "living out the implications of your songs."[3] Can you say more about that? Does that ring true today?

JAYNE: I would say so, yeah. A lot of what I'm trying to do, what I think, the way I've lived goes into my songs. The attitude that I've had over the years will go into different songs. I'm a very moody person too, and I also write songs when I'm in different moods. To get a different feeling of the song and everything. If I'm in an angry mood, if I'm mad about something, I'm really great onstage.

So a lot of the songs also have been written under different moods. If I want to sit down and write some songs and I'm in a bad mood, those are songs that'll come out mean or something like "Fuck Off." "Fuck Off" is a really mean song. It's saying to someone "If you don't want to fuck me, fuck off"—that's a mean song. It was written about someone too, somebody who used to tease me all the time. I would say that a lot of my songs are an extension of my personality.

JUDITH: That brings me to the question of one of your newer songs, "I Don't Fit in Anywhere" [with AM Taylor, released October 2020], which I think is a beautiful song.

JAYNE: I was so happy with that song.

JUDITH: I love it! It's so catchy, and it's such a great anthem. Can you tell me what prompted you to write that song?

JAYNE: It's a song about having an aversion toward society, which I'm really good at writing about. It's about someone who doesn't fit into anything that's going on. You have this type of person, and this type of scene, or you might have a religion or a philosophy . . . some people don't fit into any of that at all. They're just their own creation, and don't fit into anything that society has already laid out for us. Because we're supposed to be part of a mold, and you're supposed to be kind of the same and believe the same thing. But that song represents people who just don't fit in anywhere. There's no reason that it has to be a bad thing. Not fitting in could be a good thing, because you take what you are and watch how you're thinking—and use it. You use it for yourself. You use it to either get ahead, or to write songs with, or to make money, or anything. You use what you are. Just because you don't fit in anywhere doesn't mean you can't do something with it, because you can. If you don't fit in, write about it. If you don't fit in, do something different, create something different for the people that don't fit in. That's the way I look at it.

JUDITH: It's an inspiring message.

JAYNE: Thank you.

JUDITH: It makes me think about the bullying that is such a problem in our country, as well.

JAYNE: Oh, God. I know. It really is a horrible problem. Thank you. I'm really pleased with that song. I'm very happy with how that song came out.

JUDITH: Do you think of a song like that as political?

JAYNE: I think it's political. It's subtly political. Standing up to the powers that be, and standing up to the way our society is structured, it's a political thing. In trying to create your own state of being instead of trying to be like everyone else, I think that's very political. Definitely.

JUDITH: Do you look back on your career and think about the politics of your pioneering work?

JAYNE: Sometimes, yeah. I would like to think that other trans people or other people who don't fit in for other reasons, not just trans people, other people that don't fit in, can look to me and feel inspired, and do something with themselves, and not hate themselves. It's very important not to hate yourself. Just because you don't fit in, you don't hate yourself and go, "Oh, poor me. I don't fit in. Ohhh." Don't do that! You go: "I don't fit in. Fantastic! That's right. I don't fit in, fuck you." [*laughs*]

JUDITH: So we all need to learn how to wreck, huh?

JAYNE: Mm-hmm [*affirmative*]. That's the way I think. I think that's pretty much it. In a nutshell.

JUDITH: I'm curious to know what you think about a place like Cornell collecting punk ephemera and flyers and correspondence? And about people studying and teaching about punk?

JAYNE: I like it because it's a part of history. I'm a history buff. I love history, and punk is part of history. New York City, that whole period is part of history, and London in that period is a part of history. You had Paris in the twenties and Berlin in the thirties, and you have New York in the seventies and eighties. I think it's really important for us to let people know about our history. A lot of people think, "Oh, history. I don't understand. It's no interest to me at all," but it should be. You learn from history. You learn from your past. You really do. I love history. I love the thought of being taught in school. [*laughs*]

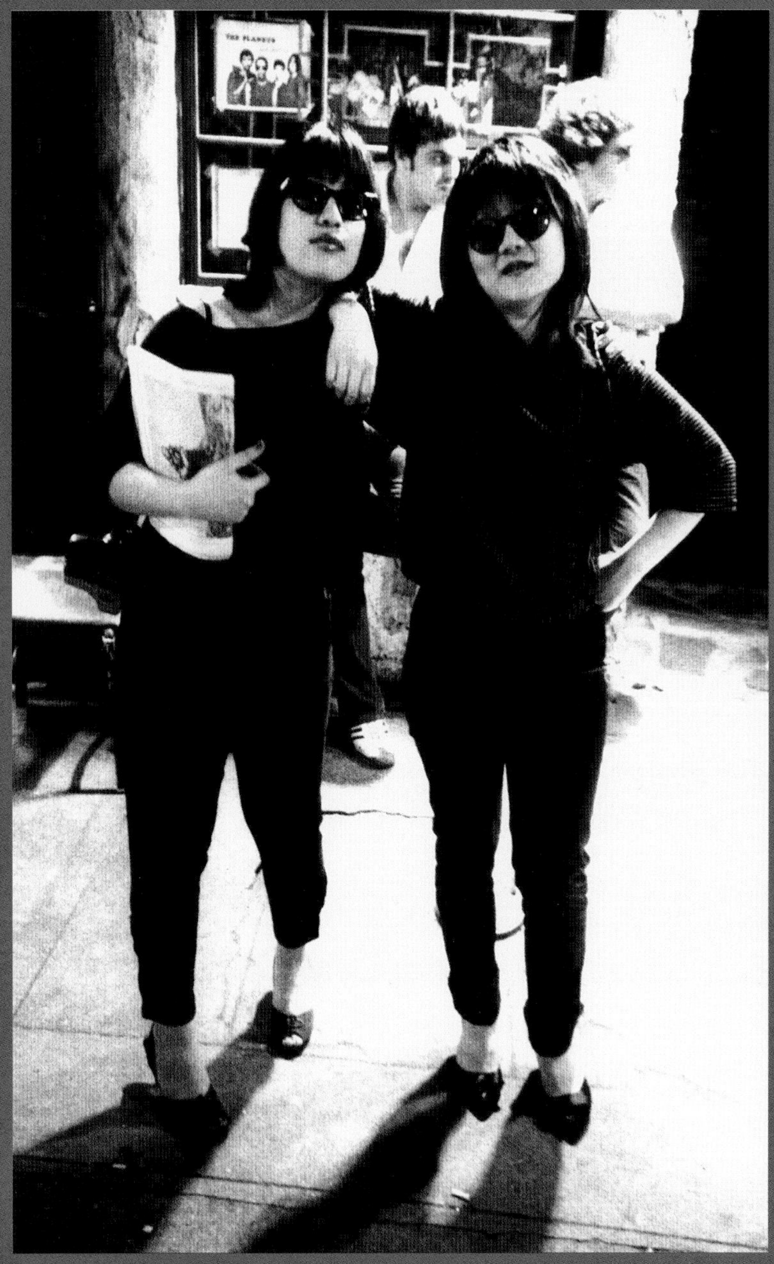

1.63. Sylvia Reed and Anya Phillips, Bowery, 1976. Photo: © GODLIS.

This photo of us in front of CB's is a favorite of mine. She and I met in Taiwan in high school, and she lived with my family for some time after that in Hawaii. We made our plans to go to NYC together, and we were inseparable during these years. —Sylvia Reed

CH. 4

“Two Chinese girls” in the NYC Punk Scene

AN INTERVIEW WITH SYLVIA REED ON ANYA PHILLIPS

Sylvia Reed (née Morales) is an artist, designer, and manager who landed in New York in 1974 and was brought into the CBGB scene by her high school companion Anya Phillips. As the business partner and second wife of Lou Reed, Sylvia was integral to his life and work from 1977 to 1994. In this interview, conducted on January 25 and 26, 2022, Sylvia discusses her long friendship with Anya, the impact Anya had on the scene through her fashion sensibility and strong persona, and Sylvia’s own perspective on the scene as a woman of color.

JUDITH: Can you tell me a little about your family background?

SYLVIA: My father was a dark-skinned Mexican man. His family—in fact I have very old photos of the great-grandparents—were indigenous looking. On my mother's side, while she was Hispanic as well, there were Spanish and European people, so lighter-skinned people. I believe she had some English background. Atkinson was the name. I remember her talking with me about trying to find Ellis Island records about Atkinsons coming, and somehow they got into Texas, so she was very fair-skinned.

I had grown up primarily in Europe, and then we did spend one eighteen-month period in Texas near my mother's family when I was a kid, when my father, who was in the Air Force, chose isolation duty to get away from the kids, I think. Isolation duty is where the serviceman is assigned somewhere that's so remote that their family can't be with them there. And he liked that just fine for that one time period. But it had been Germany—Berlin, in fact—that was a key for me later on, when I met Lou. He had done this *Berlin* album, and I had actually lived in Berlin.

JUDITH: When your father was stationed in Taiwan, you went to high school and became close friends with Anya Phillips. What do you know about her family background?

SYLVIA: Her mother had television work in Taiwan, but previously she had also existed in this arts community in China. If I recall correctly, Anya told me the story of how her mother fled China. I believe her mother was pregnant with Anya at that time, but Anya's father was not her younger brother's father. Her brother's father was an American soldier, American colonel. Her father was Chinese. But she always used the Phillips name. I met her stepfather on more than one occasion and, of course, met her mother and brother. I believe that for her there was a lot around the issue of this absent father or actual father and how Wade Phillips was not her father. It figured very heavily later into the differences between her and her brother, who became a giant pop star in China [Fei Xiang]. His fans often talk about how tall he is because his father was very tall. So this biracial look that he has is important to his fans. I think Anya definitely had feelings about this, and whatever action it was that her mother had taken to leave that prior life.

JUDITH: When you were living in Taiwan during your high school years with Anya, how did you get hold of American popular music and fashion?

SYLVIA: In Taiwan, there was a big disparity economically, of course, so if you had American money, you would be able to take a lot of advantage of the people who were working for pennies, comparatively. And in one respect, it was very significant for our high school that there were many pirated records available. As soon as an American or Western album came out, someone in Taiwan would pirate it and put it out on this very thin vinyl that was of cheap quality. I think you could play a record maybe five or six times, and then it was unplayable. So everyone would make a tape of the album when you played it the first time, so you could keep listening. But these thin vinyl records cost thirty-five cents, so the record collections that we all had as American kids were amazing. You could buy everything. If we were in the States, and had to pay stateside money for that, you certainly couldn't afford to buy fifty albums at a pop, but we could there.

In the same respect, they had wonderful and very cheap seamstresses working for a penny. The seamstresses were impoverished. I knew many of the American women living there at the time would go to seamstresses to have dresses made. There was a specific row, a street in Taiwan, and you would find a tailor or seamstress, and they would do custom clothing for very cheap. So Anya could draw something up and take it to the person that her mother used, and just have the clothing made. That gave her a real head start in that she knew things about fabric, and how it would hang, and different seams, and all of that. My mother was a big seamstress herself. She was an amateur seamstress who was always sewing at her favorite sewing machine; she loved to make clothes for herself and for me.

Anya enjoyed that. She would use my mother's sewing machine when she was living with us, and talk about her fashion ideas. And, of course, the stuff that she was doing—very different. My mom always worked from those patterns that you could buy, and Anya was just wildly creative. But she had this knowledge and background, and experience. Like I said, she loved to go shopping for fabric, and I'd go with her. She'd think about what the fabric could do. I remember sitting for hours in Anya's house, which her mother had designed, and it featured a fabulous round sunken living room. Her mother had every fashion magazine that existed delivered there. We'd sit in that sunken living room and look at these magazines, and Anya would review what she liked and what she thought was ugly. I participated mostly for her; I was not really deeply interested in that, but she would discuss what were the inspirations, etc. Regarding the music, since I didn't spend much time in the United States, I was not that well-versed in mainstream American culture. I feel like I was not present for that due to the time spent in Europe and Taiwan, which was the result of my father's various assignments in the Air Force. But New York culture was something we were specifically aiming for.

JUDITH: How did you both end up in New York?

SYLVIA: Anya had been living with me when I lived in Hawaii in 1974. She had fallen out with her mother. She managed to graduate high school early, as I recall, and I had already left and was living in Hawaii due to my father's transfer. She came and lived with my family for some months and then lived elsewhere in Honolulu. During that last year of my high school, this was when we were making the plans about where we were going to go, and what we were going to do. Of course it would be together, and we were both focused on going to New York.

For various reasons, I arrived in New York, I think it was a couple of months after her. It had to do with a plan we'd made to go to New York together. I was holding on, waiting for school acceptances in a more conventional way, and she began to believe I wasn't going to show up. She was thinking, "Oh, that's just your way of getting out of it." We'd made all these plans, and so she was emotionally caught up, and upset that I wouldn't just take off with her when she wanted to go.

When I arrived, I was caught up for the initial period in attending my art school, Pratt Institute. This first semester was filled with a lot of activity and people that had to do with Pratt. But eventually, we agreed for me to come and meet her, and see what she was doing. And once she had me back in her influence, she tried very hard to get me to leave school, because that's what she had done.

I think she had applied in a real hurry to Parsons School of Design. If I remember correctly, she was accepted instantly, because she's just very talented (1.64, 1.65). I think she had a portfolio of fashion drawings, and she was accepted, but I think within three or four days of attending, she stopped going. They had given her a full scholarship as well, but she stopped going. It

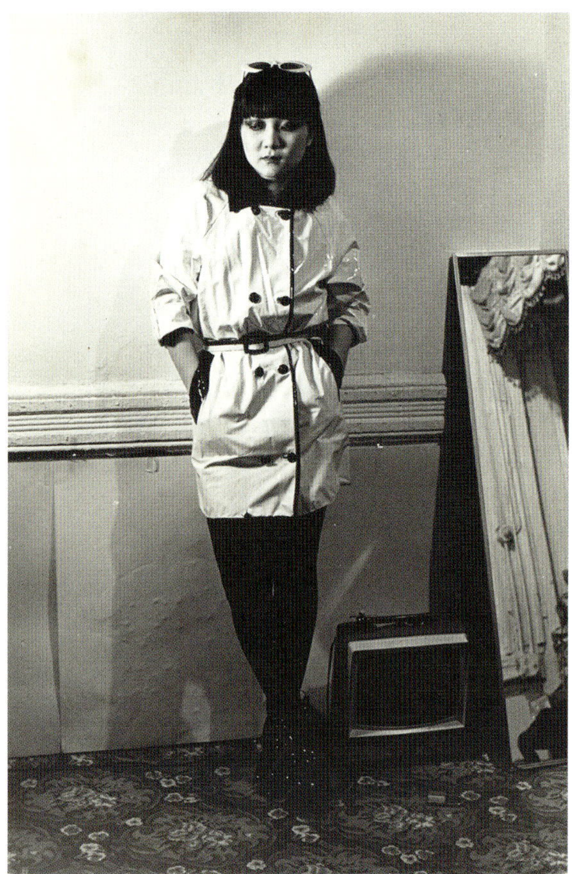

1.64. Anya Phillips, December 1976.
Photo: Sylvia Reed.

(*Below*) Anya took her chopped-up hairstyle to an extreme here. She didn't often do that with her hair. Usually, her coiffure was a little more smooth or refined. This rain jacket reminds me that she was into really graphic patterns like the polka dots, or she might say, "Gold is going to be the big color in a few months," and she would pick up vintage gold lamé items when we went thrifting. She analyzed fashion trends. She would say things like, "With black and white, polka dots are going to be the new thing as opposed to stripes." And she'd sort of plan an entire outfit around this kind of thinking. —Sylvia Reed

(*Above*) She loved doing photo sessions in our St. Mark's Place storefront apartment. Anya had a unique elegance; she looks as if she might have stepped out of a Godard film here. —Sylvia Reed

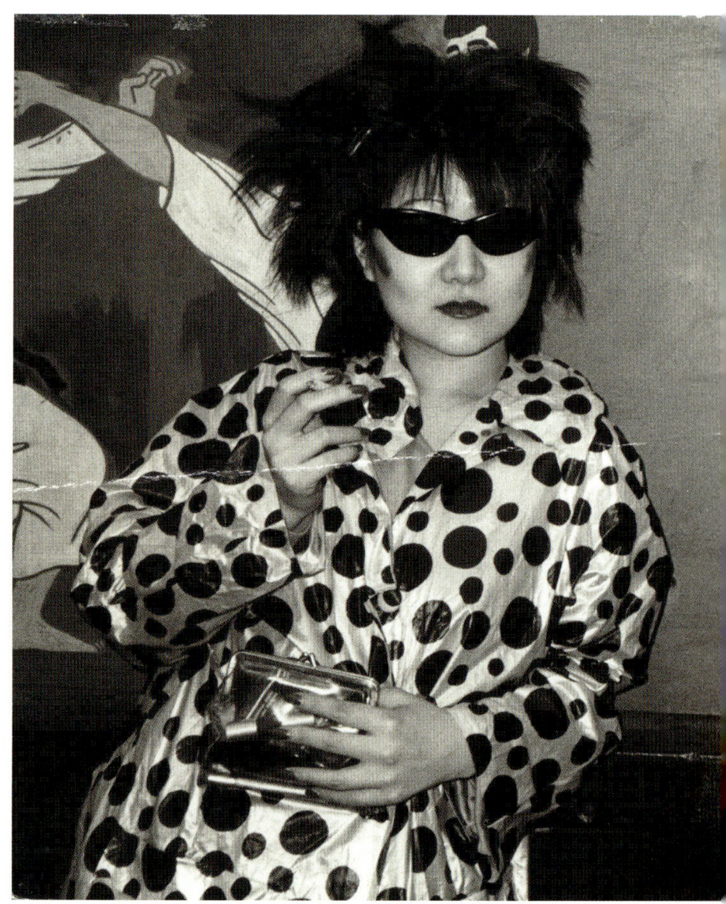

1.65. Anya Phillips, circa 1978. Photographer unknown.

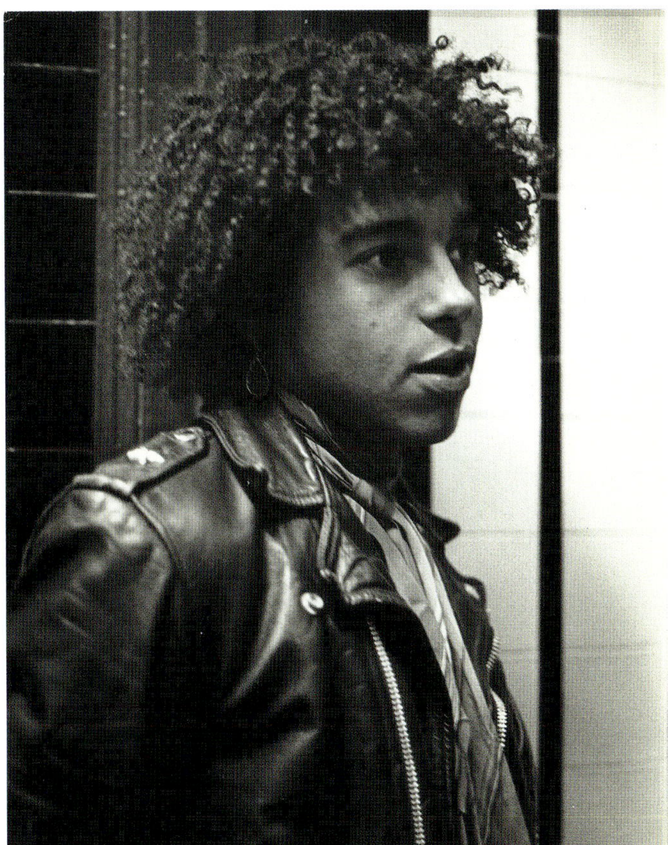

1.66. Ivan Julian (guitarist for Richard Hell and the Voidoids), 1977. Photo: Anya Phillips.

Anya and I were close friends of Ivan, who is such a warm, creative, and talented musician. We both ended up taking a lot of photos of him, but Anya's were much better than mine. —Sylvia Reed

had to do with that not being how she saw the way to develop her talent and interests. She was not going to accede to that sort of structured discipline. I think she felt that wasn't the way to do it for her. It wasn't worth her time.

I became very focused on dance, theater, and film. For Anya, it was really all about fashion and music in the sense of the music scene. I remember when she was living with me in Hawaii, we went to a record store, and she was the one who picked out from the record bin a Lou Reed album. So the first time I ever saw an image of him was her holding it up and showing it to me. I believe it was the cover of *Rock and Roll Animal*. I have a distinct memory of that. She's sort of waving this at me like, look at this guy. I think I was a bit dismissive of the image, saying something about how that artist was such an attention seeker.

JUDITH: In a conversation we had earlier, you made this remark that in the punk scene you and Anya were surrounded by an awful lot of white girls, and that in retrospect, now in this contemporary context, you have a different way of thinking and understanding what your experience was of that time. Can you elaborate on that?

SYLVIA: I think what's interesting, and this probably applies to many people who think about the arts and consider them, is to look back to see what was considered transgressive—back in the sixties or seventies, let's say—and then to see what people are calling each other out on today. It's something that I think about a lot because of the fact that Anya was notably one of the very few Asian persons who were in the scene. She made a big impact.

When I was introduced by her into the CBGB scene, I had the ability to see it from an outsider at first, and see how she had already impacted the people that she met there, and absorbed some of the creativity that she found there. As I started regularly being there with her, I overheard—and other people also mentioned it—"Oh, those two Chinese girls." I had an exotic look. It happened many times before in my life that people had thought I was either Chinese or part Chinese, because of my personal look. So when Anya and I would show up together, somehow our look caused this sort of reaction (1.63, 1.68).

So, we were sort of grouped together with this . . . I'm going to say exoticism and maybe a little bit of fetishization of "those two Chinese girls"—Anya and I. She appreciated getting attention, and I think she used that in some way. She definitely wanted to have a look, she definitely planned how she was going to look, and how her look would impact whatever event she was going to. I think she really thought about that a lot, but at the same time, I think that she was upset that that was a dismissive way to be thought about. I certainly felt that, because I was not at all the fashion plate that she was. I was not thinking deeply about my "look."

I was her blank slate. I allowed her to dress me, and do things to my hair and makeup. I was like her fit model—that's someone who designers have hang around while they create and they use that person's body to create the clothing on, and try different things. Maybe I was also a little bit of a muse, because she was really interesting in the way she would get into it, very in depth. When Anya wanted to do something, she would just have you stand there in front of a full-length mirror, naked, but you had to wear shoes because the shoes were important. And then she would drape and work as if she was working on a sewing mannequin.

She chopped my hair up one night in a way that was so obviously done just to evoke, "What happened to that girl?" She did it in such a savage way that other people spoke to me about it. I remember one of my dear friends said, when she saw this hair, "You know, I don't think Anya really wants you to look good." Because I think Anya had gone at it with big scissors. These were not in any way salon scissors. She was just hacking at it, and then taking gigantic gobs of Vaseline and shaping it. I think I was interested in it because it was sculptural, but also because she had such a strong influence on me. I basically followed her lead.

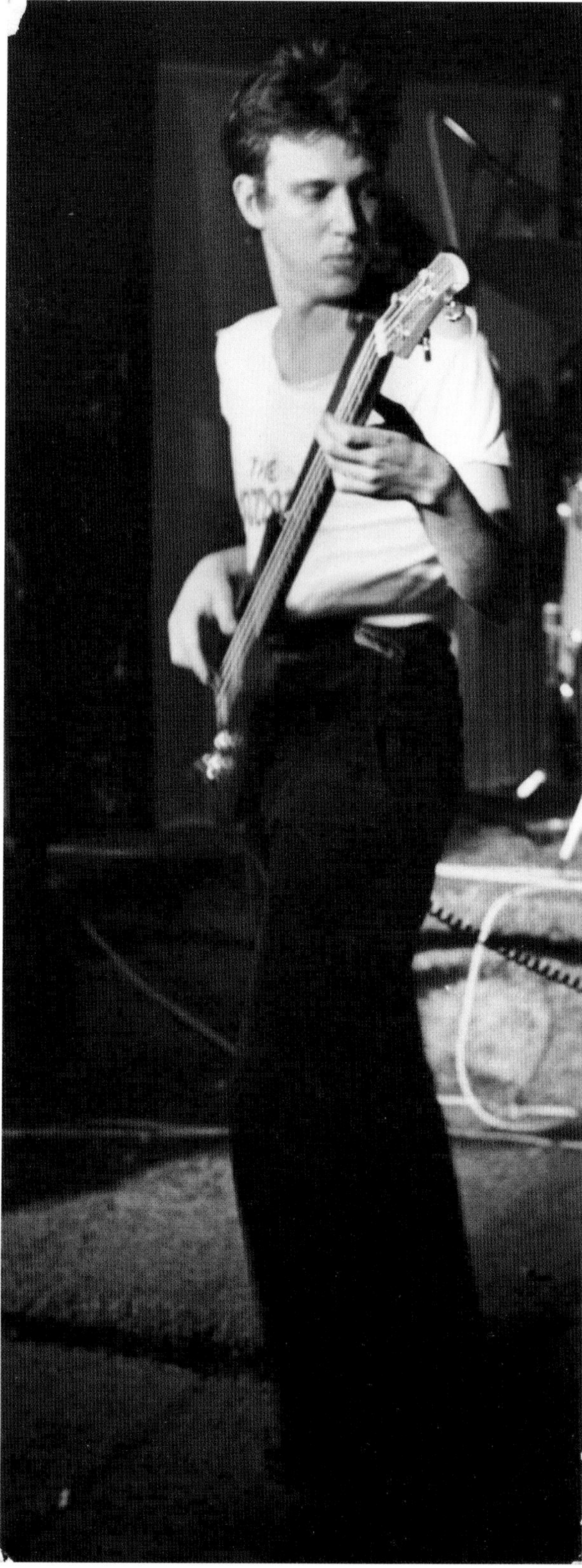

1.67. Richard Hell, 1977. Photo: Anya Phillips. Published by permission of James Chance.

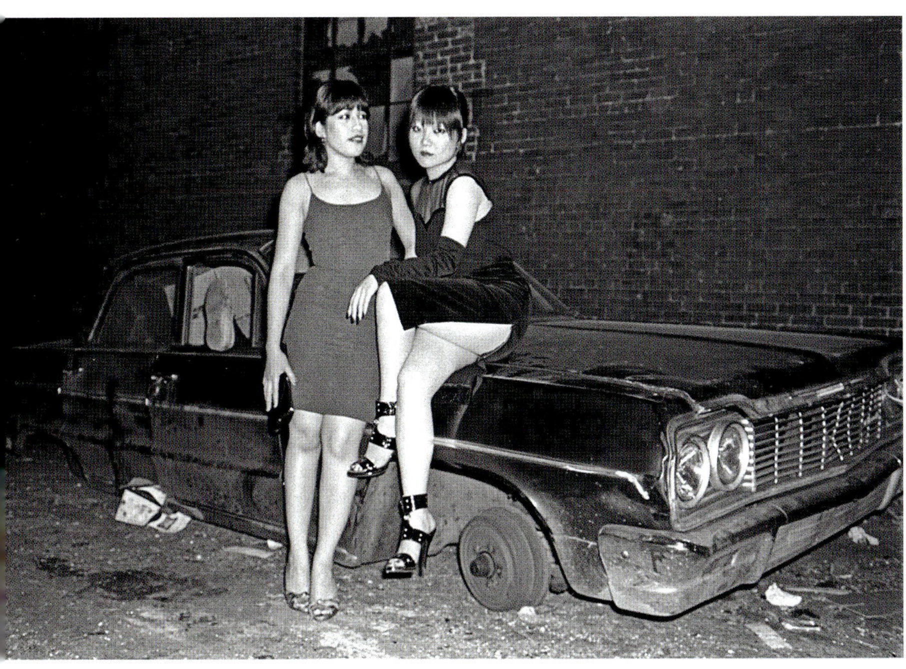

1.68. Sylvia Reed and Anya Phillips in the empty lot next to CBGB, New York, May 28, 1977. Photo: © Allan Tannenbaum.

I remember specifically her saying, as we were walking down the street, "I think gold is going to be important this year." Meaning gold, like wearing gold, metallic, gold color. I was just laughing at her because I didn't know where this thought came from—such fashion awareness and how definitive she was, as if she saw it all before anyone else. She was . . . I don't know, just very perceptive, and aware, and paying attention to that kind of thing.

Even though we were living a hardscrabble life, she found ways to do this work that she was doing. I think she wanted it to be taken seriously, and that is one of the reasons why I think the idea of being dismissed or pushed aside for a concept of, "Oh, those two Chinese girls that hang around"—it was something that she reacted against. But I would say there was a lot of interplay between wanting the attention and then really sort of demanding that she had some credibility and significance for the artist that she was.

JUDITH: It's difficult to get out of where society slots you. I think that is, in a way, a central tension within punk. What's your response to the appropriation of Hispanic names such as James Curtis [cofounder of the Mudd Club] taking the name Diego Cortez?

SYLVIA: For whatever reason, Diego wanted to take on that persona, that name, I'm not sure whether it has to do with maybe some sort of street credibility that he thought that name gave him. It's interesting because you're right. These appropriations happened all the time. One of my favorite artists or singers, Willy DeVille [born William Paul Borsey Jr.] in Mink DeVille, for a long time I thought he was Hispanic. He's not at all. But he took on this entire Hispanic persona and wrote these great songs, which were like the gorgeous Tex-Mex love songs I had heard when living in Brownsville, Texas, for a brief time. I'm correcting myself now: there were a couple of Hispanic guys in his band, but there again you see there's a sort of persona he's taking on, and we don't look at it the same way now. I think people are rightfully called on these kind of things now.

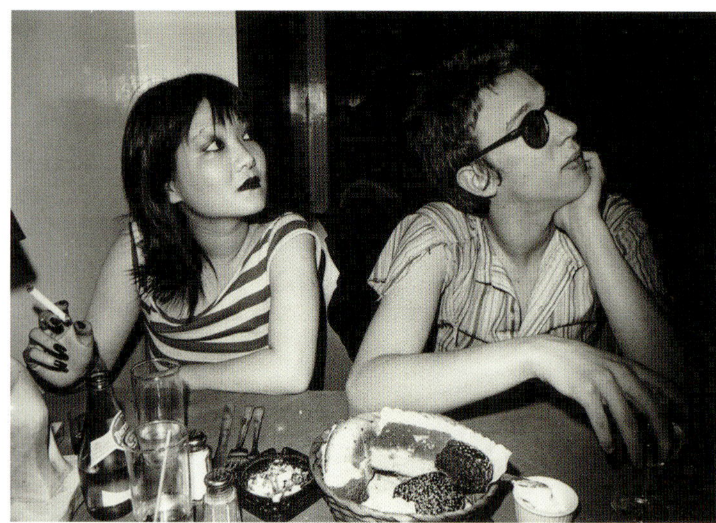

1.69. Anya Phillips with Richard Hell, circa 1977. Photo: Copyright Jimmy DeSana Trust. Courtesy of the Jimmy DeSana Trust and P·P·O·W, New York.

(*Below*) Anya found an ideal partner in James. They understood each other, and together they would turn heads when they were out in the clubs. They were truly an iconic couple. She dressed him meticulously. He was instantly noticed whenever he performed, thanks to her sense of style. She was a huge boost to his career, and she knew exactly how to promote him and his work. —Sylvia Reed

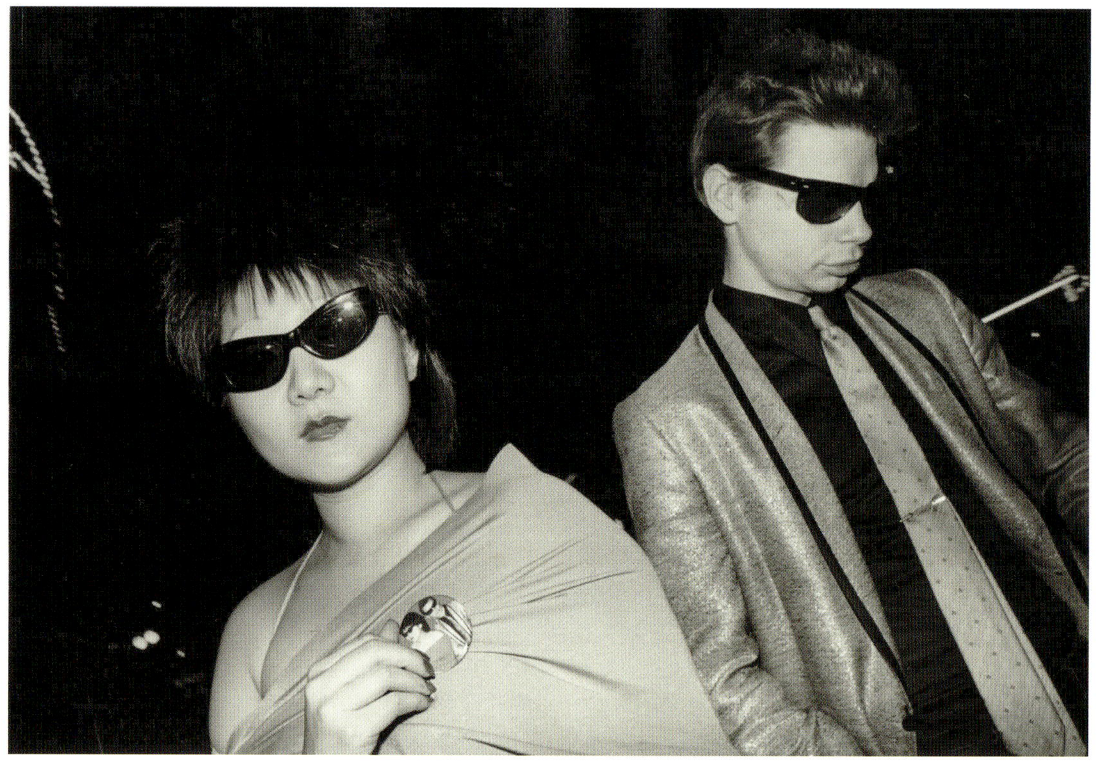

1.70. Anya Phillips and James Chance of the Contortions, circa 1978. Photo: Copyright Jimmy DeSana Trust. Courtesy of the Jimmy DeSana Trust and P·P·O·W, New York.

Esoterrorists was as an imaginary Munich punk band consisting of (*left to right*) Charlie Heil, Diego Cortez, Anya Phillips, and Harald Vogl (aka Harald V. Uccello). In another incarnation, Esoterrorists was an imaginary NYC punk band consisting of Anya Phillips, Duncan Smith, and Diego Cortez. They only existed as documented by various photos published in art and music magazines and zines in 1978–79.

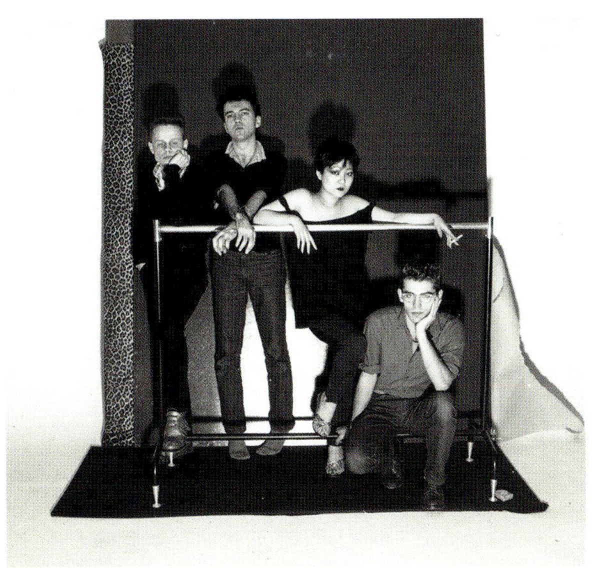

1.71. Esoterrorists, 1978. Photo: Harald Vogl.

He absorbed that whole vibe and totally became enamored of it. He was really, truly one of the most amazing performers I'd ever seen. They didn't have the fan base the way the Ramones did. Oh, and another was Alan Vega [born Boruch Alan Bermowitz]. I was a big Suicide fan, and they were so off the wall and crazy and strange that people would literally flee out the door when they came on. There was only a handful of us. He went off into some sort of trance and he would just deliver this persona that was so aggressive, and yet at the same time vulnerable.

JUDITH: The appropriation of Hispanic names and identities as part of an edgy persona connects to what you are saying about the tension within Anya using her exoticism, if that's the best word, to promote her clothing or her fashion sensibility as also cutting edge. Is that something that sounds right to you?

SYLVIA: Right. I think of it as her artwork. That's her. That's what she was doing, and I believe she saw it as a vehicle to use. She wanted that edginess. You can see from these pictures (1.69, 1.70, 1.71), it's not your typical Asian daughter; not "I'm going to listen to my family and behave appropriately." She's very much not about that. This is a scream of freedom: "This is all about me and how I want to present myself." And so it's very individualistic for her.

I also like her kind of sex-positive focus of some of the cutaway dresses that she did and how she cut and draped and wrapped that fabric on a model person, whomever she's going to do the dress on, and then sort of cut away at it and tie things and loop things. I think she wanted it to be attention getting. She had this real desire to be seen as a strong woman and almost aggressive. You'll find a lot of people who will probably say that she's scary.

In her way, what she's doing and wearing is her statement. I do think she was determined to stand out. She loved to be considered at the center of whatever was happening, and it was really important to her. And of course, she enjoyed playing a role, wearing costumes, like in the "Nick Detroit" [issue of *Punk* magazine] (1.72).

JUDITH: That reminds me of *The Foreigner*, the Amos Poe film, where she does have a role, but every time she comes on-screen, you hear the Hollywood Charlie Chan–type music.

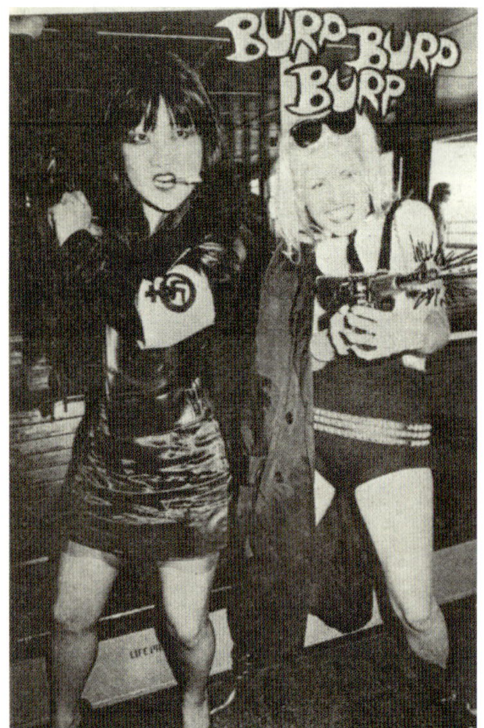

1.72. Anya Phillips and Debbie Harry playing "Nazi dykes" in the *fumetti* "The Legend of Nick Detroit," *Punk* magazine no. 6, October 1976. Photo: Chris Stein.

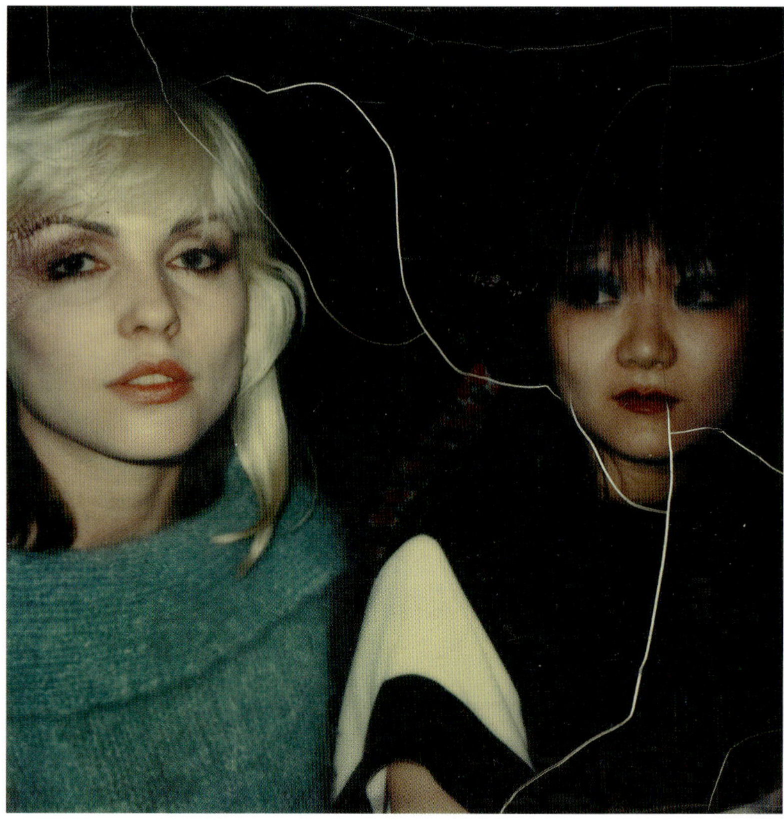

1.73. Debbie Harry and Anya Phillips, San Francisco, April 1977. Photo: Diego Cortez.

Debbie's look was so just stunning, and of course that attracted everyone to her and Anya as well. Anya saw her as a perfect kind of inspiration. I think they had a close and warm relationship. There was a vintage clothing place that was on Tenth Street somewhere in the East Village. The owner had big garbage bags full of vintage clothing that he'd collected. And so he'd just rip these bags open right there on the floor. There's nothing else in the store. It's just bare floorboards, and he would throw these bags in, and everybody would go attack the bags and pull out the different things. I think you could fill a paper bag for ten dollars or something. So that's where she'd go and she'd get things that she could either change or make over. It was a big inspiration for her. And this one particular time he had a bunch of mohair. And this picture reminds me of that. I'm wondering if that is one of the pieces that Debbie got from Anya because I got a really great couple of mohair sweaters from that place. —Sylvia Reed

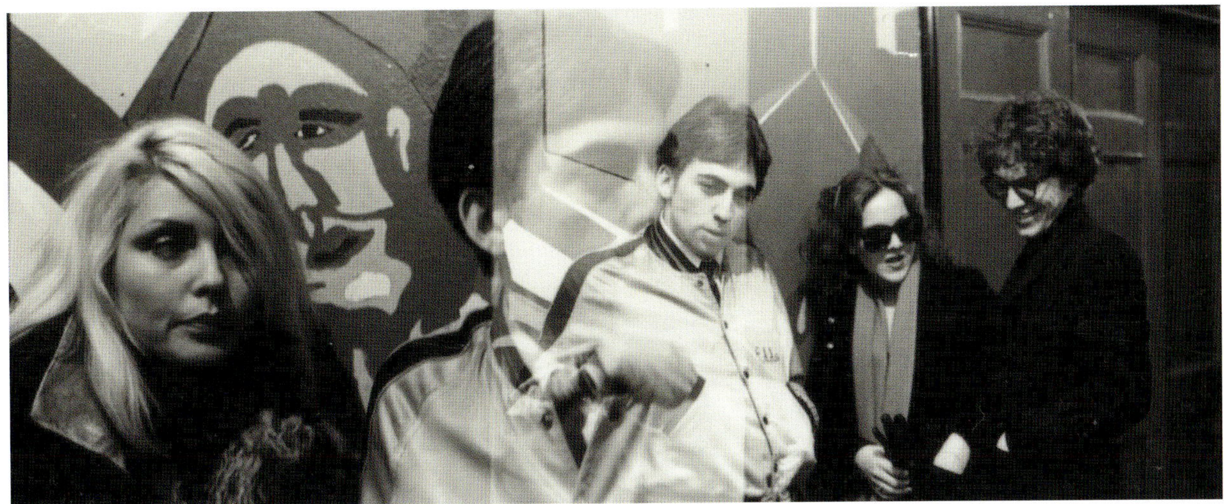

1.74. Two superimposed contact sheet frames picturing (*left to right*) Debbie Harry, Chris Stein, Lisa Jane Persky, and Gary Valentine, 1976. Photo: Anya Phillips. Published by permission of James Chance.

It's very clearly tapping into film clichés, but it is nevertheless stereotyping. In that film at one point she is wearing a body suit. . . .

SYLVIA: The latex suit.

JUDITH: Latex, right. And she says it's from Malcolm McLaren's Sex store. So was she intently watching Vivienne Westwood and what was coming out in London punk fashion? Did she feel herself to be in competition with that?

SYLVIA: Well, as I said, she was really perceptive, and she paid attention to these things. She went to London (1.75, 1.76), where I think there was a heightened sense of "let's take it to the costume level." I remember a certain orderliness about the rows of safety pins, all nicely lined up. In New York, it was very much street-level creativity. By the time you meet a person who was going to be a fashion leader and impresario, like McLaren and Westwood, they're right away developing a commercially available item.

JUDITH: Was that ever her goal, to develop a line of clothing? Or was she really just designing for herself and her immediate friends?

SYLVIA: We had long conversations about her plans, and she had always intended to do her own line. That was going to be what made her famous, her fashion line. She had it all planned out. I still wonder had she lived . . . she was so tremendously talented and ambitious, and I really believe she would've realized her idea of being a fashion designer of note, and to some, a real leader.

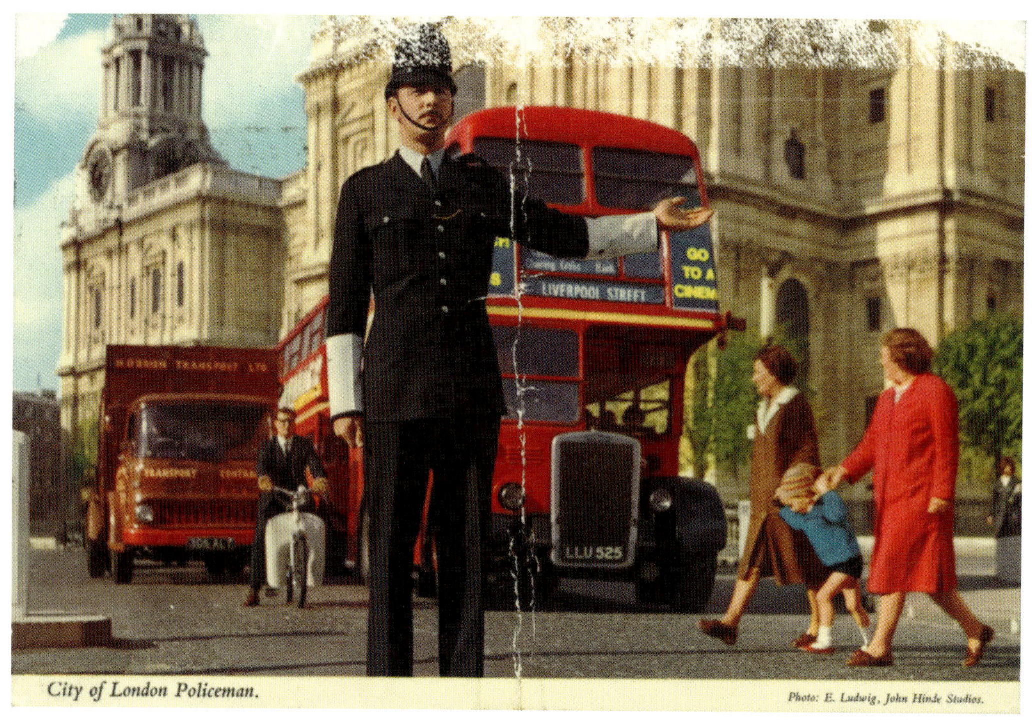

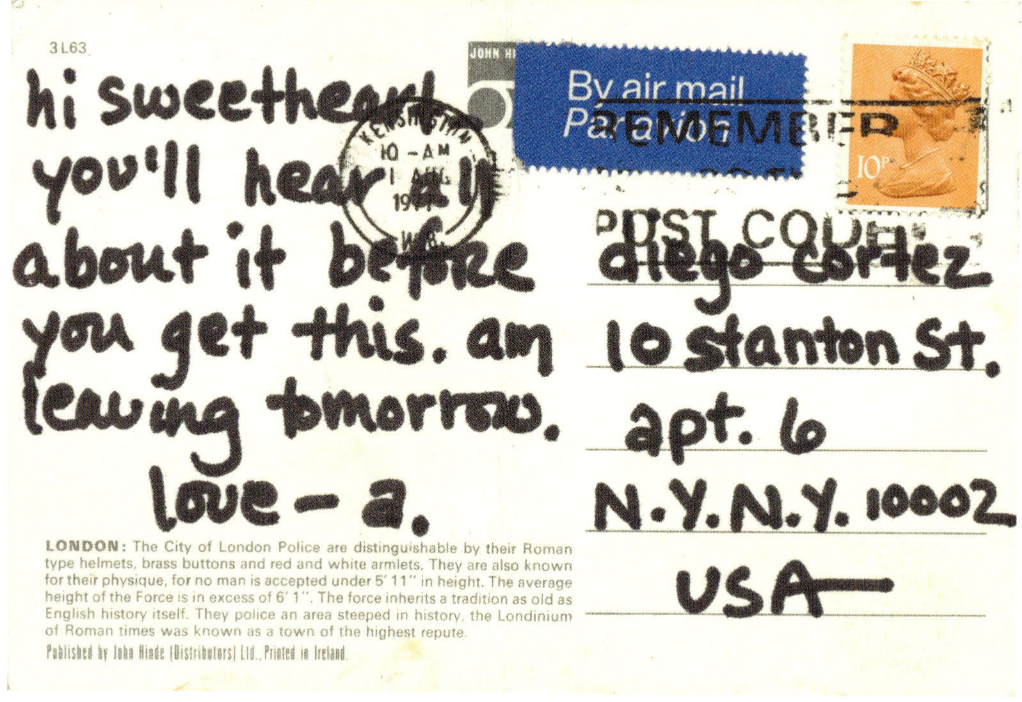

1.75 and 1.76. Front and back of a London postcard from Anya Phillips postmarked August 1977.

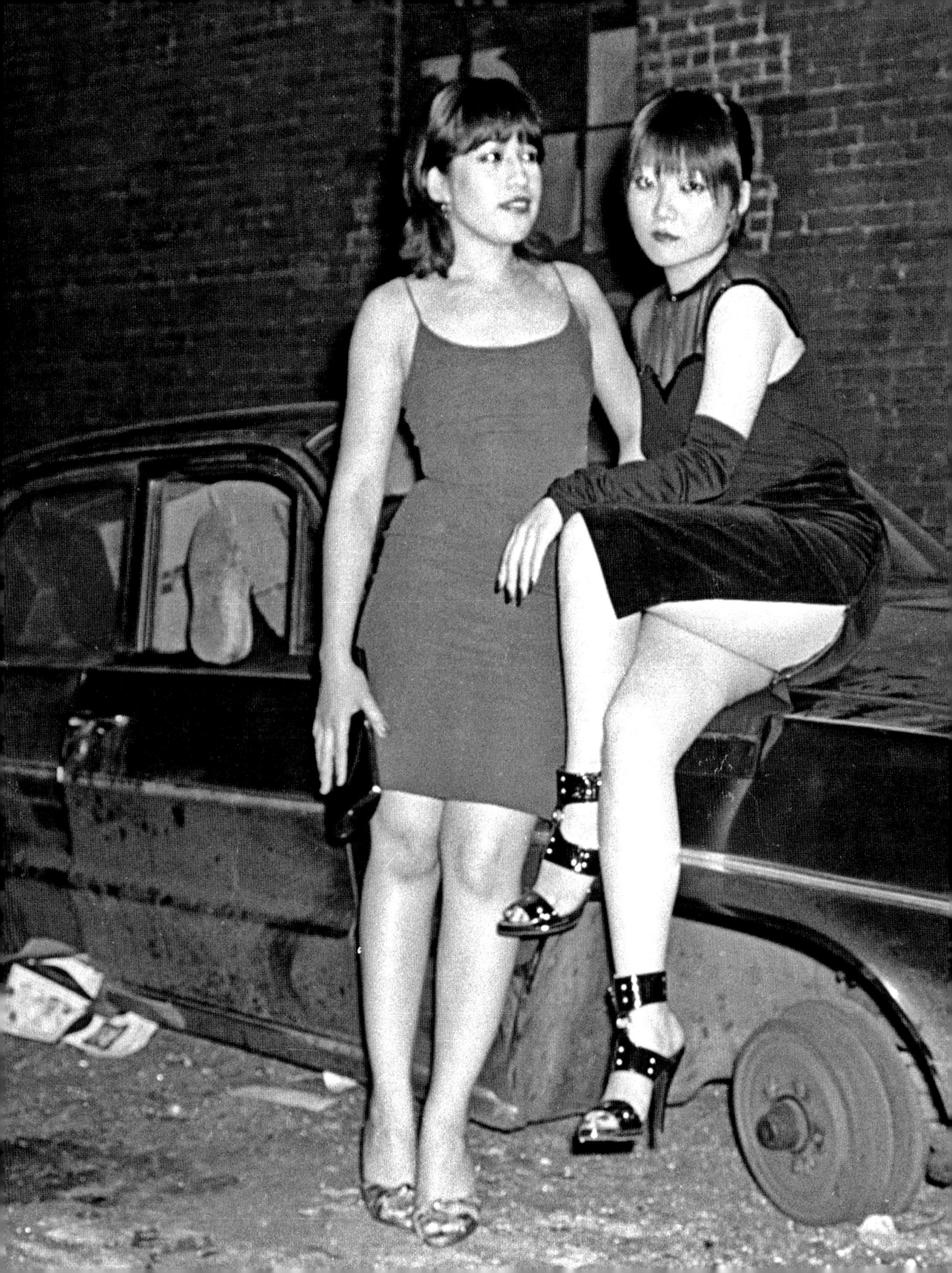

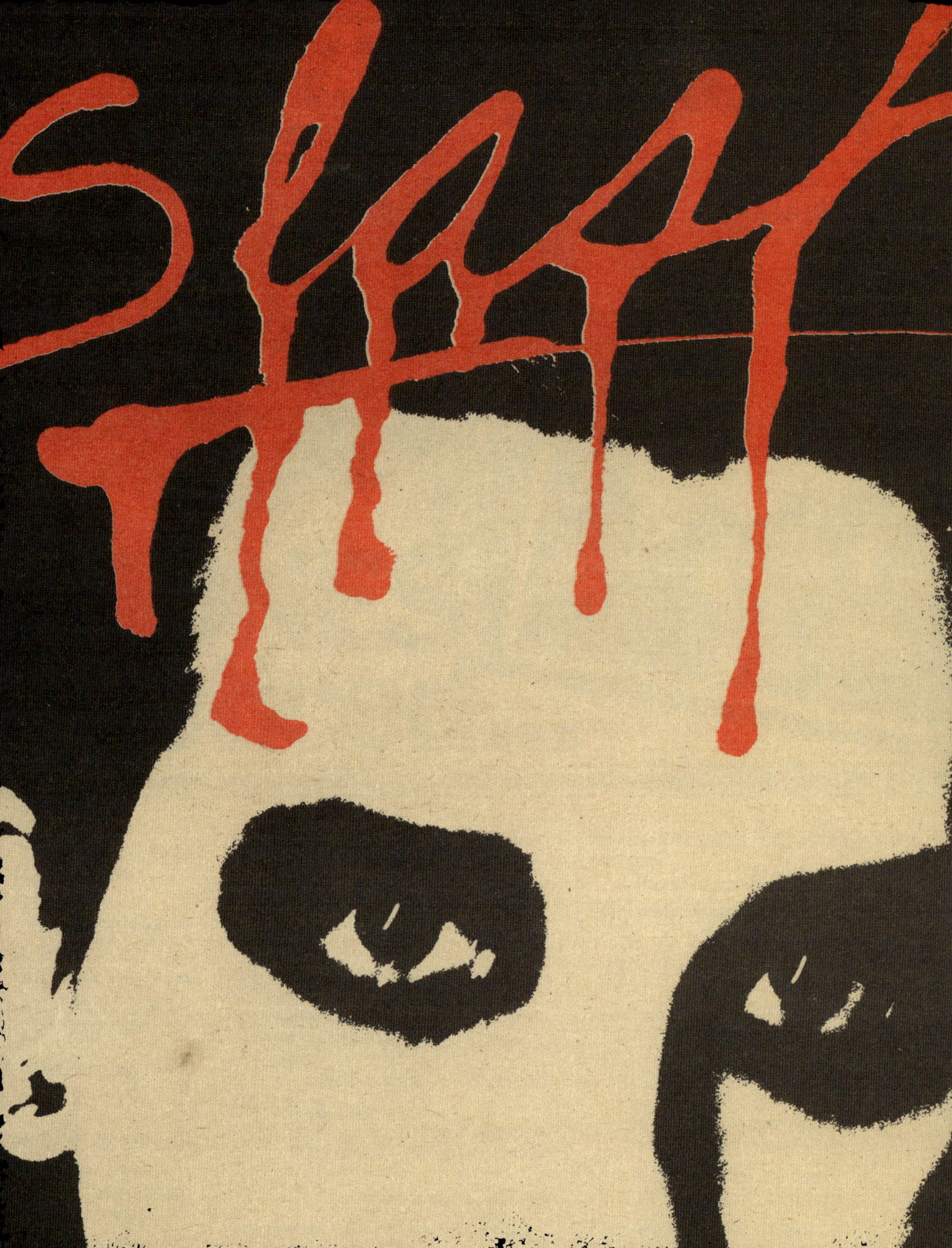

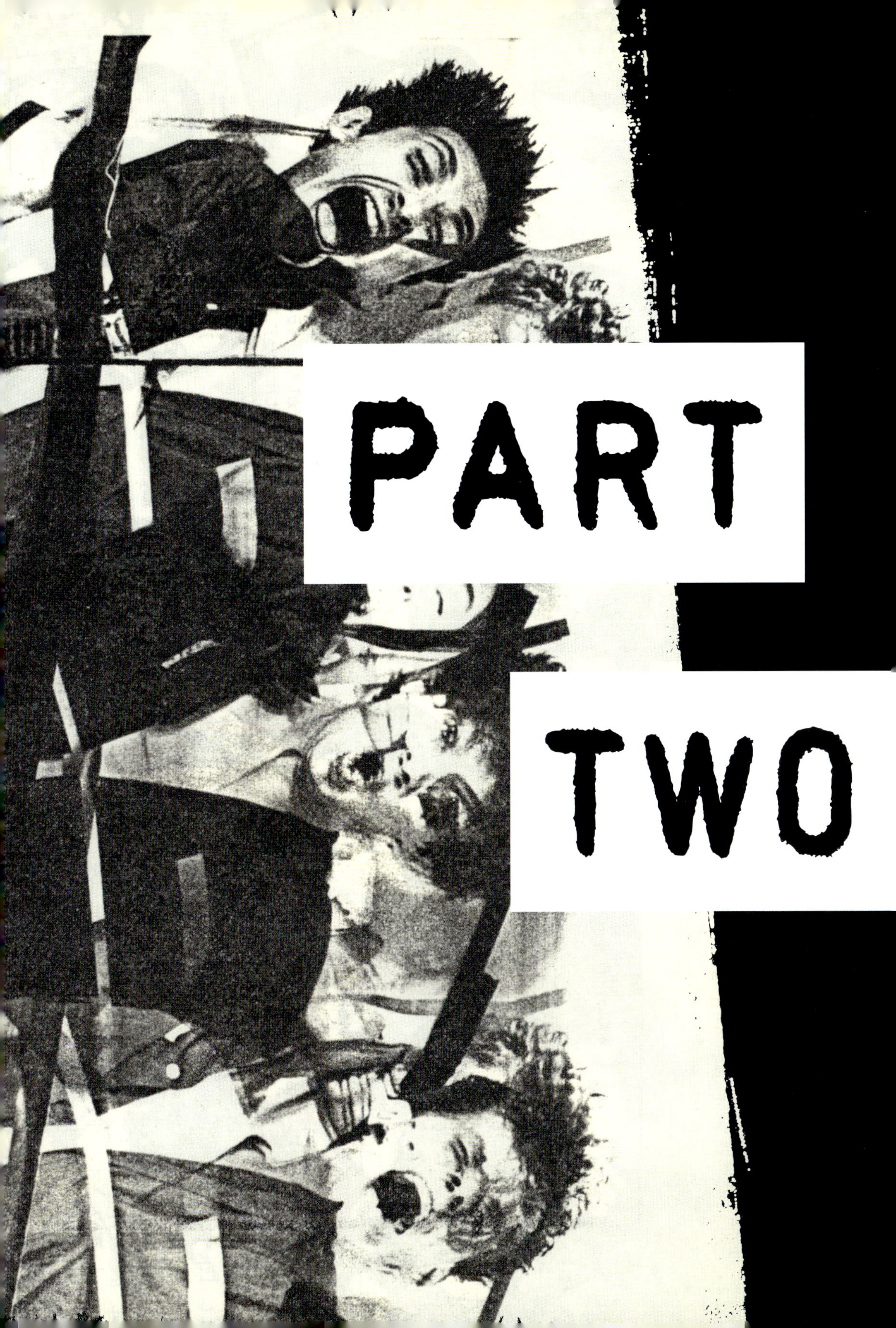

PART TWO

CH. 5 Doing the Future Yourself

THE SCREAMERS AND EARLY LOS ANGELES PUNK

Step into the Whisky on any night of the week in 1977 and you might catch the art-school punk of the Weirdos, the chaotic darkness of the Germs, the power-pop of the Zeros, and the Chicano punk of the Plugz. Where you would have seen the Doors a decade earlier, now you'd find their former keyboardist Ray Manzarek in the crowd as the producer for the rockabilly-infused punk of X. And if you happened to be there on December 17 that year, you might have noticed X's John Doe working the sound for the Screamers (2.37)—that is, if you could look away from the frantic convulsions of their wide-eyed front man Tomata du Plenty, tearing at the words to each song above Tommy Gear's distorted synthesizer riffs, Jeff McGregor's electric piano bass lines, and KK Barrett's driving drumbeat.

PART 2 digs deep into one band's brief but impactful career as punk took off and transformed in Southern California. The Screamers came together as a band in the early months of 1977, but the roots of their legendary performances reach back to the late 1960s counterculture and experimental drag and queer theater troupes in San Francisco, New York, and Seattle. The brainchild of Tomata (or Tomatâ, as he preferred to write it) and Tommy, who moved to LA together and joined forces with KK and a changing slate of keyboardists (David Brown, spring 1977–August 1977; Jeff McGregor, December 1977–April 1978; and Paul Roessler, April 1978–January 1980), the Screamers' music and image took queer performance art in a different trajectory—away from the campy ironic twist on the early 1960s pop and garage rock of Jayne County, Blondie, the Ramones, and the Mumps, and toward the manic look and performative aggression of the Sex Pistols and the Damned. While the Screamers never released a recording in their day, images and interviews in zines, bootleg tapes of their demos, and early grainy videos of their live shows and pre-MTV song videos circulated for decades—reaching fans like Ian MacKaye in DC and Martín Sorrondeguy in Chicago (see their contributions in CHAPTER 10).

FROM THE ASHES OF GLAM

Five years before the Screamers moved to Los Angeles, Rodney Bingenheimer—an acolyte of Sonny Bono and body double for Davey Jones of the Monkees—had emerged as an influential scene-maker on the Sunset Strip with his club Rodney Bingenheimer's English Disco (1972–1975). The gravitational pull of LA's thriving audience for glam rock was strong: Iggy Pop and the Stooges moved there in 1973, and David Johansen's reconstituted New York Dolls (sometimes known as the Dolls) played frequent gigs at the Whisky. By 1974, Bingenheimer's English Disco was losing ground to a new type of disco stemming from a smoothed-out funk groove and soulful vocals. In October he and producer Kim Fowley hosted a funereal celebration of glam rock's end, ironically billing it as the "First Annual Hollywood Street Revival and Trash Dance." Iggy Pop, the New York Dolls, and Los Angeles–based Zolar X and GTOs (Girls Together Outrageously—an early all-woman group produced by Frank Zappa) shared the bill (2.17).

In September 1975 a new local band called the Runaways began to make noise and generate buzz. Managed (and often abused) by Fowley, the Runaways started out as a contrived novelty act of an all-teenage-girl band, but they filled the local underground rock void with a sexualized yet tough image and searing hard-rock sound that attracted kids looking for something new and "snottier than arena rock" (as KK Barrett puts it in his caption for 2.19). Nearly a year later, in early August 1976, the Runaways found their way to CBGB, swapping places with the Ramones, who played their first West Coast shows at the Whisky around the same time. Their LA appearances made one Chicano teenager from East LA named Brian Tristan (aka Kid Congo Powers) "a true believer in the church of the Ramones."[1] Powers, who organized the band's West Coast fan club, later helped create the Screamers fan club (and went on to play guitar in the Gun Club, the Cramps, and Nick Cave and the Bad Seeds). But it would still be eight months before LA's own punk scene exploded onto local stages. In the meantime, the city attracted musicians and artists from across the country, looking for opportunity and community.

Arriving from Oklahoma in December 1976, KK Barrett had no problem finding LA's own punk underground: "Within days, I met some of these people. It seemed so easy and accessible. . . . There was this underground alternate scene of people starting bands, the same way I had started a band in Oklahoma" (see his interview in CHAPTER 8). One of these new bands, the Zeros (2.18), was an energetic group of Chicano teenagers from Chula Vista, with singer and guitarist Robert Lopez (aka El Vez) at the helm. Lopez had been inspired in part by Lance Loud and the Mumps.[2] The Zeros scored a gig with two other new bands, the Weirdos and the Germs, at the Orpheum on April 16, 1977. This now-legendary show—sandwiched between Iggy Pop and Blondie at the Santa Monica Civic Auditorium on April 15, and the Damned at the Starwood on April 17—set off a chain reaction. "The first local punk show I saw was the Weirdos, the Zeros, and the Germs at the Orpheum," recalls Alice Bag, the Chicana front woman of the Bags. "When I saw the Germs, I was surprised and outraged and excited all at once. . . . I thought, 'Wow, if they can do that, surely I can do something better.'"[3] Soon after, Bomp! Records threw a party to welcome the Runaways back as "L.A.'s own teen queens of noise," attended by "in-crowd people and local bands" including the Screamers before they had even stepped foot on a stage together (2.19).

Like the early New York punk scene rooted in queer film, theater, poetry, and visual art, the punks in Hollywood drew on the city's long association with the entertainment industry as fuel to burn in their songs and performances: X sang about it in their noirish "Sex and Dying in High Society"; the Bags put paper bags on their heads as a fuck you to the LA image machine; and a laughing Darby Crash wrapped himself in red licorice, while fans attacked him with food, markers, or glass bottles. Even LA's premiere punk zine *Slash* seemed to draw blood from the artfully photographed faces that graced its early covers. If "art damaged" became a catchphrase to describe bands like the Bags, the Germs, the Weirdos, and the Screamers, their performances also reminded everyone not to take themselves too seriously (2.20–2.24).

DOING THE FUTURE YOURSELF

The first issue of *Slash* from May 1977 featured a photo shoot and teaser copy for the Screamers, proclaiming them "THE FUTURE!" before they had played their first gig (2.30, 2.31). That would be a *Slash*-sponsored party on May 28, 1977. By many accounts, the *Slash* proclamation rang true: to see the Screamers perform was to witness a band that was ahead of its time. Pioneering a distinctive electropunk sound, they ditched guitars for an ARP Odyssey synthesizer,

Fender Rhodes electric piano, and plenty of distortion. Asked by *Slash* to describe the Screamers' sound in one word, Tomata du Plenty replied: "anxiety."[4]

Tomata's stark answer and the severe sound it describes seem a far cry from his early days in various psychedelic gender-bending cabaret troupes, including San Francisco's Cockettes, Seattle's Ze Whiz Kidz (which he founded in 1970 and where he first met Tommy), and New York's Hollywood Spit with Fayette Hauser. But as Tommy, Fayette, and KK recount in their contributions to PART 2, the Screamers emerged at a point in time when various countercultural and "freak" scenes across the country were scattering, regrouping, and absorbing the spikier edges of underground music and experimental theater.

The Screamers were not the first or only rock band to emerge from Ze Whiz Kidz. After a stint in New York with Fayette, Tomata returned to Seattle in 1975 and formed a garage-rock band called the Tupperwares with former Whiz Kid Rio de Janeiro (David Gulbransen) and Melba Toast (aka Tommy Gear). Although short-lived, they participated with two other bands—Meyce and the Telepaths—in the legendary "TMT" show on May 1, 1976, which sparked Seattle's long-lived underground music scene (see Tommy Gear's essay in CHAPTER 6). Penelope Houston, then seventeen, worked the door at the show and later became the lead singer for San Francisco punk stalwarts the Avengers. Whiz Kid Satin Sheets (aka J. Sats Beret) formed the Lewd, first in Seattle in 1977, and then with new members after relocating to San Francisco in 1978.

The Tupperwares, plotting their next move in the summer of 1976, changed their name to Gianni Bugatti and considered a move to LA.[5] During the transition to what would become the Screamers, bandmates Rio, Tomata, and Tommy communicated their ambitions and visions for the future through elaborate questionnaires (2.25–2.27): answering Rio's question about bands they might emulate, Tomata writes: "Bay City Rollers—attention, Sparks—image, Tomita—sound, Paul McCartney—longevity." Answering Tommy's question about hopes for the future, Tomata writes: "I have every confidence in TIME, we will be flying. My personal hopes for future involvement include more sophisticated equipment, therby [*sic*] allowing a fuller sound, improvement on all vocals, recording dates, tours, even if at first we are the only producers of all these efforts, also airplay a prime mover. A deeper impression into the INDUSTRY." Answering Tomata's question about his vision, Tommy describes integrating films and videos into their performances.[6]

Although Tomata continued as the Screamers' charismatic front man, the turn from campy pop to expressionist angst fit into Tommy's vision: "There is a definite need for the Screamers music today," he told *Slash* for their June 1978 feature on the band. "Anxiety, frustration and rage must be worked on constantly, underscored, brought out in the open and positively resolved . . . that is the purpose of our group."[7] Tommy's interest in psychology (as reported in the same *Slash* issue) led to this theory of the band's music and performance as mirror, agitation, and catharsis. Maybe it wasn't just a theory. In March 1978 the Screamers played a show for the residents at the Camarillo State Mental Hospital while their entourage handed out fan club applications (2.53). "The affinity was obvious," *Slash* reported, "anxiety level music for anxiety-wrought minds."[8] But as Tommy describes in his caption for the working notes on that gig (2.54), "they were one of the most authentically appreciative audiences that we'd ever encountered."

Tomata often described his performance as "a controlled nervous breakdown." "The Screamers was a highly theatrical thing," he remarked in 2000; "how could you put that on record?"[9] The band famously never obtained a record deal, though they did try (2.47). Without the resources of a record label, the Screamers did everything themselves, falling into the DIY model by default. They started off with homemade flyers, collaging photographs of the band members (2.32, 2.33, 2.43, 2.45), but eventually hired artist and scenester Gary Panter to put together a logo. By early 1978, the iconic image of a screaming man with spiked hair appeared on flyers, ads, letterhead, stickers, and almost every other publicity material the band put out (2.46, 2.50–2.52).

Flyers and posters are the most typical way to remember a show: image, band names, the venue and date, and maybe a small map to help you find the club. Tommy Gear's accounting sheets for the Screamers' gigs, on the other hand, provide time capsules that record what went on behind the scenes: the division of labor, expenses, and profits (such as they were) shared among the band members and their support team, who were often their friends. Budget calculations for the Masque show on December 17, 1977, indicate that Tommy printed and mailed flyers; Gorilla Rose and John Doe (of X) served as roadies; and Herb Wrede and Diane Grove, who managed the fan club along with Kid Congo Powers, worked as gofers (2.37). For the Whisky shows in February 1978, KK silkscreened posters; Jeff bought the paper and rented rehearsal space; Gorilla worked lights; Herb, Diane, and Brian (Powers) pitched in with printing and transportation tasks; and $100 went to "hospital"—a charge that shows up in other budgets for the Whisky (2.44). The financial record for the trip to San Francisco for the Target Video shoot in August 1978 tells a story of the band's misadventure on their drive from Los Angeles in the line item for "additional car repair expenses" (2.60).

Of course, the band didn't claim indie cred (there was none to be had in 1977 and '78). Instead, they took on all the publicity tasks that a major label would do: preparing their own press kits with a band chronology, media clippings, and quotes, and targeting key local, national, and international rock magazines such as *New York Rocker*, *Creem*, *Rock Scene*, *Variety*, *Melody Maker*, and *NME* (2.65). By the fall of 1978 they had created enough buzz to tour clubs in the eastern half of the US without releasing a single recording (2.61, 2.62). Rather than setting the model for the punk underground to come—distributing singles, albums, and cassettes through independent labels and zine networks, playing in basements or warehouses in small towns—the Screamers imagined, and began to act out, another future, anticipating the rise of MTV by several years. In the August 1978 issue, *New York Rocker* reported, "The chances of hearing the Screamers on wax, at least in the near future, are slim. They say they are holding out for a video-disc arrangement, where they can bombard their audiences visually as well as musically."

SHUT UP AND LISTEN!

After the band returned from New York at the end of 1978, they began working with the Los Angeles–based Dutch filmmaker Rene Daalder, who started to script the band's shows. Daalder had his own ambitions to create a German Expressionist–inspired "punk/disco operetta" revolving around Tomata's angst-ridden *Mensch* character. Daalder staged a version of this operetta for the Screamers' 1979 shows, cowriting a few songs and adding two violins and vocalist

Sheila Edwards to increase dramatic action and intensity (2.71–2.75). The Fayette and KK interviews, and captions from Tommy and Bianca Daalder-van Iersel, detail the Screamers' Daalder period, which culminated with the filming of *Population: 1*, but also the band's dissolution (2.67–2.70).

With the turn toward cabaret, the Screamers circled back to their queer performance roots and headed in the opposite direction of the hardcore bands in LA's South Bay suburbs (Hermosa Beach and Huntington Beach). In Dewar MacLeod's words, "art-damaged was replaced by just plain *Damaged*—the title of Black Flag's first album" (2.86).[10] MacLeod's neat division of LA punk sounds a lot like the Roessler family, where older brother Paul played keyboards in the Screamers and his younger sister Kira later played bass in Black Flag. But if the urban and suburban scenes resembled a generational divide and sibling rivalry, they could also resemble an extended family gathering.

The story of the clean break between art punk and hardcore, so often told as a shift from diversity to homogeneity, can be persuasive in part because race, gender, and sexuality seem to map easily onto geographic conflicts: Hollywood versus Hermosa Beach; East LA versus Orange County. Some punks definitely felt the transition. Robert Lopez of the Zeros remembers, "Clubs were shutting down because of the violence caused by people we didn't know, those new guys from Orange County. Punk had turned a corner. Less art and more machine, punk wasn't dead; it had just become something else" (2.80).[11] Similarly, the photographer Ann Summa felt that, for women, "when it got more hardcore, it became less welcoming."[12] Other members of the hardcore scene experienced it differently, as fan Angelita Figueroa Salas remembers: "I never really thought about being a woman in the scene. . . . Being Latina wasn't an issue. We were just all people who liked a common theme, and it was the music."[13]

It is important to remember that even the emblematic hardcore band Black Flag included at various points the Puerto Rican singer Ron Reyes, the Colombian-born drummer Robo (aka Julio Roberto Valverde Valencia), and Kira Roessler (2.84, 2.85). And with Raymond Pettibon drawing most of the band's flyers and album covers, it's hard to make the case that hardcore killed off the artiness (2.83). At the same time, hardcore didn't come so late to the scene. Greg Ginn formed his first band Panic! with Keith Morris in 1976—the same year the Screamers showed up in LA—and morphed into Black Flag in late 1977. A year later, Ginn founded the label SST Records, releasing Black Flag's first EP, *Nervous Breakdown*, in January 1979. SST soon became home to a growing roster of bands in the area: Boyle Heights' Mexican American hardcore band Stains (2.90); San Pedro's econo minded Minutemen, who mixed funk, country twang, norteño, and more into their version of punk (2.87, 2.88); and Wilmington's proto-grunge Saccharine Trust (2.80).

Beyond Black Flag and their early SST label mates, new and old punks were mixing it up in bands and on bills across Southern California. Former Screamers keyboardist Paul Roessler and former Germs drummer Don Bolles joined Dinah Cancer's goth-punk band 45 Grave in 1980; and Texacala Jones, singer for "cowpunk" stalwarts Tex & the Horseheads, played a bill with 45 Grave and a solo acoustic set by D. Boone (2.89). In East LA, a vibrant Chicano punk scene coalesced around a community arts center called the Vex, which began hosting punk shows in 1980 with a bill that included neighborhood bands the Brat, the Undertakers, the Plugz, and Los Illegals. The Brat, powered by vocalist Teresa Covarrubias and their blend of reggae, pop, and punk, became a regional favorite, sharing a bill in 1982 with an early incarnation of the Bangles, then called the Bangs (2.81). The flyers from all these shows tune any viewer into a scene more open and varied than a simple story of art versus hardcore or Hollywood versus Hermosa Beach. Despite what divisions, infighting, and violence crept into the scene, there was always room on a bill for someone new to join the eclectic mix. You only need to look at the flyer for the Vex in November 1982, when a band of kids between twelve and fifteen years old calling themselves Mad Society shared the same stage as the Circle Jerks, Black Flag, and the Plugz (2.82).

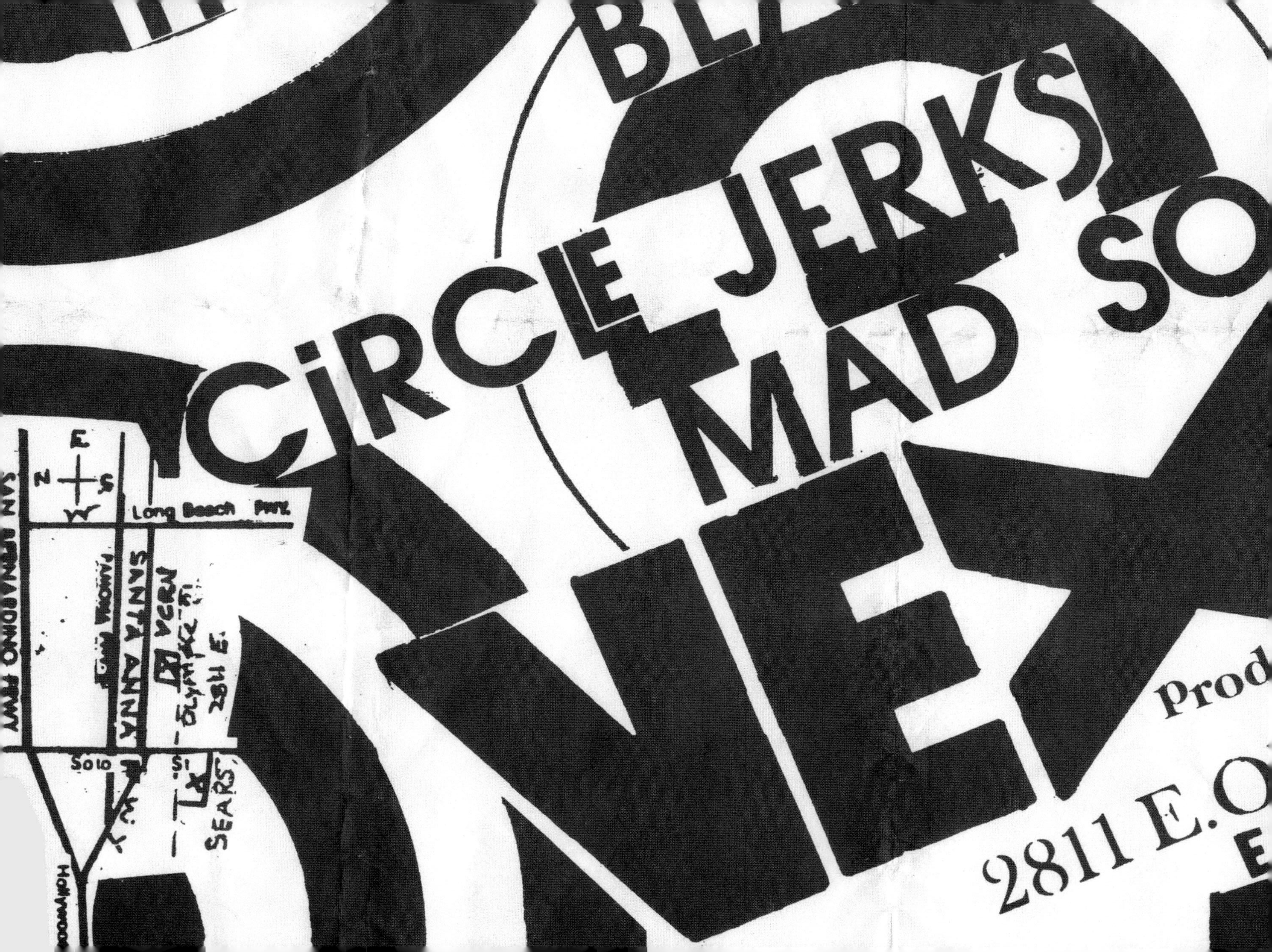

BL
CIRCLE JERKS
MAD SO
VE
Prod
2811 E. O
E
Long Beach FWY.
SANTA ANNA FWY
PAMONA FWY.
SAN BERNARDINO FRWY
VERN
OLYMPIC
2811 E.
SEARS
Solo
Hollywood
N
S
E
W

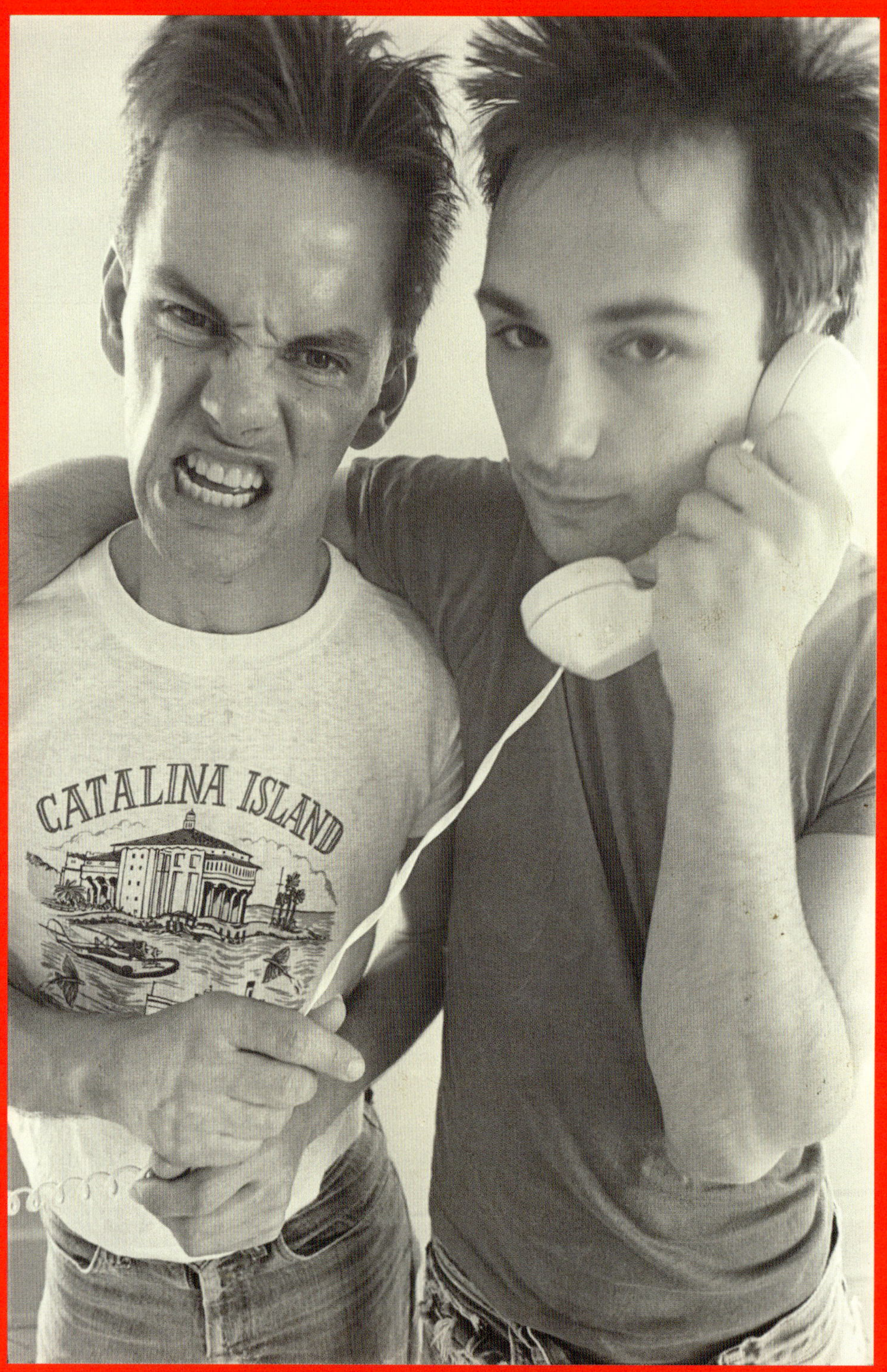

2.1. Tomata du Plenty and Tommy Gear, circa 1976. Photographer unknown.

A Punky Analepsis

CH. 6

TOMMY GEAR

A song rises, approaches, or fades away. . . .
multiplicities fill it, singularities connect with one another,
processes or becomings unfold, intensities rise and fall.

—Gilles Deleuze, "On Philosophy" (1988)

Serendipity alone cannot account for the intersecting paths that culminated in the formation of the Screamers. Living countercultural lives in the 1970s, Tomatâ du Plenty and I found ourselves ricocheting between multiple urban enclaves with underground scenes that were always in varying degrees of emergence or dissolution.

We made our initial acquaintance amid a farrago of wannabe bohemians in Seattle's Capitol Hill neighborhood, and although he was several years my senior, we both shared a Roman Catholic family background as well as the experience of leaving home as "teenage runaways," which landed him on the streets of Hollywood by the mid-1960s and me in the Haight-Ashbury in 1968. By the end of that decade the Cockettes performance troupe had formed in San Francisco (taking inspiration from forerunners such as New York's Theatre of the Ridiculous and the Living Theatre), presenting their eclectic brand of psychedelic hippie drag spectacles regularly at the Palace Theater in North Beach, events that I often frequented prior to returning to Seattle to finish high school and commence my university studies.

After my return, it quickly became apparent that Seattle's burgeoning underground/fringe scene had been succeeding to further amplify itself through local alternative media like the *Helix*, a politically leftist weekly newspaper, and the noncommercial independent radio station KRAB-FM, where listeners could hear garage bands such as the Sonics (hailing from Tacoma, Washington), the Seeds (hailing from Los Angeles), the Stooges and MC5 (hailing from Detroit)—progenitors of what later became commercialized as punk rock—along with a panoply of "progressive" rock, "art" bands, and experimental music genres ranging from the likes of Frumious Bandersnatch, Frank Zappa and the Mothers of Invention, the Velvet Underground and Nico, Yoko Ono, Captain Beefheart, Can, and Neu! among even quirkier playlists.

Tomatâ also decamped from San Francisco to Seattle around the same time, and taking a cue from the Cockettes, he soon attracted a fluid ensemble of local amateurs eager to cut their musical comedic teeth chewing the scenery in the glare of the nearest available cabaret spotlight, which opportunistically presented itself in a cramped basement dive bar (aptly christened the "Submarine Room") that offered a makeshift platform garishly festooned with glittery swags as a stage set beneath a low ceiling bedecked with hanging plastic flower garlands, which was literally located underground near Seattle's historic Pioneer Square in the Smith Tower building (the city's first skyscraper, notable for having been the tallest building west of the Mississippi when it was originally built in 1914). That ensemble made their public debut on Labor Day in 1970 as Ze Fabulous Whiz Kidz before an audience at the Sky River Rock Festival largely composed of stoned Pacific Northwest hippies. Another of their flamboyant performances followed on Halloween at downtown Seattle's premiere rock concert venue, and by the summer of 1971 Ze Whiz Kidz were billed as the opening act in Seattle for Alice Cooper's "Love It to Death" tour, mounting a melodramatic rockabilly-themed extravaganza that featured a squad of motorcycles on the Paramount Theater's lavish rococo stage.

By the fall of 1971 I had started college and decided to undertake an independent study abroad in Europe—a self-fashioned "Grand Tour" spanning several months of travel throughout England, France, Germany, the Netherlands, Switzerland, and Italy. While affording opportunities for study and research in certain academic areas of interest to me at the time, this experience of cultural immersion also proved to be creatively formative as the direct result of gaining firsthand exposure to cutting-edge Continental thinkers and artists. In particular I was drawn to contemporary experimental aesthetic practices that were exploring new forms of conceptual art, electronic music composition techniques, and nontraditional theater, with a specific interest in those influenced by Antonin Artaud's "Theater of Cruelty," Peter Brook's "Empty Space," Jerzy Grotowski's "Poor Theater," Hermann Nitsch's "Orgien Mysterien Theater," as well as Ariane Mnouchkine's epic production by Le Théâtre du Soleil of "1789" that I attended when it was presented at London's Roundhouse. My exposure to these seminal theatrical visionaries would inform the visceral performative approach that would come to fruition later in the context of the Screamers.

After returning to the US I largely remained focused over the next couple of years on my college studies, interspersed by recurrent visits with friends residing in San Francisco, Los Angeles, and New York City's Lower East Side. By late 1972 Tomatâ had relocated to New York City and was sharing a flat on the Bowery with his longtime soulmate Fayette Hauser; over time they were joined there by Michael Farris (aka Gorilla Rose), who had performed with Ze Whiz Kidz as well as others from the West Coast who would be drawn there by the cultural excitement being fomented by scenesters in downtown Manhattan at places like Andy Warhol's Factory and

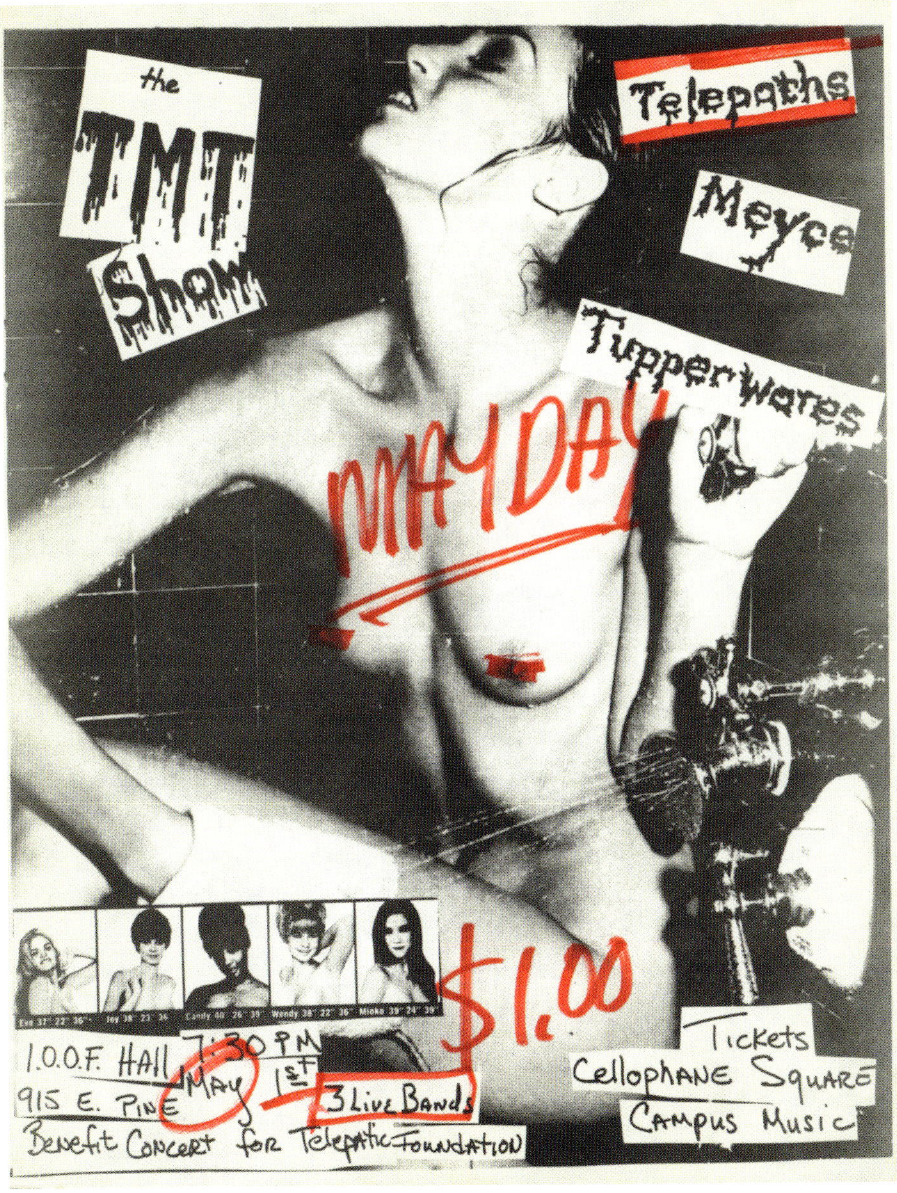

2.2 and 2.3. Flyer and ticket for the TMT Show (Telepaths, Meyce, Tupperwares) at the Independent Order of Odd Fellows Hall in Seattle, May 1976. Flyer design: Tommy Gear.

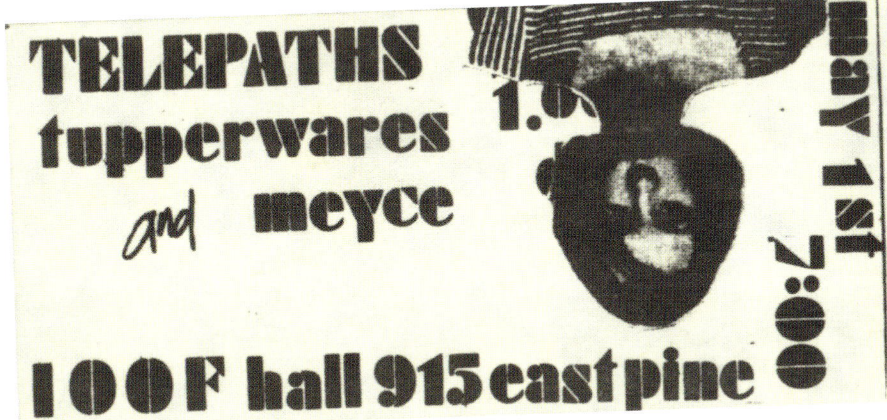

Interview magazine, Max's Kansas City, the Loft, Trude Heller's, the Continental Baths, and CBGB. During the time he resided in the Bowery, Tomatâ befriended so many others living in the vicinity as neighbors with their own aspirations for creative success—among them Debbie Harry and Chris Stein, Dee Dee and Joey Ramone, Arturo Vega and Lance Loud—a number of whom were soon to become quite notable, finding wider success a few years hence.

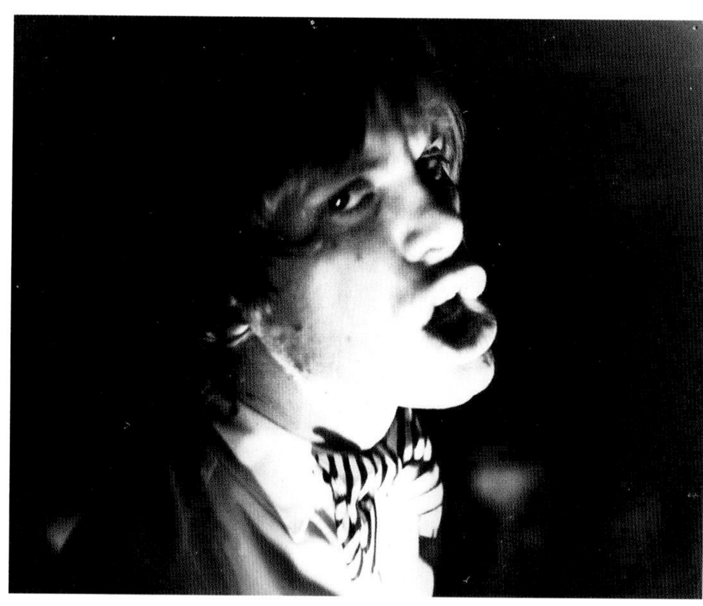

2.4. Photo of Tomata du Plenty during a Tupperwares show. Photo: © Fayette Hauser.

Meanwhile back in Seattle, having performed in larger concert venues as the opening act for touring rock bands, Ze Whiz Kidz had gradually shifted their performance style from its former reliance on staging melodramatic vignettes with improvisational histrionics toward a primarily song-based format, often spotlighting an unreservedly mannerist solo vocalist supported by a well-rehearsed backing band whose stage personas emulated those of fellow gender-bending glam rockers who were becoming popularized in that period, exemplified by David Bowie, Marc Bolan, and Jobriath, as well as the New York Dolls (for whom the troupe was the opening act at Seattle's Moore Theater in 1974). It was later that same year, occasioned by the US economy having tanked in a global energy crisis that set off a stock market crash and related recession, when many creative artists in New York were finding the demands of living in the city had become an unrelenting struggle to survive, that Tomatâ ultimately took the hard decision to withdraw back to Seattle with a view to regrouping.

After Ze Whiz Kidz's eventual dissolution in 1975, some of its former members undertook reinventing themselves, subsequently reincarnating as spinoffs in the form of harder rock bands (such as the Sixteen Year Old Virgins, the Knobs, and the Lewd) or exploring other transitional performance endeavors, such as the formation of the Tupperwares, which started out as a somewhat ad hoc songwriting trio of Tomatâ, Rio de Janeiro (aka David Gulbranson), and me (aka Melba Toast at that time). In Seattle we collaborated with a local teenage garage band (the Telepaths) to devise basic chord progressions and rhythmic paradiddles to match our idiosyncratic lyrics; at the outset their members also accompanied us playing guitar, bass, and drums as our backing band when performing live, until we later recruited our own instrumental lineup that included Pam Lillig (later with the Girls) and Ben Rabinowitz (later with the Girls and the Moberlys, and since deceased) on guitars, plus Eldon Hoke (aka El Duce, who later formed the Mentors, and since deceased) and Bill Rieflin (later of the Blackouts, Ministry, Nine Inch Nails, R.E.M., and King Crimson among others, and also since deceased) on drums.

Taking inspiration from Brian Eno's early work with Roxy Music using the EMS VCS 3 portable analog synthesizer, as well as his use of audio synthesis, effects processing, and an "oblique strategies" approach to composition and production on his first three solo albums, I acquired an ARP Odyssey Mark I (Model 2800), a duophonic analog synthesizer that I played in the Tupperwares and which was later incorporated into the Screamers' instrumental lineup along with a

Roland TR-66 drum machine and a Fender Rhodes Mark I electric piano, which I augmented with a series of analog signal processors (such as the classic Electro-Harmonix Big Muff Pi).

The Tupperwares' debut performance took place New Year's Day 1976 at Seattle's Moore Theater with a short set of original songs intended as the live opening act preceding that city's first public screening of the John Waters film *Pink Flamingos*, starring Divine. Several weeks after that show I traveled to New York to visit a friend from Seattle who had been living in Alphabet City, and I stayed at her apartment in the Christodora on Avenue B across from Tompkins Square Park. During my time there I made a point to contact some from Tomatâ's erstwhile circle of downtown friends, to check in and catch them up on what we had been doing together. One day while I was out and about, I decided to walk over to see if Arturo Vega was around. When I finally caught up with him, he was schlepping band equipment to load onto a double-parked truck; then I noticed that Joey and Johnny Ramone were anxiously milling around nearby. Arturo told me they were on their way to record their first record album at Radio City Music Hall but were running late. He asked me whether I could help them load up a couple amps and the last few boxes of cables they needed so they could finally get going. Of course I was willing to help, and once everything was securely loaded, I wished them all good luck and waved to them as they quickly headed off to Plaza Sound Studios for their recording session. By April I had been back in Seattle for a while, and we were preparing for the upcoming "T-T-Oh! Show," which would be showcasing three local bands (the Tupperwares, the Telepaths, and Oh! Henry) at Seattle's Polish Hall; however, as it turned out, the venue ended up canceling the show, most probably because they realized the night we'd planned to play there was Easter Sunday. Though somewhat disappointed, about a week later we were excited to learn that Sire was about to release the Ramones' first album, which buoyed our spirits as we focused on promoting our upcoming "TMT Show" in May, featuring the Tupperwares, the Meyce, and the Telepaths at the Odd Fellows Temple on Seattle's Capitol Hill, which had been organized by the three bands collaboratively (price of admission, one dollar). It would be the first public performance (albeit with guitars) of three early songs that would later be readapted for electronic keyboards and incorporated into the Screamers' standard repertoire ("I'm Going Steady with Twiggy," "Eva Braun," and "Magazine Love").

While the Ramones were performing on the Fourth of July in London, establishing punk rock as a global phenomenon that would change the course of music history forever, we spent the summer of 1976 finalizing our plans to relocate in Los Angeles, a sunnier destination (and epicenter of the recording industry), believing that the limited opportunities to perform or reach a wider audience would only constrain us if we were to remain in Seattle. So in the fall we loaded up a rented U-Haul van and drove down the Pacific Coast to Southern California, where each of us had made arrangements to stay with friends until we could find our own accommodations and get resettled. But soon after arriving it became apparent that our troika was in need of creative realignment, and we quickly came to a mutual understanding to break off our collaboration as the Tupperwares.

At this juncture Tomatâ and I took it upon ourselves to reassess our musical efforts to date and realized this presented us with a singular opportunity to reenvision ourselves anew.

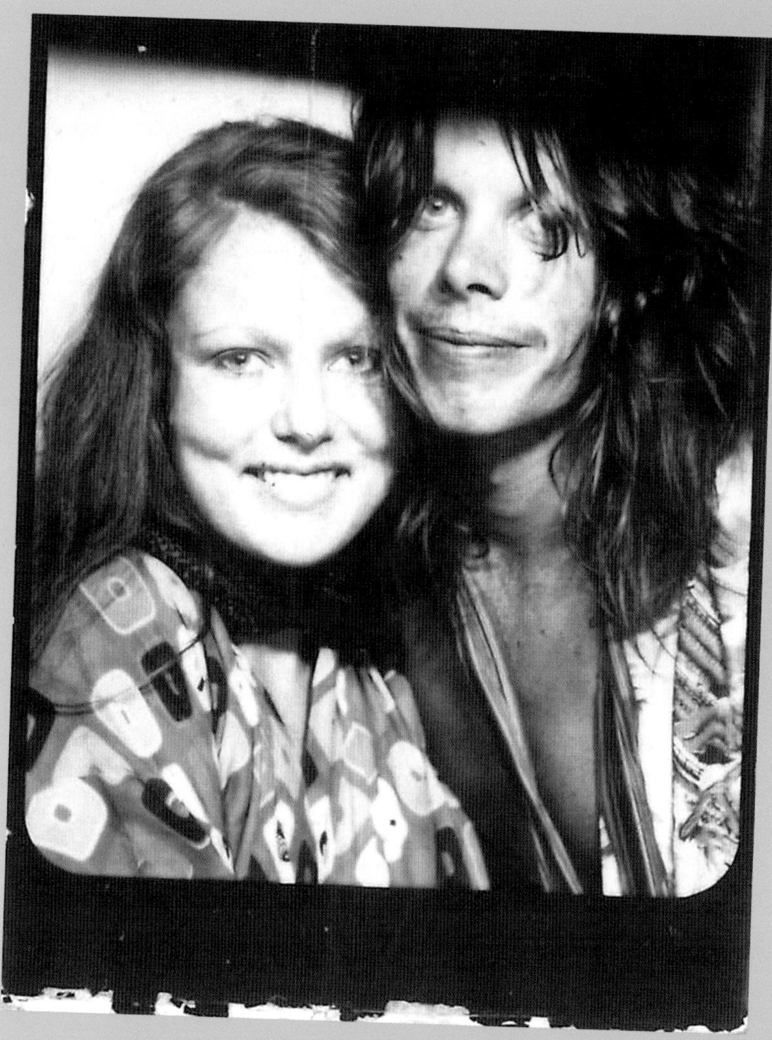

2.5. Fayette Hauser and Tomata du Plenty, photo booth picture, Seattle, 1971. Courtesy of Fayette Hauser.

CH. 7

"Punk is the last incarnation of the counter-culture"

AN INTERVIEW WITH FAYETTE HAUSER ON TOMATA DU PLENTY AND CULTURAL TRANSFORMATION

Fayette Hauser is an artist, photographer, writer, and performer and was a founding member of the acid drag cabaret troupe the Cockettes in San Francisco at the tail end of 1969. She met Tomata du Plenty in the summer of 1971 when he brought his own Seattle avant-garde drag troupe, Ze Whiz Kidz, to San Francisco. They formed a lifelong bond and performed together in New York, Seattle, and Los Angeles from 1973 into the early days of the Screamers. In this interview, conducted on January 20, 2022, Fayette shares her memories of Tomata du Plenty and discusses his importance as a bridge between the psychedelic and punk countercultures, and a mentor to young artists in the LA scene.

JUDITH: You knew Tomata du Plenty since his earliest performing career. What do you remember about those early days?

FAYETTE: Tomata started in San Francisco with the Cockettes. He grew up in Southern California. Well, he was born in New York. But then they moved to Montebello, California. He came to San Francisco, definitely by 1970. He was in one or two Cockettes shows. But I didn't meet him that summer.

JUDITH: Tell me about the Cockettes. What would Tomata have walked into when he came to San Francisco?

FAYETTE: We were so energized by the acid and the energy in the society. The society energy was incredible because everybody was talking about concepts and ideas and a future vision, like a futuristic society set in a past country. We were really a parallel world. Because people like the Diggers and the Beats had created the nesting, the groundwork. The Diggers chilled out the politics and created the free clinic and housed people in the housing there. Nobody wanted to live in the old drafty Victorians, so it was easier than you might think.

A lot of people went to San Francisco in the Summer of Love, but then a lot of people left. They had fun in the park and then left, because they wanted to go home or whatever. But so many people were alienated from their family and from society because they were different. They were artists. I mean, you know the 1950s and '60s middle-class dream was not to have your kid be a freak. So San Francisco was a petri dish for what is happening now in modern culture. Because everybody was involved in creating a new culture. Everybody who was an artist, a musician, or an intellectual was drawn to the energy of the new culture. I went to a really good art school in Boston, Boston University College of Fine Arts, and so I had a lot of art theory. Then I went to San Francisco and put it to work. All the psychedelics made that come alive for me (2.7–2.9).

JUDITH: Following up on what you are saying about San Francisco, that was clearly a lure for Tomata at some point in his life. But then he left for Seattle. Why didn't he stay in San Francisco?

FAYETTE: As hyperactive as Tomata was, I think it was a little too intense for him. When he came to San Francisco,

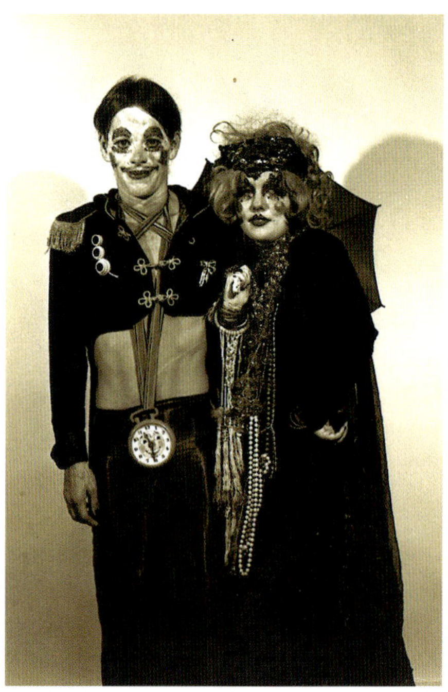

2.6. Fayette Hauser and Tomata du Plenty in Ze Whiz Kidz costumes, Seattle, circa 1971–72. Photo: Chuck Roche.

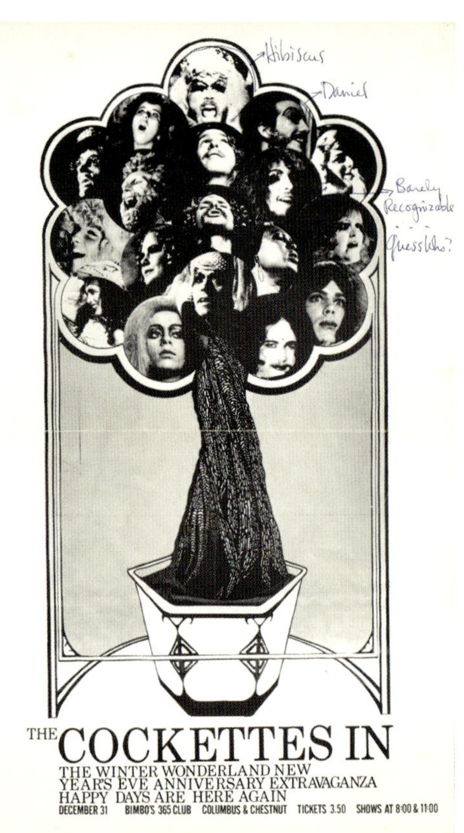

2.7. Flyer for the Cockettes' New Year's Eve show, San Francisco, 1970.

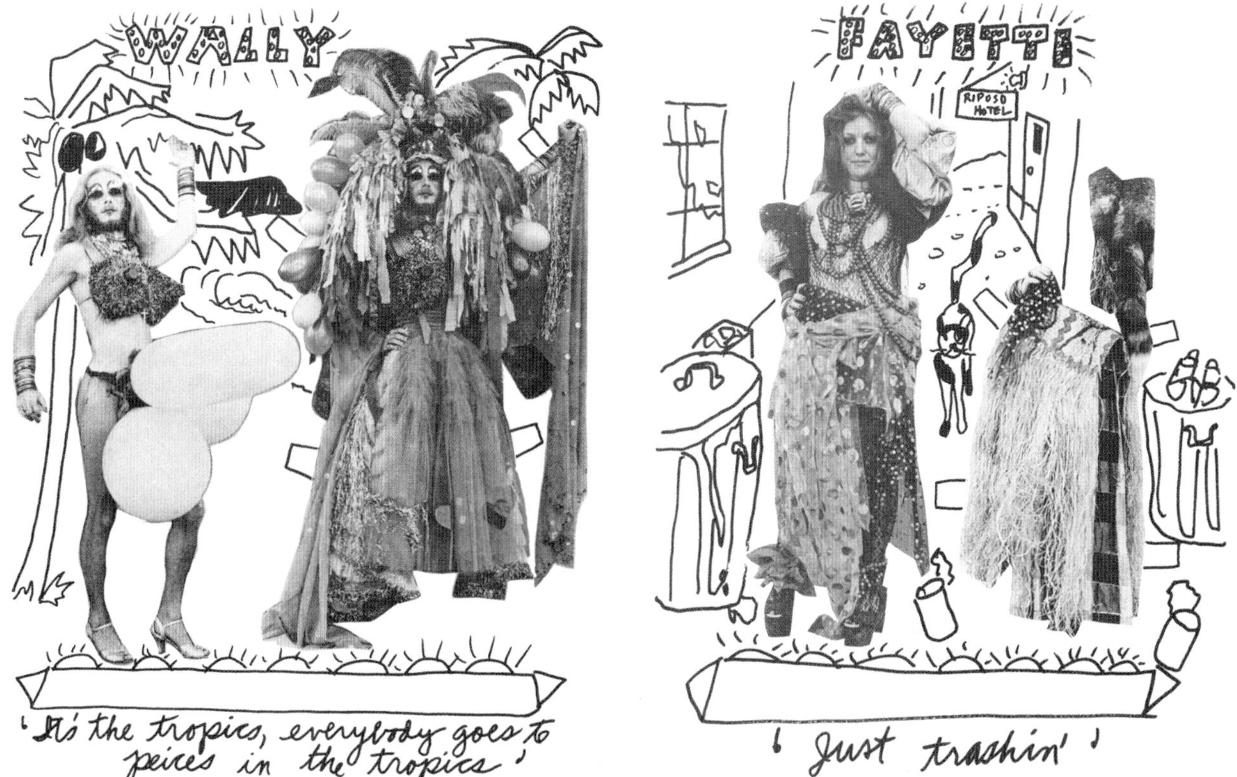

2.8 and 2.9. Two pages from *The Official Cockettes Paper Doll Book*, 1971.

Scrumbly [Richard Koldewyn] remembers him in the early shows, when he was David Harrigan. So he hadn't become Tomata. A lot of people came into the house and couldn't take it because the energy in the house was acute and intense, very "in your face." If a newcomer came to the house, we would try to trip them out even more, like a bit of a test.

Seattle was a popular place to go if you wanted something that was a little less intense. For a lot of people, San Francisco was just a bit too much. They wanted more of a country vibe. Somebody would say, "Hey, I'm going to Seattle. You want to come?" And then you'd jump in the car. So he ended up in Seattle, and it was also very cheap to live on Capitol Hill in the old houses. They lived together in various houses, as we did, and they named their houses, House of Leather, Lavender Shadows, etc. Tomata created Ze Whiz Kidz. They had a video artist, Randy [John Morris], who became Black Randy. Randy was really young and so enthusiastic. He was another one who had fabulous energy. He must have had a very high IQ. He got into video, and so he videoed their shows.

The thing is when you had a group, if you were a freak theater group, there were other groups in the country. There was Ze Whiz Kidz in Seattle. There was the Ridiculous Theatre in New York, the John Waters Family in Baltimore. We would come and visit each other, and it would be like royalty was coming to visit. And if they came by plane, you would go to the airport and greet them at the airport because we thought we were all very special. And we were! So when Ze Whiz Kidz came in the summer of 1971, they brought their videos to show us, and then they were in our next Cockettes show. That's also when they shot *Trisha's Wedding*. I was in New York for a family funeral. I was so pissed off, but Tomata and Satz [Satin Sheets] are in *Trisha's Wedding* [a satire about the wedding of Patricia Nixon, daughter of then president Richard Nixon]. Tomata is Hazel the Maid, and Satz is Joan Collins.

JUDITH: So how similar were Ze Whiz Kidz to the Cockettes?

FAYETTE: Very similar. There was a core concept to the Cockettes that was affiliated with the counterculture concept that was going on. The social core was about sharing everything, and it was about really being together. I mean, our group really loved each other, and so did Ze Whiz Kidz. They were very tight. They lived in houses together. The groundwork was totally similar. But they took it in a different aesthetic direction. Our aesthetic concept was cubistic, with a lot of satire and humor. It was completely nonlinear; we created a concept that would have different time periods involved and different references to everything—movies and different characters, personal choices—put together to become an assemblage that was difficult to define, mysterious but very appealing and cerebral. We were channeling the energy of the street and took it to an absurdist level—more of everything! It was instantly popular. So they did the same thing, but it was different people, so you had different versions of it. There's a building in Seattle called Smith Tower with a basement club called the Sub Room. It was a Mafia-run bar; the Mafia also had a strip club, I guess it was in the same building. They had a bigger theater that was a strip club. Satin Sheets found this little basement club and talked the owner into letting them perform there, and the guy said, "Well, I'll just take the bar and you can do whatever they want." So they started performing there once a week, on weekends, and they developed a lot of material. Randy videotaped their shows.

JUDITH: Was Tomata like the Hibiscus of the group? [Hibiscus was a central figure in the Cockettes.]

FAYETTE: Yes, definitely. He was the lead. He brought what inspired him in the Cockettes, what transformed him. I always say once a Cockette, you never go back, because it was a transformational experience. The Cockettes was the second incarnation. You had your first incarnation through acid and the culture of the society so that your head was blown. You had all new ideas and ways of thinking, all that shit from the past just evaporated. You didn't have to care about what people thought about you. It was such a supportive environment, coming from such an essence of love. It was totally nonviolent. It was very much about the positive, not about the negative. I mean, people would actually confront somebody who came into the group and said negative things. They would say, "Why are you talking like that? That doesn't produce anything." We supported each other in the development of our ideas, it was very much a group effort. So Ze Whiz Kidz came as a group to San Francisco in the summer of 1971, and that's when I met Tomata, and we fell in love immediately.

JUDITH: So Tomata was . . .

FAYETTE: Bisexual for one thing. Tomata loved women. That was not a problem then: many people were bisexual. Almost all of the Cockettes were. The result of the cosmic thinking that abounded in our society was that social boundaries like race and gender were irrelevant or at least of lesser importance than individuality. The individual was most important, and any particularities that were different only made you more special, more interesting. Sly and the Family Stone are the prime example of this aspect.

Bisexuality went way out of favor when AIDS came along, for sure. But there are still a lot of people who identify as bisexual. The gay community, at a certain point, said, "If you have sex with men, you're gay and you cannot fuck women." Tomata loved women, he loved everybody, and it wasn't a problem.

So I went to New York with the Cockettes in the fall of '71 for our shows at the Anderson Theatre on the Lower East Side of Manhattan. They went back to Seattle, then Tomata and I were writing to each other—Tomata was a great letter writer—and Tomata was constantly saying, "I want you to come up and be in the Whiz Kidz." The Cockettes disbanded by 1972. So then I went up to Seattle to live with Tomata and started performing in Whiz Kidz shows (2.6). Tomata and I had a relationship that I swear was so special, unique and magical. I definitely feel we had been together in a past life. I just know it because we would be together and the world would go away and we would only be in our own headspace that was completely in sync. We created our own world and talked about what we were going to create in the future.

JUDITH: What were some of the things that he talked about back then in the early days in Seattle?

FAYETTE: He would talk about just anything. He was a great reader—we all were. We were reading Flannery O'Connor. We were reading William Burroughs. Everybody had a library in their houses. And we were into old dime novels; we collected those, and we would read them. A lot of the shows came out of the dialogue of dime novels. We would collect things, ephemera, and then go over it and talk about the aesthetic, and about whatever we were discovering. We talked about the future, and Tomata said we're going to grow old and come back to Seattle so we can sit at the top of Pike Place Market and gaze at the Sound and take the ferry to Bainbridge Island.

JUDITH: When and why did he decide it was the time to go to New York?

FAYETTE: That was me. Because when the Cockettes performed in New York, when we did *Pearls over Shanghai*, which was our great show, the theater was packed every night. But it was mainly artists that came to see us, after the press panned us on opening night, which broke a record for Off-Off-Broadway opening nights because of Danny Fields. Danny Fields was the press agent. But New York was expecting something else, not our acid freak theater. All the underground artists that were inspired by us wanted us to come back—the Warhol people, the underground performers, all the Ridiculous Theatre people . . . they wanted us to come back to perform with them. So in one of our "future" talks, I said, "Tomata, we should go to New York. We could perform with all these people and keep doing it." In the fall of 1972, Tomata and I left for New York.

We found an apartment on Second Street and Bowery, a tenement. It was a city-owned building, across the street from the men's shelter. We had the top floor. The apartments were fifty dollars each. So we got two apartments that were adjacent with only a wall in between. We broke through the wall and just made a large hole in the wall that you could walk through like a door, but we never finished off the door. We hung a bark cloth curtain over the unfinished door—none of us were carpenters. Tomata and I lived on one side, and the other side, which

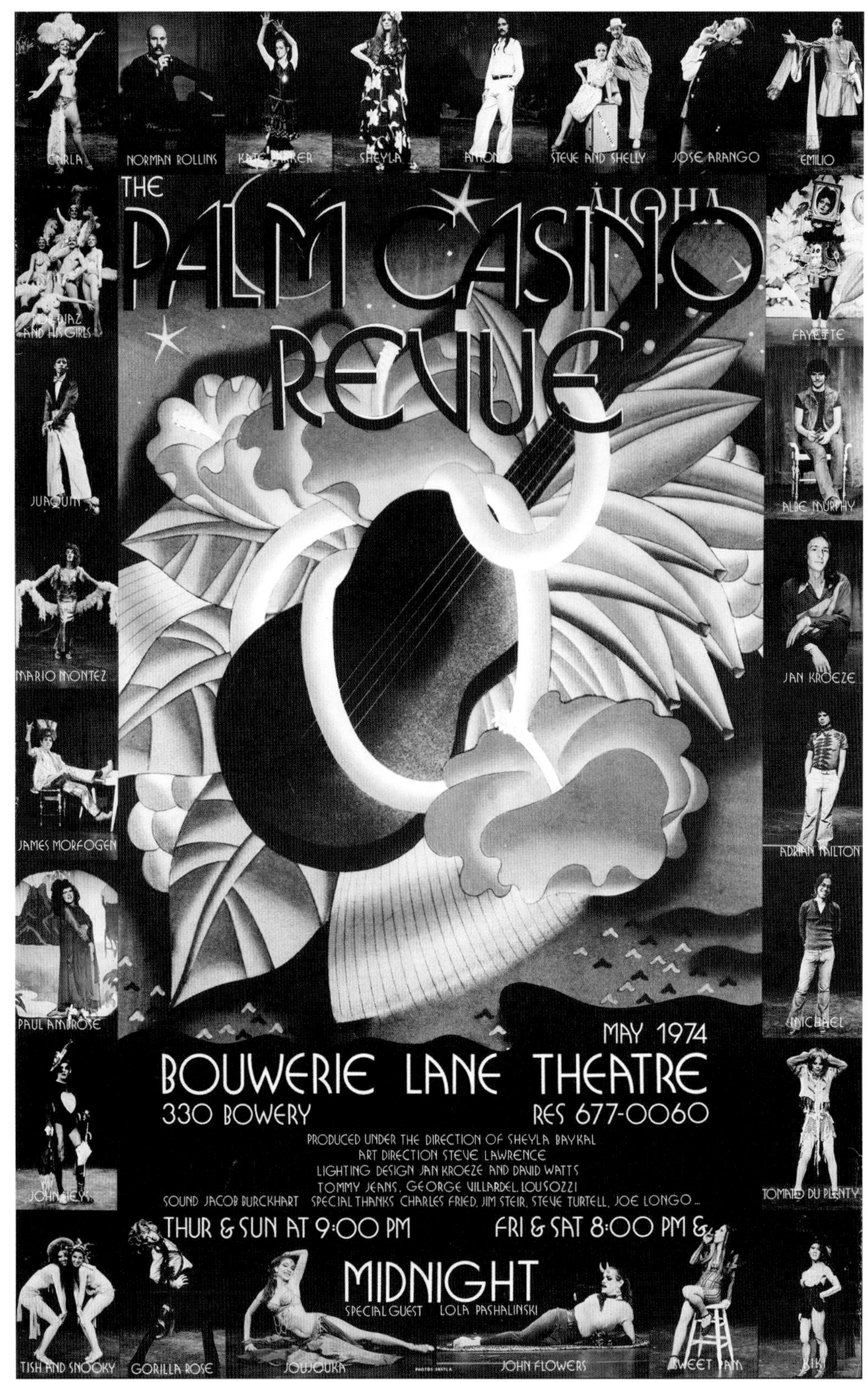

2.10. Poster for the Palm Casino Revue, May 1974.

had the kitchen and the bathtub, became occupied by Whiz Kidz and Cockettes who came later. Tomata and I started looking for small theaters. We found a café that had a small theater space and did our first show. The name of the show was "There's Egypt in Your Dreamy Eyes." There were two John Waters family people in the cast.

Tomata brought all the Whiz material with him. At first we started doing things that he had created in the Whiz Kidz. We didn't call them sketches, but they were what became "sketch comedy" on *Saturday Night Live*. So we had different small acts that we would do with one person or more, with dialogue or narration; and if people wanted to sing a song, that was good. Whatever anybody wanted to do, they would do it. We were very open to anyone's idea, as we were in our original groups.

So we did a few shows on our own. Then there was this woman Sheyla Baykal . . . she was not a performer, but she loved the underground. So she put together a revue called "The Palm Casino Revue" (2.10) that started in the summer of 1973. Anybody could do anything they wanted in the show, which was the experimental concept created by John Vaccaro. Where you had a theme, you had players, you had a starting point, but then where it went was the discovery. So she brought in people that were from Off-Broadway. There were Cockettes, Warhol family people, and other performers. It was a fucking great hit, and it ran all summer.

JUDITH: Do you remember what Tomata's bit was? What did he do in the show?

FAYETTE: We did an act called "Little Lulu and Tubby on the Moon," and he also did a solo song. This was the beginning of him as a solo performer. In that show we wrote a play called *The Titicaca Iceberg*. It was like a really old-school murder mystery—the Clue game on acid. A lot of people who were in the revue were in the play as well. There was a belly dancer. Then Gorilla Rose [Michael Farris] did a solo song too. John Flowers did a solo song. So all these people had different acts.

JUDITH: Can you tell me about "Hollywood Spit" and the cable TV show?

FAYETTE: Gorilla Rose was a graphic artist, and he came to New York after we were there. Gorilla got a job at this soft-core porn magazine called the *Naked News*. Tomata and I, we did a gossip column, which we called "Hollywood Spit," but it was all fake. I was "in California" he was "in New York." We did photo booth pictures where we had a telephone. We were way into the photo booth. There was an arcade in Times Square that was so old, and it had three old Italian photo booths. We would go with drag, and we would dress up the photo booths. So we would write this crazy column. Then we met Joey Freeman, who was a video artist. He went to high school with Chris Stein. We talked about it, and Tomata said: "Well, let's do a video magazine." It was August 1973. We did it at night on the roof of Joey's loft because it was hot as hell. Chris Stein did the sound and photographed it as well.

JUDITH: And you did how many shows?

FAYETTE: I think it was about three. And we put it on public access television in New York.

JUDITH: We have a flyer that advertises a "Spit" show at CBGB (1.21). What do you remember about performing there?

FAYETTE: We were performing at CBGB all the time. Sometimes Gorilla and Tomata would do something. We were the first people to perform there actually. We did a show, Savage Voodoo Nuns, and we did that several times at CBGB with one of the incarnations of Debbie [Harry] and Chris [Stein] that they had gotten together—either Snake, or Angel and the Snake [with Tish and Snooky Bellomo]. We created Savage Voodoo Nuns after or during the summer. Palm Casino really got us actively performing in New York and doing shows that we really liked, creating new scripts. So we were doing things at CBGB whenever we wanted. But the Club 82 was around the corner from our apartment; it was an old Deco club run by two lesbians. The Club 82 had a fabulous stage, all glass, as I remember, like in an old musical with carved metal palm trees as decor. We loved it, and they were enthusiastic about having us perform there. We did a show called "Love Dames Die Hard." Also the Manhattan Transfer [with Fayette's brother Tim Hauser] were forming. They were all about four-part harmony. Tomata and I would write stage patter for them because they didn't know what to say between songs, and I was doing their drag. . . . I was dressing them like Cockettes. We would go to their rehearsals at the Lambs Club; we loved roaming around that great old Broadway club, filled with memorabilia. That must have been 1974.

The Ramones started in '74. They opened for us. That was their first performance and our last show of Savage Voodoo Nuns. Ramones and Blondie both performed. Here is an aside to that show: my brother who by that time was on Atlantic Records, they had gotten a deal with Atlantic. Ahmet Ertegun [cofounder and president of Atlantic Records] loved to go out with the people that were on his label. He was way into hanging out with the young, the underground. So Tim brought Ahmet again to CBGB, and that was the last Savage Voodoo Nuns show he brought him to see. It was the Ramones' first show [August 14, 1974]. So after the show Tim said, "Well, what did you think, Ahmet?" And he said, "Well, they should play one less chord." He didn't get the Ramones at all. Nobody did at the beginning. So Savage Voodoo Nuns kind of were eliminated from the history because the music more or less took over CBGB, and we left by the fall of 1974.

JUDITH: That's when Tomata went back to Seattle?

FAYETTE: Not yet. After the summer of '73, Joey Freeman wanted to bring "Hollywood Spit" to public access television in LA. So he got a drive-away car, a white Lincoln Continental. When we got to LA, Tomata went back up to Seattle. The purpose of this trip was also to bring all our gear, our trunks, back to New York, as we wanted to stay there. We stayed and performed for another year, and then l left in the fall of '74. A bit later Tomata went back to Seattle and began putting together the Tupperwares.

In the fall of '74 I went to Mexico and Guatemala for six months, and when I returned to New York—well, I didn't know whether to stay in New York or not. The [Manhattan] Transfer were offered a four-part summer series on CBS, and they wanted me to come with them to LA and be a writer on the show. So I left New York for LA, but I really didn't like it. It was so straight, both the city and the TV gig. I would be crying on the phone with Tomata how much I hated it and I wanted to leave. He said, "No, no, you have to stay because I have this group, we formed the Tupperwares, and we're doing all these shows, and I want to come to LA and do the shows, and we can continue to do what we were doing." Then in the fall of 1976, he came. Then the Tupperwares immediately became the Screamers.

JUDITH: Do you know anything about the brief Gianni Bugatti phase between the Tupperwares and the Screamers (2.25–2.27)?

FAYETTE: Tomata loved playboys. That's probably where that came from because he loved these Euro-trash playboy stories. He was way into the racing car drivers and their high life; he loved to parody that ridiculous playboy lifestyle.

JUDITH: Do you know anything about him creating questionnaires for the band members?

FAYETTE: Tomata and I, every time we had an idea for a show, we would immediately get a composition book and start writing the ideas. I have all my composition books. I have our writing and Tomata's notations and how we developed the ideas. So this is all of a piece, that he would go back and forth with the people in the group.

JUDITH: It's fascinating because he lists the bands he likes, or aspires to be like.

FAYETTE: Tomata loved the Bay City Rollers, and Sparks. He was way into the pop bands then. And Tomata called the *TV Guide* the Bible. So, yeah, he was into modern pop culture all the way, but he was into everything. He could contain it all in his head and transform it into absurdist satire and just put it all into a piece that reflected all these things, but created something else so that the audience would love the new creation, all with a great deal of humor.

JUDITH: Can you talk about the turn that his performance persona takes with the Screamers from what he was doing in Ze Whiz Kidz, the New York shows, and Tupperwares?

FAYETTE: Ze Whiz Kidz was staged performance and acts—themed with performers doing certain things with a lot of drag. The Tupperwares probably, I mean, I don't know if he created it as a music group or as a performance group, but probably it was performance with music. Tommy Gear was into the synthesizer, so he probably wanted more of a music group. When

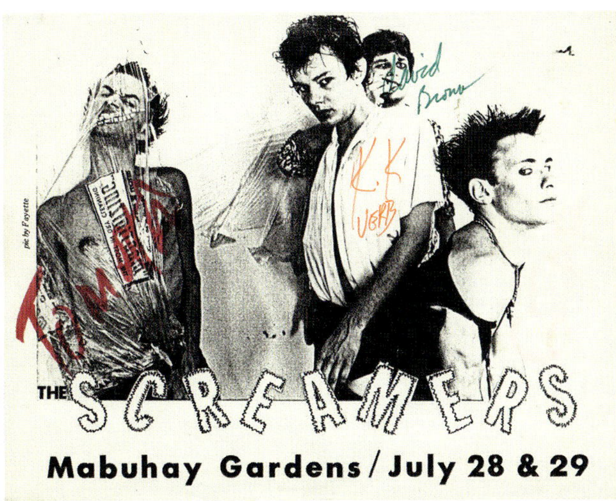

2.11. Autographed flyer for the Screamers' first show in San Francisco, July 28 and 29, 1977. Photo: © Fayette Hauser.

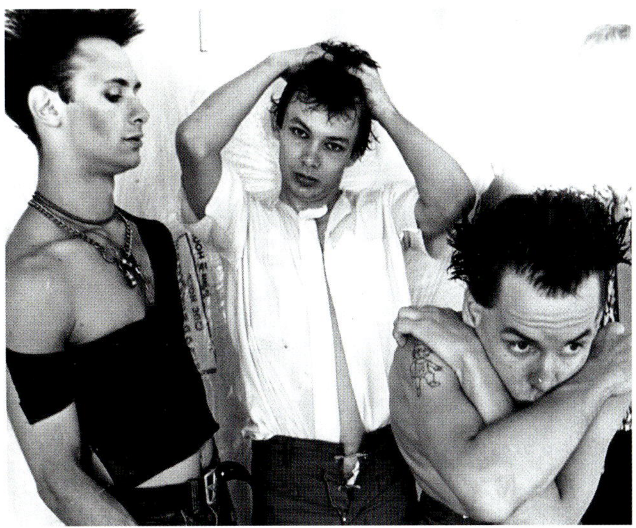

2.12. Screamers publicity photo, summer 1977. Photo: © Fayette Hauser.

they came to the scene here in LA, the bands were starting to form. Brendan Mullen, who came from London, got a funky club off of Hollywood Boulevard called the Masque, which was in a basement. It became like a cabaret; it was a version of CBGB. But it didn't have a bar—probably a good thing. But it had a bigger stage. Anyway, the punk scene was beginning when he came here with the Tupperwares. They didn't perform right away. They took time to change . . . to create the Screamers. Tomata created his stage persona. So that was a metamorphosis that was created in LA.

They lived in this 1920s Arts and Crafts house on Wilton Place. It became known as the Wilton Hilton. A lot of kids, high school kids, Kid Congo [aka Brian Tristan], who is KC Powers now. He was there. All these kids flocked to the Wilton Hilton, which was a version of our freak-hippie theater houses in SF and Seattle. Tomata was the most spiritually generous person ever. He supported people in doing whatever their dream was. That was the whole thing in San Francisco with the counterculture: you were supportive of each other. I mean, it was a total positive vibe; the counterculture was a complete support platform. Tomata brought that with him. That's why it was so attractive to all these high school kids and young people, because it was, I mean in LA, are you kidding? LA in the 1970s was so straight—please! Here was a house that contained, really, the future, and it was so hip—yeah, beyond words. Nothing that these kids had ever experienced. And it was non-drug, because Tomata was not into the drugs. He had so much brain energy that he didn't need drugs.

JUDITH: So he was a mentor . . .

FAYETTE: Oh, definitely. His spirit was so generous, and he loved these kids. He felt they were the modern energy that he wanted to express. That's who he was talking to. There was a kid in high school who really wanted to be in a band—Jeff McGregor. He was a really good musician, and he played keyboards. They were looking for somebody after David Brown left because nobody was playing the melody. So Tomata couldn't follow where they were in the song. It was just KK on drums and Tommy Gear on his synthesizer that was all over the place. They were looking for somebody who could play whatever the actual melody was, or the through-line of the song.

JUDITH: So did Tomata come up with his angsty stage persona for the Screamers?

FAYETTE: Definitely. The persona in the Screamers came from Tomata, absolutely. All the punk bands had their own version of angst, and that definitely came from London. That was a big London influence because the working class in London were fed up with their class shit. So they were angry with everything. Even though people who were in bands in America were not angry per se, it was so juicy, persuasive and appealing. Tomata was not . . . I mean, we all have angst issues, but Tomata was a real happy person and a positive person with a lot of creative energy. And so it was a character, because he was a stage performer and really could do anything. This was his persona in the Screamers. I think that at the end of the day, that persona became too much for him.

JUDITH: Did Tomata want to record songs or make an album?

FAYETTE: Tomata didn't care. Tomata was a performer, and that's what he wanted to do. Tomata was a true artist, and didn't want to compromise his art and his aesthetic. But Tomata

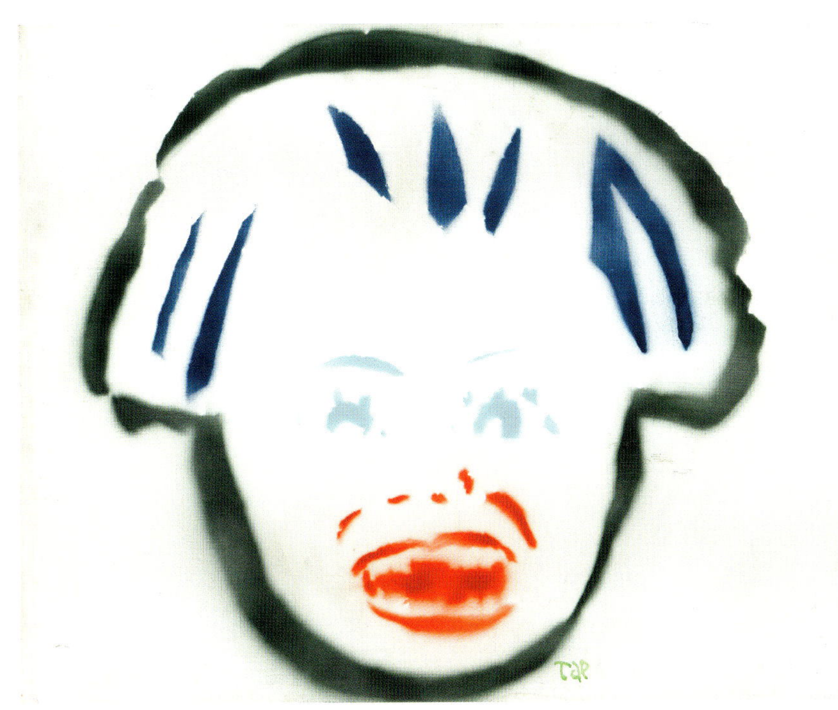

2.13 and 2.14. Original artwork by Tomata du Plenty. Stenciled spray paint on board, date unknown.

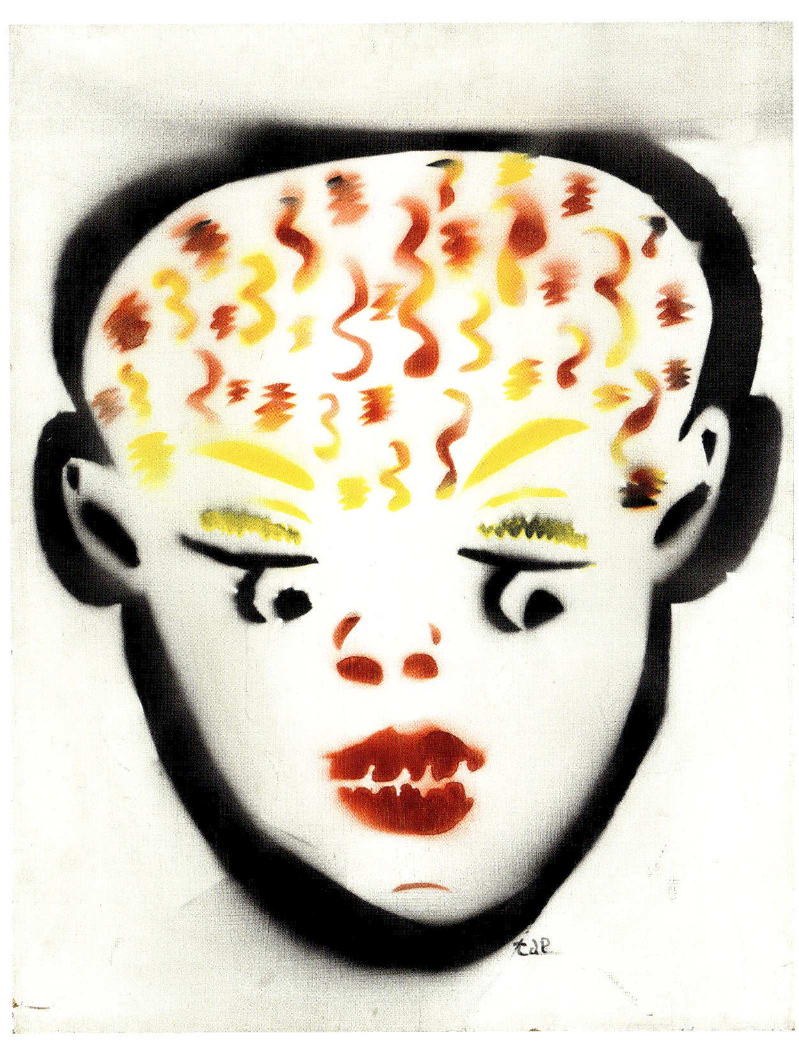

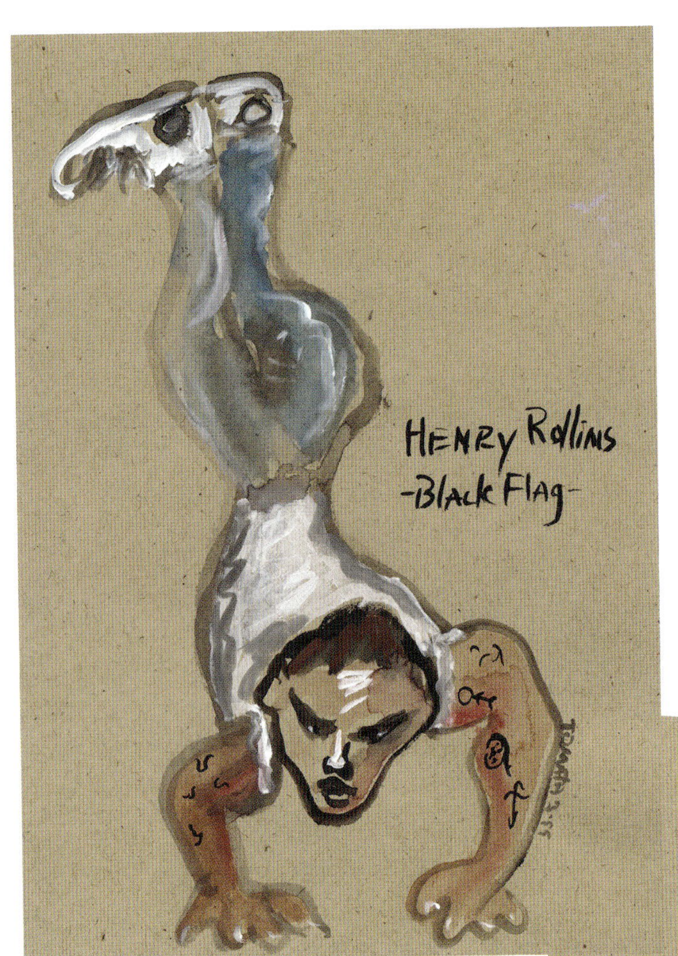

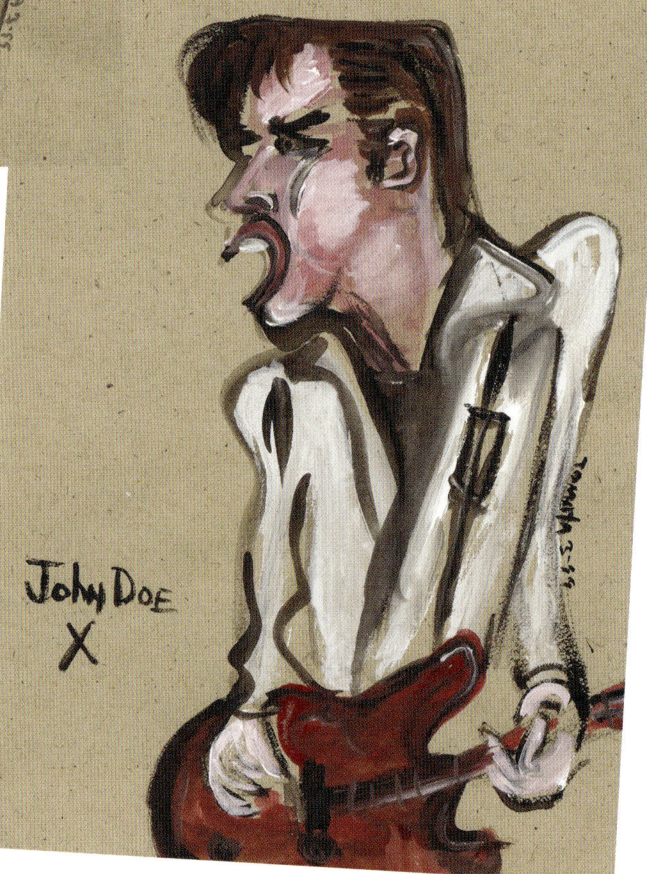

2.15 and 2.16. Original artwork by Tomata du Plenty. Watercolor on paper, 1999.

was not about the business. Punk is the last incarnation of the counterculture, which was also not about money. It was about being authentic. The authenticity of the counterculture was that your work and your life were all of a piece, uncompromised. That was the punk thing, too. People lived together and worked on their bands and their art. It was the most important thing, and it was their life. That changed in the eighties because money entered into the picture. Large money began to buy off the artists, so then it all became about selling a product. The counterculture was over.

JUDITH: What do you remember about Rene Daalder and his work with the Screamers?

FAYETTE: You know who brought Rene Daalder to them was me. OK, so Malcolm McLaren. When I was with Malcolm, he knew Rene. Rene and I became friends immediately, and he wanted to be connected to the underground in LA, and he had absolutely no connect. So, I brought him to see the Screamers and into the whole scene. Then he came up with his ideas. He had a whole idea about America—what America was à la a Dutch intellectual. He loved Sheila [Edwards]. Sheila was all over the place. Rene was trying to re-create the Screamers in this way, and they did *Population: 1*. Some people liked it, some people didn't like it. Penelope [Houston] was in it. But I think as far as Tomata was concerned, that was over for him. He pulled away to do his own thing, and it became his artwork (2.13–2.16). When he died in 2000, he was just beginning to show at the major art galleries. He was on the verge of having a show in New York. It was a great tragedy.

JUDITH: Do you have any final thoughts about Tomata that you want to share?

FAYETTE: Tomata went so successfully through so many mediums that it really is . . . I don't know how to put it. It really shows what a great artist he was because of his vision in his artistry. In his paintings, he reinterpreted people through his vision. His vision was so positive. He saw the best in everyone, and his enlightenment only broadened that view.

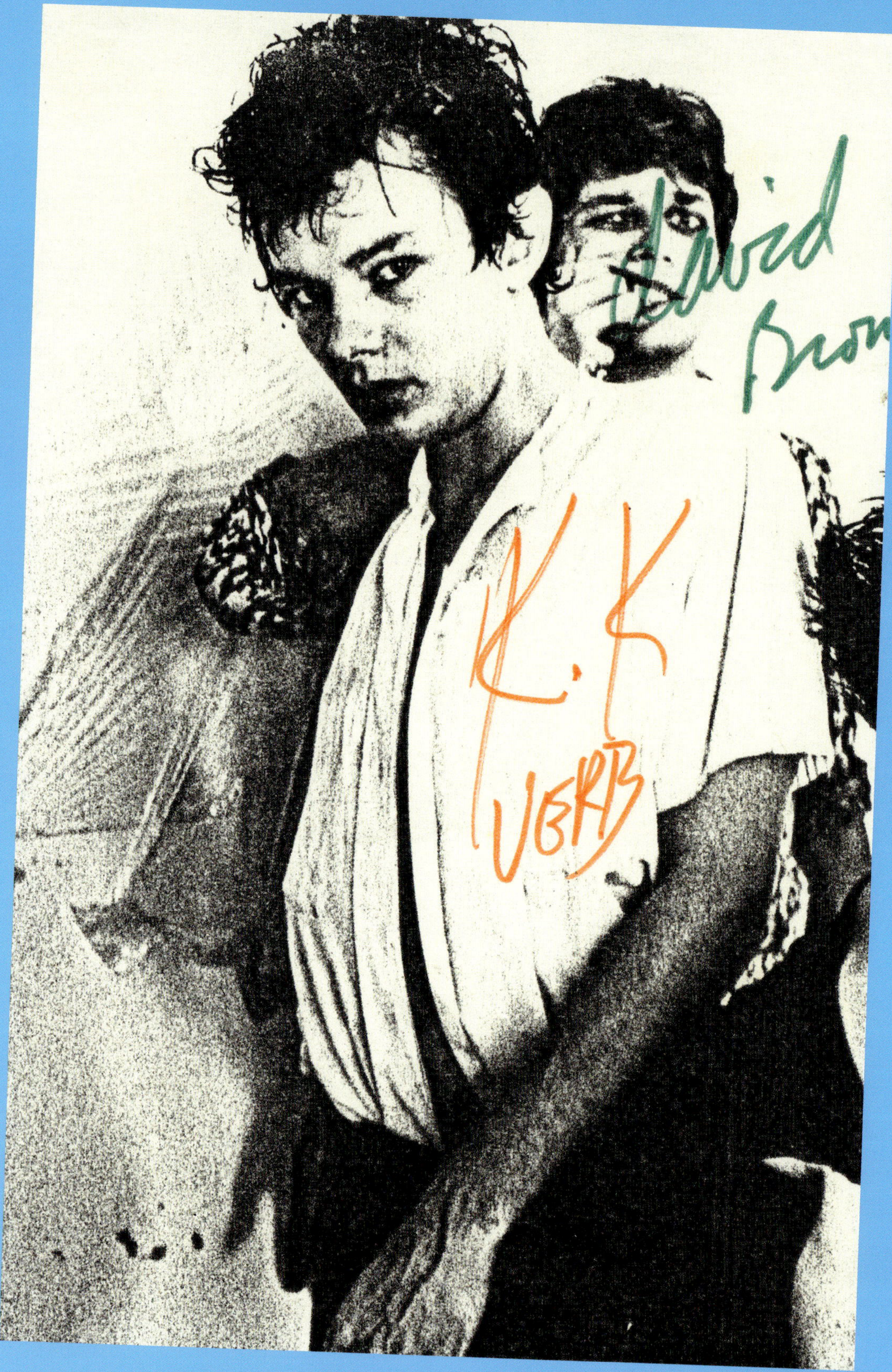

CH. 8

"We wanted to *de-codify* it"

AN INTERVIEW WITH KK BARRETT ON THE SCREAMERS

KK Barrett served as the drummer for the Screamers from their inception in late 1976 to their final projects in 1981. After the Screamers disbanded, KK and his wife Trudie Arguelles-Barrett opened an all-ages hip hop club called Radio. Getting a taste for film production while working with director Rene Daalder on Screamers-related projects, KK eventually became an award-winning production designer whose films include *Being John Malkovich* (1999), *Adaptation* (2002), and *Her* (2013), among many others. In this interview conducted on November 16, 2021, KK discusses growing up in the Midwest, his art college days in Oklahoma, and the self-empowered creative community of Los Angeles in which the Screamers developed their distinctive image and sound.

JUDITH: You grew up in the "Heartland," as they call it, Oklahoma and Nebraska. What was that like for you in terms of thinking about musical possibilities or even identity possibilities?

KK: I've never heard it called the Heartland, but it's less confusing than the Midwest. I was probably more Southwest: born in Nebraska, moved at six to Missouri to the Ozarks, and then moved at eight or nine to Oklahoma City. I was brought up in the sixties—I was born in 1952—and so I was aware as a kid of the birth of radio, which meant the birth of transportable radio, transistor radios, where you could take music with you to the beach or anywhere. We had beaches at lakes in the Midwest. But I was aware of music coming out of people's cars. We got our first transistor radio in 1960 or '61 or something like that. Being able to change channels and listen to music was my own self-exposure, really, just turning an ear toward something that I was curious about.

I spent fifteen years in Oklahoma until I finished college, and decided to come to Los Angeles. The thing about the Heartland at that time was that it was very free. It was very much like any of these scenes that I've been part of where you could make anything out of it that you wanted. There wasn't the polarization that we experience now. I went to a very free-range college, Oklahoma State University, where a lot of my art professors were from San Francisco, from the Ken Kesey world and from the Beats. They were self-empowering. They weren't trying to teach you any certain doctrine to follow. They just wanted you to make sure that you were yourself. So, it was definitely a sixties-leaning liberal education. I remember having gay professors. We, in the art department, would know of the gay professors, likely because some of our fellow art students were gay, opening the door to acknowledgment within our clique, even though they couldn't share their identity with some of their fellow professors. It wasn't very racially mixed, though. Except I went to high school with indigenous people, and I was exposed to all that. I remember we had this old Oklahoma history book, and all of a sudden it was replaced midsemester, and a lot of the history of the Trail of Tears and things like that just were gone. They updated it, and they erased it.

But back to your question about the music: I was curious. I think that's always been my education, just being curious and following the radio. I also grew up in the era in high school when radio went from AM only to an FM focus as well. That was a huge shift as far as musicians being able to put out things that weren't tailored just for fast consumption, singles as opposed to album sides and longer songs. I was attuned to all that stuff. Eventually, I used up the Midwest and left.

JUDITH: I've read online that you went to California because your parents had moved there.

KK: My parents left Oklahoma before I did. I still had a year of college to finish. They had moved to California, but I wanted to go. I was a painter and a sculptor in college and wanted to continue doing that. But in the last two years of college, I began playing music with my roommates, who were also painters, and recording original songs and performing live. I realized that this was much more exciting than being solo in a studio, working on something. I'd rather be engaging with people my own age out in nightclubs and performing. The painter side of me wanted to move to New York. But it was in the middle of winter, and I didn't really have a connection there. I had never been there before, and I needed to get out of the snow in Oklahoma. Finally, I just said, "I'm going to leave. I'm done." I at least had a stopover if I moved to

California, which was my parents. I moved just before Christmas in 1976. And I also had a car accident and my leg was banged up. I spent a month there, and then a band member that I played with in Oklahoma came out and stayed with me as well. We both moved to Hollywood in January '77.

JUDITH: How did you find the shift between Oklahoma and the LA area?

KK: Surprisingly seamless. I was reading cultural magazines like *Rock Scene* and *Creem* and things like that, and dreaming about playing music in these scenes or meeting these people. Within days I met some of these people. It seemed so easy and accessible. It was a very small scene. There were two scenes: there was the commercial rock and roll scene, which had been around since the sixties and was kind of dying. But it was doing very well for itself. And then there was this underground alternate scene of people starting bands, the same way I had started a band in Oklahoma.

You found other pockets of people doing the same thing, aligned, coming out of the curiosity of the Detroit Stooges. The lineage of Doors, Stooges, and then the English lineage of Bowie, Roxy Music, Brian Eno, the collision of those two. It seemed like everybody had those two scenes and music sources in their back pocket, as well as the Velvet Underground, the New York Dolls. By the time we started playing music, *Horses*, Patti Smith's album, had just come out; and the Ramones' first album came out just before I left Oklahoma.

JUDITH: So when you landed in LA and started to circulate within the scene, was it already calling itself punk?

KK: Well, punk was a media term, and it was out there. I think the first time anybody said they saw it was on a flyer for a Suicide gig [in 1970] they called themselves punk music. But, yeah, we were aware of New York, and we were aware of England because they were parallel—January '77, late '76—it was happening at the same time. We didn't think of what the name meant until everybody started calling a sidebar set of musicians "new wave." And then we thought that is such a nice way of saying that they're not part of the rock establishment; they're trying something different, but they are not very adventurous. We hated that term for its namby-pamby-ness and said, well, I guess we're more punk than that, but we didn't really want to be labeled at all.

We were really an art band. And a kind of a performance assault band. It doesn't hurt when there's a bunch of you. You're not just one outcast, hard to label. It works well for the press, but it also works well for the collective of musicians who respect each other in like terms that you're grouped in this category. And then to the consumer, or the fan, I think it helps a little bit, because they know a little bit of what to expect if they're calling you that. Before it becomes detrimental and confining and kind of lockstep in its rules.

JUDITH: You brought up the labels "art band" and "assault rock" for the Screamers. That could describe Suicide as well. I was wondering if Suicide was lurking in the background of what you were putting together with the Screamers. Or were they not a well-known element of the New York scene?

KK: We loved that record [*Suicide*, released 1977]. The great thing about any early kind of rock music is that it celebrates its clumsiness. It's important that it has to be awkward because once it's refined it's kind of done. Like painters when they're experimental. Then all of a sudden they find something that sells and they just keep making that for the rest of their lives. They don't explore anymore, and it's not part of the game, which it should be, constantly.

I think for the Screamers, our strength and our downfall is that we just kept changing so fast that we changed right out of what we were once we got good at it, and that most people hadn't caught up with yet. Then we were done with it, which was fine. So, yeah, we were definitely aware of Suicide. In '75 when we started recording music in Oklahoma, we already recorded with early synthesizers and drum machines and things like that. It was part of the lazy language. If you had it and it did something for you automatically, you could always make your falling-down-the-stairs elements on top of that, and humanize it. It wasn't like it was looked at as cold. It was looked at as a tool. It's a tool that helps get to the end faster and do something that I can't do as well, so that I can concentrate on the other things that humanize it. So we were definitely aware of Suicide. I hadn't seen them. Tomata had seen them because he was in New York at that same time at the beginning. He was well aware of them. Even though, at the time he was doing comedy, a kind of skit comedy with Fayette Hauser.

JUDITH: How did the Screamers form?

KK: I'd met Tommy and Tomata at a show at the Starwood or the Whisky, which had just reopened in the late seventies after being closed toward the end of the sixties. There were shows like John Cale and Cheap Trick on the same night—funny billings, like the Ramones and the Quick. The Quick were a local Sparks-like band produced by Beck Hansen's father [David Campbell], who we would later work with as well.

So landing here in Los Angeles, all of the people that ended up in these bands and in this scene—Bobby Pyn [later Darby Crash], and Pat Smear from the Germs, and the Go-Go's, and the guys in the Weirdos—we were all out at these shows. I ran into Tommy and Tomata, who had just moved there, I think in December '76 as well, and they were intentionally done up, definitely embracing what you would call a punk look at the time of their reinvention. I thought, "Well, I want to meet these guys!" So I went out and talked to them, and they said, "Oh, what are you doing? We've got this band." They were very friendly.

I said that I was in a band. Somehow it came about that they were looking for a drummer, and I said "I'm a drummer." I met them again a week later and gave them a tape of these original songs that were kind of New York Dolls-ish and Brian Eno-ish and Stooges-like. I guess they liked what they heard, and so I was in the band before I ever played any music with them. Two weeks in, or something like that, all of a sudden I was in a band and my idea of being an artist was put aside, because this is what was happening right now, in my mind. This was being an artist—a musical one. I think that all of us approached that in different ways.

I came into the situation. Tomata and Tommy had a place to live in Los Angeles. They had bought a piano and a drum machine. I don't think the intention was to use the drum machine other than thinking: we don't have a drummer, so how are we going to do this? It's a great tool for the moment. But nobody had used it in this punk thing that seemed to be guitar, bass, vocals, drums—from the Ramones, from the New York Dolls, from the Stooges, from the Velvets. So anyway, in terms of that, it was breaking the mold a little bit. But Suicide had broken that mold as well. So it wasn't intentional. They had the piano, they had drum machine, they had a PA, they bought their microphones. I don't know what they were like before, but it seems like they had improved. Somewhere along the way, they decided not to have guitars.

As you see again and again, and actually with punk that happens later, everybody just wanted to be the same. They thought that they had to codify it. We wanted to *de-codify* it. We wanted to start our own genre, and coming from an art background and the way I thought, it was the only choice. No copying. You had to be completely separate or you didn't begin to make a statement.

JUDITH: What I hear in the Screamers is this intense use of the keyboards and the synthesizers as melodic instruments, because Tomata isn't himself singing tunefully. You hear the tune through the synthesizer, and you hear this interesting sonority with his rhythmic shouting on top of the tune that the synthesizer is playing or the Fender Rhodes is playing. But the keyboards aren't playing harmonies, or chords.

KK: Well, I mean there were no harmonies, but there were many, many overtones. And that is harmony in a way, but it's not intentional or formal. We also usually reduced the chords down to playing fifths, a first and a fifth rather than a first, third, and fifth, so that it came through stronger with less stray overtones, more of a pure sonic overtone. It also made the Fender Rhodes piano blend in with the synthesizer's single monophonic tones better. In guitar these are called power chords. Although the different piano players played different ways. You know, David Brown [aka David Braun] was a Berklee-schooled musician, and he was quite adept at playing pretty radical melodic structures and adding all of these different bits and sevenths in; and then Jeff McGregor, who was an interim piano player, was pretty basic, mainly because he was so young. Then Paul Roessler was also an educated musician. He had to be a little bit deconstructed, whereas David Brown had already deconstructed himself. Paul was more classical, and coming to this new scene, he had to get raw, as it were.

JUDITH: How did he do that? Did the rest of the band coach him on things to do? To mess with his technique somehow?

KK: Yeah. Well, Paul was my friend—I had met him at the Masque. It was a small scene of maybe forty or fifty people. He and I worked a lot by ourselves. We very rarely rehearsed, but he and I made other music on the side. When he got in the band, we became a unit together. So we would play and strip down things and talk about stuff like that. It was just like: "Let's make it simpler, let's get to the pure melody line." And then: "Now let's build it up stronger until it's more powerful." He would play left-hand bass, which helped me a lot because there was no bass player. I was having to play the tom-toms to try to get some low end.

JUDITH: Tomata had also transformed from the drag and camp humor of Ze Whiz Kidz and his shows in New York to a harder, more austere, less overtly queer style.

KK: I don't think it was an intentional thing. Now you got to remember that the ashes of glam were very nearby.

JUDITH: So, passé?

KK: It wasn't quite passé yet, it was still embraced, as opposed to arena rock and things like that. We all liked glam. It was on the border of camp all the time. From T-Rex to Roxy Music and Bowie, they were very campy. Some people didn't know what to do with that, other bands would take the look, but not add the ambisexuality of it, or the innuendo. And it came off as a little bit flatter. Even the New York Dolls were campy. It was Pop Art. We were just doing it and making decisions: well, let's not do that, let's do this. But it wasn't like a dogma. It was just decision making about how we present ourselves onstage. Each show had to be different to surprise the audience and make them wonder what we're going to do next. We felt like it was the bargain with performing that you have to deliver something unexpected that will keep them curious because we didn't know recording at the time. We only knew performing.

JUDITH: What were some of the ways you would change it up?

KK: We decided one night to open the show behind black plastic. This is from stories of bands in Texas and Oklahoma playing behind chicken wire, because people would throw things at you, onstage. We set the whole thing up at the little punk club, the Masque, where it was very egalitarian and the stage was one foot off the ground. It was a kind of snobby elite thing to say that we're going to play behind black plastic and you can't see us. But we knew that they were going to rip it down, and they instantly did. So then you've got the audience participating in the act. Just little gamesmanship like that.

JUDITH: Were you thinking in terms of the fourth wall and theater theory?

KK: Yeah. Tommy was big on [Antonin] Artaud and amused by *Winning through Intimidation* [by Robert Ringer, 1974] and books like that. So campy or theatrical—theatrical, meaning you're presenting something in a nondocumentary way that is going to be absorbed and in concert with the audience participation. I think that we were all interested in that. That was the artful performance part of it.

JUDITH: How self-conscious was the connection with the German Expressionist stylings? Egon Schiele?

KK: I was very aware of that from my art background and from the films, from the 1930s. I think that parallel of what Tomata looked like in his poses—not intentional. I think it was just coincidental and lucky. Everybody was aware of Egon Schiele's etchings and drawings, and Ernst Kirchner—all of these different artists from that time. And also, it's hard to get access to films and things prior to cable TV, so if the midnight movie house showed *The Cabinet of Dr. Caligari* or *M* or *Nosferatu*, then everybody that was in this same interest group would go and know that stuff from that.

JUDITH: How important was Gary Panter's logo to the band's image and publicity?

KK: Gary moved from Texas about the same time that I moved there [to LA], and about the same time that Devo moved out as well. So we were all coming from different places and arriving in the same scene. I met Gary at the show that we did at the *Slash* party, the opening of *Slash* magazine [May 28, 1977]. So me and Gary always knew each other from our "art damage" backgrounds. He was a big music fan, and his wife, Nicole at the time, was also managing the Germs. We were just all in the scene together. You know, we all knew each other.

Let's talk about image control for a second. I mean, I obviously had an artistic sense. Tommy as well. And Tomata. At the beginning, the band's image from the personal players down to the flyer presentation was a little bit generic. Like, oh, this is what punk is and people would just throw something together. Anybody could make a collage. Sometimes the booker designed the flyers, or a friend.

But then we cleaned up our act and became more strenuous about making a bold statement rather than a slapdash statement. We started dressing in different ways, but it wasn't something we talked about. Once we got that image from Gary, it was iconic in the same way that Black Flag had their image or the Germs circle. It's just more powerful when you have something. It's branding—another Warhol lesson.

JUDITH: Were Tomata and Tommy both writing songs? And were they writing together or separately?

KK: Sometimes both ways. It's funny, when I was asking Tommy about the lyric or the song authorship credit for the songs that we put out [*Screamers Demo Hollywood, 1977*, released by Superior Viaduct, 2021], he wasn't sure. Usually I could tell. I always thought of the more bubblegum stuff as Tomata's, and the more brutalist stuff as Tommy's. I think at one time I did an interview for the *LA Weekly* and I said if it was all Tommy we'd be Rammstein, and if it was all Tomata it would be "[I'm Going Steady with] Twiggy" all the time.

JUDITH: It seems to me that there's not a lot of that bubblegum stuff that made its way through to the Screamers, at least what's preserved on the internet and the demos.

KK: Well, "Twiggy" was a leftover from the Tupperwares, "Magazine Love" was a leftover from the Tupperwares. That's playing with Pop Art—all the magazine titles, and the fashion models. So it's like consumer-aware.

JUDITH: Right. But "122 Hours of Fear," that would be a Tommy song?

KK: Yeah, it is grabbed from the headlines [from the *Los Angeles Herald-Examiner* reporting on the hijacking of Lufthansa flight 181 in 1977]. But then again, we had magazines, like there were these great newsstands where you got your information at the time, and there were these great East LA magazines, low rider magazine, and some Cholita magazines, and *fumetti*, which are like photo storyboards of a film with the bubble captions, like cartoon captions of the dialogue. They were always torrid and violent. We'd have magazines from Mexico where the front page would be somebody with their head cut off. It was so drastically violent. So it was just cultural absorption. Reflection.

JUDITH: On one of the sites that I've been reading ("You Better Shut Up and Listen!" by David Jones), you make a comment, at least you're credited as making a comment, that half the songs are about "Catholic damage."

KK: That was a fun term to bandy about at the time. Everything was "damaged." I don't know where I came up with that, but it was like Catholic damage, art damage. You're wearing your influences on your sleeve in the best way, trying to turn something that you've been indoctrinated with, then spinning it to your own perspective.

JUDITH: And Tomata was Irish Catholic.

KK: Yeah. He was Catholic. Nobody was practicing, that's for sure. I was an atheist from way back. If anything, we really appreciated how, especially coming out of glam, how the Catholic Church really had ceremony and presentation down. It was high camp.

JUDITH: I am thinking of the song "Mater Dolores," which hits that Catholic damage element plus speaks to the Latino community in LA and their own Catholicism. It's a brilliantly placed song for the community, it seems.

KK: Yeah. I think that was Tomata's and Gorilla's cleverness, but maybe more Tomata's. Gorilla Rose was always around. I wonder what influence he had on the lyric writing because he was very clever, and sometimes I'll read press blurbs about us and I can say Gorilla wrote that, like he's feeding the quotes into situations because he would do that. Especially in the fan club letter and things like that. He also helped us with lights. We had a number of different people who helped us in staging and set up equipment. They were just our friends. John Doe did it, Kira Roessler did it, my wife Trudie did it, Gorilla did it. Just different people that were always around helping on the periphery.

JUDITH: Were the bits of Spanish that got into your lyrics a nod to the Latino population in LA?

KK: Yeah, definitely. That's also Tomata's upbringing, between Coney Island and Far Rockaway, New York, and Montebello, California. Also when you live in Los Angeles, you learn a lot of billboard Spanish. The magical thing about it was, because we're in Los Angeles, there's such a Latino influence of all the different neighborhoods. It wasn't New York, it was car culture. You'd have some beat-up car and you would drive to these shows. There was a lot of kids from East LA and El Monte, La Puente—like Kid Congo Powers [Brian Tristan], who later played with the Cramps and with Nick Cave, and the Gun Club. A lot of girls starting to play music too. And then there was the gay faction. I mean, there was a lot of kids who were gay as well, guys and girls. And it was like, nothing.

JUDITH: Are you saying in all the punk shows or in yours in particular?

KK:: All the punk shows that I went to. This is the pre-militaristic punk.

JUDITH: Before Black Flag.

KK: Yeah. And what we called HB, Huntington Beach. That was a little harder, because there was a bit more machismo going on and a lack in multicultural education, say. They just didn't grow up with people that were different from them.

JUDITH: So there was a "big tent" feel to your shows.

KK: Yeah. I can't speak for everybody, and I don't know how well everybody felt comfortable in the scene, but I think they felt more comfortable there than many places they had been, maybe even in school. Because it was creative first, and it was coming of age, and it was coming out. And then also not being thought of as just Mexican or just gay or all of these things. So I think it was empowering. I think anytime you find yourself in a real creative crowd, you're going to find that same mix.

JUDITH: Can you talk about the 1979 shows, which are more like cabaret or musical theater?

KK: After the Target Video period, Rene Daalder staged a couple of shows with us. It was more like releasing ourselves to say: why don't you stage us and see what you do? Some of the songs were written with Rene, and some of the songs were written with David Campbell, musically, and some other people. I think Paul wrote "Friends" and "I Go for You" musically, just on a piano, because they're simpler. I don't mean simple as far as the melody lines. I mean simple as far as the instrumentation. Pretty much just solo piano and Tomata.

This was Rene's idea. Tomata to me is a front man. When you're performing live and you want to make an impact with an audience, I wouldn't trade a front man for somebody who had vocal chops, anytime. Even in theater, you would rather have somebody that's a great live performer than somebody that can sing in a musical well. Some of these songs ask more of a singer than Tomata probably had in his chops, so he ended up talk-singing like in a later Lou Reed style, because that was his range. He had more of a staccato delivery of lyrics rather than so much a singer of a melody line.

So this wasn't really that successful, but it was different. Nobody else was doing it, and it was something different for us. It was an adventure. This was also when we brought Sheila Edwards in to sing on a couple songs, to do a duet on "I Want to Hurt" and "She Frightens," songs that we'd performed by ourselves before. It was an attempt to try to build a tempo and an arc to a musical set, a performance set. I always thought that a song is built in the same way as a set is, or a set is built in the same way a song is. You come in, you introduce a theme, you hit the theme harder, you change and bring it to an apex. And then you taper out carefully and leave them happy when they leave. The ending is very important. It's something that I'm very aware of in film as well. That each moment has its place and you have to tease forward, tease forward, cliff-hanger, and then free fall, and then summarize in the end.

We were always careful to deliver this kind of performance, but this was really like a stage play. I think it was a little bit clumsier, actually, than what we were doing of our own instinct. I was never impressed with it, but I went along for the ride because I'd never done it before. I was willing to learn and willing to explore.

JUDITH: The Screamers also worked with Daalder on a few film projects, which get folded into *Population: 1* later.

KK: We began by making what they now call music videos or musical shorts. At the time this was before MTV, so there was no outlet for this stuff, and they were not connected in a story. Then we started making these different short films, these short musicals. There's two for Sheila, "10 Cents a Dance" and "Jazz Vampire"; then "Mensch" and "Nervous" are Tomata's versions, all within this same film structure. I designed the sets, which was my first stab at designing sets, which were a bit expressionistic and *Caligari*-like, even though it was bright colors. Tommy was also a character in the film; Al Hansen—Beck's grandfather—was also a character in the film. And Robert Lopez [from the Zeros], as well as Penelope Houston [from the Avengers], who Tommy and Tomata knew in Seattle.

The Rene Daalder period was kind of the end of the Screamers and the beginning of a different project that was his. It wasn't a Screamers film. It was a Rene film that the Screamers participated in by writing some songs. Tomata was the star of it. I did the sets—just by volunteering. It was the beginning of my film career. But again, I'd never done it before, so I was glad to participate and go with the gamble. Never afraid to try something and fail, but well aware to walk away and try something else if it didn't feel right.

All of the things that I got into, each time I would start, whether we'd start the hip hop club Radio or whatever, it was very Andy Hardy "Let's put on a show, we can do this!" It was not intimidating. It was like: we just need to get a couple hundred dollars together and we can rent this place and do this. Find this guy named Ice-T and pay him thirty bucks a night and we can make it happen. So even in film, it's all the same.

It's my life's creative thread of, well, let's just take this and this and put it together—we can do this. Nobody's saying we can't do this. That's the thing that's hard to capture, to figure out a way of saying how this stuff sprung up and where the energy came from, and how it empowered everybody to participate in it. It was really self-owned.

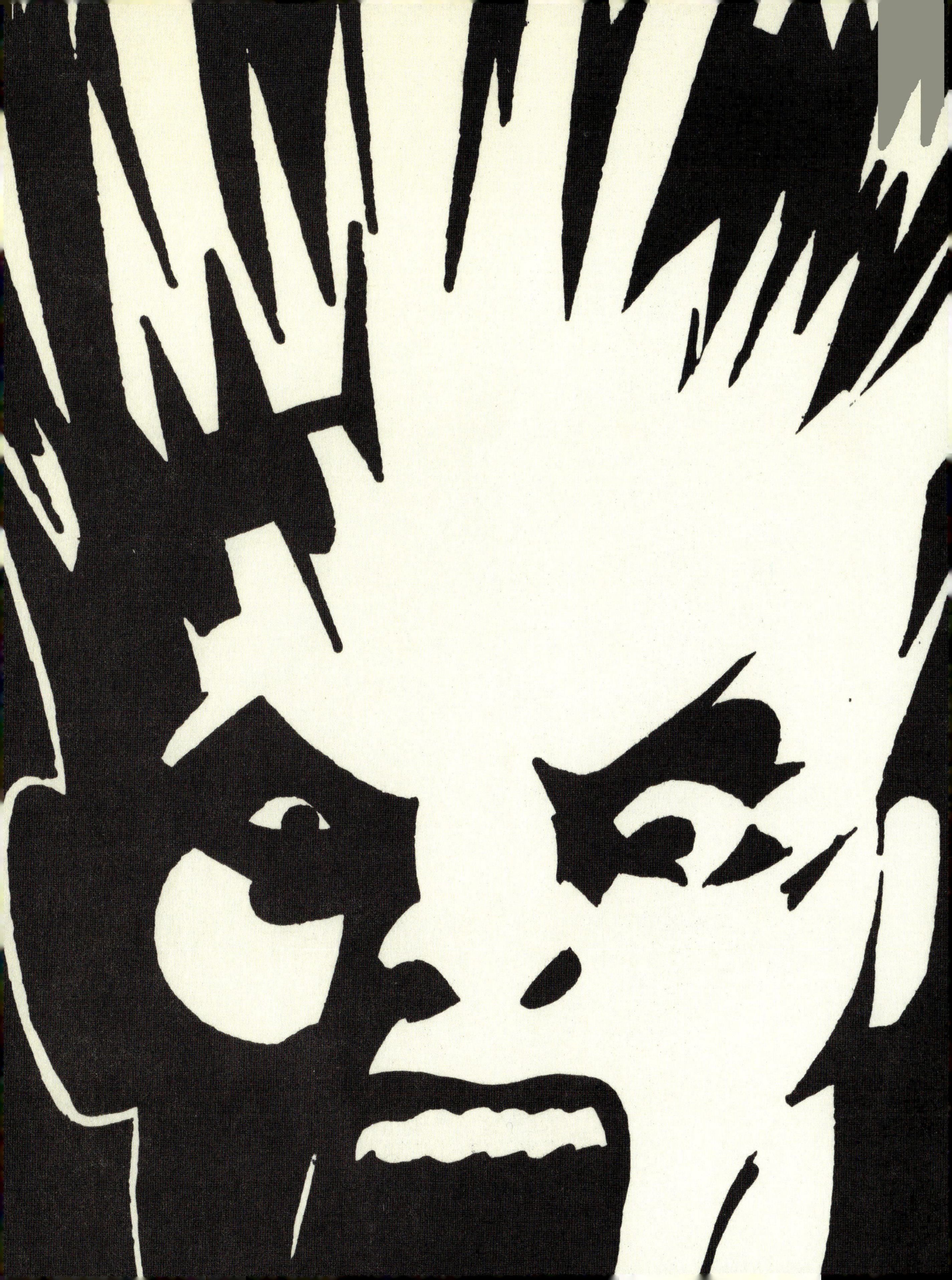

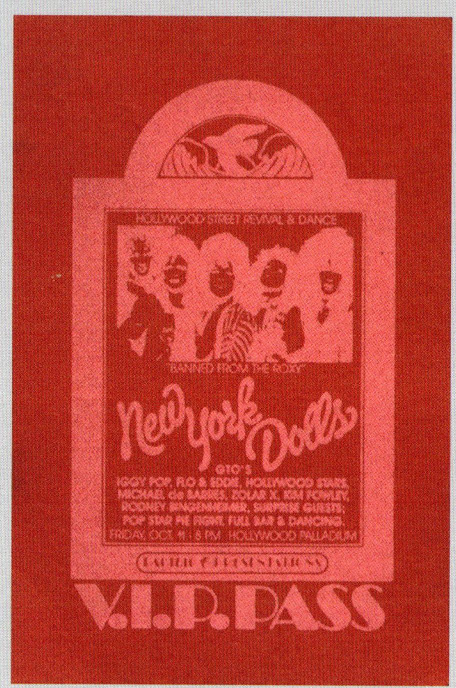

2.17. VIP pass to First Annual Hollywood Street Revival and Trash Dance, 1974.

One of my heroes of the scene was Tomata du Plenty. To me he was the man—funny, witty, irreverent, always trying new things but still rooted in vaudevillian showmanship and old-style Hollywood glamour (via the punk-shattered mirror). The Screamers. They were my favorite!
—Robert Lopez, *Under the Big Black Sun*

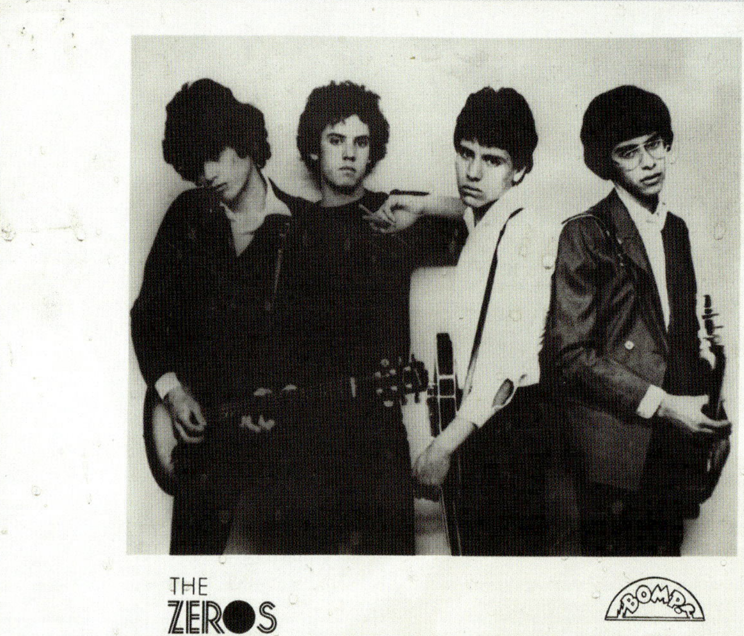

2.18. The Zeros publicity photo for their first single on Bomp! Records, 1977. *Left to right*, Javier Escovedo, Baba Chenelle, Hector Penalosa, Robert Lopez (later known as El Vez).

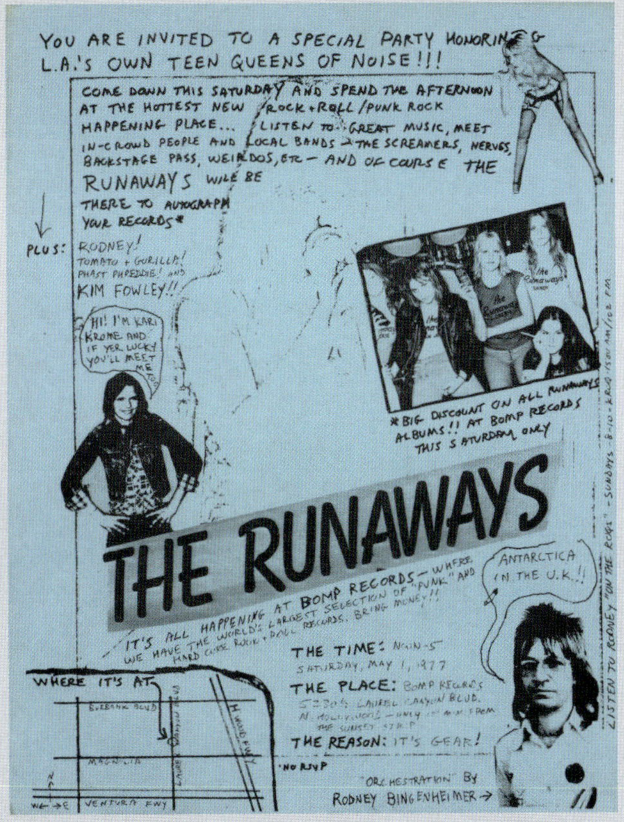

2.19. Flyer for party honoring the Runaways at Bomp! Records, May 1977. Attendees included the Screamers, the Nerves, Backstage Pass, and the Weirdos.

One of the bands I was curious about when I was in Oklahoma, by reading in magazine articles and hearing the record, was the Runaways, and Joan Jett was one of the first people I met when I moved here. We all knew who they were because we were curious and we thought it was cool too, to see an all-girl band playing something between glam and some other kind of snottier rock than arena rock. But you're coming from the Midwest and they're stars because they've got a record out. You read about somebody and then you meet them. It was a different thing then. —KK Barrett

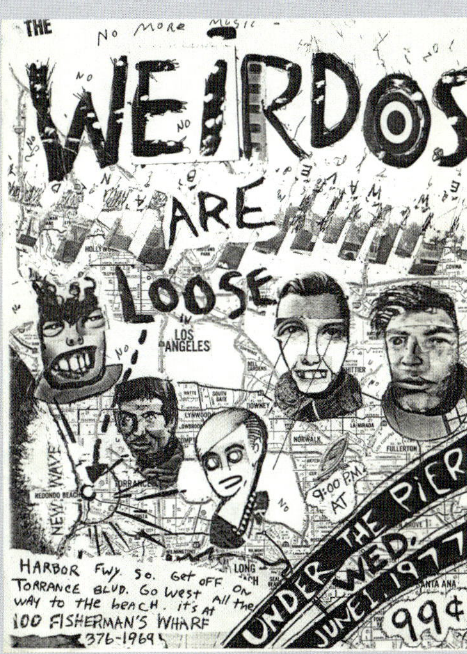

2.20. Flyer for the Weirdos show at Under the Pier, Redondo Beach, June 1977.

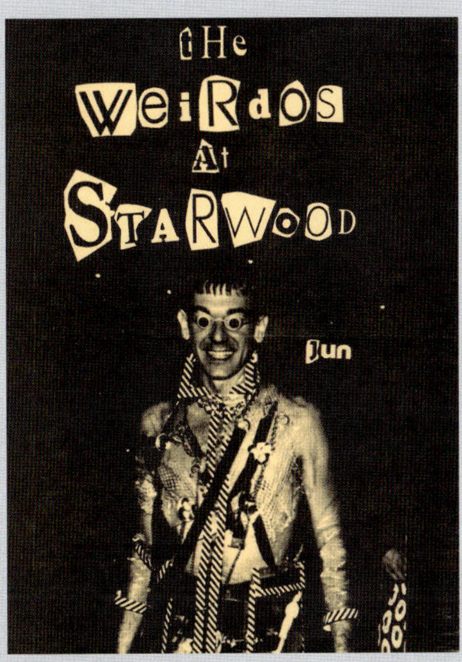

2.21. Flyer for the Weirdos show at the Starwood, June 1977.

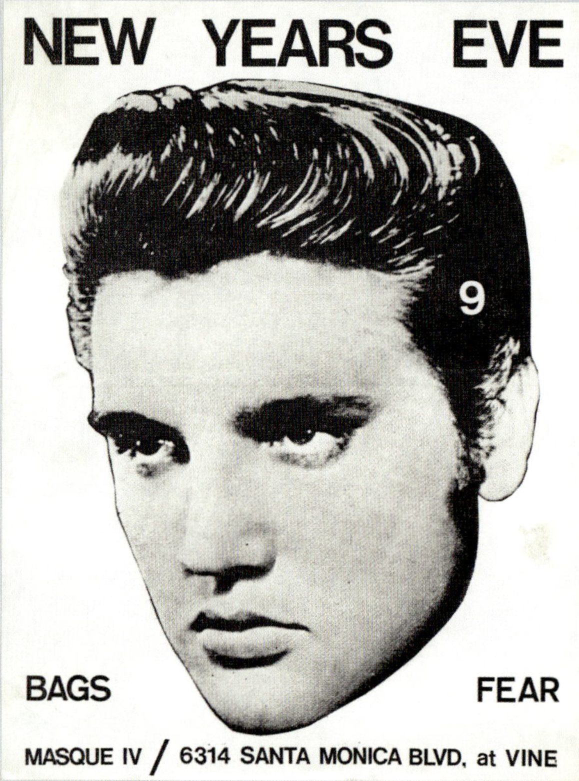

2.22. Flyer for the Bags show at the Masque, December 1978.

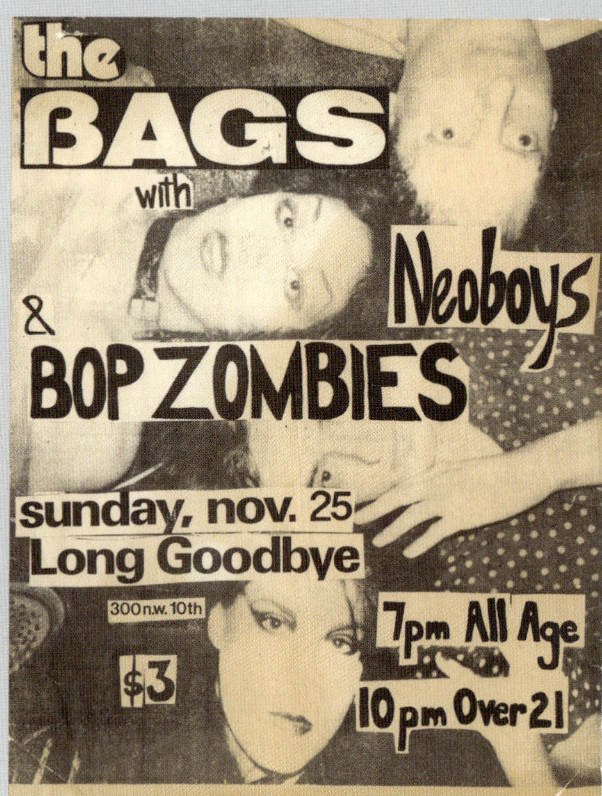

2.23. Flyer for the Bags show at Long Goodbye, Portland, Oregon, November 1979.

[Tomata] was a little older than some of the other punks. Perhaps noticing that I was still sort of fresh-faced, he asked me where I'd gone to school. When I told him I'd gone to a small Catholic school called Sacred Heart of Mary in Montebello, he surprised me by having heard of it, telling me that he used to live in Montebello. His accent was East Side Manhattan, not LA Eastside. . . . I couldn't believe that this odd duck could have survived on the Eastside, but indeed he had.
—Alice Bag, *Violence Girl*

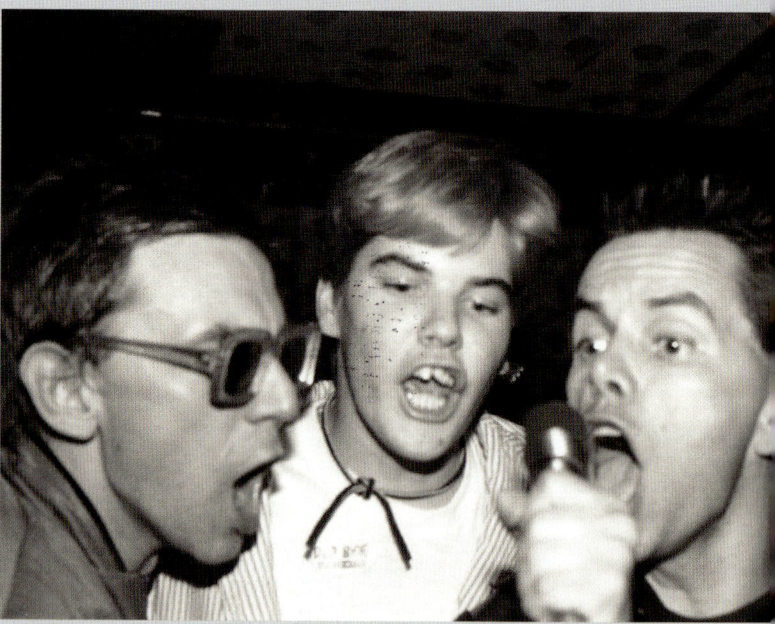

2.24. John Denney (Weirdos), Darby Crash (Germs), and Tomata du Plenty (Screamers) sharing a microphone, circa 1977. Photo: Diane Grove.

2

DECEMBER 1976
GIANNI BUGATTI
QUIZ No 1

GIANNI BUGATTI TO BE REFERRED TO AS "G.B."

① DO YOU FEEL THAT, WHEN ECONOMICALLY FEASABLE, MORE EMPHASIS SHOULD BE MADE ON PERSONAL IMPROVEMENT AS AN AID TO GROUP REHEARSAL?

Yes, Yes, Yes, – but not as to remove personality, kill creativity, or to conform to other standards or laws of music. We can break the rules, if we pull it off with distinction & CLASS.

② IF YOU WERE OFFERED AN OPPORTUNITY TO BECOME A MEMBER OF ONE OF THE TOP TEN GROUPS IN THE WORLD, WOULD YOU ACCEPT?

No, For selfish reasons mainly. I have to feel the instigator of something NEW. or instigators.

③ IF G.B. WAS TO BREAK UP TOMMOROW, WHAT WOULD YOU DO? Take a vacation. Start anew with a new group. Stay in L.A. This Question has been on my mind constantly now. It's never to late to pick up and start again and I'm almost 40.

OVER

④ WHAT WOULD YOUR REACTION BE IF G.B. BECAME EXCLUSIVELY AN INSTRUMENTAL GROUP (NOTEING THAT YOUR MEMBERSHIP IS GUARANTEED)

Leave the group. No regrets. No tears. It was swell.

⑤ IF IT WAS NECCESARY FOR GB TO EXACTLY COPY ONE GROUP OR INDIVIDUAL, WHO WOULD YOU CHOOSE?

toss-up
Bay City Rollers — attention
Sparks — image
Tomita — sound
Paul McCartney — longevity

⑥ IS THIS GLASS HALF-FULL OR HALF-EMPTY?

©1976 RIO

2.25 and 2.26. Two-page quiz for the other members of Gianni Bugatti, December 1976. Designed by Rio in blue pen, with answers in red pen by Tomata du Plenty.

Questionaire

1. What does Gianni Bugatti mean to you? (10 words or less)

3/4 ______________________________

2. Is a hit record essential? (Yes or No)

3, Do you feel you have an objective outllook on G.B., AND can you integrate your personal goals into the total goal of the group? Yes or No

4. How would you deal with a drug, alchol or sex dilemna in the group when these 3 afflictions are affecting sales, performance, and image?

____

____

5. What would you look for in a manager? ______________________________

____

6. If the going gets rough, would you step aside from the decision making process of the band, but continue to devote yourself? Could you manage this transition gracefully? ______________________________

____

____

7. What performers would you like to see you rated against? Multiple choise

Aerowsmith Rolling Stones Tavarres Donna Summers Roxy Abba LaBelle

Peter Frampton/Bruce Springsten Cher Sammy Davis and Mink de Ville

8. What if one of the 3 original Buggattis walked out for good, wouldnit just kill you? or would it? ______________________________

____

9. Io years from today do you want to be retired on a farm in Scotland, on your 3rd annual farewell tour, doind hair at the Smart Men's Boutique, jamming with muscians twice as young as you or doing Whiz Shows with Dena in that Sub room in the sky?

10. When the curtain opens and the lights go up what do you see as Bugatti? (visually and otherwise) ______________________________

____

____

____

2.27. Typed questionnaire on back of a 1974 “Hollywood Spit” CBGB show flyer (see 1.21 for front), designed by Tomata du Plenty for the members of Gianni Bugatti, summer 1976.

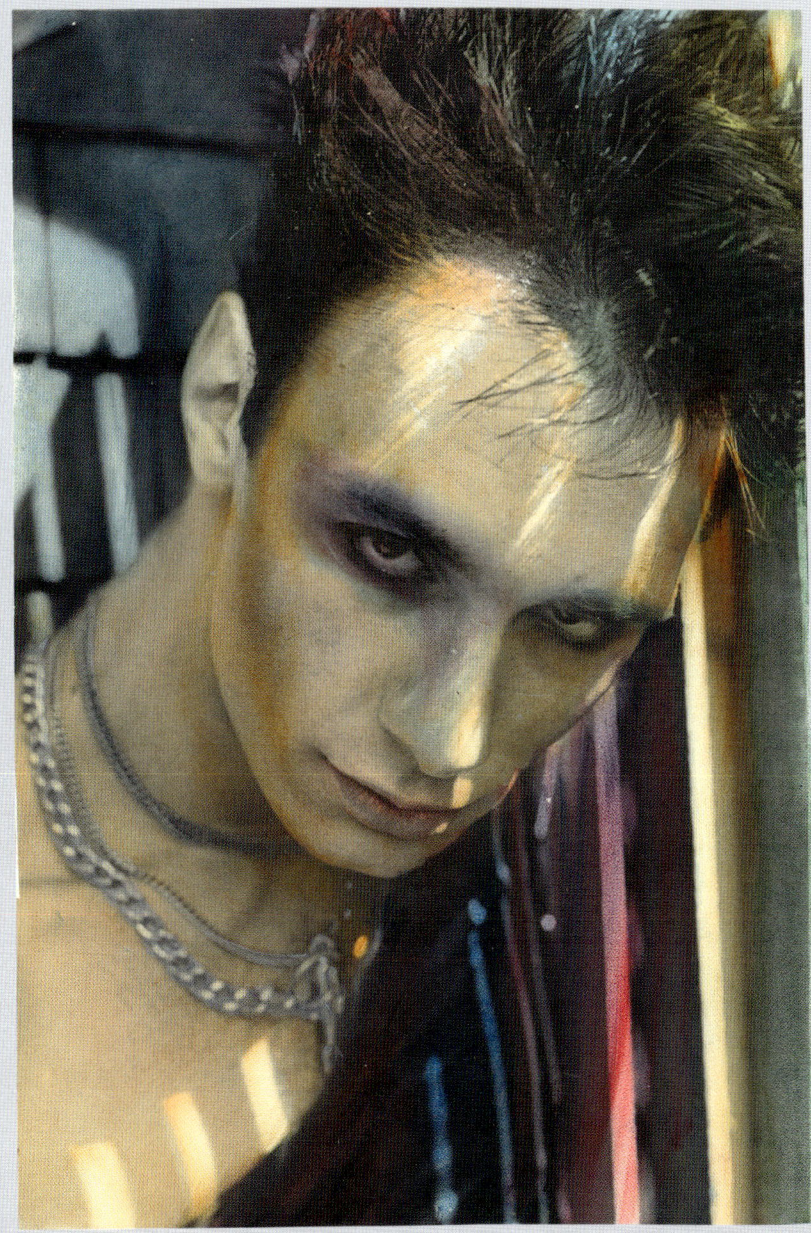

2.28. Hand-tinted black-and-white photograph of Tommy Gear, summer 1977. Photo: © Fayette Hauser.

After Tomatâ and I moved to LA in 1976, when people saw us walking around on the streets they'd be fascinated, often reacting quite strongly to our everyday appearance, which wasn't just a stage look—it was an expressive statement (as well as a form of self-promotion). One time a young woman stopped me on the street and said, "I really like the *gear*!" I decided to take that as my moniker—I liked the way it sounded, plus it's polysemous: as a noun it can mean clothing or a moving part that transforms energy into motion or something purposive; as a verb it can mean to be in a state of readiness; as an adjective it means to be stylish.
—Tommy Gear

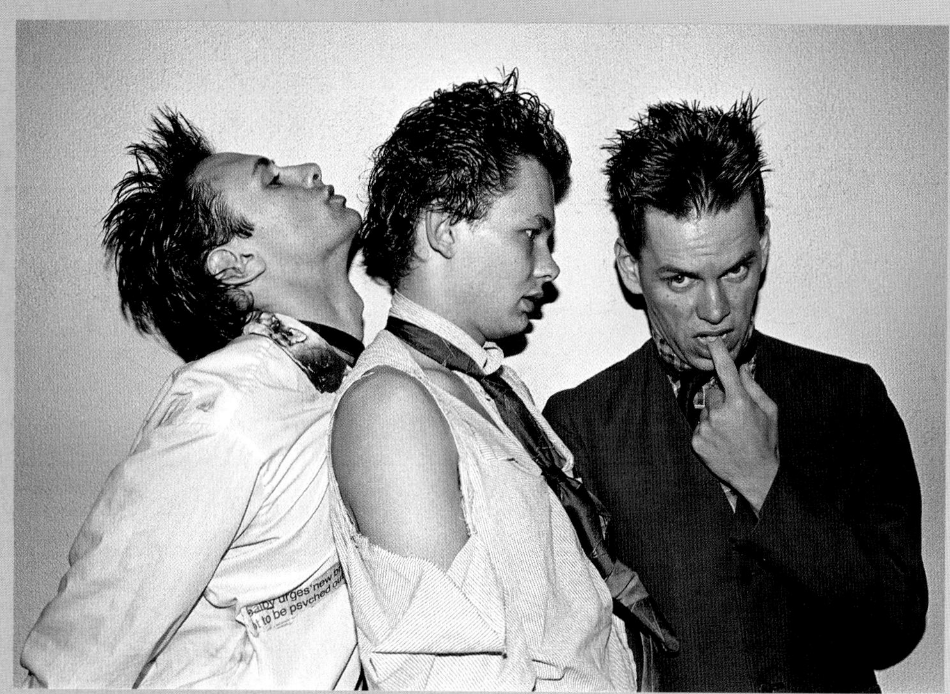

2.29. Tommy Gear, KK Barrett, Tomata du Plenty, North Hollywood, April 9, 1977. Photo: Jenny Lens, 1977.

I created this Screamers Trio portrait outside Bomp! Records Store, North Hollywood, opening day, April 9, 1977. It was the first big social gathering of LA punk. Tomata had introduced himself and Tommy to me at the Whisky, February 1977 during Blondie's LA debut and the Ramones' triumphant return to LA. They created the *most* fun, amazing party for the Ramones and Blondie. I took some of my most favorite photos just hanging out with the Screamers. Truly a most remarkable and uniquely memorable live band. —Jenny Lens

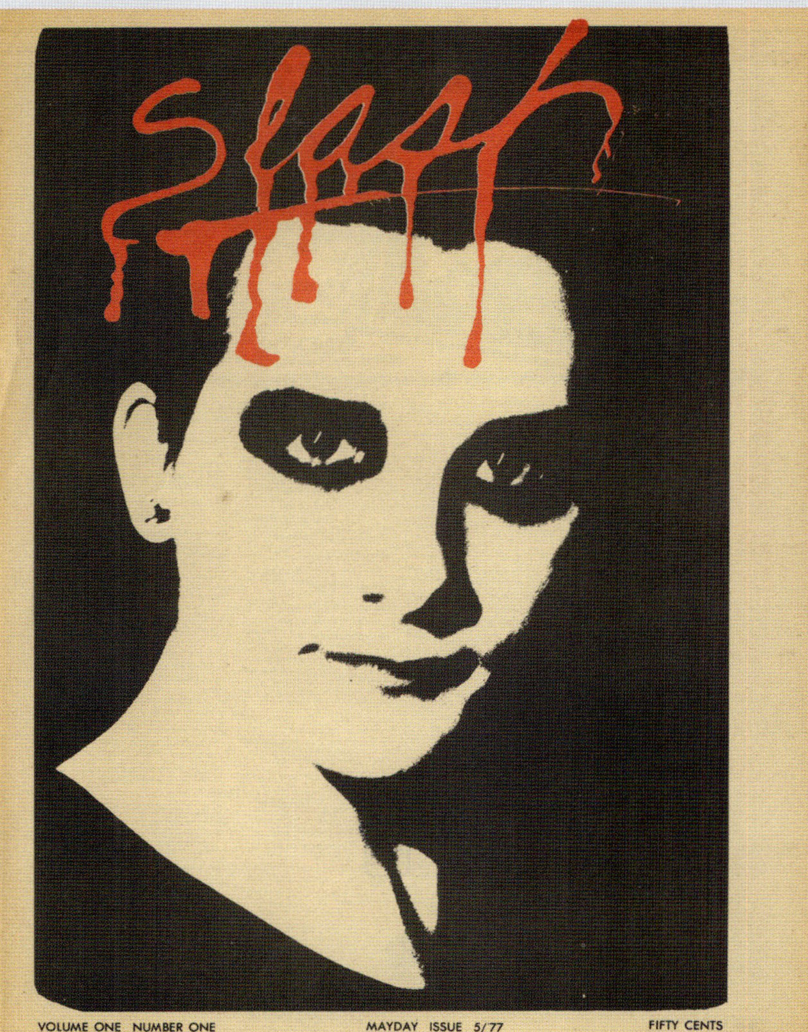

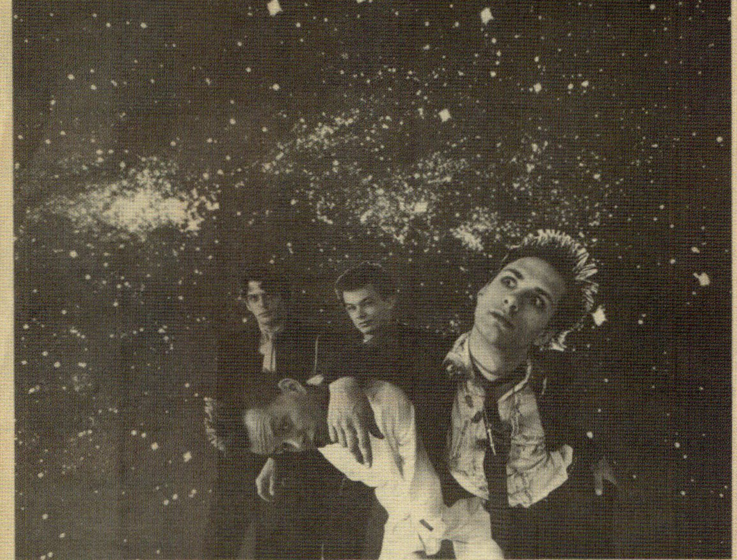

Screamers

SLASH PRESENTS ... THE FUTURE!

They start with their love song, "Eva Braun", then they do some of their greatest hits, "Going steady with Twiggy", "You don't love me, you love magazine", "Peer Pressure", and the infamous "Master De Dolores". Still don't know who we're talking about, do you? Relax, neither does the rest of the world. But not for long, kiddes! Because Slash, always on the crest of the wave in all avant-garde matters, is proudly announcing an upcoming interview with THE SCREAMERS, L.A's most underground combo. The group that, asked to discribe thie sound in one word answered "anxiety!", the one and only group in this galaxy to have done away with guitars and other lame gimmicks will very soon chat with us in these very pages, discussing everything from their stage act ("a very controlled nervous breakdown") to punk noise to the Monkees!

They might not look like your average rock n' roll outfit (see the following pages) and may be their song won't hit the charts for a few months but they ARE the future, and the whole deranged SLASH staff would rather sober up for the rest of their lives than ignore new musical directions! So, kiddes, stick with us and learn all about Tomata, Gear, K.K. and David, pioneers of what one of them calls the "NOUVEAU VAGUE SOUND" ...IN SLASH #2.

SLASH PAGE NINE

2.30 and 2.31. *Slash* vol. 1, no. 1 (May 1977) cover and page 9 teaser for the Screamers' first show.

The Screamers' first Los Angeles club performance took place at the Starwood, in West Hollywood, on July 4, 1977. One week prior, on June 25, the NBC television network news magazine *Weekend* aired a program titled "The New Elizabethans," which profiled the UK punk rock scene on US television for the first time. Many in the Starwood's audience had seen that broadcast and were primed to act out based on its portrayal. Since it was the Fourth of July holiday, concertgoers had smuggled firecrackers into the club. After the band took to the stage, looking the way we looked, the audience began throwing lit firecrackers, and as we played they were exploding all around us. We continuously had to dodge them as we ran through our set—it was crazy! As a consequence of that show, the Starwood banned the Screamers—they wouldn't book us—and we never performed there again. That first public performance in LA contributed early on to the band's punk reputation and mystique. —Tommy Gear

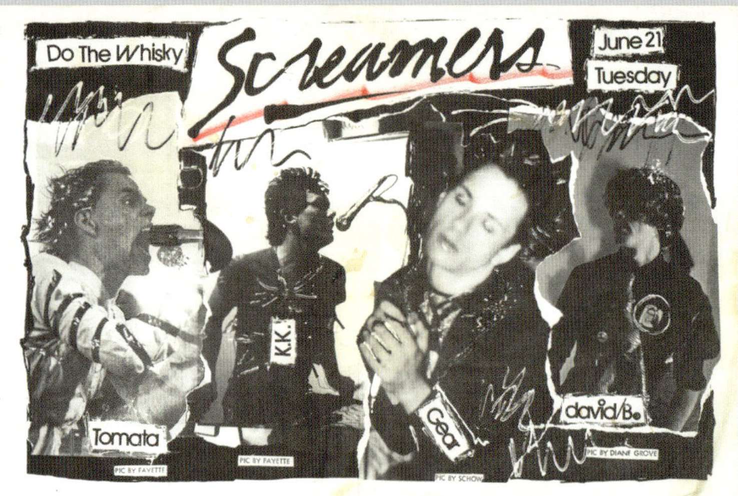

2.32. (*Above*) Flyer for canceled Screamers show at the Whisky, June 1977.

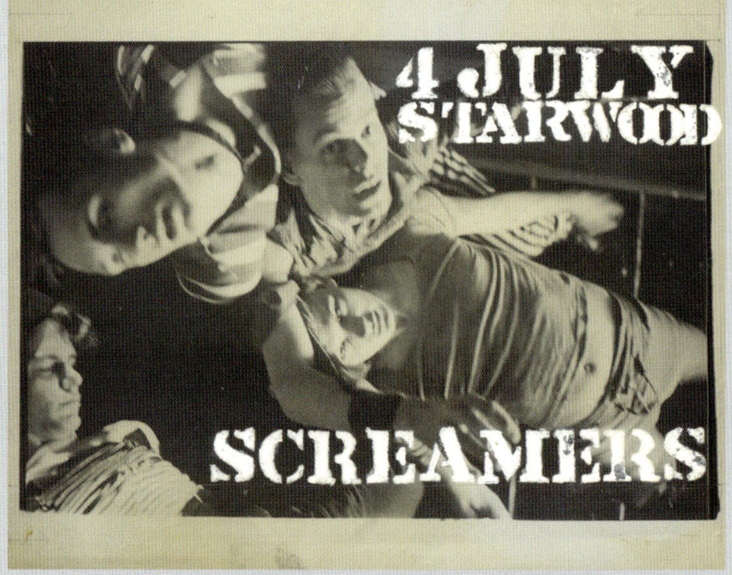

2.33. (*Right*) Screamers flyer with hand-stenciled lettering for first club show at Starwood, July 1977. Design: Tommy Gear; photographer unknown.

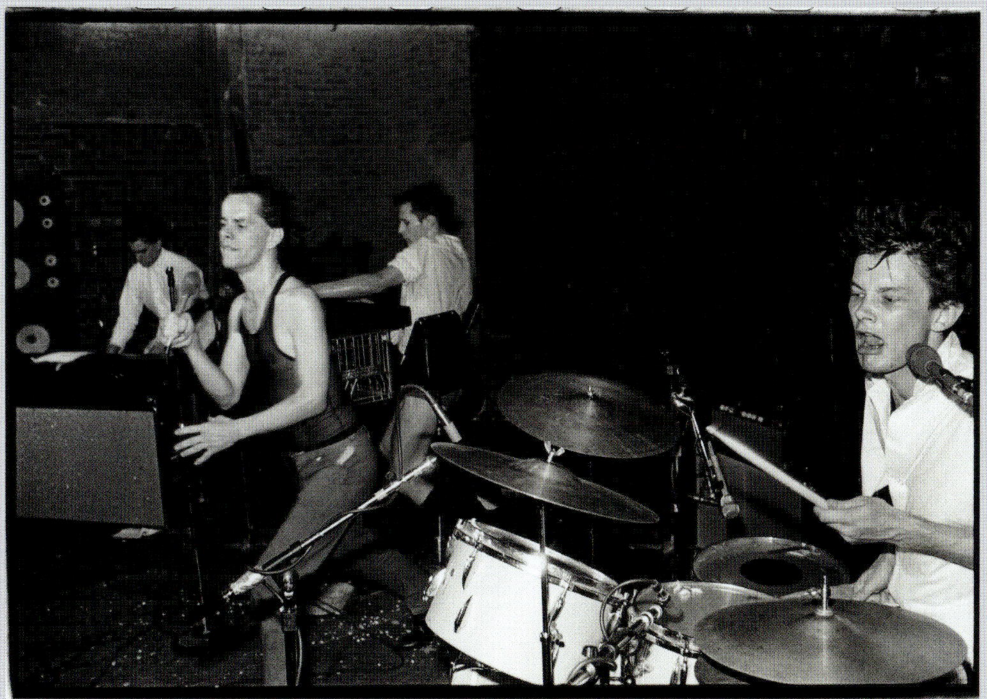

2.34. Screamers performing with Paul Roessler on Fender Rhodes, Mabuhay Gardens, San Francisco, 1977. Photo: Kamera Zie.

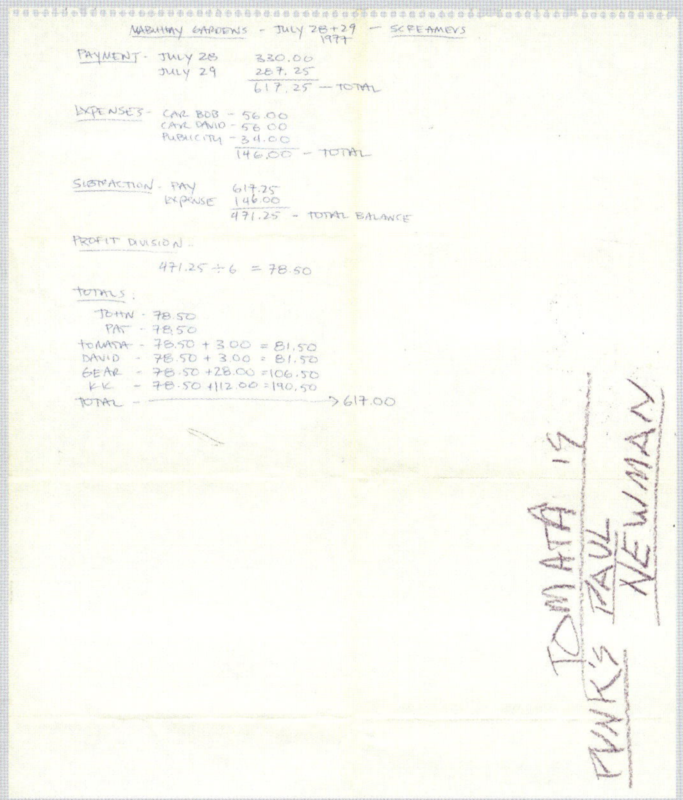

MABUHAY GARDENS - JULY 28+29 1977 - SCREAMERS

PAYMENT - JULY 28 330.00
JULY 29 287.25
617.25 — TOTAL

EXPENSES - CAR BOB - 56.00
CAR DAVID - 56.00
PUBLICITY - 34.00
146.00 - TOTAL

SUBTRACTION - PAY 617.25
EXPENSE 146.00
471.25 - TOTAL BALANCE

PROFIT DIVISION:

471.25 ÷ 6 = 78.50

TOTALS:

JOHN - 78.50
PAT - 78.50
TOMATA - 78.50 + 3.00 = 81.50
DAVID - 78.50 + 3.00 = 81.50
GEAR - 78.50 + 28.00 = 106.50
KK - 78.50 + 112.00 = 190.50
TOTAL — → 617.00

TOMATA IS PUNK'S PAUL NEWMAN

2.35. Accounting for shows on July 28 and 29, 1977 at Mabuhay Gardens, San Francisco. Annotation possibly by Gorilla Rose.

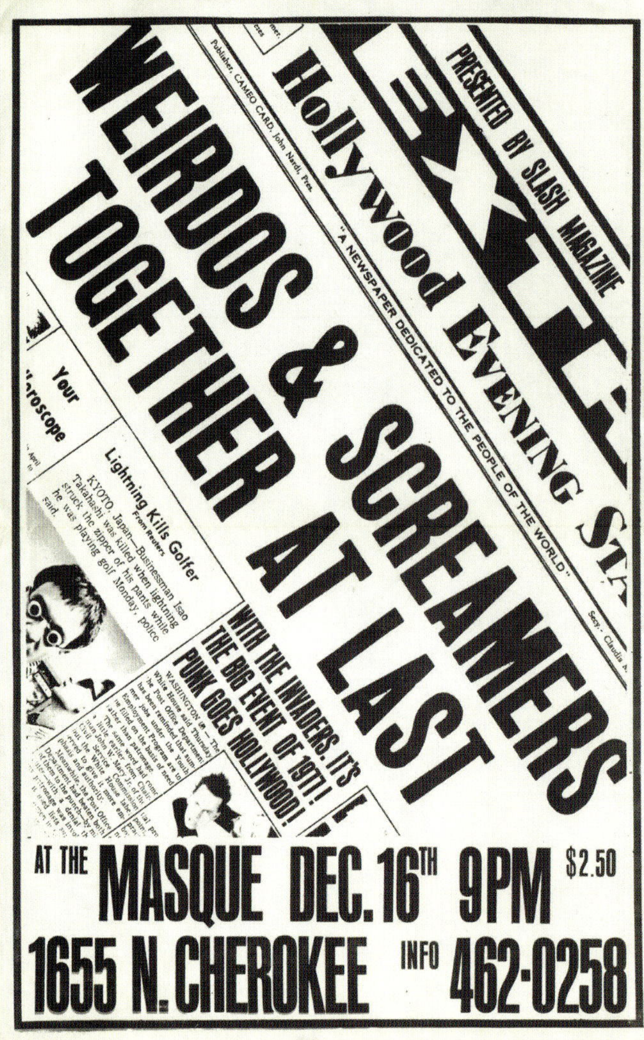

2.36. Poster for Weirdos and Screamers show at the Masque, December 16, 1977. Design: Paul Lesperance (from the band Shock). This was Jeff McGregor's first show with the Screamers. The lineup for December 17 was the Screamers, the Weirdos, the Deadbeats, the Bags, and the Plugz.

The Screamers played at the Masque in late 1977 on a bill that included the Weirdos and Skulls. At that point we thought, since it's a completely raw space, let's play around with the staging. So in a theatrical gesture (and to make a sly commentary on what happened earlier that year at the Starwood), across the front of the stage area we strung chicken wire fencing—as if to protect us from the audience (or vice versa). Being a somewhat flimsy barrier, it offered an inviting provocation for the audience, as rabid as they were, to destroy what was separating them from us. As soon as we started playing they immediately tore it down, becoming inherent participants in our first and only performance at the Masque! —Tommy Gear

LA SHOW - MASQUE - DEC 17

EXPENSES; (TO BE PAID BACK)

35.00 JEFF (REHEARSAL)
13.67 TOMMY (PRINTING)
14.00 HERB + DIANE FENCE
3.00 WIRE + STAPLES
2.00 PRINTING
1.00 TAPE
68.67
- 5.00 for recording TAPE T+T ONLY.
63.67

PAYMENT ~~PROFIT~~ ESTIMATE: (MONEY TO BE MADE)

180.00 BASED ON ADMISSION 3.00 X 200 PEOPLE @ 30% OF TOTAL.

Additional expenses;

ROADIES — GORILLA - 10.00
STU - 10.00
SOUND — JOHN - 20.00
EQUIP - 50.00
90.00

2.37. Itemization of expenses for the Screamers show at the Masque, December 17, 1977. John Doe of X worked sound.

(*Below*) A couple of the Screamers' young fans [Herb Wrede and Diane Grove] took it upon themselves to produce a Xeroxed fanzine. They'd interview each of us then develop what we said into clever content and add collaged photos. The reference to "Mama du Plenty" comes straight from Tomatâ—he was known to bring a dish like potato salad to a potluck or dinner party and present it as being Mama du Plenty's recipe. Those dishes were usually very Americana—but I'm not sure he ever used an actual recipe. —Tommy Gear

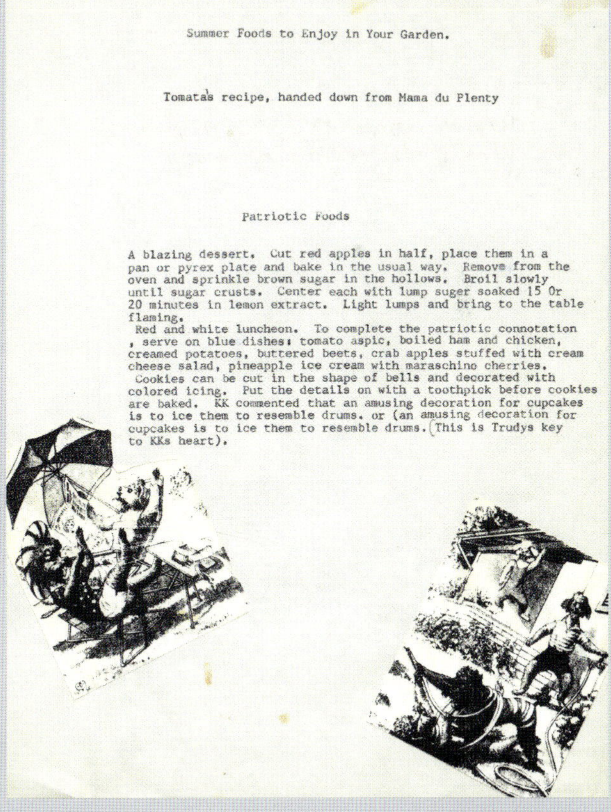

Summer Foods to Enjoy in Your Garden.

Tomatas recipe, handed down from Mama du Plenty

Patriotic Foods

A blazing dessert. Cut red apples in half, place them in a pan or pyrex plate and bake in the usual way. Remove from the oven and sprinkle brown sugar in the hollows. Broil slowly until sugar crusts. Center each with lump suger soaked 15 Or 20 minutes in lemon extract. Light lumps and bring to the table flaming.

Red and white luncheon. To complete the patriotic connotation , serve on blue dishes: tomato aspic, boiled ham and chicken, creamed potatoes, buttered beets, crab apples stuffed with cream cheese salad, pineapple ice cream with maraschino cherries.

Cookies can be cut in the shape of bells and decorated with colored icing. Put the details on with a toothpick before cookies are baked. KK commented that an amusing decoration for cupcakes is to ice them to resemble drums. or (an amusing decoration for cupcakes is to ice them to resemble drums. (This is Trudys key to KKs heart).

2.38. Page pasteup from a Screamers Fan Club newsletter, produced by Herb Wrede and Diane Grove (undated).

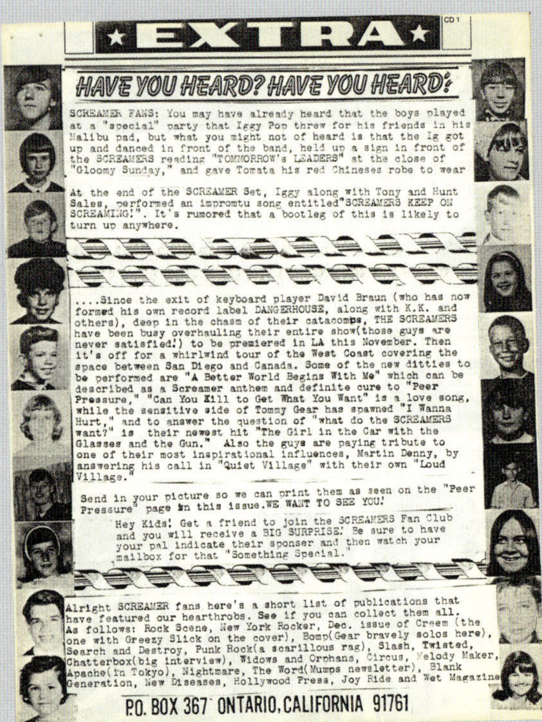

★ EXTRA ★ CD1

HAVE YOU HEARD? HAVE YOU HEARD?

SCREAMER FANS: You may have already heard that the boys played at a "special" party that Iggy Pop threw for his friends in his Malibu pad, but what you might not of heard is that the Ig got up and danced in front of the band, held up a sign in front of the SCREAMERS reading "TOMMORROW's LEADERS" at the close of "Gloomy Sunday," and gave Tomata his red Chineses robe to wear

At the end of the SCREAMER Set, Iggy along with Tony and Hunt Sales, performed an impromtu song entitled"SCREAMERS KEEP ON SCREAMING!". It's rumored that a bootleg of this is likely to turn up anywhere.

....Since the exit of keyboard player David Braun (who has now formed his own record label DANGERHOUSE, along with K.K. and others), deep in the chasm of their catacombs, THE SCREAMERS have been busy overhauling their entire show(those guys are never satisfied!) to be premiered in LA this November. Then it's off for a whirlwind tour of the West Coast covering the space between San Diego and Canada. Some of the new ditties to be performed are "A Better World Begins With Me" which can be described as a Screamer anthem and definite cure to "Peer Pressure," "Can You Kill to Get What You Want" is a love song, while the sensitive side of Tommy Gear has spawned "I Wanna Hurt," and to answer the question of "what do the SCREAMERS want?" is their newest hit "The Girl in the Car with the Glasses and the Gun." Also the guys are paying tribute to one of their most inspirational influences, Martin Denny, by answering his call in "Quiet Village" with their own "Loud Village."

Send in your picture so we can print them as seen on the "Peer Pressure" page in this issue.WE WANT TO SEE YOU!

Hey Kids! Get a friend to join the SCREAMERS Fan Club and you will receive a BIG SURPRISE! Be sure to have your pal indicate their sponser and then watch your mailbox for that "Something Special."

Alright SCREAMER fans here's a short list of publications that have featured our hearthrobs. See if you can collect them all. As follows: Rock Scene, New York Rocker, Dec. issue of Creem (the one with Greezy Slick on the cover), Bomp(Gear bravely solos here), Search and Destroy, Punk Rock(a scarillous rag), Slash, Twisted, Chatterbox(big interview), Widows and Orphans, Circus, Melody Maker, Apache(in Tokyo), Nightmare, The Word(Mumps newsletter), Blank Generation, New Diseases, Hollywood Press, Joy Ride and Wet Magazine

P.O. BOX 367 ONTARIO, CALIFORNIA 91761

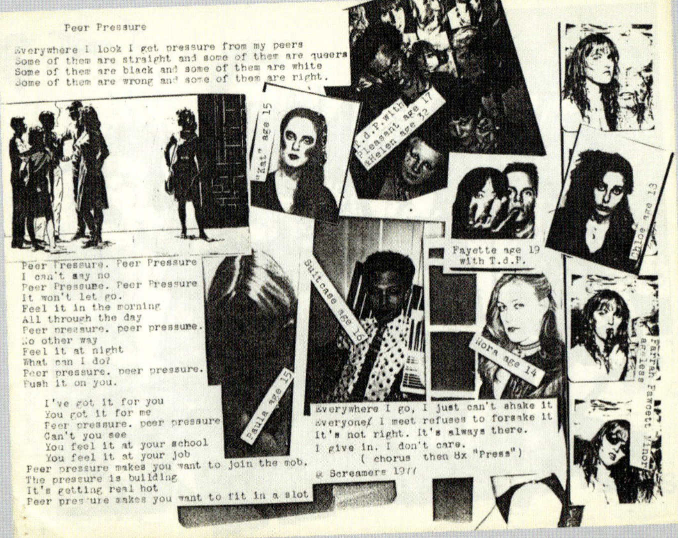

Peer Pressure

Everywhere I look I get pressure from my peers
Some of them are straight and some of them are queers
Some of them are black and some of them are white
Some of them are wrong and some of them are right.

Peer Pressure. Peer Pressure
I can't say no
Peer Pressure. Peer Pressure
It won't let go.
Feel it in the morning
All through the day
Peer pressure. peer pressure.
No other way
Feel it at night
What can I do?
Peer pressure. peer pressure.
Push it on you.

I've got it for you
You got it for me
Peer pressure. peer pressure
Can't you see
You feel it at your school
You feel it at your job
Peer pressure makes you want to join the mob.
The pressure is building
It's getting real hot
Peer pressure makes you want to fit in a slot

Everywhere I go, I just can't shake it
Everyone I meet refuses to forsake it
It's not right. It's always there.
I give in. I don't care.
(chorus then 8x "Press")
@ Screamers 1977

"Kat" age 15
T.d.P. with Pleasant age 17 & Helen age 32
Chloe age 13
Fayette age 19 with T.d.P.
Paula age 15
Suitcase age 16
Nora age 14
Farrah Fawcett Minor ageless

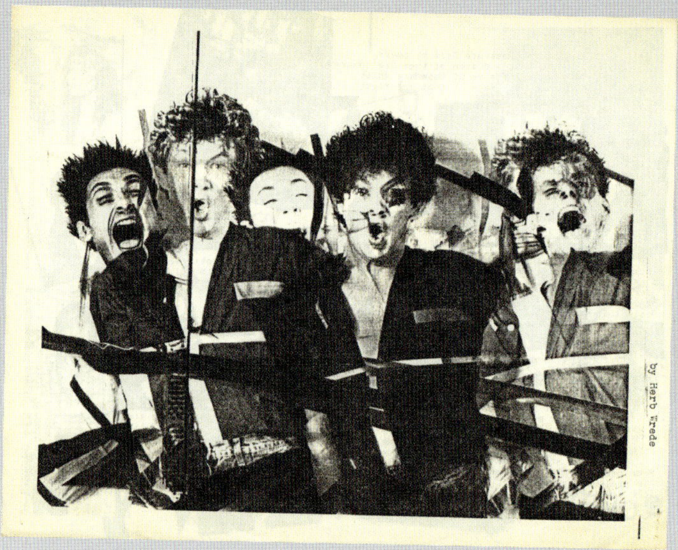

2.39–2.41. Pages from the Screamers Fan Club newsletter issue 2, circa October 1977, created by Herb Wrede and Diane Grove.

To promote his new album *The Idiot* in 1977, Iggy Pop went on a world concert tour (with David Bowie on backing vocals and piano). I saw that show on April 15 when he played at the Santa Monica Civic Auditorium. After the tour ended he was staying in a Malibu beach house for the summer. He called me and invited the Screamers to come over and play. We lugged our equipment up the Pacific Coast Highway and set up in his living room with the Pacific Ocean as a backdrop. It ended up being a bespoke Screamers performance for Iggy and the Sales brothers, Tony and Hunt, who had been in his backing band for the tour. As we were playing he called David Bowie in Berlin, held up the phone and said "Listen to this!" Then at one point between songs he handed me the phone and I was like, "Hello . . . David?" —Tommy Gear

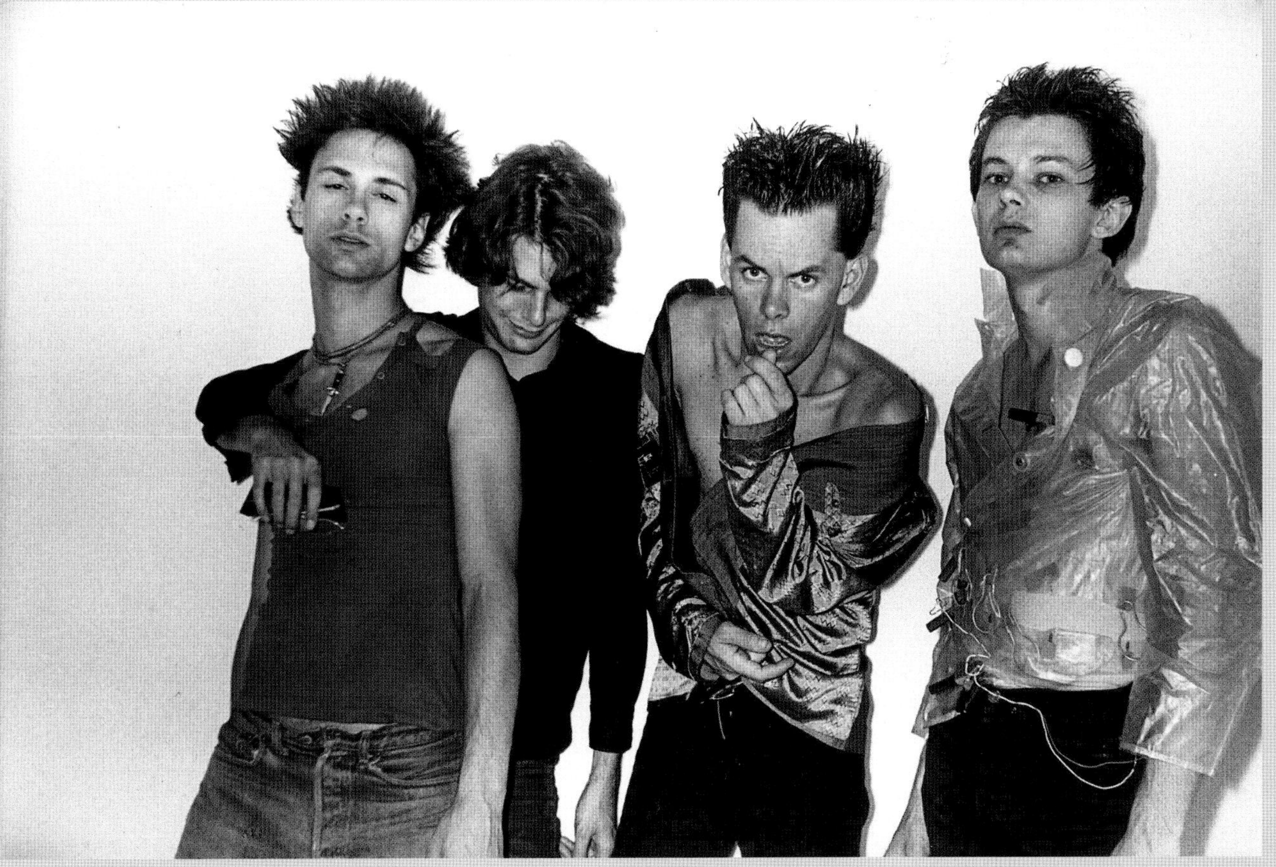

2.42. Screamers circa early 1978 with Jeff McGregor. Photo © Fayette Hauser.

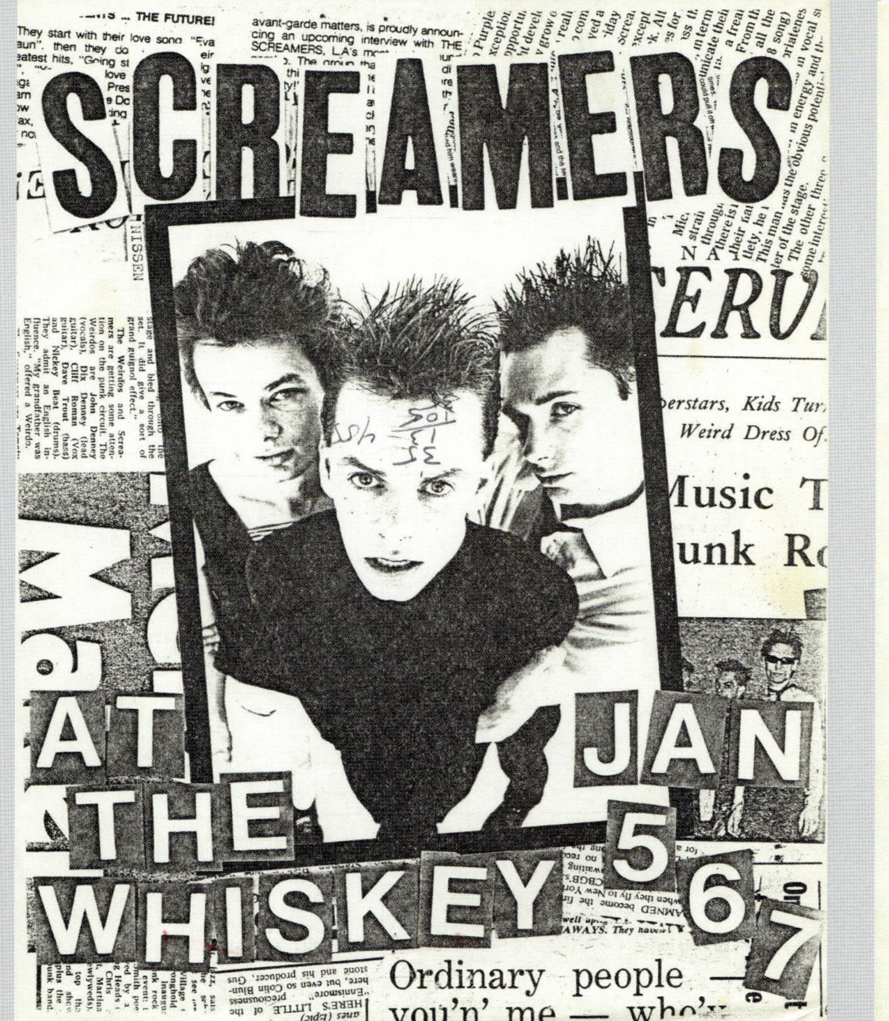

2.43. Front of Screamers flyer for shows at the Whisky, February 16–19, 1978.

WHISKEY SHOW FEB. 16,17,18&19th. (Thurs-Sun)

PUBLICITY : Silkscreen -K.K.

~~paper thru Jeff $24.~~
other costs
mail outs $10. maximum
Slash ad.

4.55 POST
2.00 GAS
18.02 PRINTING TO D+H

Fan Club manpower

REHEARSELS 2½ weeks prior to shows
Jeff paid $21. towards it
HE owed (74.) OWED TO JEFF

FAN CLUB $50. DEDUCTION.

Sound man - RAND? ($40.)
Roadie [DUTCH?] ($100 maximum)
Costs

Lights - Gorilla ($40.)
(rentals) ?
(note: talk to Marshall about light change)

Agent - Phil ~~$100.~~ 10%

Hospital ($100.)

Additional Props ~~$30.~~
(use of rizers)

Back-up Bands
DEADBEATS
F-Word

2.44. Back of Screamers flyer showing accounting for shows at the Whisky, February 16–19, 1978. Expenses include a $100 "hospital" charge, which was a deposit for potential liability costs.

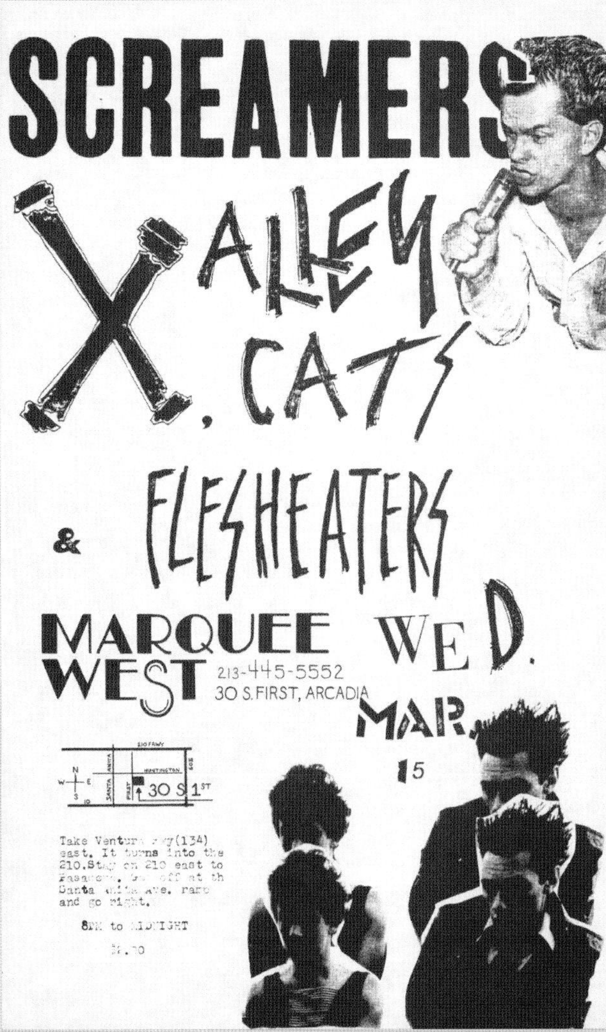

2.45. Flyer for Screamers show with X, Alley Cats, and Flesheaters at the Marquee West, Arcadia, California, March 15, 1978.

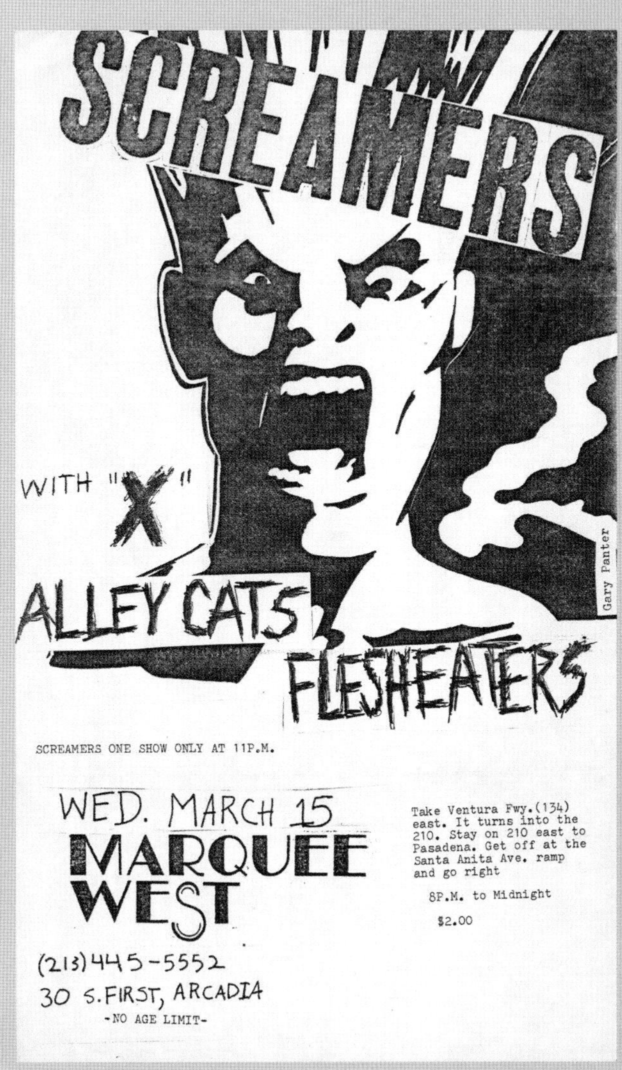

2.46. Second flyer for the Marquee West show on March 15, 1978, with one of the earliest appearances of the Screamers logo by Gary Panter.

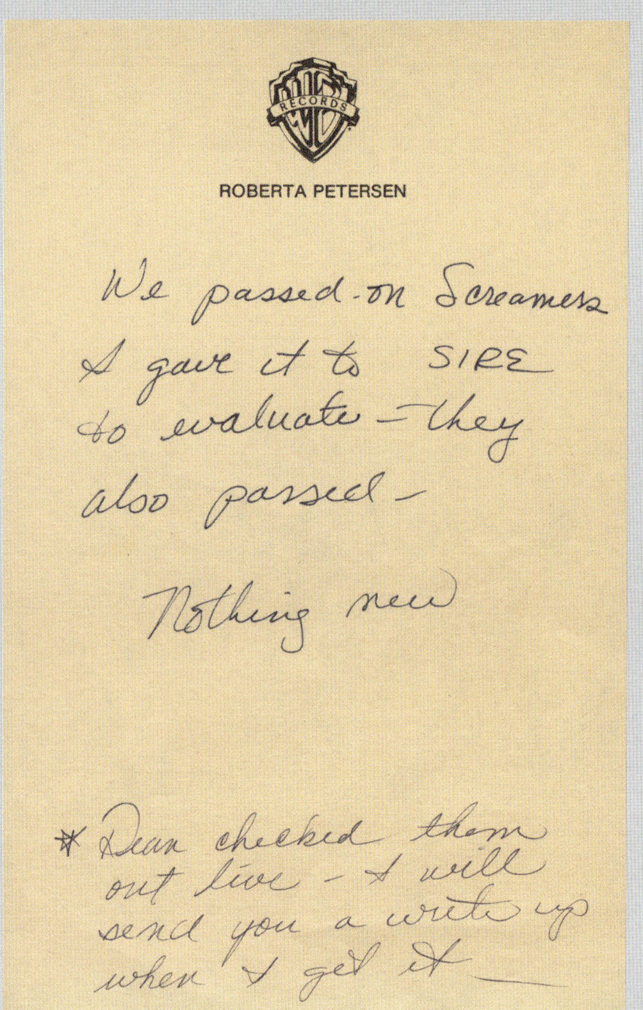
ROBERTA PETERSEN

We passed on Screamers
I gave it to SIRE
to evaluate – they
also passed –

Nothing new

* Dean checked them
out live – I will
send you a write up
when I get it –

2.47. Note from Roberta Peterson, Warner Bros. Records general manager of A&R (artists and repertoire), January 1978.

The Screamers had a devoted and growing fan base; when we played at the Whisky a Go Go we performed three weekend nights straight, two shows a night, and they were all usually sold out. We had no guitars, and our lead singer couldn't really carry a tune—Tomatâ's distinctive vocalizations had more in common with singers like Tom Waits or even Captain Beefheart. I'd consider him to be more of a "song stylist" whose vocals were a performative sonic expression, highly integral with our electronic instrumentation—Screamers performance as *Gesamtkunstwerk*. But we couldn't get any traction from the major record labels to consider signing us; their A&R staff was conditioned by what typically got picked up for radio airplay at the time, and they seemingly couldn't make any sense of us. At one point the Ramones' manager Danny Fields introduced me to Sire Records founder Seymour Stein, which was one of several avenues we explored that didn't work out. Early on there was Dangerhouse, an independent label largely run by Pat Garrett, who moved to LA from Oklahoma around the same time as our drummer KK. He produced the earliest releases by local punk bands such as the Alley Cats, the Avengers, the Bags, Black Randy, the Dils, the Weirdos, and X. Although they were interested in recording us, at the time we decided to hold out rather than go with a smaller label. —Tommy Gear

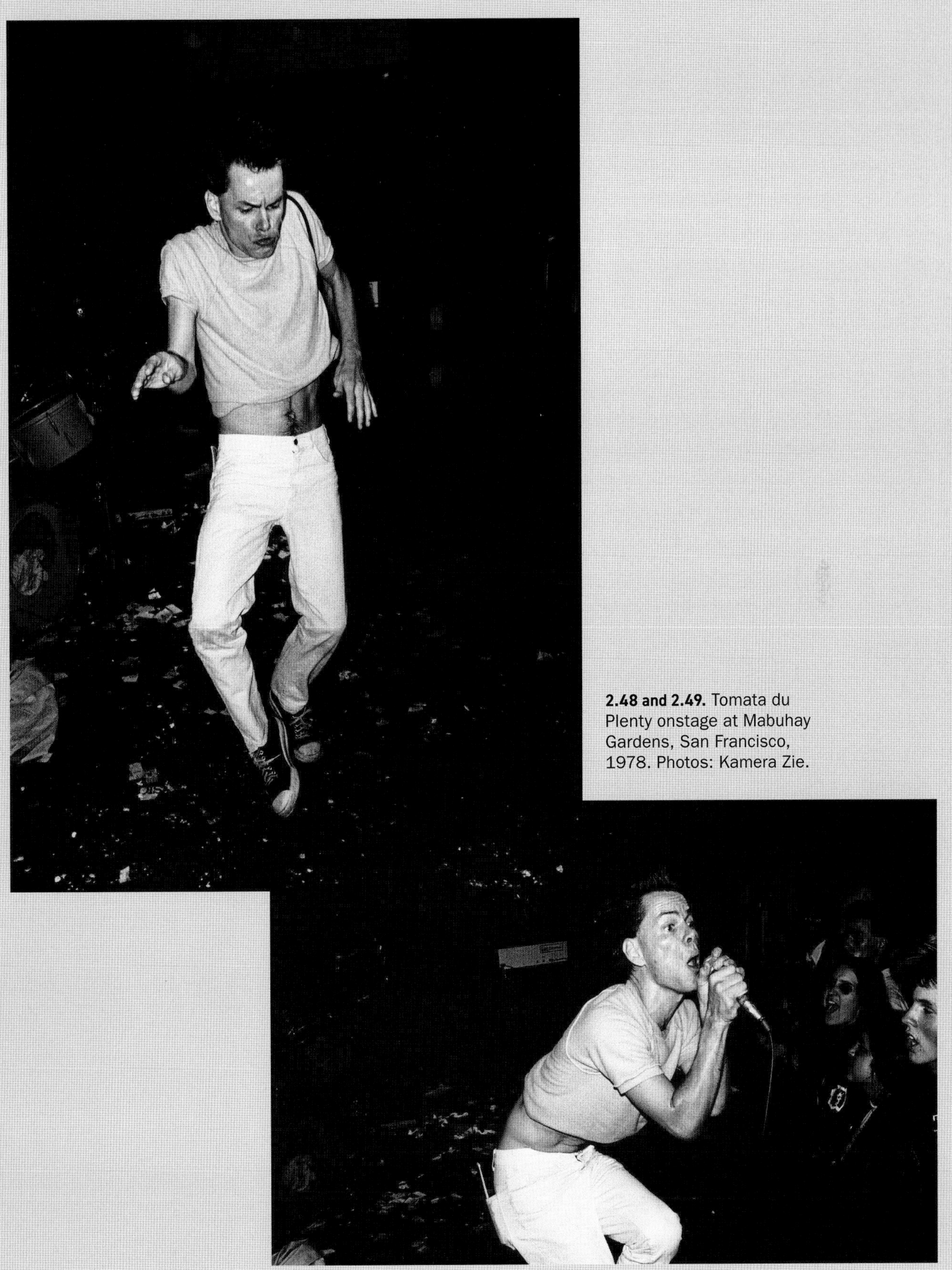

2.48 and 2.49. Tomata du Plenty onstage at Mabuhay Gardens, San Francisco, 1978. Photos: Kamera Zie.

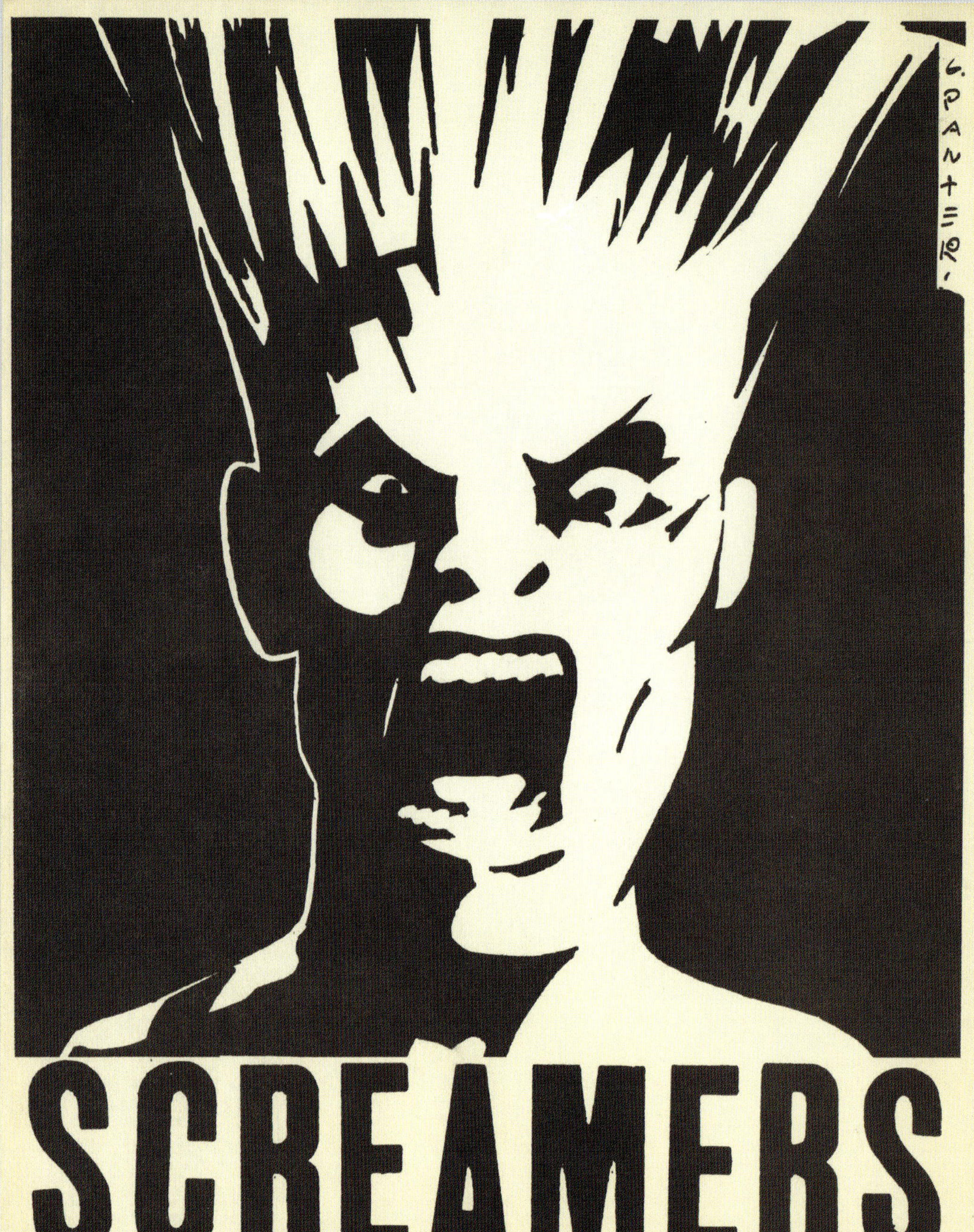

2.50. Blank poster with printed Screamers logo.

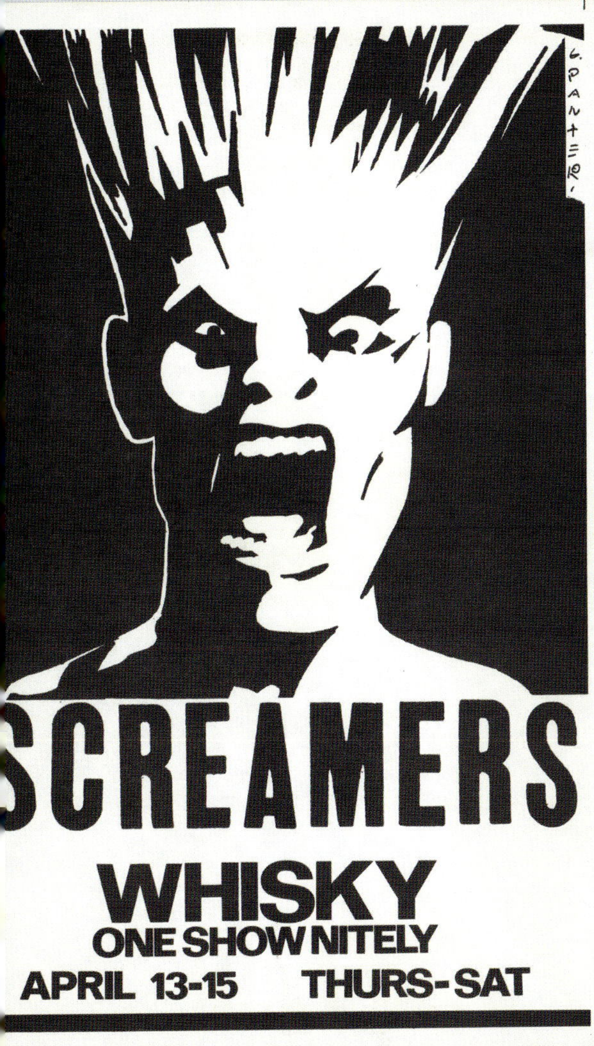

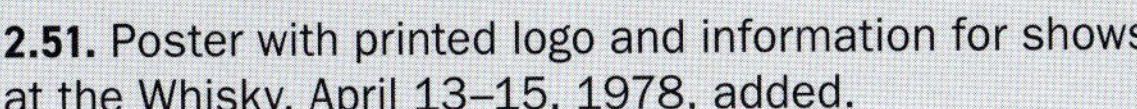

2.51. Poster with printed logo and information for shows at the Whisky, April 13–15, 1978, added.

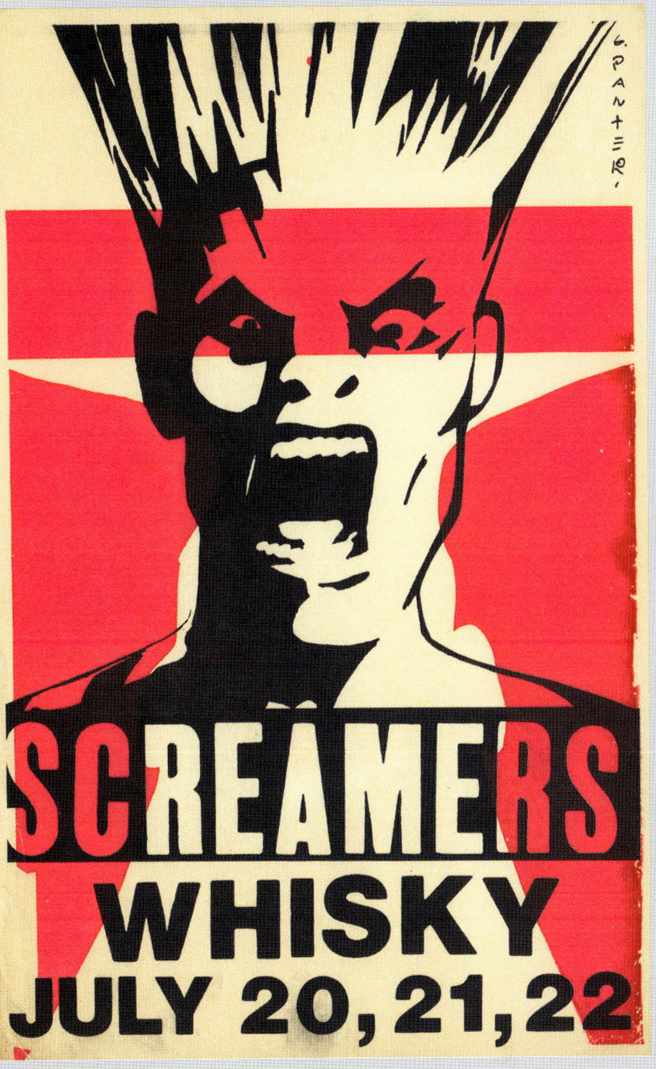

2.52. Poster with printed logo and pink upside-down logo silhouette silk screen overlay, July 1978.

The image of the Screamer came out of sketchbook work and unpublished false starts at making comics when I was in Dallas before moving to LA in '76. I had been making work I was excited by since a revelatory year in '72 and in general at the inspiring atmosphere and teachers I had at East Texas State University, now called Texas A&M University, in Commerce, Texas, from '69 to '74. It was a very rich place to accidentally land sixteen miles from my hometown. The image was not a specific portrait of Tomata but of the impression the Screamers made walking into a room looking the way they did. —Gary Panter

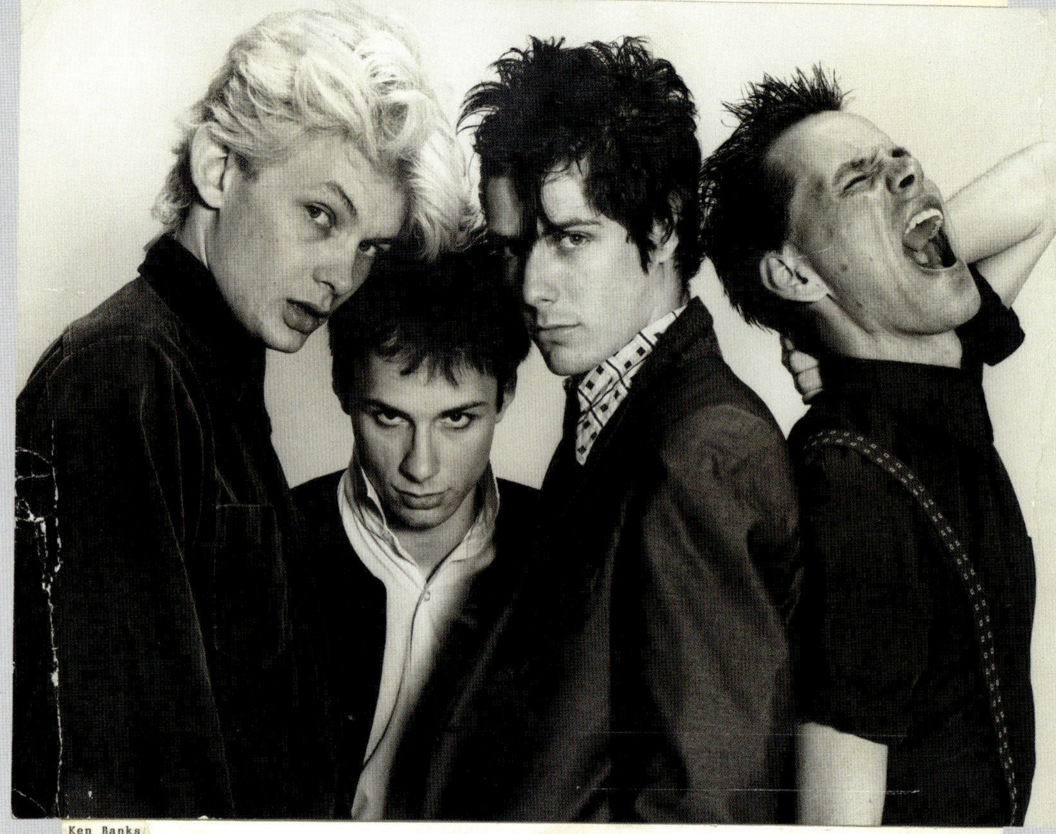

ALL YOU NEED TO JOIN THE OFFICIAL SCREAMERS FAN CLUB! EXCLUSIVE NEWSLETTER, CRAMMED WITH FABULOUS FAX & FOTOS, THE INSIDE NEWS, SPECIAL OFFERS— ALL YOURS FOR ONLY $2. PER YEAR. JOIN NOW AND GET A BONUS BUTTON FREE! MAIL THIS FORM ALONG WITH CHECK OR MONEY ORDER TO:

SCREAMERS ASSAULT!/BOX 330/1626 N. WILCOX/HOLLYWOOD, CA 90028/U.S.A.

NAME ____________ ADDRESS ____________

CITY ____________ STATE ____________ ZIP ____________

FAVORITE THING ____________ SHOE SIZE ____________

PHONE # ____________ AMBITION IN LIFE ____________

2.53. Pasteup for Screamers Fan Club application, circa April 1978. Photo: Ken Banks.

The patients filtered into the recreational building, introducing themselves to the Screamer-affiliated ranks with much zealous hand-shaking. An amiable bunch, they mingled and exchanged small talk as Screamer Fan Club applications were distributed. Many were quizzical as to how to fill out the form, particularly the spaces designated for "shoe size" and "ambition in life." —Bob Taylor, *Slash* no. 10, reporting on the Screamers show at the Camarillo State Mental Hospital on March 23, 1978

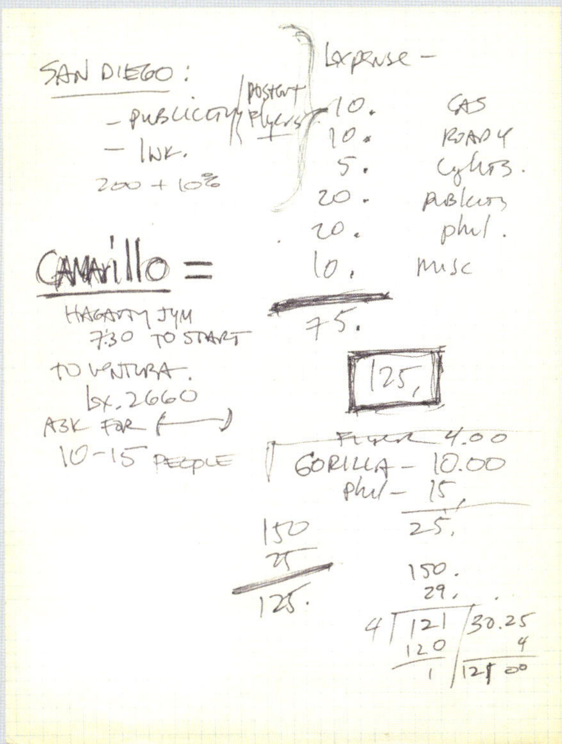

2.54. Working notes for Screamers performances: contact for show at Camarillo State Mental Hospital held on March 23, 1978, and itemization of expenses for show in San Diego held on March 25, 1978.

I had been rereading Michel Foucault's *Discipline and Punish: The Birth of the Prison*. Knowing what a Screamers performance could be like, I started imagining what it would be like to do a show in a carceral environment and how an audience of prison inmates would respond. So I started to initiate inquiries to identify a penitentiary that might be open to having the band perform there, but unfortunately nothing ever came of that. Instead, we were able to a get a gig playing at the California State Mental Hospital in Camarillo, which had recently been reorganized and was beginning to implement current biopsychosocial treatment approaches with its adult patients, allowing them to leave their closed living units to attend therapy groups, educational programs, and other group activities, such as a music performance by the Screamers in this case (though at the time I don't think anyone running that facility was familiar with the band or punk rock). Upon our arrival we were ushered into an empty, bare auditorium with a raised proscenium stage on which we set up our equipment to play. As soon as we were ready, the hospital staff began ushering in residents that weren't under lockdown. From the stage, we could see the semi-darkened space was starting to fill with people ranging from young adults to those more elderly. There was no seating, so some of them stood close together in small clusters or in dyads holding hands, others stood by themselves keeping a distance from anyone else. It was also readily apparent that the audience reflected a diverse range of diagnoses, ranging from psychiatric disorders to autism to Down syndrome to developmental disabilities.

As we began performing our regular set, moving through one song to another, I noticed that each person in the audience was responding differently to the music. As the music started, some began reacting immediately, agitatedly jumping up and down or flailing their arms wildly; others coupled together in a ballroom dance pose, slowly moving around in a circle as if waltzing; yet others merely swayed languidly or barely moved at all, standing perfectly still while looking toward the stage or gazing uninterestedly into the space around them. In contrast to hypermanic punks always trying to outdo one another in the mosh pit, this seemed like a relatively benign bedlam, with everyone ensconced in their own private world. For me, the most moving part of the experience occurred after the show was over while we were packing up our equipment. Some of the audience still remained milling around, and a bunch of them came to the edge of the stage. Smiling and friendly, they approached, simply wanting to connect with us, reaching out to hold our hands and to gently embrace us, to have direct human contact in a sweet and loving way. I was quite touched by their uncontrived gesture of gratitude for what we had to offer—they weren't trying to be a punk or a fan or a groupie, or to conform or to pander. They were one of the most authentically appreciative audiences that we'd ever encountered. —Tommy Gear

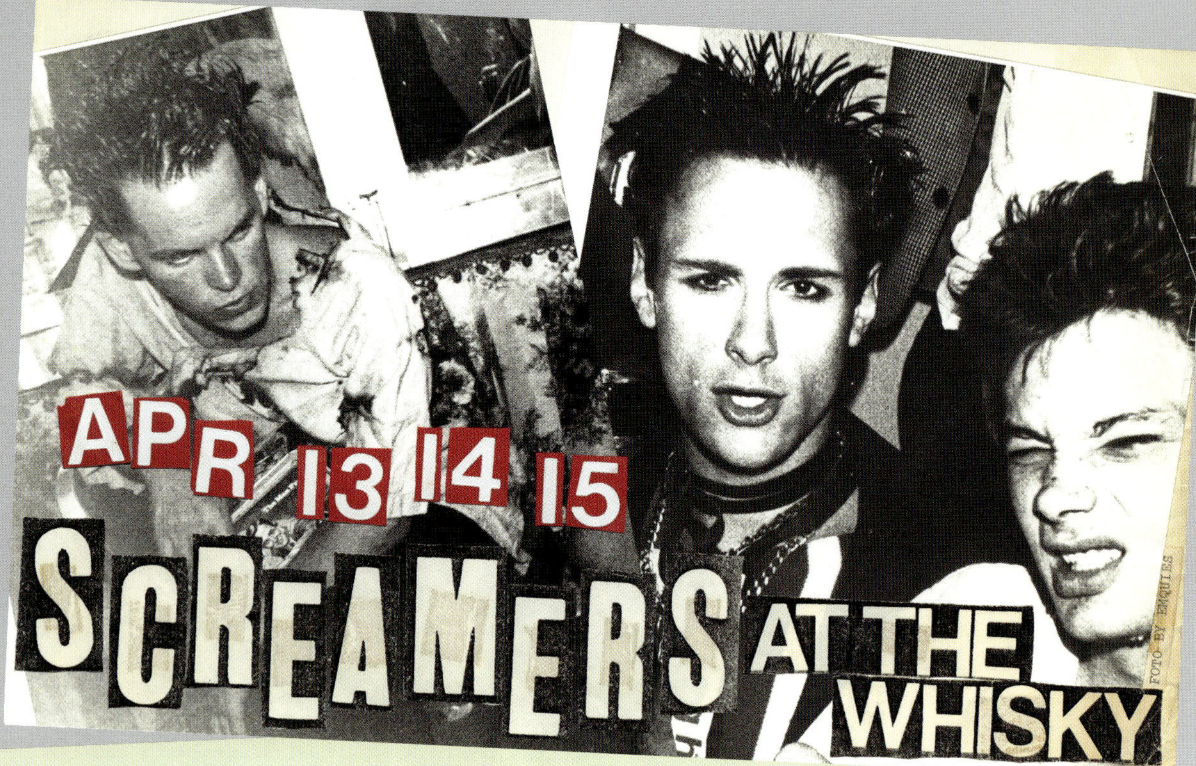

MARCH 1978 LOS ANGELES

PERIOD ______ TO ______

EMPLOYEE	BASIS	EARNINGS TOTAL	DEDUCTIONS	AMOUNT OF CHECK	DISTRIBUTION	AMOUNT	
MARQUEE WEST ARCADIA CAL. 3/15/78	PAY	150.00	PHIL'S PERCENTAGE (10%)	15.00	TO PHIL	15.00	PAID
			GORILLA PAY – LIGHTS	10.00	TO GORILLA	10.00	PAID
			FLYER	4.00	TO TOMATA	4.00	PAID
				29.00			
BALANCE AFTER DEDUCTIONS		121.00	→		TO TOMATA	30.25	PAID
					TO GEAR	30.25	PAID
					TO KK	30.25	PAID
					TO JEFF	30.25	
APRIL 1978 LA WHISKEY 4/13–15/78	PAY	1803.00	PHIL'S PERCENTAGE (10%)	180.00	TO PHIL	180.00	PAID
			GORILLA PAY – LIGHTS	65.00	TO GORILLA	65.00	PAID
			GEZA PAY – SOUND	40.00	TO GEZA	40.00	PAID
			KIRA PAY – ROADIE	25.00	TO KIRA	25.00	PAID
			SCAFFOLDING	53.00			PAID
			PUBLICITY (FLYERS ETC)	48.50			PAID
			POSTAGE	25.00			PAID
			HOSPITAL DEDUCTION	100.00			PAID
			TOTAL	536.50			
BALANCE AFTER DEDUCTION:		1266.50	PERCENTAGE DISTRIBUTION →		13% TO TOMATA	165.00	PAID
					13% TO GEAR	165.00	PAID
					20% TO KK	253.00	PAID
					20% TO JEFF	253.00	PAID
					34% TO FUND	431.00	PAID
			TOTALS		100%	1267.00	
						ROUNDED TO HIGHER DOLLAR	

DELUXE CHECK PRINTERS MASTER PAYROLL SHEET

2.55. (*Top*) Flyer pasteup for Screamers show at the Whisky, April 13–15, 1978. Photography by Salomon Emquies.

2.56. (*Bottom*) Accounting for the Marquee West (March 15, 1978) and Whisky (April 13–15, 1978) shows. Crew for the Whisky show included Gorilla Rose, Kira Roessler, Geza X, and Phil Miller.

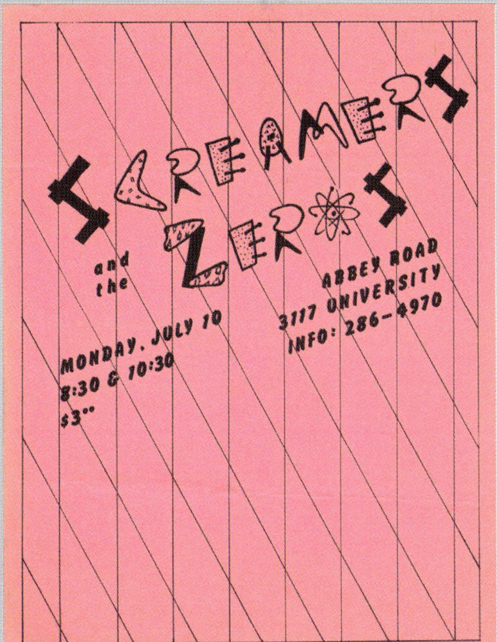

2.57. Flyer for Screamers and the Zeros show at Abbey Road, San Diego, July 1978.

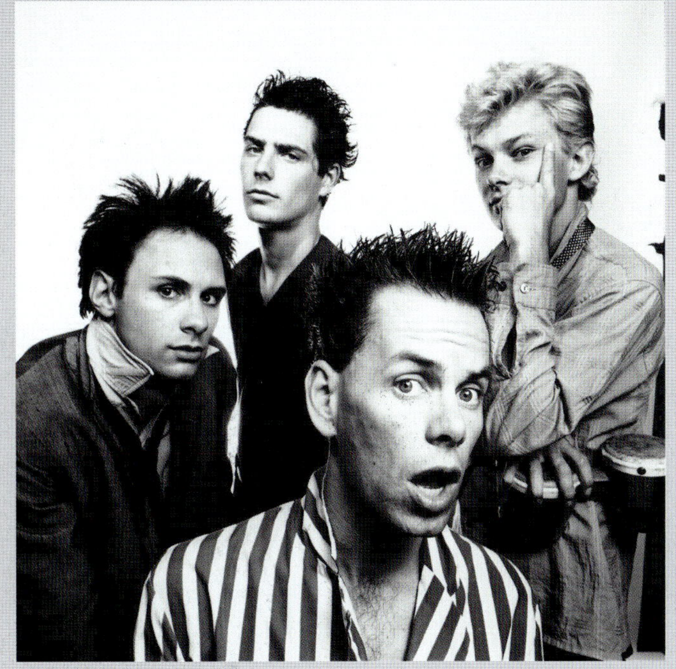

2.58. Publicity photo (with Paul Roessler), after April 1978. Photo: Eric Blum, 1978.

'Nazi,' 15, Kills Schoolmate Over Taunt

LANSING, Mich. (AP)—When 15-year-old Roger E. Needham showed up at Everett High School wearing a Nazi party pin and talking quietly about Adolf Hitler, his classmates jeered.

When Needham heard one taunt too many, he pulled a .22-caliber, Luger-style pistol in a crowded school hallway and shot two teasing classmates. One of the boys died.

Today, the frail, slender Needham was brought from Ingham County Jail to answer for his no-contest plea on a murder charge. Probate Judge Donald Owens ordered him held temporarily at the county juvenile home until authorities could complete a nationwide search for an appropriate mental institution where he could receive sophisticated therapy.

Owens, who set another hearing for Aug. 16, also ordered the juvenile home to add a full-time staff member simply to watch over Needham.

Needham, who is being dealt with as a juvenile and could therefore be released once he turns 19, sat silently in the courtroom, dressed in blue jeans and a red- and yellow-striped T-shirt. His father sat next to him.

The court proceedings did nothing to answer the deeper questions asked at Everett High School about Roger Needham. But for his Nazi pin, he looked like any other student.

When exactly did he slip from a perhaps unnatural interest in war into a belief in Nazism that could cause him to kill?

Authorities described Needham as a brilliant loner. They said he once made a detailed blueprint of a Nazi extermination camp complete with gas chambers. A psychiatrist characterized him as "highly intelligent, hostile, intensely angry at everyone."

After the shootings on Feb. 22, authorities found a diary in which the boy had written about his school experiences. One entry read:

"I almost abandoned Hitler last night—out of being pushed too far by my colleagues. I almost went to school without my Nazi party pin in my jacket. But luckily again I had a burst of courage and never again will I think about abandoning Mein Fuhrer and Nazism."

Roger E. Needham

AP Wirephoto

The diary, entitled "My Struggle" after Hitler's "Mein Kampf," also contained this passage: "While I in no way forgive my enemies, I will refrain from killing them for the moment."

The entry was written two days before Needham fatally shot Bill Draher, 15, and wounded Kevin Jones, 16. Jones, whose head was grazed by a bullet, later admitted he had been looking for a fight with Needham "because of the Nazi deal."

Curiously, Everett Vice Principal Robert Dingman said, the victims were probably as close friends as Needham had. "He was probably hurt that they were the ones who had done some of the heckling," he said.

He said Needham had taken part in no school activities after a brief stint on the track team. He was considered an excellent builder of models, such as tanks and armored personnel carriers. He took the usual sophomore subjects and was considered intelligent. He got an A in science but did not excel in social studies or history.

"He generally didn't apply himself in school," Dingman said. "He was too engulfed in this Nazi thing."

In the semester before the shooting, Dingman said, Needham was absent a lot.

Daniel McLellan, chief assistant prosecutor, said Needham probably became aware of Nazism because his father, a Cooley Law School professor, is a World War II history buff. The pistol used by the youth belonged to his father, McLellan said.

Needham's parents are divorced and the youth lived with his father. The elder Needham has refused to discuss the case.

The boy's interest in Nazism "was apparently quite accidental. He took whatever interest his father had and perverted it. Hitler was the perfect symbol for his feelings," McLellan said.

Dr. Ames Robey, the psychiatrist who examined Needham, concluded the boy suffers from a rare mental illness that makes him a "true paranoiac." McLellan said the illness causes "a feeling that I am better and everybody else is no good, that they are the cause of my problems and if I can get rid of them I get rid of my problems."

It is a sickness, he said, "which leads to murder."

Under Michigan law, juvenile court retains jurisdiction until the person is 19 and then Needham could be released. "Once he's 19, he walks unless we can prove he's still dangerous," McLellan said.

"He's a terribly dangerous person whose only disappointment was that he didn't kill more people when he had the opportunity. He feels no remorse."

SCREAMERS

JULY 15 & 16

MABUHAY

2.59. Flyer pasteup for Screamers shows at Mabuhay Gardens, San Francisco, July 1978.

The Screamers headlined several times at the Mabuhay Gardens in San Francisco in 1977–78. The opening band for the Mabuhay shows in July 1978 included the Snot Puppies, a Los Angeles–based band comprised of teenagers who attended Beverly Hills High School. This Mabuhay show flyer is a mockup, repurposed from a previous flyer that I put together to promote a Screamers performance organized by Snot Puppies' band members to take place at their high school campus during the students' lunch period on June 15. That performance never occurred; it was canceled by the school's administration as a result of the flyer's illustration, which they deemed to be controversial. The flyer reproduced a news clipping of a widely published report of a school shooting by a fifteen-year-old student that took place in Lansing, Michigan, on February 22, 1978. The use of this clipping on the promotional flyer was intended to bring awareness to the rise of right-wing neo-Nazism, gun violence, and mass shootings by high school teenagers in the US. —Tommy Gear

SF VIDEO TRIP FINANCIAL

84.05 GAS.
42.71 ADDITIONAL CAR REPAIR EXPENSES.
45.00 MUSC (EATING)
5.00 GEZA EATING
100.00 CAM—VAN
65.00 VIDEO RENTAL (MABUHAY)
30.00 VIDEO TAPE.
10.00 MABUHAY ROADIE.
20.00 GEZA DRAW
10.00 ADDED GAS FOR SAM
401.76 TOTAL EXPENDITURE.
20.00 ADDITIONAL *
421.76 REVISED TOTAL

MABUHAY TOTAL = 365.50
PHIL = 36.00
329.50 TOTAL

ADD EXPENSES:
34.95 Trailer rental

* i.e. ELECTRONICS EXPENSES. 9.67 recording tape
7.48 ADAPTORS
2.64 MAGNA ADAPTOR
20.00

2.60. Accounting for trip to San Francisco for Target Video shoot, August 1978. Includes car repair expense.

MY TOUR.

1. CBGB (Thu + Wed) 300.00 + 168.60 = 468.60
2. ARTEMUS (~~Fri + Sat~~ Mon + Tue) = 75, + 50.
3. PHASE III (Fri + Sat) = 400.
4. HORSESHOE (Halloween) = 250 (205.25)
5. Hurrah (Fri + Sat) = 844.
= 671.
6 THE RAT (Wed) = 152.
7. HOTEL NELSON (SAT + SUN ~~Fri + Sat~~) = 613.00
= 169.80 (78.28)
782.80 − 10% TX. = 704.52 CANADIAN $
= 592.00
8. Hurrah (THANKSGIVING)

2.61. Accounting for the fall 1978 tour. Stops listed: 1. CBGB (New York), 2. Artemis (Philadelphia), 3. Phase III (Swissvale, PA), 4. Horseshoe (Toronto), 5. Hurrah (New York), 6. The Rat (Boston), 7. Hotel Nelson (Montreal), 8. Hurrah (New York).

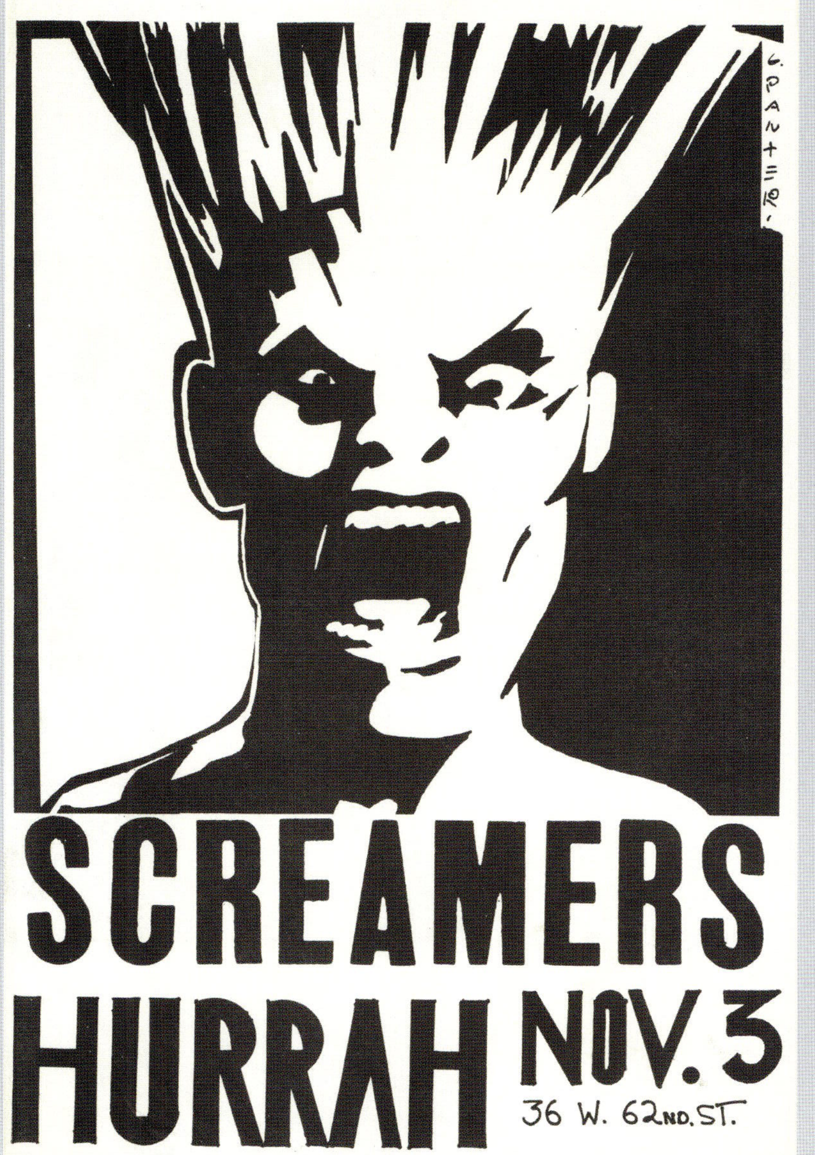

2.62. Flyer for Screamers show at Hurrah, 1978. Robert Fripp joined them onstage for "Eva Braun."

SCREAMERS
SCREAMERS
SCREAMERS
SCREAMERS
SCREAMERS
SCREAMERS
JULY 5•6•7•8
WITH LOUNGE LIZARDS THURS. & SUN.
HURRAH
36 WEST 62ND ST., N.Y.C.

2.63. Poster for Screamers shows at Hurrah, July 5–8, 1979.

SCREAMER DATES

5-28-77 SLASH PARTY

7-4-77 STARWOOD

7-28-77 MABUHAY GARDEN

8-8/9-77 WHISKEY

8-16/17-77 SLASH BENEFIT AT LARCHMONT

8-7-77 AT IGGY'S MALIBU

12-16/17-77 BENEFIT AT THE MASQUE

12-18/19-77 AT THE MABUHAY

1-5,6&7-78 AT THE WHISKEY

2-16,17&18&19-78 AT THE WHISKEY

2-28-78 BENEFIT AT ~~XXXXX~~ ELKS HALL FOR MASQUE

3-15-78 AT THE MARQUEE CLUB IN ARCADIA

3-23-78 CAMARILLO STATE

3-25-78 SAN DIEGO AT STRAIGHTA HEAD BALLROOM

4-8-78 ELKS LODGE FOR ARTIST AND LAWYERS BALL

4-13,14 &15-78 AT THE WHISKEY

6-22-78 ROCK CORPORATION

5-13/14-78 AT MABUHAY

5-18 AT BEAVER BLDG. IN PORTLAND

5-19 seattle (SOME HALL?)

5-20 KRAB RADIO STATION

5-21-78 AT DREAMLAND

5-23-78 AT MABUHAY

7-3-78 STARTDUST BALLROOM MASQUE PRESENTS

7- -78 AT ABBEY ROAD

7-20,21& 22-78 AT THE WHISKEY

7/ -78 AT THE MABUHAY 2 NIGHTS WITH SNOT PUPPIES

2.64. List of Screamers performance dates through July 1978, including a live radio show on KRAB in Seattle on May 20, 1978.

From 1977 to 1979 the Screamers toured, playing clubs in California (Los Angeles, San Francisco, San Diego, Arcadia), New York City, Boston, Philadelphia, Pittsburgh, Montreal, Toronto, Portland (Oregon), and Seattle. While in Seattle, we had an invitation to play a live broadcast on KRAB, a local independent noncommercial radio station. We set up our electronic keyboards and drums in the station's recording booth. There's an interlude in our song "Eva Braun" where we'd program the analog synthesizer and drum machine to play themselves in a loop indefinitely (this was before MIDI or digital sampling). Then we would exit the stage for an indeterminate period of time while the instruments continued playing, leaving the audience uncertain as to whether we would be returning or if the show was actually over. When we performed that song live on the air in Seattle, we left the radio station while the looping segment played, got in the car and drove around Capitol Hill for a while listening to the looped song play on the car radio before returning to the station and finishing our set. It turned out to be a great live performance, plus we actually got to hear ourselves played on the radio! —Tommy Gear

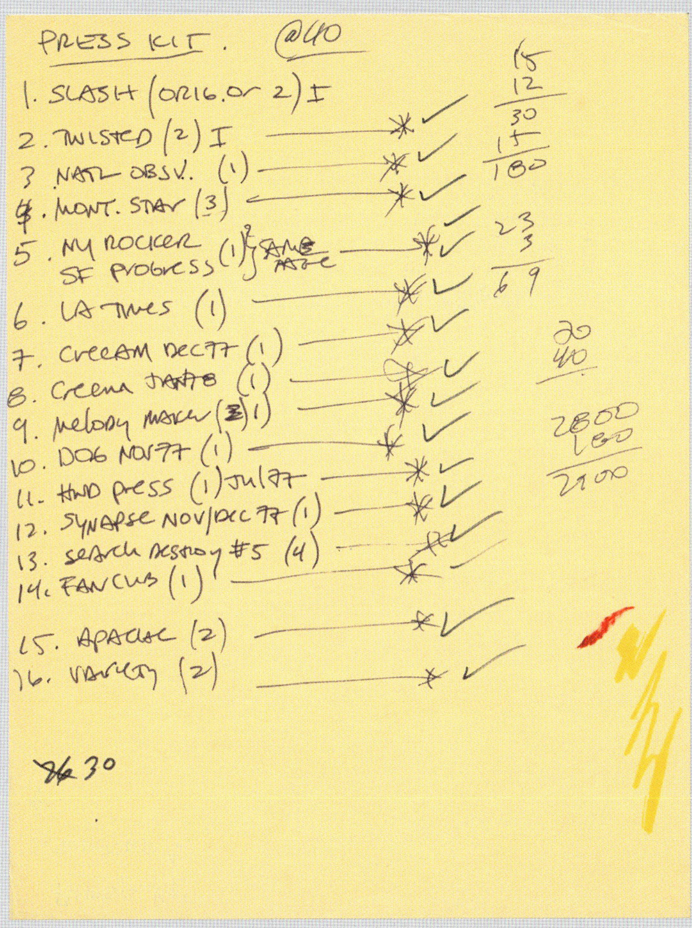
PRESS KIT. @40

1. SLASH (ORIG. or 2) I
2. TWISTED (2) I
3. NAT'L OBSV. (1)
4. MONT. STAR (3)
5. MY ROCKER / SF PROGRESS (1) SAME PAGE
6. LA TIMES (1)
7. CREEM DEC77 (1)
8. Creem JAN78 (1)
9. Melody Maker (1)
10. DOG NOV77 (1)
11. HWD press (1) JUL77
12. SYNAPSE NOV/DEC 77 (1)
13. search destroy #5 (4)
14. FAN CLUB (1)
15. APACHE (2)
16. VARIETY (2)

$30

2.65. Checklist of recipients for Screamers press kit, 1977 to January 1978.

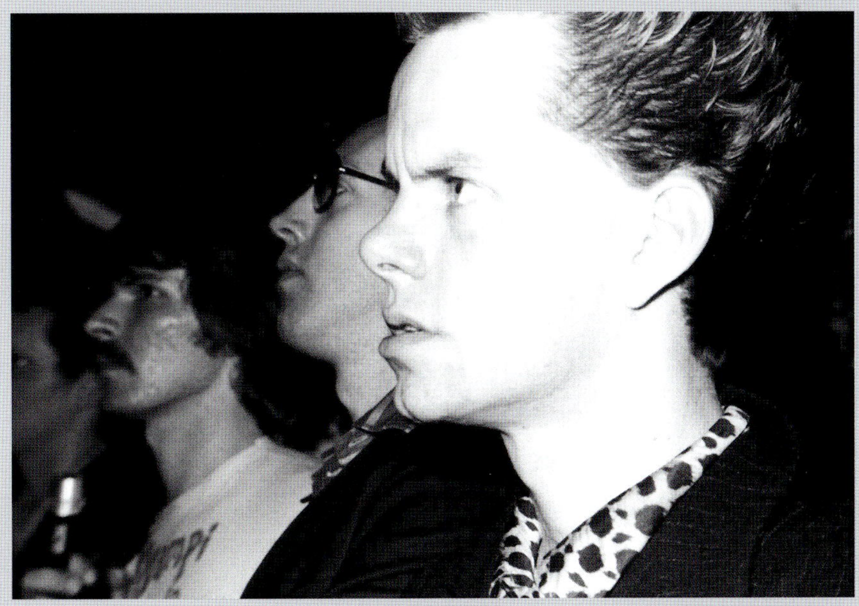

2.66. Tomata du Plenty and Gorilla Rose (with glasses) at the Whisky during the Nico show on June 5, 1979. Photo: Lisa Jane Persky.

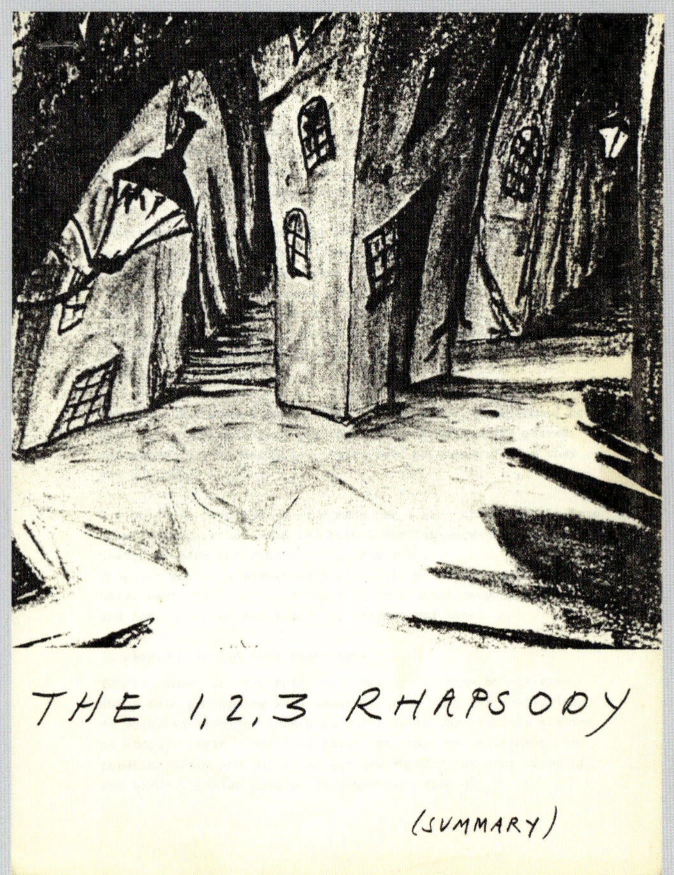

S U M M A R Y

THE 1, 2, 3 RHAPSODY will be made in the spirit of low budget features. The cost-cutting, innovative techniques of this genre are essential in achieving the spontaneity, vibrancy and raw emotionality of our project and story.

This story, and the themes it revolves around, have been dictated by the personalities joined together in the project and the sensibilities of a generation in the process of creating its own brand of excitement. We will not utilise actors in the lesd roles; not impersonators, but the real thing - stars of such bands as the SCREAMERS and AVENGERS, who've already demonstrated their deep impression on and fanatic rapport with their audience.

These are not actors but already trained stars whose school of performing arts has been the countless stages they've played and shows they've headlined, their acts as theatrical as they are musical.

Our movie is populated by and made for a generation that is into heavy dramatizations and the primal battles between life and death, freedom and control, good and evil.
Thus our movie is essentially a classic melodramatic fairy tale, performed as a vaudeville entertainment composed of music and dance, terror and violence, passion and love.

It revolves around four characters:

TOMATA, known as "The Prince of Anxiety" by some of his fans, whose main performing goal seems to be to keep everybody always on edge, to involve as many as possible in the reckless schemes he stages, their cause less important than the excitement, unpredictability and thrill of getting through the next curve of the psychic roller coaster ride he takes them on.

2.67–2.70. Plot summary for *The 1, 2, 3, Rhapsody* by Rene Daalder, 1979.

PENELOPE, the essential American Wholesome Blonde, super sensuous yet with the strength of the classic frontiers woman. At any time this soft spoken creature is capable of erupting into screaming tantrums or fervid oratory.

JEFF, the quasi punk fascist, whose high I.Q. and disillusioned disgust with the brain ravaged, proselytising former hippies of the previous generation have driven him into the arms of a philosophy that opts for superlative design and does away with all "degenerates", in the process turning him into a sadly confused killer.

ROBERT, the youngest but truest teenage idol of the picture, the first tragic victim of JEFF's misguided ideology.

And weaving his web around them all is HANSEN, the aging "hipster", veteran of every cultural wave in three tumultuous decades, now a government functionary in charge of a desperate program to recapture the authority now vested in the countless cults, sects and rock & roll gurus that have invested the land. This clandestine mission - to scrutinize the brainwashers, trend-setters and their respective manipulative tools, and then become the great deprogrammer, reigniting the spirit of independent, non-congested minds. But he himself is ultimately undone, a victim of his study of man's natural drives, the contradictions of imposing control, discipline and liberation, and above all, his maddening lust for and fascination with the unfathomable PENELOPE.

Their odyssey takes them from an urban youth "cabaret of the macabre", where HANSEN first discovers the wildly performing TOMATA and PENELOPE, to an apartment-hotel populated by musicians, performers, idiosyncratic characters of every stripe and age, living in a riotous peaceful co-existence which eventually self-destructs, then on to a surreal journey on a madly careening bus heading towards the Pacific Northwest, during which TOMATA, the clown of urban angst, plays Pied Piper to the passengers who soon forget time, place and destination, then a trek across the snowy wastelands, over glaciers and through avalanches, finally ending up at "Disco Caligari", a mock Bavarian trendy ski-resort nightspot which is actually the central headquarters for HANSEN's mind-control experiments.

The film ends with a violent, confession-laden, justice-meting denouement which leaves TOMATA and PENELOPE as the only human survivors lost in the snowy expanse surrounding what was once HANSEN's disco cum concentration camp.
They break into song -----------

Although the craftsmanship and high technologies (both musically and cinematically) employed in the film will be on the highest standard of today's state of the art, the end result will appear as alive, simple and full of gusto as a bedazzling vaudeville entertainment, full of song and dance, rowdy and infectious.

The 1, 2, 3, Rhapsody is the first draft of the idea for the movie that ended up with the name of *Population: 1*. We built a small soundstage and audio studio in an old warehouse on Melrose and Hyperion in Los Angeles. KK Barrett and Carel Struycken were the hands-on team doing most of the actual building work. We shot and recorded three-quarters of the movie there [changing the title to *Mensch*] but ended up with an incomplete story when a financier pulled out. During that time we also organized two live shows with the Screamers and Sheila Edwards in the Whisky and Roxy. Later the set of a bunker was built in Tomata's apartment in Hollywood, where the scenes were shot with Tomata personifying the last living person on earth. We made a lot of use of the then still experimental early blue and green screens [Chroma Key]. *Population: 1* was shot on film and edited on 2-inch video at the audio/visual studio of Todd Rundgren in Bearsville, New York. With all the stops and starts, *Population: 1* took nearly ten years to complete. —Bianca Daalder-van Iersel, producer of *Population: 1*

SCREAMERS AT THE ROXY

On July 19, 20, and 21 at the Roxy in Los Angeles, the SCREAMERS will present twice nitely their unique combination of songs and dramatics that wowed capacity crowds at the Whisky last May. Having taken the show to San Francisco (presented by Bill Graham) and to New York, the SCREAMERS return to Los Angeles in their first appearance at the Roxy.

Specially presented with a sideshow of violinists and a one-girl chorus, their performance transports one into a world of passion, love,,terror and violence, to a place where the confrontation between good and evil is visable and omnipresent.

Undisputably the most popular and daring of the newer bands to surface in Los Angeles, the SCREAMERS, following these Roxy dates, will take a hiatus from live performing to begin production on two videodisks, a record album and a feature length film to be produced by Rene Daalder, film director and provocateur.

The press says:

"One of LA's most important and most popular bands."
BAM Magazine - David Gillerman

"The SCREAMERS have much to offer this sloppy, indiscreet and out to lunch planet."
Andy Warhol's Interview

"The songs are simply about how damn tough it is to be human...some provocative and sensitive artistry."
LA Reader - Chris Morris

"Their performance goes beyond the realm of entertainment into primal experience...they were so good they were scary."
Los Angeles Times - Kristine McKenna

2.71. Press release for Screamers show at the Roxy, July 1979.

Roxy July 79

CREWLIST SCREAMERS

Tomata du Plenty
Tommy Gear
K.K.
Paul
Sheila

Russell Howard Goldstein	violinists
Geza X Kira Roesler	sound
Donne Daniels	light
Paul Problem Joe Kaufman	stage
Cloe	make up
Trudi	wardrobe
Chase Rick van Zaten + 2	fanclub
Rene Daalder Tommy Gear	management
Bianca Daalder Nick Wechsler + 1	--- contact for any questions or informatior
Rory Johnston	assistant

2.72. Band and crew list for Screamers shows at the Roxy, July 1979.

The Screamers returned to Los Angeles from our first US East Coast tour at the end of 1978. Among other cities, we played in New York City at CBGB and at Hurrah (where we were joined onstage by Robert Fripp). We started working in Los Angeles on an initial set of music demos (coproduced by David Campbell, father of Beck Hansen), each having an accompanying film short (directed by Rene Daalder) in anticipation of the impending launch in 1981 of MTV. Previously, club performances integrated aleatory elements that contributed to the band's mercurial spontaneity. Bringing in a film director impacted the band's previous working dynamic in irrevocable ways: antecedent expressive elements (in lyrics, musical arrangements, performative staging) were subsumed by diegesis; earlier repertoire became relegated to feedstock for narrative reworkings fabricated in service of expanding character-driven scenarios. In due course, by the end of 1979, this shift in representational bearing fostered increasing dissipation of the group's former creative momentum. —Tommy Gear

Tynes

WHY THE WORLD

NERVOUS

short

VIOLENT WORLD

MENSCH layout after stop

8

SHE FRIGHTENS

4 x 8

I WANNA HURT

I GO FOR YOU

FRIENDS

VERTIGO

PUNISH OR BE DAMNED

122

FOR OLD TIMES' SAKE

2.73. Set list with annotations for 1979 show.

The Screamers relied on two keyboard instruments to produce their distinctive sound: an ARP Odyssey Mark I analog synthesizer and a Fender Rhodes portable electric piano, whose internal action is primarily mechanical, which can be further augmented with external analog signal processing devices. The Rhodes keyboard triggers internal hammers (like traditional pianos), but instead of striking internal strings to produce sound as in an acoustic instrument, the Rhodes hammers strike thin steel rods (called tines, each of which acts like an individual tuning fork), then their tuned vibrations are amplified by an electromagnetic pickup (similar to the pickups used on electric guitars). The output of each pickup's tonal vibration is routed to a built-in amplifier and speaker, the amplitude of which can be manually controlled. Invented by Harold Rhodes during World War II, this particular method of producing sound in a keyboard instrument was further developed for wider use by professional musicians from 1959 on. And because the mechanical vibration of each tine is converted into an electric current for amplification, it can also be routed through external signal processing devices prior to output through a speaker. Furthermore, in order to generate the Screamers' distinctive sound with the Rhodes, keyboard players would have to cultivate a particular playing style that often necessitated depressing the keys connected to the tines repeatedly in close succession with inordinate force. Consequently, after continuous playing, in time the steel rods would gradually weaken and eventually break, necessitating replacement to ensure each key can produce the note associated with it. Prior to a show and while on tour, it was always necessary to have a stock of "tynes" [*sic*] on hand in the event of any breakage to ensure that the complete range of keyboard notes would be audibly amplified and performances unfold smoothly. —Tommy Gear

I AM A MENSCH!

(Disco base drum introduces new song, Tomata in sudden protest turns to the band and interrupts)

STOP THE BEAT!

STOP! (to K.K.)

(irresponsive layers of music build nonetheless)

I AM A MENSCH!

I AM A MENSCH!

I ONLY DANCE WHEN I WANNA DANCE!

(music continues - strong dance beat. Tomata's response is an "anti-dance" routine, going totally against the beat)

TO THE SOUND OF A DISTANT DRUM

I AM A MENSCH!

I AM A MENSCH!

I STEP OUT OF LINE

I STEP OUT OF LINE

YOU FOLLOW THE BEAT

(laughter) I DANCE AGAINST IT 'CAUSE I AM A MENSCH!!

(musically K.K. plays the sound of a drum kit falling apart - as he has always been an extension on Tomata's stage persona; on stage of course, Tomata's "dance" becomes a hopeless tragic-comic routine)

STOP THE BEAT!

(the beat in effect stops)

I AM A MENSCH!!!

AND RIGHT NOW I WANT TO DANCE

-2-

(the beat picks up again - triggering off a superb disco dance routine; every time Tomata pauses he repeats: "I AM A MENSCH")

(laughter) I AM A MENSCH!

I AM A MENSCH!!!!

(finally the music comes to a logical conclusion - Tomata though decides on his own conclusion, ranting and raving on and dancing and jumping; in short celebrating his nerve and proof of being a free spirit)

I AM A MENSCH!

I AM A MENSCH -------- etc.

(K.K. fills in an occasional drum hit or roll)

(Tomata hits the cymbals - laughs)

(laughter)

2.74 and 2.75. Staging script for "I Am a Mensch!" Written by Rene Daalder and Tomata du Plenty, 1979.

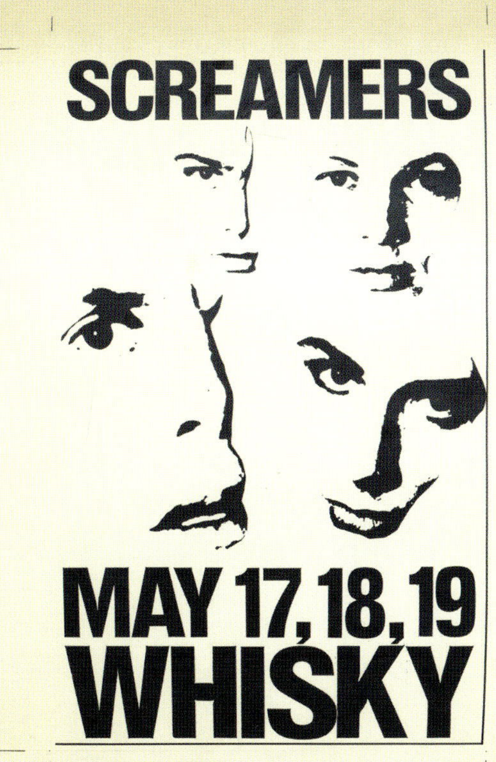

2.76. (*Left*) Printer's proof for Screamers shows at the Whisky, May 1979.

2.77. (*Below*) Magazine ad pasteup for Screamers shows at the Roxy, July 1979.

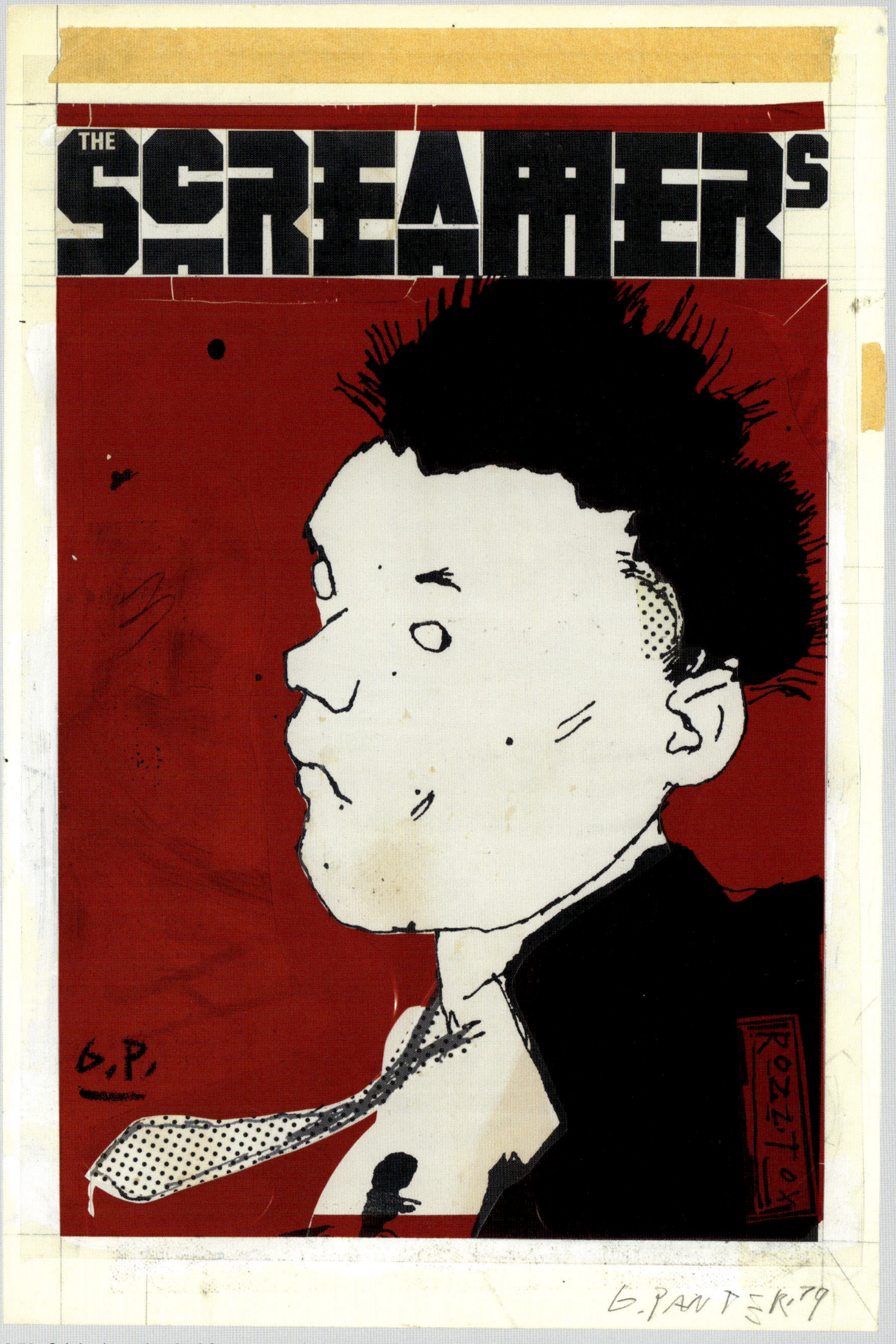

2.78. Original mechanical for poster with an alternative image for the Screamers. Design: Gary Panter, 1979.

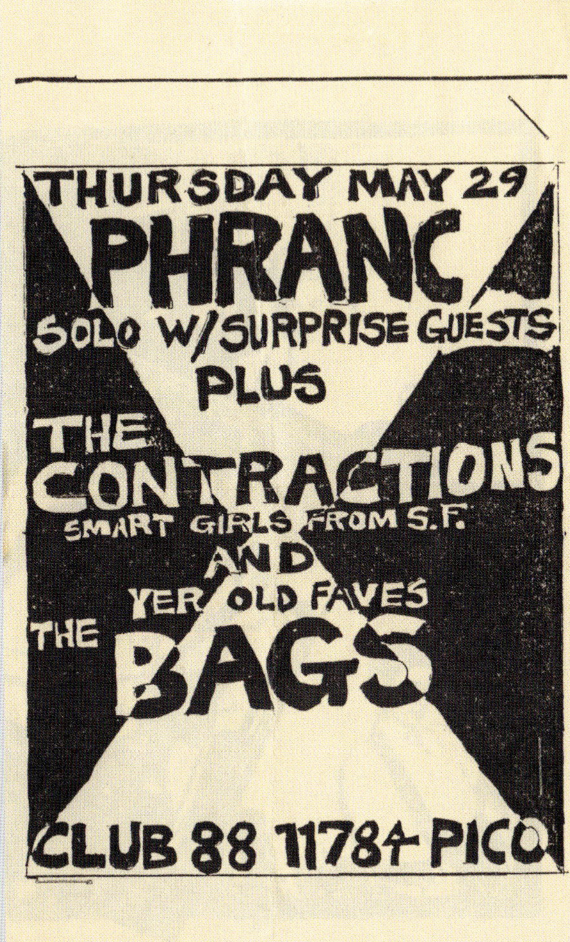

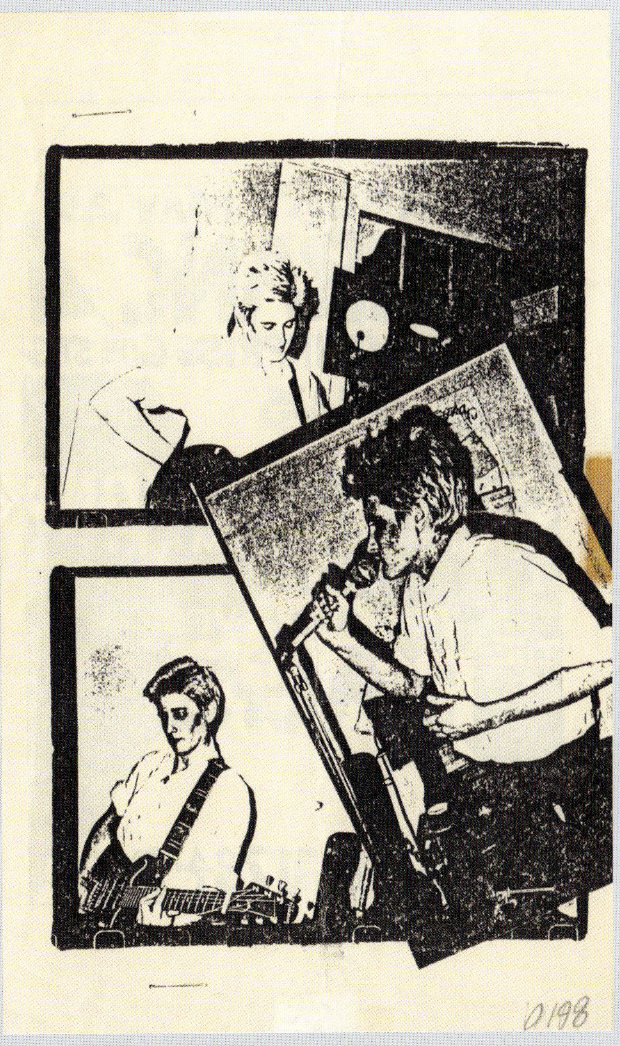

2.79. Flyer advertising a show with bands from the SF and LA punk scenes, Pico, California, 1980.

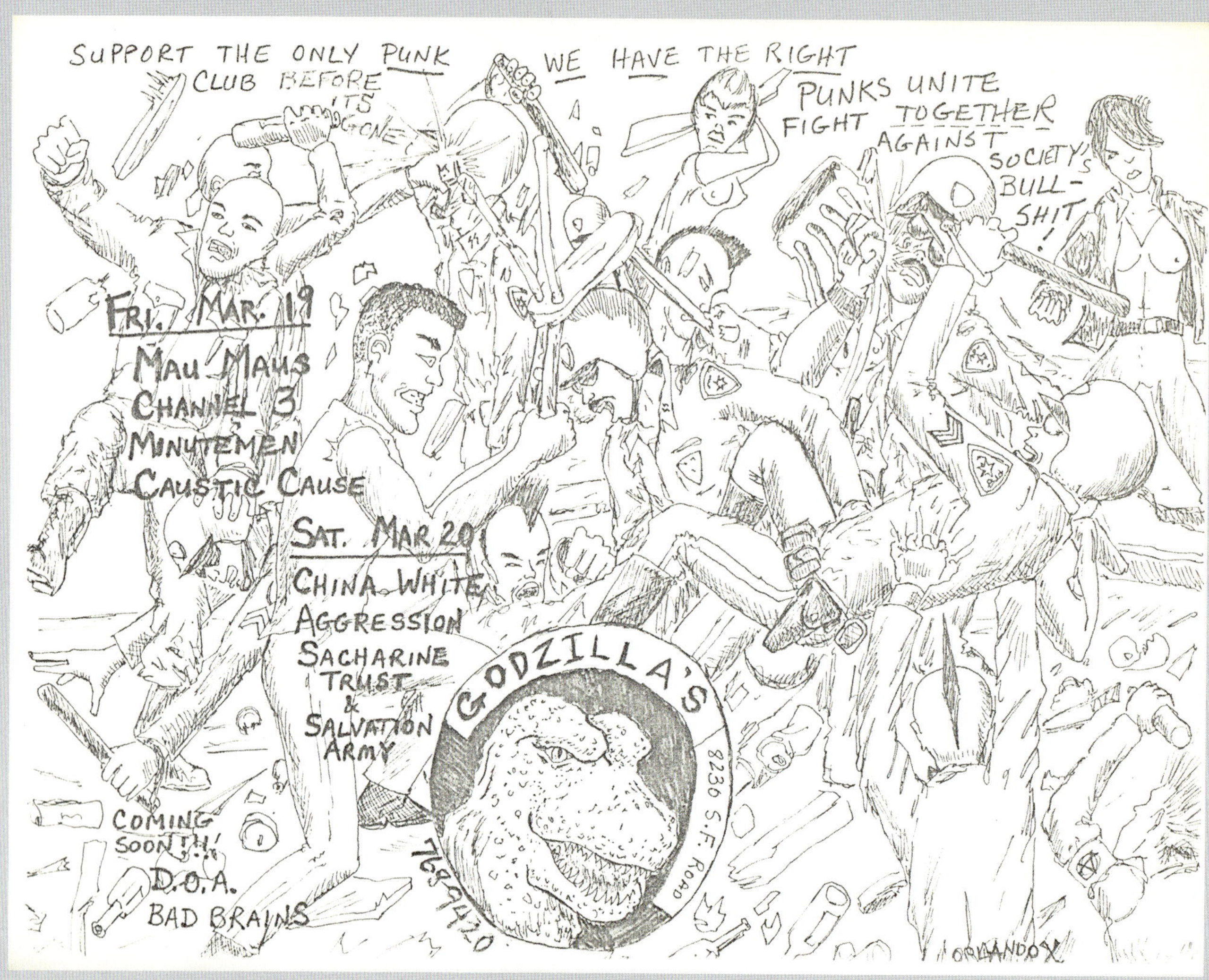

2.80. Flyer for shows at Godzilla's, Sun Valley, California, March 1982, depicting conflicts with the police in the suburban hardcore scene.

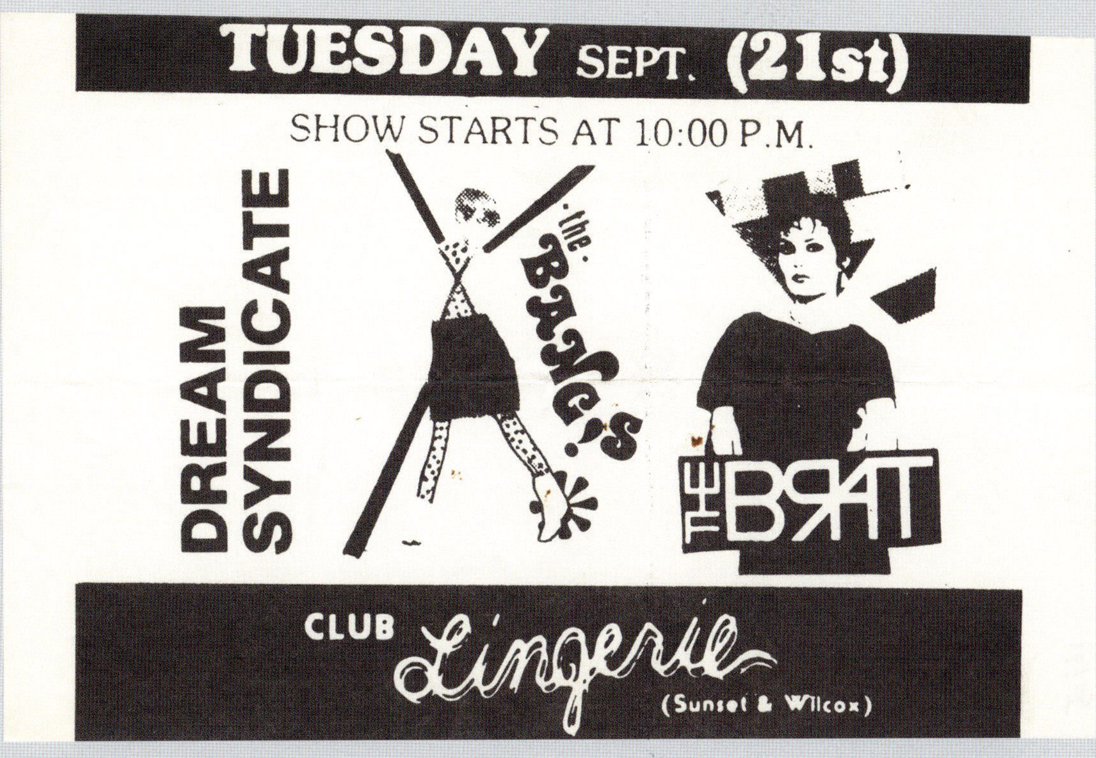

2.81. Flyer for show at Club Lingerie, Los Angeles, September 1982.

2.82. Flyer for show at the Vex, November 1982.

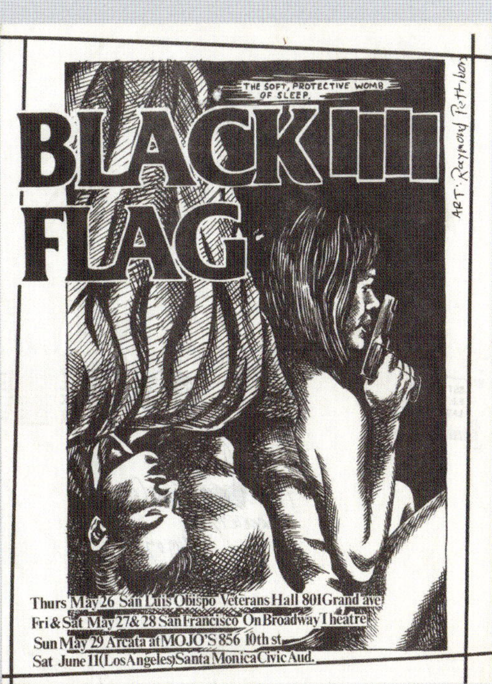

2.83. Flyer for Black Flag shows, May 1983. Design: Raymond Pettibon.

2.84. (*Right*) Black Flag circa 1980. *Left to right,* Greg Ginn, Robo, Dez Cadena singing, and Chuck Dukowski on bass. Photographer unknown.

2.85. (*Below*) Black Flag, April 2, 1985. *Left to right,* Ginn, Bill Stevenson, Henry Rollins singing, and Kira Roessler on bass. Photo: Klik Abstrakt.

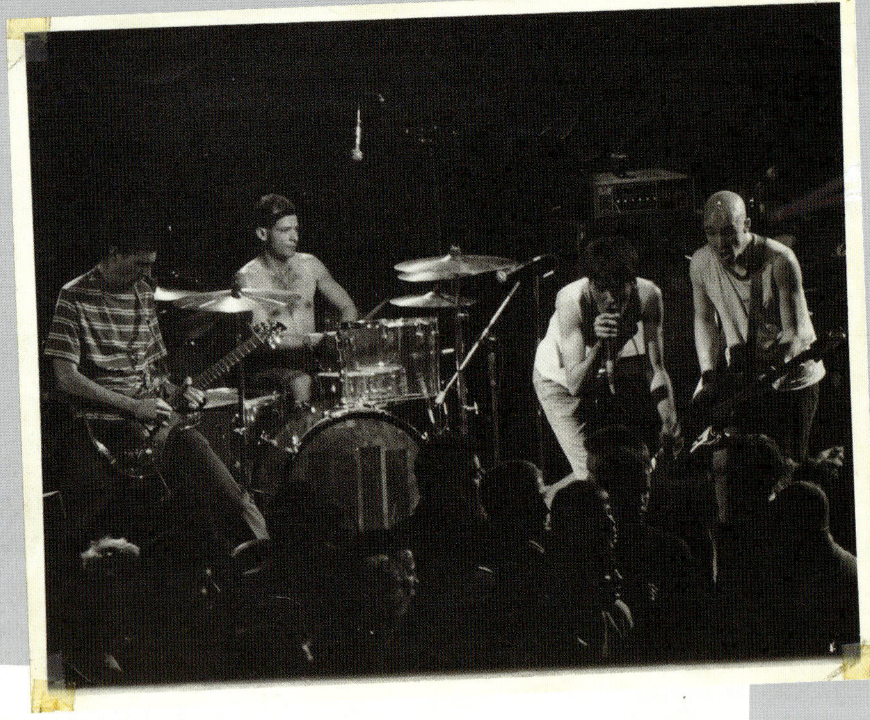

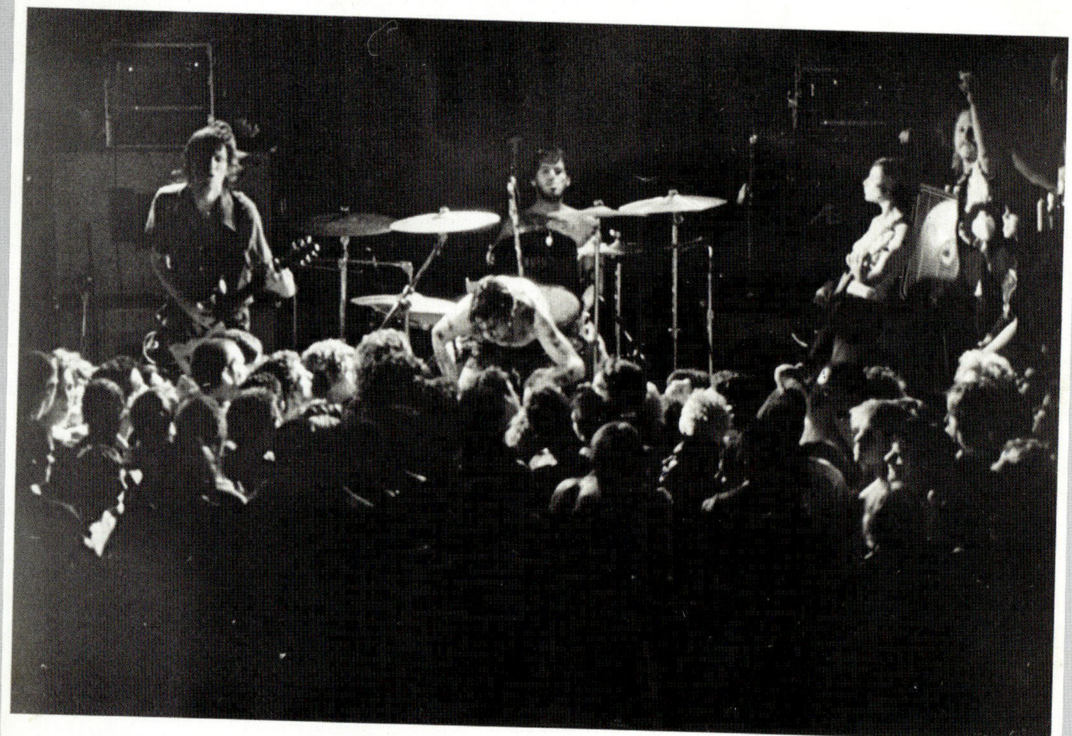

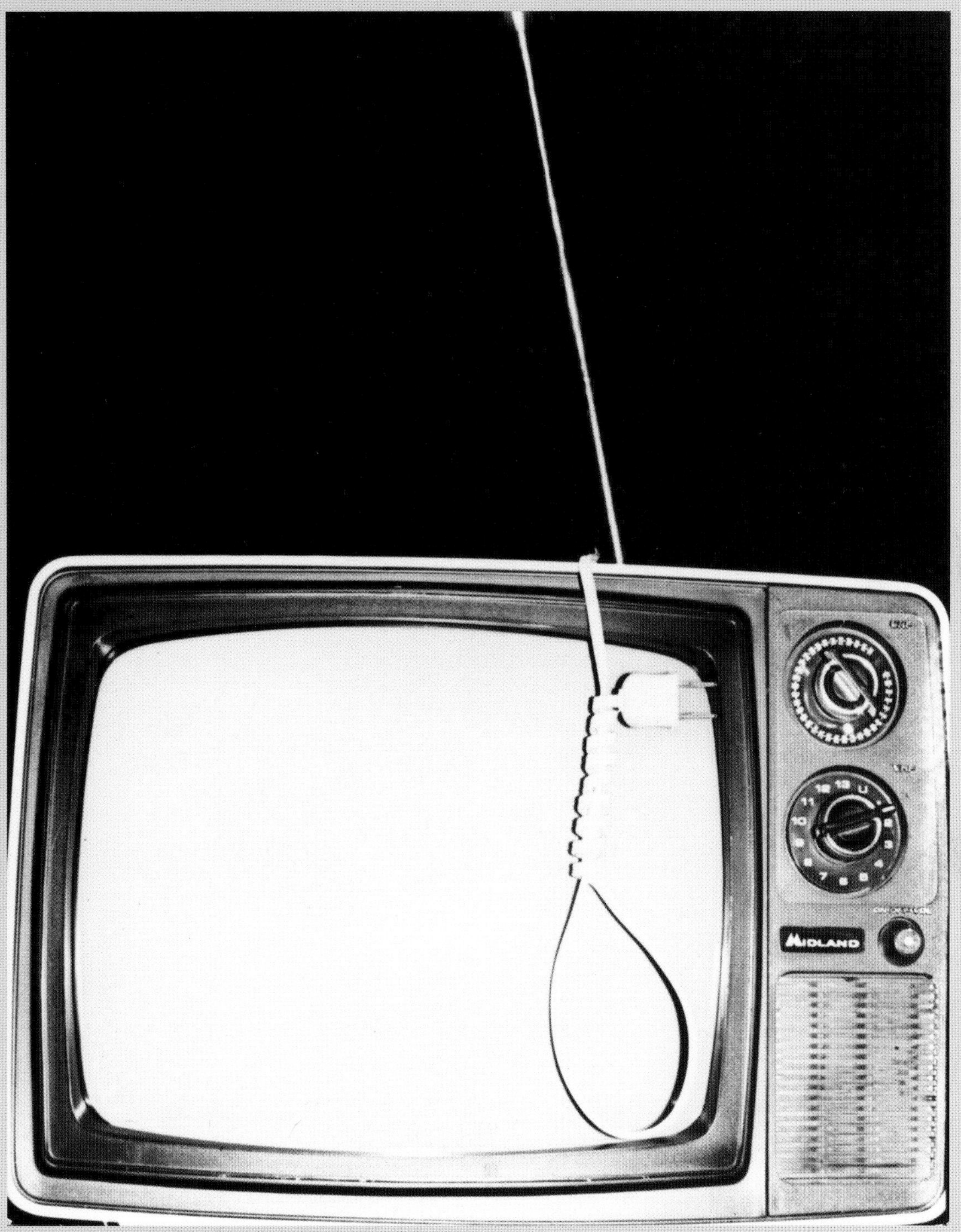

2.86. One of several alternative images for Black Flag's *Damaged* album cover (1981). Photography by Edward Colver.

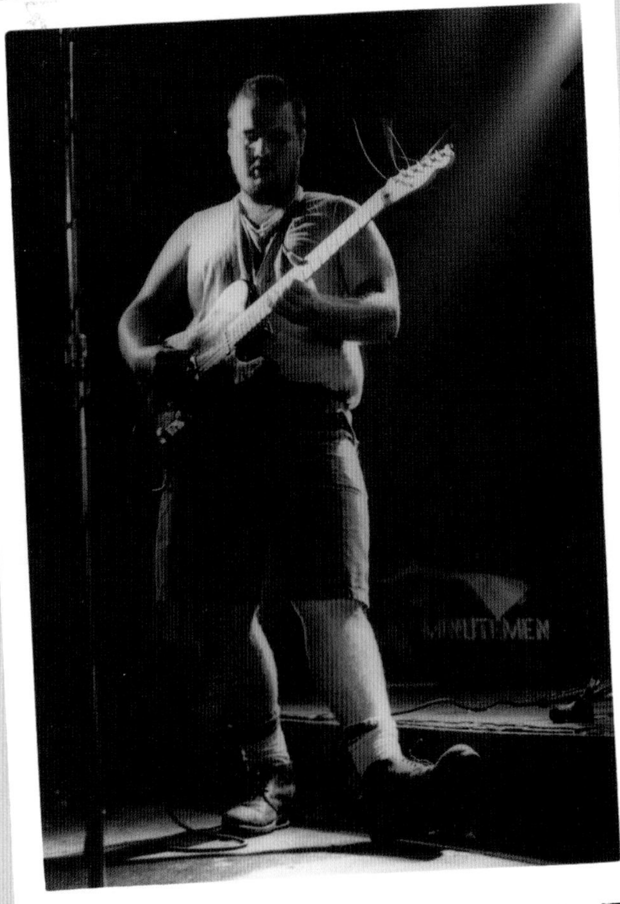

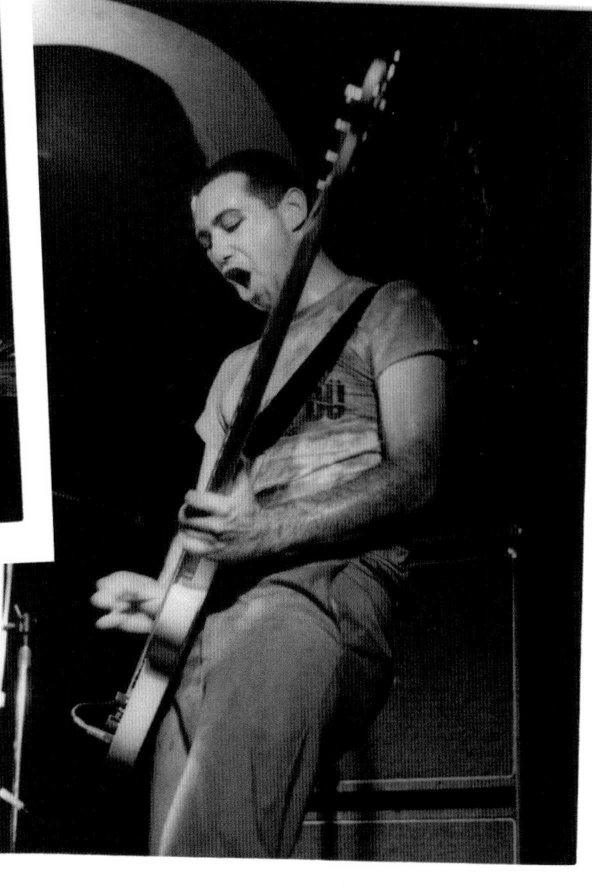

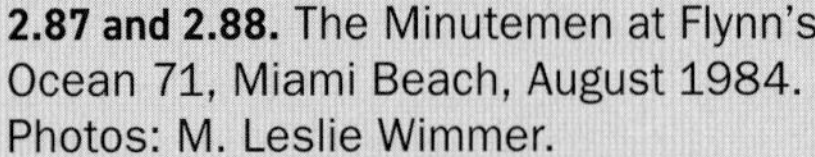

2.87 and 2.88. The Minutemen at Flynn's Ocean 71, Miami Beach, August 1984. Photos: M. Leslie Wimmer.

I remember that night well. Our South Florida scene was soooo excited that we were blessed with not one, but two nights of the Minutemen! Wednesday and Thursday August 1st and 2nd, 1984, at Flynn's Ocean 71 on Miami Beach, Florida. A local band called Gay Cowboys in Bondage opened for them both nights. I took these two pictures of D. Boon and Mike Watt on the second night, Thursday. —M. Leslie Wimmer

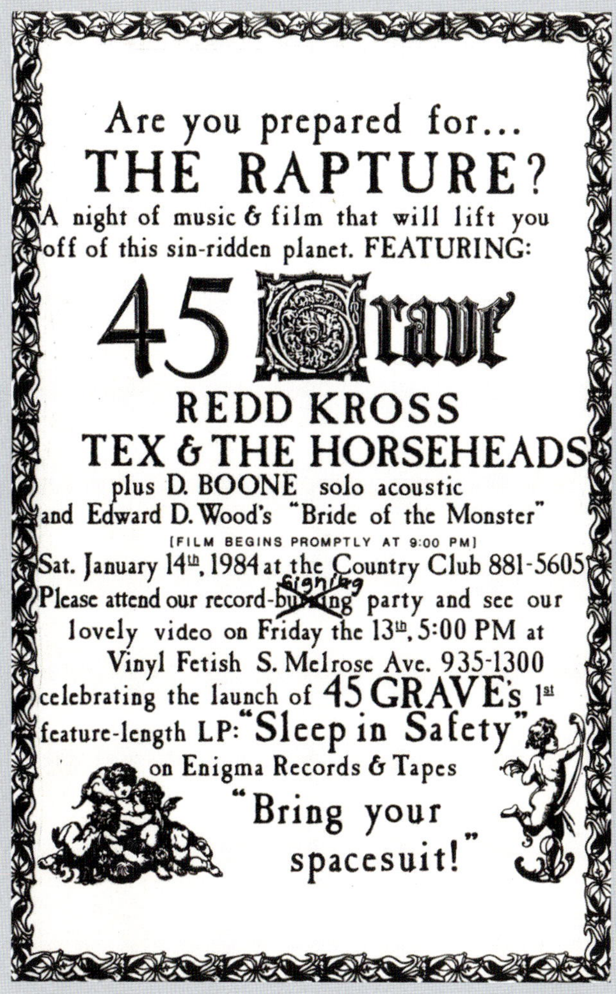

2.89. Flyer for "a night of music and film" at the Country Club, Los Angeles, January 1984.

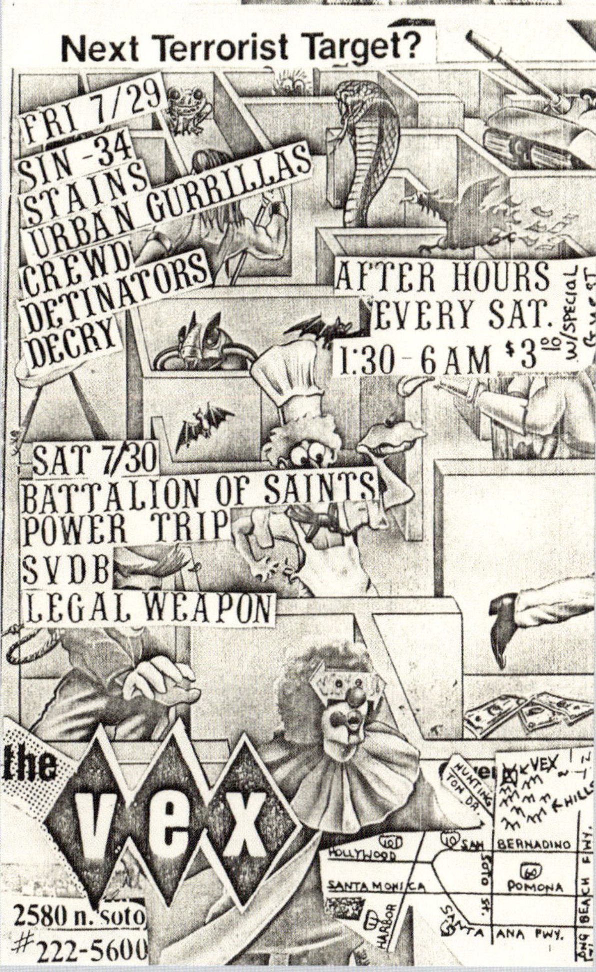

2.90. Flyer for shows at the Vex, July 1984.

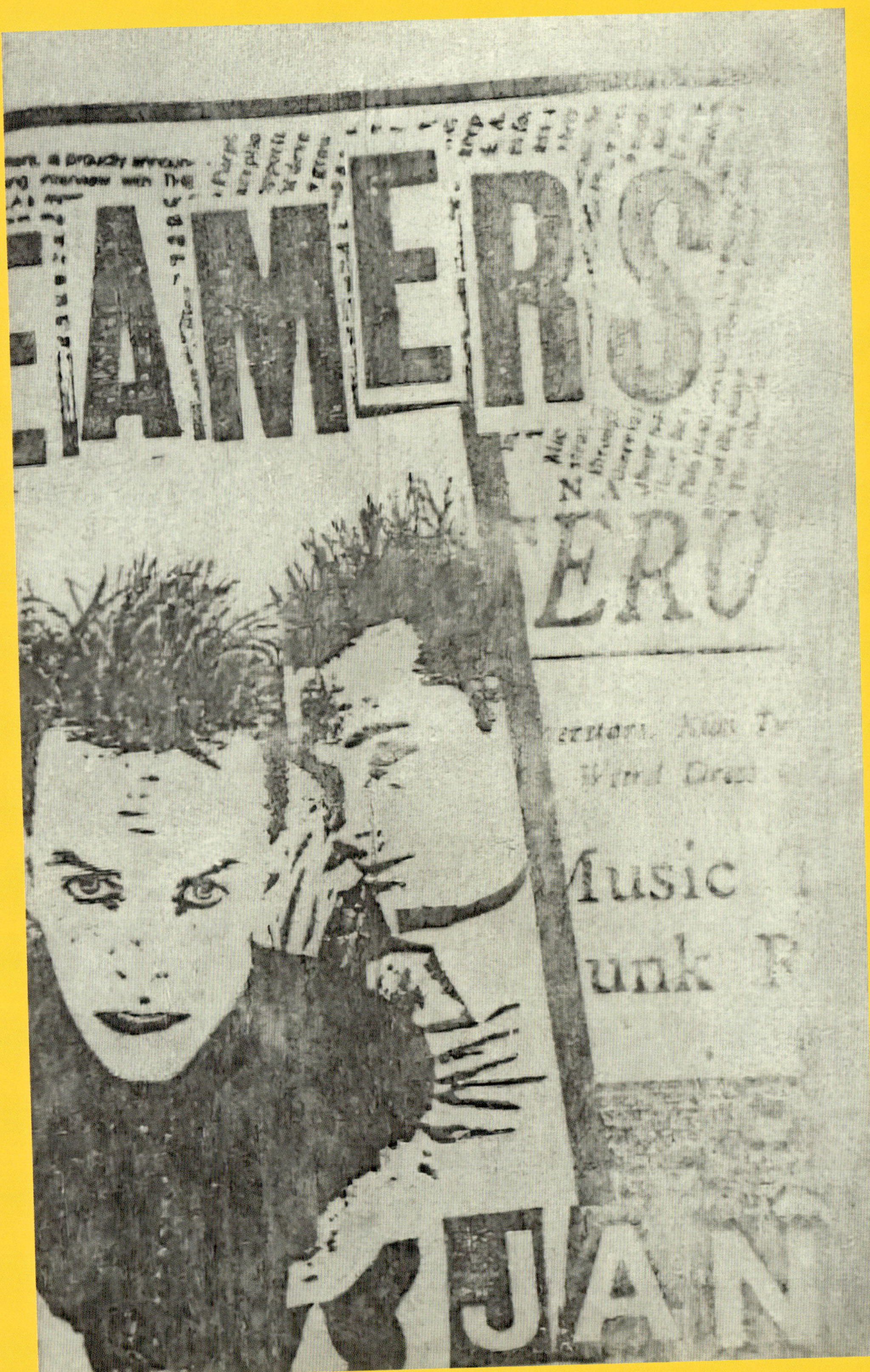

EAMERS
ERO
Music
unk
JAN

Magazine Love

CH. 10

IAN MACKAYE AND MARTÍN SORRONDEGUY ON DISCOVERING THE SCREAMERS

IAN MACKAYE

The most notable thing for me about the Screamers was that there was no sound. They didn't make records, and it would be years before any of us in DC ever heard them. We read that they only did videos, but even if that was the case, there was no way that we could ever see these videos or films because they weren't being screened in DC. The band did look incredible in the photos we saw of them, and their legend was so mighty. LA people spoke about the Screamers with reverence in the pages of *Slash* magazine.

Very early on, probably '79, I was buying *Slash* magazine from what we called "import stores." They were basically shops that were bringing in punk and new wave records from England as well as working with independent distributors that carried underground music—

distributors like Bomp! Systematic, Important, Dutch East, and Greenworld. These were smaller distributors that carried independent or alternative releases. The mainstream major record companies had set up something akin to their own private fiefdoms. They had their own pressing plants and distribution companies, who primarily worked with larger chain stores. Smaller shops usually weren't able to establish direct accounts with these distributors, so they usually had to buy major label titles from companies called "one stops," intermediate operations that were more expensive.

A store like Yesterday and Today in Rockville, Maryland, is a good example of an import shop. It was owned and operated by Skip Groff, a local radio DJ who had worked in the music industry for years. He opened the shop in 1977 and had a focus on independent and imported records. The shop also had an enormous used section. Skip would regularly fly to London with giant empty suitcases, returning with thousands of records, mostly seven-inch records. The shop carried the British music papers, *Sounds*, *Melody Maker*, *NME*, as well as the *New York Rocker*, *Boston Rock*, and LA's *Slash*.

Slash seems to have been largely modeled on Warhol's *Interview* magazine—really beautifully laid out and full of great photos. We read it closely and learned so much about what was happening out on the West Coast. It was in *Slash* that I first encountered Black Flag, who became hugely important and influential to me in the early eighties. The live review of Black Flag that I read in *Slash* said something about how the band members looked like guys that hang around in 7-Eleven parking lots. This really resonated with me and my friends here in DC.

We liked hearing about a band that didn't put a lot of emphasis on their appearance. So much of punk rock had been boiled down to fashion, and we just didn't give a fuck about that. We didn't feel we needed to adhere to a scripted look.

When I first got into underground music there seemed to be two camps: "new wave," which was kind of goofy or lighthearted with bands like Devo or B-52s, and "punk rock," which was more nihilistic or self-destructive, think Sid Vicious. Both forms had strong fashion elements, but neither really fit where we were coming from. We decided that we would just wear our street clothes and call ourselves "hardcore punks."

One aspect of the Screamers that definitely had a profound impact on us was their use of graphics. Dischord had a serious aesthetic when it came to our sleeves and advertisements, and I think the strong clean stuff we saw coming from LA, like the Screamers flyers and Dangerhouse Records covers, really inspired us. Again, a band that we never heard, but whose graphics won us over.

The Screamers were a little scary. They were older and clearly a level or two above where we were with punk. Of course, I never met any of them, and didn't really have any real sense of what was going on. If I speak about them with any authority, it's really just the authority of a fan. Someone who had studied them from afar and thought a lot about punk. There was so much to take in at that point in time, and we were just trying to get our minds around all of it. We were sixteen or seventeen years old and feeling overwhelmed with the new.

MARTÍN SORRONDEGUY

The Screamers were a band that if you weren't really around for that time when they existed, and prior to the internet, it came to you in the weirdest of ways. And when you found it, it had an impact.

I want to say I first saw the Target Video of "122 Hours of Fear." That video was so wild to me. When I think I saw that, I was like, "Who are these really gaunt, skinny dudes doing this music?" And it was just keyboard, the way it was shot. It was really grainy. Because I think I saw it on a video that had been copied off videos and duplicated and duplicated. So when it got to me, it was so degraded, it looked like some really avant-garde art film or something, which on top of what it originally is, made it even more interesting and weird. But it was extremely grainy. I got that video, I want to say it was around '86, '87, that video came to me, and it had a lot of stuff. It had a lot of the early San Francisco stuff. Somebody had packed—you know when you can control the amount of time you can stretch a VHS out, recording it depending on the quality—it was about six hours of punk videos. So the Screamers one was on one of those.

There were no Screamers records. The video was the thing that you recall seeing, and there was a bootleg that came out, but I want to say it came out a few years after that, if I'm not mistaken. They were really one of those bands who I think were very popular at the time. Then you didn't hear about them. And then boom! The Screamers! Now, who doesn't love the Screamers? They're an amazing band. I think they're awesome.

So much material started to surface after a while. The imagery is so iconic, the Gary Panter drawing, that's something that you saw throughout. Even in the mid-eighties somebody might've used that as a flyer. Or you'd see it show up in a *Maximumrocknroll*, or a *Flipside*, or in a zine somewhere—that graphic. So I think this is where the visuals of punk go beyond the sound of punk, because the records, sometimes the sounds were so rare that your chances of seeing the visual of the band was more likely than hearing the band, unless somebody gave you the tape.

This commentary has been excerpted from an interview conducted by Judith Peraino on July 15, 2021.

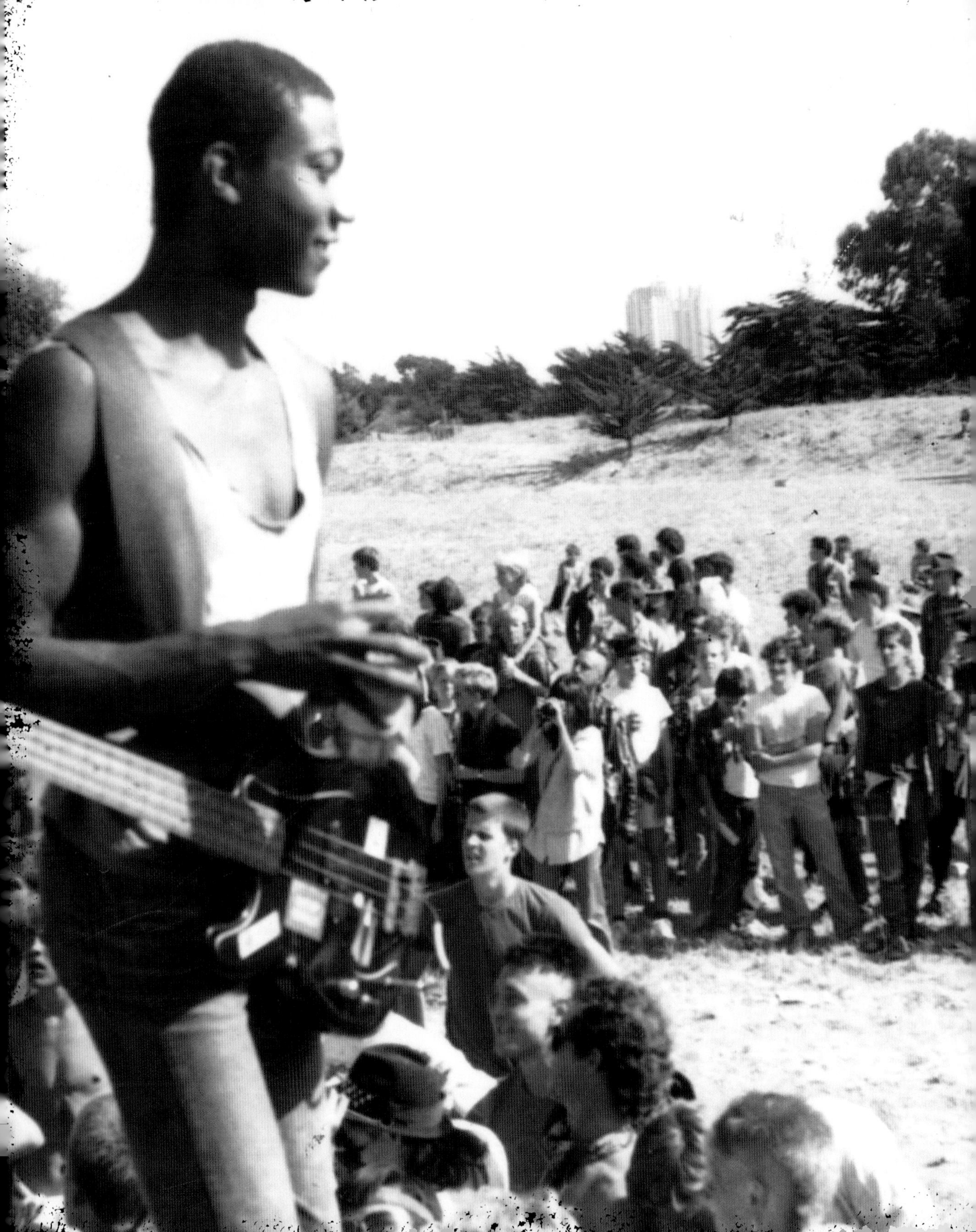

PART THREE

CH. 11

Peace or Annihilation

THE POLITICS OF PUNK IN THE BAY AREA

When the Sex Pistols played their last show at San Francisco's Winterland Ballroom on January 14, 1978, Johnny Rotten ended their set and career with a now legendary sneer: "Ever get the feeling you've been cheated?" Rotten's boredom and disgust (tinged with lament) only exhilarated the crowd, sending them into the streets, which brought an early end to the show. But while the Pistols left the stage, the evening's two opening bands, the Avengers and the Nuns, and the swindled closing act Negative Trend, had already made San Francisco punk their own: the Avengers' Penelope Houston shouted out a new anthem in the biting lyrics to "The American in Me" where she fused the city's long-standing left-wing politics with punk's rejection of failed 1960s idealism: "Ask not what you can do for your country. What's your country been doing to you?"

By 1978 San Francisco and the greater Bay Area were eleven years past the Summer of Love, and the Avengers' words channeled the disappointment and fury of a younger generation witnessing an onslaught of local horrors that only amplified a national catastrophe, as the killing of Martin Luther King Jr., Robert Kennedy, and students at Kent State University set the backdrop for the murders of Black Panther Bobby Hutton by the Oakland police and Meredith Hunter at Altamont by the Hell's Angels, Patty Hearst's kidnapping by the SLA, the terror of the Zodiac killer, and the Golden Dragon massacre in San Francisco's Chinatown. The year ended with the Jonestown massacre and the assassination of Harvey Milk and George Moscone, followed by the White Night Riots several months later. All the while the political machine kept churning. Eight years of Ronald Reagan as California's governor had laid waste to social welfare programs, which along with the country's economic recession and deindustrialization produced the massive rise of an unhoused population in San Francisco. This is the muck in which Bay Area punk was born. But while others ran for the hills (or the suburbs), punks felt the thrill of history moving in the mess; they understood the chaos and had something to say about it.

If you wanted to hear the chaos documented in real time you headed to the home of early San Francisco punk at the Mabuhay Gardens (the Mab), a Filipino restaurant and nightclub just two blocks from Beat Generation bookseller City Lights in North Beach, which funded the scene's first fanzine, *Search and Destroy* (3.1–3.2). Another North Beach staple, the Savoy Tivoli, lit the fuse for the scene when it hosted the Ramones in August of 1976 supported by locals Mary Monday and the Bitches (whose second vocalist Vermillion later wrote for *Search and Destroy*). Mab promoter Dirk Dirksen kept things burning with local bands like Flipper, the Offs, the Mutants, and Crime (3.3). More bands played upstairs at the club On Broadway, and beyond North Beach other venues put their own mark on the scene with spaces like the experimental artpunk Club Foot, the deaf association's Deaf Club (3.5), the sweatbox basement of Tool & Die, the Polk Street gay bar Hinckley's, or the multipurpose warehouse of Target Video. And 1839 Geary (3.7), a former synagogue wedged between Jim Jones's People's Temple and the original Fillmore (rechristened the Elite Club), hosted locals like the Dead Kennedys and the Offs as well as out-of-towners like Jim Carroll, the Plugz, and the Clash. Other venues, plus squats and public protests, made punk audible across the streets of San Francisco.

No one quite channeled the city's political history and the time's head-spinning descent like the Dead Kennedys' surreal and sophisticated satire, propelled by front man Jello Biafra's cabaret caterwauling. To the left of the left, in "California Über Alles" Biafra called then (and future) governor Jerry Brown a "zen fascist," and he channeled Jonathan Swift and Charles Baudelaire to mock the Carter administration's neutron bomb in "Kill the Poor." Amidst it all he found time to run against Dianne Feinstein for mayor (3.8).

But while the Dead Kennedys grabbed national press, powerful women also commanded attention on SF stages: the Nuns, the Avengers (3.4), and Mary Monday and the Bitches were joined by Pink Section's singer Judy Gittelsohn and drummer Carol Detweiler, the female experimental duo Noh Mercy, consisting of just Tony Hotel on drums and Esmerelda (Kent) on vocals—no guitars or keyboards—and the all-women Vs. (3.5), featuring Amy Unger on guitar, Jane Weems on drums, and Olga de Volga on bass. Olga also played in the Offs and the Lewd; as an anchor point in three bands, her speedy dynamic bass lines were a generator for the city's scene.

By 1982 most of these bands were gone: AIDS and drug overdoses took their toll. The Dead Kennedys' "Nazi Punks Fuck Off" called out the influx of bullying jocks in the pit, and eventually the song became a rallying cry against the neo-Nazi postures of the local BASH boys and SF Skins. Flyers for curfew shows at the Mab in the mid-1980s, sponsored by *Maximumrocknroll* (*MRR*), testify to the impact of Mayor Feinstein's "tough on crime" police violence against punks (3.21). The closure of the Mab, On Broadway, and other clubs in San Francisco as the decade rolled on ultimately changed the location of the scene's energy. At the same time, Rock Against Reagan and Rock Against Rent protests (3.22) brought music out of the clubs and into the streets. And when traditional venues closed, shows moved to the Farm (3.59–3.60), a 1970s co-op in the Mission District that transformed an abandoned area next to the 101 freeway into a working farm that hosted punk shows alongside the robotic warfare of Mark Pauline's Survival Research Laboratories (3.23). All the while a new generation of kids was making more noise across the bay (3.15–3.16).

"THIS IS BERKELEY, NOT WEST BAY"

One counter to the country's rightward swing in the early '80s was the rise of "peace punk" taking root in West Oakland and Emeryville, especially at the New Method warehouse, and stretching up to the campus of UC Berkeley. That's not to say aging hippies would have recognized the black-clad and spike-laden members of Crucifix, and later bands like A State of Mind, Atrocity, Treason, Trial, and P.L.H., as continuing the sixties vibe if they saw them on the street or heard the stunning ferocity of their songs (3.28–3.33). These bands, often including the same members or members of the same family, agitated for peace through brutal sound, apocalyptic imagery, and earnest lyrics that placed antinuclear protests, animal rights activism, and anti-imperialism at the heart of punk. Crucifix front man and Cambodian refugee Sothira Peng took on his personal experience of authoritarianism and colonialism. Cyrnai (Carolyn Fok) played in Treason and Trial, and released her own solo LP, alternating from charging distortion to the brooding side of peace punk with reverb-heavy, flange-laden guitars. Atrocity's singers Sarah Borruso and Katherine Harris gave voice not only to animal rights but also, with "Abandoned," to the environmental disaster of drought and starvation. As a collective, peace punk channeled opposition to dehumanizing regimes and industrial slaughter into a sonic force that bands like Christ on Parade (made up of three former members of Treason) and Neurosis would carry forward in the second half of the 1980s (3.27).

At the same time, the sound of Bay Area punk was transforming in other ways, opening up to a wide range of influences. While bands like Special Forces (see singer Orlando Xavier's interview in CHAPTER 15) continued the high velocity of hardcore, Fang (3.18–3.20) slowed into a midtempo trudge for most of their album *Landshark!* (1982). Whipping Boy's (3.24) album *Muru Muru* (1984) dove into the noiser, darker, and more experimental music that singer Eugene Robinson and guitarist Niko Wenner continued to explore in their band Oxbow. And Beatnigs (3.63) brought industrial punk into a dancier condemnation of capitalism. (Singer Michael Franti would go on to work in hip hop and funk with Charlie Hunter, and reggae with Spearhead). Meanwhile, Wes Robinson, the promoter and booker at Ruthie's Inn, brought the thrash, metal, and hardcore scenes together and ushered in yet another new sound spinning off from the fire of punk (3.43). The sonic and racial diversity in these bands and this scene spoke to a moment in which many joined antiapartheid protests at UC Berkeley (3.139), where they used a zine, flyers, and occupation to rename the university's Sproul Plaza as Biko Plaza after South African activist Steve Biko (3.36–3.37). Bay Area punks didn't so much have to forget their local history of protests as claim their own place in struggles echoing from the Black Panthers, the Free Speech Movement, and countless demonstrations and occupations along Telegraph Avenue from Oakland to Berkeley.

The most intentional call for a transformation in punk community ("the re-generation of our culture," as an early flyer puts it) was the founding of the Gilman Street Project in a West Berkeley space next to a caning shop. Gilman was by design all ages, volunteer run, and alcohol free. The now legendary venue emerged from efforts on both sides of the Bay: *MRR* founder and KPFA radio host Tim Yohannon (3.6, 3.47–3.58), who had moved offices from North Oakland to San Francisco in July 1985, joined forces with a group of East Bay kids seeking to establish a more permanent home for punk.

Gilman's first full year of shows (1987) intersected with the rise of Lookout Records, which released debut vinyl from Blatz, Crimpshrine (3.68–3.71), Corrupted Morals, Filth, Green Day (3.79–3.83), Isocracy, the Mr. T Experience (3.45–3.46), Operation Ivy (3.73–3.78), and a dozen other scene-defining bands in the label's first five years. And yet this convergence of *MRR*, Gilman, and Lookout represents only one node in an entire punk infrastructure, both visible and invisible, identified or anonymous, that powered punk across the greater Bay Area (3.85). Sound engineers like Kevin Army and Andy Ernst, and studios like Dangerous Rhythm (3.34) and Art of Ears, and many other independent record labels besides the better-known Lookout and Alternative Tentacles helped get the scene's music into people's hands. Steve List handed out copies of *The List*—on one folded-over eight-and-a-half-by-eleven sheet—so people knew where to go to shows at clubs, vets halls, student housing co-ops (Barrington, Cloyne Court), church basements, and house parties. Photographers, especially Murray Bowles, caught freeze frames of the wild energy that passed in a flash (3.39–3.67). Countless local zines—like *Cometbus* (3.10–3.11), *Ripper* (3.14), *Slingshot* (3.86), *Can of Worms* (3.88), and all of the forgotten pages in copy machines—provided a platform for direct communication (long before social media) where opinions, scene reports, creative writing and graphic design could get out to the community and maybe even beyond it. Sometimes it all revealed that the bands were the alibi to hang out, make secret art, start a revolution (of the mind or on the street), silkscreen patches with images and slogans that had nothing to do with music, imagine government takeovers, share food (and stop bombs!), subvert property rights (squat, copy tapes, win court battles with the FCC) (3.90), and a thousand other actions hidden or openly referenced in the items scattered across these pages.

The confluence of Gilman and the local bands associated with Lookout did a lot to change what sounded punk: emphasizing more melodic (Crimpshrine, Isocracy) or pop punk (Green Day, MTX); fusing melody with crust screams (Filth); setting the template for high-speed ska-punk (Op Ivy) and avant-garde metal (Neurosis); or forgetting all the rules to interlace three singers and multiple tempos in one song (Blatz). However, even more than the music, these locals helped shift the attitude of punk. Some criticized the scene, and especially Tim Yohannan, for setting up an unofficial rule book for punks (3.91). But while East Coast hardcore bands might have called Gilman "Romper Room" when they witnessed Isocracy's prankish takeovers of the club with confetti (3.64) or kitty litter, the scene's emphasis on positivity paralleled what straight edge hardcore bands like Youth of Today were calling for in New York, and the new direction in DC's Revolution Summer of Embrace, Rites of Spring, and Beefeater at roughly the same time. Punk reinvented itself across the country in the mid-1980s, negating punk's original negation, transforming "no future" into a future. Gilman put a local stamp on that change.

"THERE'S A DYKE IN THE PIT": QUEERCORE

Anna Joy Springer makes clear in her essay that this transformation wouldn't have happened without the energy of queer punks. As the AIDS epidemic raged on in the 1980s, Tom Jennings created the *Homocore* zine—one of the first to focus on queer identities in San Francisco punk. Bands like Tribe 8, the Popstitutes, and Pansy Division soon followed, as did Matt Wobensmith's *Outpunk*, which filled the void when *Homocore* folded. *Outpunk* also served as a record label, releasing a slate of queercore and riot grrrl bands (3.93–3.94). Queercore bands changed the topic of punk from what other bands sang about, even when they sang the same songs. In the hands of Tribe 8, Black Flag's "Rise Above" became a thunderous anthem for resisting homophobia and sexism. And they acted out that change onstage too: performing shirtless, roleplaying BDSM with volunteers from the audience, and chain-sawing dildos.

The following pages show how scenes specific to the Bay Area unfolded, in continuity and discontinuity, building on what had come before but also ripping it up to start again. From Pink Section to Spitboy, Atrocity to Blatz, Dead Kennedys to Green Day, the Mab to Gilman, Tim Tonooka's *Ripper* to *Cometbus*, Bay Area punk repeatedly forged itself in the crucible of left-wing thought, street violence, and hilarity that has fueled generations of punks to jump into the fray.

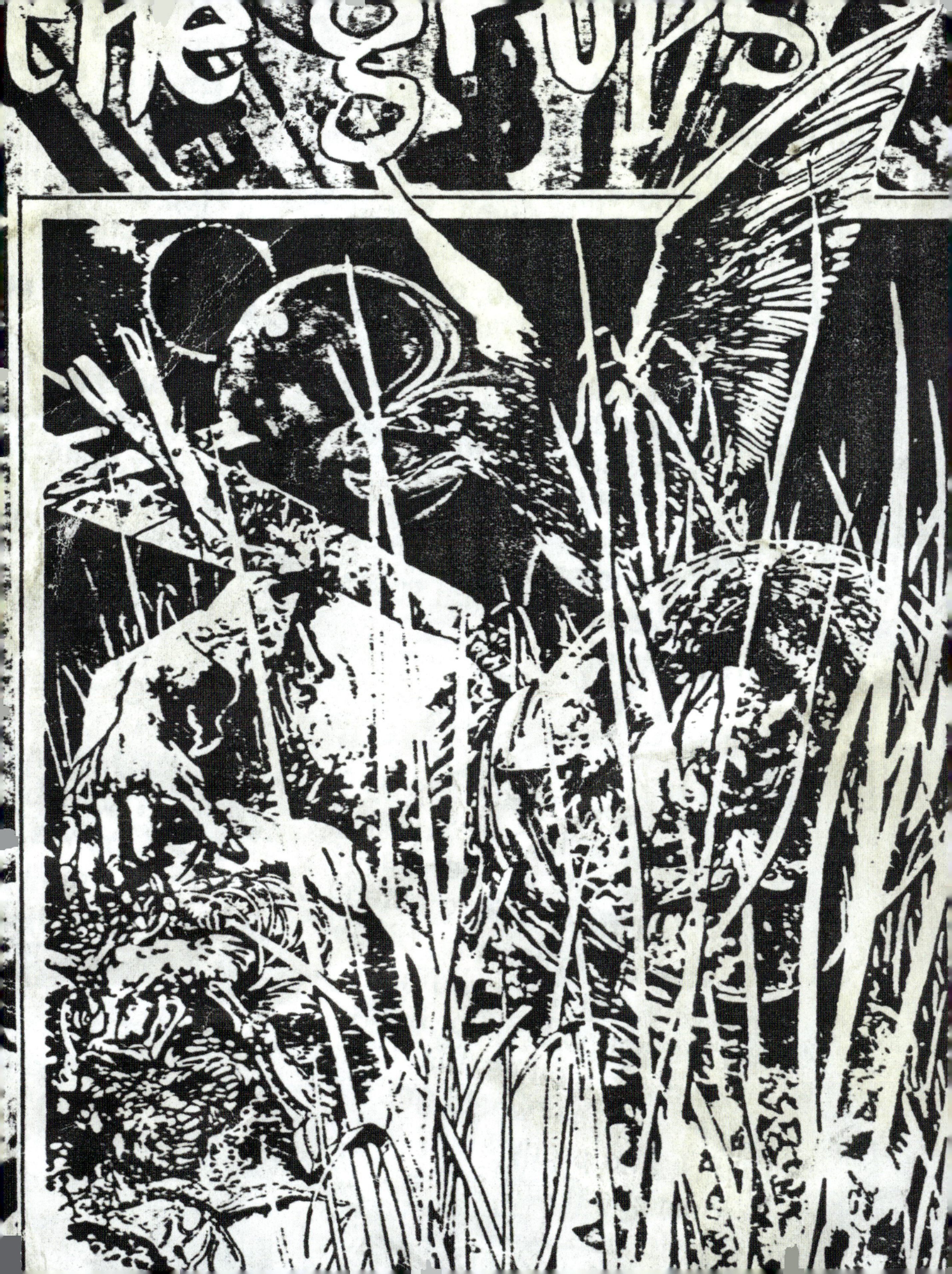
the grubs

CH. 12 IMAGE GALLERY

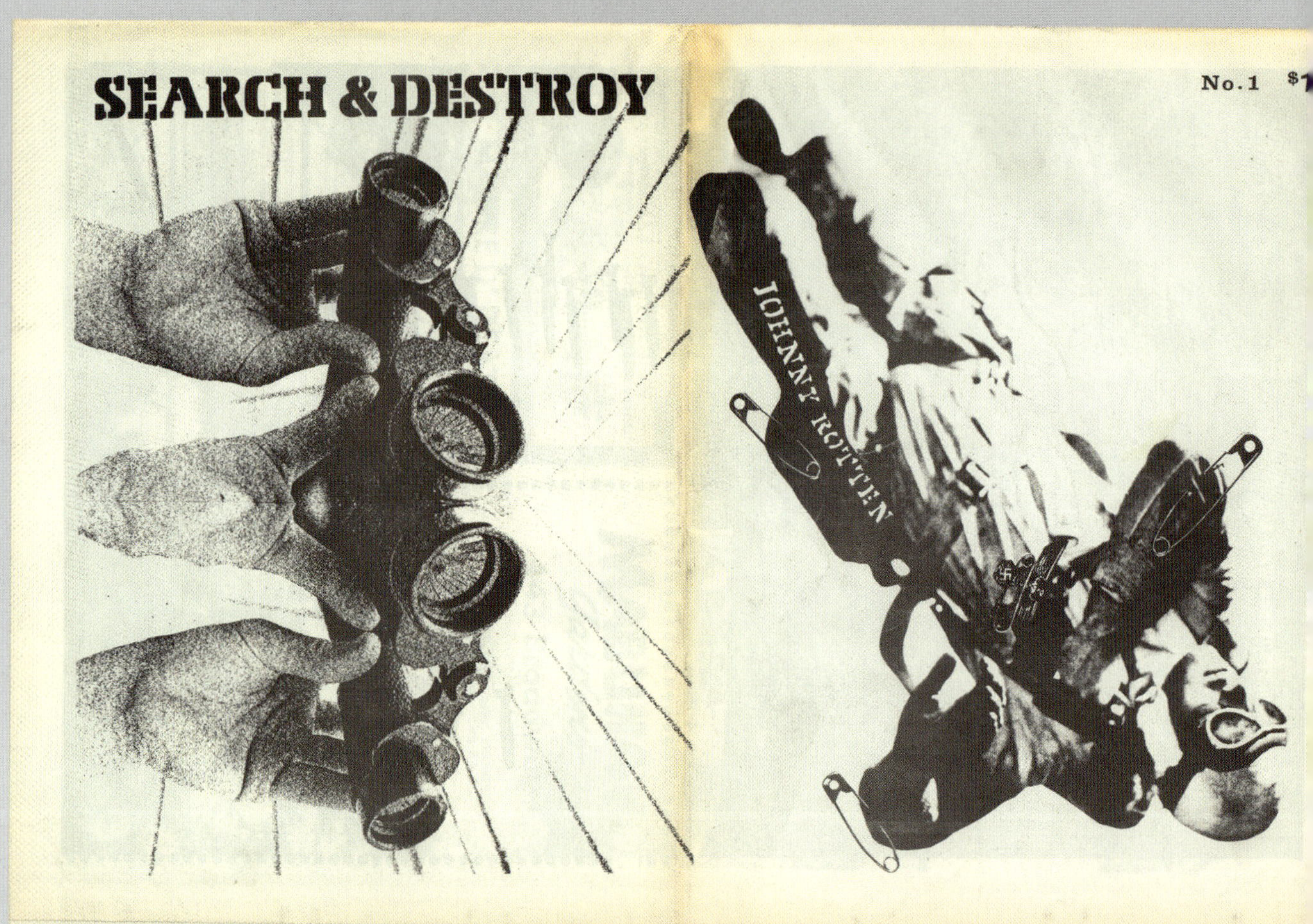

3.1. Cover for *Search and Destroy* no. 1, 1977.

Return of the 45

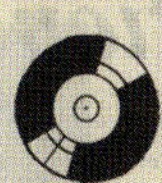

Among the waking dreams and smouldering ruins of 45's a song occasionally ignites my aural imagination, and confirms a total commitment to ecstatic expression without which my will to live might diminish. What is at stake at such moments is my own authenticity. Often my life has been transformed by 45's, e.g., involving rebellion and high school life as in Billy Harlan's SCHOOL OF ROCK 'N' ROLL, mad love and its defiance of death in Magic Sam's ALL NIGHT LONG, or social utopia versus human fragility in the Wailers' DREAMLAND....

I am grateful for the existence of the 45. What about its form makes it so personable? And, in a jukebox, so affecting? Why does the obsessional replay of my aural consciousness take its libidinal stance before the first chords of HEARTBREAK HOTEL and its lyrics about feeling so lonely I could die? Dreams break on through to other dreams; some permutate for what seems to be forever. At times I have found myself revulsed at HEARTBREAK HOTEL and its self-dramatizing detachment, but its obsessional justification keeps recurring in life.

If no other song was ever recorded, if all music as we know it today save this one song was unaccountably destroyed, the destiny of the 45 would have been fulfilled by Carl Perkins' HER LOVE RUBBED OFF. No question here, as with HEARTBREAK HOTEL,of authenticity -- singer and listener unite at the dual center of cyclone and rose.

It's impossible to paraphrase what so effortlessly exists as an unquestionable artifact of the ear. Suffice it to say that HER LOVE RUBBED OFF begins MURKILY. Some of the best intro's of 50's rock 'n' roll seem to have no relationships with music, but are entrances to unseen worlds of blinding attractions. Carl strolls through a city park and meets his girl standing in the shadows. Toward the end of the song Carl slips into an irresistibly obsessional recall about that woman and that moment when her love rubbed off is memorialized as his closing and truly sensuous warble (turn the speakers up here) is eclipsed by night and fade out...

Several years ago some of us in San Francisco had the good fortune to stumble upon Trenchtown Records (then Kingston Records) which today still flourishes at Bush & Fillmore. Rows of reggae singles hang in suspension about wooden spindles. The labels themselves, the names of the groups, the song titles, and, at first, even the music itself appear strange and exotic. For a time we were transported elsewhere. Private collections of 45's began to grow. Local distribution, though, became (and sadly continues to be) a critical problem, because supply for the demand is sporadic. The crest of the reggae wave seemingly has peaked within a frozen frame, but it surely will continue on for the natural force of reggae is permanent -- it is veritable music for the primal scene.

Today at the best two record stores in the area, Aquarius Records, SF, and Rather Ripped Records Berkeley, for those who search, there are rows upon rows of 45's in predominantly red, black and white picture sleeves. The music they represent has been identified as "punk rock" here in the U.S. press, but the English have preferred to use the term "NEW WAVE." (By the way, in each of these stores you can ask them to play a 45 that you are interested in hearing).

The indisputable classic of New Wave 45's, the Originating Spark, is the Sex Pistols' ANARCHY IN THE U.K. ("I am an antichrist/ I am an anarchist..."). The notorious recording-company snafus of the Sex Pistols (they are currently signed with their third company -- Virgin Records) has so far restricted their recorded work exclusively to 45's, but what 45's! Their second 45, just now available, is a devastating put-down of the Silver Jubilee called GOD SAVE THE QUEEN ("God save the queen/ the fascist regime/ that made you a moron, a potential H-Bomb/ God save the Queen/ She ain't no human being/ There is no future in England's dream").

Although ANARCHY IN THE UK and GOD SAVE THE QUEEN are, in some ways the best 45's, so far, from the New Wave, the ongoing output already embraces many divergencies. The Damned have issued at least one classic 45 in NEW ROSE which can be heard on their great import album DAMNED DAMNED DAMNED. The Clash have issued several intriguing 45's in WHITE RIOT/"1977" and REMOTE CONTROL/LONDON'S BURNING, but these are basically duplicated on their album, THE CLASH -- an instant classic of working-class insurgency. Domestically an incomparable Iggy and the Stooges' reissue of I GOT A RIGHT/ GIMME SOME SKIN is a walkaway fave. Locally the best New Wave 45 has been Crime's HOT WIRE MY HEART/BABY YOU'RE SO REPULSIVE. Crime will have another 45 out shortly: FRUSTRATION/MURDER BY GUITAR.

Since the beginning of the 70's the 45 had waned. A soul album (substitute "disco" for today) harnessed with only one good song on it, that being its sole hit, often managed to sell better than the original hit single. Of course, the record collectors and those who are really into a musical life-style will always go on collecting and buying singles, for the history of early rock, doowop, R'n'B, rockabilly, reggae, etc. is a history of 45's. Indeed when the demand for a popular music is great, the focus is inevitably put back on 45's as the most accessible indicator of where the music's at. Hopefully the New Wave deluge is only beginning. Although, so far, very few groups in the U.S. are out-and-out New Wave (The Ramones, Crime), many New Wave groups in England are about to release their first 45's. For those who continue to believe in 45's,New Wave and reggae are where the music's at. LONG MAY THEY WAVE!

Politics of PUNK

by Nico Ordway

It would be easy and predictable to call Punk fascist.

Rhetoric aside, however,there are some interesting things to be said about Punk politically.

First, there's the basic difference between UK Punk and US Punk.

UK Punk comes out of rage, the total rage of people in a collapsing society, where anarchy is all that seems to be on the horizon. But don't forget, "The passion for destruction is a creative passion."

UK Punk is in the ruins. US Punk comes out of something totally different: the aesthetic boredom of the middle class rather than the anger of the stepped-on. Though here too hasty judgments are NOT in order.

But no matter where Punk finds its fans, including the idiots with money, for musicians Punk has another meaning, here in the US.

Bill Graham has said off the record that the potentially richest rock'n'roll market in the country is New York-New England. Why no big concerts there any more? CROWD CONTROL.

As Graham has said, "You get 55,000 New Yorkers in one place and watch the fences go down."

Punk is to some extent a reaction to that. I.e., realizing they have no hope as mass performers in a place where industry powers will not encourage mass audiences, some Eastern bands have taken the opportunity to push their public faces as far as possible in the direction of the bizarre, since an entertainment industry unable to satisfy musicians' needs and fantasies by maintaining mass audiences cannot expect to hold onto musicians' aesthetic loyalties.

In this regard Punk is also something of a reaction to Disco, probably the worst excuse for music ever to appear, anywhere.

Disco is one way of getting around mass audiences. Punk is another. This issue also provides a contrast UK vs. US: In the UK Punk's audience is mass; here it's elite.

Will it stay that way?

Ginsberg SEZ:

I like the Nuns. They're like Kabuki Theatre. I don't think the term NEW WAVE has reached the East Coast yet. I've been to CBGB's 15 or 20 times -- Denise Mercedes, Peter Orlovsky's girlfriend who's really a rocker, first took me there. But now I think the Mabuhay is a better scene. CBGB's a bit tired. The main result of protest music is usually more sexual liberation. The New Wave music is protest music, but its chief concern seems to be the Mockery of television, machinery, and decadence....

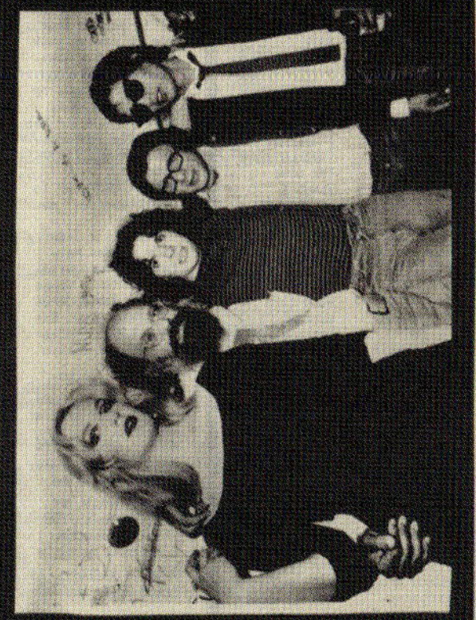

3.2. Page 1 of *Search and Destroy* no. 1, featuring a photo with Jennifer Miro of the Nuns and Allen Ginsberg.

A DIRKSEN-MILLER PRODUCTION

MABUHAY

FRIDAY 11 PM 5/26

THE NUNS
THE OFFS
& NEW WAVE
FILM 10 PM

3.3. Flyer for show at Mabuhay Gardens, San Francisco, May 1978.

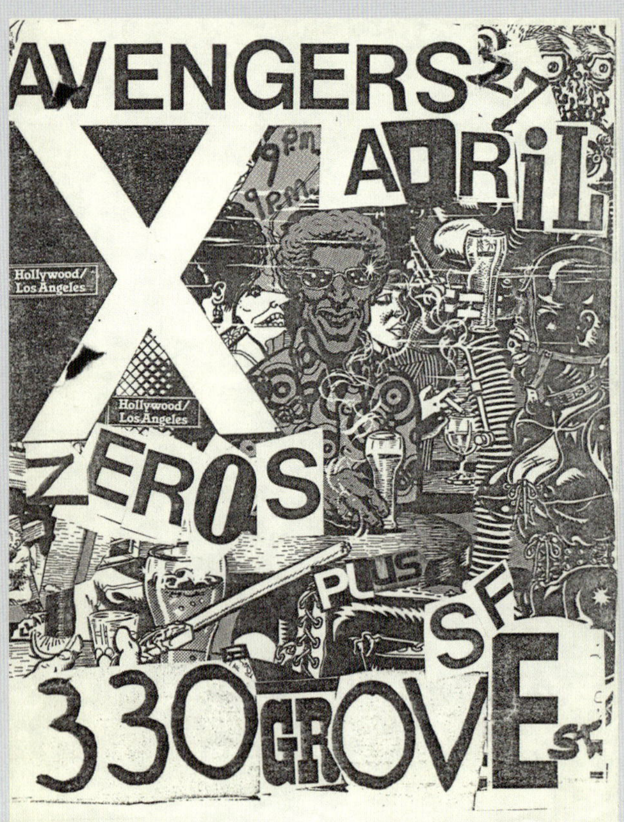

3.4. Flyer for show at 330 Grove, San Francisco, circa 1979.

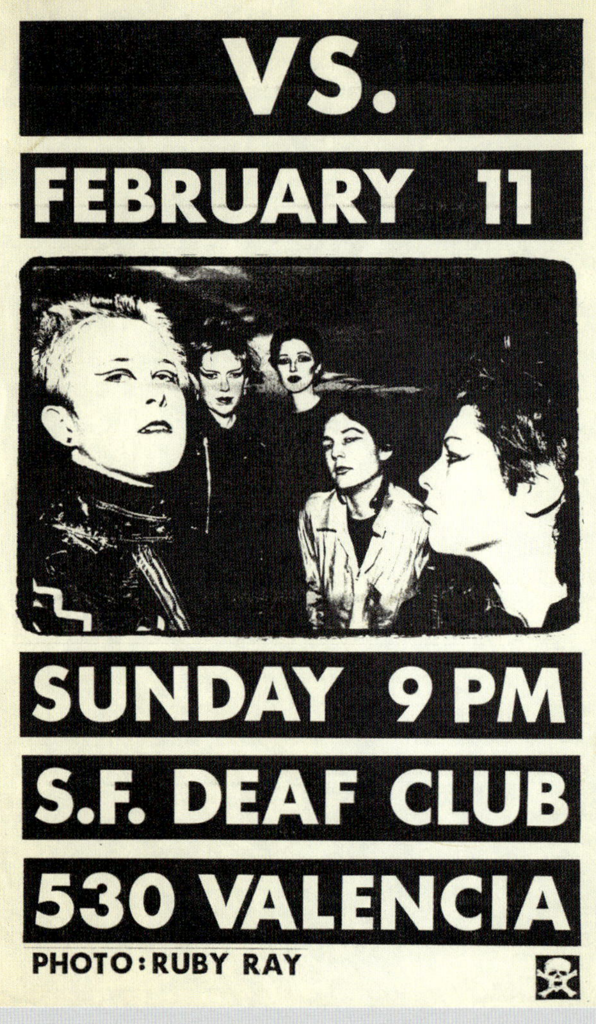

3.5. Flyer for show at the Deaf Club, San Francisco, February 1979.

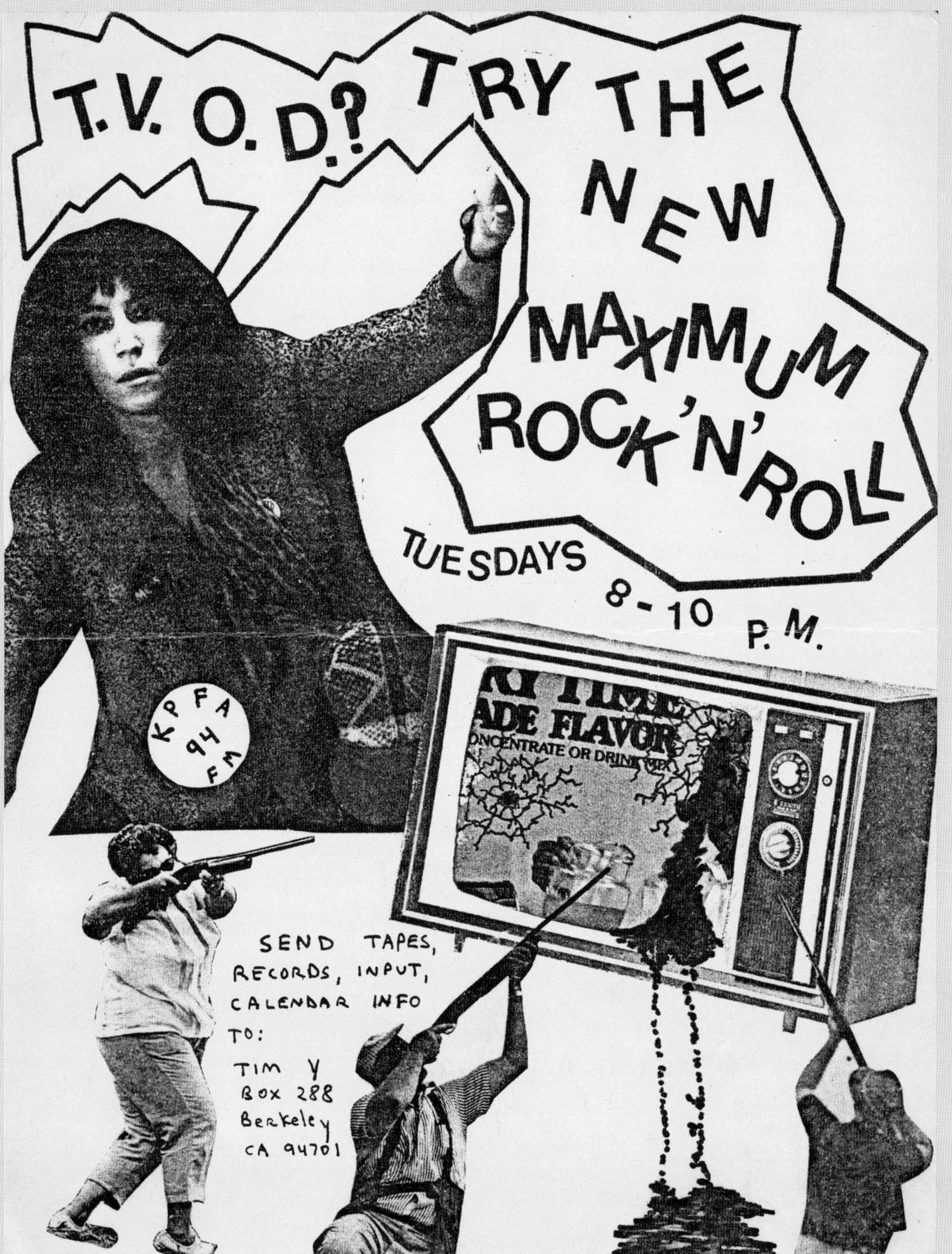

3.6. Flyer for Tim Yohannan's radio show on KPFA, circa 1977.

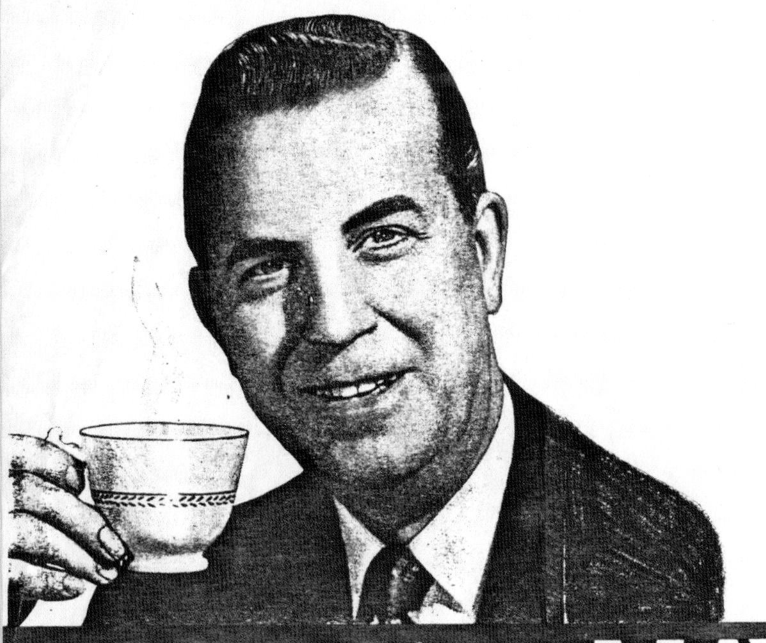

3.8. Campaign poster for Jello Biafra designed by Winston Smith, 1979.

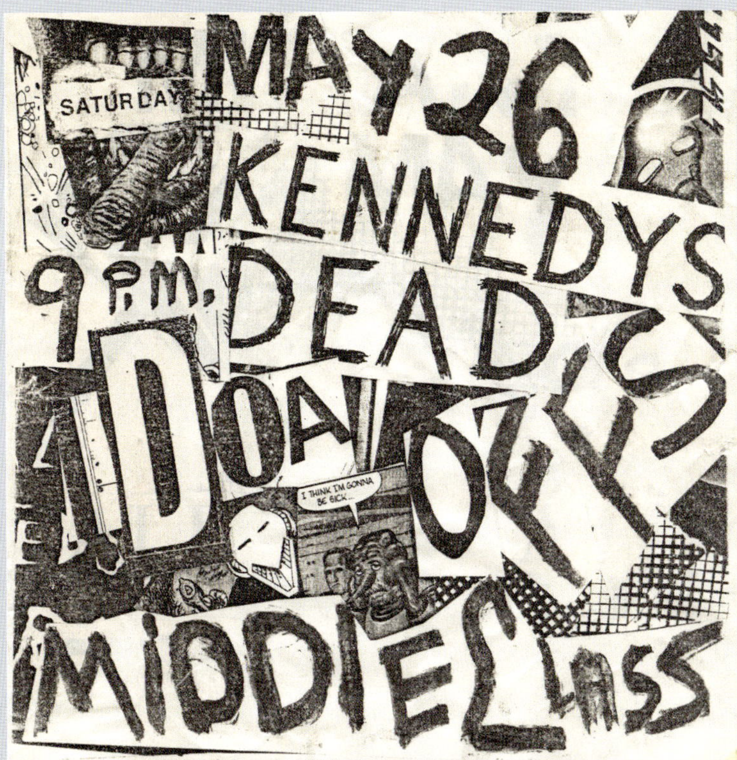

3.7. (*Above*) Flyer for show at 1839 Geary St. (aka Temple Beautiful), San Francisco, May 1979.

3.9. (*Below*) Wedding invitation for Therese Soder and Jello Biafra, October 1981.

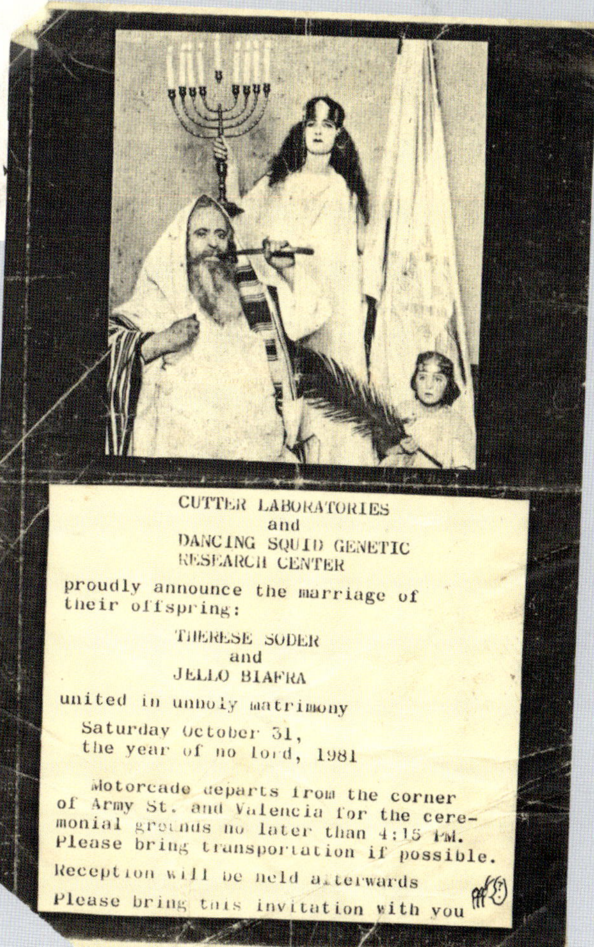

CUTTER LABORATORIES
and
DANCING SQUID GENETIC
RESEARCH CENTER

proudly announce the marriage of their offspring:

THERESE SODER
and
JELLO BIAFRA

united in unholy matrimony

Saturday October 31,
the year of no lord, 1981

Motorcade departs from the corner of Army St. and Valencia for the ceremonial grounds no later than 4:15 PM. Please bring transportation if possible.

Reception will be held afterwards

Please bring this invitation with you

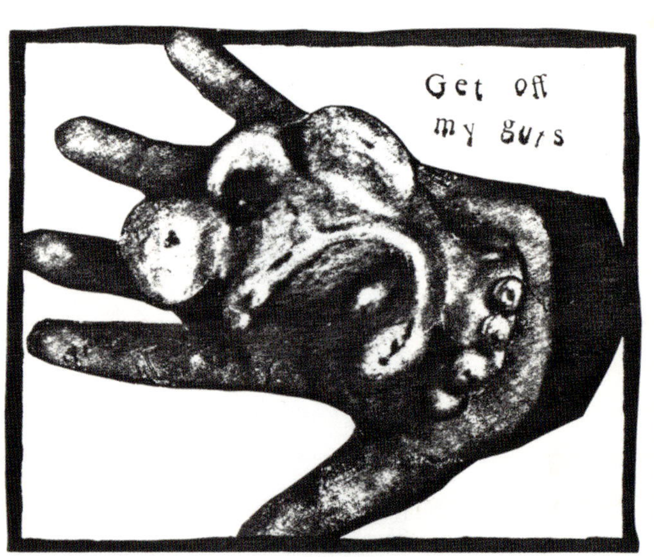

3.11. J-card design for *Get off My Guts*, the first Cometbus compilation tape (BBT 01, 1982).

3.10. *Outlash* no. 6, Summer 1982. Before Aaron Cometbus decided on *Cometbus* as his fanzine's name, he produced small-format zines like this one, sometimes with his friend and future singer for Operation Ivy, Jesse Michaels.

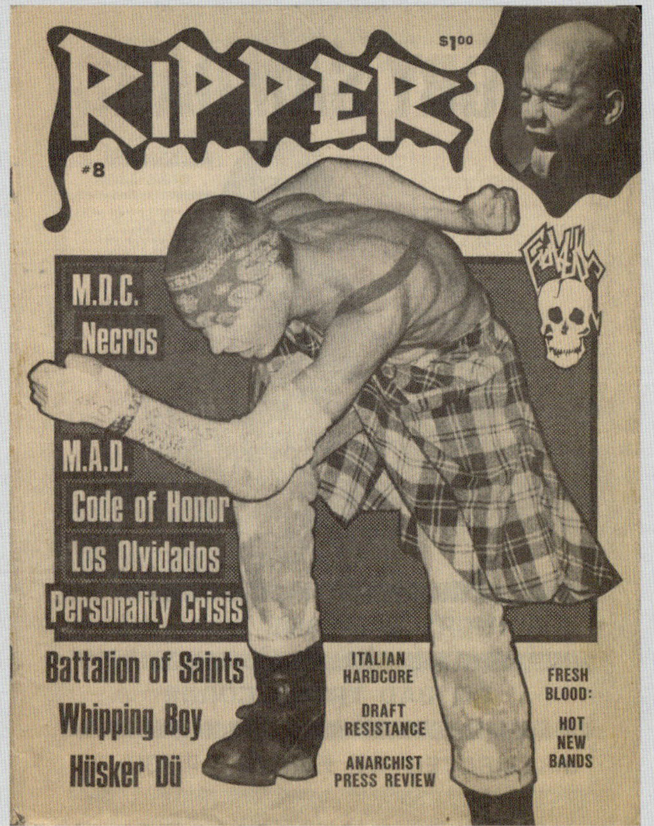

3.14. Tim Tonooka's *Ripper* no. 8, 1983.

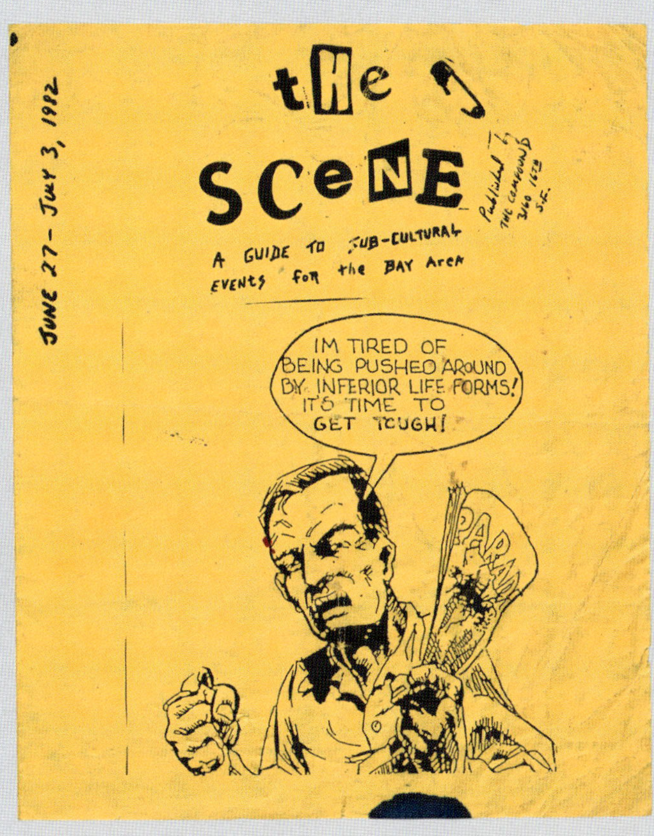

3.12 and 3.13. Front and back of *The Scene: A Guide to Sub-cultural Events for the Bay Area*, June 27–July 3, 1982.

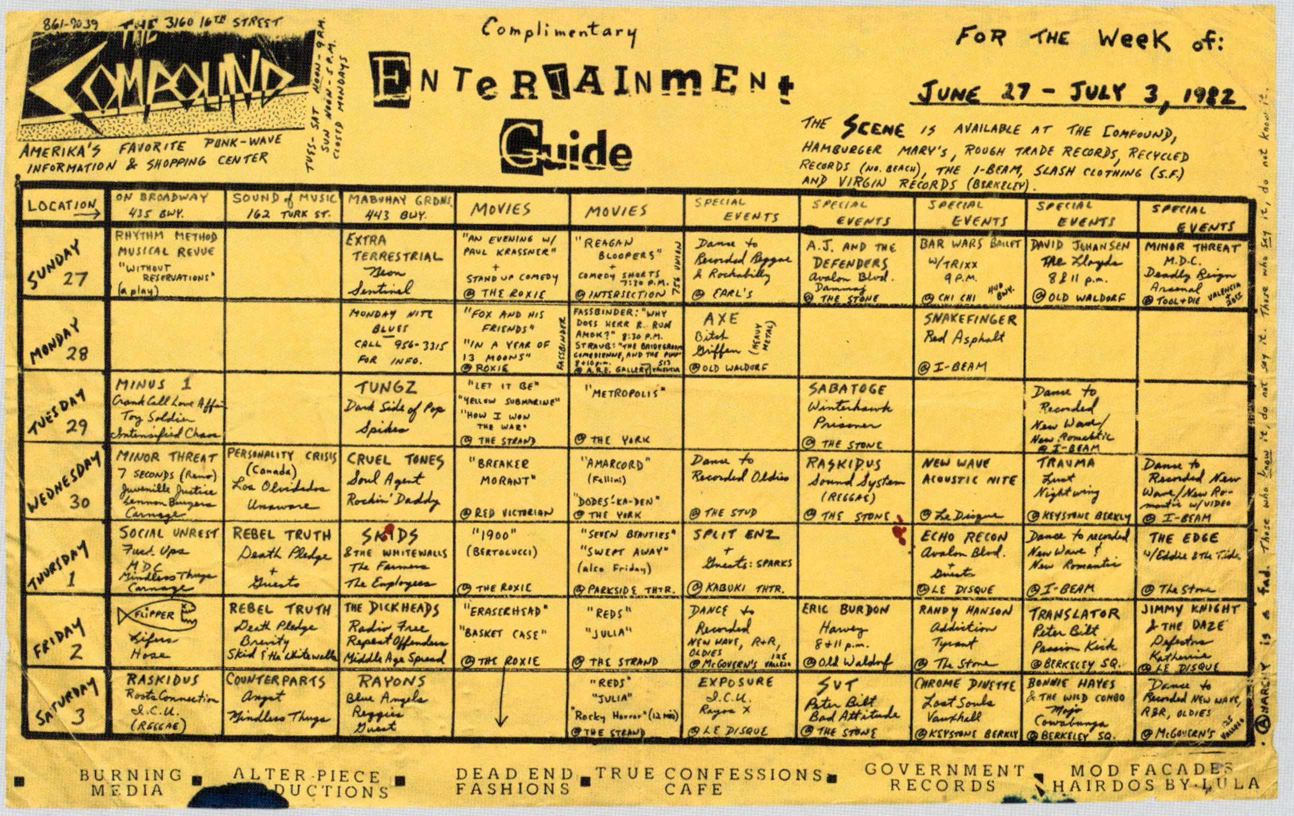

861-9039 THE 3160 16TH STREET
THE COMPOUND
AMERIKA'S FAVORITE PUNK-WAVE INFORMATION & SHOPPING CENTER
TUES-SAT NOON-9P.M. SUN NOON-5P.M. CLOSED MONDAYS

Complimentary

ENTERTAINMENT Guide

FOR THE Week of:

JUNE 27 – JULY 3, 1982

THE SCENE IS AVAILABLE AT THE COMPOUND, HAMBURGER MARY'S, ROUGH TRADE RECORDS, RECYCLED RECORDS (NO. BEACH), THE I-BEAM, SLASH CLOTHING (S.F.) AND VIRGIN RECORDS (BERKELEY).

LOCATION →	ON BROADWAY 435 BWY.	SOUND of MUSIC 162 TURK ST.	MABUHAY GRDNS 443 BWY.	MOVIES	MOVIES	SPECIAL EVENTS	SPECIAL EVENTS	SPECIAL EVENTS	SPECIAL EVENTS	SPECIAL EVENTS
SUNDAY 27	RHYTHM METHOD MUSICAL REVUE "WITHOUT RESERVATIONS" (a play)		EXTRA TERRESTRIAL Neon Sentinel	"AN EVENING W/ PAUL KRASSNER" + STAND UP COMEDY @ THE ROXIE	"REAGAN BLOOPERS" + COMEDY SHORTS 7:30 P.M. @ INTERSECTION 756 UNION	Dance to Recorded Reggae & Rockabilly @ EARL'S	A.J. AND THE DEFENDERS Avalon Blvd. Dammaj @ THE STONE	BAR WARS BALLET W/TRIXX 9 P.M. @ CHI CHI 440 BWY.	DAVID JOHANSEN The Lloyds 8 & 11 p.m. @ OLD WALDORF	MINOR THREAT M.D.C. Deadly Reign Arsenal @ TOOL+DIE VALENCIA + 20TH
MONDAY 28			MONDAY NITE BLUES CALL 956-3315 FOR INFO.	"FOX AND HIS FRIENDS" "IN A YEAR OF 13 MOONS" @ ROXIE FASSBINDER	FASSBINDER: "WHY DOES HERR R. RUN AMOK?" 8:30 P.M. STRAUB: "THE BRIDEGROOM, COMEDIENNE, AND THE PIMP" 8+10 p.m. @ A.R.E. GALLERY 513 VALENCIA	AXE Bitch Griffen (HEAVY METAL) @ OLD WALDORF		SNAKEFINGER Red Asphalt @ I-BEAM		
TUESDAY 29	MINUS 1 Crank Call Love Affair Toy Soldier Intensified Chaos		TUNGZ Dark Side of Pop Spikes	"LET IT BE" "YELLOW SUBMARINE" "HOW I WON THE WAR" @ THE STRAND	"METROPOLIS" @ THE YORK		SABATOGE Winterhawk Prisoner @ THE STONE		Dance to Recorded New Wave/ New Romantic @ I-BEAM	
WEDNESDAY 30	MINOR THREAT 7 SECONDS (Reno) Juvenille Justice Lennon Burgers Carnage	PERSONALITY CRISIS (Canada) Los Olvidados Unaware	CRUEL TONES Soul Agent Rockin' Daddy	"BREAKER MORANT" @ RED VICTORIAN	"AMARCORD" (Fellini) "DODES'-KA-DEN" @ THE YORK	Dance to Recorded Oldies @ THE STUD	RASKIDUS Sound System (REGGAE) @ THE STONE	NEW WAVE ACOUSTIC NITE @ Le Disque	TRAUMA Lust Nightwing @ KEYSTONE BERKLY	Dance to Recorded New Wave/New Romantic w/VIDEO @ I-BEAM
THURSDAY 1	SOCIAL UNREST Fuck Ups MDC Mindless Thugs Carnage	REBEL TRUTH Death Pledge + Guests	SKIDS & THE WHITEWALLS The Farmers The Employees	"1900" (BERTOLUCCI) @ THE ROXIE	"SEVEN BEAUTIES" "SWEPT AWAY" (also Friday) @ PARKSIDE THTR.	SPLIT ENZ + Guests: SPARKS @ KABUKI THTR.		ECHO RECON Avalon Blvd. + Guests @ LE DISQUE	Dance to recorded New Wave & New Romantic @ I-BEAM	THE EDGE w/Eddie & the Tide @ The Stone
FRIDAY 2	FLIPPER Lifers Hose	REBEL TRUTH Death Pledge Brevity Skid & the Whitewalls	THE DICKHEADS Radio Free Repeat Offenders Middle Age Spread	"ERASERHEAD" "BASKET CASE" @ THE ROXIE	"REDS" "JULIA" @ THE STRAND	DANCE to Recorded NEW WAVE, R+R, OLDIES @ McGOVERN'S 125 VALLEJO	ERIC BURDON Harvey 8+11 p.m. @ Old Waldorf	RANDY HANSON Addiction Tyrant @ The Stone	TRANSLATOR Peter Bilt Passion Kick @ BERKELEY SQ.	JIMMY KNIGHT & THE DAZE Defectors Katharine @ LE DISQUE
SATURDAY 3	RASKIDUS Roots Connection I.C.U. (REGGAE)	COUNTERPARTS Angst Mindless Thugs	RAYONS Blue Angels Reggies Guest	↓	"REDS" "JULIA" "Rocky Horror" (12 mid) @ THE STRAND	EXPOSURE I.C.U. Rayon X @ LE DISQUE	SVT Peter Bilt Bad Attitude @ THE STONE	CHROME DINETTE Lost Souls Vauxhall @ KEYSTONE BERKLY	BONNIE HAYES & THE WILD COMBO Mojo Cowabunga @ BERKELEY SQ.	Dance to Recorded NEW WAVE, R&R, OLDIES @ McGOVERN'S 125 VALLEJO

Ⓐ ANARCHY is a fad. Those who know it, do not say it. Those who say it, do not know it.

BURNING MEDIA ▪ ALTER-PIECE PRODUCTIONS ▪ DEAD END FASHIONS ▪ TRUE CONFESSIONS CAFE ▪ GOVERNMENT RECORDS ▪ MOD FACADES HAIRDOS BY LULA

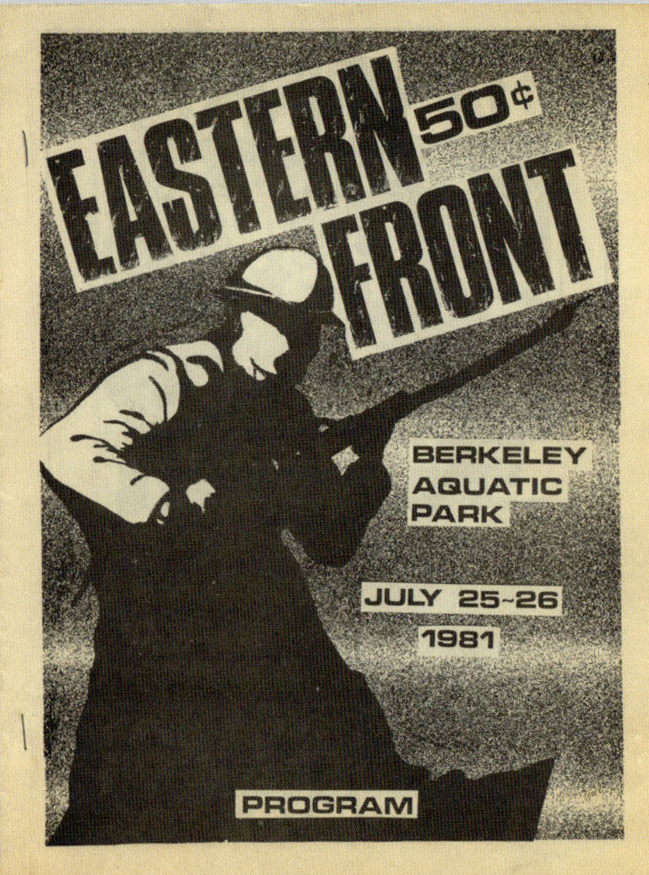

3.15. Program for the first Eastern Front festival, Berkeley, July 25–26, 1981.

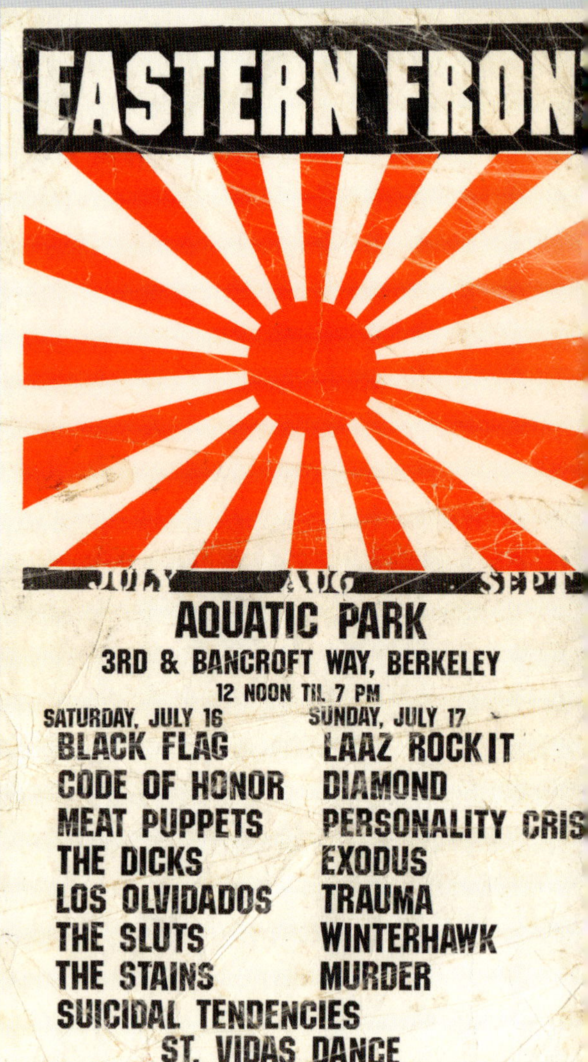

3.16. Poster for the third Eastern Front festival, Berkeley, 1983.

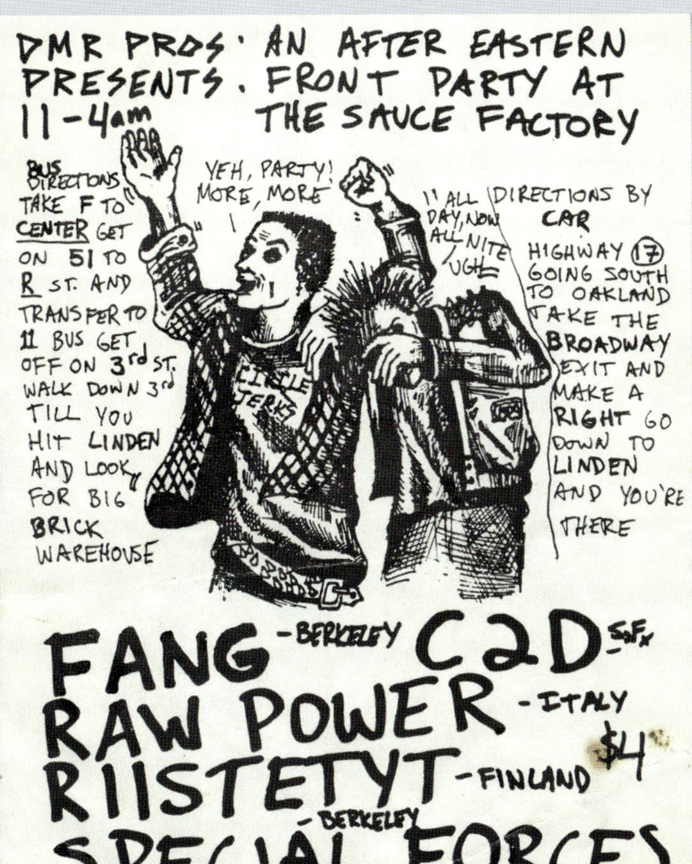

3.17. Flyer for an Eastern Front after-party hosted by DMR Productions, early 1980s.

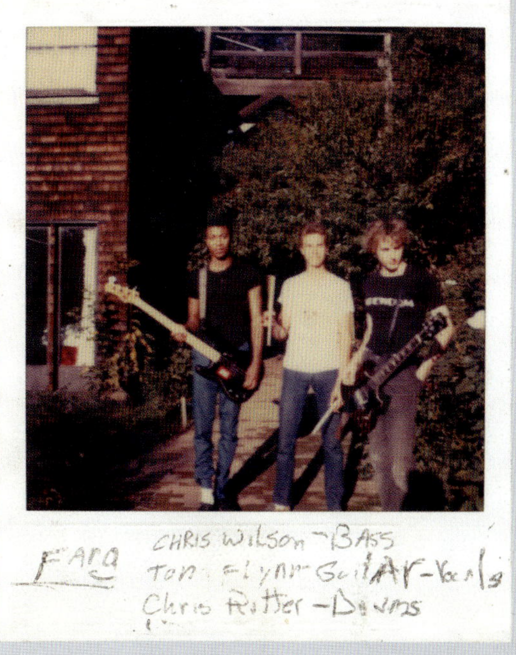

3.19. Polaroid photograph of early Fang before Sammytown (Sam McBride). *Left to right*, Chris Wilson, Tom Flynn, Chris Ritter, circa 1981. Photographer unknown.

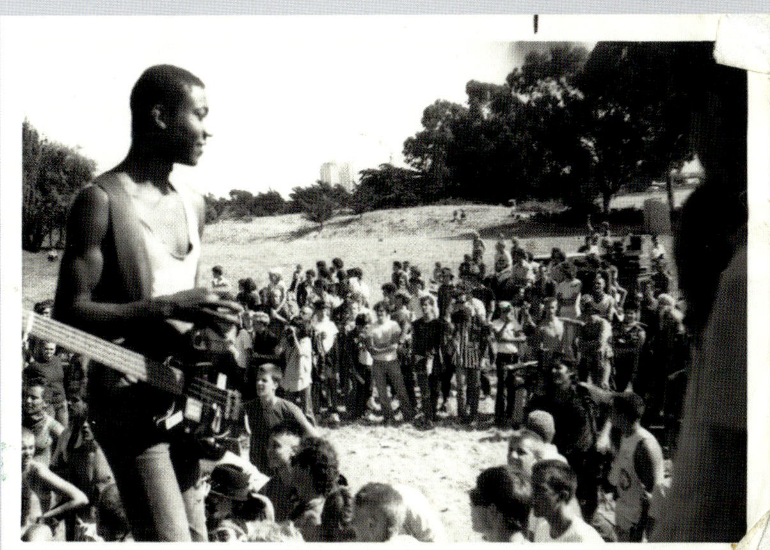

3.18. Chris Wilson of Fang at 1983 Eastern Front, Aquatic Park, Berkeley. Photo: Aaron Cometbus.

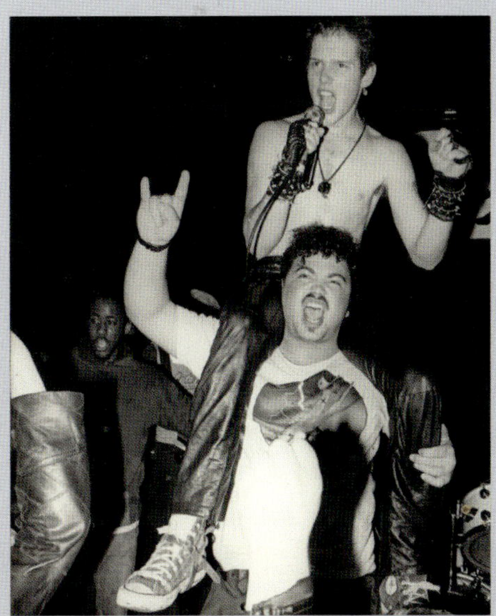

3.20. Sammytown riding on the shoulders of Max Fox, circa 1984. Photo: © Murray Bowles.

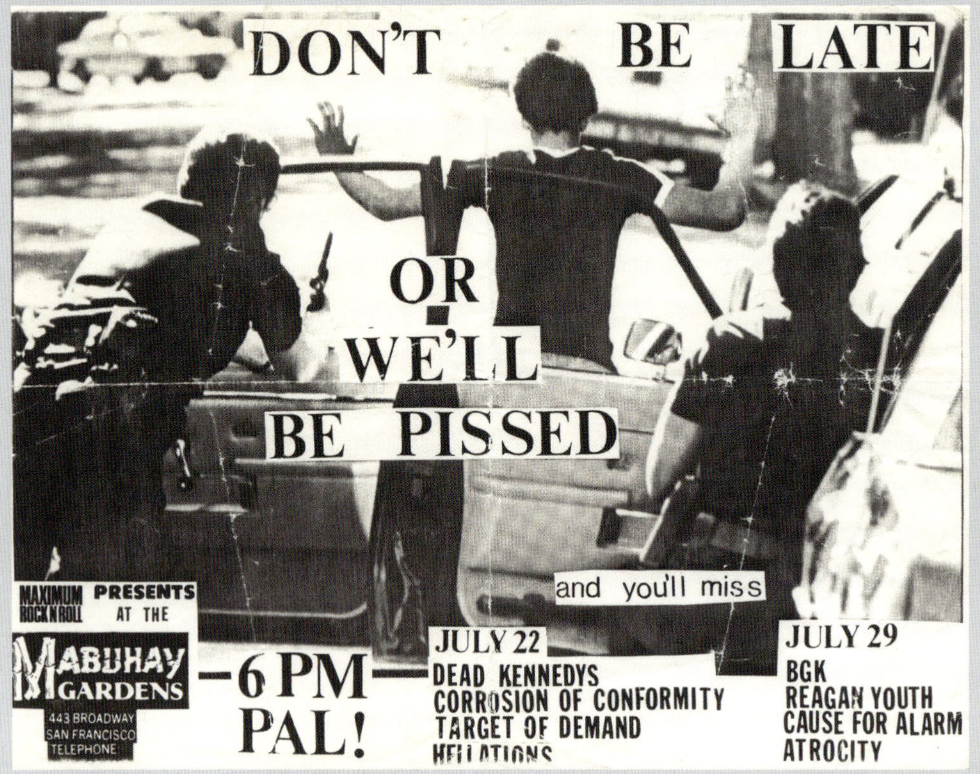

3.21. Mabuhay Gardens curfew flyer, 1984.

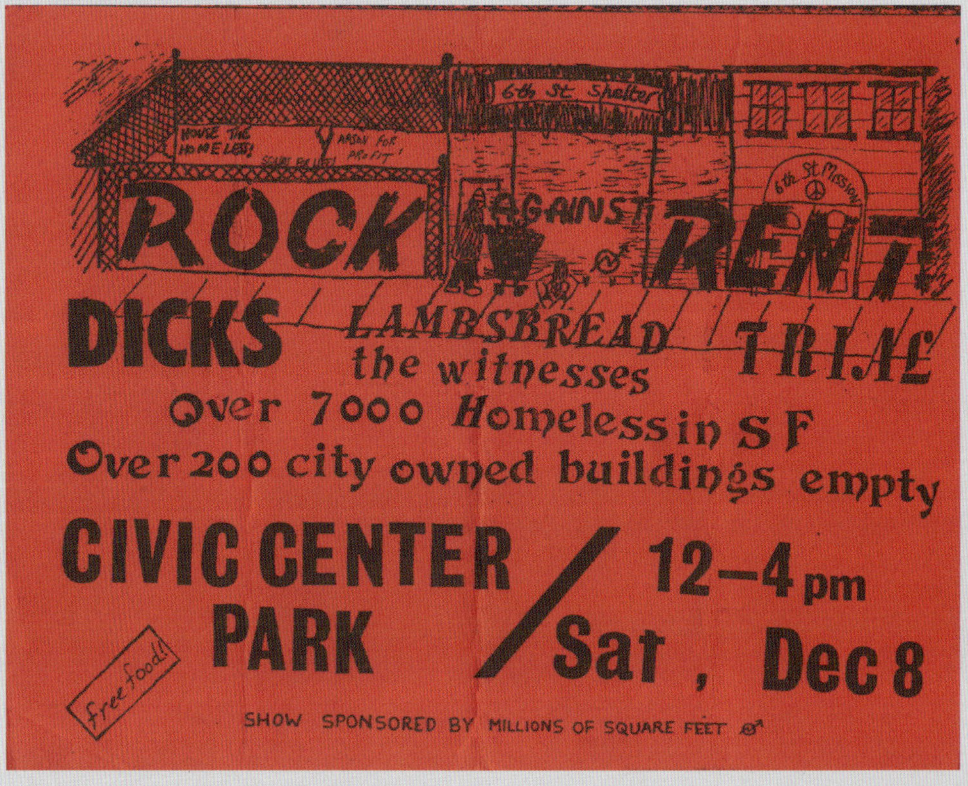

3.22. Flyer for Rock against Rent show at Civic Center Park, San Francisco, December 1984.

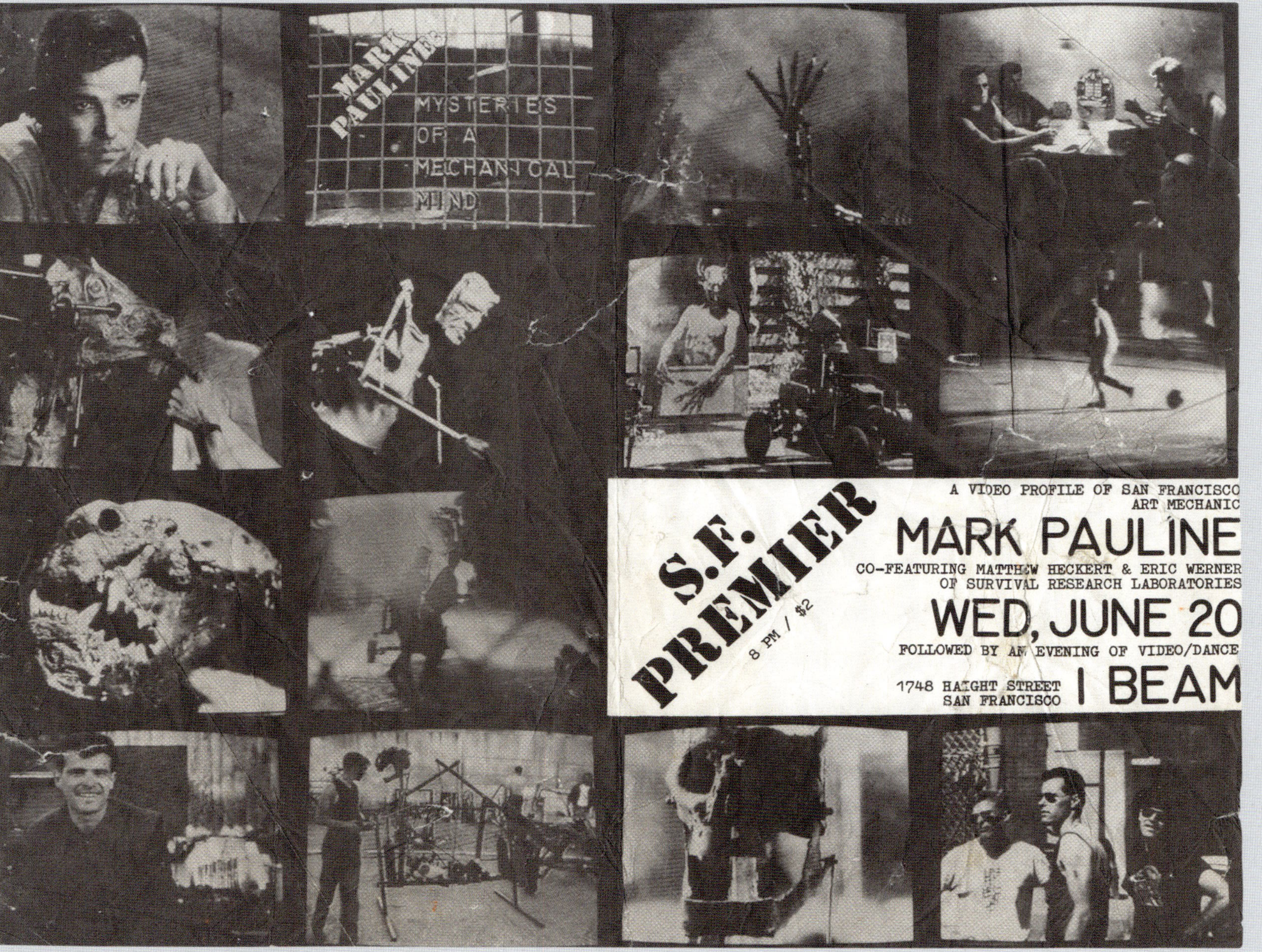

3.23. Flyer for Mark Pauline of Survival Research Laboratories at I-Beam, San Francisco, 1984.

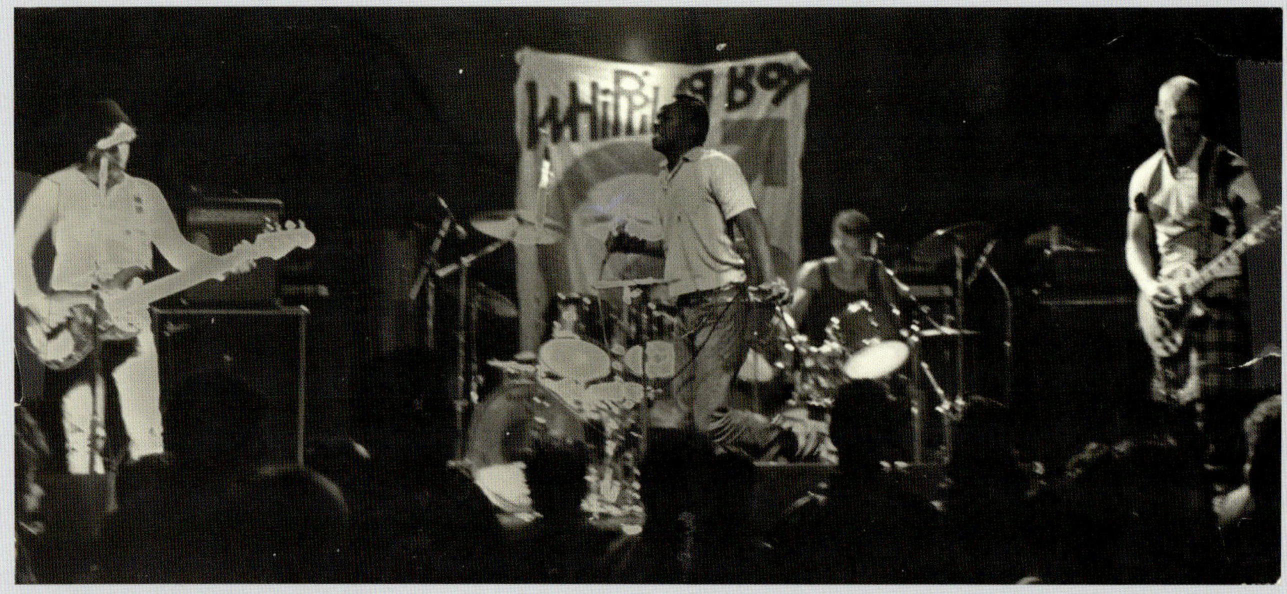

3.24. Whipping Boy. *Left to right*, Dave Owens, Eugene Robinson, Sam Smoot, Steve Ballinger, early 1980s. Photographer unknown.

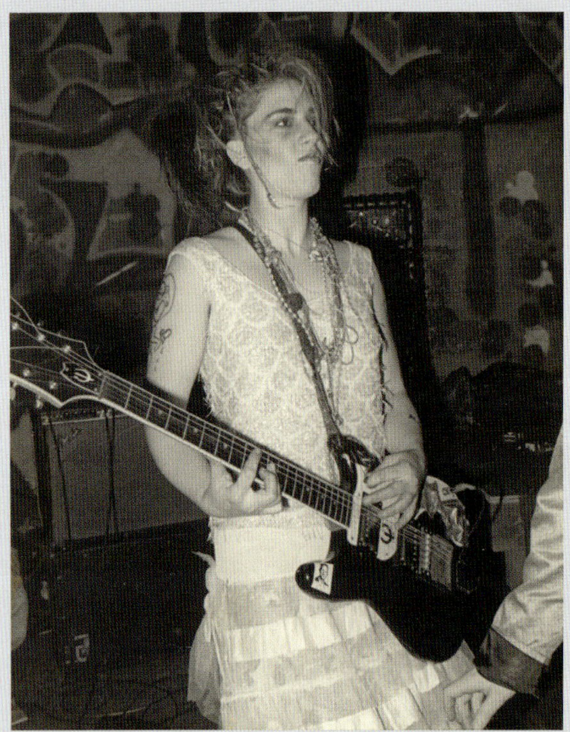

3.25. Mia d'Bruzzi of Frightwig, circa 1984. Photo: © Murray Bowles.

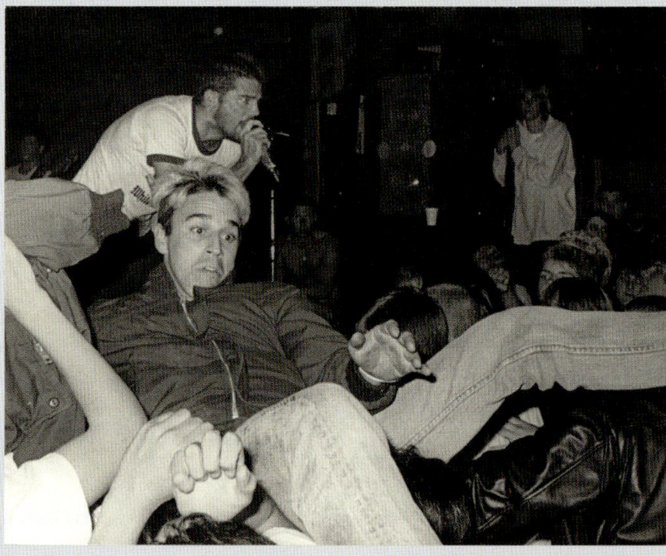

3.26. Descendents, circa 1984. Bay Area skater Jim Thiebaud stagediving. Photo: © Murray Bowles.

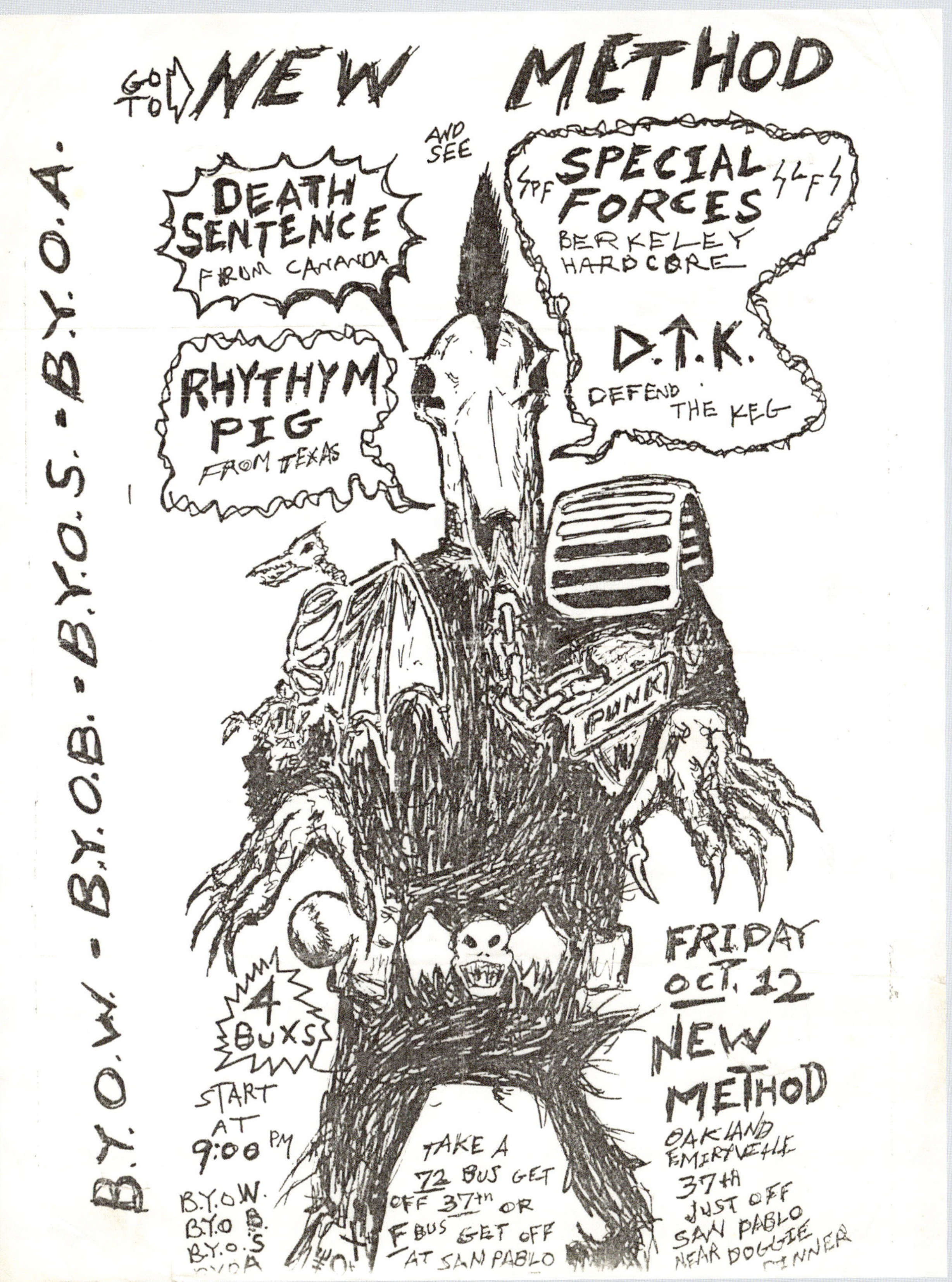

3.27. Flyer for show at the New Method warehouse, Emeryville, April 1982. New Method was home to members of Christ on Parade, Crucifix, and Neurosis and a key venue in the East Bay scene of the early to mid-1980s.

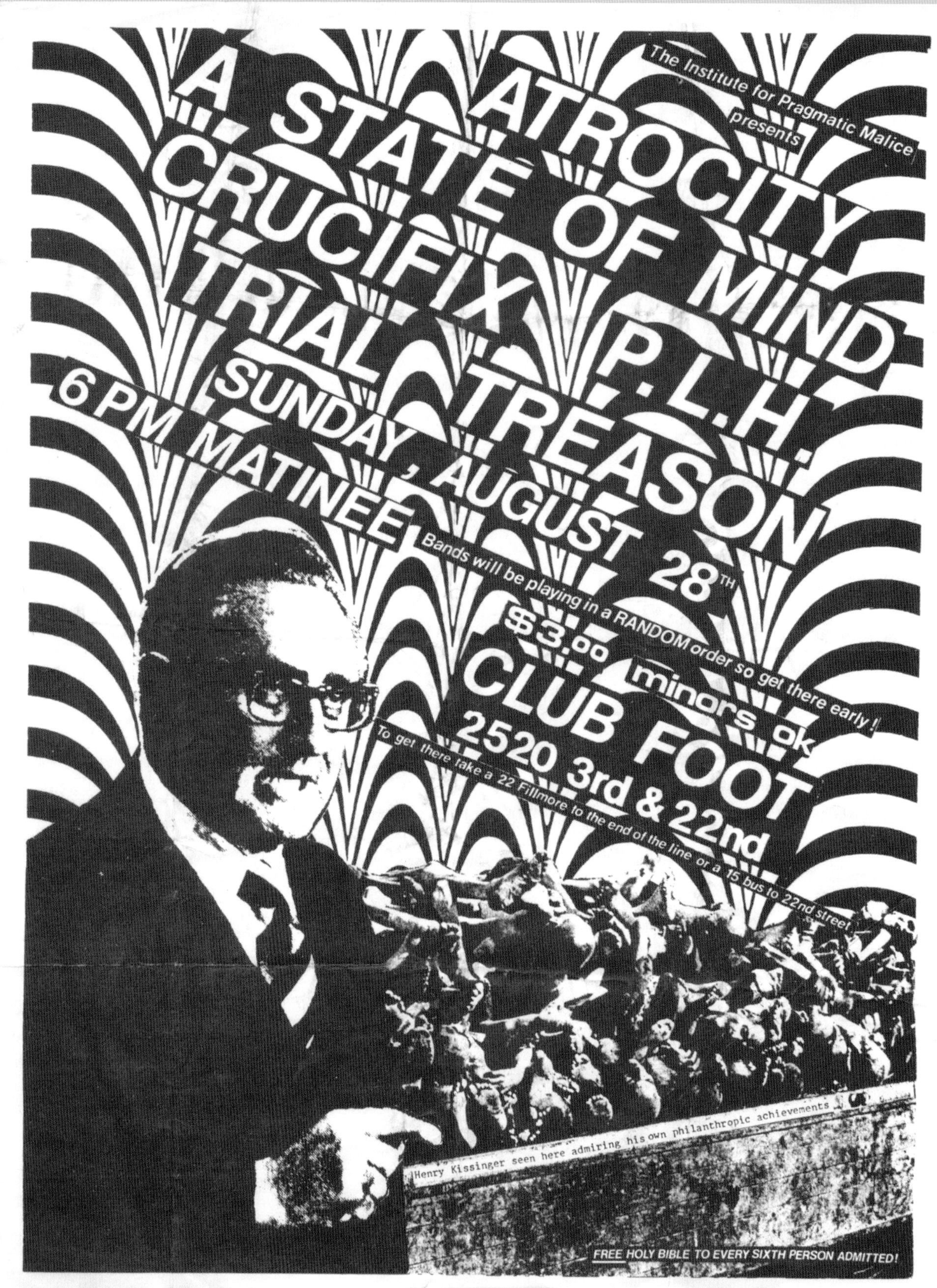

3.29. Flyer for show at Club Foot, San Francisco, 1982.

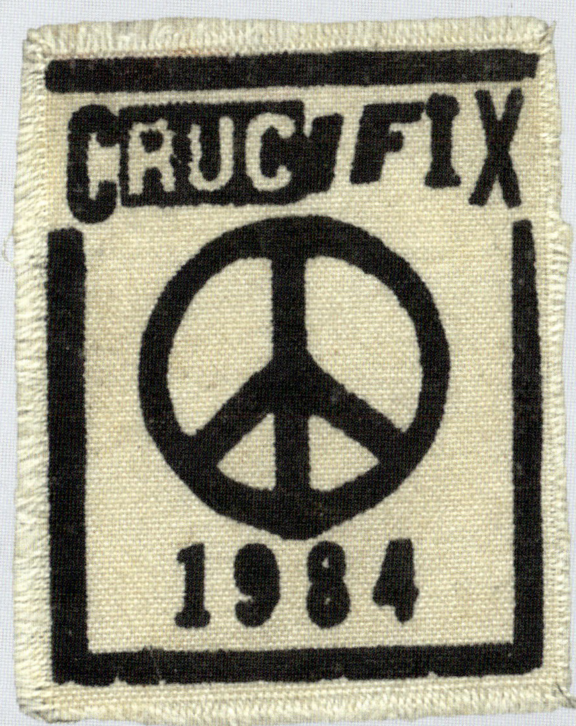

3.28. Cloth patch for Crucifix, 1984.

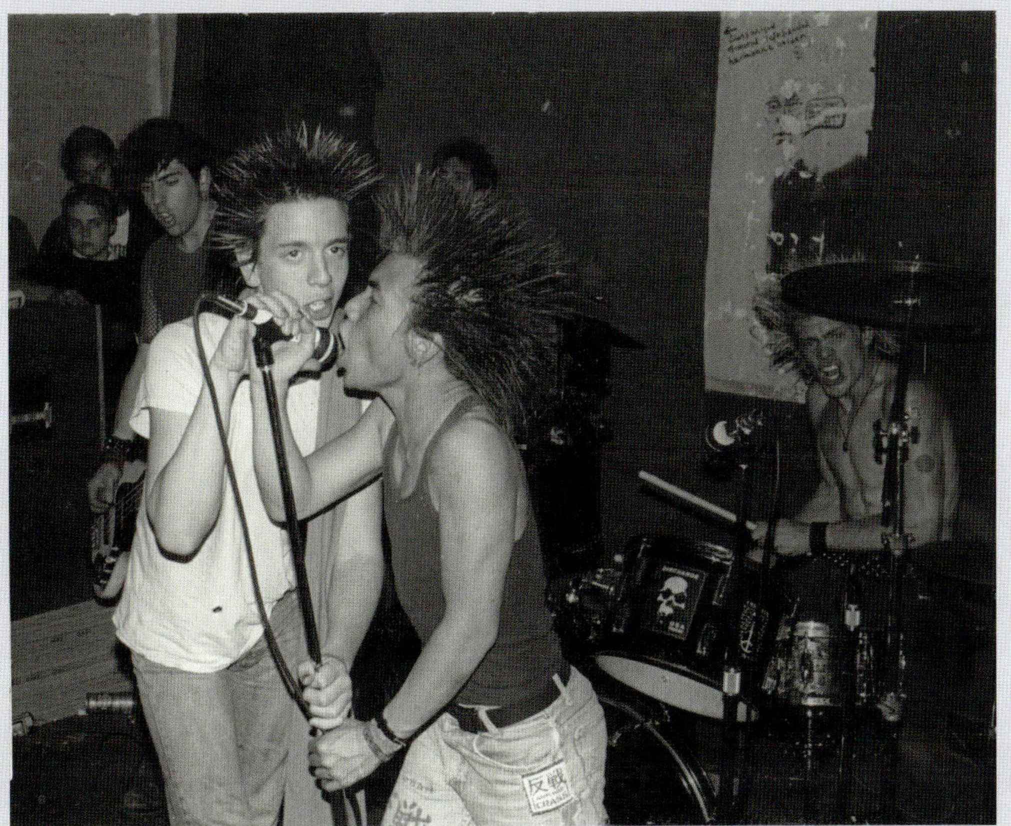

3.30. Crucifix, early 1980s. Photo: © Murray Bowles.

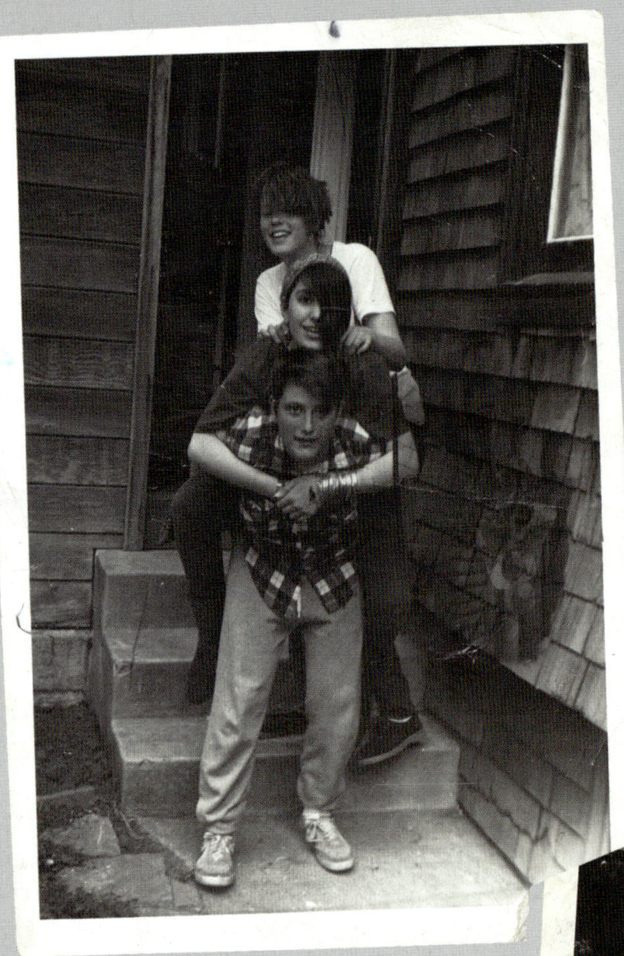

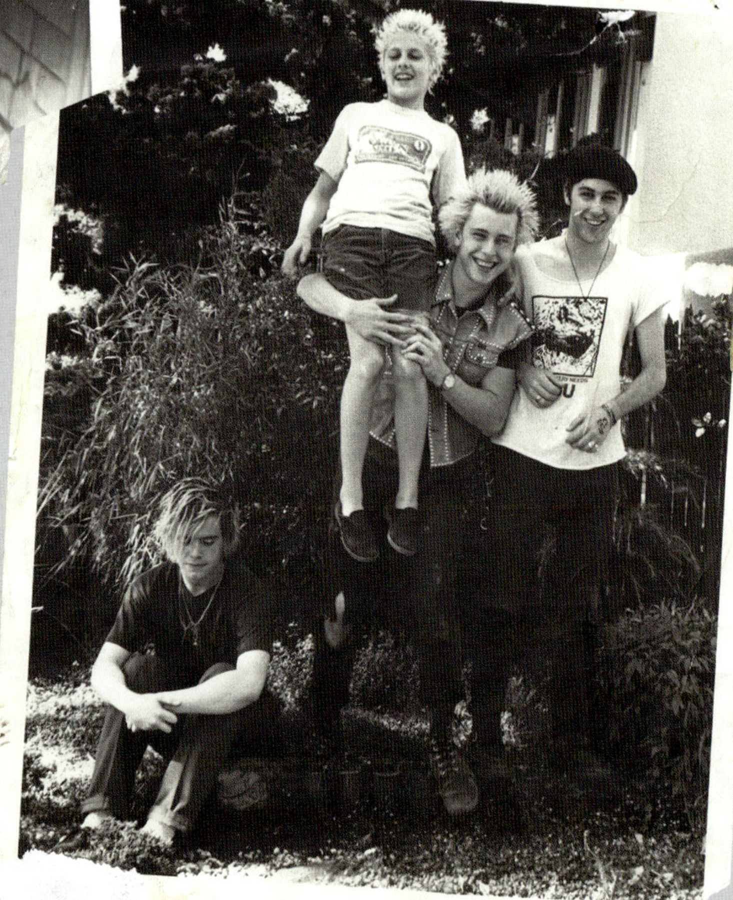

3.31. (*Above*) Atrocity, early 1980s.
Photo: Aaron Cometbus.

3.32. (*Right*) Trial, early 1980s.
Photo: Aaron Cometbus.

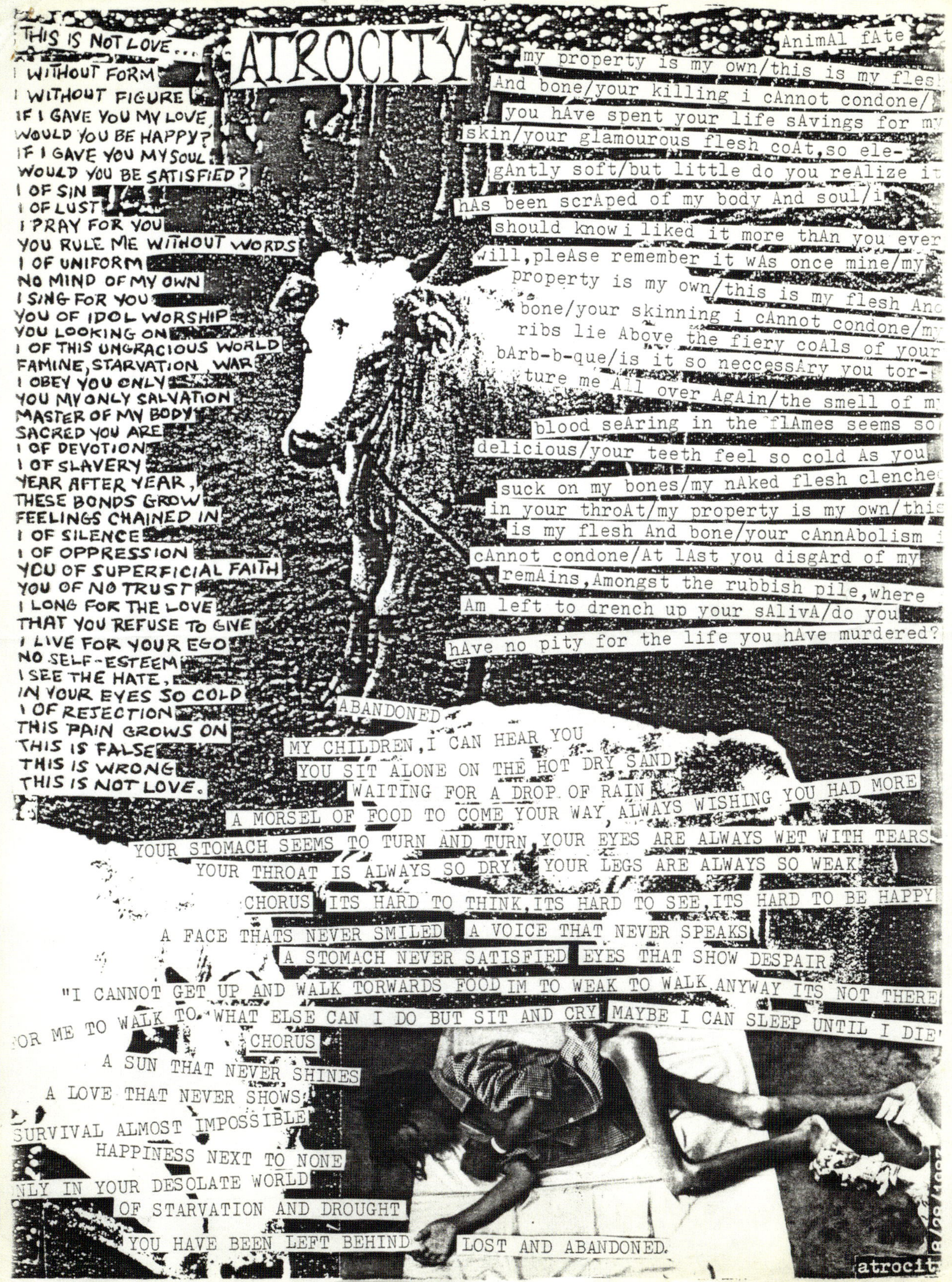

3.33. Atrocity lyric sheet, early 1980s.

anyway we just want the world to know that old dangerous rhythm is still the same as it"s always been except kevin and bill just bought three new couches since matt took the old couches away (matt is still around in his own ubiquitous way) we still have big rooms smiling engineers and the famous bathroom snare pounding away driving the guy upstairs crazy at two in the morning and also low rates (16 dollars an hour) special graveyard rates and day block-out rates and that same old crazy phone number(huh) (415)261-9150 so like let's all make some monsterous sounds and trash these couches so we have a good excuse for going to garage sales again

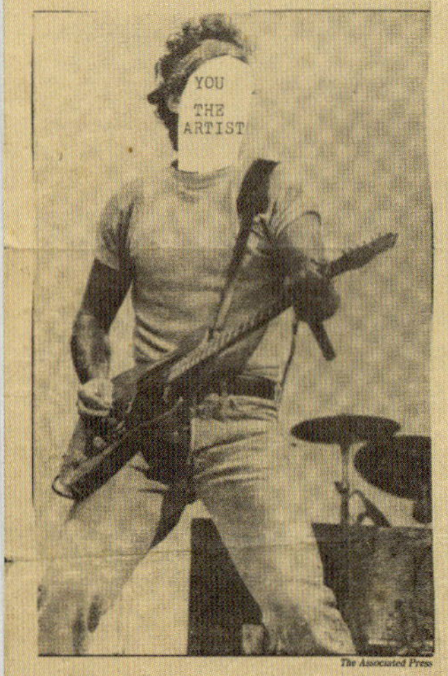

DANGEROUS
RHYTHM
8-TRACK
RECORDING
STUDIOS

WHERE YOU"RE THE BOSS

(415) 261-9150

Le boss

American rock star and famous newlywed You, The Artist performs for 60,000 French fans Saturday in the first of two concerts at La Courneuve ground north of Paris. You, The Artist are completing a tour of European cities.

3.34. Flyer for Dangerous Rhythm Recording Studios, Oakland, early 1980s. Many of the early East Bay punk bands recorded here.

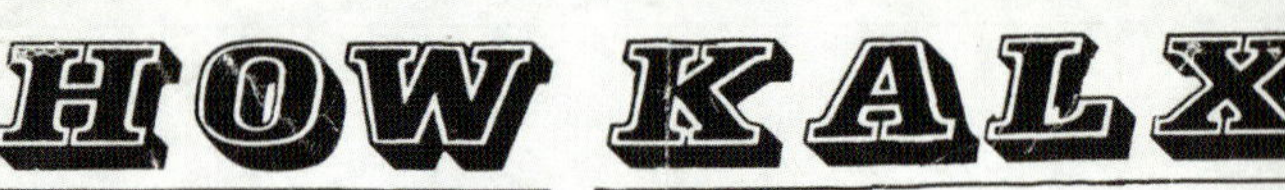

MADE A MAN
OUT OF
ME

ONE DAY....

HEY! QUIT KICKING THAT SAND IN OUR FACES!
THAT MAN IS THE WORST NUISANCE ON THE BEACH
LISTEN HERE, I'D SMASH YOUR FACE...ONLY YOU'RE SO SKINNY YOU MIGHT DRY UP AND BLOW AWAY.
THE BIG BULLY! I'LL GET EVEN SOME DAY
OH DON'T LET IT BOTHER YOU, LITTLE BOY!
DARN IT! I'M SICK AND TIRED OF BEING A SCARECROW! I'M GOING TO VOLUNTEER FOR KALX! THEY'LL KNOW HOW TO MAKE A REAL MAN OUT OF ME!
BOY! IT DIDN'T TAKE KALX LONG TO DO THIS FOR ME! WHAT MUSCLES! THAT BULLY WON'T SHOVE ME AROUND AGAIN!
THERE'S THAT BIG STIFF AGAIN SHOWING OFF IN FRONT OF GRACE AND THE CROWD. WELL IT'S MY TURN THIS TIME!
WHAM! - NOW IT'S YOUR TURN TO DRY UP AND BLOW AWAY!
OH MAC! YOU ARE A REAL MAN AFTER ALL!

MONEY BACK GUARANTEE.

IT WORKS!

RECRUITMENT MEETIN

ON-AIR TRAINING
NEWS
SPORTS
PUBLICITY
PUBLIC AFFAIRS

COME TO:
2311 BOWDITCH
7:30
TUES: SEPTEMBER 11, 1984

3.35. Flyer for KALX recruitment meeting, Berkeley, 1984.

BIKO PLAZA NEWS

VOL 2. NO23 BERKELEY, CALIFORNIA FRI. SEP. 6, 1985

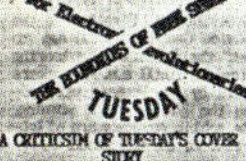

A CRITICISM OF TUESDAY'S COVER STORY

BAD JOURNALISM, RIGHT-ON POLITICS

by Steve Masover

The front cover of Tuesday's BPN featured a diagram of a 'timing device' for igniting outdoor barbecues and, I am afraid, 'Molotov Cocktails.'

We have subsequently learned that this 'timing device' is sound-sensitive, and is therefore a bad choice for anyone interested in a time-delay fuse. For the BPN to have printed such instructions was, to say the very least, irresponsible to our readership.

But aside from techical considerations, printing the timer instructions was a foolish thing to do. Many campus activists have told us so, for a variety of reasons. Those reasons range from 'bad tactics' to 'you'll alienate the moderate/pacifist elements of your readership.'

Printing the instructions was certainly bad tactics. Anybody who wants to build a timing device can figure out how to do so for him/herself. The placement of the instructions — which were lousy instructions to begin with — was itself inflammatory (pardon the pun), and the information serves no useful purpose to the advancement of left/progressive politics on the Berkeley campus. If the purpose of the BPN is to get students to plug into campus activism, Tuesday's front page was a big step backwards.

But it is important to acknowledge, despite the serious errors in judgement that went into the 'timer' cover, that the political motive that inspired the article's inclusion is perfectly valid, and requires serious consideration.

One of the BPN staff, responding to one campus activist's criticism that the article would alienate pacifists who have participated in recent activity, said that it is more than a little hypocritical for us (leftists in

(cont. on p. 5)

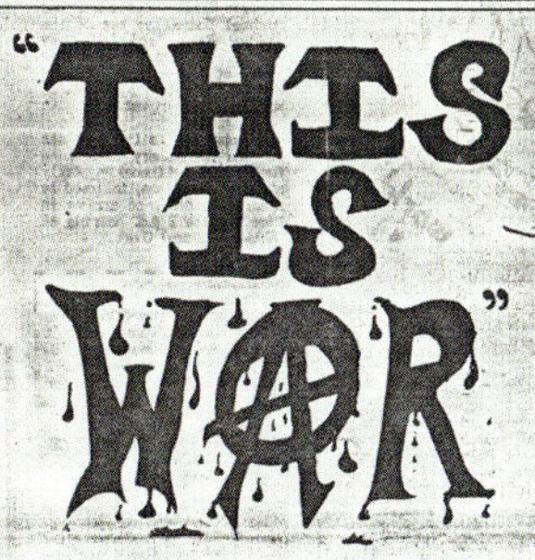

Asst. D.A. Nancy O'Malley to David Lukas' Lawyer.

IN MEMORIUM: FREDY PERLMAN

I want to tell youabout a friend of mine named Fredy Perlman. I found out yesterday that he died in Detroit on July 26, about one month shy of his 51st birthday.

All of you who care about making the world a better place should know about him. He was a very unusual person, with great intelligence and great integrity, and a sense of humor. Luckily he wrote a fair amount and left behind a lot of stuff for the rest of us to think about and act on.

He was born in Czechoslovakia in 1934. His family escaped to Bolivia in 1938 and when he was eleven, they moved to the U.S.A. I remember him saying that he grew up with the Indians in Bolivia and not here in this country. It was very important to him. He lived in many places and went to all different kinds of schools.

(cont. on p. 6)

Affirmative Action

(from Disorientation)

by Pedro Noguera

In order to understand why affirmative action programs exist and why they fail to address the denial of access to higher education for Third World people, we must first understand how they came into being.

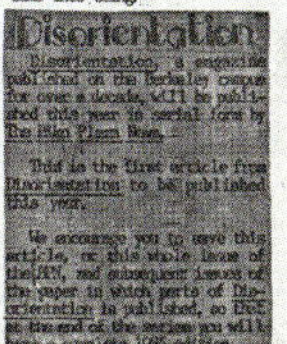

It may come as a surprise to some, but people of color did not suddently gain the intelligence to succeed in American colleges in 1965. Prior to that time, American-styled apartheid kept all ethnic minorities out of higher education except for the priviliged and fortunate. What opened the doors in 1965 was the protests of the Civil Rights Movement and the massive uprisings which took place in several American cities.

The doors were opened reluctantly, sometimes only under the pressure o' the national guard. Slowly, B' acks, Latinos, Asians and Nativ. Americans were being admitted and integrated into American universities. During the late sixties and early seventies, the pioneering Third World college students militantly demanded their confirmed right to an education, and the creation of academic programs consisting of multi-disciplinary approaches to the study of their cultures.

(cont. on p. 4)

3.36. *Biko Plaza News* vol. 2, no. 23, September 6, 1985. The *Biko Plaza News* was distributed during the antiapartheid occupation of UC Berkeley when protesters renamed the university's Sproul Plaza "Biko Plaza" in honor of slain South African anti-apartheid activist Steve Biko.

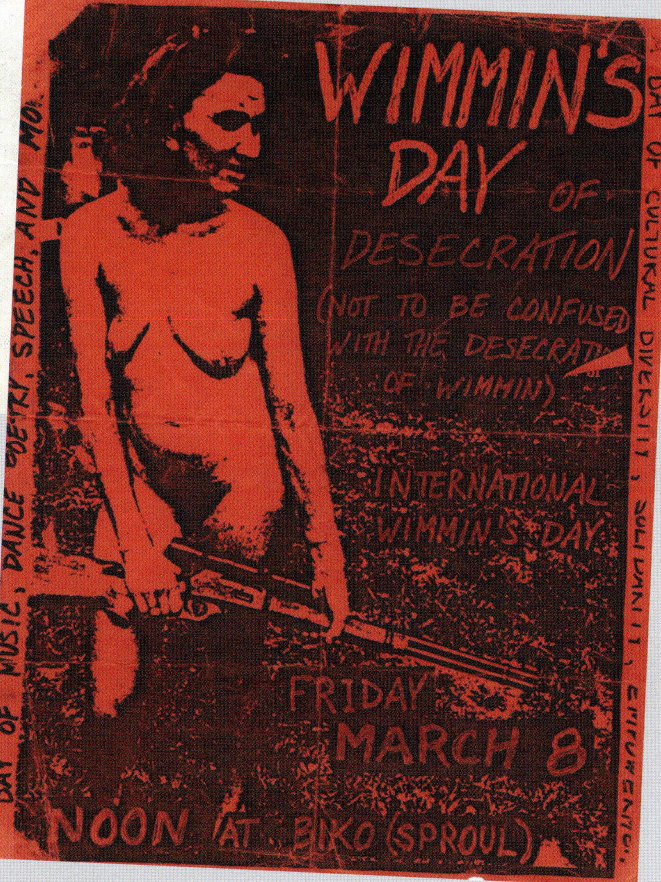

3.37. Flyer for International Wimmin's Day rally at Biko (Sproul) plaza on the UC Berkeley campus, March 1985.

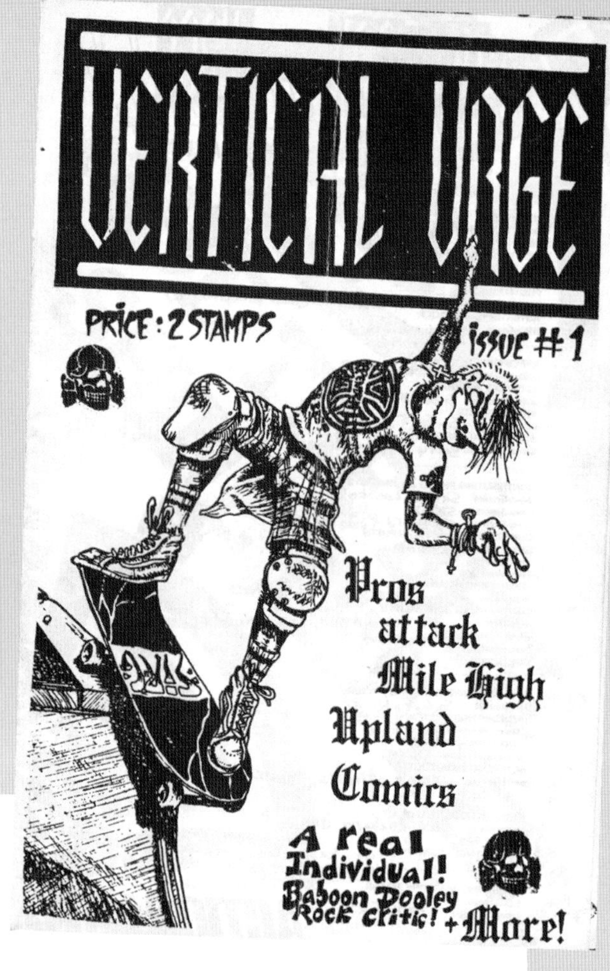

3.38. (*Right*) *Vertical Urge* no. 1, 1985.

3.39. (*Below*) Sluglords at People's Park, circa 1984. Photo: © Murray Bowles.

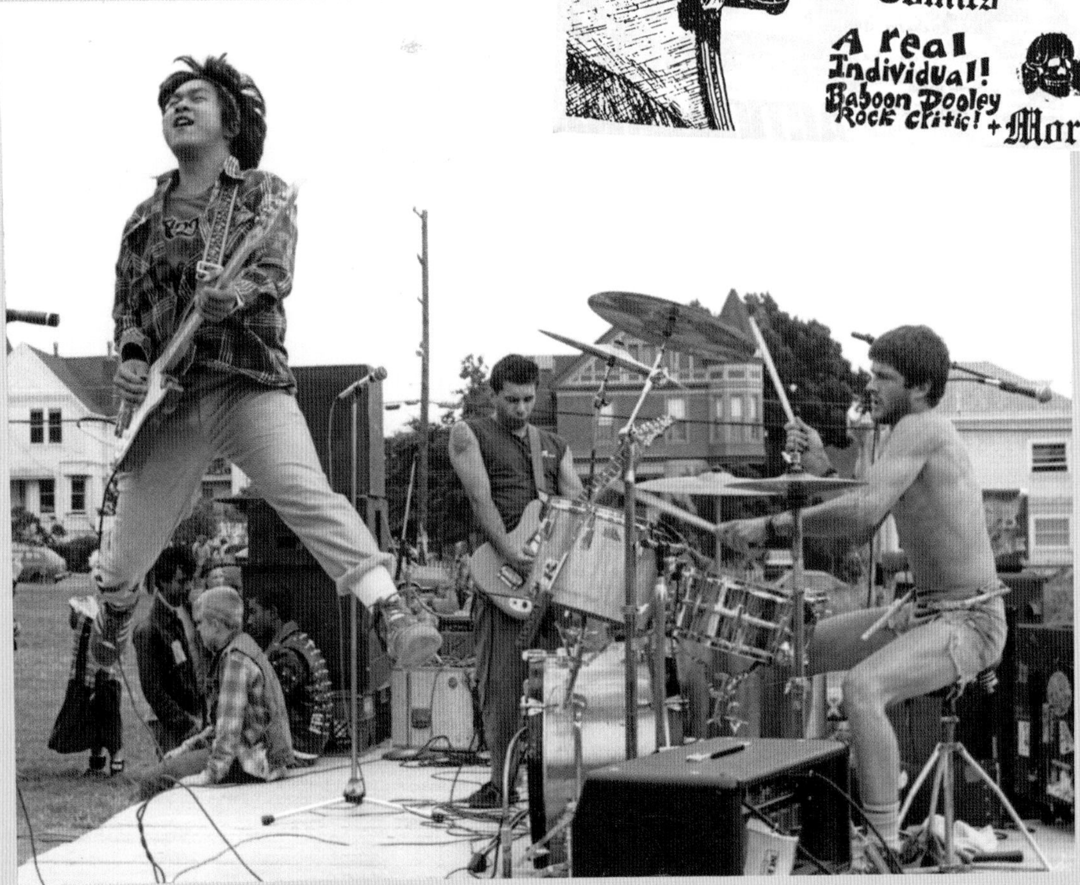

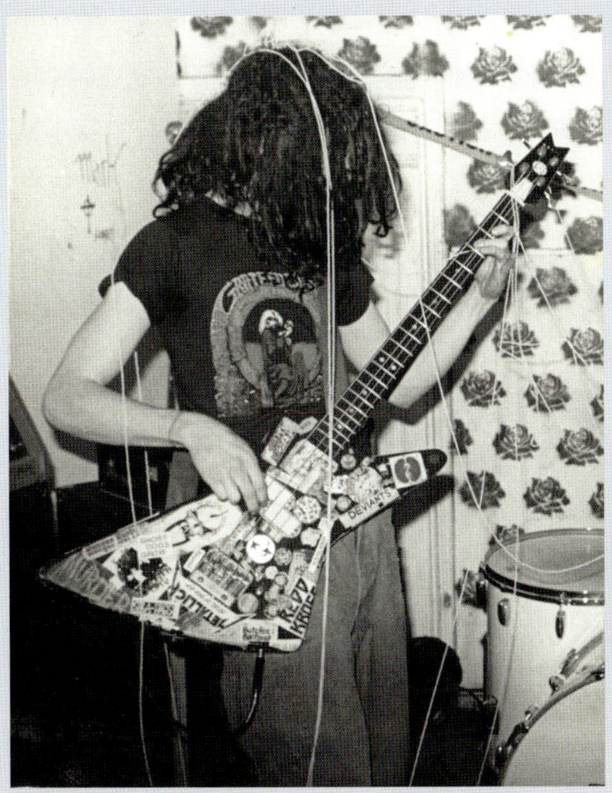

3.40. Larry Boothroyd from Victims Family at Club Foot, San Francisco, 1985. Photo: © Murray Bowles.

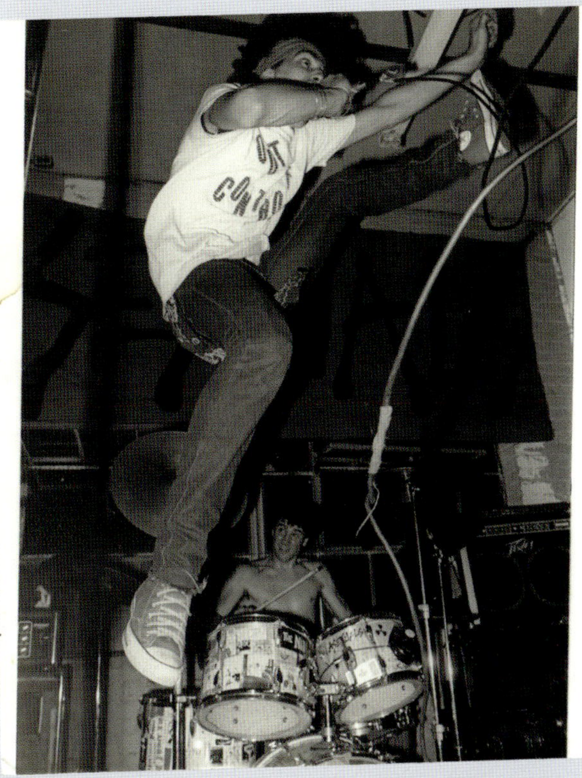

3.42. Asexuals at New Method, Emeryville, 1986. Photo: © Murray Bowles.

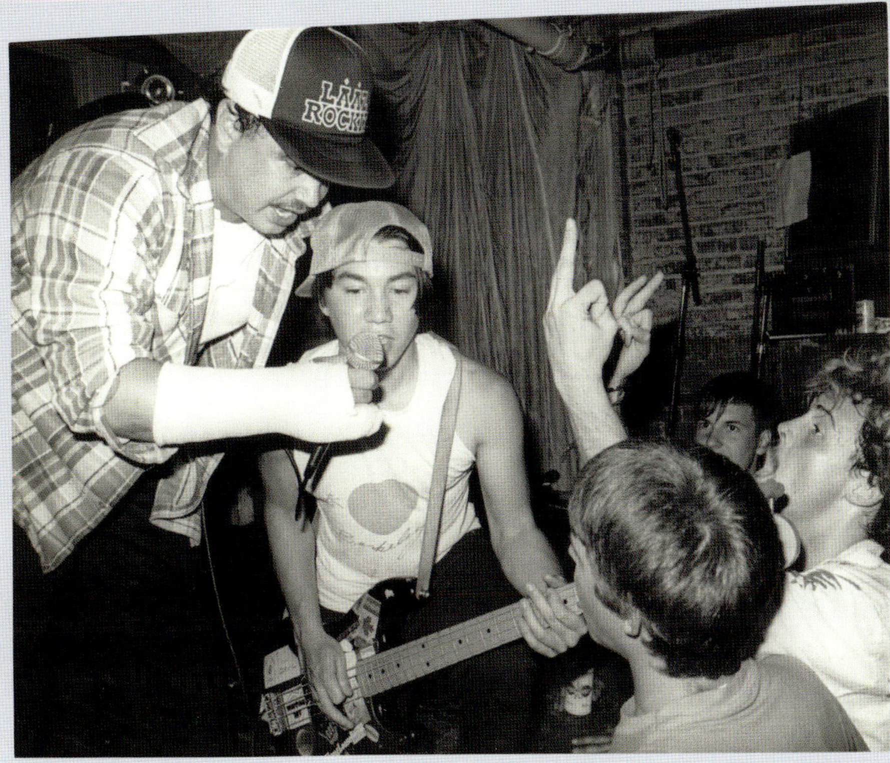

3.43. Max Fox and Troy Takaki of the Boneless Ones at Ruthie's Inn, Berkeley, circa 1986. Photo: © Murray Bowles.

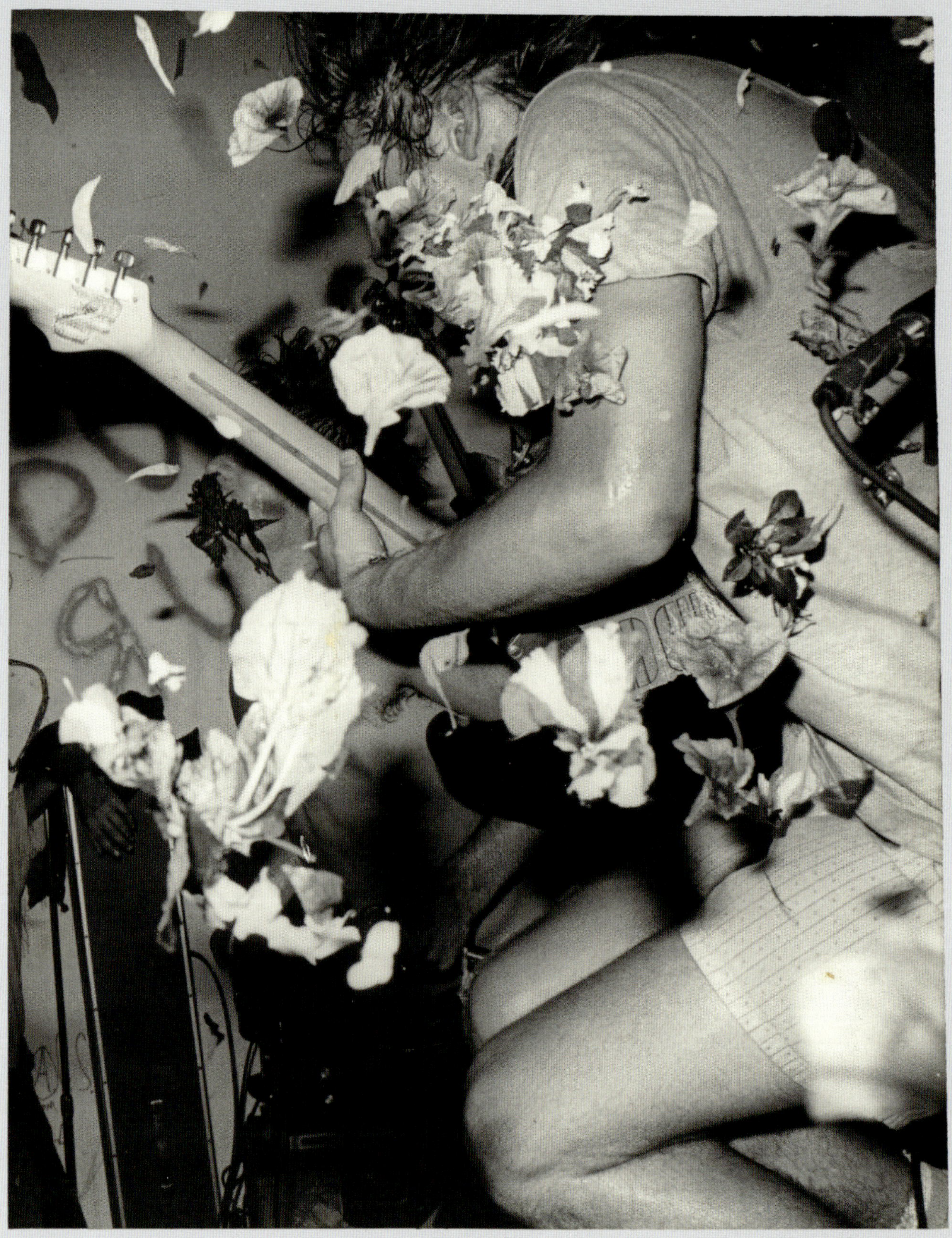

3.41. Short Dogs Grow at Club Foot, San Francisco, 1986. Photo: © Murray Bowles.

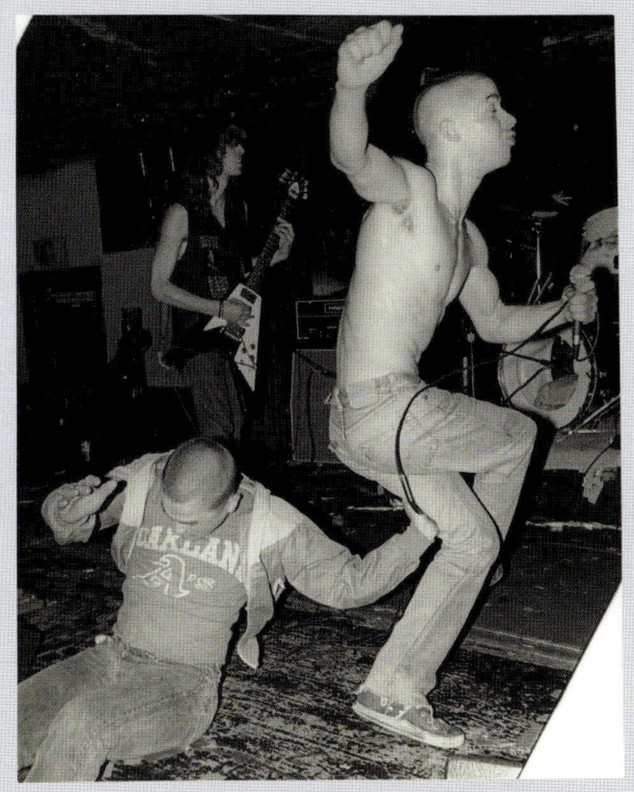

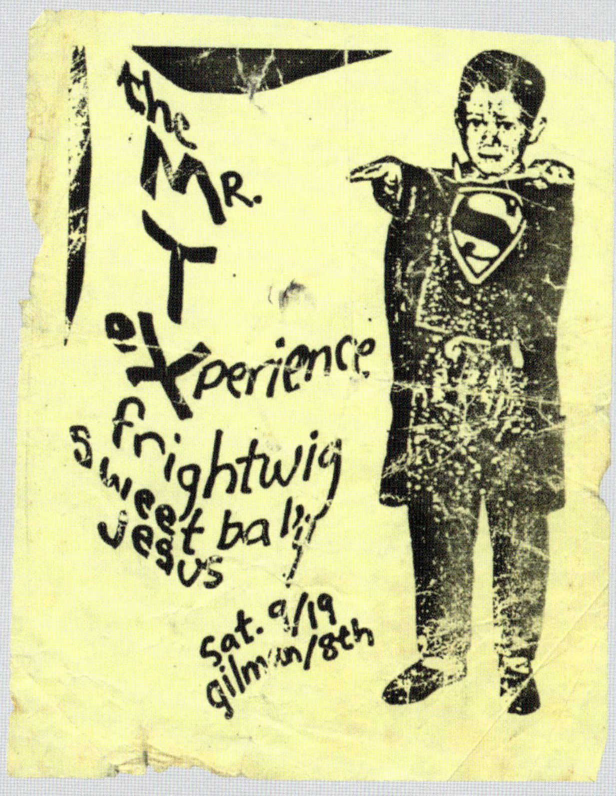

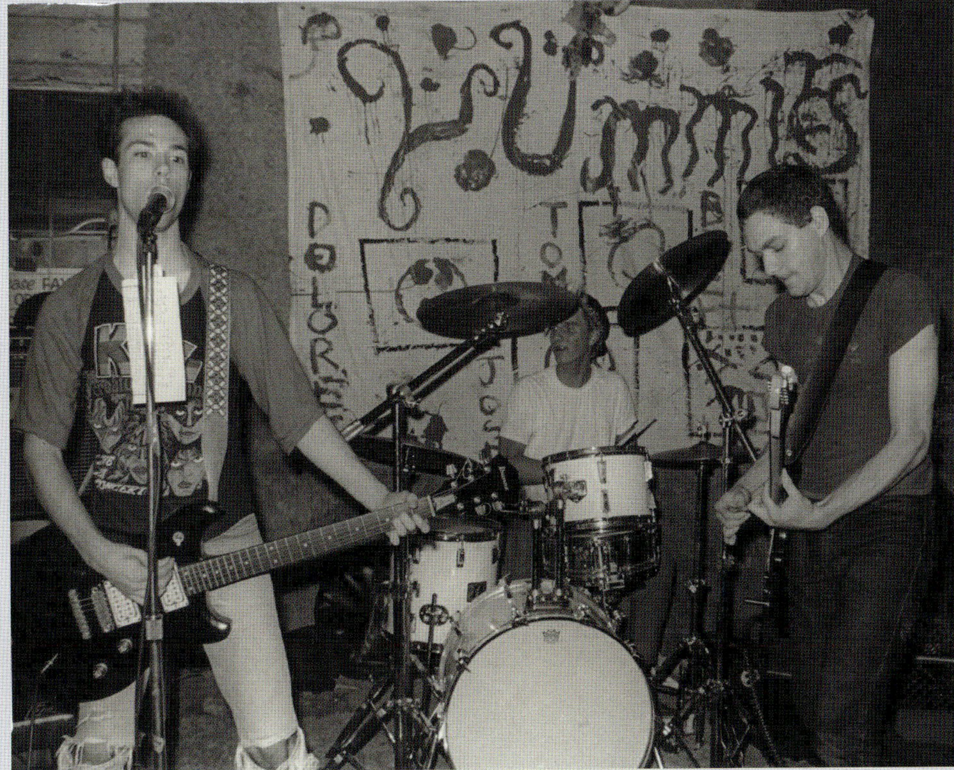

3.44. (*Above left*) Death From Above, circa 1986. Photo: © Murray Bowles.

3.45. (*Above right*) Flyer for the Mr. T Experience, Frightwig, and Sweet Baby Jesus show at Gilman, Berkeley, September 1987.

3.46. (*Left*) The Mr. T Experience at New Method, Emeryville, late 1980s. Photo: © Murray Bowles.

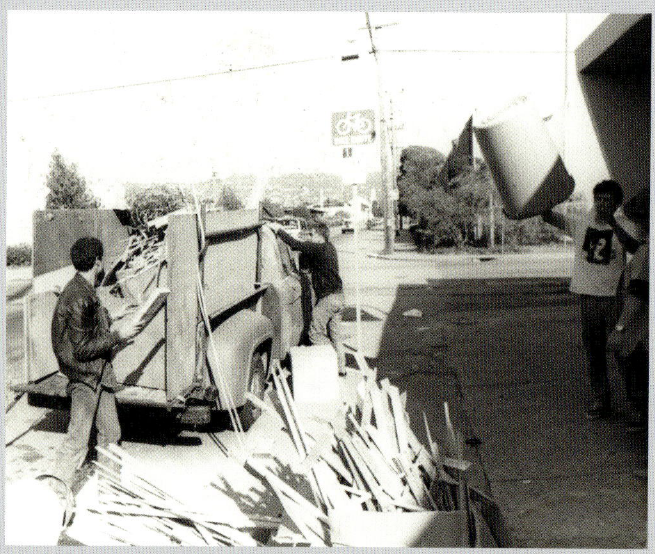

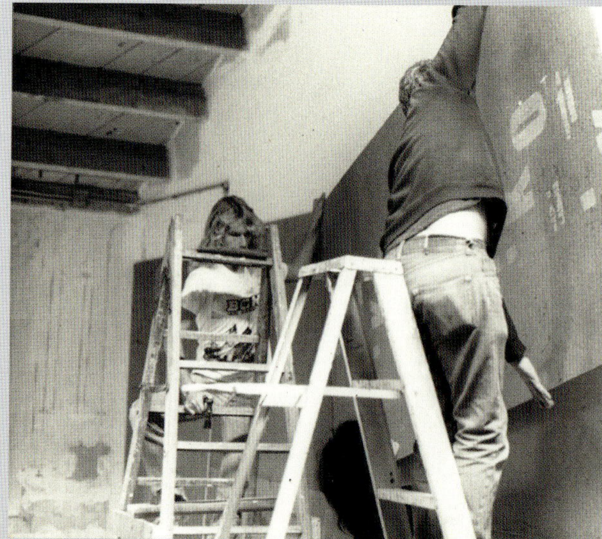

3.47 and 3.48. Photographs of the early construction of the Gilman Street Project at 924 Gilman Street, Berkeley. Photo: © Murray Bowles.

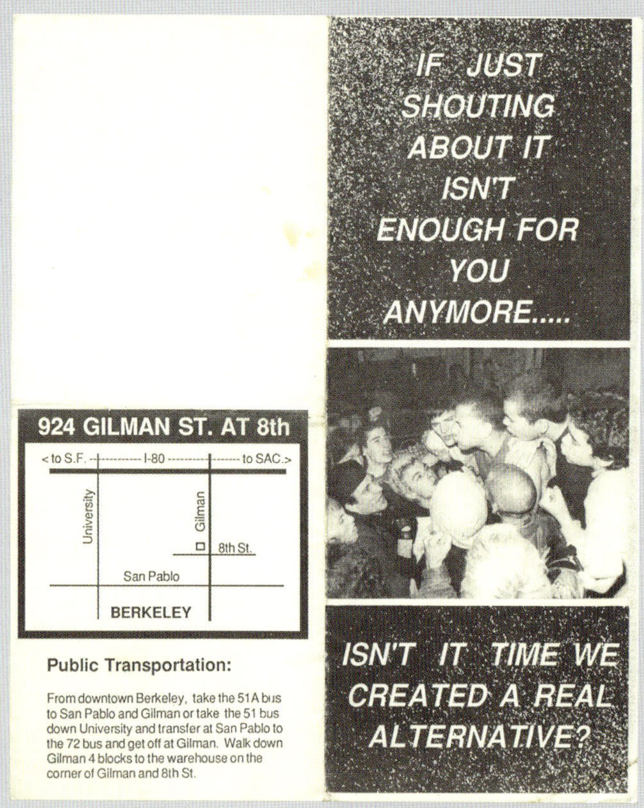

3.49. Flyer announcing the Gilman Street Project, Berkeley. Printed by Mike Miro, late 1986.

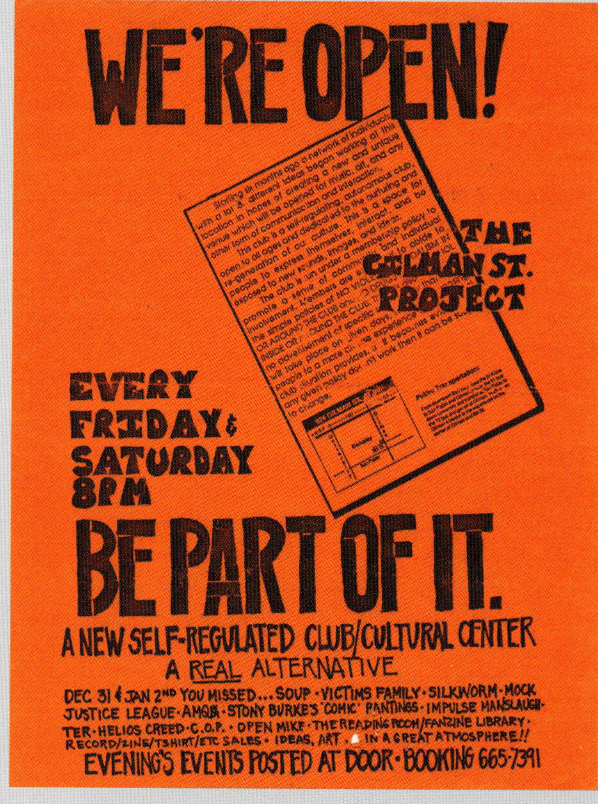

3.50. Flyer for opening of the Gilman Street Project, Berkeley, 1987.

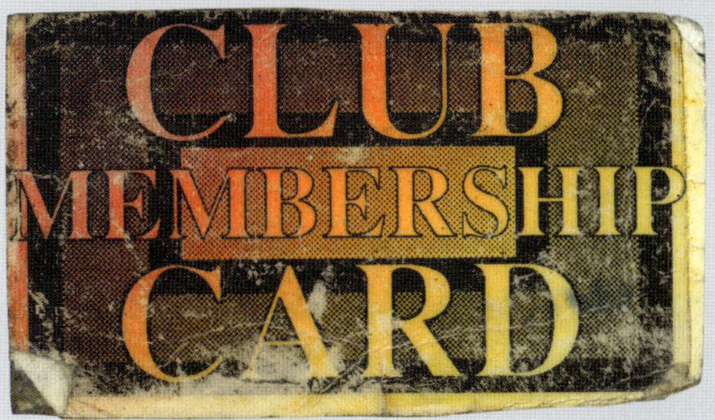

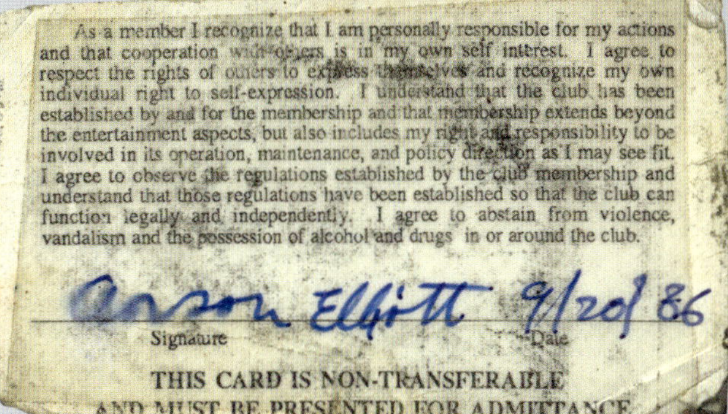
As a member I recognize that I am personally responsible for my actions and that cooperation with others is in my own self interest. I agree to respect the rights of others to express themselves and recognize my own individual right to self-expression. I understand that the club has been established by and for the membership and that membership extends beyond the entertainment aspects, but also includes my right and responsibility to be involved in its operation, maintenance, and policy direction as I may see fit. I agree to observe the regulations established by the club membership and understand that those regulations have been established so that the club can function legally and independently. I agree to abstain from violence, vandalism and the possession of alcohol and drugs in or around the club.

Aaron Elliott 9/20/86

Signature Date

THIS CARD IS NON-TRANSFERABLE
AND MUST BE PRESENTED FOR ADMITTANCE

3.51 and 3.52. Front and back of Gilman membership card from 1986, signed by Aaron Elliott (aka Aaron Cometbus) in August 1986. The date shows that members gathered at the club months before it opened for performances.

924 GILMAN STREET

TRIAL MEMBERSHIP CARD

This card is proof of membership in 924 Gilman St. Membership is required for admission to all events. Members agree to follow all rules of the club including: No drinking, drug use, or vandalism in or around the club, and no stagediving or excessively violent dancing during the show. Membership is yearly, except for one night only trial memberships (which is what you have if you have one of these cards), and non transferable. 924 Gilman street is based on the fact that bands, audience and staff are all equally important to the success of a show, and this card is warrant to the role of audience. For show info, call (510) 525-9926. 924 Gilman is an all ages volunteer corporation. *THIS CARD IS A TEMPORARY, TRIAL, MEMBERSHIP CARD, GOOD ON THE DAY ISSUED ONLY. IT ENTITLES YOU TO FULL MEMBERSHIP PRIVILEGES FOR THAT DAY ONLY.*
We hope you like what you see enough to come back, and get a full year membership card. Have a good time.

3.53. Gilman one-day membership card.

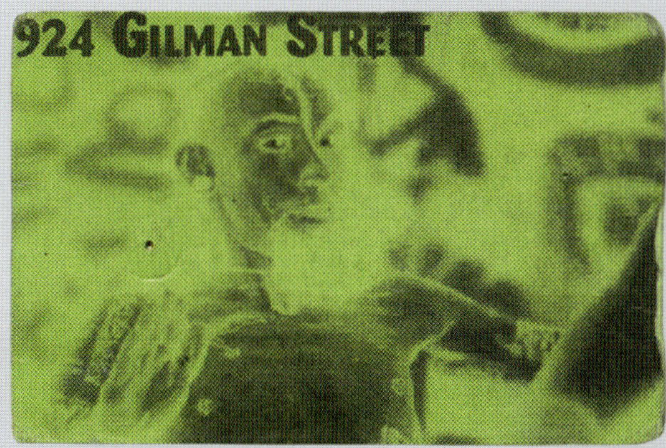

3.54. Gilman membership card from 1994 to 1996.

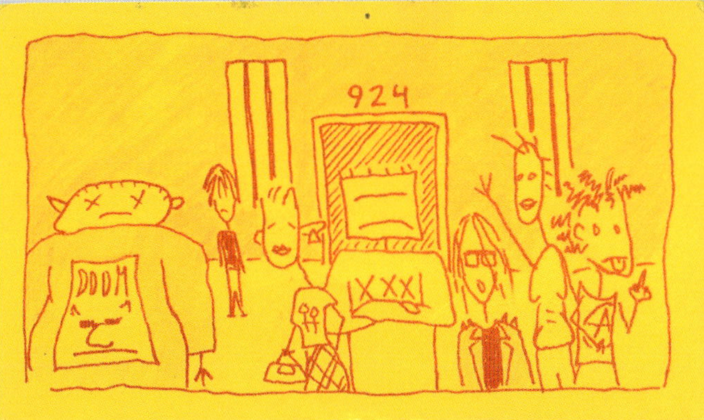

3.55. Gilman membership card from 2002 to 2004.

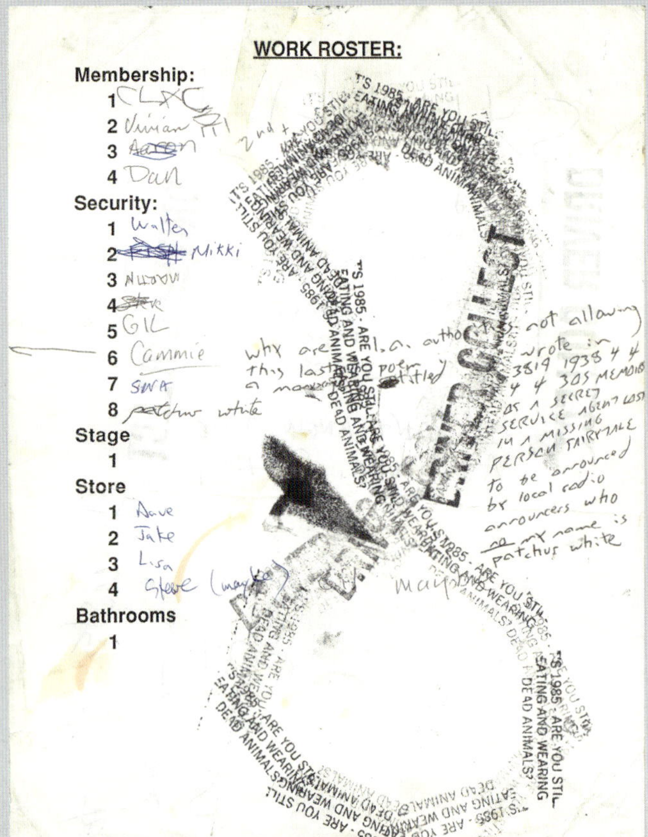

3.56. Gilman volunteer sign-up list, circa 1987.

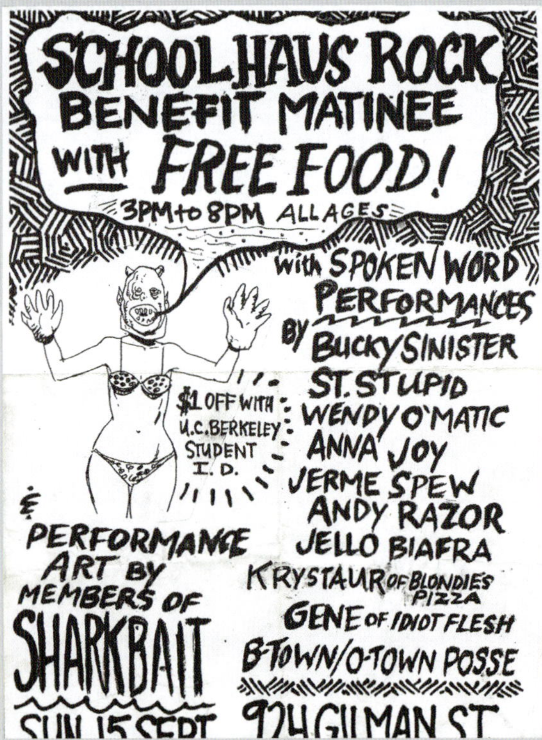

3.57. Flyer for benefit poetry reading and performance art show at Gilman, Berkeley, 1991.

3.58. Flyer for a rummage sale at Gilman, Berkeley, 1993.

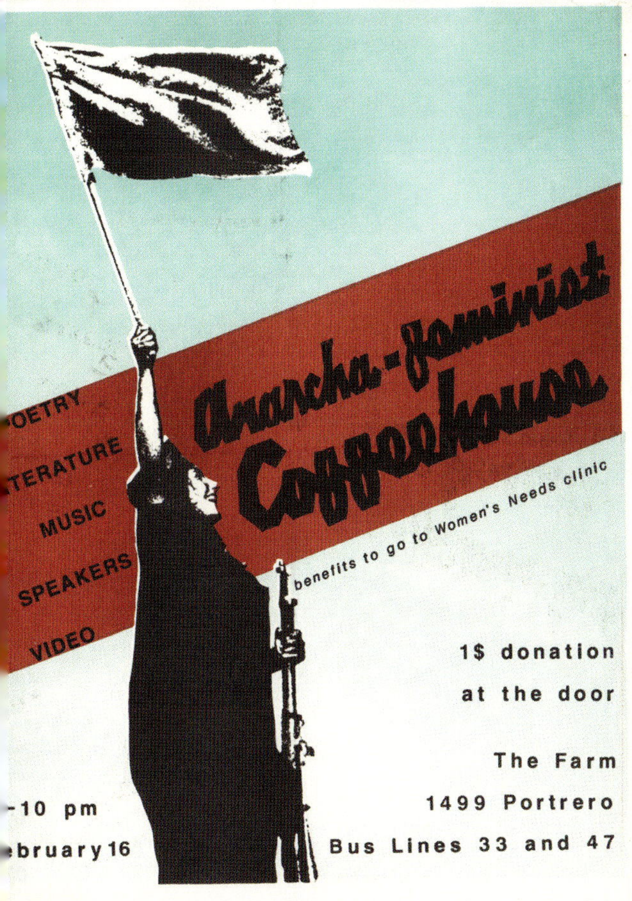

3.59. Flyer for event at the Farm, San Francisco, mid-1980s.

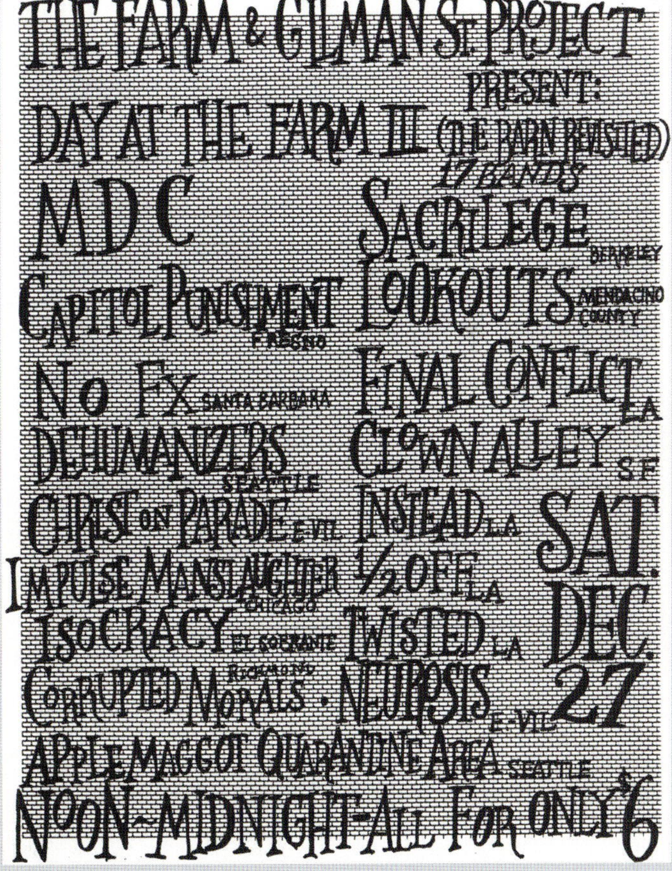

3.60. Flyer for a collaboration show between Gilman in Berkeley and the Farm in San Francisco, 1986

THE GILMAN STREET PROJECT CALENDER
MAY '87

FRI.	SAT.	SUN.
9PM FRI. 1 — "HORROR SHOW" LETHAL GOSPEL (COME EARLY!), TIMES², SID TERROR & THE UNDEAD, CELEBRITY SKIN, plus HORROR/SCI-FI MOVIE TRAILERS & FILM CLIPS — $4	9PM SAT. 2 — BLAST!, NOMEANSNO CANADA, MR. T EXPERIENCE, PRIMAL SCREAM, UNIT PRIDE — $5	
9PM FRI. 8 — BWANA DEVILS, ESKIMO, SICK TO DEATH OREGON, PLUS SPECIAL GUESTS T.B.A. — $4	9PM SAT. 9 — SOCIAL UNREST, SWEET BABY JESUS, ANGST, I AM THE HAMSTER L.A., VIOLATION — $5	6PM SUN. 10 — RUBELLA BALLET U.K., LAST STAND BOSTON, ISOCRACY, EL SOBRANTE, BRAIN RUST — $4
9PM FRI. 15 — SCHRÖDINGERS CAT, GORK, AKOUSMA SANTA CRUZ, THE WEB, plus PERFORMANCE and/or SLIDE SHOW BY: HYENA CABARET — $4	9PM SAT. 16 — FRIGHTWIG, BULIMIA BANQUET L.A., DIDJITS ILLINOIS, NATION ON FIRE MONTEREY, PSA — $5	6PM SUN. 17 — BENEFIT for "DIET FOR A SMALL PLANET" with: M.D.C., OPERATION IVY, GANGREEN — $4
9PM FRI. 22 — FREE FALL NOW, ACID RAIN, "FLIGHT NIGHT" participatory visionary experience, "BRING BACK THE 90'S" — $4	9PM SAT. 23 — RUIN PHILADELPHIA, FINAL CONFLICT L.A., CONDEMNED ATTITUDE, FREESINGER BAND, NO DOGS — $5	6PM SUN. 24 — "COMPOSERS CAFETERIA" — $4
9PM FRI. 29 — OPHELIAS, TYPHOON, CHILD SUPPORT SOCIAL CLUB, plus HORROR/SCI-FI FILM CLIPS & MOVIE TRAILERS — $4	9PM SAT. 30 — CAPITOL PUNISHMENT, T.B.A., CRIMPSHRINE, ASSASSINS OF GOD, SMA — $5	6PM SUN. 31 — BENEFIT for ANIMAL LIBERATION FRONT, CHRIST ON PARADE, Ⓐ STATE of MIND, CAROLINER, CONDEMNED ATTITUDE, TOTENTAN — $5

924 GILMAN ST. AT 8TH IN BERKELEY - $2 LIFETIME MEMBERSHIP FEE

3.61. Calendar for Gilman, Berkeley, May 1987.

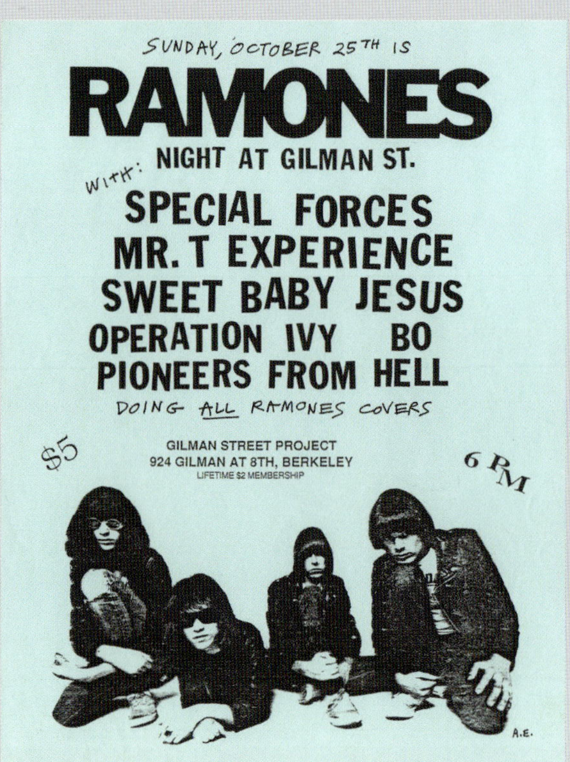

3.62. Flyer for Ramones tribute show at Gilman, Berkeley, 1987.

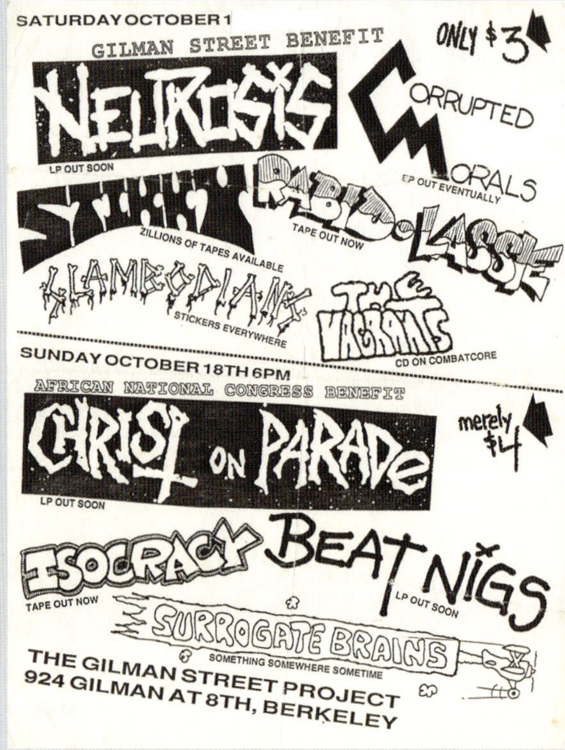

3.63. Flyer for Gilman and African National Congress benefit shows at Gilman, Berkeley October 1987.

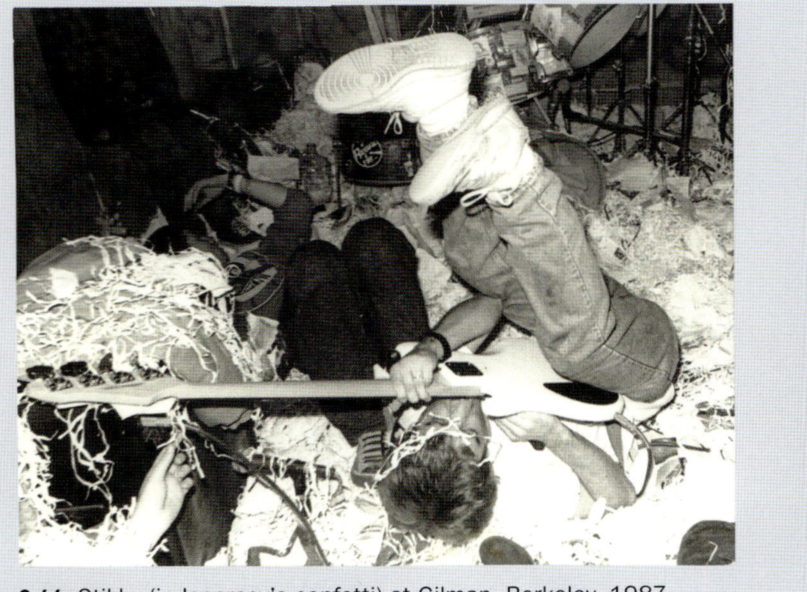

3.64. Stikky (in Isocracy's confetti) at Gilman, Berkeley, 1987. Photo: © Murray Bowles.

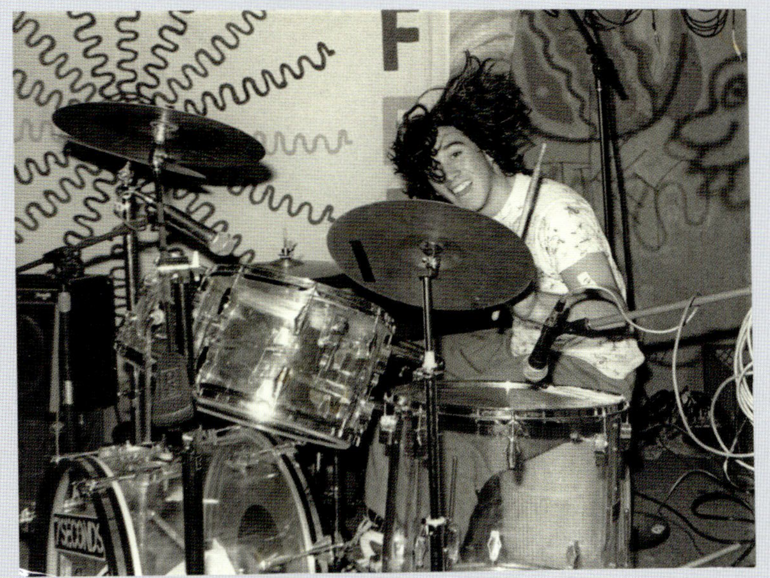

3.65. Empty Offer at Gilman, Berkeley, 1987. Photo: © Murray Bowles.

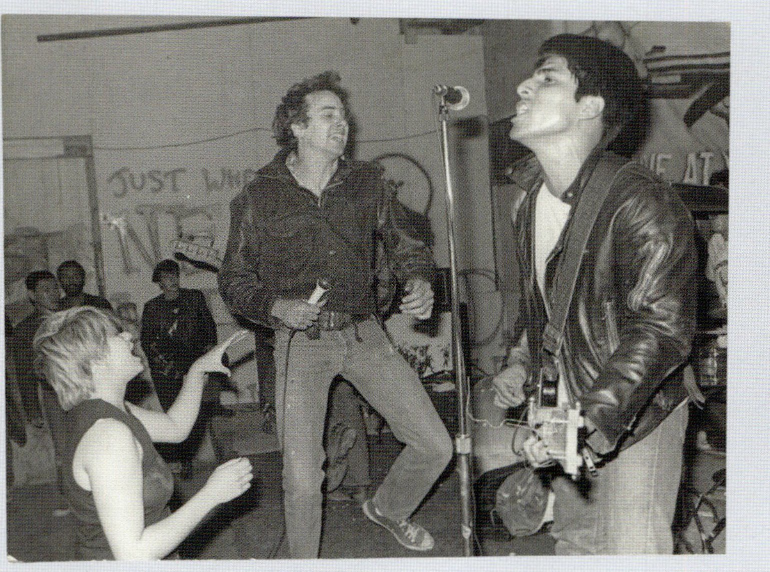

3.66. Detonators at Gilman (Kamala Parks in the audience), Berkeley, 1987. Photo: © Murray Bowles.

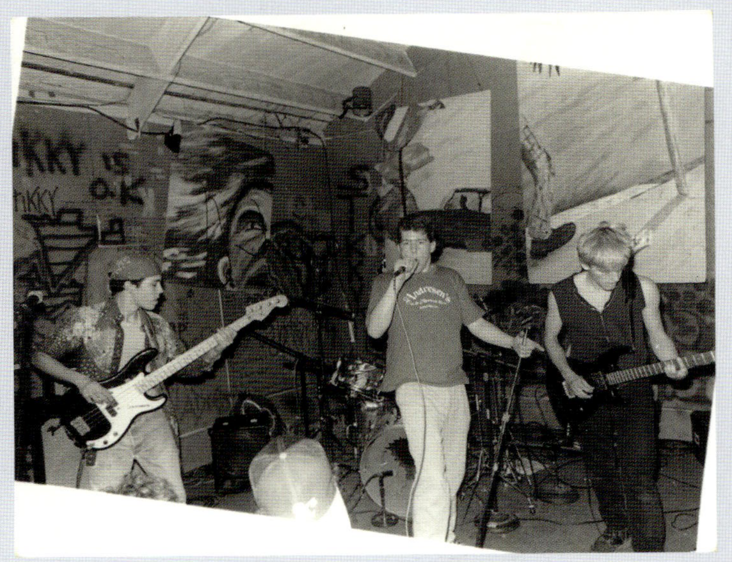

3.67. Trap A Poodle at Gilman, Berkeley, 1987. Photo: © Murray Bowles.

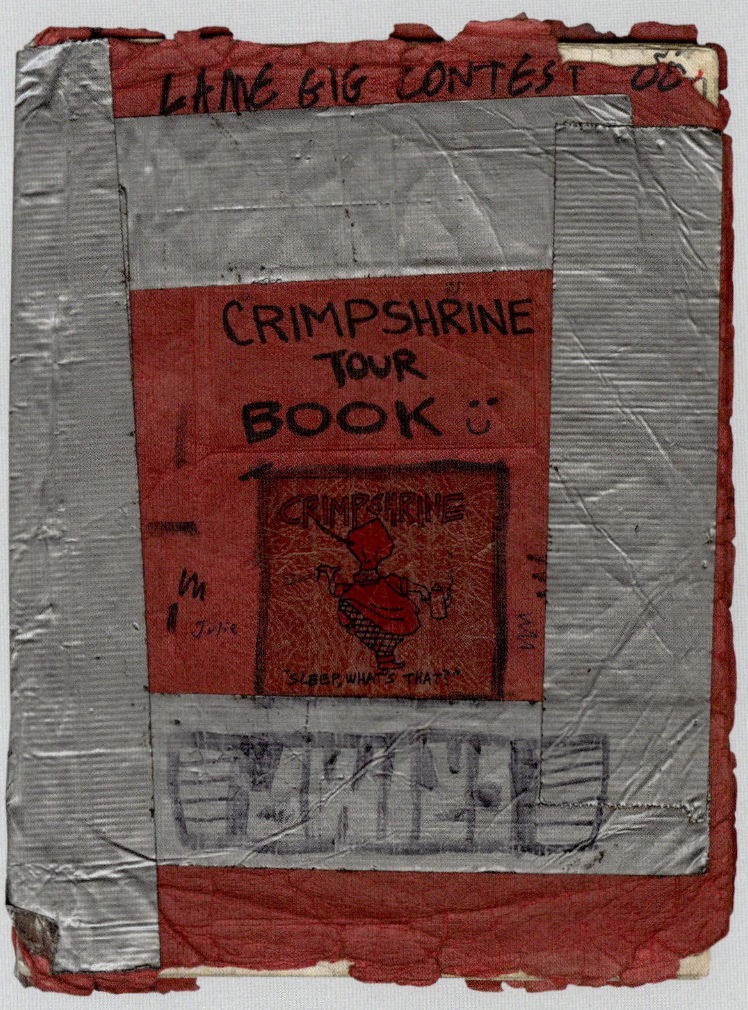

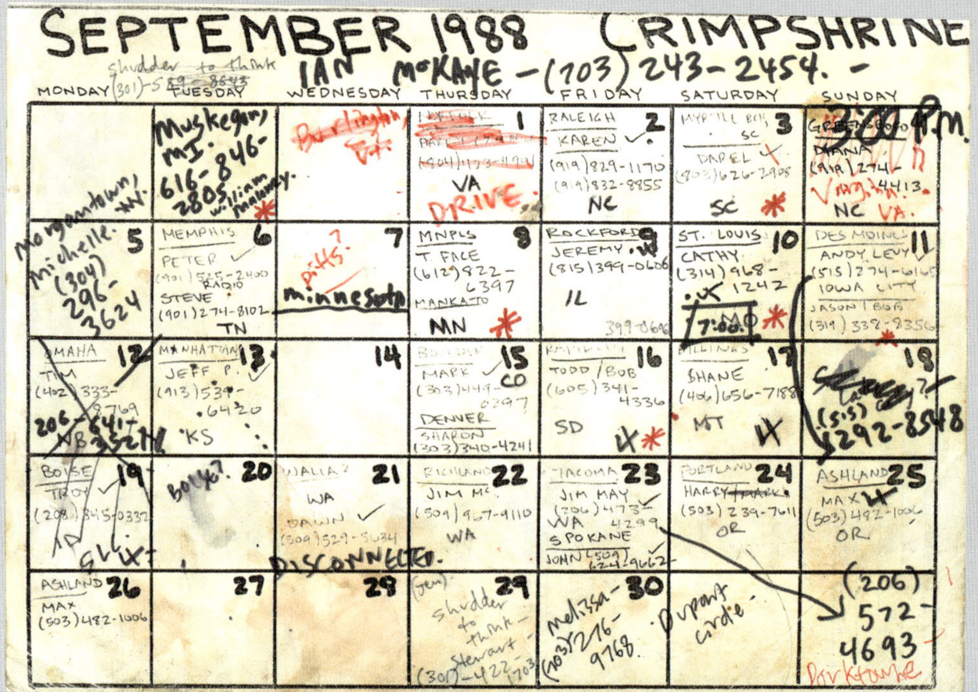

3.68 and 3.69.
Cover and inside page from Crimpshrine tour book, 1988.

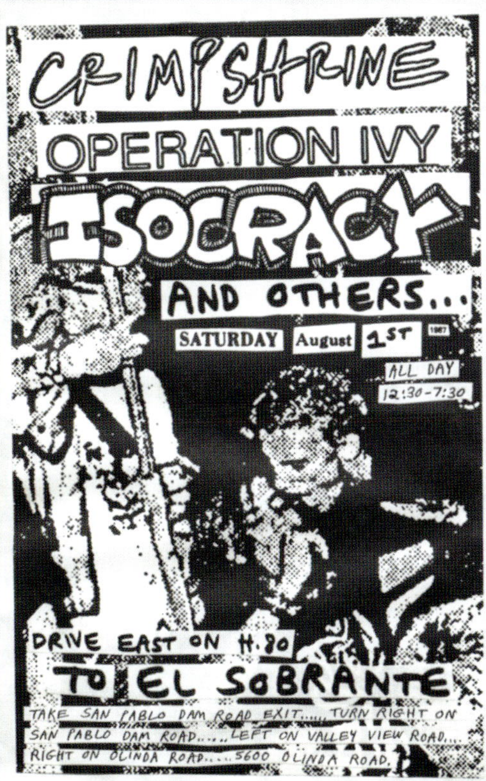

3.70. Flyer for Crimpshrine, Operation Ivy, and Isocracy show in El Sobrante, California, 1987. Design: Aaron Cometbus.

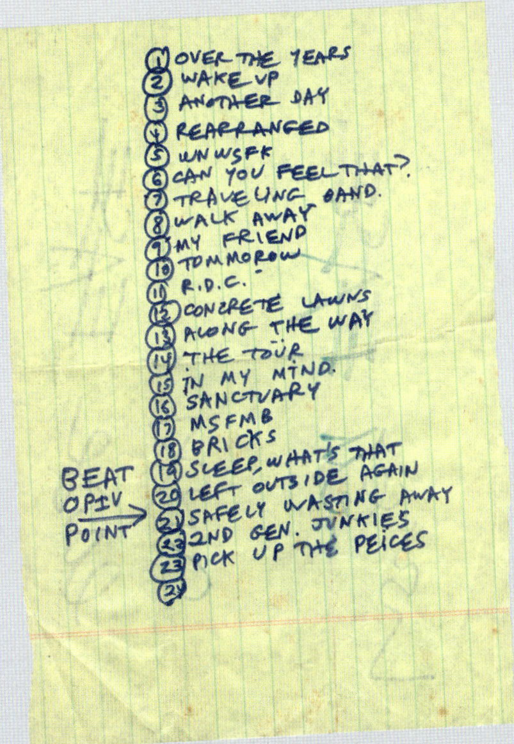

3.71. Crimpshrine set list with "Beat Oplv point" annotation, circa 1987.

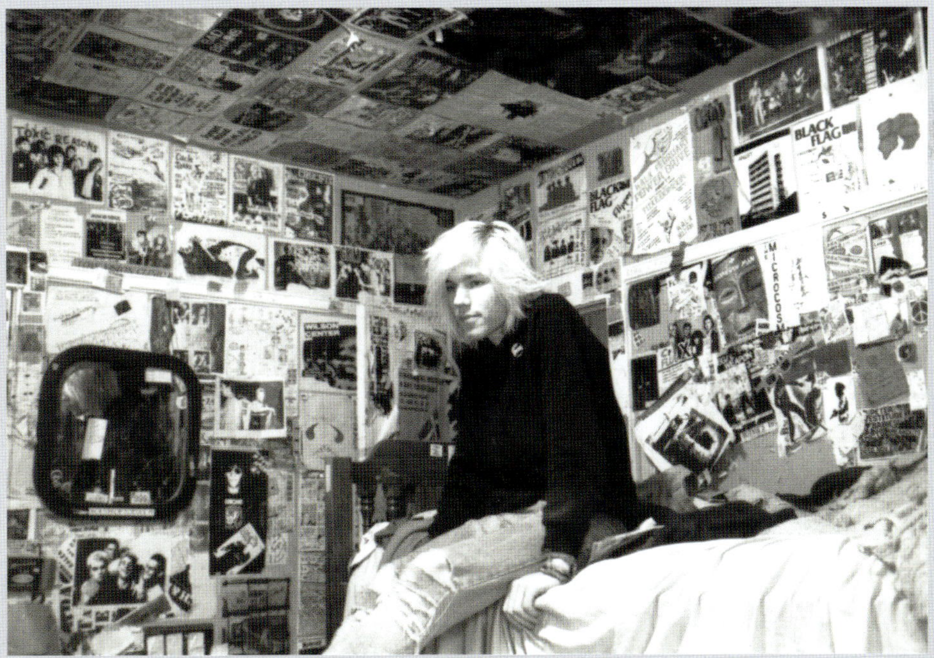

3.72. Aaron Cometbus's room, circa 1986. Photo: Lilian Elliott.

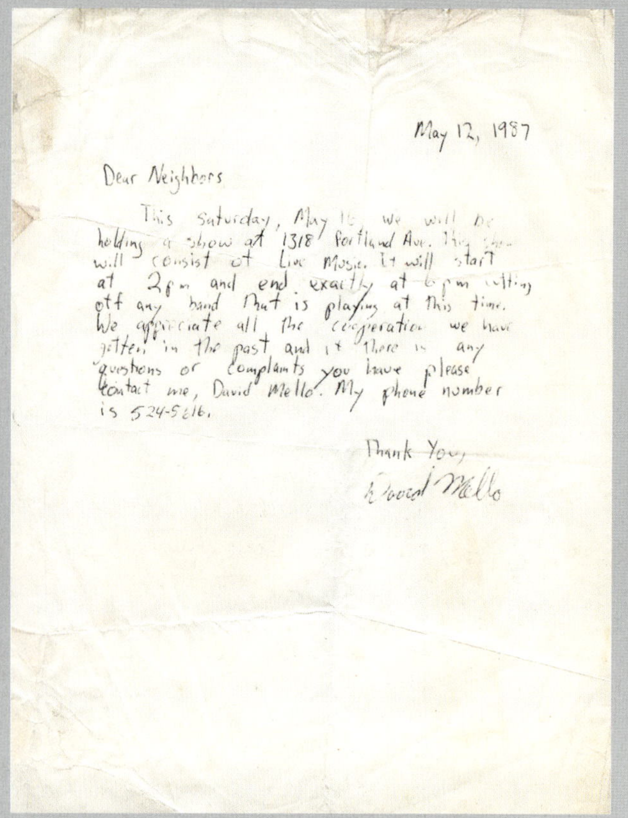

May 12, 1987

Dear Neighbors

This saturday, May 16, we will be holding a show at 1318 Portland Ave. This show will consist of Live Music. It will start at 2pm and end exactly at 6pm cutting off any band that is playing at this time. We appreciate all the cooperation we have gotten in the past and if there is any questions or complaints you have please contact me, David Mello. My phone number is 524-5616.

Thank You,
David Mello

3.73. Letter to Operation Ivy drummer Dave Mello's neighbors about one of the band's first shows, 1987.

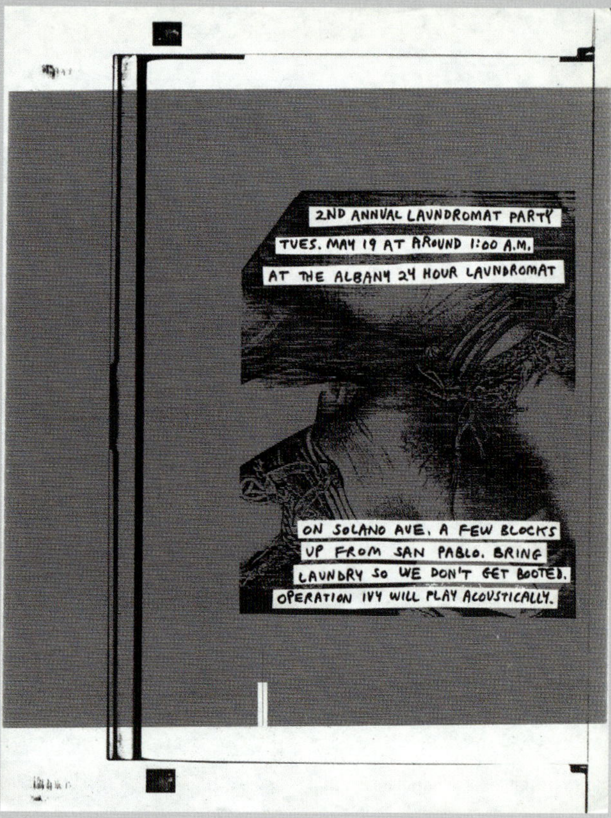

3.74. Flyer for the 2nd Annual Laundromat Party with Operation Ivy, Albany, California, 1987. The first Laundromat Party was their first show.

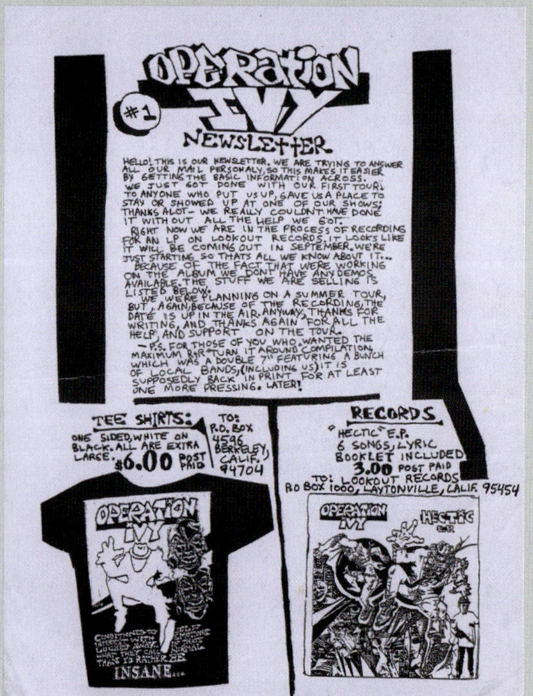

OPERATION IVY
#1
NEWSLETTER

HELLO! THIS IS OUR NEWSLETTER. WE ARE TRYING TO ANSWER ALL OUR MAIL PERSONALY, SO THIS MAKES IT EASIER BY GETTING THE BASIC INFORMATION ACROSS.
WE JUST GOT DONE WITH OUR FIRST TOUR. TO ANYONE WHO PUT US UP, GAVE US A PLACE TO STAY OR SHOWED UP AT ONE OF OUR SHOWS: THANKS ALOT– WE REALLY COULDN'T HAVE DONE IT WITH OUT ALL THE HELP WE GOT.
RIGHT NOW WE ARE IN THE PROCESS OF RECORDING FOR AN LP ON LOOKOUT RECORDS. IT LOOKS LIKE IT WILL BE COMING OUT IN SEPTEMBER. WE'RE JUST STARTING SO THATS ALL WE KNOW ABOUT IT...
BECAUSE OF THE FACT THAT WERE WORKING ON THE ALBUM WE DONT HAVE ANY DEMOS AVAILABLE. THE STUFF WE ARE SELLING IS LISTED BELOW.
WE WERE PLANNING ON A SUMMER TOUR, BUT, AGAIN, BECAUSE OF THE RECORDING, THE DATE IS UP IN THE AIR. ANYWAY, THANKS FOR WRITING, AND THANKS AGAIN FOR ALL THE HELP, AND SUPPORT ON THE TOUR.
–P.S. FOR THOSE OF YOU WHO WANTED THE MAXIMUM R+R "TURN IT AROUND" COMPILATION, WHICH WAS A DOUBLE 7" FEATURING A BUNCH OF LOCAL BANDS, (INCLUDING US) IT IS SUPPOSEDLY BACK IN PRINT FOR AT LEAST ONE MORE PRESSING. LATER!

TEE SHIRTS:
ONE SIDED, WHITE ON BLACK. ALL ARE EXTRA LARGE. $6.00 POST PAID
TO: P.O. BOX 4596 BERKELEY, CALIF. 94704

RECORDS
"HECTIC" E.P.
6 SONGS, LYRIC BOOKLET INCLUDED
3.00 POST PAID
TO: LOOKOUT RECORDS
P.O BOX 1000, LAYTONVILLE, CALIF. 95454

3.75. *Operation Ivy Newsletter* no. 1, circa 1987.

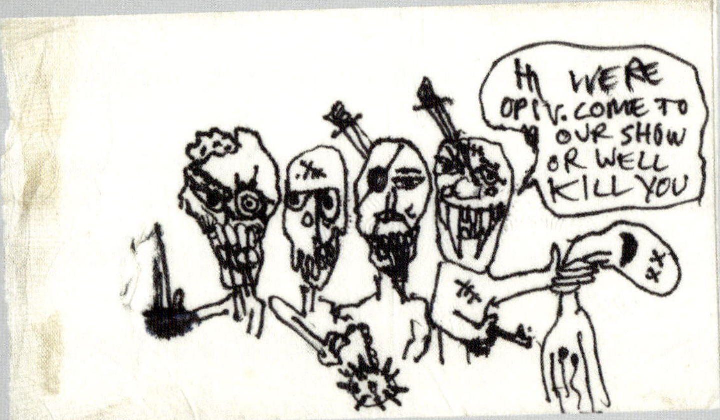

3.76. Napkin drawing by Jesse Michaels, singer of Operation Ivy, circa 1987.

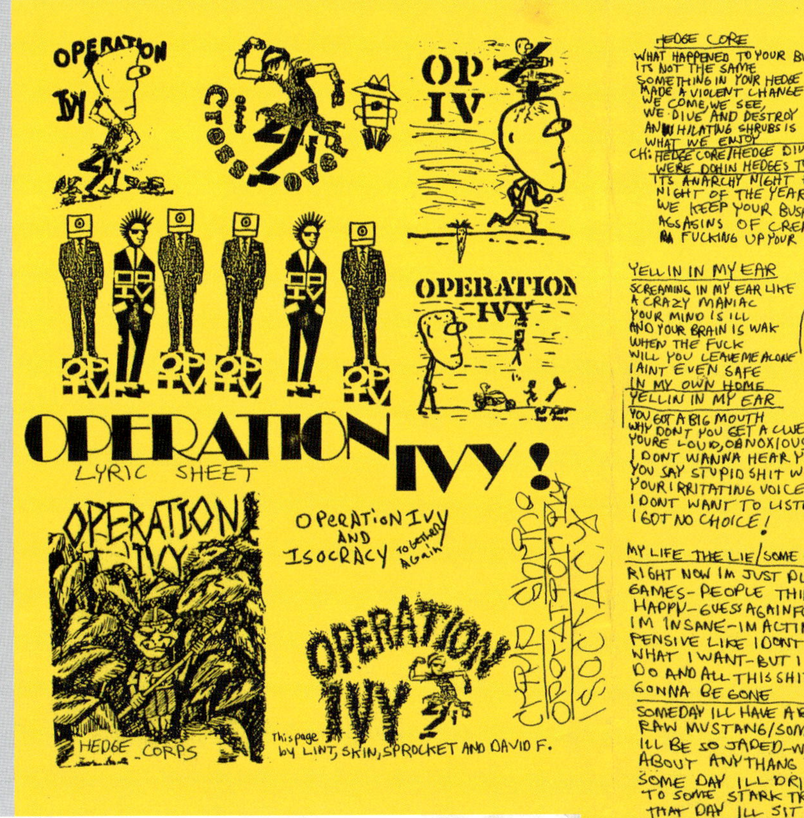

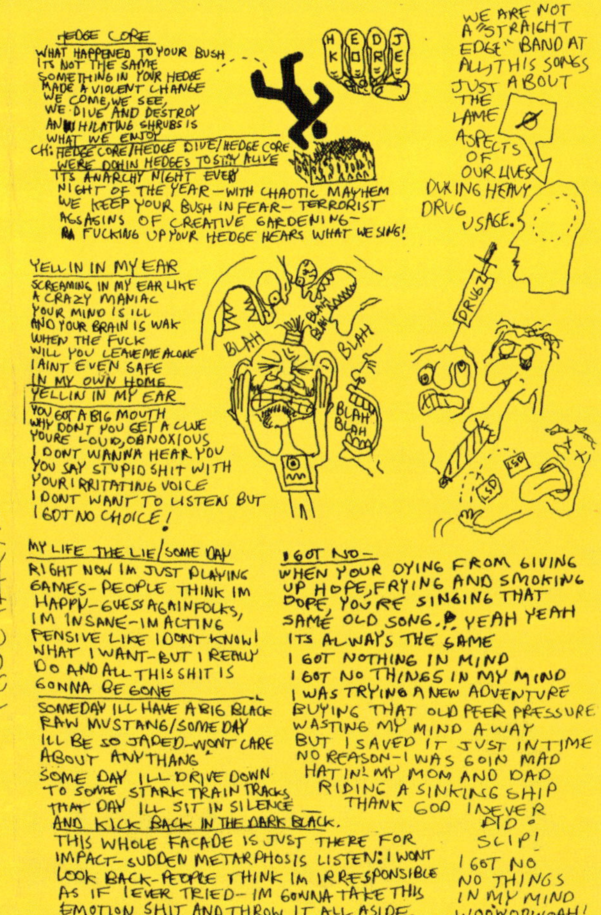

HEDGE CORE

WHAT HAPPENED TO YOUR BUSH
ITS NOT THE SAME
SOMETHING IN YOUR HEDGE
MADE A VIOLENT CHANGE
WE COME, WE SEE,
WE DIVE AND DESTROY
ANNIHILATING SHRUBS IS
WHAT WE ENJOY
CH: HEDGE CORE/HEDGE DIVE/HEDGE CORE
WERE DOHIN HEDGES TO STAY ALIVE
ITS ANARCHY NIGHT EVERY
NIGHT OF THE YEAR—WITH CHAOTIC MAYHEM
WE KEEP YOUR BUSH IN FEAR—TERRORIST
ASSASINS OF CREATIVE GARDENING—
FUCKING UP YOUR HEDGE HEARS WHAT WE SING!

WE ARE NOT A "STRAIGHT EDGE" BAND AT ALL, THIS SONGS JUST ABOUT THE LAME ASPECTS OF OUR LIVES DURING HEAVY DRUG USAGE.

YELLIN IN MY EAR

SCREAMING IN MY EAR LIKE
A CRAZY MANIAC
YOUR MIND IS ILL
AND YOUR BRAIN IS WAK
WHEN THE FUCK
WILL YOU LEAVE ME ALONE
I AINT EVEN SAFE
IN MY OWN HOME
YELLIN IN MY EAR
YOU GOT A BIG MOUTH
WHY DONT YOU GET A CLUE
YOURE LOUD, OBNOXIOUS
I DONT WANNA HEAR YOU
YOU SAY STUPID SHIT WITH
YOUR IRRITATING VOICE
I DONT WANT TO LISTEN BUT
I GOT NO CHOICE!

MY LIFE THE LIE/SOME DAY

RIGHT NOW IM JUST PLAYING
GAMES—PEOPLE THINK IM
HAPPY—GUESS AGAIN FOLKS,
IM INSANE—IM ACTING
PENSIVE LIKE I DONT KNOW
WHAT I WANT—BUT I REALLY
DO AND ALL THIS SHIT IS
GONNA BE GONE
SOMEDAY ILL HAVE A BIG BLACK
RAW MUSTANG/SOMEDAY
ILL BE SO JADED—WONT CARE
ABOUT ANYTHANG
SOME DAY ILL DRIVE DOWN
TO SOME STARK TRAIN TRACKS
THAT DAY ILL SIT IN SILENCE
AND KICK BACK IN THE DARK BLACK.
THIS WHOLE FACADE IS JUST THERE FOR
IMPACT—SUDDEN METARPHOSIS LISTEN: I WONT
LOOK BACK—PEOPLE THINK IM IRRESPONSIBLE
AS IF I EVER TRIED—IM GONNA TAKE THIS
EMOTION SHIT AND THROW IT ALL ASIDE.

I GOT NO—

WHEN YOUR DYING FROM GIVING
UP HOPE, FRYING AND SMOKING
DOPE, YOU'RE SINGING THAT
SAME OLD SONG. YEAH YEAH
ITS ALWAYS THE SAME
I GOT NOTHING IN MIND
I GOT NO THINGS IN MY MIND
I WAS TRYING A NEW ADVENTURE
BUYING THAT OLD PEER PRESSURE
WASTING MY MIND AWAY
BUT I SAVED IT JUST IN TIME
NO REASON—I WAS GOIN MAD
HATIN' MY MOM AND DAD
RIDING A SINKING SHIP
THANK GOD I NEVER
DID SLIP!
I GOT NO
NO THINGS
IN MY MIND
WOOWOOWOAH!

Dear Jeff,

Thank you for your interest in Hedgediving. Hedgediving was first introduced to me by Noah Landis from the band Christ On Parade way back in the early 80s. Later I took it up with some friends, including Aaron, as a latenight, after-the-show activity. It basically involved getting a bit drunk, wandering around the suburbs and diving into the hedges. Aaron Cometbus was by far the most extreme practitioner, rarely emerging from a hedge without some kind of permanent injury. ~~Although the band~~ That song was a goofy song about our sport.

yours,
Jesse Michael

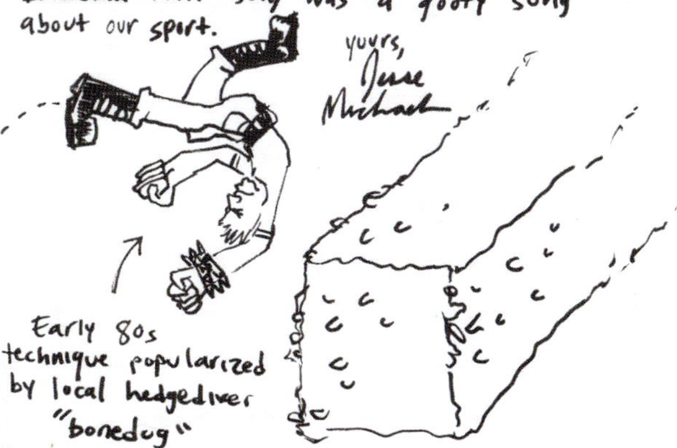

3.77. (*Above*) Operation Ivy lyric book page 1, circa 1987.

3.78. (*Left*) Letter by Operation Ivy's Jesse Michaels explaining "hedgediving."

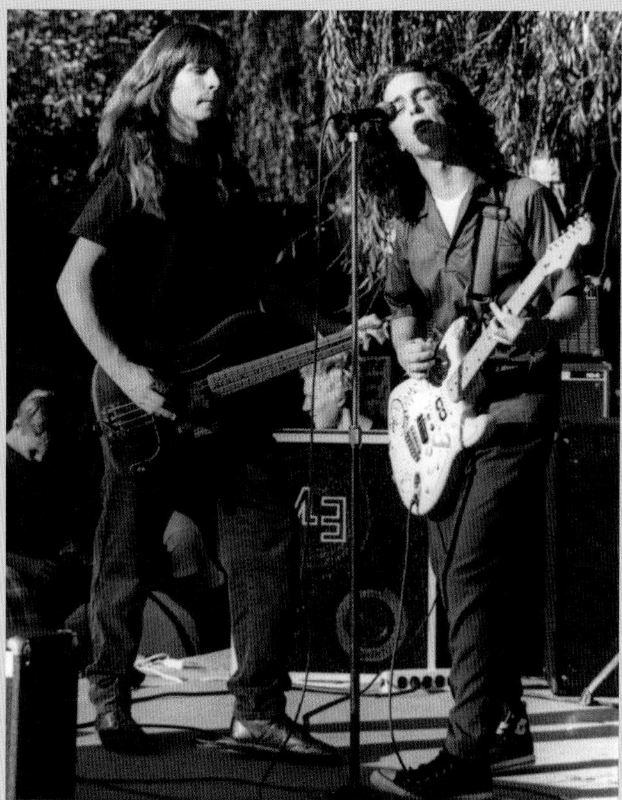

3.79. Green Day live show, circa 1987.
Photo: © Murray Bowles.

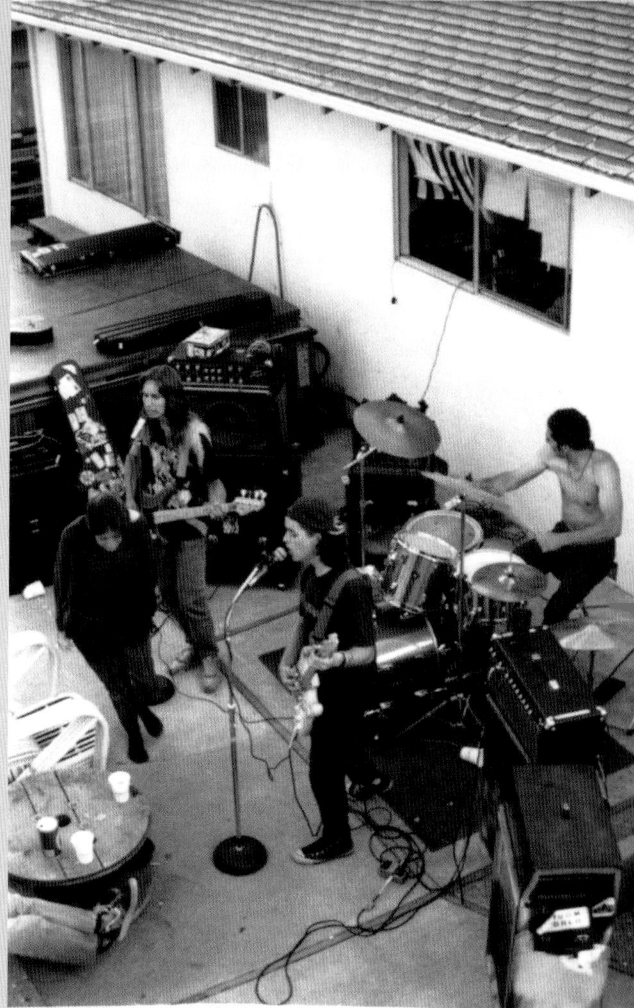

3.80. Green Day live show in Robert Eggplant's backyard, circa 1988. Photographer unknown.

THIS IS NOT A CONTRACT

(It is more like a list of desires)

Thanks for booking **Green Day**. This is **Green Day's** first tour and we hope it will be fun. We are asking for a few things that will make our trip a little easier. you do not have to give us any of these things, of course we don't have to tune before we play either.

We are asking for $100, more if you can spare it. This is not a guarantee, we are only asking.

We are asking that you do not book us with the band **ALL**

More important than money is food and a place to stay. We have one vegetarian and four guys who will eat just about anything. A place to stay would be nice, but a secure place to park the van overnight will do.

Please make flyers. What good is a show that no one knows about?

We have three vocals, two guitars and a drum set. We can get by with two vocals. We will have microphones with us but no P.A.

Info on a good place to get coffee and a place to buy cheap T-shirts would be greatly appreciated.

Green Day needs WATER on stage. This may sound funny, but we find ourselves on stage without water too often. If the hall or club does not have water could you please bring some.

We are not a straitedge band, so don't be afraid to offer us a beer.

Once again, thanks for having us play your town and we hope you'll want us back sometime.

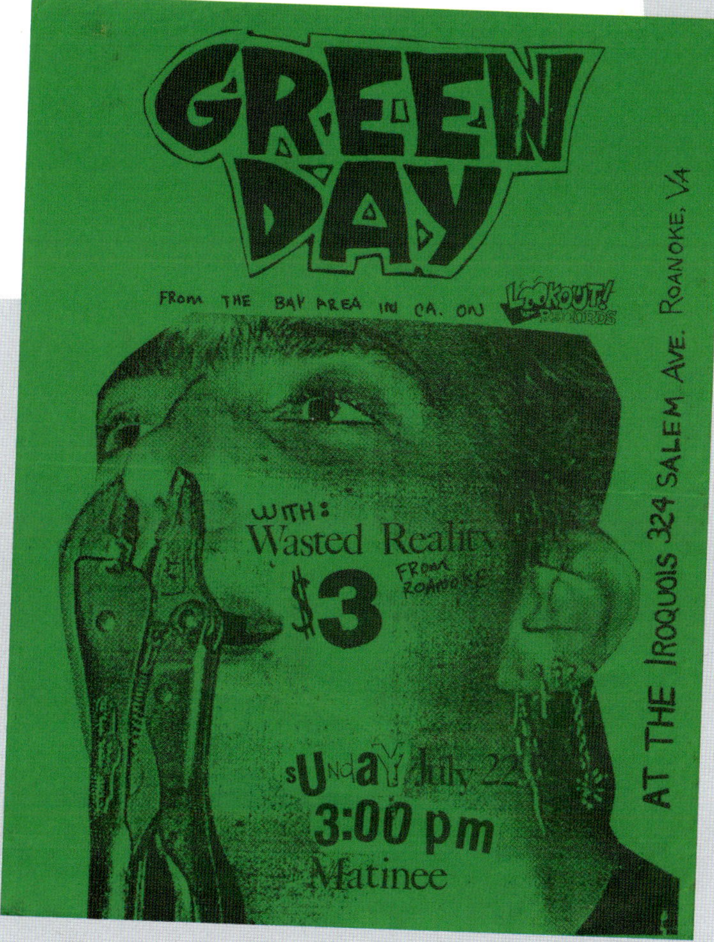

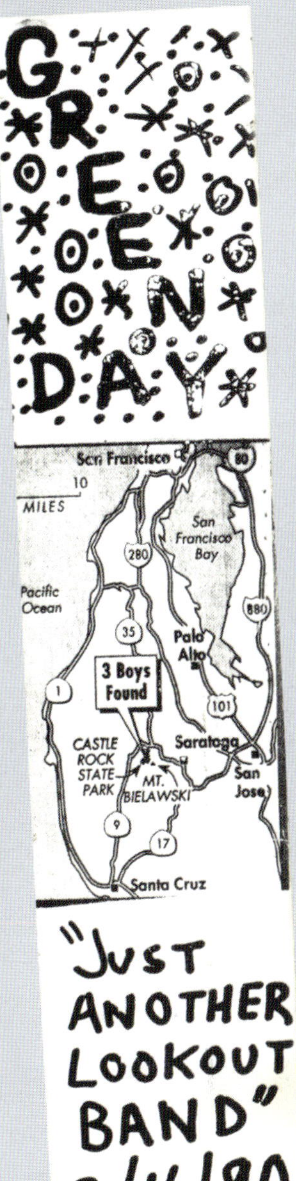

3.81. (*Above left*) Green Day's "anti-rider," circa 1990.

3.82. (*Above right*) Green Day sticker, 1990.

3.83. (*Bottom left*) Flyer from the first Green Day tour, 1990.

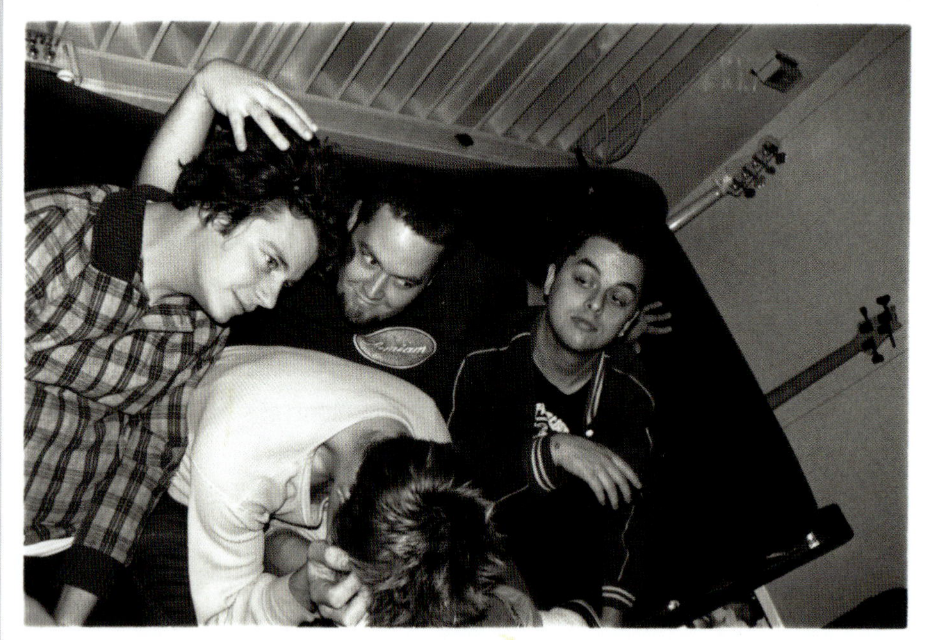

3.84. Pinhead Gunpowder, circa 1998. Photo: © Adrienne Armstrong.

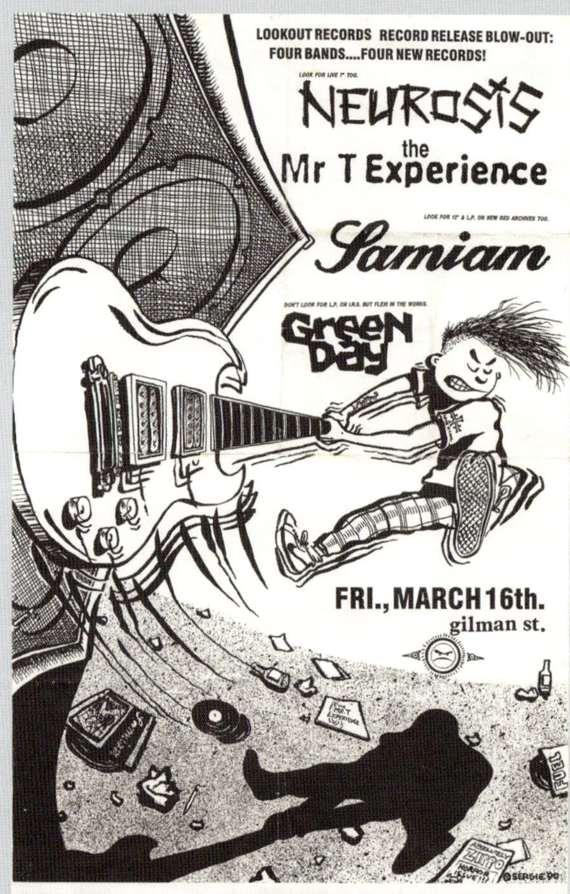

3.85. Flyer for Lookout Records artists at Gilman, Berkeley, March 1990.

"They won. They proved they can take the streets by force. Basically, there is nothing we can do."
-Sgt. Conrad T. Craig

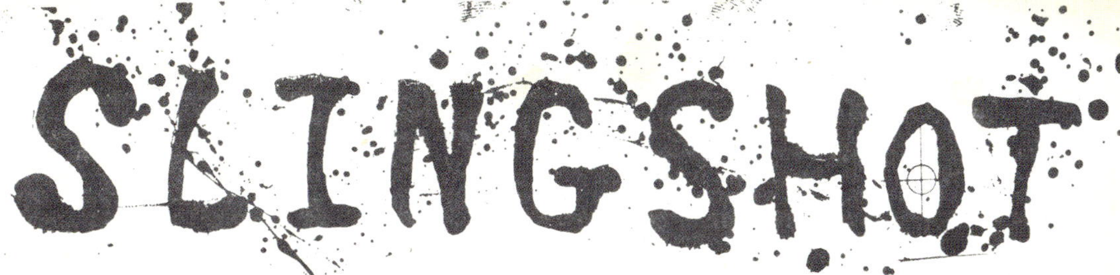

Volume 1, Number 28 June, 1989 Berkeley, California

TOO HOT TO HANDLE

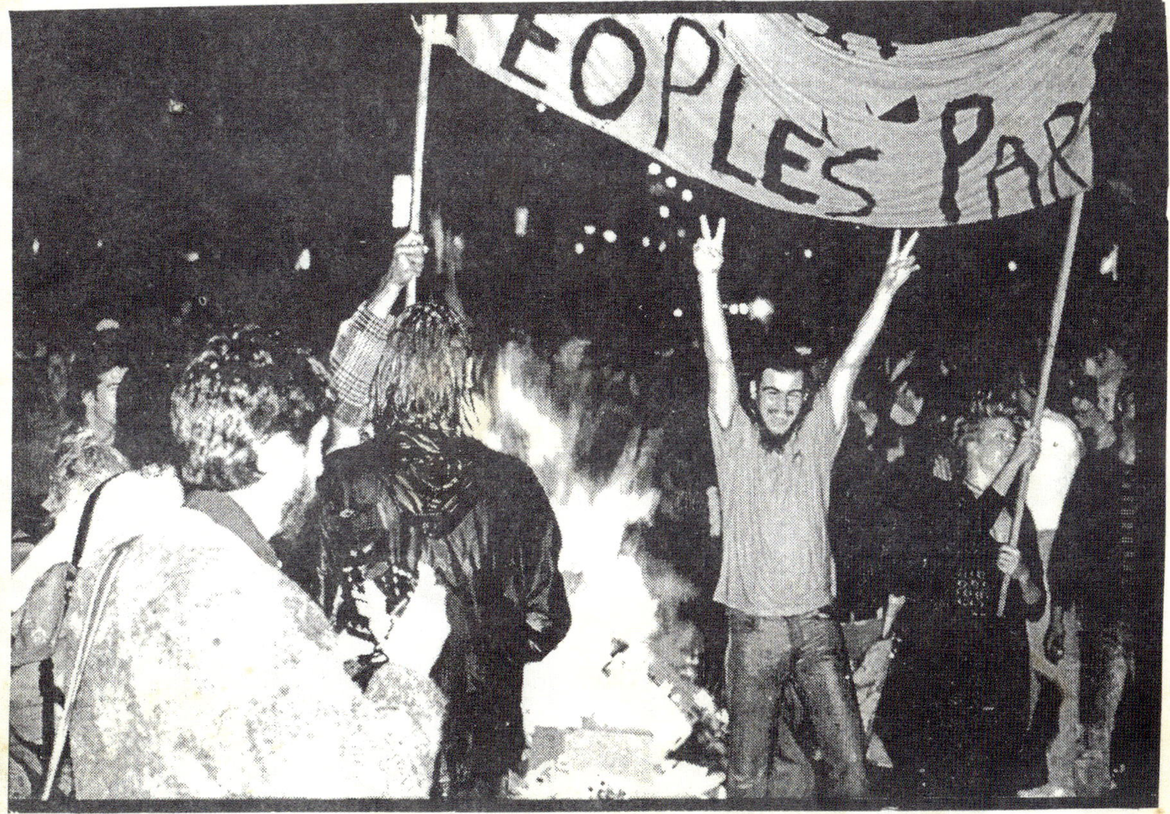

-SPECIAL RIOT ISSUE-

3.86. *Slingshot* vol. 1, no. 28, June 1989.

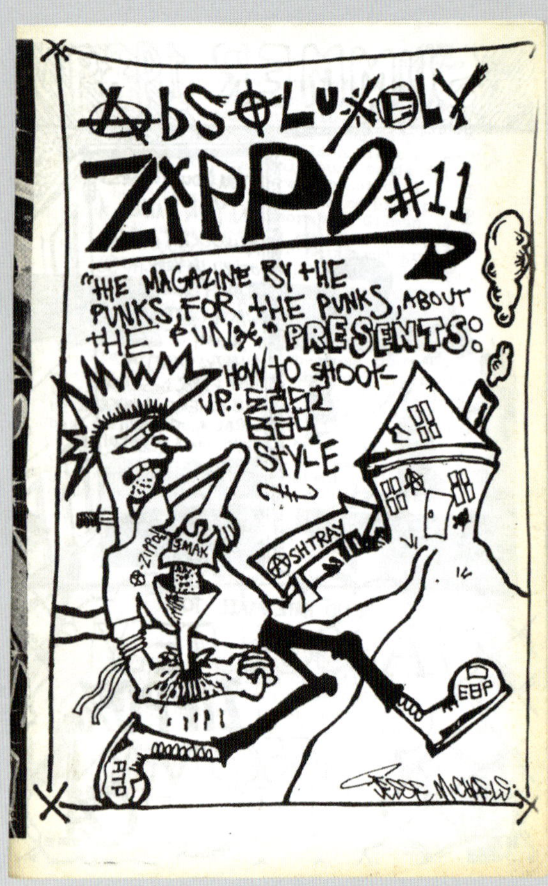

3.87. *Absolutely Zippo* no. 11, summer 1989. Absolutely Zippo was a fanzine started in 1988 by Robert Eggplant, guitarist for Blatz. This cover is drawn by Operation Ivy's Jesse Michaels.

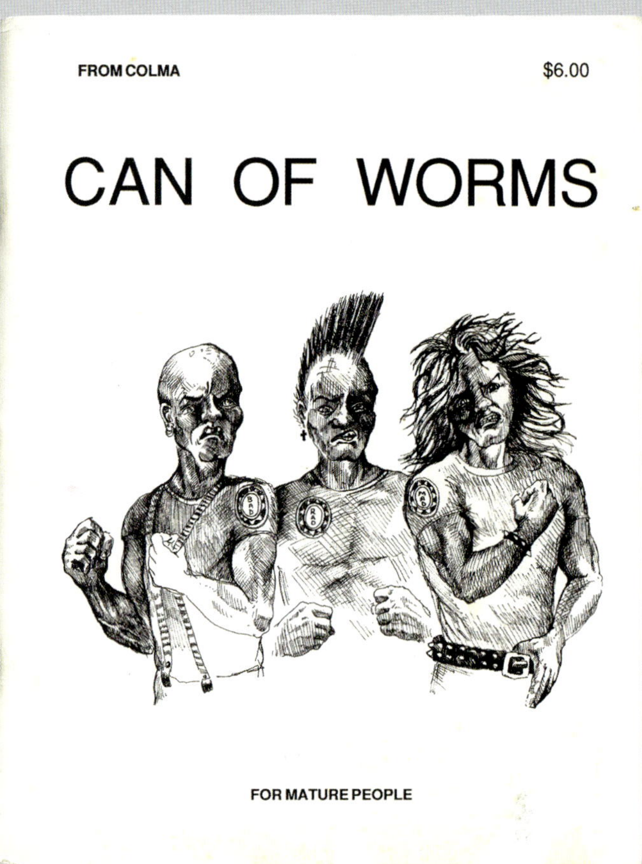

3.88. *Can of Worms* zine from Colma, California, 1990.

The PUNX -VS- The Berkeley PIGS

VOLLEYBALL

The second.

NORTH BERKELEY BART IS CLOSEST STA

THURS. OCT. 15TH AT 4:45 Pm! Stoopid!

THEY FLED THE COURT IN TERROR AT OUR FIRST GAME ATTEMPT. NOW THEY THINK THEY CAN HANDLE A REMATCH! SHINE YOUR DR. MARTINS FER THIS ONE!

Hey wich Side ARE YOU ON ANYWAY The PUNX, OR THE PIGS!

TACO BELL

NORTH

UNIVERSITY AVE.

ADDISON

BONAR

BREAD FACTORY

GRASS

STRAWBERRY CREEK

ALLSTON

PLAY GROUND

BASKET BALL

TENNIS

BONAR

VOLLEYBALL

BACROFT WY.

3.89. Flyer for volleyball match between local punks and the Berkeley police, 1992.

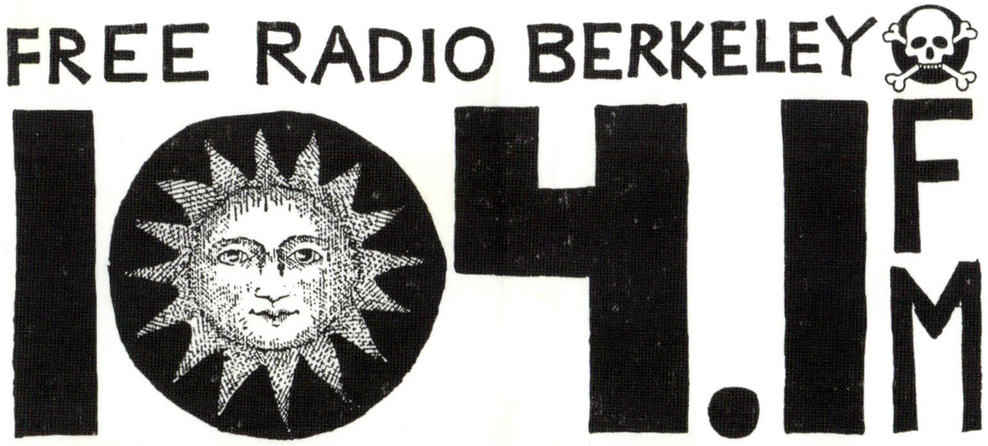

3.90. Sticker for Free Radio Berkeley, the only pirate radio station to win in court against the FCC. Bay Area punks hosted many of the shows.

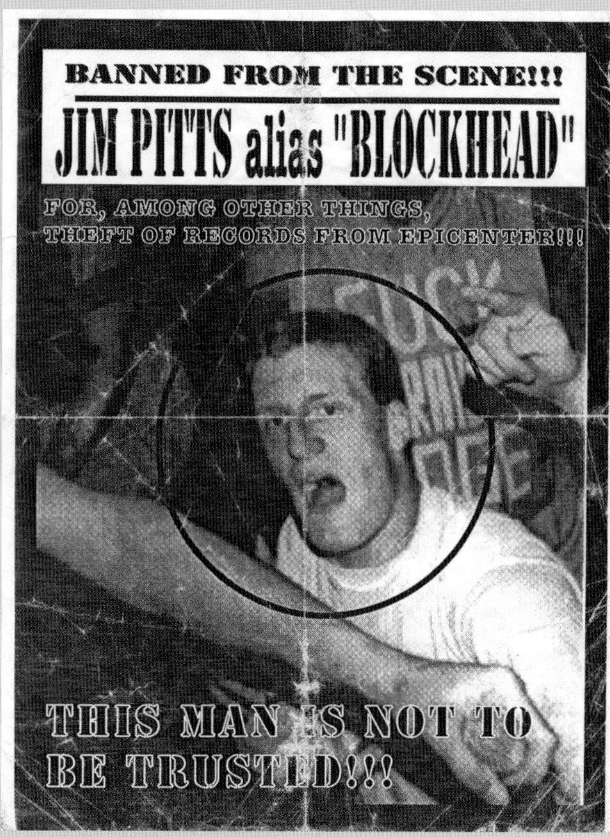

3.91. Flyer published by Tim Yohannan, 1992. Who says punk rock doesn't have rules?

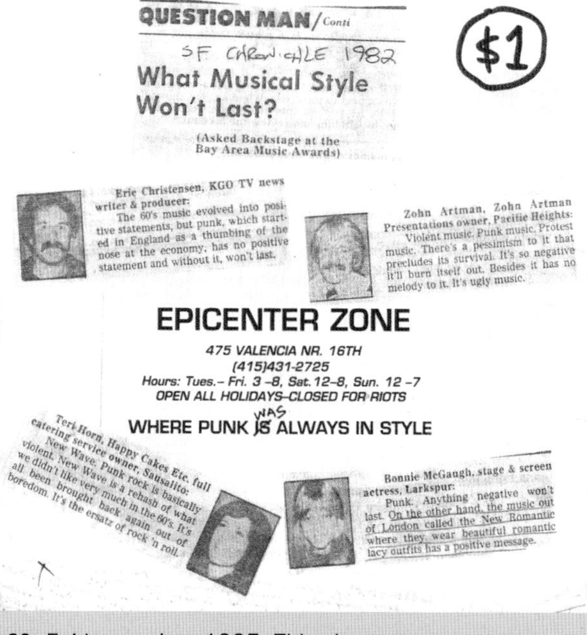

EPI-LOGUE

The Zine of Epicenter Zone's Demise

QUESTION MAN/Conti

SF CHRONICLE 1982

$1

What Musical Style Won't Last?

(Asked Backstage at the Bay Area Music Awards)

Eric Christensen, KGO TV news writer & producer:
The 60's music evolved into positive statements, but punk, which started in England as a thumbing of the nose at the economy, has no positive statement and without it, won't last.

Zohn Artman, Zohn Artman Presentations owner, Pacific Heights:
Violent music. Punk music. Protest music. There's a pessimism to it that precludes its survival. It's so negative it'll burn itself out. Besides it has no melody to it. It's ugly music.

EPICENTER ZONE

475 VALENCIA NR. 16TH
(415)431-2725
Hours: Tues.– Fri. 3 –8, Sat. 12–8, Sun. 12 –7
OPEN ALL HOLIDAYS–CLOSED FOR RIOTS

WHERE PUNK ~~IS~~ WAS ALWAYS IN STYLE

Teri Horn, Happy Cakes Etc. full catering service owner, Sausalito:
New Wave. Punk rock is basically violent. New Wave is a rehash of what we didn't like very much in the 60's. It's all been brought back again out of boredom. It's the ersatz of rock 'n roll.

Bonnie McGaugh, stage & screen actress, Larkspur:
Punk. Anything negative won't last. On the other hand, the music out of London called the New Romantic where they wear beautiful romantic lacy outfits has a positive message.

3.92. *Epi-Logue* zine, 1995. This zine commemorates the end of the San Francisco record store, venue, and community space founded with *MRR*'s help in 1989 and closed in 1995.

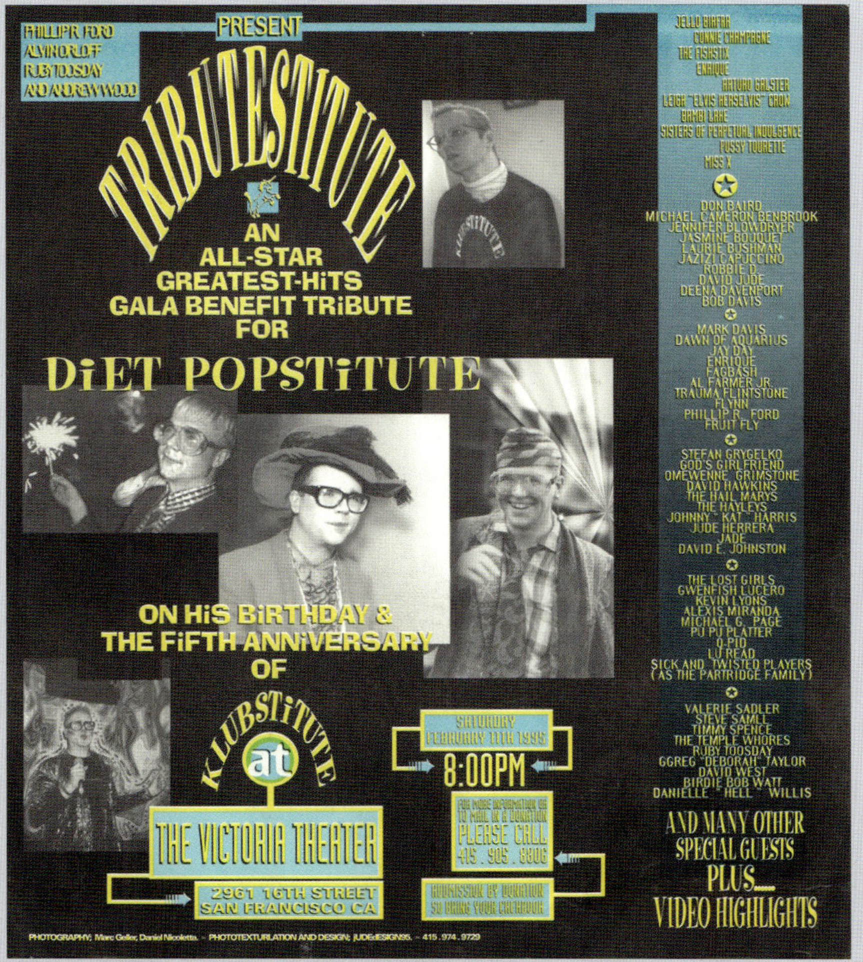

3.93. Poster for benefit concert for Michael Collins (aka Diet Popstitute), February 1995. Michael Collins led the queer punk band and performance group the Popstitutes and hosted the floating queer-oriented club and cabaret Klubstitute until his death from AIDS in August 1995.

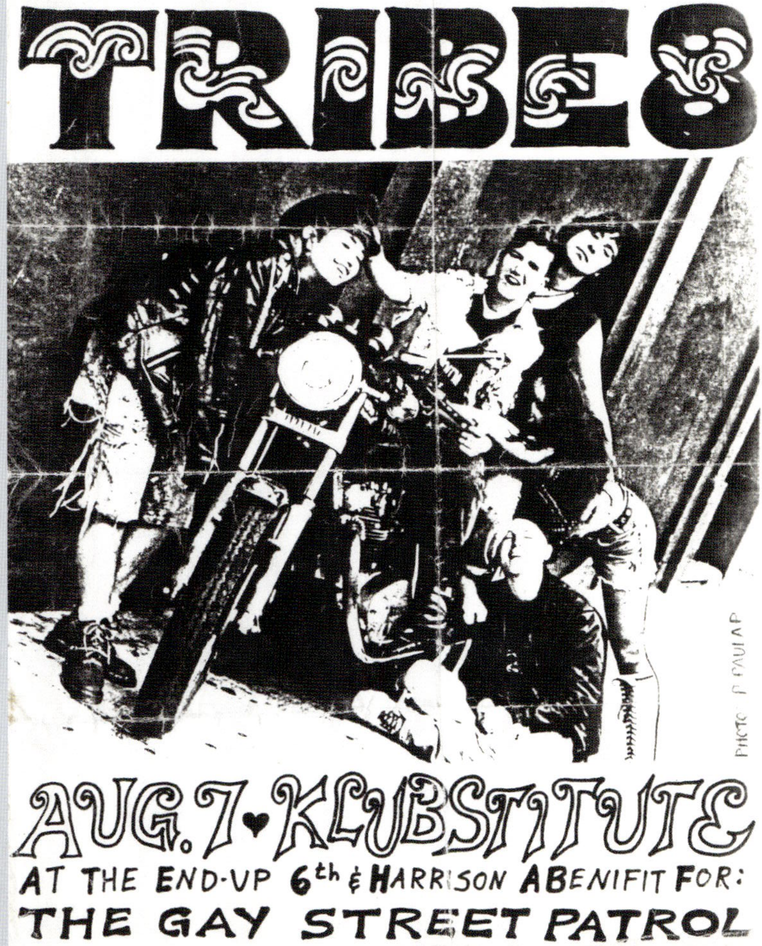

3.94. Flyer for Tribe 8 at Klubstitute, San Francisco, early 1990s.

NEW EL SALVADOR TODAY (NEST) AND
STUDENTS AGAINST INTERVENTION IN CENTRAL AMERICA (SAICA — formerly SAINTES)
PRESENT:

THE "BOOKS NOT BOMBS"

DANCE-A-THON BENEFIT

TO PROVIDE EDUCATIONAL MATERIALS FOR BERKELEY'S SALVADOREAN SISTER-CITY, SAN ANTONIO LOS RANCHOS

SAT., FEB. 25

8 P.M. - DAWN

BERKELEY HIGH CAFETERIA

(ALLSTON AND MILVIA)

THE LOOTERS
"HARD FUNK"
THE CLIQUE
"NEW ROCK"
BIG CITY
"AFRICAN HIGHLIFE, CALYPSO AND FUNK"
THE DICKS
"PUNK ROCK"
THE GREASE MONKEYS
"RED HOT ROCKABILLY"
WILL PROVIDE THE BEAT,

WE NEED YOU TO DANCE!

ENTRY FORMS AND SPONSORSHEETS AVAILABLE AT:
SAICA (formerly SAINTES), 613 ESHLEMAN, UCB (642-7783)
NEST: 1720 OREGON ST., BERKELEY (549-2114)
OLD MOLE BOOKS: 1942 UNIVERSITY AVE., BERKELEY
TERRY DORAN B144

NON-SPONSORED ADMISSION:
STUDENT: $4.00
OTHER: $5.00
ADVANCE TICKETS: $3.00

ASUC

Ticker Tape from the Punk Parade

CH. 13

AARON COMETBUS

Let me start by explaining that I was never a collector; I just had parents who never threw anything away, so growing up, I did the same. Whatever I found on the street or at a show, I brought home. Steadily the piles grew, and so did I, until there was no more room. So I moved out, with the piles in tow, and for thirty years I sorted and sifted, trying to make sense of it all.

Had the mess been mine alone, I might've dispatched it all to the dump, but my slovenliness had accidentally caused a whole community's efforts to be preserved. Not only had I saved thousands of flyers, but also the paperwork involved in setting up shows. I'd kept the fanzines and demo tapes, the set lists and guest lists, the stickers and lyric sheets. I'd brought home the handwritten signs pinned up outside of gigs saying which bands were playing that night, and which bands had broken up, or broken down, on the way. I even had the leases from a few clubs, the front door keys, and in the case of CBGBs, a chunk of the dressing room wall.

The surprise was just how much energy this pile of kindling contained. The punk documentary films and coffee table books seemed dull in comparison, always narrowly focused on the stage and on the handful of bands that achieved some level of fame. Most portrayed punk as a rags-to-riches story, a battle for success. The American Dream, with a mohawk for effect.

What I'd saved presented a different picture. It was the paper equivalent of the bruises and hickeys, the ringing in your ears, and the smell of smoke and sweat that hung on your clothes after a show. It captured the passion that remained after all the bands had packed up—the tiny germ or flame you carried home, which sustained you in your isolation, and braced you against oppression, until you could be in a like-minded crowd again.

It was a meaningful, historical mess. Still, I had to get it out of my room. My goal was twofold: to preserve the material in an accessible place, and to present it as if it were evidence in a case. I wanted to challenge the common misunderstandings about punk—both the mainstream media clichés and the reductive narratives gaining ground in college lecture halls.

The archive speaks for itself, but let me just say this: ours is a participation-based movement, and that's how its failure or success should be judged. Not by the photos of bands, but by the level of involvement of the women and men *behind* the lens. Not simply by the music, but by the network of people who helped get the message out. They were and are our stars.

Now let's take a peek at some of the paper trail, and I'll explain how it came to live at Cornell.

HARDCORE BUSINESS CARDS

Punk's sense of urgency is well documented; less so its emphasis on network building. Malcolm McLaren used the cynical slogan "cash for chaos" to market punk to a mainstream audience, but "poverty through productivity" would be closer to the truth. My collection of punk business cards is proof.

What makes these interesting isn't just the obvious paradox. Punks have always had mixed feelings about business. Traditional methods were frowned upon; so was success. Yet what other movement produced as many cottage industries and resourceful entrepreneurs? Punks enjoyed the contradiction, poking fun at themselves with drawings mixing spiky hair and three-piece suits.

These cards are from long before punk was considered a viable career. But was the intention behind them serious, or tongue-in-cheek? A bit of both, I'd guess.

Let's start with the fanzines. *Savage Pink* wasn't "Philly's only subversive fanzine," as their card claims. How could *Savage Pink*'s editor Allison overlook *Anarchy for Punks and Skins*, published by Robbie from the Sadistic Exploits? Perhaps the cold shoulder approach masked a simmering, forbidden passion, for it wasn't

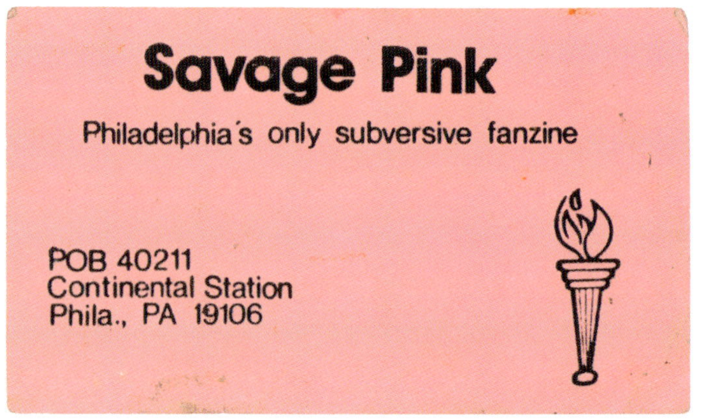

3.95. Business card for *Savage Pink*.

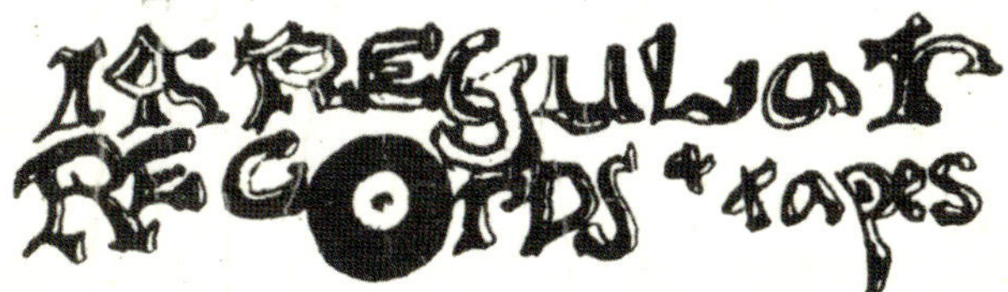

INDEPENDENTS • IMPORTS • RARE • POPULAR
NEW, USED ~~& RENTALS~~

SAT. & SUN. 10 TO 8
TUES.—FRIDAY
5:30 P.M.—8:00

4655 APPIAN WAY
EL SOBRANTE, CA. 94803
(415) 223-5800

3.96. Business card for Irregular Records.

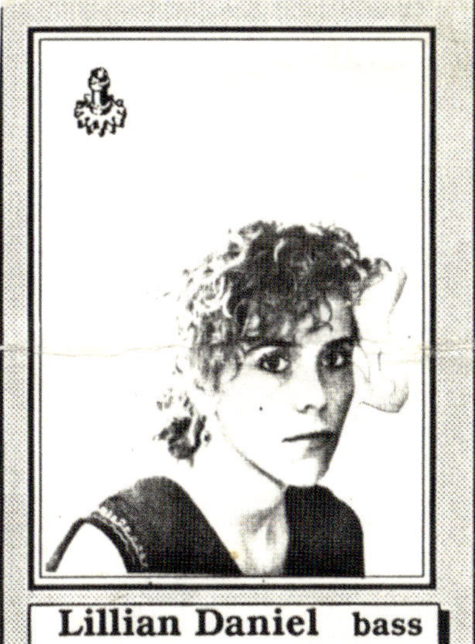

LILLIAN DANIEL
no stagename, thank-you
Personal Description: businessman, philanthropist, humanitarian
Instrument: fretless p.bass with buzz
Secret Geeky Thing: wears waist-high underwear
Three Favorites:
1. Saint- St. Teresa of Avila
2. Poet - Brother Antoninus
3. Food - Nacho Cheese Corn Nuts

All time best makeout tune: "When U Were Mine" by Prince
Fantasy Gig: Performance art/Arena rock/ Tap and Mime extravaganza with Seachunk, Superweed and the Geeks
Quote: "You can not say when a wolf eats another wolf that it breaks the law." - Georges Bataille

3.97–3.100. Front and back of punk trading cards for members of Geek, 1990.

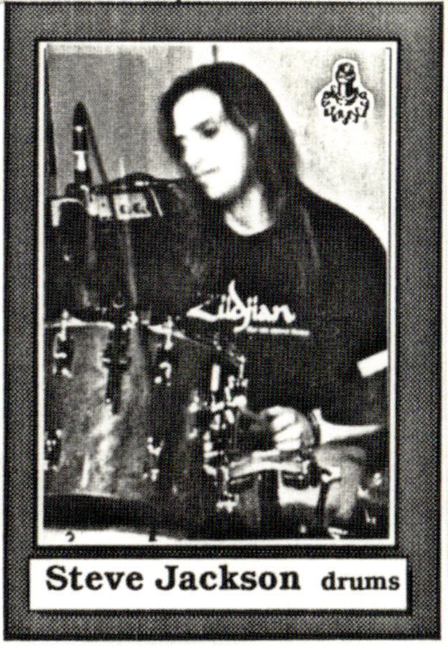

STEVE JACKSON
a.k.a. "moist boy "or "butt pirate"
Personal Description: giver god fashion plate saint
Instrument: drums and Ziljan Rock Crash cymbals, but only while wearing Animal t-shirt from the Muppets
Secret Geeky Thing: always sits down when he pees
Three Favorite Things:
1. camping
2. bowling
3. Mac Rock Magazine

All time favorite makeout tune: "Cashmere" by Led Zeppelin
Fantasy Gig: opening for New Kids On The Block
Quote: "One foot in the grave and one foot on a banana peel."

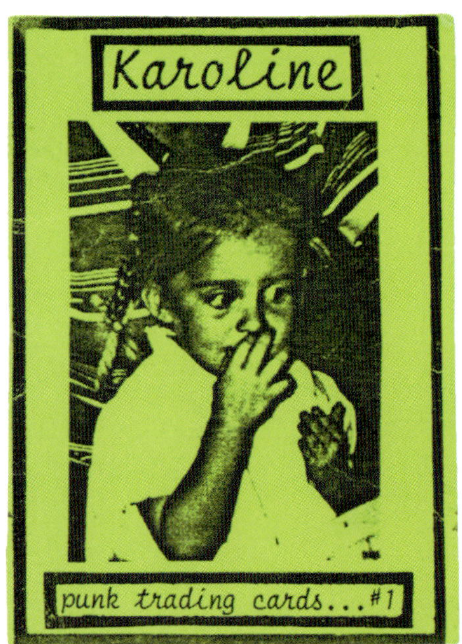

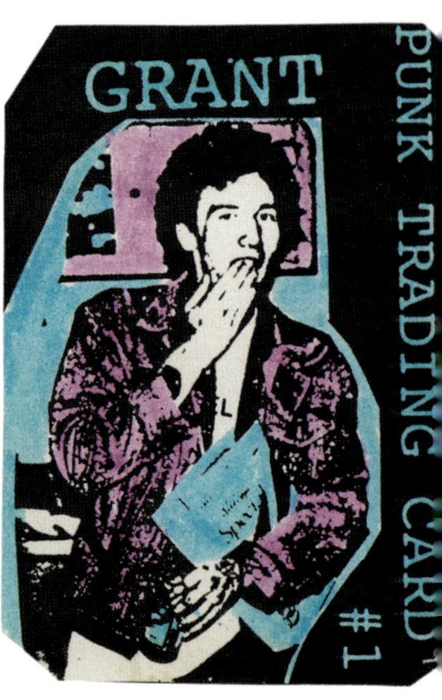

3.101–3.104. Front and back of Milwaukee punk trading cards, made by each person, 1995.

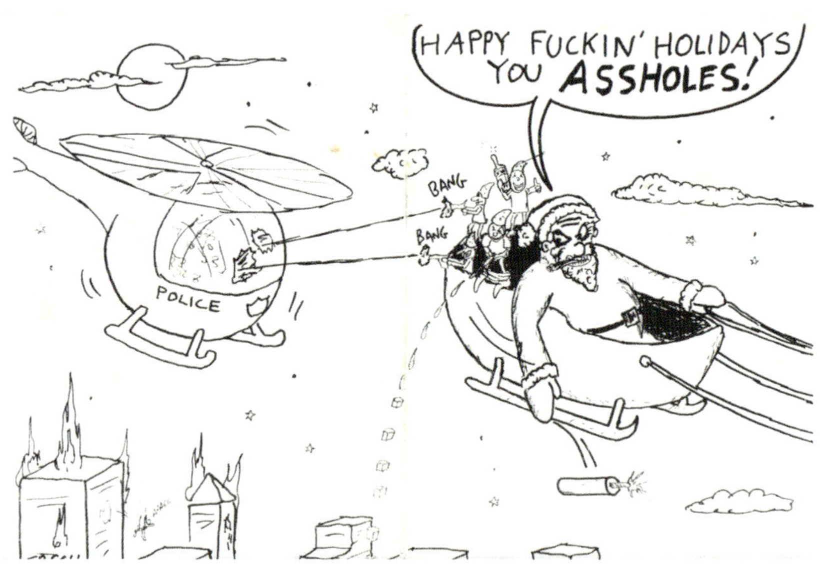

3.105 and 3.106. Front and interior of punk greeting card from Kwik Way.

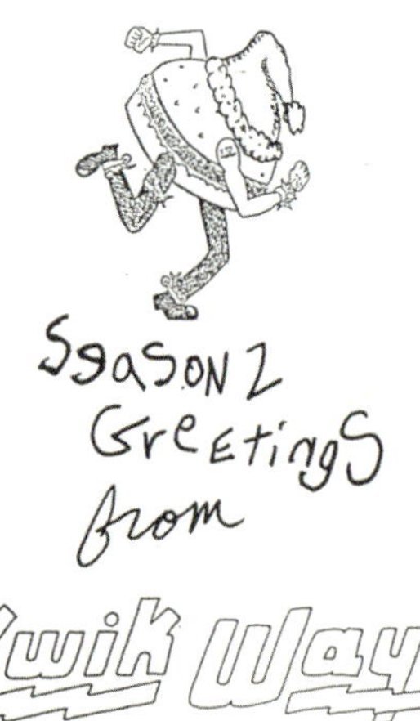

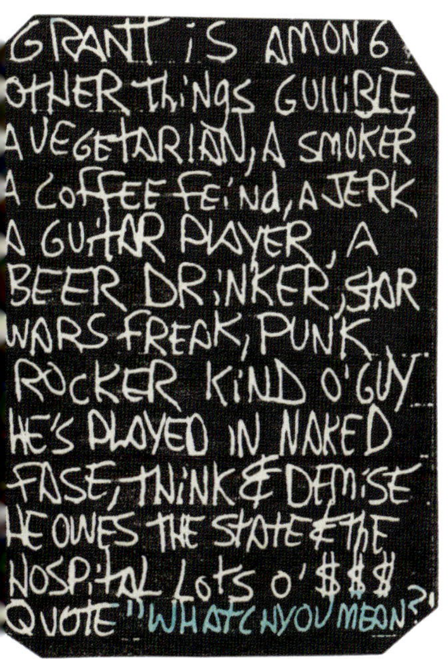

long before Robbie and Allison eloped together to Oakland, where both sang in the fantastic peace punk band A State of Mind.

Business cards aren't unusual for stores, but some businesses are unusual in their own right. Burning Media was one example: the first fanzine store in the world, years before Quimby's or See Hear. It was located in the Compound, a punk shopping mall on 16th Street in San Francisco's Mission District. Its only customer, or so it seemed, was me. Because my allowance was two dollars a week, Burning Media didn't last long, and the owners—Robin and Naomi of *Revolutionary Wanker* mag—soon dropped out of sight.

Another wonderful and nonsensical woman-owned shop was Irregular Records. Nan opened a punk record store in El Sobrante, the most oppressive of all the backwater towns in the East Bay. A boon for local punks, had there been any, which was not the case. But build it and they will come. Irregular, just by existing, created a whole scene. It gave birth to Isocracy, who gave birth to Filth, Samiam, and Green Day.

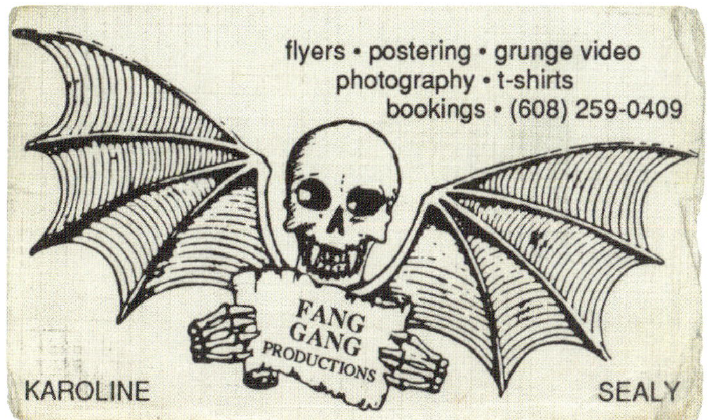

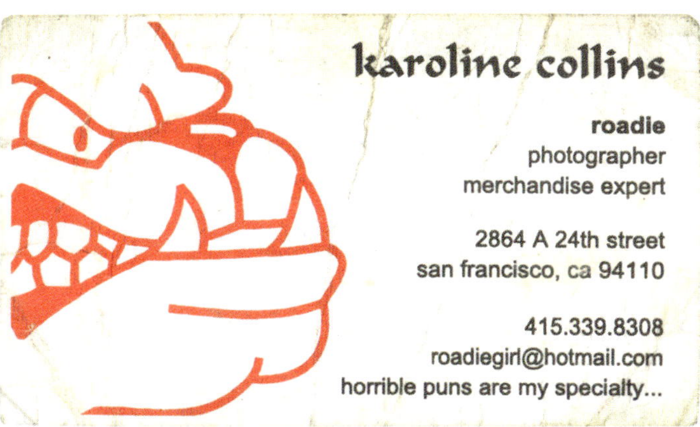

3.107 and 3.108. Two business cards for Karoline Collins.

There are several related species that I'll touch on just briefly. My archive includes two sets of punk trading cards—one for the mid-nineties Milwaukee scene, and one from the Chunk (later Superchunk), Seaweed, and Geek tour. If I recall correctly, the pack even came with a stale stick of gum.

Punk greeting cards ("Sincere best wishes for the new year from Rebel Truth") and bookmarks have their own files, representing the scene's sentimental and literary sides.

There were also personal calling cards, the same size and shape as for business, but with no services involved, like the one for A-head, "gutter punk and idiot extraordinaire." For legendary roadie Karoline Collins, I have not one card but two. The earlier and later versions make for an interesting comparison, tracing changes in the underground. In a few brief years "flyers, postering, grunge video" morphed into "photography and merchandising."

Merch was a word unheard just a decade before, when fewer records or shirts were made, and none hawked at gigs.

Looking into the past, it's easy to see foreboding signs which at the time were not clear. The early eighties all-woman band G.O.D. was one such example. Self-fulfilling prophecies are best to avoid when choosing a name. Sure enough, Girls on Drugs suffered at least one fatal overdose. Somehow, the innocently christened Battalion of Saints fared even worse, with only one or two survivors in the bunch. Their card shows punk's emphasis on shared responsibility, with each band member assigned a specific duty.

I've saved the very best for last, the crown jewel atop the heap of punk trash: Dead Kennedys at San Francisco's Russian Center in the spring of '83. It's the only specimen I've seen of a business card for a show.

3.109. Battalion of Saints business card.

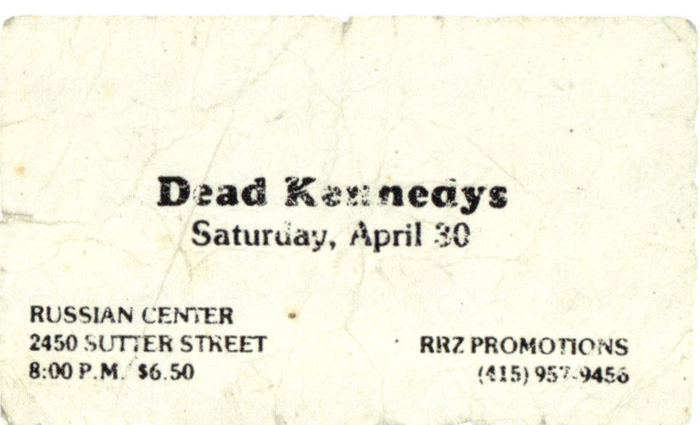

3.110. Card for Dead Kennedys show at the Russian Center, San Francisco, 1983.

BUTTHOLE SURFERS ART

Punk had its own regional rivalries. The classic *No New York* compilation album was followed by *Yes LA* and *Maybe Contra Costa*. Not only was there *This Is Boston, Not LA* but also *This Is Phoenix, Not the Circle Jerks*. The Bay Area's best band, Code of Honor, advocated California seceding from the union. San Francisco even had a band called Anti-LA.

These feuds were mostly playful. The point was less about the superiority of one particular region and more about the decentralized, antiauthoritarian nature of punk.

Flipside, the best and most popular punk fanzine of its time, caused a stir in 1982 when it ceased publishing scene reports. The reason? The reports were inaccurate, since one person couldn't sum up a whole state or country in a few short paragraphs. Worse, having a central voice took power away from the regional zines. *Flipside* printed a long list of them, urging readers to go straight to the source.

It was a bold move. Unfortunately, *Maximumrocknroll* started a few months later to fill the gap and create the centralized voice which *Flipside* strove to avoid.

Cometbus already covered only local bands, but that was half accidental. After *Flipside*'s decision, it became policy. I met and loved many touring bands, but it was only the local ones—plus the Ramones—who made it into the mag.

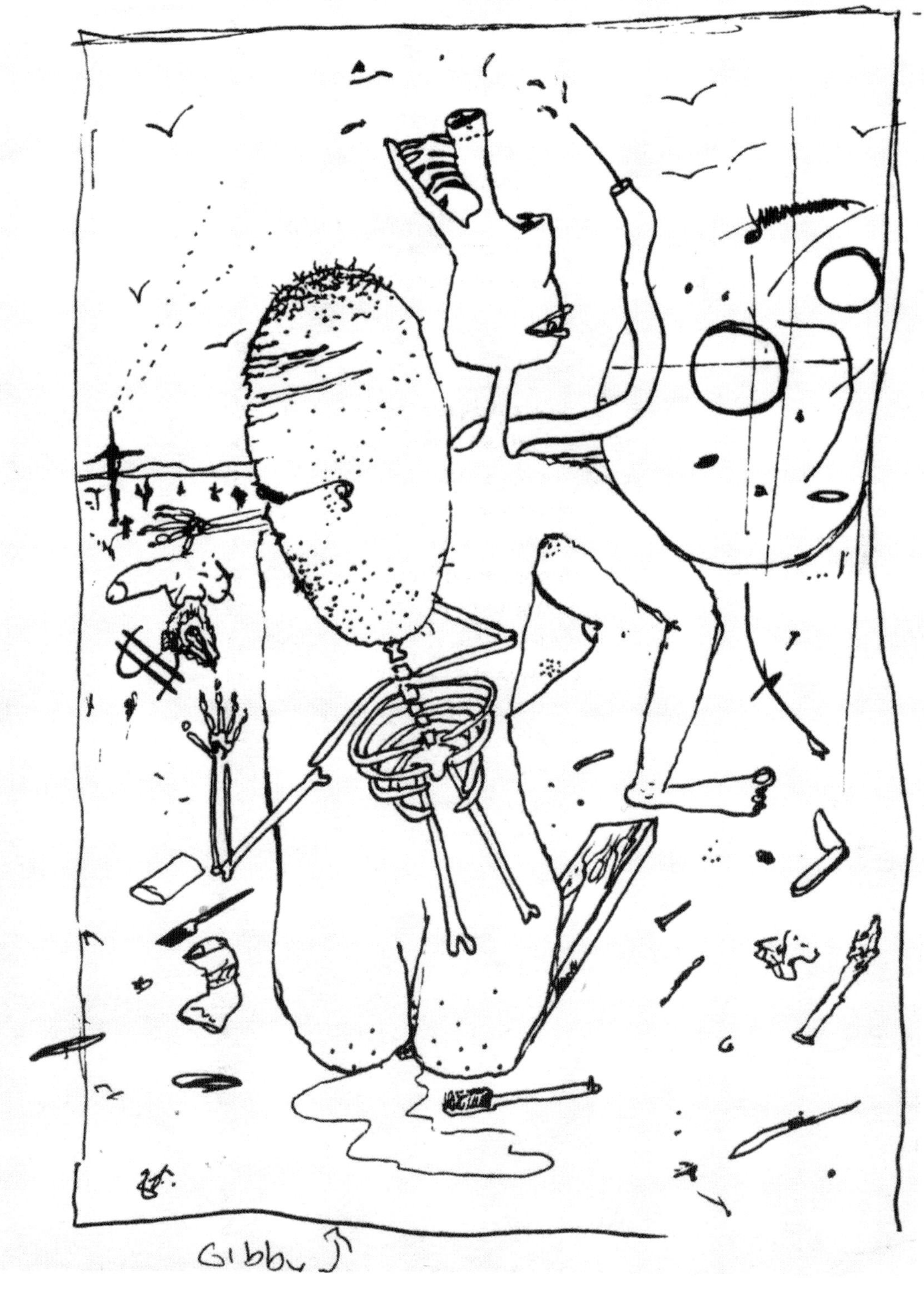

3.111. Butthole Surfers original art.

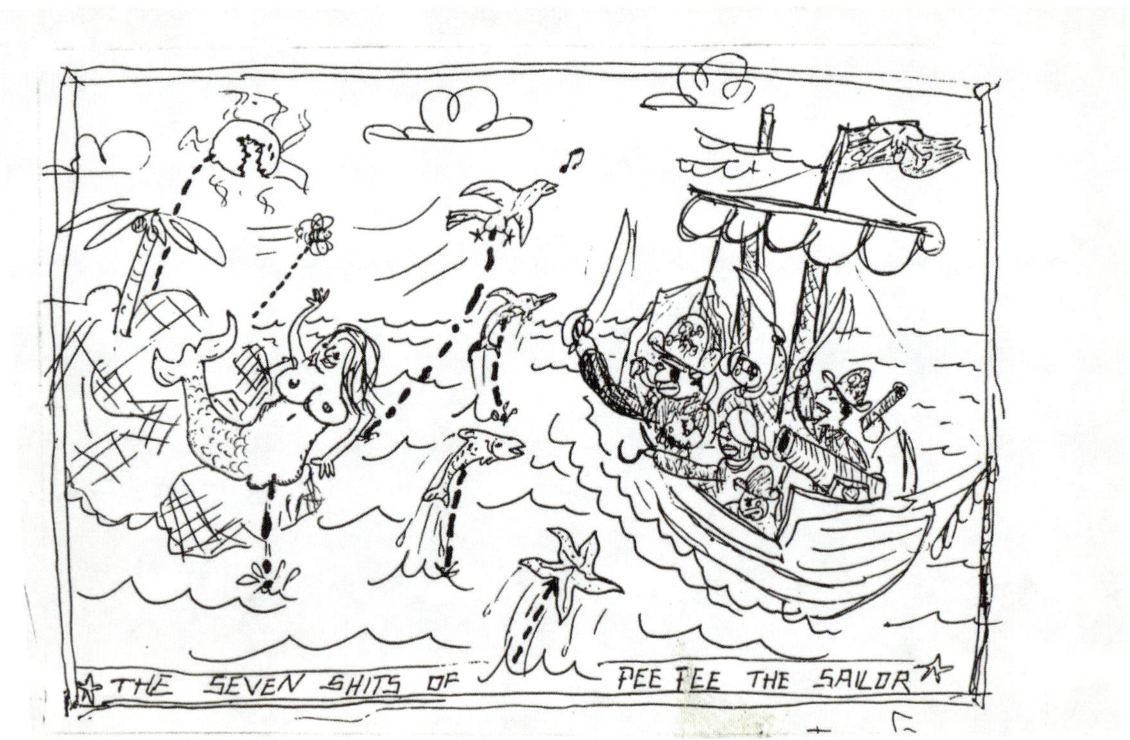

3.112. Butthole Surfers original art.

Then came the Butthole Surfers. Every couple of years a band would arrive and turn the Bay Area on its ear, making everyone hot and bothered, and pulling all the wash-ups out of the woodwork. Soon the band had girlfriends, boyfriends, a record label, and a slew of imitators. They settled right in and grew roots.

The Buttholes were the exception, feeling at home in the Bay long enough to sample every soup kitchen in town and pronounce the quality higher than restaurants back home, yet choosing not to stay. Even still, they were exciting enough to break my locals-only rule. Grux interviewed them for *Cometbus*, not once but twice, with accompanying drawings by each member of the band.

I've mentioned the mess I grew up in, and my severe lack of organization and discipline. Grux made me promise to return the original art to him. When I didn't, he stopped speaking to me, which hurt, because he was a friend. What could I do? The art was lost somewhere in the knee-high piles I waded through every time I crossed my room, the punkest fire hazard in town.

I uncovered those drawings twenty years too late—a memento of a great band in its prime, before subsequent fame. Also a memento of a friendship lost to the pitfalls of hoarding. I don't blame Grux for being sore.

BRAPH SMEARS DEMO

I've known folks who despise the phrase "demo tape," just like I've had bandmates who scoff at the words "practice" and "rehearse." They don't want to equate music with a drill or test—something they have to get *right*. Or in the case of these cassettes, to demonstrate.

Point taken, but what should we call them instead? "Mix tapes" is a much later expression, and inaccurate even for the compilations included in the archive. Most were handmade, but they weren't personalized. Dozens or even hundreds of identical copies were duplicated.

Neither does "demo" infer a lesser quality than a vinyl release. In fact, the opposite is true. I can't count the times I've heard someone say, "Their demo was way better, before they got overproduced."

Previously, cassettes had been used solely for promotional purposes—to pass on to club owners, labels, and DJs. Suddenly in the early eighties they seemed poised to revolutionize the music industry, democratizing it the way paperbacks had publishing. Bow Wow Wow's first release, issued only on tape, made the band an overnight success in the UK. On a smaller scale, cassette-only labels like ROIR and BCT were generating the same excitement in the US. Compilations like *Charred Remains*, *No Core*, *Kitten*, and *New York Thrash* helped spotlight regional scenes that had been overlooked. Audio magazines like *Non* and *YCAM* started popping up.

Bands began selling their own tapes at gigs as if it was the most natural thing on earth, which it was. Yet despite the increasing popularity of cassettes, most groups expected to follow up their demo with a "proper" vinyl debut. This was wishful thinking. Few slated projects got recorded, and only a handful of those ever saw release. Most bands disappeared without a trace, except for maybe an appearance on a local compilation tape. These weren't just the obscure bands, but also the most popular groups of the time, who missed the chance to do it themselves because they were so busy trying to get signed.

One treasure of a cassette is by the Braph Smears, an almost entirely forgotten all-woman group from early eighties Portland who are an important missing link in punk history. Mish Bondage went on to sing for Sado-Nation, while Angie Mima and Shellee moved to SF and formed

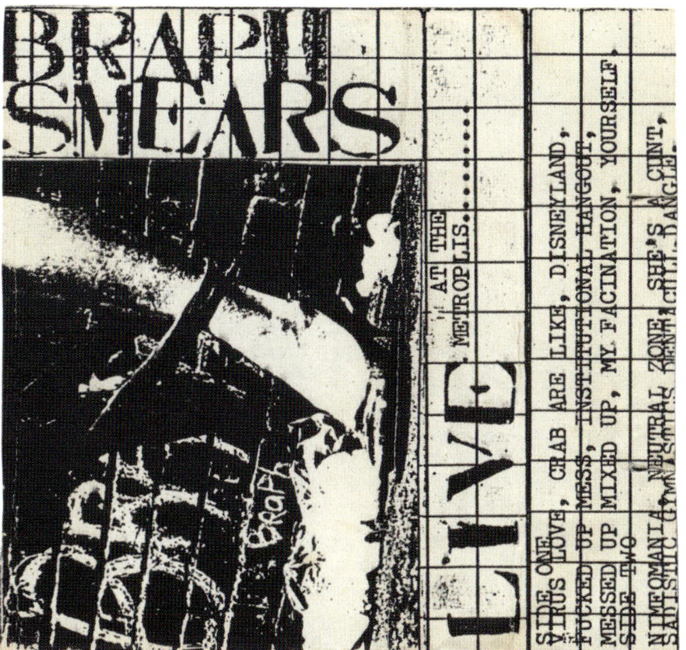

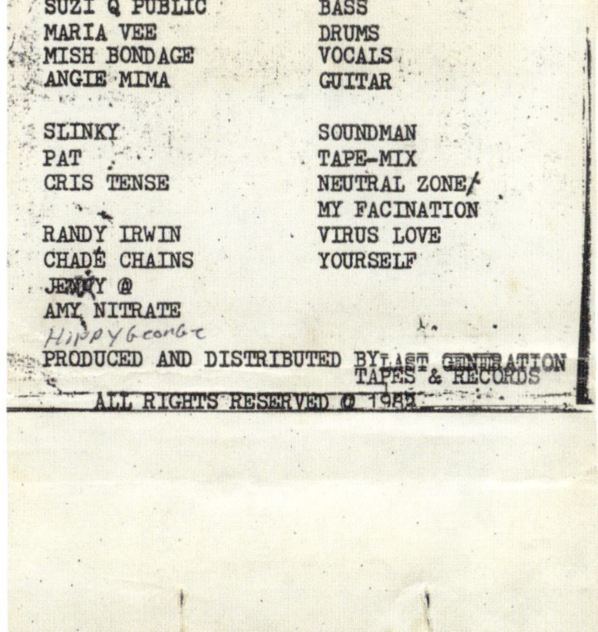

3.113 and 3.114. Exterior and interior of Braph Smears demo J-card.

Hello Impending Doom zine —

Saw your zine listed in Flipside and thought I'd write. I live way out in the boondocks in western Kentucky and mailorder records and zines are about all that keeps me functional! We have a small scene here, 2 bands in the garage here in Paducah & maybe the same in Carbondale Illinois where the only club that will book HC regularly is. I'm in one band, Box Lunch, playing bass and I manage the other, the Drooling Idiots (who have a couple of cassettes out and really rip).

We've all been thinking of moving out your way, San Francisco actually (although from what I've heard about rents in the city we might end up in Berkeley or some other nearby town just to prevent starvation). All we have here is each other - nowhere jobs or no jobs, noplace to play 90% of the time, more societal pressure than a normal person can deal with to settle down, get married, and mortgage your life away. I don't know about you, but my goal in life is not a brand new pickup truck with a Red Man sticker on the back bumper and a sixpack under the seat! I realize (after living 4 years in Albuquerque N.M., where there's a fairly big scene & a bigger city) that moving doesn't solve everything but my patience has limits. This place is driving me and all the other punks here totally fucking crazy!! So if you've got the time, tell me a little about the bay area and what you think of it in a letter. We'd all appreciate it!

I didn't send a stamp or money since you were listed as free but if you need it let me know for next time you get an issue out. Thanx— Mitzi Waltz

3910 Sunset Av. Paducah KY 42001

P.S.-Here's a Peace Core sticker. They're a cool band from Denver who played at the club I used to run (the Bash & Mash) in Albuquerque.

3.115. Letter from Mitzi Waltz to Aaron Cometbus, 1984.

Barely Human. Angie also howled for the amazing Green Hell, who played only one show before going down in a self-destructive blaze. Now there's a band that could actually be your life!

There was nothing tentative or shy about this crew. They were dirty and nasty, absolutely hardcore yet unafraid to experiment and make beautiful music as well. Their songs, however, were less important than the example they set. Bands were an attempt to create new and better families—more supportive, more expressive, and more egalitarian than the families we'd grown up in. Each band was a miniature version of what we were trying to create on a much larger scale: a group that worked together despite our differences, for little or no reward, and regardless of the fact that we sometimes hated each other's guts.

That, Dear Reader, was punk. It wasn't a particular sound. Nor was it simply an attitude, because you had to include yourself in a group. It wasn't just about doing-it-yourself—it was about doing it *together* and helping each other out.

MITZI WALTZ LETTER

A letter arrived in 1984 from a young woman in Paducah, Kentucky, asking for advice. Should she keep the home fires burning, or move to more fertile ground where her talents might be better appreciated and put to use? I printed her letter in *Cometbus* #15, asking the readers to weigh in. Surprisingly, they did—surprising because at the time the mag received very little response. Publishing a fanzine was like being a late night disc jockey, which I also did. You put your heart into it, but couldn't tell if anyone was out there listening.

Mitzi received opinionated letters from a funny variety of folks. The verdict was split: half encouraging her to move, and half urging her to stay put. Predictably, perhaps, she packed her bags and headed west. Less predictable was the fact that she stayed and thrived. I saw her around town for the next several years, then continued to see her name in print. First it was attached to bands and fanzines, then journalism, and finally studies of bipolar disorders and autism, on which she became an expert.

Mitzi's letter is a reminder for me that even when no one seems to be listening, the effects of your broadcast can be life changing.

OFFSPRING CHECK

I knew the Offspring. Not well, but we were part of the same scene in the mid-to-late-eighties. They were widely regarded as TSOL clones, which wasn't such a bad thing. Had TSOL stuck to their classic formula, they'd have been playing to teeming crowds instead of mostly empty rooms.

There was a lot of talk about moving forward in punk, but the truth was that no one's second album was as good as the first. Punk bands were often great right out the gate, yet in the long haul, not so hot. Where the Offspring ended up fitting into this equation I can't say, having not seen or heard them besides an occasional radio hit in almost thirty years.

I remember them, however, as being nice, earnest, and rather wholesome guys. After their Bay Area shows, we would sometimes go bowling at an all-night alley in Pinole. They must have stopped by one of my annual laundromat parties, for what else would explain the birthday card I later unearthed?

KEVIN J. WASSERMAN
5411 PARK AVE. 714-897-9705
GARDEN GROVE, CA 92645
250
Vernal Equinox 1999
16-7021/114
3220
Pay to the Order of AARON ELLIOT
$ 250000000
250 Million Fuckin Bones Dollars
COAST SAVINGS AND LOAN
GARDEN GROVE OFFICE
12555 VALLEY VIEW STREET
GARDEN GROVE, CALIFORNIA 92645
Memo Warm Water/No Starch
Noodles Offspring

3.116. Offspring check made out to Aaron Elliot, 1987.

In 1987 the idea of punk millionaires was inconceivable, and the new century seemed impossibly far away. As a joke, they made out a check for a fortune and wrote "Vernal Equinox, 1999" as the date. Good timing—I found it while cleaning my room at the end of the century and deposited it on New Year's Eve. I hoped they would take the whole thing in good humor after the initial shock. I planned to return every penny if it cleared. It didn't. As a result, we can deduce that the Offspring are not millionaires.

CRASS SKETCH

Historians like their eras clearly defined, especially when it comes to punk. Borders are drawn. Timelines too. Anything after the arbitrary cutoff date is dismissed as homogeneous, commercial, or fake.

But real life isn't so easily contained. It's messy and complicated, and so is our scene.

Recently, I read and enjoyed Thurston Moore's *No Wave*. The book is an obsessive look at late seventies New York, including groups that never even played a gig. There's only one band so mysterious that no information could be found. I smiled when I saw their name: Arsenal.

Moore declares No Wave dead by 1980, but he was looking in the wrong place. Arsenal was still alive and well three years later, playing in a dingy basement in San Francisco's Mission District, opening up for Minor Threat. They were producing a dizzying array of fanzines, flyers, music, and film—and bassist Dionne carried a bag of saltwater taffy which she dispensed to punk kids like me, making every day like Halloween.

When I interviewed them, they spoke about the dull audiences back in New York and their upcoming cut on a compilation released by Crass. Dave the drummer drew a sketch on my binder. It was the Crass logo—which it turned out he'd designed.

I was shocked, but shouldn't have been surprised. There are always people who straddle different eras and scenes, and apply themselves wherever the action is.

DICKS AT BHS FLYER

Berkeley High was unlike other schools. Swahili was taught. So was Crime in the Streets, which I took. The teacher was an ex-con and ex-cop, as well as a former 49ers quarterback. Instead of a final, he screened old Jackson Five footage as a special treat.

The school's uniqueness did not, however, keep it from being an oppressive environment where creativity thrived only when it was hidden from sight. The casual beatings of junior high were gone, but there was no support to take their place. Our bands weren't invited to play the talent show or interviewed in the school paper. The extremely talented punk artists weren't taken seriously on their own terms. And I certainly didn't get credit—or any kind of encouragement—for doing *Cometbus*. Which seemed fine at the time. We were accustomed to avoiding official attention and making our own fun. Only in hindsight does it seem like a wasted opportunity and a shame.

Considering the unwelcoming or, at best, indifferent climate, the last thing we expected was the flyer that greeted us when we trudged onto campus one day. A dance-a-thon in our school cafeteria was weird enough, but our young minds were blown when we got to the small print halfway down the page. The Dicks—who *Maximumrocknroll* accurately described as a "commie faggot band"—were playing.

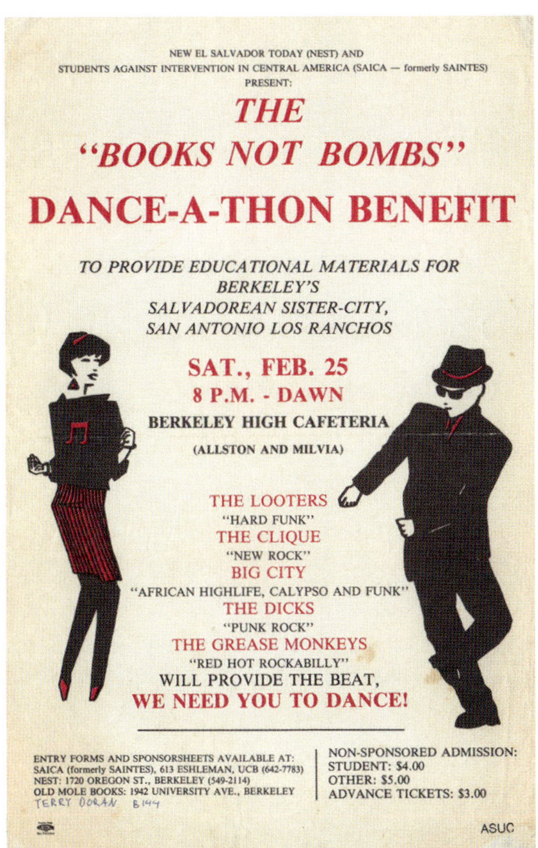

3.117. Flyer for the Dicks show at Berkeley High School, 1984.

We stared in disbelief. Instead of the stone-faced cafeteria staff, it would be Gary Floyd in a nurse's outfit belting out "Little Boys' Feet" while he ladeled greasy slop onto plastic trays. Even the flyer alone was hard to comprehend. Not only was the band's name uncensored, but the description of their music was accurate. "Punk rock," like that was just some normal thing.

You have to understand, Berkeley was a liberal city, but it was heavily regulated as a result, which made DIY creativity difficult. The chance of punks booking a local punk band to play the high school was nil. When I'd tried with MDC a few years earlier at our junior high, I'd described them as a string quartet, and even that was rejected out of hand.

So how had this miracle come to pass? There was a logical explanation—logical in local terms, at least—and I pieced it together in the weeks preceding the event, as we waited for the Dicks with bated breath.

The band, you see, had unusual ties. They had allied themselves with the Revolutionary Communist Party, our slovenly, conniving, embarrassing local Maoist army. For this the Dicks could be forgiven, having only recently arrived from out of state. All self-respecting commies and anarchists considered the RCP a joke, yet they had some mysterious pull with the older armchair radicals in town. With a Berkeley High alumnus as chairman, they were the closest we had to a home team, if a Pol Pot–style takeover was your end game.

Our school's Black Studies department included some fellow travelers. This I knew, having run into them at planning meetings for No Business as Usual, one of the many promising movements the RCP had hijacked and ruined. It seemed crazy that this pair of militant, dashiki-wearing educators had conspired with a bumbling Maoist army to book the fattest, gayest, greatest punk band of all time to play our high school's lunchroom—and at 3 a.m., no less. Yet that appeared to be the case.

This story has no satisfying conclusion, I'm sorry to say. The long-awaited date arrived, and the Berkeley punks queued up outside. But the Dicks were a no-show. They had accidentally double-booked themselves and were playing elsewhere that night. The usually enjoyable Grease Monkeys (featuring a young Charlie Hunter) were cold comfort in this case.

This flyer is the only proof of what might have been.

BOBBY MADNESS ART

New York City, London, and California may have had the best-known scenes, but we would be remiss if we didn't also look closer to home—in this case, right down the hill from the campus at Cornell.

Strange to say, but coming of age in Berkeley, it was Ithaca punk that was legendary to me. I studied its style and slang. I knew the graffiti under the local bridges and the cut of the waitresses' uniforms at the State Diner. I even knew how many refills you were likely to receive before getting kicked out. All from three thousand miles away.

My romantic ideas about the place didn't come from records, photos, or films, but from the comics of Ithaca-born artist Bobby Madness. His stories were action-packed enough to seem exotic, but they were familiar, too—certainly more so than the hackneyed tales of bar bands in the metropolitan capitals. After all, I was from a college town myself. Like Bobby, I was a townie in a town where the university played an oversize role.

His illustrations were unapologetically bleak yet still bursting with hope, the basic recipe for punk. They were particular *and* universal, like all great art. Only his scenery seemed exaggeratedly grand and lush, which I chalked up to too much weed. Funny, then, to arrive in Ithaca and already know my way around. Turns out he hadn't exaggerated a thing.

The only piece missing was Bobby himself. We missed each other by a single day, and continued to miss each other on every subsequent trip I made. Finally we simply traded coasts, Bobby settling in Portland and me in New York. By then, the college library I'd taken refuge in on my visits to Ithaca felt like an old friend, albeit an uncommonly quiet and reliable one. It was always welcoming, kept late hours, and was open to the public, in stark contrast to its counterpart in Berkeley. A warm spot to study and read is a friend indeed. So when it came time to place my archives, the Cornell library was a natural choice.

Best of all, I could preserve in its permanent collection the wonderfully evocative, irreverent art that had led me there in the first place.

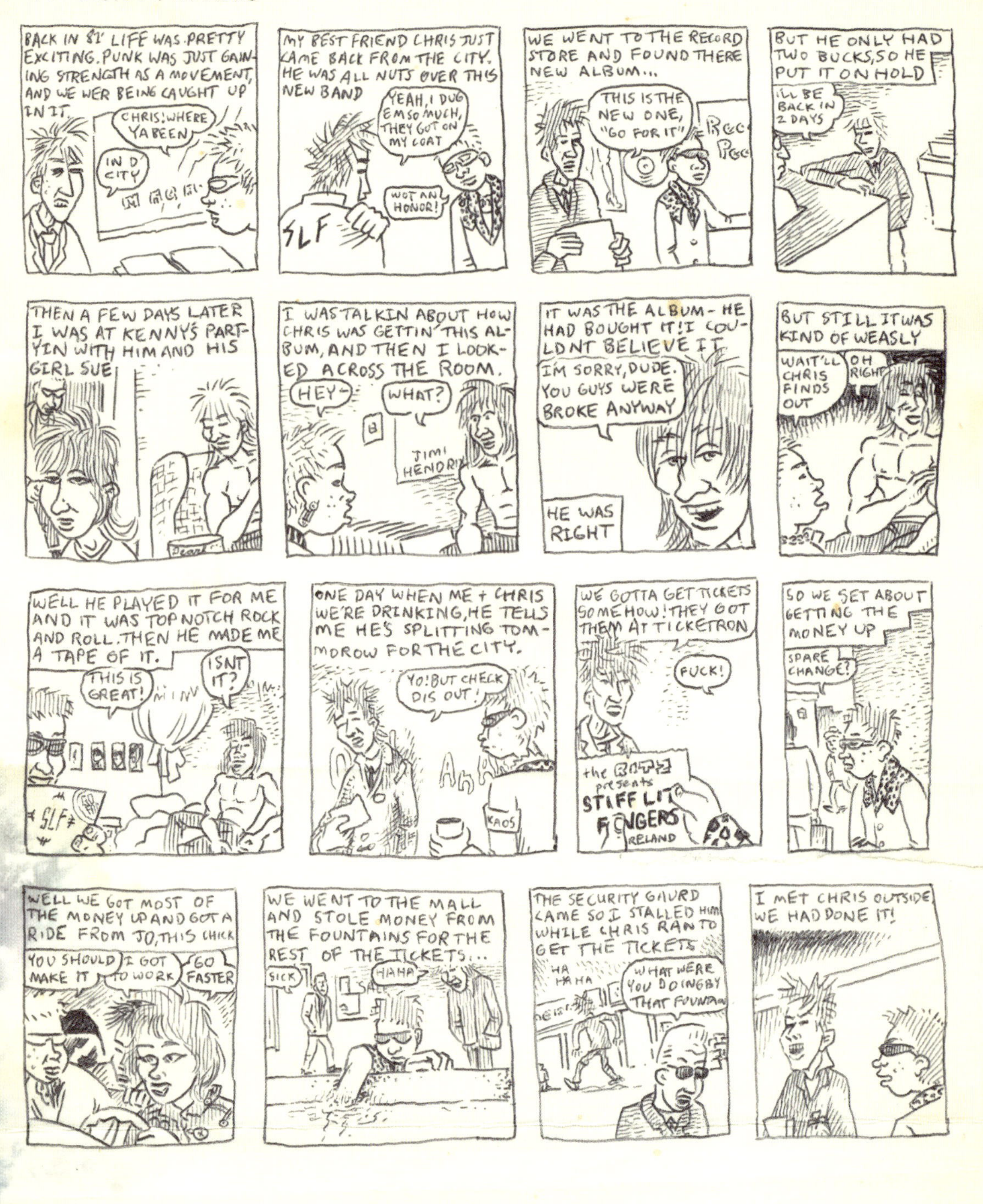

3.118 and 3.119. Previously unpublished two-page story about a road trip from Ithaca to see Stiff Little Fingers in New York City. © Bobby Madness.

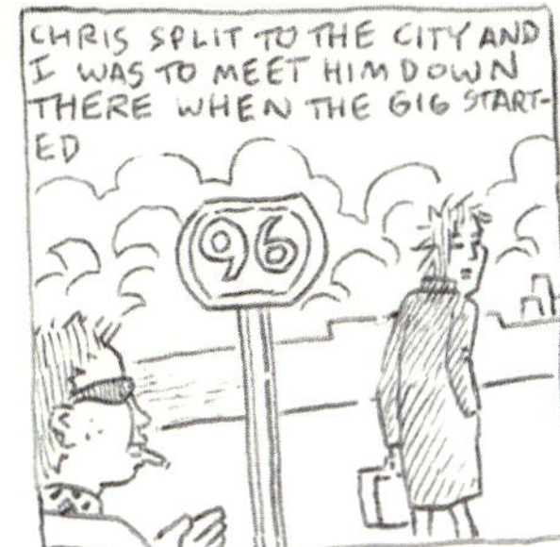

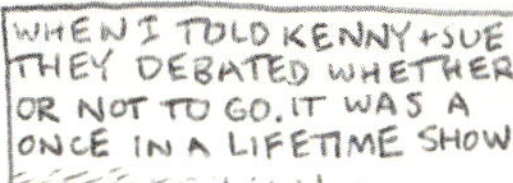

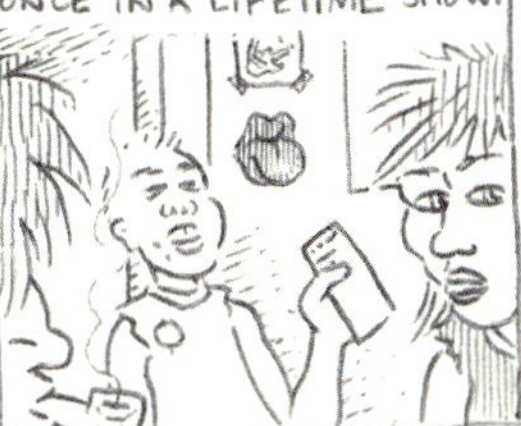

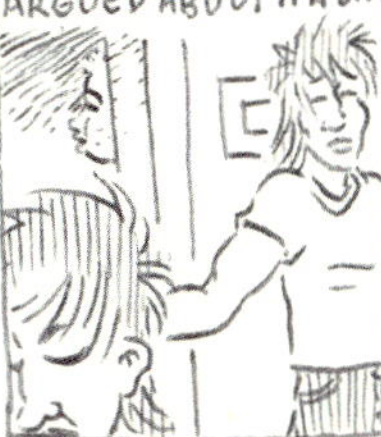

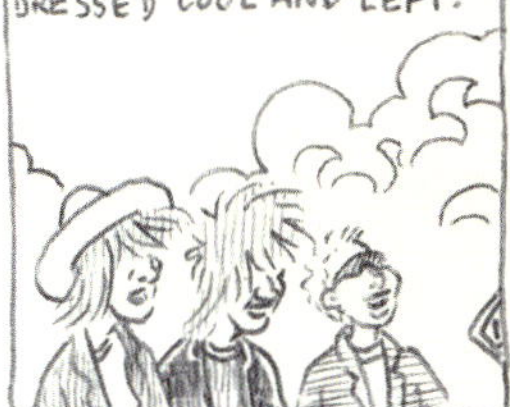

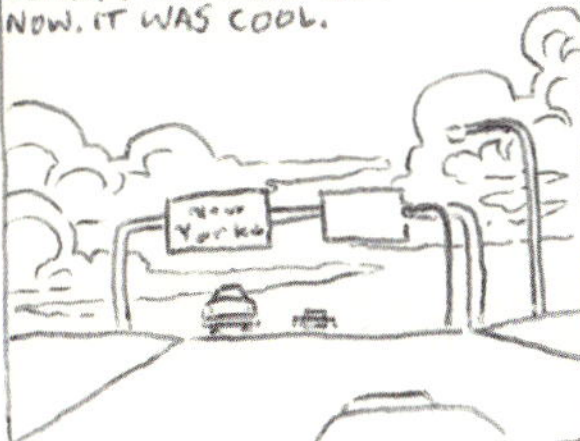

WHEN WE GOT THERE WE TRAIPED AROUND CLUE-LESSLY. WE DIDNT KNOW WHERE CHRIS WAS, ONLY THAT HE WAS ON THE LOWER EAST SIDE

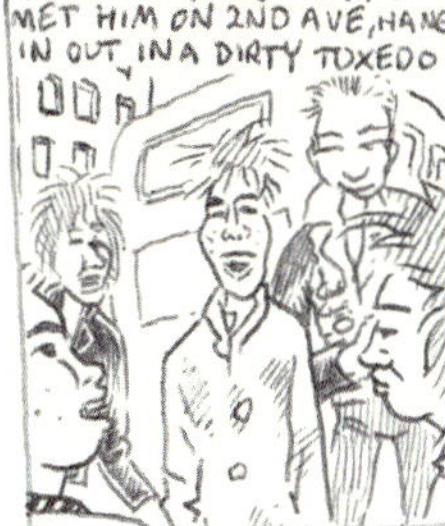

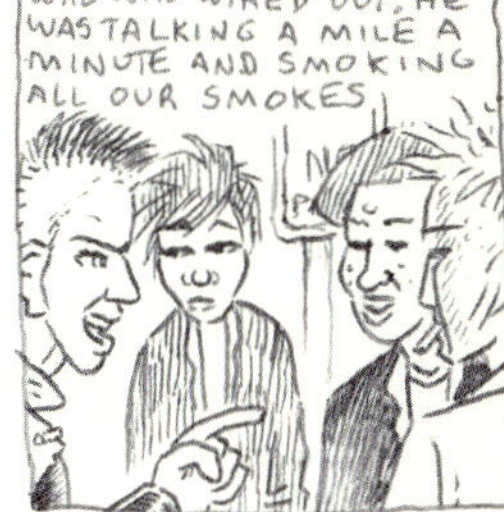

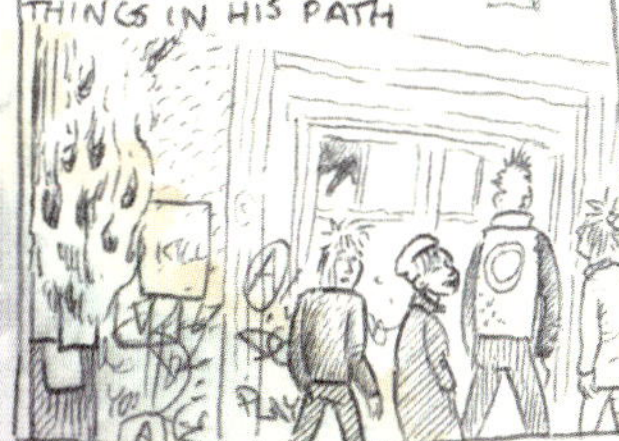

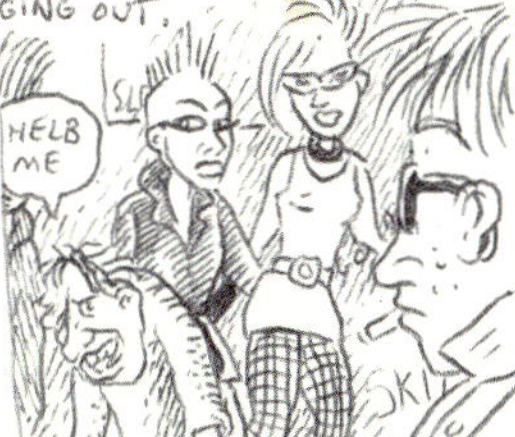

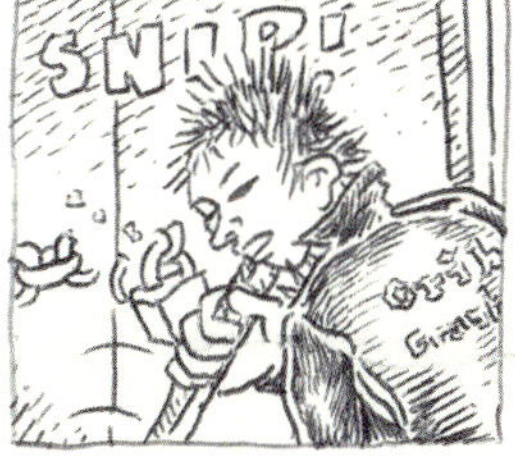

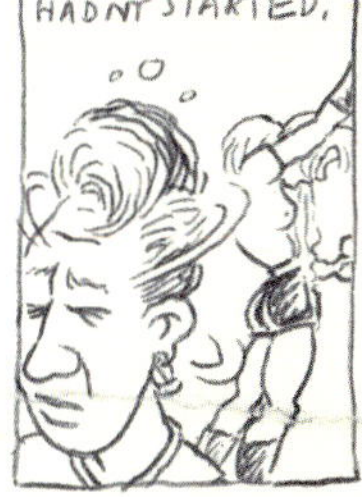

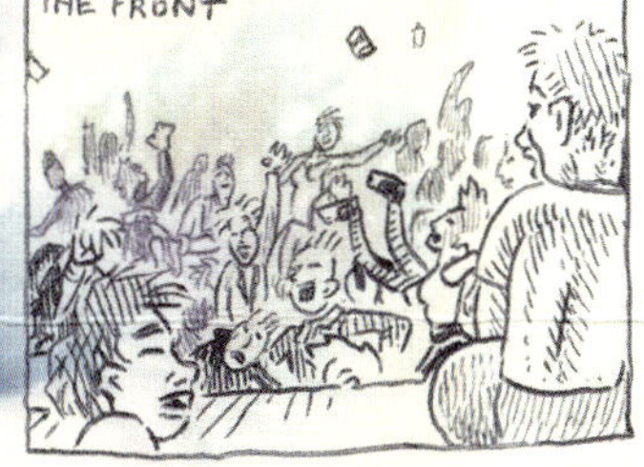

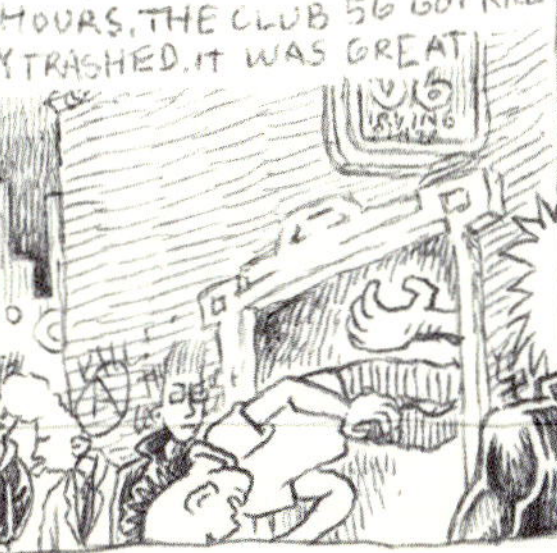

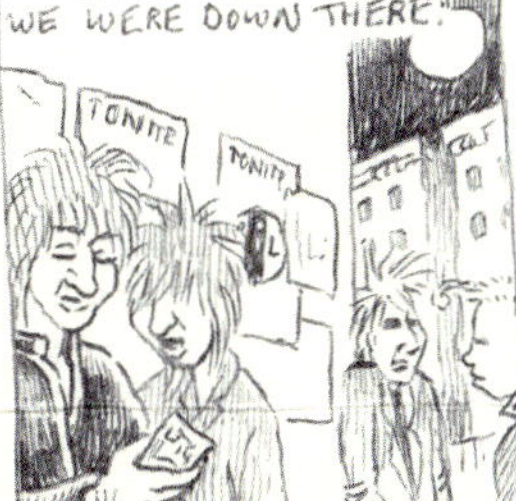

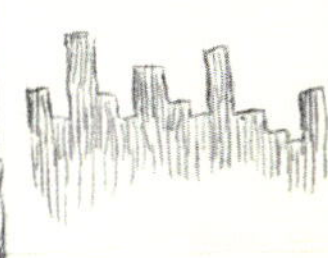

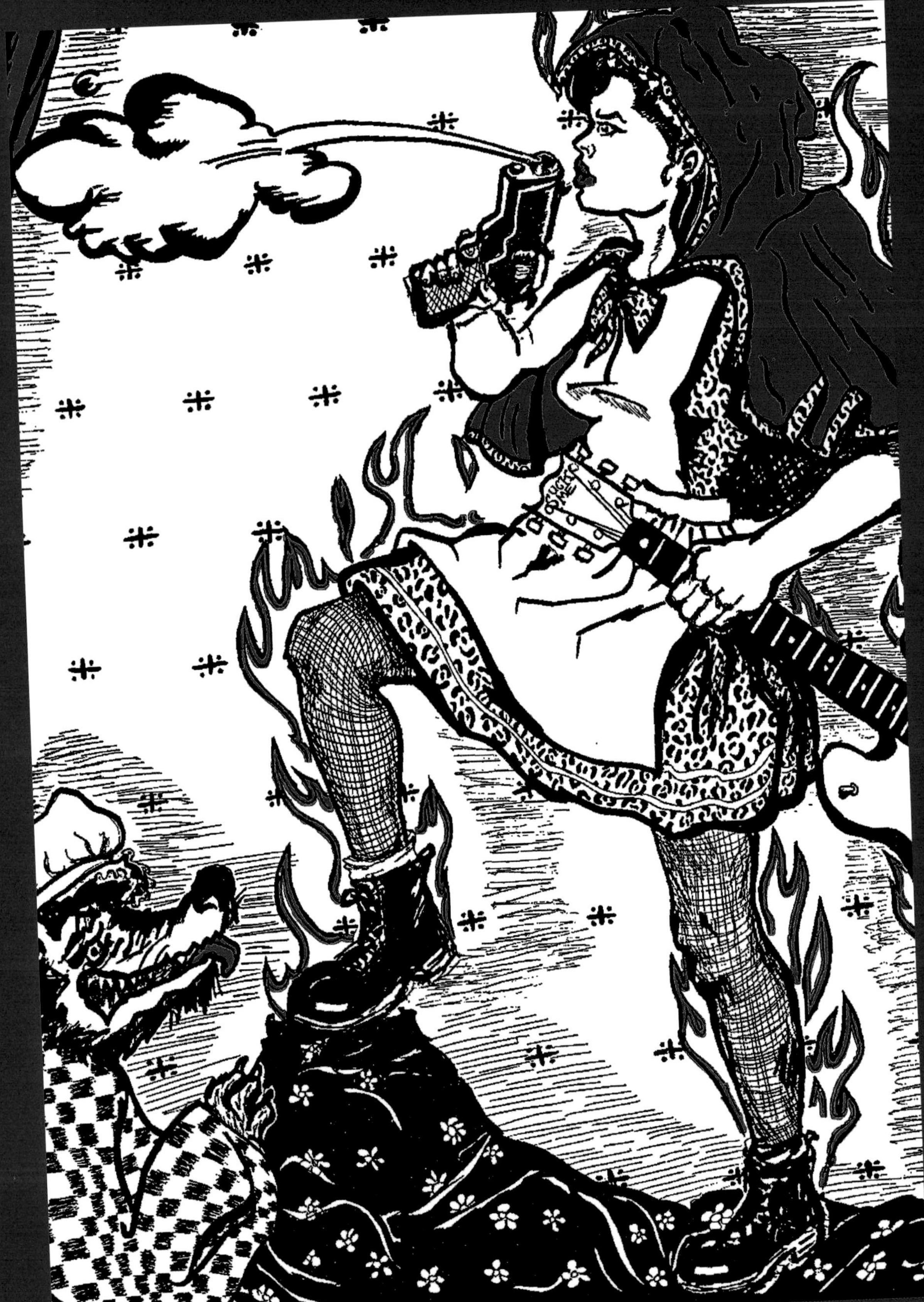

Maps for the Groundless

CH. 14

ANNA JOY SPRINGER

In my late teens and twenties I was a vocalist in California Bay Area punk bands Blatz, the Gr'ups, and Cypher in the Snow. I also performed with Sister Spit, a queer feminist group of punk writers who first began touring the US in the nineties. Now at fifty, I'm an artist, writer, and tenured professor with a framed and hand-gilded certificate praising my contributions to punk performance. Given the social value of work done by that year's other winners (one colleague proved neuroplasticity and another helped establish a new democracy's first nationwide voting procedures), I'm astonished and even a little worried to have received this honor for crashing about onstage shouting provocations like, "Kill 'em all and let the Goddess sort 'em out!"

After twenty years of teaching, I know we don't replace previous incarnations of ourselves with new models. Developmental phases accrue. The part of me that's confused by prizes honoring conceivably dishonorable activities feels teenagerish. Increasingly aware of prevalent adult hypocrisy, this younger me has more trouble with paradox than I do now. Despite throbbing sensitivity, she's determined not to care about anything but the most gruesome social and interpersonal injustices. This young protector remains a living part of the current, older me. I feel her slam to the front of my chest at any hint that our nemesis, Wolf-in-Sheepsuit, may be nearby.

FROM THE CRADLE TO THE STAGE

Our personal threshold-crossing into punk possibility came at fourteen on a back-to-school shopping trip to Santa Cruz. Dusty and mean, my hometown Merced featured the sweet bile smell of fruit-processing factories, wasted Air Force dads cruising Main in lowered trucks, and unofficial segregation by railroad tracks. Two hours west, Santa Cruz was a university/beach town with a transgressively virtuous counterculture. There angular-haired bisexual girls sold used books and vintage clothes at shops where bundles of *Poetry Flash* confettied doorways near stacks of *Maximumrocknroll*—a magazine, it seemed, for angry boys.

Self-consciously scuttling through a record store, having only ever bought cassettes from Kmart and Musicland, I flipped through LPs with muted urgency, not knowing what I was looking for. Striking cover design led me to Subhumans' *From the Cradle to the Grave*. On the front, a giant hand descends from clouds toward Earth, an infant scaling its palm crawling away from the cow pasture where it's being deposited. The record opened in a gatefold, with all the lyrics on the inner covers, so anyone could read them without having to buy the record first. The writing was churchy but self-critical and secular, warning against the cruel designs of ruling-class grownups and their flunky-making institutions in shrewd lyrics penned by singer Dick Lucas.

I couldn't have predicted that in a few short years I'd be touring Europe in my band the Gr'ups with Dick Lucas and other members of Subhumans, who'd regrouped as Citizen Fish.

What happened between that first record purchase and the tour bus? I got saved, derailed from a full-speed trajectory toward marriage, motherhood, bathtub crank, and multiple jobs when I got a scholarship to a state-funded summer arts program for California high schoolers. There I found punk girls. They took me through the portal to a parallel world where I encountered the height of teenage intellectual civilization: espresso, Operation Ivy, Crimpshrine, the Yeastie Girlz, powder drugs, and a magical Denny's crowded with potential boyfriends. One of these punk girls, a poet, was Annie. In a year we'd be singing together in Blatz, dodging wet cat food and spit.

It's a funny story, how we became bandmates. Jesse, the new singer, had misunderstood guitarist Robert "Eggplant" when he'd suggested Annie as a possible "girl singer" for Blatz. A freshman at Mills College, I'd been volunteering with Jesse at Gilman booking shows for a few weeks. Jesse believed Eggplant wanted to recruit me, though I, a chubby, opinionated college girl from nowhere was hardly on anyone's radar. Annie and I showed up for tryouts at the same time, delighted to see each other! Until we realized we were in competition for the same "girl singer" spot.

I yelled; Annie screamed. We left together and devised a plan upstairs at Café Med: if the band wanted one of us, they'd have to keep us both. Jesse backed us up. We showed up at rehearsal the following week, daring them to make either of us leave. Which, although grouchy for months, they didn't do. That is the true story of how Blatz ended up with three vocalists, as we would sometimes posit, "like Crass." As for division of vocals and lyrics, my primary rule was that I wouldn't sing it if I didn't mean it. On the perplexing song "Fuk New York," for instance, I only ever yelled, "Fuck." It took several shows and a first EP to prove we weren't "backup singers." Between "Berkeley Is My Baby" and "Lullaby" (a song I wrote for the infant I was babysitting at the time), Annie and I became known as full members of Blatz.

Origin stories remain central to both punk and feminist testimony, maybe more so when they overlap. But origin stories ideally precede subsequent quests, reversals, and sometimes even moments of emotional and intellectual resolution. That said, until I began to write this essay, I didn't register the complexity and persistence of my emotional connection to my youth in punk bands. The old "everything's fine, as long as I don't care" stance regularly sneaks back in as an unconscious defense. Yet clearly I *do* care. It's through the filter of this hazily remembered, sometimes skeptical tenderness that I discuss writings, recordings, and other ephemera that I made (or otherwise touched) held in the punk archive at Cornell University in both the "Aaron Cometbus Punk and Underground Press Collection, ca. 1977–2018" and Matt Wobensmith's "Riot Grrrl Zine and Music Collection, circa 1989–1997."

MARGINALIA IS THE MESSAGE

Cornell Library's "Wake the Form: Artists' Books in Context" exhibition page displays the 1993 zine *Diseaster Now for Future Love* vol. 1, no. 3 (3.120 AND 3.121).

As I began to look through materials in the archive, I became excited about this particular zine for personal reasons. The back cover shows a gag-style line drawing of two white characters

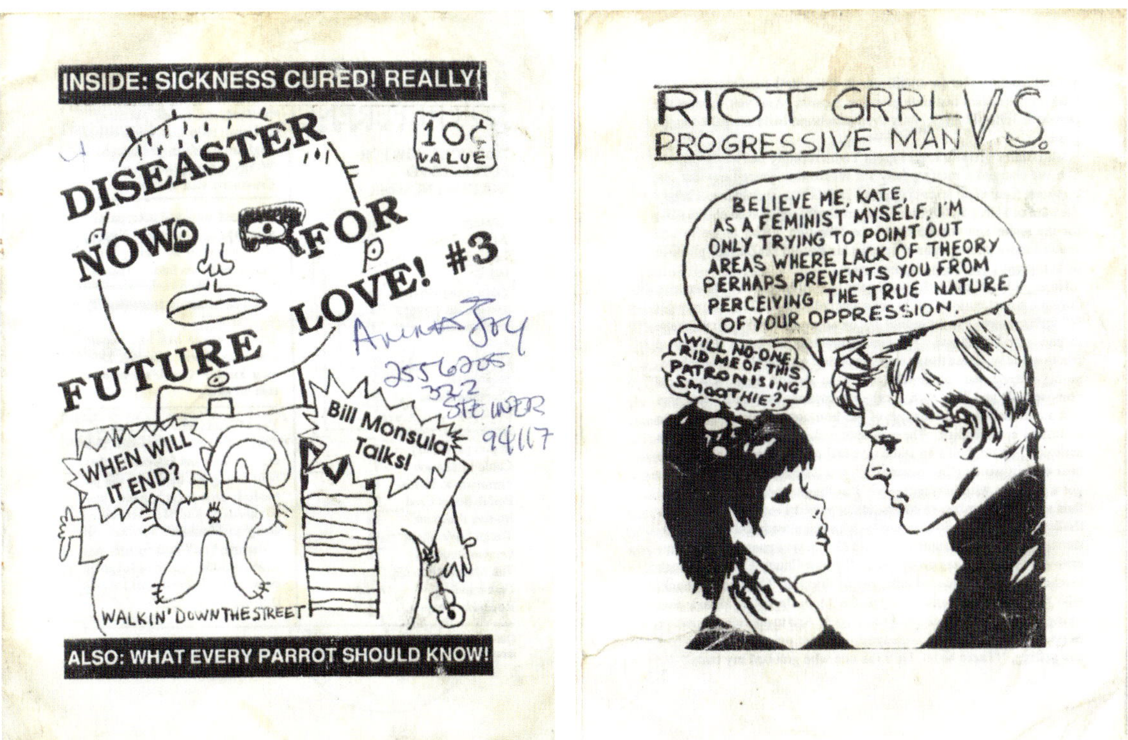

3.120 and 3.121. Front and back pages of the zine Diseaster Now for Future Love vol. 1, no. 3, 1993.

facing each other in profile coded as "Riot Grrrl" and "Progressive Man," art seemingly made either by someone unfamiliar with basic feminist agency, someone accusing riot grrrl of producing polite, ineffectual straight women, or someone, more likely, in a process of publicly learning through the complexities of something they deeply cared about. On the front cover in blue ballpoint pen is my name and contact information. I had just moved to the Lower Haight, and a new address meant a new phone number, which I'd written onto the zine cover offered up by my guy friend Aaron Cometbus. By then, I was deeply into school, work, and the dyke punk scene in San Francisco, enjoying life as a pseudo-separatist. Aaron was an exception that proved the rule. Now, twenty-five years later, I was reintroduced to my old handwriting (how long had it been since I'd *written down* a phone number?) on *Diseaster Now*. . . . I got a flash of Aaron and me back in my room on Steiner arguing the night away, our thousands of cigarette butts overflowing a giant pink ashtray moonlit against my velvet bedspread.

PLAYERS AND PLAYTHINGS

In thinking about subcultures that produce exciting entertainment like the ones represented in Cornell's punk archive, it's easy to focus on performers and products, the entrepreneurs, labels, the minor, anti- or full-on celebrities. But, as Aaron writes in his introduction to the Cometbus Collection (BOX 1, FOLDER A), during this period of punk cultural history, much of the most vibrant and dedicated manifestations of punk community happened offstage. The rock part of punk is just one aspect of a participatory rhizomatic experience made by all sorts of people doing all sorts of things, including not doing much but hanging out and talking. Bullshitting and joking, yes, but also talking with passionate intelligence. In punk culture, it's mostly OK to be smart and show it; to speculate wildly, read, and argue ideas. In my experience, this emphasis on dynamic conversation and a general respect for intellect is as at least as significant an expression of community life as are music and debauchery. At the same time, in the punk scenes I knew, certain self-aggrandizing displays of moral righteousness might be seen as masculinist-authoritarian and kind of embarrassing. Unlike the passionate seriousness of other contemporary scenes, silliness, clowning, pop, and camp frequently defined late twentieth-century Bay Area punk aesthetics.

It stands to reason that a culture that extends as unofficial rites both (a) walking around all night barefoot in torn fishnets and (b) touring the country in a $500 van without cellphones would need to make its own guidebooks and specialized maps. Some, like the "Book Your Own Fucking Life" project, shared accurate, practical information, while other hand-drawn maps faithfully misrepresent their territory. (See, for instance the original poster for "The Cometbus Traveling Archive" boasting "Maps Guaranteed to Get You Lost" (3.122).

The archived Blatz board game is a functionally useless but perfectly safe ethnographic adventure game and material object of self-mockery in the form of a multidirectional map with game cards and spinner (3.123, 3.124, 3.125).

Created collaboratively by Blatz bandmate Jesse Lucious and his extremely awake friends Kevin Pickle, Ken Wisconsin, and Salerinda Sometimes (and unnamed others), board and cards refer parodically to mythical punk activities like blowing up police stations, shooting up in bathrooms, and beating up ska fans, which no one involved in making the game had any intention of doing. I remain vaguely upset by the many enthusiastic allusions to intravenous drug use in Blatz, even as equally fictitious references to looting, cannibalism, and infanticide delight me.

3.122. Poster for "The Cometbus Traveling Archive."

The game board locates some of the first venues Blatz had played in 1989 and 1990, including two Bay Area–adjacent towns where Blatz ran amok. The first, a pizza place in Redwood City, had banned Blatz from ever returning, as documented in our demo cassette *Banned in R.C.*[1] Blatz's first seven-inch "Cheaper Than the Beer" quotes the pizza place manager's main reason for pulling the plug: "You know honey, it ain't nice to spit in the customer's face." That statement was directed at me. It is just as true today as it ever was.

At the top of the game board is Davis, rural college suburb of Sacramento and site of our April 6, 1990, show at the Vets' Hall with the Mr. T Experience, Monsula, and Nasal Sex, another accidental comedy that led to Blatz's early, outsize sense of self-esteem. In Davis, singer Jesse was stripped naked by other ostensibly straight guys in the dance pit, as was normal. Having enjoyed this liberatory form of communal expression many times before, Jesse had developed a system of tucking his clothes into the bass drum to avoid losing them in the melee that would inevitably escalate toward the end of the set when the band might be, for example, pseudo-consensually pelted with old McMuffins, kidnapped from stage, or buried in garbage. But after this show, Jesse was surprised to discover that bandmates had already loaded the equipment into the van. As Jesse streaked across the parking lot toward the van to retrieve his pants, an offended skinhead outside the venue asked a cop working security at the show to intervene. The security cop was, no lie, related to the skinhead, and Jesse was arrested. By some strange providence, local celebrity columnist Herb Caen wrote about the fiasco in his column. Some item buried in the archive, maybe in the Lawrence Livermore Papers, should corroborate my story.

On a seemingly tangential note, it was in game-maker Salarinda's room at the famous Oakland Genoa Street punkhouse (where I lived in the carriage house) that I found Kathy Acker's novel *Don Quixote*. This discovery of punk feminist literature and Kathy Acker herself would have incalculable impact on my future.

BONDAGE BELTS AND WOLF'S HEAD HAT

My experience of punk was shaped by coming of age in a very specific literary Bay Area counterculture. In 1991 it seemed that everywhere I turned, from the window displays of Artists'

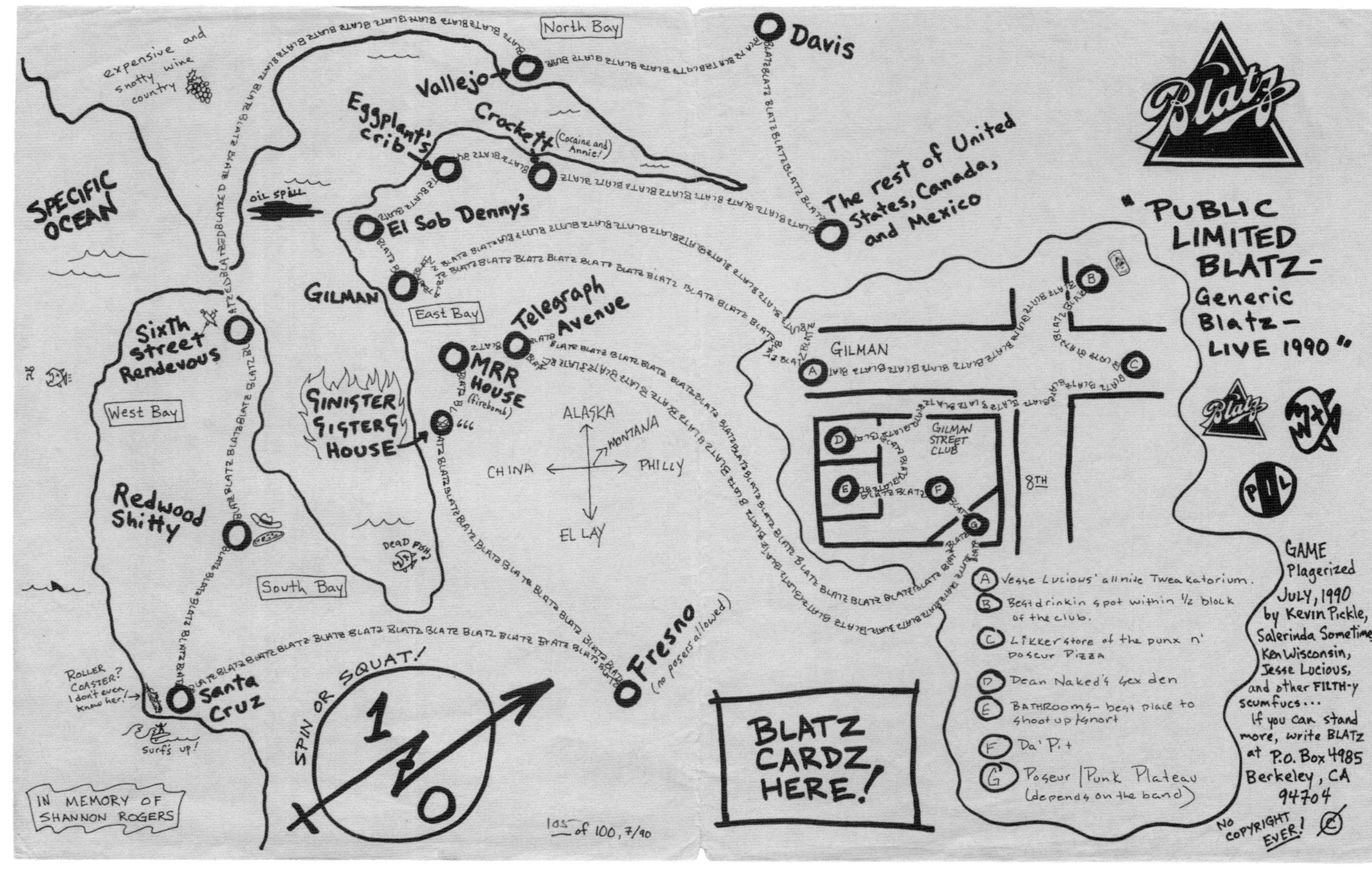

Blatz
"PUBLIC LIMITED BLATZ- Generic Blatz- LIVE 1990"
PIL
Davis
The rest of United States, Canada, and Mexico
North Bay
Vallejo
Crockett (Cocaine and Annie!)
Eggplant's crib
El Sob Denny's
GILMAN
East Bay
Telegraph Avenue
MRR HOUSE (firebomb)
666
SINISTER SISTERS HOUSE
DEAD FISH
South Bay
ALASKA
MONTANA
CHINA
PHILLY
EL LAY
Fresno (no posers allowed)
expensive and snotty wine country
SPECIFIC OCEAN
OIL SPILL
Sixth Street Rendevous
West Bay
Redwood Shitty
ROLLER COASTER? I don't even know her!
Santa Cruz
Surf's up!
SPIN OR SQUAT!
1
0
IN MEMORY OF SHANNON ROGERS
105 of 100, 7/90
BLATZ CARDZ HERE!
GILMAN
GILMAN STREET CLUB
8TH
A Vesse Lucious' allnite Tweakatorium.
B Best drinkin spot within 1/2 block of the club.
C Likker store of the punx n' poseur Pizza
D Dean Naked's sex den
E BATHROOMS- best place to shoot up/snort
F Da' Pit
G Poseur/Punk Plateau (depends on the band)
GAME Plagerized JULY, 1990 by Kevin Pickle, Salerinda Sometime, Ken Wisconsin, Jesse Lucious, and other FILTH-y scumfucs...
If you can stand more, write BLATZ at P.O. Box 4985 Berkeley, CA 94704
NO COPYRIGHT EVER!

Blatz

PUBLIC LIMITED BLATZ

Generic Blatz

Live 1990"

Yo! Cut out the pointer + the game pieces on the dotted lines (---) and fold on the dots (..........). Pin the Pointer on the spinnersquat thang on the lower left of the ~~bored~~ board. Put yer piece anywhere and spin, move, and pick up a card every turn. Go in any direction for however long you want to play. Ya might want to keep track of your punk points on another piece of paper. Have a shitty time, we always do.

POINTER

BLATZ

pin →

pointer →

game board →

PICKLE

SYRINGE

SALAMANDER

HAIR DYE

RENT A COP

RAZOR

USED RUBBER Yum!

GAME PIECES ↑ (make yer own if ya want, You lazy shit!)

Get into a ska show put on by Lou for free, set off stink bombs, and write "DIRTY LOU" graffitti. +30 PUNK P+Z.	You catch Dean Naked drinking COORS - Stop Hallucinating, ya trippy hippy! -10 PUNK POINTZ	OP Ivy reunites with the other Jesse singing, they sign to EMI. Lose 47 points
Almost die driving home from riot by driving thru construction site, and not get caught! +10 PUNK POINTZ	GILMAN profiled in "FACE-IT" long hairs show up for 2 weeks afterwards. TAKE A VACATION IN EL SOB.	CRIMPSHRINE plays reunion show at Sixth Street Rendevous, 3 People show up for SLAM ATM who open +7 PUNK POINTZ
Marshall plays BLATZ + FILTH on Magic 61, keeps job. 357 of S.F.'s elderly have fatal heart attacks. +20 PUNK PTZ.	Marshall caught shaving chest in girl's bathroom. You figure. No POINTS.	ANNA BLATZ returns from Europe months early AND beats up Mr. Hayes. +30 P+Z.
DAVE M.D.C. rallies crowd against skinheads but misses fight cuz he's autographing M.D.C. cd's. SWITCH POINTS WITH POSEUR TO YOUR LEFT	Discover Joey BLATZ's nipple ring is a clip-on. -10 PUNK POINTZ (5 for each nipple)	Each GARGOYLE gets sex change, become ugly enough to work as San Pablo hos. Yikes! +17 PUNK POINTZ
LENNY from FILTH shows you his secret MORRISEY shrine. You slit your wrists but survive. -5 POINTS, ya PUNK...	Witness Eggplant lose virginity, sell photos to "National Geographic" +18 PUNK POINTZ	TIM Yo roadies for DANZIG + PENELOPE HOUSTON sings for THE FUCKUPS. PLUS 15 for Penelope, MINUS 15 for TIM.
ECONOCHRIST new LP's NOT on colored vinyl! +10 PUNK POINTS	You know more about drugs than Claude. Lose 27½ points for lying and lose a turn	In Europe, Annie o.d.'s in Amsterdam, but lives to shatter all the windows in the Sistine Chapel singing for spare change +2 PTZ
If you can name the BLATZ member with a nipple ring, plus 10 punk pointz. If not, give yourself 10 ptz. anyway, ya brain-dead putz...	Photograph Jake exiting "D.R.I.'s Stone" show. Blackmail him sucessfully for months. +20 PUNK P+Z.	FRIGHTWIG plays "Punk Rock Jailbait" at Gazzari's in El-Lay. Take your neighbor's turn!

3.123–3.125. Blatz board game map, instructions, and sheet of game cards, 1990.

Television Access, La Raza Gallery, and Old Wives' Tales bookstore on Valencia, to the massive Rodney King protests and poles stickered in Act Up! slogans, to everyday arguments about cultural appropriation in cafés, meetings, and peepshow dressing rooms, my dominant culture's "let's-pretend-this-is-real-at-gunpoint" belief system around identity, social rank, and cultural progress was being "deconstructed" as a multifaceted bullshit myth.

I had been sitting in on Kathy Acker's SF Art Institute classes since learning she was there from my Genoa Street House roommate and Blatz board game artist Salerinda. Acker's writing put at shrill and productive dissonance a particularly feminine intellectualized combination of childishness, brutality, despair, and lust; she wrote speculative criti-fictions made partially of other people's writing as a way to slash at the imperialist project of canonized English literature, while redefining avant-garde prose as punk-inflected and red with cunts. Kathy let me attend her classes without paying and became my champion and mentor.

Now a student at New College of California, I learned about childhood as social construct. Innocent or evil, blank slate or garbage heap, the definition of childhood always supported broader ideas of social order established by adults and the ruling class. The regulation of children by a system of rules and laws they could not affect was a form of institutionalized oppression that everyone had experienced. In a mandatory humanities course, instructors opened our investigation of institutionalized oppression on the foundation of "ageism" as a rhetorical basis for subsequent lessons on classism, sexism, racism, anti-Semitism, homophobia, and some of their complicated touch points. What I'd been learning informally with my friends was now being taught in classes.

My lyrics, singing, and performance style arose at this unique historical moment when punk rediscovered itself in relation to the broader politics of identity-based oppression, which progressive instructors were keen to unpack even as ideological battles over canon protection and equitable inclusion began to rage in colleges and universities across the world. On the side of canon-disruption, Kathy Acker piqued my interest in feminist intertextuality and metafiction, while poet Lyn Hejinian introduced "phallogocentrism" and "l'écriture féminine." David Meltzer encouraged a critically perverse approach to reading stories that included rewriting them to "heighten the contradictions" implicit within the original tale. This artistic approach to analysis has proven endlessly practical in my art and teaching, beginning with my second band, the Gr'ups.

The Gr'ups began as an unironic, theme-related project with songs derived from fairy tales. Our first song, "Almond Tree," was a response to a critical reading assignment in David Meltzer's Children's Literature course. I based the lyrics on a favorite childhood bedtime story, a deeply troubling Grimm's tale that my mother loved to scare me with and I, in turn, perversely enjoyed. Folklore is always pregnant with political and interpersonal history, sometimes overt and sometimes staged as allegory. For instance, in the Grimms' times, lots of women died in childbirth. The "wicked stepmother" trope responds to this cultural moment when widowers brought in replacement wives, often recent immigrants, to manage the domestic sphere. Though I would not learn this until I began teaching fairy tales and folktales myself, the "wicked stepmother" reference is likely a nationalist dog whistle corresponding to the Grimms' nation-building project of collecting and standardizing native folktales. In the version of the story I'd learned as a child, a psychopath stepmom murders her husband's heir, blames his little sister for the death, then feeds the dead boy to his unsuspecting father for supper. The dead boy's

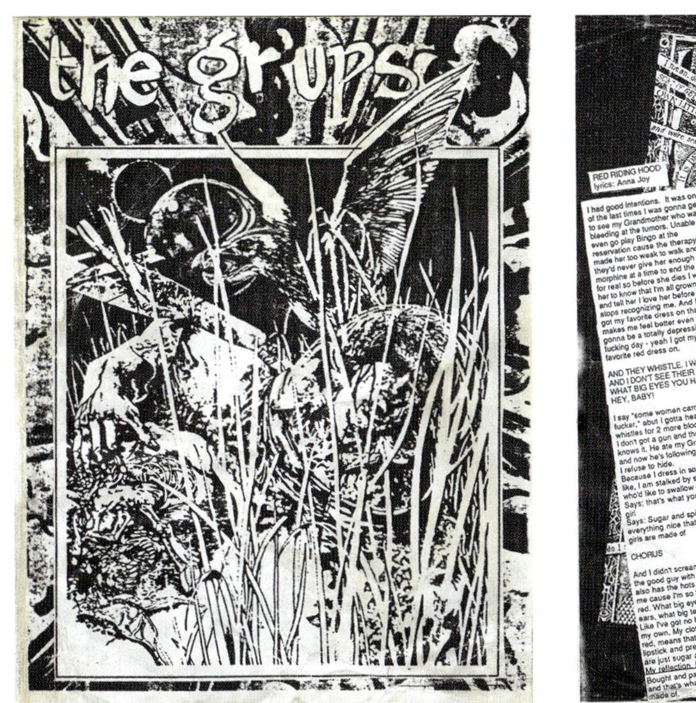

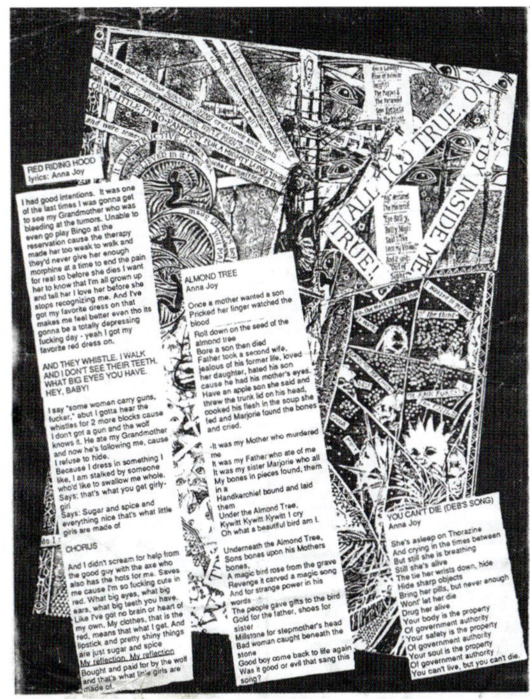

RED RIDING HOOD
lyrics: Anna Joy

I had good intentions. It was one of the last times I was gonna get to see my Grandmother who was bleeding at the tumors. Unable to even go play Bingo at the reservation cause the therapy made her too weak to walk and they'd never give her enough morphine at a time to end the pain for real so before she dies I want her to know that I'm all grown up and tell her I love her before she stops recognizing me. And I've got my favorite dress on that makes me feel better even tho its gonna be a totally depressing fucking day - yeah I got my favorite red dress on.

AND THEY WHISTLE. I WALK
AND I DON'T SEE THEIR TEETH.
WHAT BIG EYES YOU HAVE.
HEY, BABY!

I say "some women carry guns, fucker," abut I gotta hear the whistles for 2 more blocks cause I don't got a gun and the wolf knows it. He ate my Grandmother and now he's following me, cause I refuse to hide.
Because I dress in something I like, I am stalked by someone who'd like to swallow me whole.
Says: that's what you get girly-girl
Says: Sugar and spice and everything nice that's what little girls are made of

CHORUS

And I didn't scream for help from the good guy with the axe who also has the hots for me. Saves me cause I'm so fucking cute in red. What big eyes, what big ears, what big teeth you have. Like I've got no brain or heart of my own. My clothes, that is the red, means that what I get. And lipstick and pretty shiny things are just sugar and spice
My reflection. My reflection
Bought and paid for by the wolf and that's what little girls are made of.

ALMOND TREE
Anna Joy

Once a mother wanted a son
Pricked her finger watched the blood
Roll down on the seed of the almond tree
Bore a son then died
Father took a second wife,
jealous of his former life, loved her daughter, hated his son cause he had his mother's eyes.
Have an apple son she said and threw the trunk lid on his head, cooked his flesh in the soup she fed and Marjorie found the bones and cried.

-It was my Mother who murdered me
It was my Father who ate of me
It was my sister Marjorie who all
My bones in pieces found, them in a
Handkerchief bound and laid them
Under the Almond Tree.
Kywitt Kywitt Kywitt I cry
Oh what a beautiful bird am I.

Underneath the Almond Tree,
Sons bones upon his Mothers bones,
A magic bird rose from the grave
Revenge it carved a magic song
And for strange power in his words
The people gave gifts to the bird
Gold for the father, shoes for sister
Millstone for stepmother's head
Bad woman caught beneath the stone
Good boy come back to life again
Was it good or evil that sang this song?

YOU CAN'T DIE (DEB'S SONG)
Anna Joy

She's asleep on Thorazine
And crying in the times between
But still she is breathing
Still she's alive
The tie her wrists down, hide
Hide sharp objects
Bring her pills, but never enough
Wont' let her die
Drug her alive
Your body is the property
Of government authority
Your safety is the property
Of government authority
Your soul is the property
Of government authority
You can't live, but you can't die.

3.126 and 3.127. Front and back of the Gr'ups lyric sheet, circa 1992.

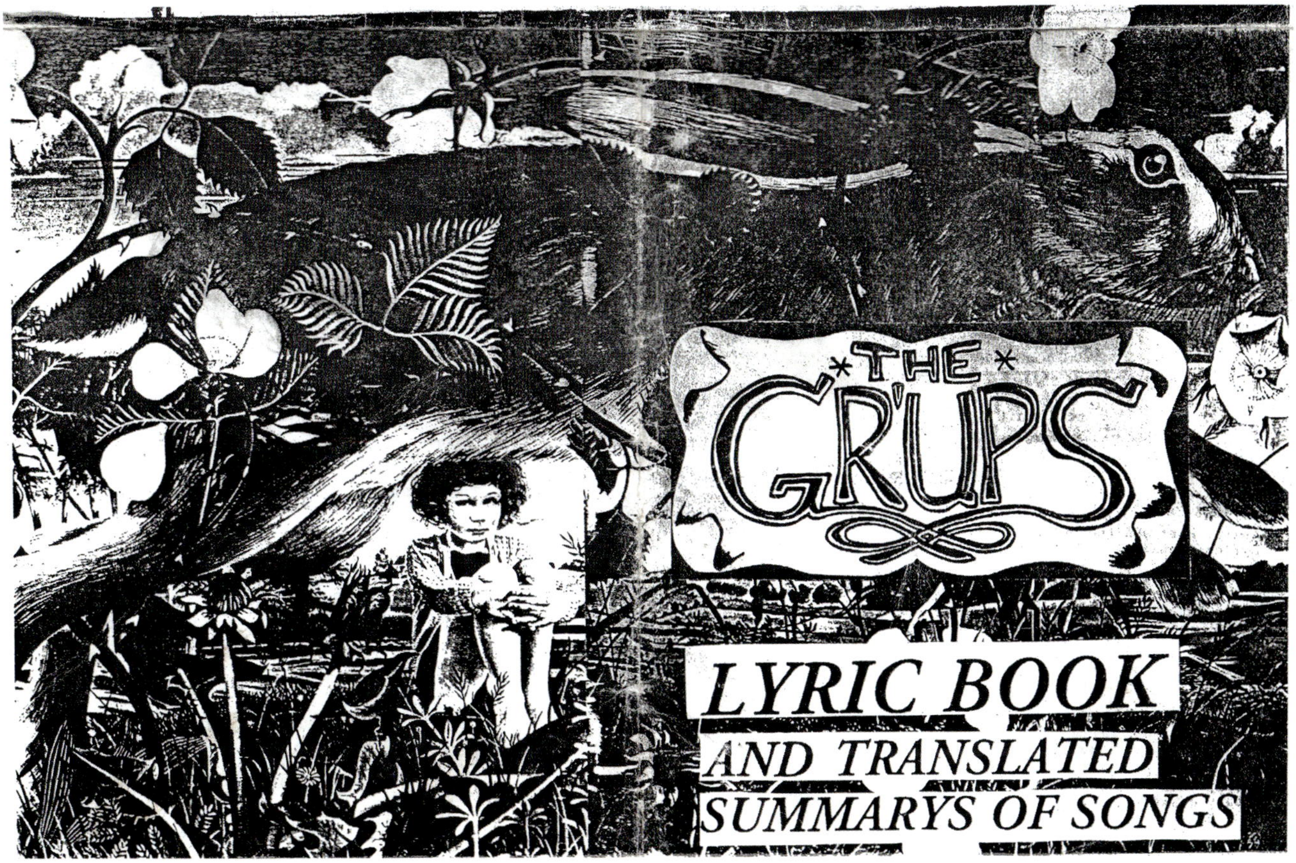

THE
GR'UPS
LYRIC BOOK
AND TRANSLATED
SUMMARYS OF SONGS

3.128. *The Gr'ups Lyric Book*, 1993.

sister buries his bones under an almond (or juniper) tree, and magic tears make the bones turn into a living bird whose song prompts villagers to give the bird expensive gifts and a weapon to kill his murderous stepmother, after which the child will return to life.

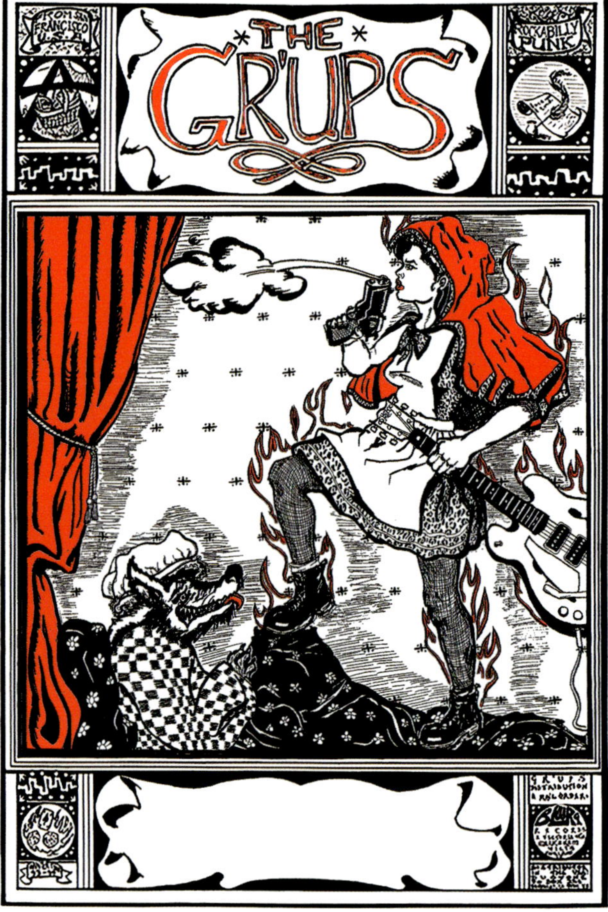

3.129. The Gr'ups European tour 1993 poster, drawn by Anna Joy and other Gr'ups based on a British Doc Martens ad.

The Gr'ups' first guitarist, Matt Freeman, arranged most of the songs with bassist Deb Disaster and drummer Kamala Parks, both of whom also did tons of offstage cultural work, as did co-singer Jesse Luscious, who'd migrated with me from Blatz. Jesse wrote the lyrics to "Snow White," the charming (autobiographical?) tale of a wealthy suburban runaway who becomes a tweaking urban squatter with lots of friends. I finished out my semester with the feminist recitative "RR Hood," a song about enjoying my excellent femme style while being enraged by intrusive macho gawkers (see lyric sheets 3.127, 3.130, 3.131).

After Matt left for Rancid, we got a new guitarist, Daniela Sea, who's featured on *Buildings Are the Purtiest Trees I've Seen*, named after a song I wrote for my one required science class, "Nature as a Concept." The Gr'ups became a full-on concept band, and everyone in it wore bespoke fairy tale costumes (including a stuffed wolf's-head hat for Jesse and an awkwardly eighties red pleather bondage outfit for me, along with various capes, tulle skirts, and gossamer wings) all through Europe in 1993, when the Gr'ups toured with Citizen Fish, as I mentioned earlier after describing the inciting Subhumans' record cover designed by Dick Lucas.

Dick Lucas also designed the original cover for *Buildings Are the Purtiest Trees I've Seen*, which I would have considered a supreme honor, had I not been so annoyed that he'd chosen such masculine imagery for the cover (3.132).

I revised Dick's original masculine-noir cover design by adding illustrations of the bloodthirsty man-killing Goddess referenced in our song "Kali Is Your Bad-Ass Mutha" (3.133). The song was yet another class assignment, this time for Erotic Poetries, taught by Rose Troche. In creating both song and art, I was ignorant of the complexities of cultural appropriation by those of us aiming for progressive feminist representation. I was hungry for alternatives to a pervasive belief that feminine power was only ever empathetic and nurturing, everywhere since the dawn of time. Today I have mixed feelings about some of the musical references in the song, but for all the ways I didn't understand this icon of the Hindu pantheon in cultural context, what I learned about her made me want to tell everyone around me that feminine destructive power was not only recognized as normal, but also worshipped. Though queer

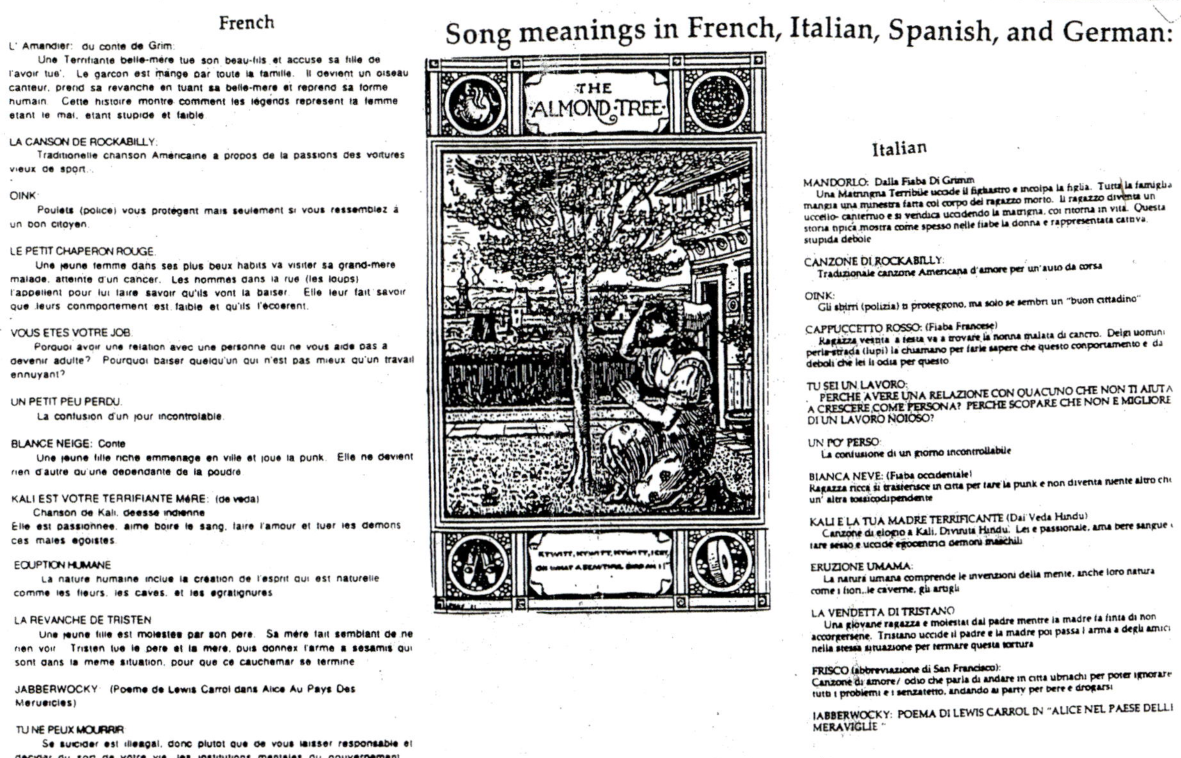

Song meanings in French, Italian, Spanish, and German:

French

L' Amandier: du conte de Grim:
Une Terrifiante belle-mére tue son beau-fils et accuse sa fille de l'avoir tue'. Le garcon est mangé par toute la famille. Il devient un oiseau canteur, prend sa revanche en tuant sa belle-mere et reprend sa forme humain. Cette histoire montre comment les légends represent la femme etant le mal, etant stupide et faible.

LA CANSON DE ROCKABILLY:
Traditionelle chanson Américaine a propos de la passions des voitures vieux de sport.

OINK:
Poulets (police) vous protégent mais seulement si vous ressembiez à un bon citoyen.

LE PETIT CHAPERON ROUGE.
Une jeune femme dans ses plus beux habits va visiter sa grand-mere malade, atteinte d'un cancer. Les hommes dans la rue (les loups) l'appellent pour lui faire savoir qu'ils vont la baiser. Elle leur fait savoir que leurs conmportement est faible et qu'ils l'écoerent.

VOUS ETES VOTRE JOB.
Porquoi avoir une relation avec une personne qui ne vous aide pas a devenir adulte? Pourquoi baiser quelqu'un qui n'est pas mieux qu'un travail ennuyant?

UN PETIT PEU PERDU.
La confusion d'un jour incontrolable.

BLANCE NEIGE: Conte
Une jeune fille riche emmenage en ville et joue la punk. Elle ne devient rien d'autre qu'une dependante de la poudre.

KALI EST VOTRE TERRIFIANTE MéRE: (de veda)
Chanson de Kali, deesse indienne
Elle est passionnee, aime boire le sang, faire l'amour et tuer les demons ces males egoistes.

EDUPTION HUMANE
La nature humaine inclue la création de l'esprit qui est naturelle comme les fleurs, les caves, et les egratignures.

LA REVANCHE DE TRISTEN
Une jeune fille est molestee par son pere. Sa mére fait semblant de ne rien voir. Tristen tue le pere et la mere, puis donnex l'arme a sesamis qui sont dans la meme situation, pour que ce cauchemar se termine.

JABBERWOCKY (Poeme de Lewis Carrol dans Alice Au Pays Des Merueicles)

TU NE PEUX MOURRIR
Se suicider est illeagal, donc plutot que de vous laisser responsable et decidar du sort de votre vie, les institutions mentales ou gouvernement vous donne des drogues qui vous laisse comme un zombie ce qui est pire que d'etre mort.

Italian

MANDORLO: Dalla Fiaba Di Grimm
Una Matringna Terribile uccide il figliastro e incolpa la figlia. Tutta la famiglia mangia una minestra fatta col corpo del ragazzo morto. Il ragazzo diventa un uccello- canterino e si vendica uccidendo la matrigna, coi ritorna in vita. Questa storia tipica mostra come spesso nelle fiabe la donna e rappresentata cattiva, stupida debole

CANZONE DI ROCKABILLY:
Tradizionale canzone Americana d'amore per un'auto da corsa

OINK:
Gli sbirri (polizia) ti proteggono, ma solo se sembri un "buon cittadino"

CAPPUCCETTO ROSSO: (Fiaba Francese)
Ragazza vestita a festa va a trovare la nonna malata di cancro. Degli uomini per-la-strada (lupi) la chiamano per farle sapere che questo conportamento e da deboli che lei li odia per questo

TU SEI UN LAVORO:
PERCHE AVERE UNA RELAZIONE CON QUACUNO CHE NON TI AIUTA A CRESCERE COME PERSONA? PERCHE SCOPARE CHE NON E MIGLIORE DI UN LAVORO NOIOSO?

UN PO' PERSO:
La confusione di un giorno incontrollabile

BIANCA NEVE: (Fiaba occidentale)
Ragazza ricca si trasferisce in citta per fare la punk e non diventa niente altro che un' altra tossicodipendente

KALI E LA TUA MADRE TERRIFICANTE (Dai Veda Hindu)
Canzone di elogio a Kali, Divinita Hindu. Lei e passionale, ama bere sangue e fare sesso e uccide egocentrici demoni maschili

ERUZIONE UMAMA:
La natura umana comprende le invenzioni della mente, anche loro natura come i fiori..le caverne, gli artigli

LA VENDETTA DI TRISTANO
Una giovane ragazza e molestat dal padre mentre la madre fa finta di non accorgersene. Tristano uccide il padre e la madre poi passa l arma a degli amici nella stessa situazione per termare questa tortura

FRISCO (abbreviazione di San Francisco):
Canzone di amore/ odio che parla di andare in citta ubriachi per poter ignorare tutti i problemi e i senzatetto, andando ai party per bere e drogarsi

JABBERWOCKY: POEMA DI LEWIS CARROL IN "ALICE NEL PAESE DELLE MERAVIGLIE"

3.130. *The Gr'ups Lyric Book* translations of song synopses, 1992.

feminist punk worship songs were, to say the least, *uncommon* (Bikini Kill's "Rebel Girl" being an obvious exception), I sang "Kali Is Your Bad-Ass Mutha" earnestly, in praise.

My formal and spiritual education corresponded with the anomalous flourishing of radical queer arts and politics in dyke punk subcultures in San Francisco, where both basic safety and pleasurable danger seemed more possible than anywhere else, and where deconstructive methods and destructive aesthetics allowed for expression of ugly-beauty in new feminist forms. In this largely entrepreneurial, creative, educated, and syncretic punk scene men were peripheral, and nobody cared whether a popular boy band "sold out" by signing to a major label.

ONE IS NOT BORN (BUT RATHER BECOMES) A GRRRL

From what I have seen of the Riot Grrrl Zine and Music Collection, circa 1989–1997, this set of archives appears to feature dyke punk materials *at least as much* as work by people involved in riot grrrl activities.[2] But "riot grrrl" and the as-yet-unnamed dyke punk part of homocore are notably different. While the various iterations of dyke, riot grrrl, and other punk feminisms share certain aesthetic/political similarities, and because some people moved between these communities, several historians have mistakenly collapsed both scenes into one and named it after the straighter one, riot grrrl. Single chapters in punk histories devoted to both riot grrrl and queercore miss exciting material and tend to divert attention away from the way both

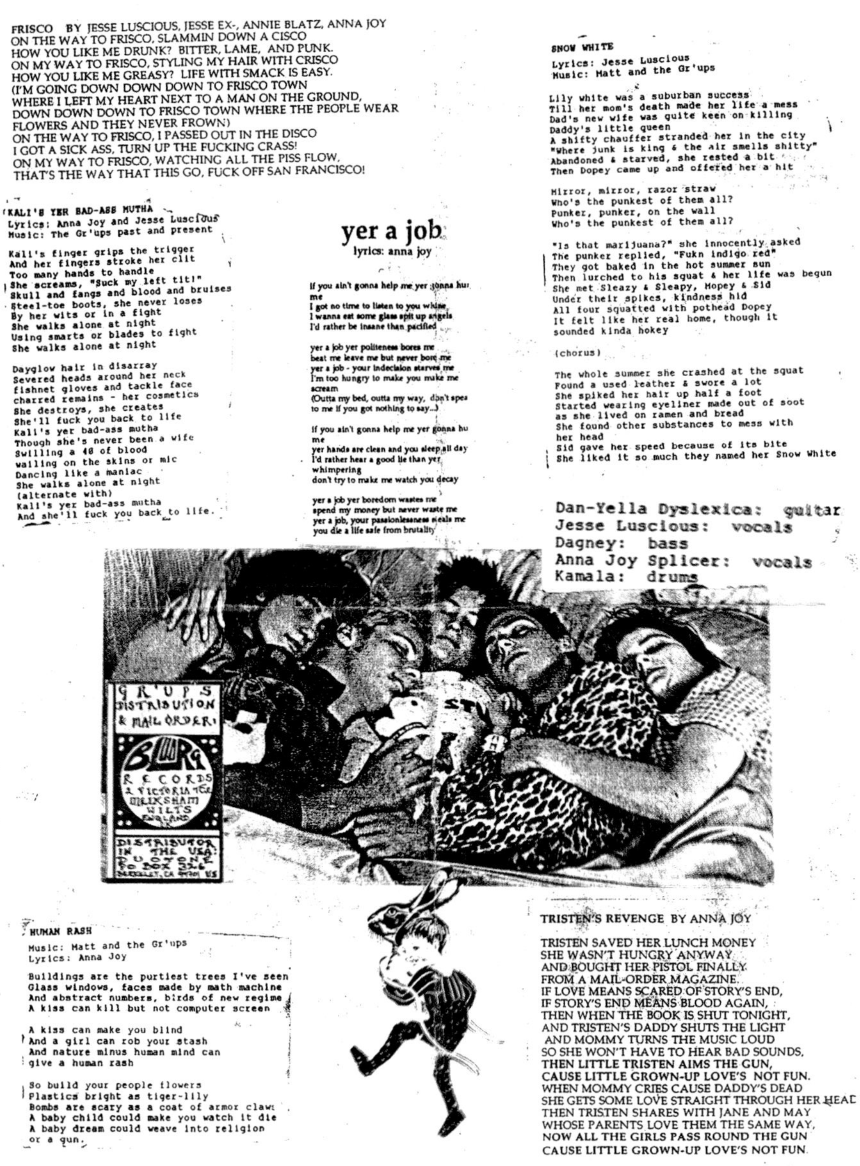

FRISCO BY JESSE LUSCIOUS, JESSE EX-, ANNIE BLATZ, ANNA JOY
ON THE WAY TO FRISCO, SLAMMIN DOWN A CISCO
HOW YOU LIKE ME DRUNK? BITTER, LAME, AND PUNK.
ON MY WAY TO FRISCO, STYLING MY HAIR WITH CRISCO
HOW YOU LIKE ME GREASY? LIFE WITH SMACK IS EASY.
(I'M GOING DOWN DOWN DOWN TO FRISCO TOWN
WHERE I LEFT MY HEART NEXT TO A MAN ON THE GROUND,
DOWN DOWN DOWN TO FRISCO TOWN WHERE THE PEOPLE WEAR
FLOWERS AND THEY NEVER FROWN)
ON THE WAY TO FRISCO, I PASSED OUT IN THE DISCO
I GOT A SICK ASS, TURN UP THE FUCKING CRASS!
ON MY WAY TO FRISCO, WATCHING ALL THE PISS FLOW,
THAT'S THE WAY THAT THIS GO, FUCK OFF SAN FRANCISCO!

KALI'S YER BAD-ASS MUTHA
Lyrics: Anna Joy and Jesse Luscious
Music: The Gr'ups past and present

Kali's finger grips the trigger
And her fingers stroke her clit
Too many hands to handle
She screams, "Suck my left tit!"
Skull and fangs and blood and bruises
Steel-toe boots, she never loses
By her wits or in a fight
She walks alone at night
Using smarts or blades to fight
She walks alone at night

Dayglow hair in disarray
Severed heads around her neck
fishnet gloves and tackle face
charred remains - her cosmetics
She destroys, she creates
She'll fuck you back to life
Kali's yer bad-ass mutha
Though she's never been a wife
Swilling a 40 of blood
wailing on the skins or mic
Dancing like a maniac
She walks alone at night
(alternate with)
Kali's yer bad-ass mutha
And she'll fuck you back to life.

yer a job
lyrics: anna joy

If you ain't gonna help me yer gonna hurt me
I got no time to listen to you whine,
I wanna eat some glass spit up angels
I'd rather be insane than pacified

yer a job yer politeness bores me
beat me leave me but never bore me
yer a job - your indecision starves me
I'm too hungry to make you make me scream
(Outta my bed, outta my way, don't speak to me if you got nothing to say...)

If you ain't gonna help me yer gonna hurt me
yer hands are clean and you sleep all day
I'd rather hear a good lie than yer whimpering
don't try to make me watch you decay

yer a job yer boredom wastes me
spend my money but never waste me
yer a job, your passionlessness steals me
you die a life safe from brutality

SNOW WHITE
Lyrics: Jesse Luscious
Music: Matt and the Gr'ups

Lily white was a suburban success
Till her mom's death made her life a mess
Dad's new wife was quite keen on killing
Daddy's little queen
A shifty chauffer stranded her in the city
"Where junk is king & the air smells shitty"
Abandoned & starved, she rested a bit
Then Dopey came up and offered her a hit

Mirror, mirror, razor straw
Who's the punkest of them all?
Punker, punker, on the wall
Who's the punkest of them all?

"Is that marijuana?" she innocently asked
The punker replied, "Fukn indigo red"
They got baked in the hot summer sun
Then lurched to his squat & her life was begun
She met Sleazy & Sleapy, Mopey & Sid
Under their spikes, kindness hid
All four squatted with pothead Dopey
It felt like her real home, though it
sounded kinda hokey

(chorus)

The whole summer she crashed at the squat
Found a used leather & swore a lot
She spiked her hair up half a foot
Started wearing eyeliner made out of soot
as she lived on ramen and bread
She found other substances to mess with
her head
Sid gave her speed because of its bite
She liked it so much they named her Snow White

Dan-Yella Dyslexica: guitar
Jesse Luscious: vocals
Dagney: bass
Anna Joy Splicer: vocals
Kamala: drums

HUMAN RASH
Music: Matt and the Gr'ups
Lyrics: Anna Joy

Buildings are the purtiest trees I've seen
Glass windows, faces made by math machine
And abstract numbers, birds of new regime
A kiss can kill but not computer screen

A kiss can make you blind
And a girl can rob your stash
And nature minus human mind can
give a human rash

So build your people flowers
Plastics bright as tiger-lily
Bombs are scary as a coat of armor claws
A baby child could make you watch it die
A baby dream could weave into religion
or a gun.

TRISTEN'S REVENGE BY ANNA JOY

TRISTEN SAVED HER LUNCH MONEY
SHE WASN'T HUNGRY ANYWAY
AND BOUGHT HER PISTOL FINALLY
FROM A MAIL-ORDER MAGAZINE.
IF LOVE MEANS SCARED OF STORY'S END,
IF STORY'S END MEANS BLOOD AGAIN,
THEN WHEN THE BOOK IS SHUT TONIGHT,
AND TRISTEN'S DADDY SHUTS THE LIGHT
AND MOMMY TURNS THE MUSIC LOUD
SO SHE WON'T HAVE TO HEAR BAD SOUNDS,
THEN LITTLE TRISTEN AIMS THE GUN,
CAUSE LITTLE GROWN-UP LOVE'S NOT FUN.
WHEN MOMMY CRIES CAUSE DADDY'S DEAD
SHE GETS SOME LOVE STRAIGHT THROUGH HER HEAD
THEN TRISTEN SHARES WITH JANE AND MAY
WHOSE PARENTS LOVE THEM THE SAME WAY,
NOW ALL THE GIRLS PASS ROUND THE GUN
CAUSE LITTLE GROWN-UP LOVE'S NOT FUN.

3.131. Gr'ups Lyric Book (English) with anti-industrial promo photo, 1992.

nonstandard genders and illegible sexualities shaped and were shaped by punk culture. And while dyke and other punk feminisms shouldn't be historically subsumed under the sign of riot grrrl, they shouldn't be framed as rivals either, even as competing community approaches are explored.

I want to go out on a bit of a limb here as a participant rather than a true historian to distinguish these feminist punk subcultures. First, my qualifications: I was identifying as a femme dyke in the Gr'ups, and in 1991 began an epic romance with Lynn Breedlove, the shirtless, knife-wielding, dildo-slashing front person of the infamous dyke band Tribe 8 after a dispute about cultural appropriation and cover art on Blatz and Tribe 8's split EP, *Bitches and Brew*. At a Blatz / Tribe 8 show at Gilman before we were a couple, Lynn connected me with folks at the SF homocore house known as "Shred of Dignity." I started my third band, Cypher in the

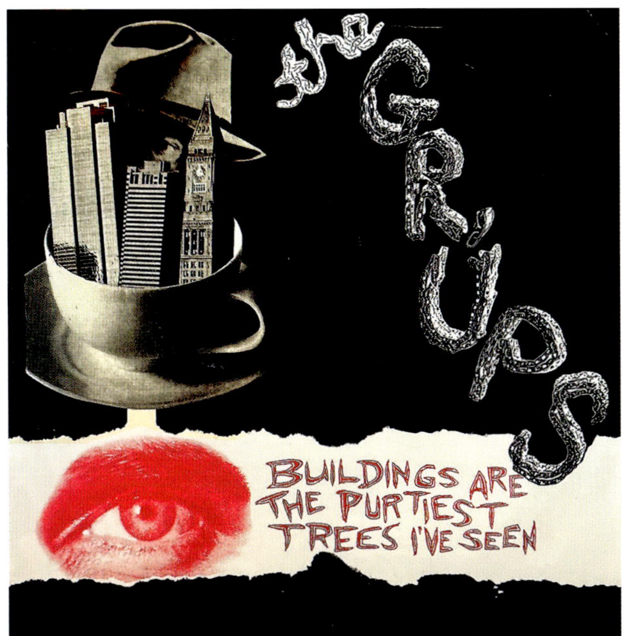

3.132. The Gr'ups' *Buildings Are the Purtiest Trees I've Seen*, front cover, 1993.

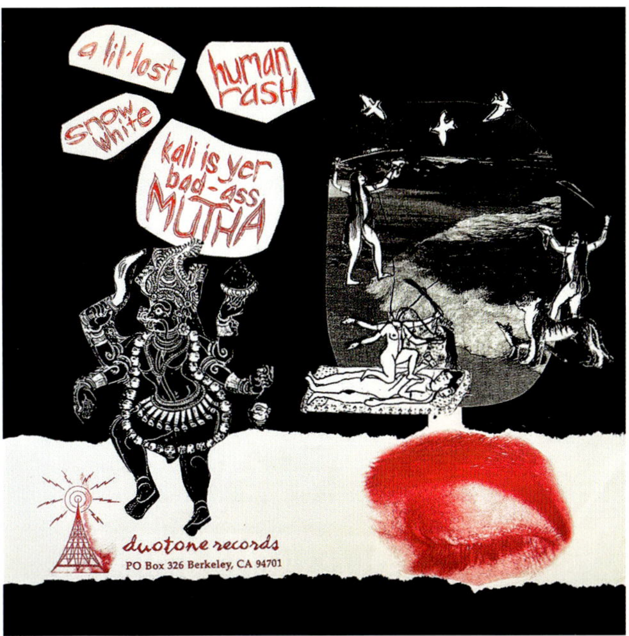

3.133. The Gr'ups' *Buildings Are the Purtiest Trees I've Seen*, back cover, featuring Hindu deities Durga/Kali, 1993.

Cypher in the Snow

Cypher in the Snow
2336 Market St. #140
San Francisco, CA USA
94114

415-224-4098

available for weddings and bar mitzvahs

3.134. Business card for Cypher in the Snow.

Snow, with former Gr'ups guitarist Daniela Sea, a couple femmes whose girlfriends also were in Tribe 8, and three other people who identified as dykes.

Cypher in the Snow remains the favorite of my bands because it was the weirdest and queerest. The cultural genre that Tribe 8 and Cypher in the Snow helped define was called homocore, a name derived from a zine that spread fantastical rumors about gay punk scenes in Toronto and San Francisco that didn't actually exist, until suddenly they did. Almost immediately homocore became synonymous with queercore. I became vaguely aware of queercore within a few months of hearing Bikini Kill's new demo tape, *Revolution Girl Style Now* (1991). The Gr'ups had at times three women and four queer people in it, but the Gr'ups was not designated a riot grrrl band or homocore band at the time it was active; since two cisgender men played in the Gr'ups, it wasn't a dyke band. However, the Gr'ups was considered by many a feminist band.

Riot grrrl and dyke punk bands might look alike to outsiders who weren't looking closely and might therefore be considered as a single category solely because they aren't made up of men. This absence of presumably cisgender, presumably straight men may come across as a singular defining feature to people who have come to perceive punk as a uniquely masculine form made almost entirely by cisgender men.

But while riot grrrl projects frequently tackle social dynamics between women and men (think, "girls to the front") and among women trained to compete for men's acceptance and protection, dyke punk largely avoids centering heterosexually inflected daily and/or intimate politics between women and men. In fact, many punk dykes lived as pseudo-separatists.

Legacies of patriarchy and misogyny saturate every social fabric, but living apart from cis-het guys allowed for a natural reconfiguration of ideological priorities and interpersonal dynamics within specifically dyke and queer punk subcultures, especially those energized by brazen femininity and masculine camp. During a time when, in responding to murderous conditions of both institutionalized medical discrimination and inadequate civil rights, most outward-facing "gay and lesbian" activism tried to convince the other 90 percent that same-sex lovers were everyday folk with money to burn. The very self-designation of the adjectives "queer," "trans," "butch," "femme," "fag," and "dyke" signaled antiestablishment politics. Those of us sheltering under the umbrella of these combative terms experienced sorts of unwanted gender-related encounters very different from those of women whose lives involved or prioritized cisgender heterosexual men. With different things to convey, we created new content in culturally distinctive forms.

FROCKCORE 11.12.93
PROFOUND VICTIMS
(LEEDS TEENCORE)
THISTLE FAIRIES
(BRADFORD APPLECORE)
COPING SAW
(LEEDS ODDCORE)
WITCHKNOT
(BRADFORD MAGICORE)
DELICATE VOMIT
(NEWCASTLE MADCORE)
GR'UPS
(SAN FRANCISCO RADCORE)
SISTER GEORGE
(LONDON QUEERCORE)
LINUS
(LONDON GRRRLCORE)
11.30 ish ONWARDS...
VIY VINYLCORE'S DISCO!
ALL 4 ONLY £3/£3.50 !

3.135. Flyer from 1993 feminist punk festival in Leeds, England.

At the same time, interpersonal, political, and aesthetic crossover did occur between homocore, dyke, riot grrrl, and other punk antimasculinist projects. We had friendships, affairs, argued, wrote. We put on shows together, played in each other's bands.

Focusing on bands alone, in her article "Making Waves: Other Punk Feminisms," Mimi Thi Nguyen observes, "In the 1990s, riot grrrl spawned fiercely feminist bands . . . but feminisms (and proto-feminisms) were not then new to punk. . . . Other punk feminisms before or contemporaneous with but perhaps outside of the riot grrrl movement . . . might help us consider alternate genealogies of punk feminisms through anti-imperialism, economic justice, and queer anti-assimilationist politics."[3] Again, bands and music are just one aspect of punk culture. Before her full-time academic career, Dr. Nguyen, a zine maker and compiler of the influential *Evolution of a Race Riot*, worked at Epicenter Zone, the volunteer-run urban resource and punk community center. "Making Waves" lists Nguyen's "soundtrack of personal favorites and also representative bands from these other punk feminisms," featuring annotated entries for the Bags, Au Pairs, Crass, Yeastie Girlz, Sta-Prest, and Team Dresch, followed by a long list of other favorites like Frightwig, Spitboy, Nervous Gender, Raooul, and Blatz, and including several of

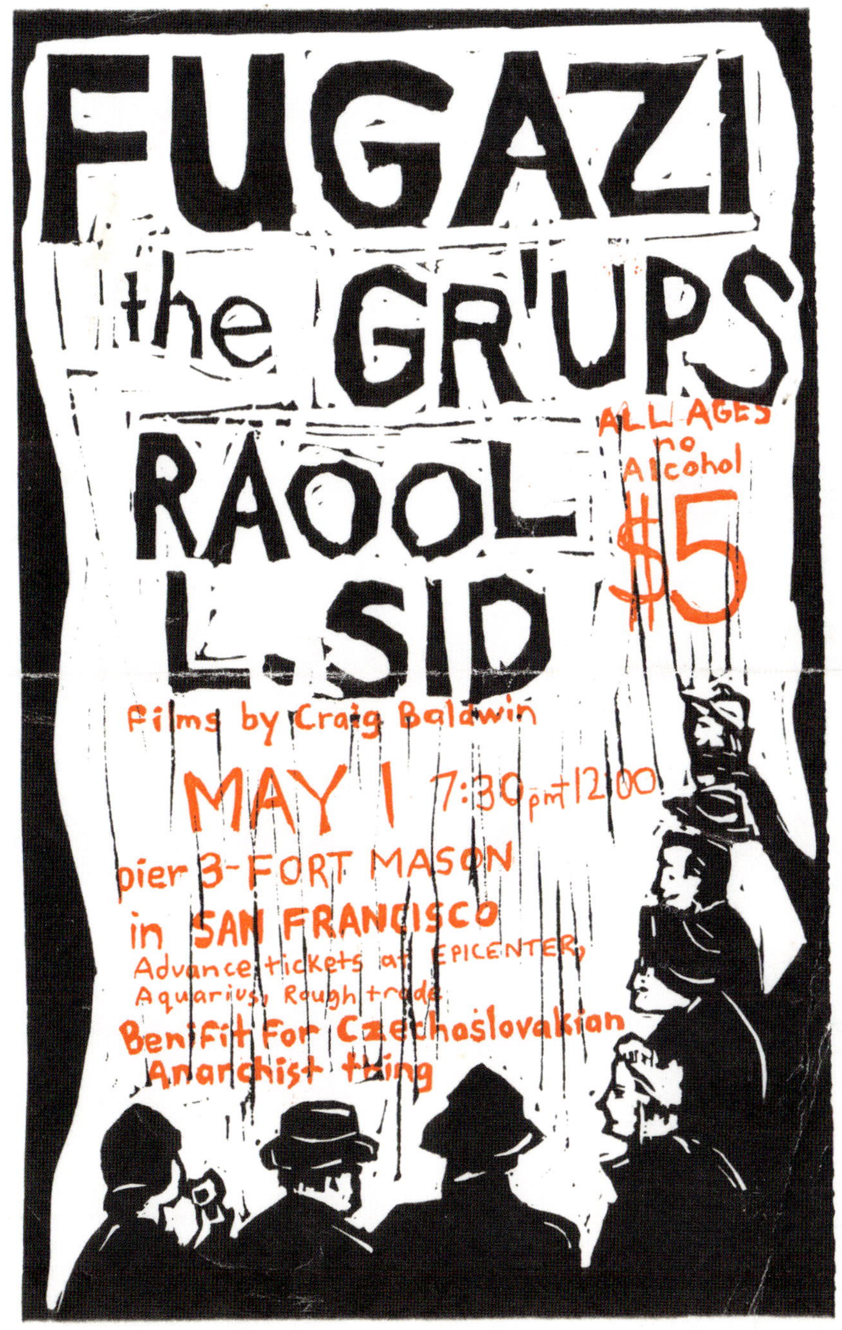

3.136. Flyer for Fugazi and the Gr'ups show in San Francisco, 1993.

the bands on Matt Wobensmith's Outpunk label compilation, *There's a Dyke in the Pit*, and on the recording *Bunch of Fucking Feminists*.

Dyke punk, queercore, and other iterations of feminist punk materials already infiltrate much of Cornell's Riot Grrrl collection, and numerous other projects could be added to the branching cosmology of punk feminisms, with several notable recordings and papers held in both punk archives (see 3.137, *Ring of Fire* by E. T. Russian, among others) and the Human Sexuality Collection.[4]

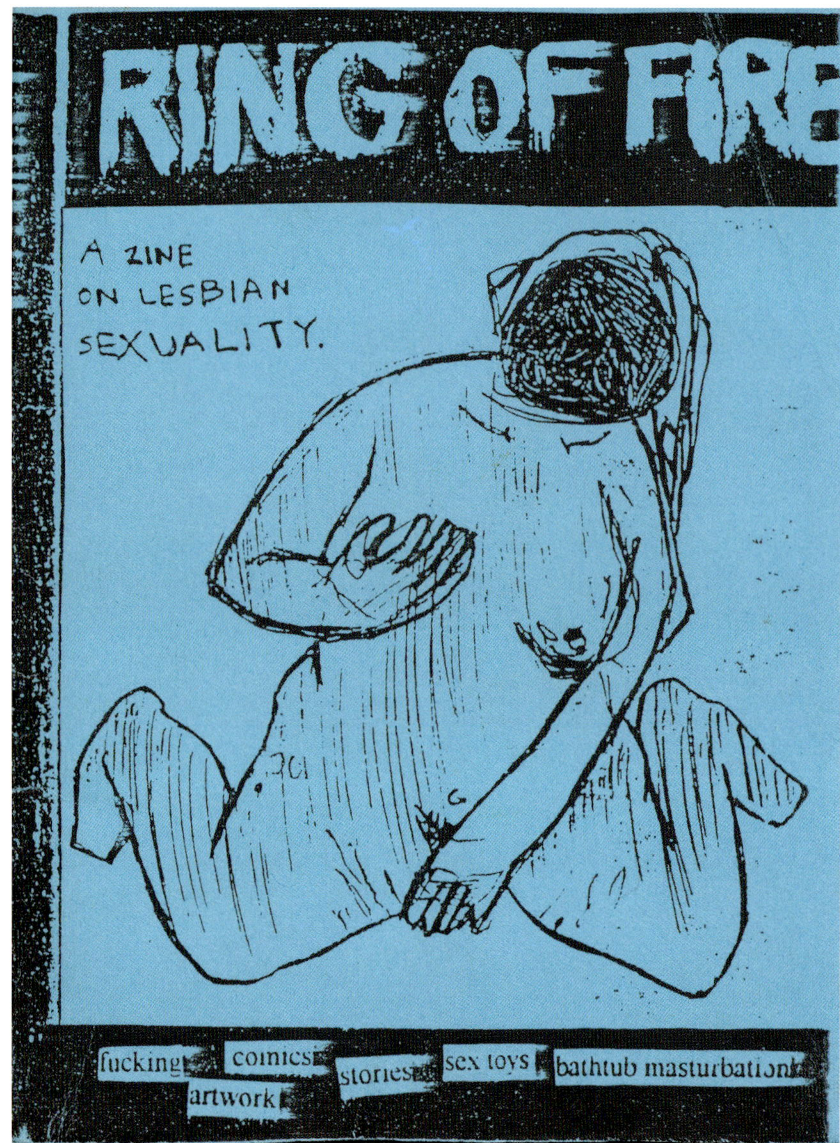

3.137. E. T. Russian's zine *Ring of Fire*, 1996–97.

PUNK'S NOT DEAD TILL NEOLIBERAL WHITE SUPREMACIST EXTRACTIVE CAPITALIST PATRIARCHY IS DEAD

The story line of a recent documentary on East Bay Punk struck me as following a common but less-than-thorough historiological template: a cross between Oedipus and Scooby Doo. In this trope, the visionary-but-controlling patriarch (Tim Yohannan) is dethroned by talented hard-working kids, who restore order. It's a mythical bloodline story about heredity rights and new regimes, not entirely unlike those wicked-stepmother folk and fairy stories from nineteenth-century Germany.

In the movie's final scene, the guitarist from Blatz tramps off-path overlooking a shimmering East Bay cityscape and into the woods. He retreats from the complexities of culture into the simplicity of nature with quiet confidence, performing the outsider role of the Romantic always-boy, a liberal masculinist fantasy of being a solitary and bounded self, separate from culture and history, not defined by relationships. He's purely himself and practically free. He's the seagull flying into the cloud and the flapping flag on the TV screen before the color bars. I'd seen this lonesome American hero trope, this existential midlife dad before. He's the bittersweet denouement. His slow-fade into sunset / stormy sea / faceless crowd / outer space signals the end of the story.

But exactly which story is over? Gilman remains active; its volunteers continue to wrangle complexities of nonprofit community arts and liberatory justice work at the same time university libraries establish punk archives full of contributions created by living, accessible people. Those of us who first learned how to get things done as young punks are meeting up at the dog park to hear each other's fifth steps between tours, running zine-making workshops for kids, texting each other about integrative medicine, smoking outside the meditation center, canvassing for voters, editing journals on vexed participation in progressive subcultures, raising pretty cool teenagers, drumming and writing poems. Some things have shifted, and some things have ended. Others have taken more subtle or outrageous forms. During this current swell of racist backlash, gender policing, and global totalitarianism, it's high time to drop the story of punk as a late twentieth-century clubhouse-tomb for destroyed, combative yet enterprising kids.

LOVE AND SURVIVAL

East Bay punk culture took me in and let me be smart, fat, slutty, rude, and profoundly upset. I ended up in a band with Annie (one of the art school punk girls who helped reroute my trajectory away from teenage wifedom) plus four Gilman guys including Eggplant and Joey, who were in high school. Marshall was an older guy who had a radio show and was quiet about both his former military experience and his love life, and Jesse was one of several punks who'd come from Philadelphia for the Anarchist Convention and stayed.

Later Annie and I wrote "Lullaby" together in Caffe Mediterraneum, the "cockroach café." A few days after writing the lyrics we recorded "Lullaby" for our first EP, *Cheaper Than the Beer*. That square bright yellow cover was photographed in the Mills College photography studios, just weeks before the 1990 strike to keep the college from becoming co-ed, where I was joined by Aaron, who sometimes played second drums in Blatz. I'd secretly professed my love for him through the recording studio glass to where he stood before we recorded vocals. For years and years, I had no idea that this confession had been taped and had ended up on the record as a sort of aural accidental marginalia, largely unnoticed. At some point in our thirties, Aaron brought this little love note from the past to my attention, having assumed it was intentional. But neither accidents nor intentions are as alive as outcomes, which keep rolling forward and producing further outcomes.

Origin stories are central to punk and feminist testimony. Shouldn't our tales of surviving be too?

THE BLATZ BEFORE CHRISTMAS

Blatz got together for a reunion show at Gilman at the end of 2013 to raise money for a friend with a bad diagnosis and big medical bills. It was Christmastime, and we hadn't been all together in more than twenty years. I was forty-two and had just gotten tenure. Annie, now a devout Catholic who was worried about Blatz lyrics swearing and making light of abortion, was going through an enormous family challenge with her teenage daughter. Gilman has no backstage, so we sat in my car down the road and listened to Bach's cello suites to calm down before the show. We were both in shitty, scary relationships. The car faced Gilman Street, and through the front window we watched excited happy Blatz fans cross the street and join the insanely long line of people waiting to get into the show. Annie didn't want to do the show. She didn't want people to throw things at her, afraid of being hit in the face or going home smelling like fish. I told her we'd make sure that didn't happen. I told her that we thought we were fierce back when we were teenagers, singing our brains out in Blatz, needing so badly to yell and scream and flail about in the face of all the horror of the world, but that really we needed to yell more than ever now as middle-aged ladies with big giant grown-up life things happening, both of us teachers in fucked-up relationships, both in a state of light panic about the size of the crowd, both now sober, overwhelmed, and utterly fierce.

Every time I'd ever sung "Lullaby," I'd meant it. On that Christmas Eve, I meant it as much as ever, but in new ways, ways I could only express after having been through the deaths of both parents, then my horrific divorce, sobriety, the elections of President Obama, the accelerating global climate emergency, social media and its famous trolls, etc. Maybe that night more than ever before we needed to sing in Blatz. So, with no idea what would happen next, we did.

MENOPAUSE MOHAWK

In early November 2016 I attended Punkfest Cornell and the opening reception for the exhibition "Anarchy in the Archives" displaying artifacts from its punk collections. I had rerouted a research trip to the New York Public Library to join Aaron and his partner Elizabeth in celebrating the acquisition and display of the Cometbus archives. A few days later the 2016 election happened. The meeting of these two moments (the Ivy League punk conference-festival and an election of an unspeakably disgusting game-show celebrity and supervillain materially supported by the leader of Russia, a former Soviet KGB official) may not strike readers now as especially dissonant, but the election results shocked many Punkfest participants.

I'd watched the first part of the election coverage at Sini Anderson's birthday party in Manhattan, which we'd all stupidly expected to coincide with the election of the first woman president. I'd known Sini since the 1990s in San Francisco, where she and Michelle Tea cohosted the first incarnation of Sister Spit, a local reading series that evolved into a rotating group of feminist poets and writers that toured the US. I traveled with Sister Spit in 1999 and 2000. Both Matt Wobensmith and Aaron were fans, so traces of this first-generation Sister Spit material are lodged with the punk archives in both Cometbus and Riot Grrrl Collections. After her time cohosting Sister Spit, Sini Andersen made the documentary *The Punk Singer* (2013), a movie about Kathleen Hanna's multidisciplinary artistic trajectory from college to midlife, including her collaborations with Johanna Fateman, known for intellectually sharp zines, culture writing, and visual art along with her sound design and performance in the bands Le Tigre (with Kathleen) and MEN. Johanna, Sini's girlfriend, had organized the election-night birthday party at a bar with good food and TVs. After candles were blown, we sickened and dispersed.

On April 26, 2019, two and a half years into this terrifying, destructive, and truly nihilistic presidency, Bikini Kill had a reunion show in Hollywood. I was at the show with my new girlfriend, who'd never been to a rock concert. It was my forty-eighth birthday, and I was PMS-ing my brains out near a woman I used to smoke with outside Gilman. She too was chugging tincture for perimenopausal mood swings and panic, and we bonded over this jagged new puberty that no one talked about. Between the bright vapid faces of "influencers" taking self-portraits, I watched Tobi Vail beat the living shit out of her drums and sing like she totally meant it. I watched Kathleen, bright with hard-won health, spark and sparkle the crowd with crystalline vocal power. Kathi's melodic bass growled my heart to life, and their new guitarist, the longtime zine-maker Erika Dawn Lyle, made me swell with an unanticipated pride that wasn't mine to feel but couldn't be stopped. Blocking my view, muffling the vibe, the influencers complimented each other with their backs to the stage.

Fueled by an ancient rage, a tiny spark of life leapt up inside: Start a scene! Bust past the security guards and shame the influencers! Squash past them to the edge of the balcony above the stage! Let them try to kick us out! I ached to crush the moral paradox. To crush even the part of it that included me, gratefully unjostled there in my free spot in the VIP section, feeling separate and irritated above the joyous energy of the crowd, reintegrating the version of myself that needed to feel so sharply alone in a crowd of happy, angry, sweaty girls, to experience that unique form of alienated connection.

I left after the last song, not waiting for the band to come up and hang out after the show. On the way out of the club my date refused to give her backstage pass to a friend's kid even after I explained why she should. Even though she didn't like the show or the band, she wanted the souvenir because Bikini Kill is famous, which is ultimately why I had to end our relationship even though she was nice. Maybe the satin sticker with its hilariously anachronistic sharpie-drawn "fetch this" dog-flipping-the-bird illustration went into her personal scrapbook, maybe the trash. It bears repeating, the music is one part of the story. The bands, zines, record covers, etc., are another. But the primacy of awkward collectivism over individual status beats the heart of punk history and leaves (almost) no trace.

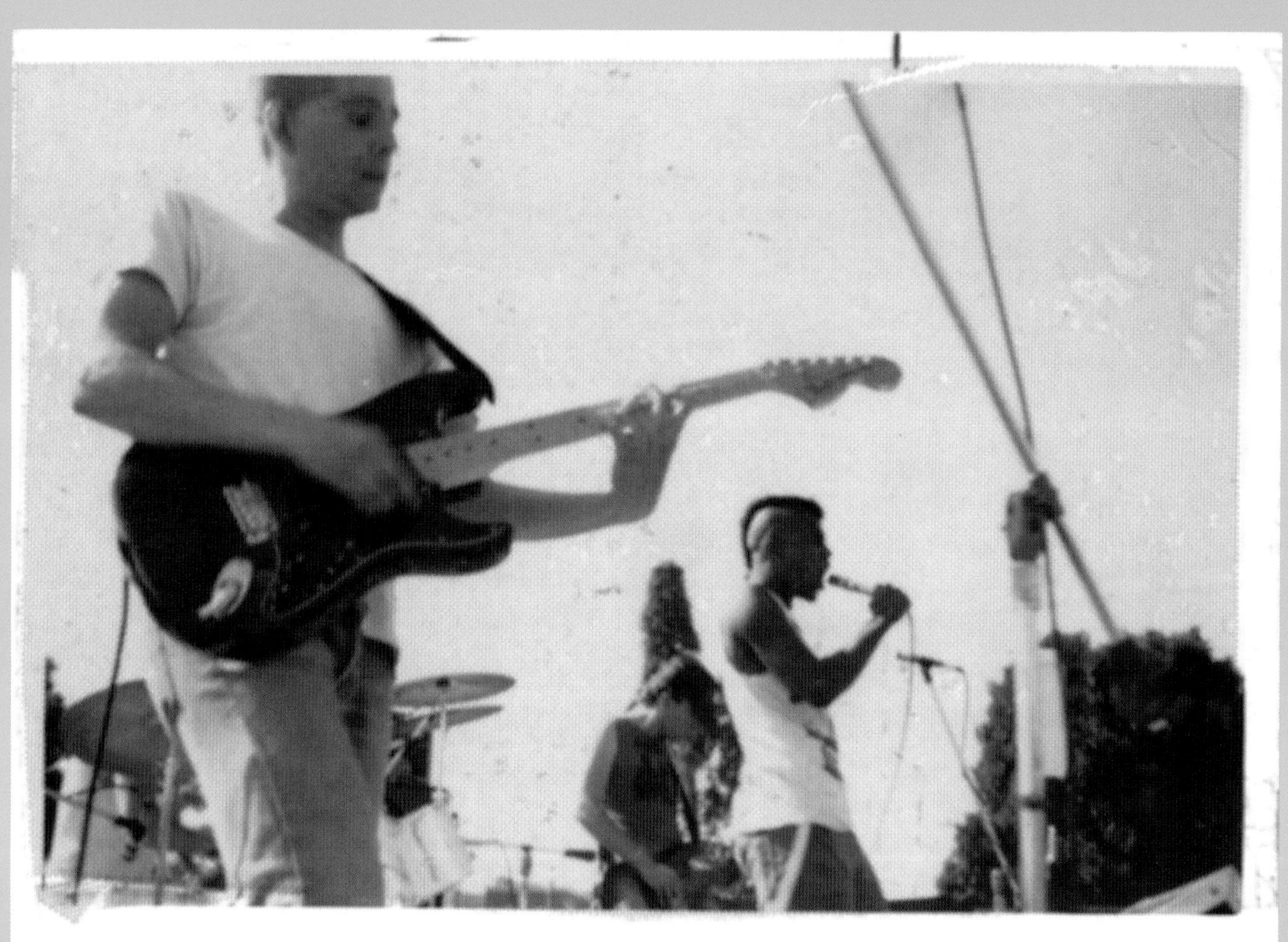

3.138. Special Forces, circa 1984. Photo: Aaron Cometbus.

"I was a very timid child"

CH. 15

AN INTERVIEW WITH ORLANDO XAVIER

Orlando Xavier was the front man for the Berkeley hardcore band Special Forces, active from 1983 to 1987, and in the late 1990s performed with United Blood and Intrepid A.A.F. In this interview conducted on November 27, 2021 Orlando discusses his experience finding common cause with his fellow misfits in the Bay Area scene, his memories of the DMR girls, performing shows at Ruthie's Inn and Gilman, and how to get through a set singing in a hardcore band.

ORLANDO: I was born in Oakland. I was the third child of five kids, so I'm right in the middle. But, yeah, 1959. My parents, before they got separated then divorced, we had a house in North Berkeley. As children growing up in Berkeley, me and my younger brother and friends would go on our bicycles and ride around all over Berkeley. We saw all the stuff going on back then. So I feel kind of blessed I grew up in the Bay Area. Blessed and cursed, but we'll get to the cursed part later.

My mother was an amazing woman. My father was an asshole. But my mom, a great, great woman. They both came from Pine Bluff, Arkansas. Moved here. Dad started running a business, he was a construction guy, and my mother was a nurse. My older brother, he wound up going to Vietnam, but luckily enough he was in the Navy and served on an aircraft carrier.

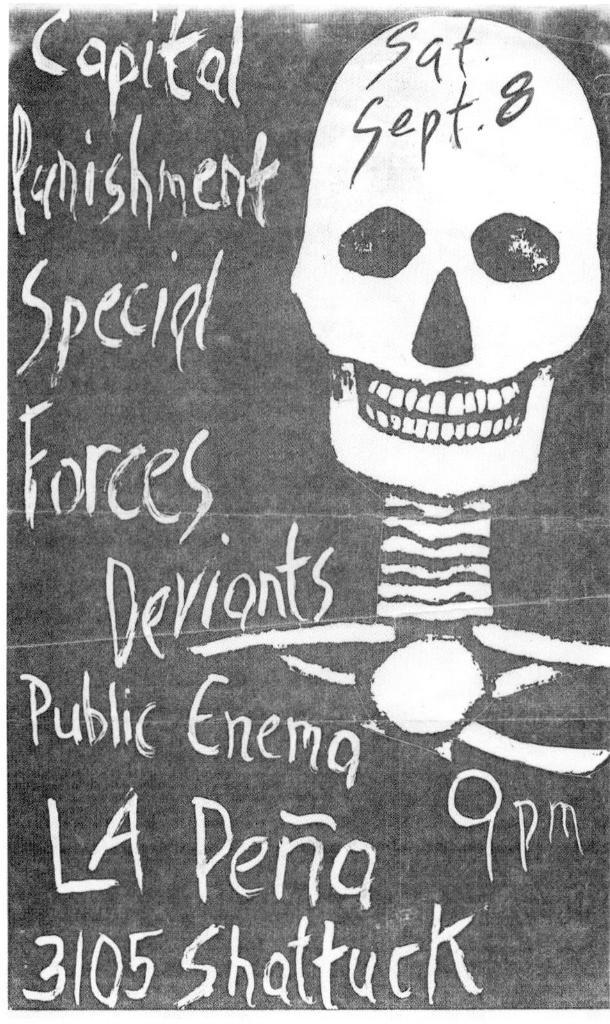

3.139. Flyer for 1984 show at La Peña, a cultural center in Berkeley founded by refugees from the regime of the Chilean dictator Augusto Pinochet.

Kennedy got killed and Martin Luther King. I was maybe four or five years old then. I barely remember what was going on, but I knew something really terrible had happened in the country. It was crazy times. I grew up in the sixties.

I got picked on a lot in school. I had a few friends. I used to wear glasses, I had bad vision. I actually got held back a year in fourth grade because they thought I was stupid. Yeah, I was stupid, but it was because I couldn't see, and I needed glasses. But I thought at the time, that's how humans normally see. I got glasses and I realized, "Oh, this is how humans are supposed to see. Interesting."

I was a very timid child. Not calm. I was bullied. It was just years, years of being picked on. Finally, in seventh grade, one big jock guy that was on the football team threw something at me. And then I just lost it. Actually went crazy. I turned around, and I told him, "If you don't stop throwing those rocks at me, I'm going to kill you." That was the first time I went red. If you've ever gotten so mad, so mad where you do actually see red. It actually happens. Everything just goes red. It's like the blood rushing because of the pain. Blood just rushing into your eye. That's why you see it red. Now you're so angry. Adrenaline's going and everything. I attacked this guy. I leapt up on the guy. Big old chopper. Jumped on him and grabbed him by his throat and banged his head. I just went crazy. Three people physically had to restrain me, my arms, and my legs. And all I can say, "I'm going to kill you." My glasses had flown off.

JUDITH: So that was a formative event for you, figuring out that you had that violence in you?

ORLANDO: It changed everything. I definitely got less bullied at the school. They called me "the Strangler."

JUDITH: Can I ask, was there any racial component to you being bullied?

ORLANDO: No. It was another Black guy. Here's the great thing about coming from the Bay Area. Yeah, sure, there was racism around, but in Berkeley everybody's mixed together. One of my best friends when I was a kid was an Asian kid—Glen. The history of the Bay Area, going to World War II and the bases, and then going into the fifties, when I was born, and into the sixties, the mixture got even more. If I had to worry about anything, it's like police forces were mostly white. So you had to deal with definitely racist cops.

TOM: So were you listening to music at this time? Was punk something that absorbed a lot of rage for you, or transformed it?

ORLANDO: So I was listening to a lot of stuff. I grew up listening to a lot of R&B stuff. And my mother, she loved the Beatles. My dad was like, "Why are you playing that crap?" I was like, "Because my mom liked it." One of her favorite bands was Squeeze. If it weren't for my mother, I tell you. I love her. My father was an asshole. My mother, thank goodness for her. If it wasn't for her, I'd probably be in San Quentin now, or dead. That's where punk rock comes in.

Actually, the first time I saw punks was when I was doing a work furlough because I was in jail in Oakland. Before I went to jail I actually shaved the sides of my head. I didn't get a mohawk until later on, but these punks were trying to talk to me, and they thought I was some rude asshole because I'd just say "I have to go sweep." It wasn't until I went back after I got out of jail, and I explained what was going on, and some of those people became really great friends. One of them would become my very closest, dearest friend. We actually played in a band together. Torrance Tang [from Special Forces and Intensified Chaos]. Turner Babcock was his nickname, because we all had to have punk rock names. Great musician. He later died, which was devastating to me.

I got out of being incarcerated in December of '78, just a little bit before the New Year. Punk rock had already been in the Bay Area. There were a lot of venues. And the Sex Pistols had played Winterland. You would notice people differently on the streets. The Sex Pistols thing was huge. There were all these crazy stories in the paper from 1977 on up to probably 1980, '85, '89. Articles about violence in the clubs, and ambulances coming back and forth, carrying people from these violent shows. I'm reading this stuff at the time, saying, "Wow! This sounds dangerous. Why would anybody go to something like that? It's crazy."

But when I got out, I met this girl, Tanya Morris, at a party. Now she was already in the punk scene and the mod scene. All the scenes were kind of blending together at that time. So Tanya takes me to my very first show, which was the Mabuhay Gardens in San Francisco—a place I would frequent quite a bit after that. I won't tell you what clothing I was wearing back then because it was so embarrassing. She told me, "You can't wear that. Let's try to dress you a little bit more punk rock." Three weeks later I had a mohawk, a T-shirt, and some boots.

This was a very important time in history. But at that time no one thought it would be historic, just like no one thought stuff that was going on in the sixties in the Bay Area would be historic. It was just what was going on at the time. So I went to the Mabuhay Gardens. You actually had a strange mix of people in there. Because the disco scene was just dying out. There was a disco place across the street, which would later become the Stone. And Dirk Dirksen was doing his thing, talking to the audience at the Mabuhay Gardens, and you'd think, "Who the fuck is this jerk?" But I later just fell in love with that man. He was a great, great man, and pivotal, uniting the American scene and the European, and UK scenes.

Pogo and thrash were going on at the same time. Thrash started in America, and pogo started in England. So I started pogoing and jumping around getting ready to go out there, and then this fight broke out. These three young kids, and this big biker guy. This guy was gigantic, long hair and leather coat. He just punched this poor, bald kid really hard, and knocked him down, and he was bleeding and stuff. And then his other three friends leapt on the biker. These three little guys were able to beat the crap out of the big guy. It was just crazy, and the band's still playing. The band didn't even stop. I wish I could remember what band it was, dammit. I've told people it was the Teen Idles, but they didn't play the Mabuhay Gardens until 1980.

JUDITH: Your very first show, and you're seeing this violence happen. What was that like?

ORLANDO: Oh, I was scared. I didn't want to actually fight. And, well, I thought it was also quite exciting. You know what I did? Two nights later, I went back to the Mabuhay Gardens by myself. That was another great thing about the Bay Area. There was a time from 1979 to 1985 that you could go out any night, seven days a week, to a show. You had shows going on in Berkeley and Oakland and San Francisco.

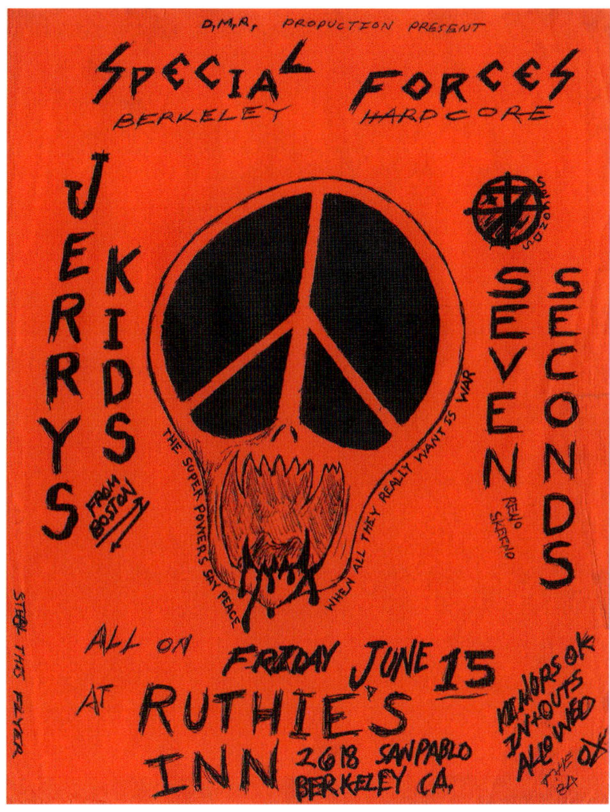

3.140. Flyer for Special Forces show at Ruthie's Inn, Berkeley, 1984.

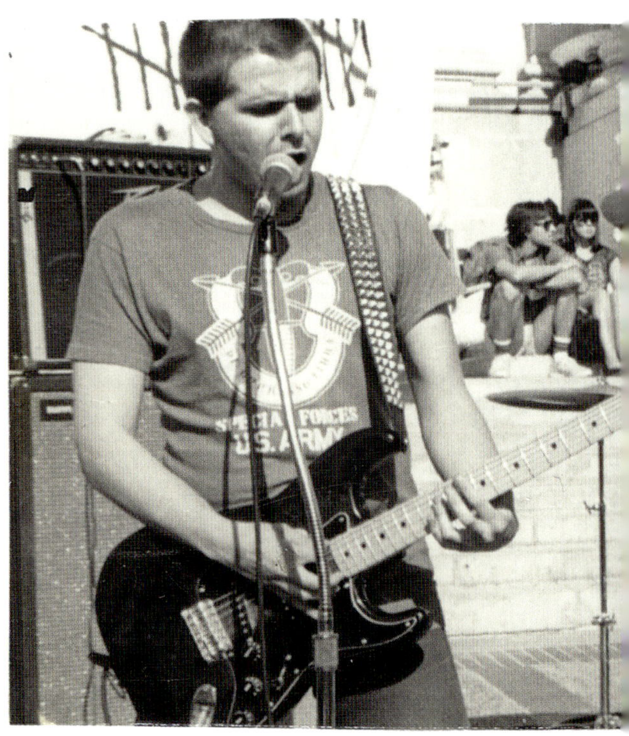

You literally could go to three shows in one night. In Berkeley you had the Berkeley Square. And there was this place up on Telegraph, I can't remember the name of, but across the street where they had a punk rock movie night. That's where I first saw *Mad Max*.

But by '79 or '80 I was working at two 7-Elevens, on Sacramento and on Parker Street in Berkeley. So that's when I was starting to meet a lot of the Berkeley punks. Already before I went to jail things were changing, and people were already starting to hang out on Telegraph and Durant.

JUDITH: So when did you get the inspiration to hook up with people for a band?

ORLANDO: In '83 I joined my first band. I was hanging out at this café, Au Coquelet. It was another place where a lot of punks would hang out from time to time. By this time, I'd just started working at Rasputin's Records. I'd just been laid off by this hot tub place I was working at because I had a mohawk. I met Kirk Hammet there, way before Metallica. Anyway, a friend told me, "Hey, this guy is looking for a singer, a front man for his band." And then I met Bill Collins. He had a place just up the street from the UC Theater. This building was famous because the blueprints were drawn up for the atomic bomb on the fifth or sixth floor. This building in Berkeley. And we were practicing down in the basement.

TOM: So you'd never sung before or anything?

ORLANDO: No, never. I had been talking about it for years, since 1980: "I would like to be in a band." And I jammed with some friends, doing some stuff, but we were too busy doing drugs and alcohol to actually get together and do a band. Anyway, that's how people formed bands.

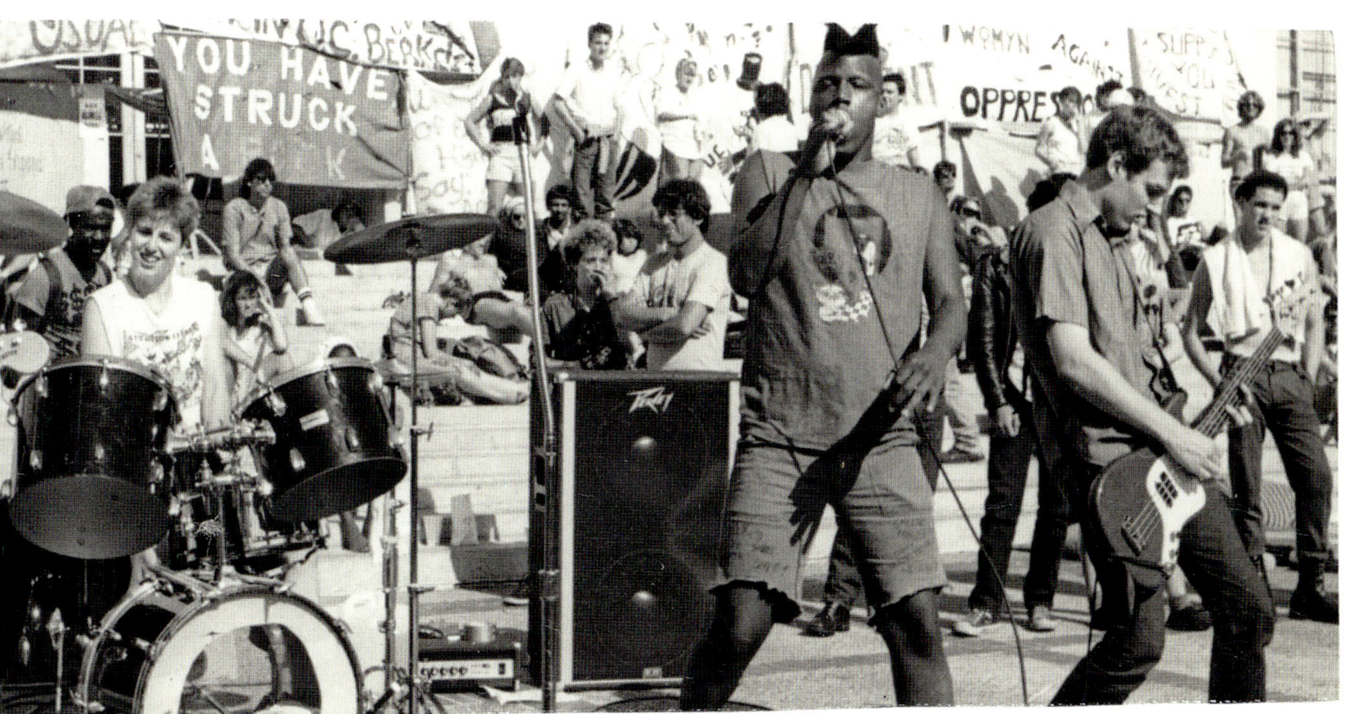

3.141. Special Forces (Bill Collins, Anna Chapman, Orlando X, Tom Flynn) at Biko Plaza, circa 1986. Photo: © Murray Bowles.

People would just start playing an instrument, drums or guitar or bass, and three or four weeks later, they'd say, "Let's do a band!" The people could barely play their instruments, but they were playing this sound. There was this sound punk had, that made . . . you didn't have to be a great musician. You learned as you went along and got better and better. And some people were excellent. Like Bill. He was writing some songs, so he gave me a tape with, I believe, three or four songs. I went home and listened to it, wrote down some lyrics, then I said, "Okay!" I called him up a couple weeks later, went down to his place. He already had a drummer and a bass player he was playing with. And that was it. In 1983, we were doing a band.

We'd practice, practice, practice. We knew our parts so well that we would get up on stage and play totally wasted and sound fantastic. It becomes so automatic. Bill and also our bass player at the time, Kirby, and also our second drummer, Steve Bragg, they were already professionals. Pretty much all those guys were professional musicians. Bill Collins definitely was a driving force. I mean he definitely dialed me up. Oh, Bill wrote some genius music. The music Bill wrote for the *World Domination* album was fantastic because of the way it progresses.

JUDITH: I wanted to ask you about "Hurt Me" from that album. It's a brilliant song because it goes through all these different tempo changes.

ORLANDO: That's right, the progression!

JUDITH: The progression is amazing. Starts out slow—

ORLANDO: And has that fast part. Oh yeah, that's one of Bill's finest. It actually was a hard one to sing because of the progression. There were some songs that we did on our album that we later didn't play anymore because we were a faster band back then with some of that stuff. And then there was another one on "Death Squad" that was a really fast, superhard one to sing because of the progression. I had to think about breathing when I sung that. See the secret of singing is: if you're being amplified you can tone it down and not burn yourself out. Another trick, the greatest thing I love, is when the audience knows your lyrics and they want to sing them, you don't have to work as hard because you're singing all together. You can back it down even more and save your voice and strength. People are singing the lyrics and you're holding the mike out to their singing. You look like you're screaming but you're toning it down, you're saying to yourself, "OK, I've got to save myself for the next song." I used to calculate all these things to get through the set so I can breathe.

TOM: It's like this photo we have of you in the archives (3.142).

JUDITH: Right, you're holding the mike to the kid to sing in that photo. You look like you're singing, but he's got the mike.

ORLANDO: It was a singer's greatest relief when you've got fans that know the lyrics to the song. Three seconds of a breather when you're live onstage for a vocalist is the greatest thing. All you need is three to five seconds. Yeah, that's Ruthie's Inn, most definitely, because I remember this kid here. The first time at Ruthie's Inn. I believe it was our third show, and Discharge was headlining. We got put on that bill. That was like, "Whoo!" But we played a terrible set. Our set was OK, but our first drummer liked to smoke the weed a little too much. He was

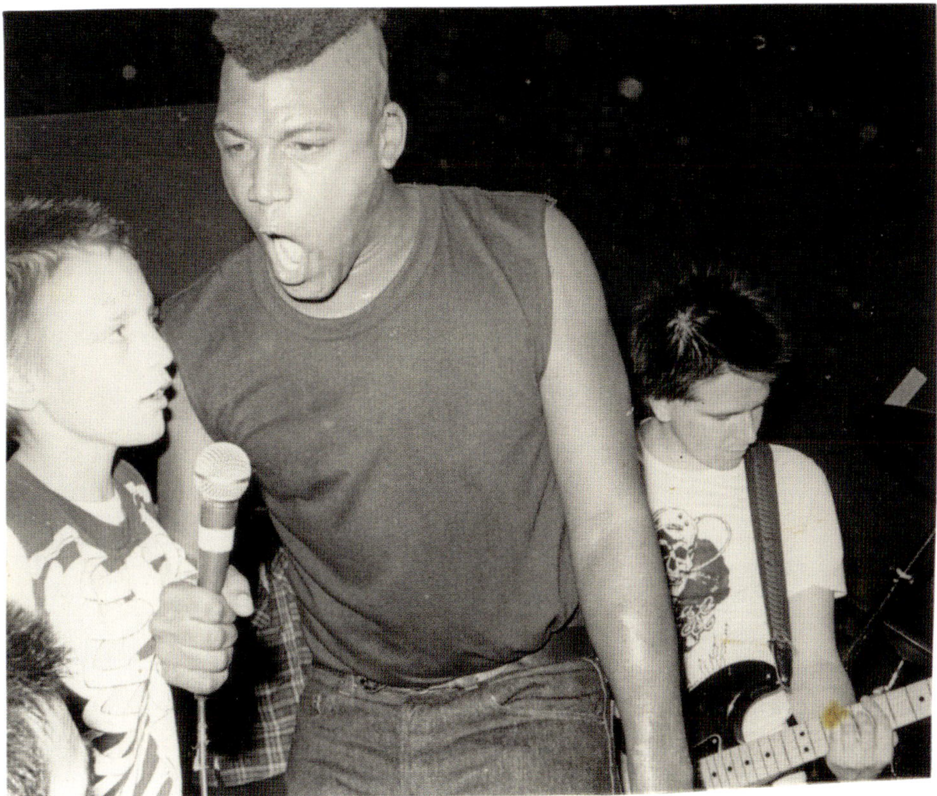

3.142. Orlando X and Bill Collins of Special Forces at Ruthie's Inn with unknown young audience member. Photo: © Murray Bowles.

a great guy. But at our next practice, I was so mad about the show, and I said, "You're playing with Discharge, right? We're opening for Discharge!" I wanted something like Discharge, because Discharge, at that time, when you had a party, at all the many punk rock parties, Discharge was one of the sing-along bands. If you get drunk, you stand around the turntable singing their songs and drinking.

And the scene toward the mid-eighties was really interesting because it was also fun, because you had the metal stuff start to really take off, and some of the punks and metalheads were hanging out together. It was pretty cool actually.

TOM: And it seems like Ruthie's was a place where that was happening more than other places?

ORLANDO: It was quite a bit, at Ruthie's, yeah. Everybody was friends. And the ska thing was starting to happen. So then it got a little confused because in the earlier eighties, some of the ska punk skinheads weren't racist at all, and there were even some gay skinheads in San Francisco, and they all got hassled by the mid-eighties because if you looked like a skinhead, you were bad. And some people got attacked for that. The thing is, we all got along really great early on. We were going to the same shows. It's kind of weird because like then, I guess, they decided they wanted to be racist skinheads or Nazi skinheads. It started to get really bizarre by '82, '83. I was like, "Wait a minute, they're starting fights with people in the pit." And I would

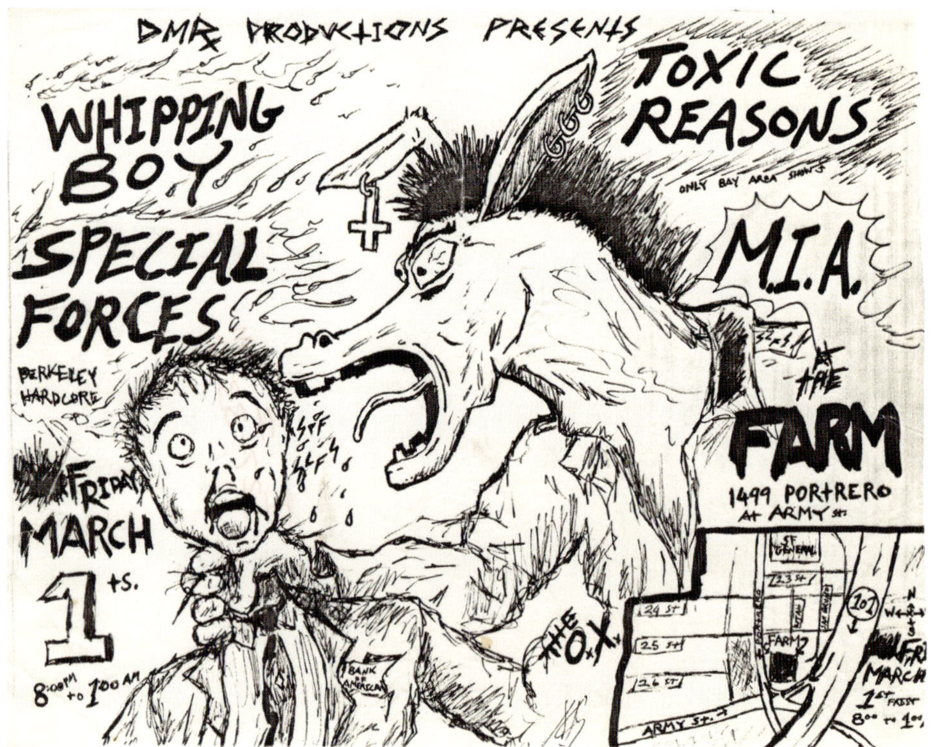

3.143. Flyer for DMR Productions show at the Farm, San Francisco, 1985.

go and stand up to them and say, “Why are you attacking people? Like what the fuck?” And I said, “What has changed with you cats, in this short period of time?” I’m sure there’s a couple of newer skinheads coming into the scene, but like why?

JUDITH: As one of the few African Americans in this punk scene, did you feel yourself to be a kind of representative . . . ?

ORLANDO: Here’s the interesting thing about the scene, because there was a lot of different mix of people who were Asians and Blacks. Mostly it was a white scene, but the thing is, when we all got together, we never thought about that. There were shows or places where, in a big group, I was literally the only Black guy there. I never thought of it. I’m just going to a show. And to this very day I don’t think about it.

JUDITH: So there’s something within the punk scene itself that allowed you to feel that way.

ORLANDO: Yes, it is, in my personal opinion. See, when we all got together, when we first started, when everybody starts getting involved in the scene, each person has something that’s happening in their separate life, something that has happened, whether it be negative or bad for me. It was like some negative stuff that happened in my life, and what you do is get together with other people that have problems with different things, and so it was a bunch of misfits. We all got together and had common issues and became friends. We found a group where we could dress the way we wanted, listen to music we wanted, and hang out. We formed these friendships and groups together.

JUDITH: So speaking of friendships and going back to what you were saying about Discharge and sing-along songs, I wanted to ask you about a song on, I think it's *World Domination*, that album. It's the cover of "Rollercoaster" by the Ohio Players.

ORLANDO: OK, so that was my idea because I saw the Ohio Players when I was a kid in Oakland in the seventies. And then I just kind of had this drunk idea, it's like, "OK, bro, Rollercoaster!" I had just seen a movie. I think it was Irwin Allen's *Rollercoaster* [a 1977 disaster film, directed by James Goldstone and featuring "Sensurround" with bass frequencies to make audiences feel the vibrations of the coaster scenes]. Irwin Allen did one of my favorite series, *Lost in Space*. The movie had nothing to do with the Ohio Players song. Of course, the Ohio Players song, "Love Rollercoaster," had come out years before that movie. But I was watching that movie with some friends, and I was thinking about the Ohio Players, and I thought, "What if you did a fun version of 'Rollercoaster'? And let's change the lyrics to sound like 'Death Rollercoaster.'" Oh, man, that was such a fun song to record. I remember that. It was their music. We just punked it up a little bit.

JUDITH: It's a great cover. Were you into that rumor about that little scream embedded in the Ohio Players' song? There's this whole controversy about whether that scream is actually a woman being murdered or something.

ORLANDO: You know, I heard that. I think it's an urban legend. We did have our screaming women—the DMR girls. It was so fantastic having them there, a great honor. DMR. Whoo! They were the two tough girls at the time. They were a bit of a terror. You did not want to ever cross them. You wanted to be their friends, because they broke Dirk's arm. Yeah. It's not the first bones they had broken, but they broke his arm.

I'm telling you someone is missing out on doing a punk rock soap opera. If I was better at writing, if I could get someone to write this, you can do a series. I mean you got romance and death and violence and gloom and music. I saw the *American Idiot* play on my fiftieth birthday with Wendy-O-Matik. I'd never really been a fan of Green Day's earlier stuff, but I think *American Idiot* was Green Day's *Sandinista*. Every song on *American Idiot* is fantastic to me. Every single one. The music and the acting, it was amazing.

JUDITH: So are you surprised that punk has become such a historical anchor point?

ORLANDO: I'll say my surprise came more around the late eighties, early nineties. The writing was already there definitely by then. "Oh, this is historic now." Look at Gilman. About the time Gilman opened, there were only a handful of places for bands to play. San Francisco went from where you had four or five places you could go to and see two or three shows in one night and then to where, boom, there's nothing. So, Gilman, at the time it opened up, it gave a new breath where bands could play. I thought Gilman wouldn't last three years. I used to talk a lot of crap about Gilman Street. But I'm so impressed considering all the different things that have happened over the years that could have closed them down. They have weathered through it somehow. And now it's like, what, the oldest surviving punk club in America? It's amazing. It's just different groups of people kept it going because enough people believe. When the pandemic happened, I was really worried, but Gilman has weathered through it again. It will continue all the way until the sun goes nova.

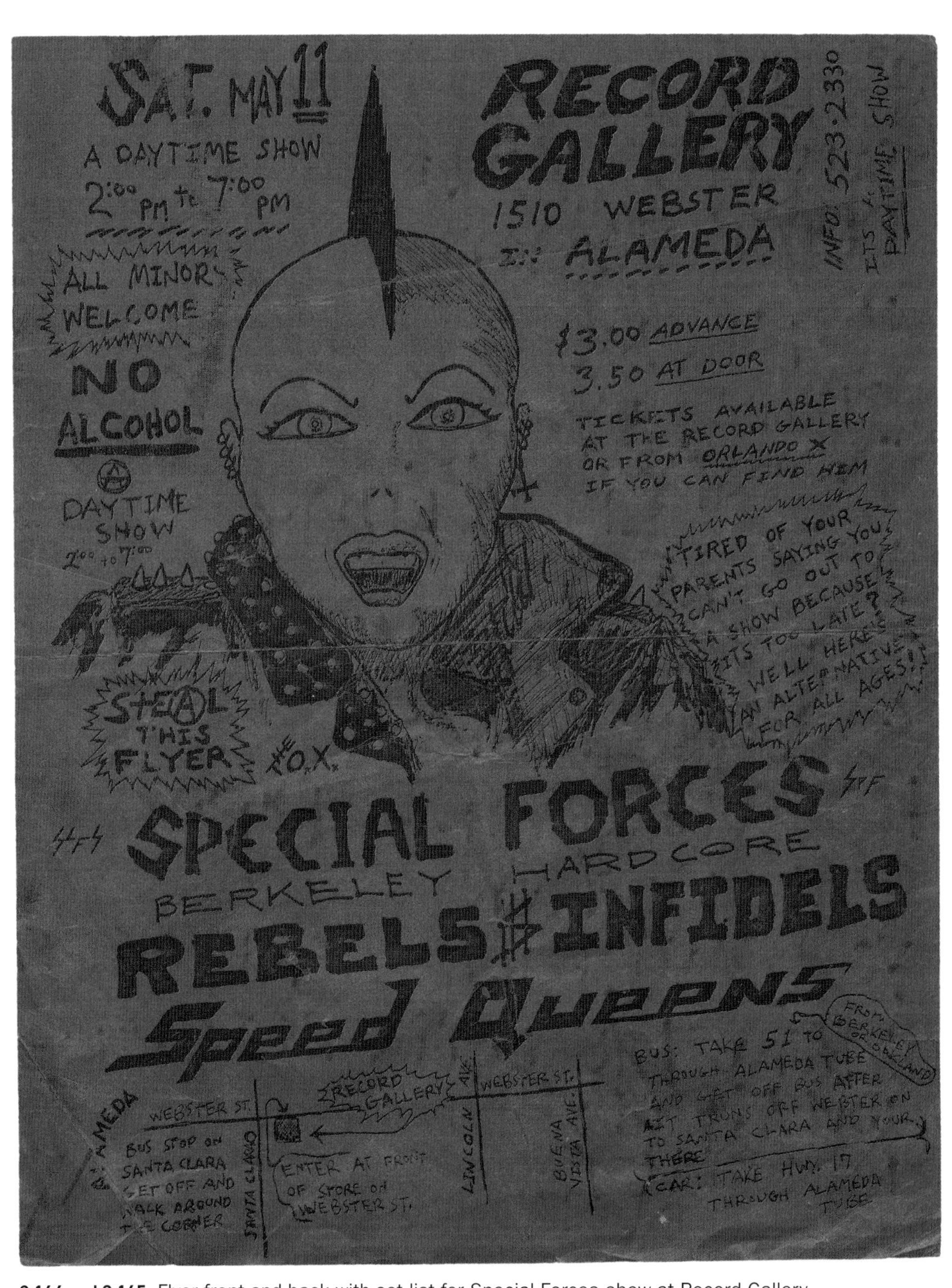

3.144 and 3.145. Flyer front and back with set list for Special Forces show at Record Gallery, Alameda, May 1985.

BONERANZA
STREET HASSLE
DEATH SQUAD
HURT ME
BERKELEY H.C
DEATH ON HOLIDAY
IN S. AFRKA
SPECIAL FORCES
GENERIC THRASH
HOUSEWRECKING PARTY
COCKROCKER
YOU CANT KILL COCKROACHES
MAKE THE WIDDERS FIGHT
WHATS THIS
MULEMEAT

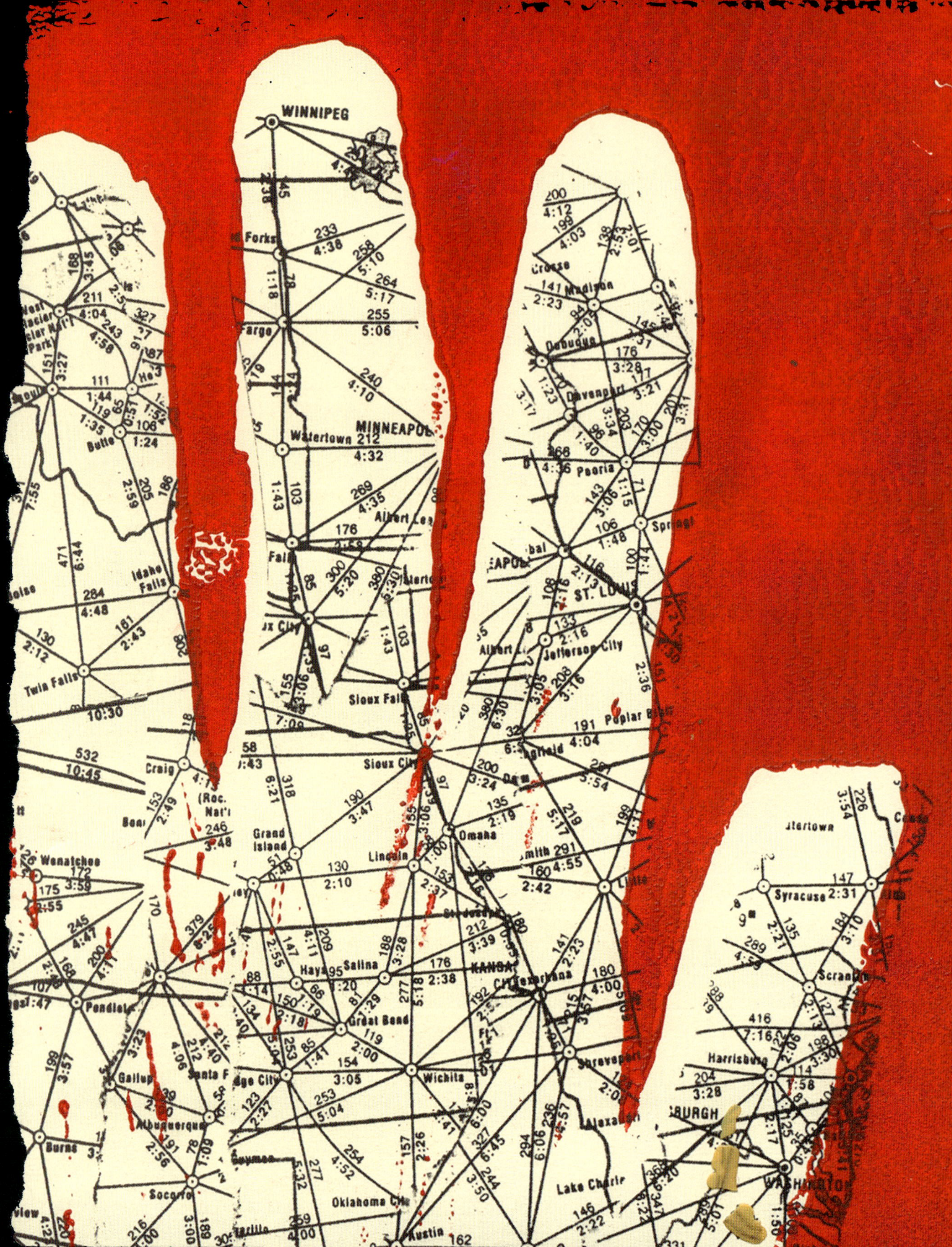
WINNIPEG
Forks
Fargo
Watertown
Sioux Falls
Sioux City
Grand Island
Lincoln
Omaha
Hays
Salina
Great Bend
Wichita
Oklahoma City
Austin
Madison
Dubuque
Davenport
Peoria
ST. LOUIS
Jefferson City
Texarkana
Shreveport
Syracuse
Harrisburg
Twin Falls
Butte
Idaho Falls
Wenatchee
Gallup
Albuquerque
Socorro
Burns

PART FOUR

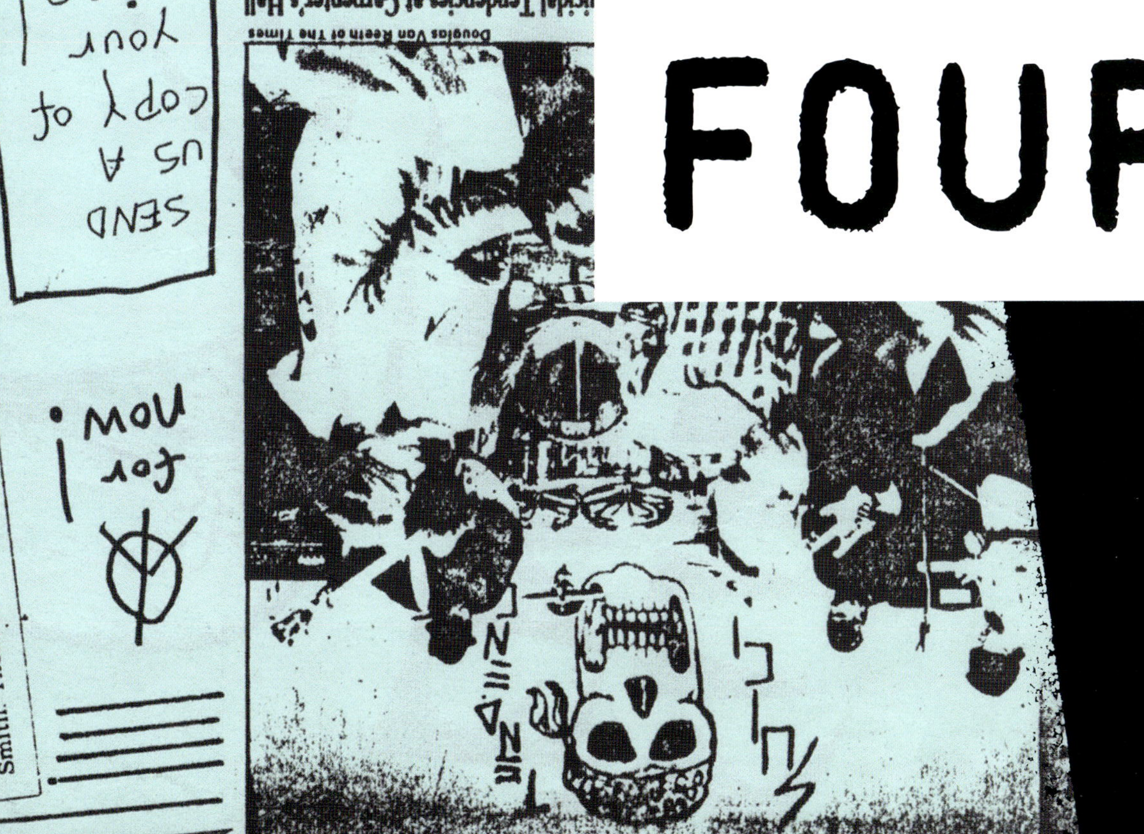

CH. 16 Be a Crossroads!

PUNK BEYOND BORDERS

There's no flyover country in punk. Bands start everywhere, not just on the coasts. Scenes don't need much more than a couple dozen creative misfits who aren't waiting around for someone else to tell them how to get things done. And when bands go on tour, they get in the van, crisscross the country, and play the majority of their shows in garages, basements, and small clubs in towns or medium-size cities.

This is all to say that the Midwest, South, and Southwest don't get enough recognition in general histories of punk, although they're central to it. KK Barrett of the Screamers found his first music scene in Stillwater, Oklahoma; Akron, Ohio, spawned Devo; Dead Boys and Pere Ubu rose from the ashes of Cleveland-based Rocket from the Tombs (4.1 AND 4.2), and the Stooges represented the anarchic side of Detroit rock. Yet it's true that for these first-gen punks, the coasts had a magnetic pull: Iggy, KK, and Devo decamped to Los Angeles (4.3), and Dead Boys and Pere Ubu became regulars in New York clubs (1.30). But others stayed put. Tesco Vee and Dave Stimson started Touch and Go first as a fanzine in East Lansing, Michigan, and later as a record label operating out of Chicago starting in 1981, which released a slew of groundbreaking bands from so-called "regional" scenes: Ohio's Necros, Michigan's the Fix, Wisconsin's Killdozer, Kentucky's Slint, and Texas's Butthole Surfers and Scratch Acid.

There are too many of these less heralded first-wave scenes for us to list here, but as punk entered its second wave in the 1980s, even the most provincial New Yorker or Angeleno had to recognize the energy distributed across the country as more fanzines and tapes were passed around, reaching new eyes and ears (with images 4.4 TO 4.17 in the next chapter's gallery, you'll see a sampling of zines and flyers from Florida to Alaska and places in between). And then there was Black Flag's relentless touring. Dubbed "the Lewis and Clarks of the punk rock touring circuit,"[1] Black Flag established DIY hardcore outposts everywhere they went, and Greg Ginn's SST label enlarged the regional span of punks on record: Bad Brains from DC, Hüsker Dü from Saint Paul, the Meat Puppets from Phoenix, and the Dicks from Austin.

Chicago's burgeoning punk scene in the 1980s and '90s took the local further into the global. Late starters compared to New York, LA, and San Francisco, Chicago punks danced to imports before they formed their own bands; DJs spun punk records alongside soul and reggae at a gay bar called La Mere Vipere in the North Side neighborhood of Lincoln Park. In the same area, life partners Jim Nash and Dannie Flesher opened Wax Trax Records in 1978, after selling their store of the same name in Denver. The Chicago store provided a center for the punk and industrial scenes in the city and access to the latest imports (records, clothing, pins, posters, and zines). This international sensibility was later matched by Wax Trax's own record label's roster of Chicagoland and European bands. Meanwhile, venues like Oz and O'Banion's, two other gay-turned-punk bars, hosted early breakout bands such as Strike Under, whose eclectic EP *Immediate Action* was an early Wax Trax's release; the Effigies, who melded melodic riffs with punchy vocals; the "loudly leftist" Articles of Faith (4.4), who drew inspiration from the Bad Brains;[2] and Naked Raygun (4.5), whose 1985 album *Throb Throb* threaded political lyrics into an eclectic field of piercing distortion. Members of Naked Raygun also joined forces with a young Montana transplant named Steve Albini to form Big Black, a band that pushed punk toward industrial and noise rock, with lyrics that Michael Azerrad describes as "bilious misanthropy."[3] Despite their often open animosity toward one another, these bands shaped a Chicago punk scene in the first half of the 1980s. However, in the early '90s, with a shift from the North Side to Pilsen on the South Side, Uruguayan-born Martín Sorrondeguy would turn Chicago punk in a new direction by taking the distinctly Latine perspective of his band Los Crudos to Mexico, South America, and Japan.

FROM LOCAL TO GLOBAL: MARTÍN SORRONDEGUY AND LATINE PUNK

Of course, Sorrondeguy was far from the first Latine punk. Whether or not you believe that punk really starts with the Peruvian garage band Los Saicos in the 1960s, Latine-powered punk bands propelled the sound of early LA punk and hardcore from Hollywood to Boyle Heights, San Pedro, and Hermosa Beach. Just up the coast, the early 1980s "nardcore" scene in the Southern California suburb of Oxnard crossed into Mexico to play bills with Tijuana hardcore bands (4.19 AND 4.20), and dozens of other Latine musicians, artists, and zine makers, in and around LA and across the country, kept scenes energized as punk entered its second and third decades.

Moreover, punk bands from Latin America, like Argentina's Los Violadores and Fun People (4.62), and later Spanish-language hardcore bands from the US, like Dogma Mundista, or Latin American hardcore like Alerta Roja (Argentina), Narcosis (Peru), and Masacre 68 (Mexico), and the entire *subte* movement put punk *en español* on the front lines confronting dictatorships, government massacres, poverty, and drug wars, revealing the lived realities linking punk and revolution. Los Crudos channeled the energy of these other histories and broadened the audience for punk through songs like "Hardcoregoismo" or "Somos los mojados" (We're the wetbacks) that criticized the xenophobic and Anglocentric members of any scene.

The 1994 passage of both California's Proposition 187, which denied social services to undocumented immigrants, and NAFTA, which ignored and exacerbated labor exploitation in Mexico, raised the political stakes for Latine punks like Los Crudos as they mobilized punk's history of antiauthoritarianism to voice resistance in songs like "La Caída de Latinoamérica" (The Fall of Latin America), "Levántate" (Rise Up), and "Unidad Prohibida" (Unity Prohibited).

Sorrondeguy's lyrics, activism, filmmaking, photography, and writing, and his record label Lengua Armada created a supportive foundation for other Latine punks, from sharing an album with fellow hardcore band Huasipungo (*Nunca nada cambia . . . a menos que lo hagamos cambiar*) or the feminist punk of Spitboy (*Viviendo asperamete*), to inspiring Downtown Boys vocalist Victoria Ruiz and providing sleeve and poster art for the queer, multiracial dance-punk band Special Interest.

Los Crudos played their last gig in 1998 (4.67), just as the internet, digital archiving, and file sharing began to alter the way punks (and everyone else) accessed music and information. As much as supporting your local scene mattered—people still needed venues and bands to go to a show—now the kid in Milwaukee could listen live to Berkeley's KALX, or the Berkeley punk could tune in to Milwaukee's WMSE. If the old punk DIY infrastructure created zines, scene reports, mail order, pen pals, etc., to keep people connected to places far from their own towns, then the rise of social media platforms meant that the once hard-earned access to local underground secrets was now available to someone four thousand miles away. Many punks embraced the new reality to become post-regional. This was true for Sorrondeguy's next band, Limp Wrist, which formed in Philadelphia but whose members lived all over the United States.

TEARING DOWN WALLS: PUNK'S INTERSECTIONAL IDENTITIES

Sorrondeguy's shift from the imposing straight edge singer of Los Crudos to the front man for Limp Wrist not only broke out from a regional identity, but emphatically turned hardcore queer. Limp Wrist's queer bear bondage look calls back to NYC's gay leather bar the Eagle's Nest, where Arturo Vega found inspiration for the Ramones' logo to match their leather-clad hustler uniform (1.38, 1.41). But as their name implies, Limp Wrist revised the outrageous camp humor of Jayne County to celebrate the homoeroticism of hardcore in songs like "I Love Hardcore Boys / I Love Boys Hardcore" and "Cruisin' at the Show," and in the many flyers designed by Sorronedguy featured in his interview chapter.

Limp Wrist's fearless queercore also stemmed from an earlier scene that formed in another region far from the coasts—Austin, Texas. In the early 1980s, the Big Boys and the Dicks reigned as the "undisputed kings," according to Gretchen Phillips (Meat Joy, Two Nice Girls, Girls in the Nose). "I first saw the Big Boys at Club Foot when they were opening for the Go-Go's [in 1981]. They were all in drag, and they were calling themselves the Short Girls."[4] (They also called themselves Kaye Mart and the Shoppers in those days.) David Yow (Scratch Acid), remembers "the Dicks were arguably the best and most rousing band ever to come out of Texas. . . . Gary Floyd, the singer of the Dicks, was brazen and truly formidable, a portly cross-dressed madhouse of a man."[5] Other Austin bands counted queer men and women in their ranks: the Jitters, Meat Joy, Jerry's Kids, and Whoom Elements, among others (4.21–4.26). For Phillips, having moved from Houston to Austin fresh out of high school, queer people were so prevalent in the scene that "punk equaled queer" in her mind. In the conservative context of Reagan-era Texas, being overtly queer came with great risks; but it also became a beacon of punk strength and defiance that encompassed antiracism, antipolice, and anti-Reagan politics, signaling how "regional" bands were thinking well beyond their regions.

At the turn of the 1990s, another politicized regional group of queer-allied feminist punks in the Pacific Northwest came together under a collective identity of riot grrrl, which became a movement of sorts, forging networks of punk women across the country. Riot grrrl emerged within the college town environment in Olympia, Washington, where radical ideas, local bands, and the indie label K Records all found a home. One foundational event involved Evergreen State student Kathleen Hanna's encounter with her hero, the experimental author Kathy Acker (4.29), who made a fateful remark to the aspiring writer: "Why are you writing? . . . You should be in a band."[6] Hanna took half of her advice and joined forces with drummer Tobi Vail, who had been publishing her own zine *Jigsaw* since 1988, to write their zine *Bikini Kill*, but also start the band of the same name (4.30–4.34). Zines brought other projects together: by the early 1990s, Molly Neuman (DC) and Allison Wolfe (Olympia) published their zine *Girl Germs* (4.35) and formed Bratmobile. Down the coast in Berkeley, Mimi Thi Nguyen and Marike put out the zine *Aim Your Dick* (4.36), and across the Bay in San Francisco Michelle Tea and Sini Anderson started the queer-feminist zine *Sister Spit* as part of their spoken-word collective formed in 1994 (4.37, 4.38).

Riot grrrl, feminist punk, and queercore represent distinct but overlapping scenes; their strong alliances can be seen in some of the materials in this section. As late as 1996, Kathleen Hanna, six years into the band Bikini Kill, exchanged zines and letters with Aaron Cometbus and suggested he consider how he wrote about any girlfriends in his zine because "there's obviously already a male/female power imbalance situation" (4.39, 4.40). The group Riot Grrrl NYC sent a postcard announcement for their convention to Matt Wobensmith's queercore zine *Outpunk* (4.41, 4.42). Meanwhile, Adee Roberson's zine *Finger on the Trigger* (4.45 TO 4.49) drew on her experiences as a Black woman in the punk scene in Pensacola, Florida, and helped lay the groundwork for James Spooner's spotlight on Afropunk a couple of years later (4.50). Alongside these voices, zines like *Xicanistas and Punkeristas Say It Loud!* insisted on the intersection of identities in punk politics and exhorted readers to "be a crossroads" (4.51, 4.52).

This is the surging wave of history that has carried forward to Downtown Boys, whose members reach from San José, California, to Providence, Rhode Island. Their activism on vinyl, on the page, and in the street calls on the resources of punk's archives across the country and across time. They generate a soundtrack for protest with their albums *Full Communism* and *Cost of Living*; they march in picket lines for labor rights, speak out against anti-LGBTQ foundations, and work to organize and unionize independent musicians.[7] To listen to Downtown Boys is to listen to punk's past striking the present. You can hear the echoes of Youth of Today's New York hardcore anthem "Break Down the Walls" (1986) and Johnny Rotten's verbal takedown of the Berlin Wall that ends "Holidays in the Sun" (1977) resounding in the voice of the band's singer Victoria Ruiz on "A Wall" (2017). Against Trump's ethno-nationalist obsession with a border wall, Ruiz transforms those earlier punk rallying calls in a new context, "from the broad side, to the hidden side . . . a wall is a wall, and nothing more at all."

As Ruiz herself writes in this book's closing essay, "Perhaps the most anti-authority way to practice punk is to recognize that there is no perfect narrative of history." Citing Alice Bag, Poly Styrene, Kathleen Hanna, and her own grandmother, Ruiz creates a solar system for punk, but one without a sun. Instead, it's a universe of rogue planets, brought together by each other's gravity, circulating, as she writes, "collectively": "we are the night that never ends." The images in the following chapters are a reminder of punk's improbable collectivity, an identity made from a communal energy of difference and resistance, a certain dark gravity that keeps pulling people together in a circle with no center.

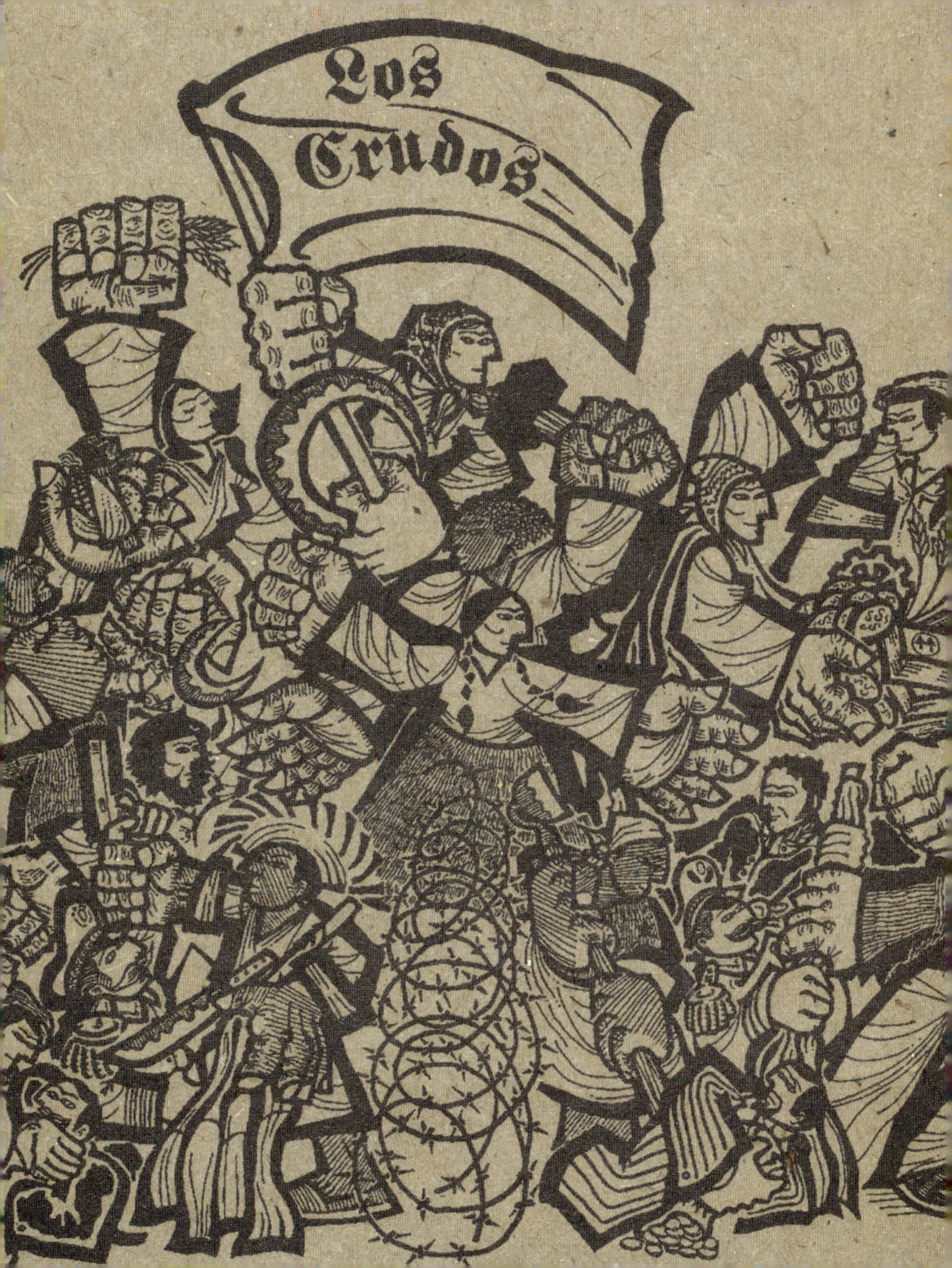
Los Crudos

CH. 17 IMAGE GALLERY

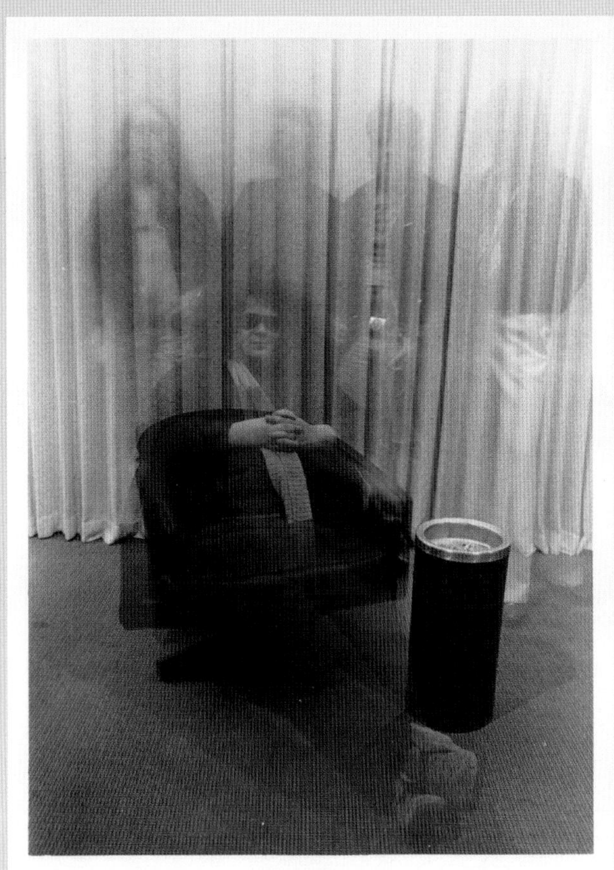

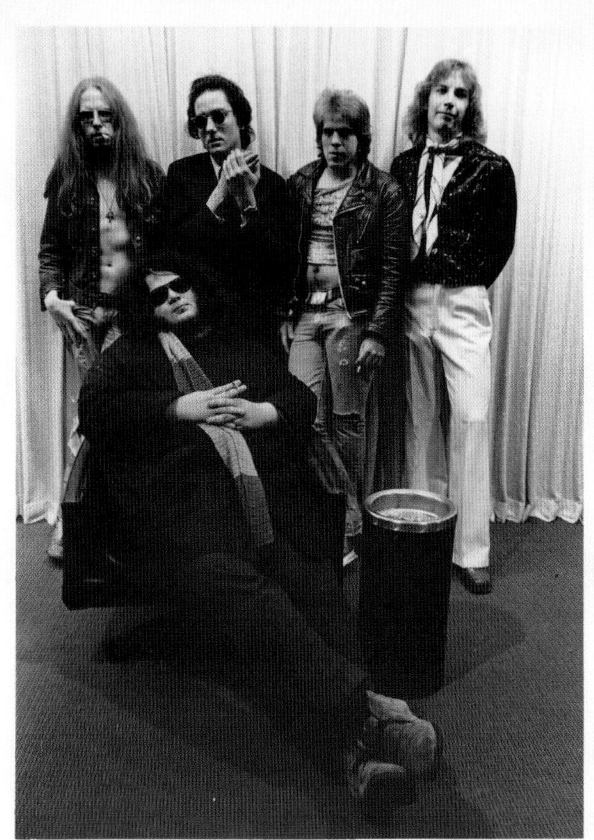

4.1 and 4.2. Rocket from the Tombs, 1975. Photo: Fred Toedtman.

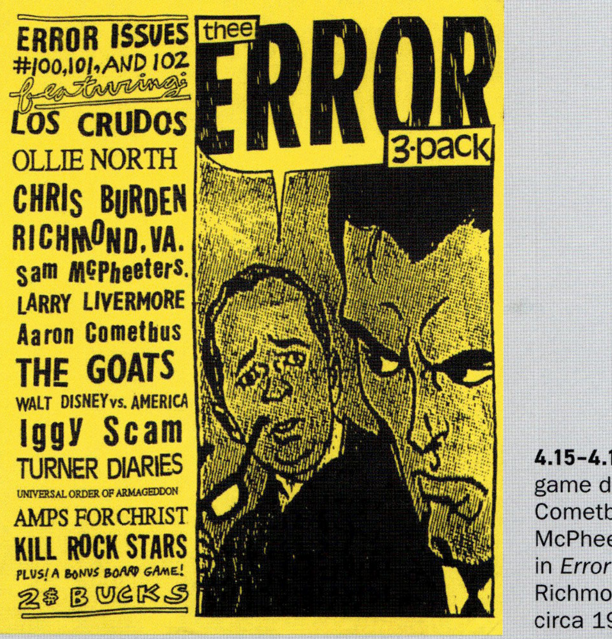

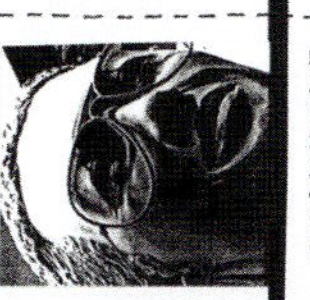
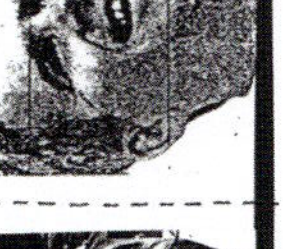
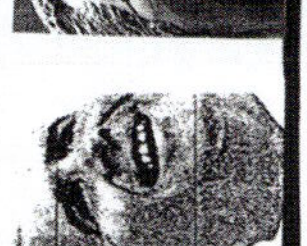
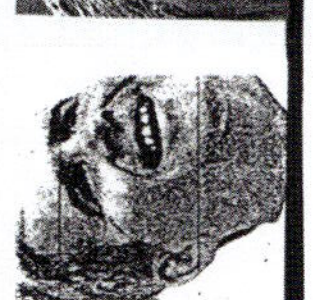
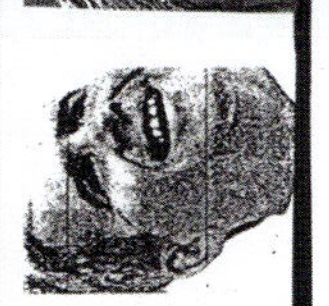
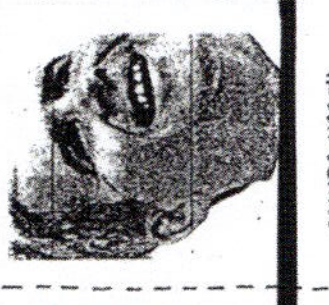
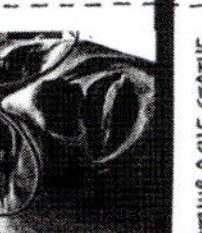

OLIVER NORTH

EDGAR ALLEN POE

ARTHUR ASHE STATUE

THOMAS JEFFERSON

RULES

HINTS: BET! CHEAT!

① CUT OUT PLAYING PIECES, FOLD BACK THE BASE FROM BLACK LINE AND TAPE A PENNY TO THE BOTTOM FOLD.

② CUT OUT CARDS AND OPEN ERROR 101 TO RICHMOND MAP AND MAP GUIDE.

③ NO DICE NEEDED. JUST START AT SQUARE #1, THE 6TH STREET MARKETPLACE, AND TAKE ONE CARD PER TURN PER PLAYER, FOLLOWING THE SPACE NUMBERS AND OBEYING THE CARD INSTRUCTIONS.

④ THE WINNER IS THE FIRST PLAYER TO MAKE IT TO SPACE 62, FROM THERE TO THE GREYHOUND STATION AND ON TO THE REST OF THE WAITING WORLD, WHILE THE LOSERS MUST FORM SEVERAL INCOMPREHENSIBLY SHITTY BANDS, APPLY FOR JOBS AT STEAK-N-EGG AND DIE OBSCURE, VIOLENT DEATHS.

⑤ GAME ENDS WHEN YOU RUN OUT OF CARDS. NO WINNERS? CLOSE TO LEAVING BUT NEVER QUITE MAKE IT? SICK OF GOING TO THE SAME STUPID PLACES OVER + OVER? YES, YOU'RE GETTING THE IDEA NOW.

OLIVER NORTH

EDGAR ALLEN POE

ARTHUR ASHE STATUE

THOMAS JEFFERSON

RULES

HINTS: BET! CHEAT!

① CUT OUT PLAYING PIECES, FOLD BACK THE BASE FROM BLACK LINE AND TAPE A PENNY TO THE BOTTOM FOLD.

② CUT OUT CARDS AND OPEN ERROR 101 TO RICHMOND MAP AND MAP GUIDE.

③ NO DICE NEEDED. JUST START AT SQUARE #1, THE 6TH STREET MARKETPLACE, AND TAKE ONE CARD PER TURN PER PLAYER, FOLLOWING THE SPACE NUMBERS AND OBEYING THE CARD INSTRUCTIONS.

④ THE WINNER IS THE FIRST PLAYER TO MAKE IT TO SPACE 62, FROM THERE TO THE GREYHOUND STATION AND ON TO THE REST OF THE WAITING WORLD, WHILE THE LOSERS MUST FORM SEVERAL INCOMPREHENSIBLY SHITTY BANDS, APPLY FOR JOBS AT STEAK-N-EGG AND DIE OBSCURE, VIOLENT DEATHS.

⑤ GAME ENDS WHEN YOU RUN OUT OF CARDS. NO WINNERS? CLOSE TO LEAVING BUT NEVER QUITE MAKE IT? SICK OF GOING TO THE SAME STUPID PLACES OVER + OVER? YES, YOU'RE GETTING THE IDEA NOW.

4.15–4.17. Punk board game designed by Aaron Cometbus and Sam McPheeters, included in *Error* fanzine from Richmond, Virginia, circa 1994–1996.

KEY

= AFRICAN AMERICAN IMPORT STORE.

= 7-11.

$ = PAWN SHOP.

= PROSTHETIC LIMB CLINIC.

MAIN

GRACE

BROAD

CARY

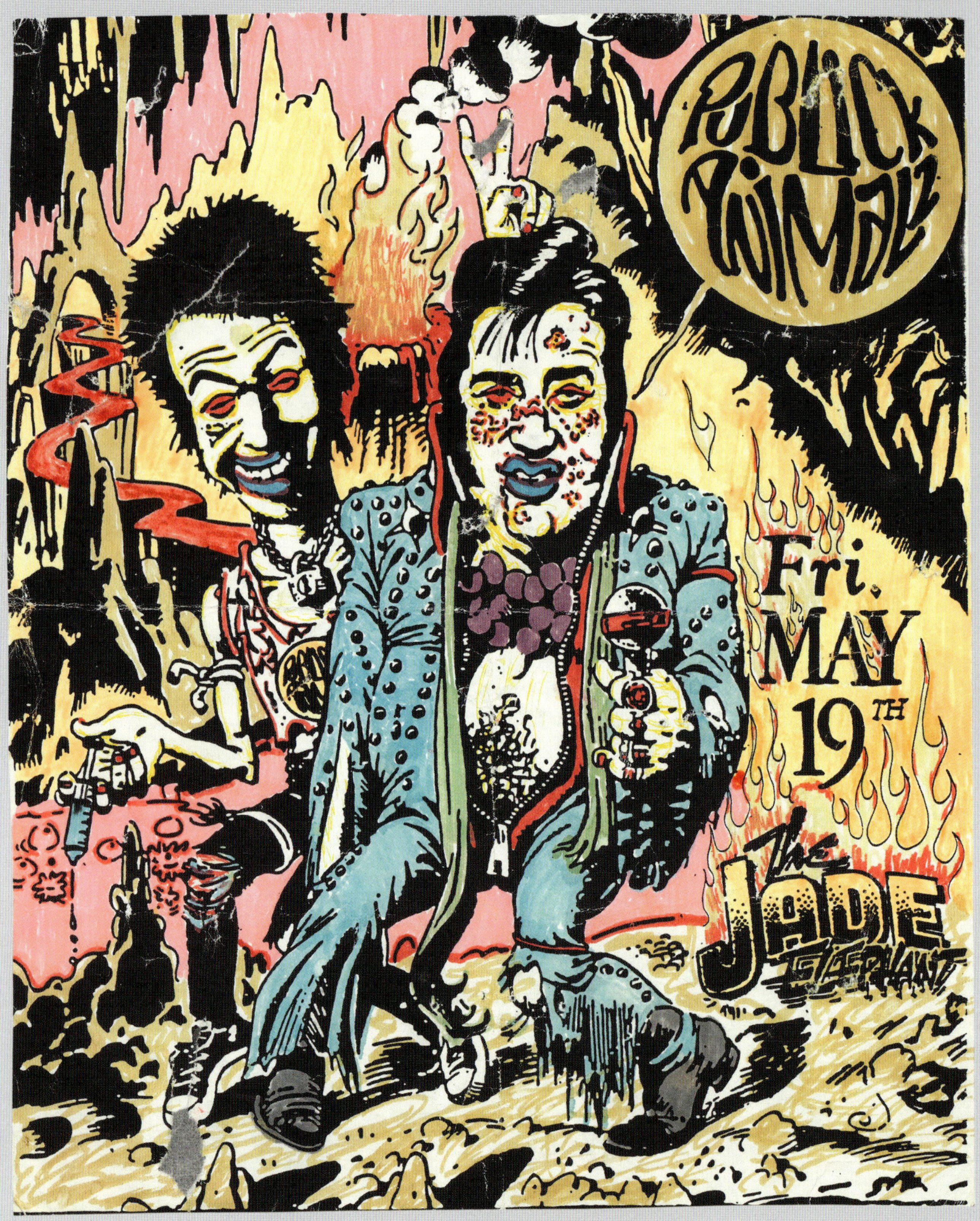

4.18. Flyer for Publick Animalz at the Jade Elephant, Richmond, Virginia, May 1989.

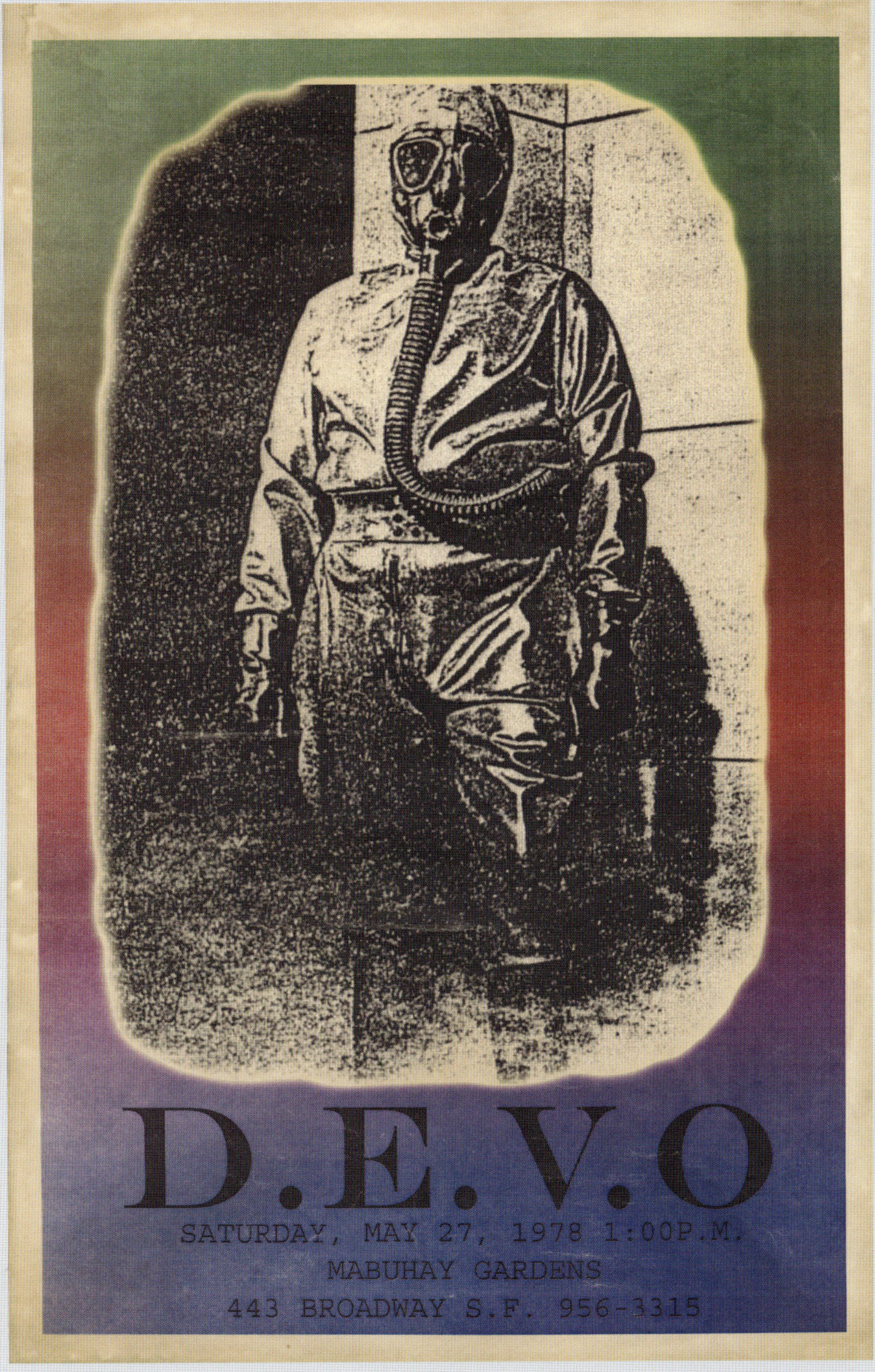

4.3. Flyer for Devo at Mabuhay Gardens, San Francisco, May 1978.

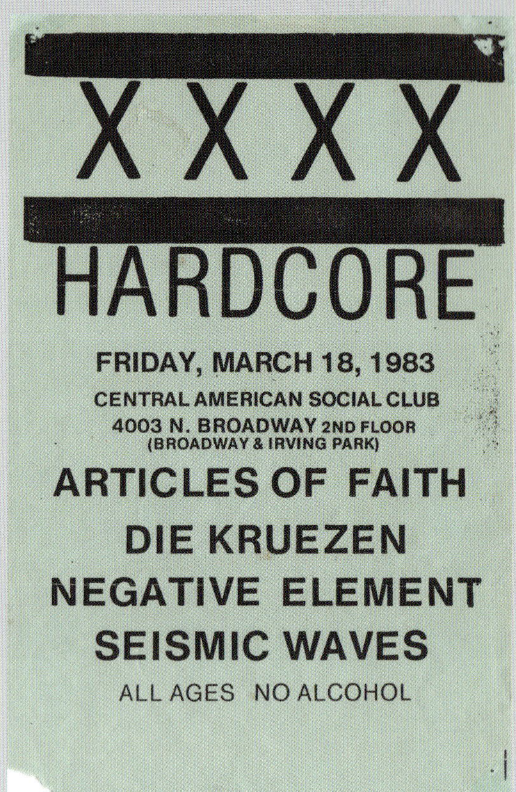

4.4. Flyer for Chicago hardcore show at the Central American Social Club, March 1983.

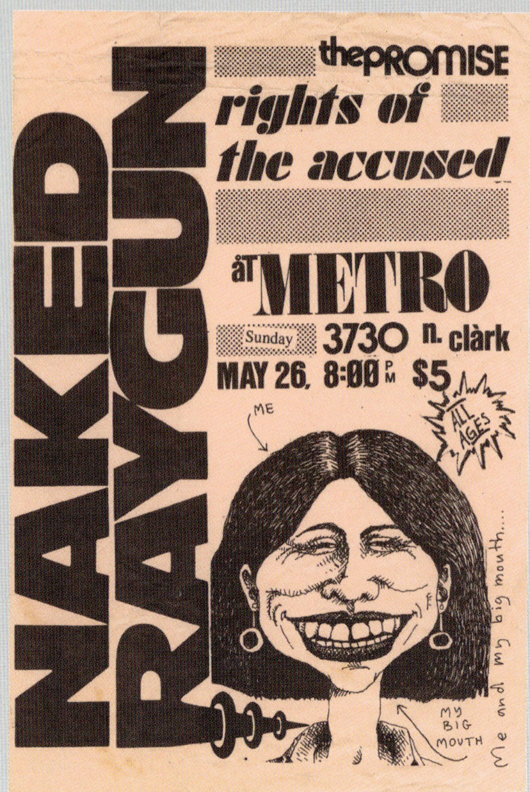

4.5. Flyer for Naked Raygun at Metro, Chicago, May 1985.

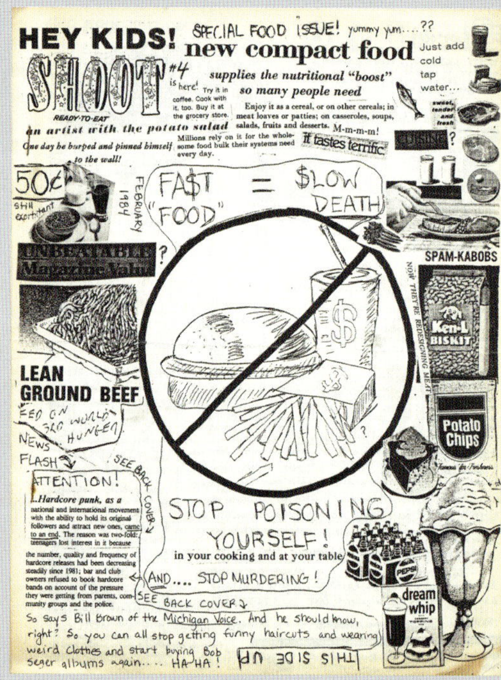

4.6. Special food issue of *Shoot* no. 4 from Lansing, Michigan, circa 1983.

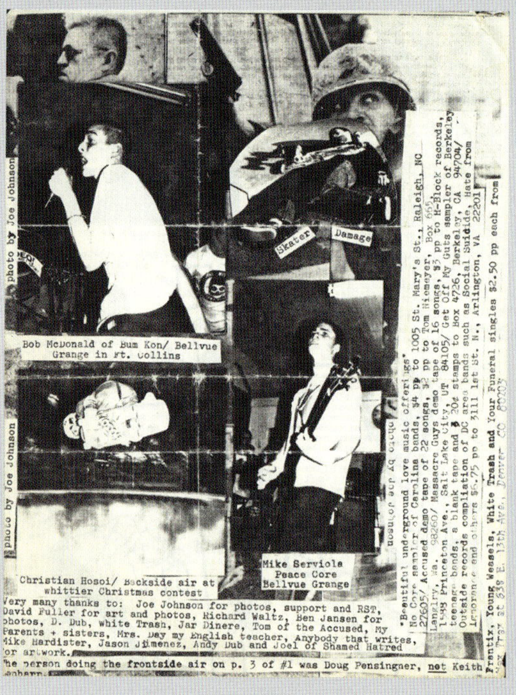

4.7. Back page from *Revenge Against Boredom* zine from Estes Park, Colorado, 1983, thanking "Parents + sisters, Mrs. Day my English teacher, Anybody that writes."

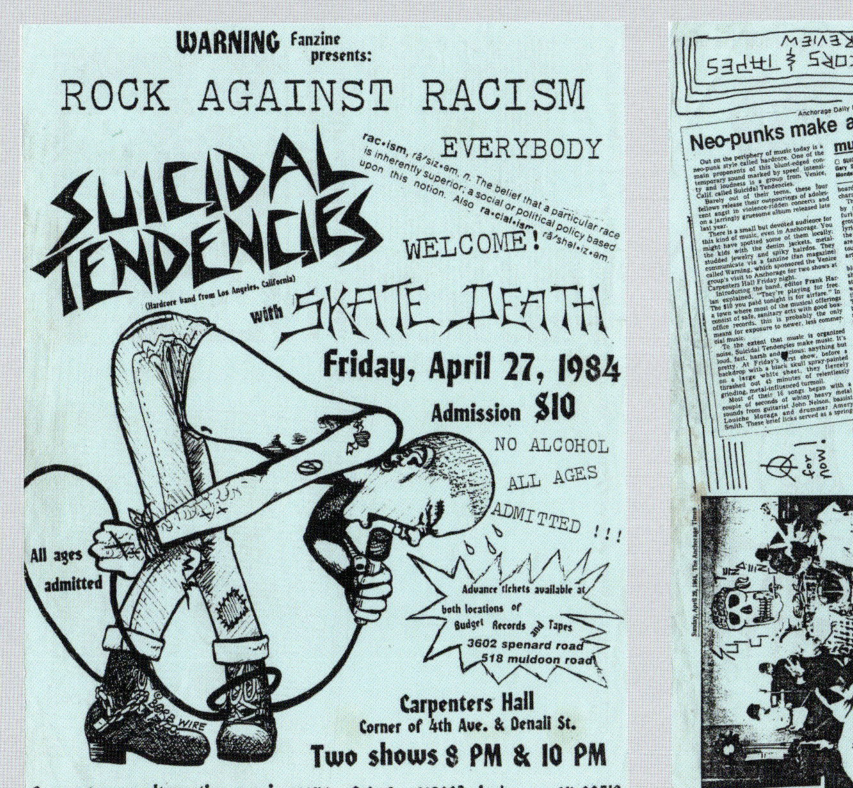

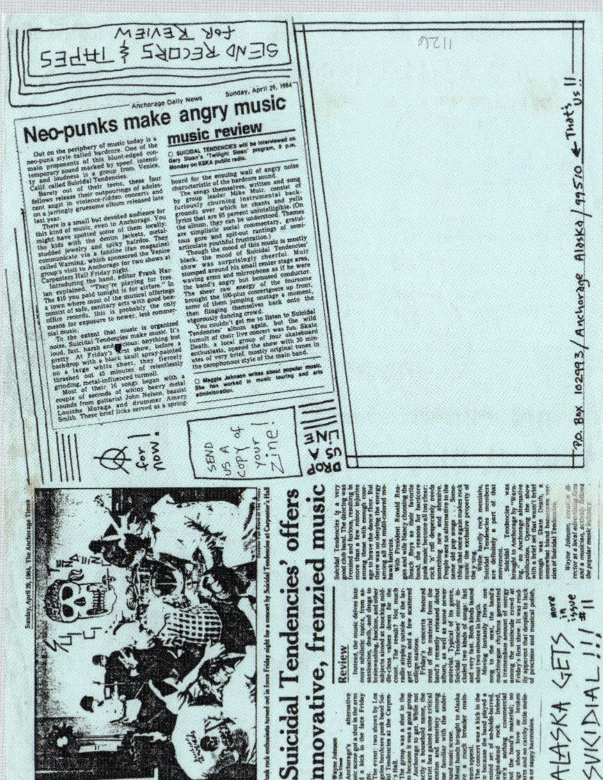

4.8 and 4.9. Front and back of flyer for Rock Against Racism show featuring Suicidal Tendencies, at Carpenter's Hall, Anchorage, Alaska, April 1984.

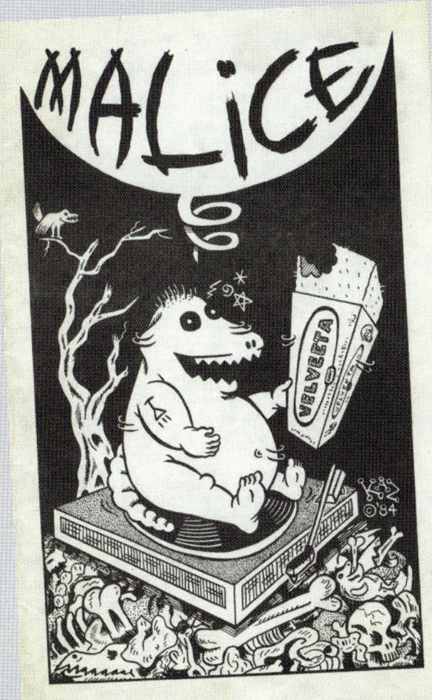

4.10. *Malice* zine from Memphis, Tennessee, circa 1983–84.

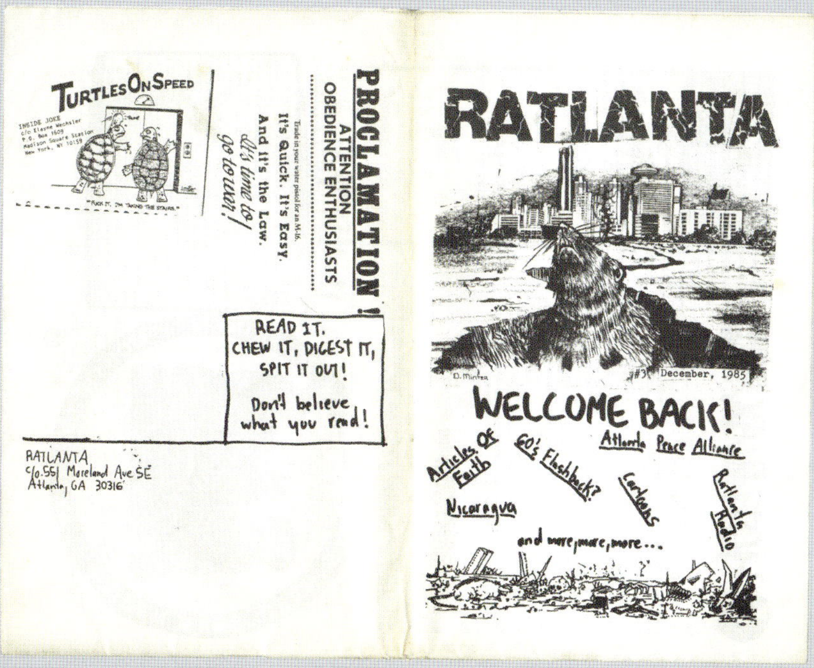

4.11. *Ratlanta* zine from Atlanta, December 1985.

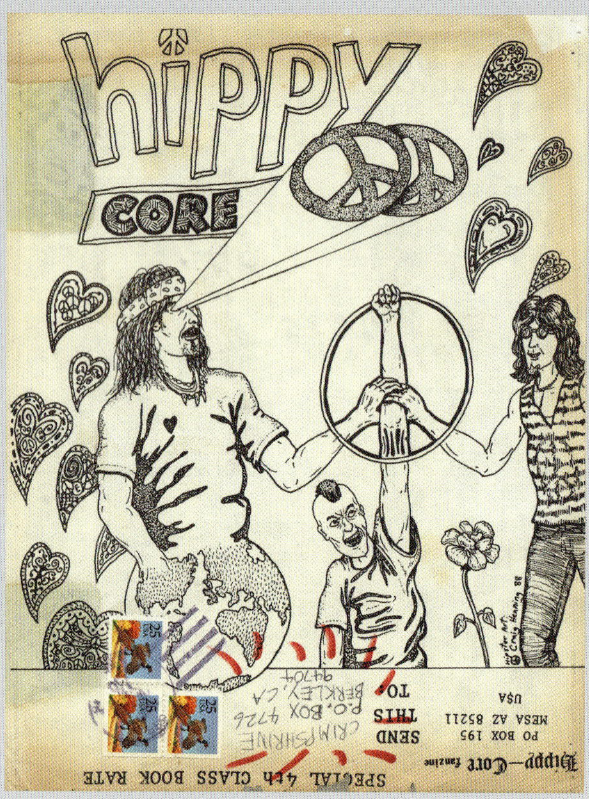

4.12. *Hippycore* zine from Mesa, Arizona, 1988.

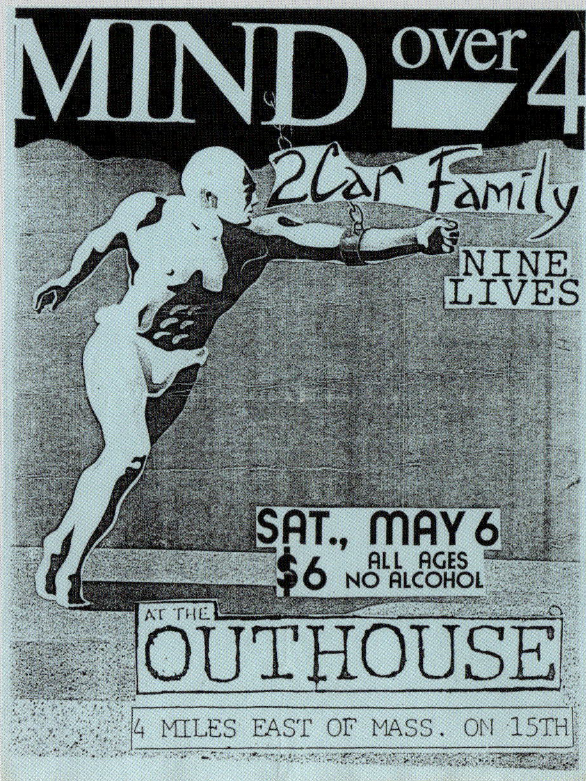

4.13. Flyer for a show at the Outhouse, Lawrence, Kansas, 1989.

4.14. *Another Pair of Shoes* zine from Minneapolis, Minnesota, 1993.

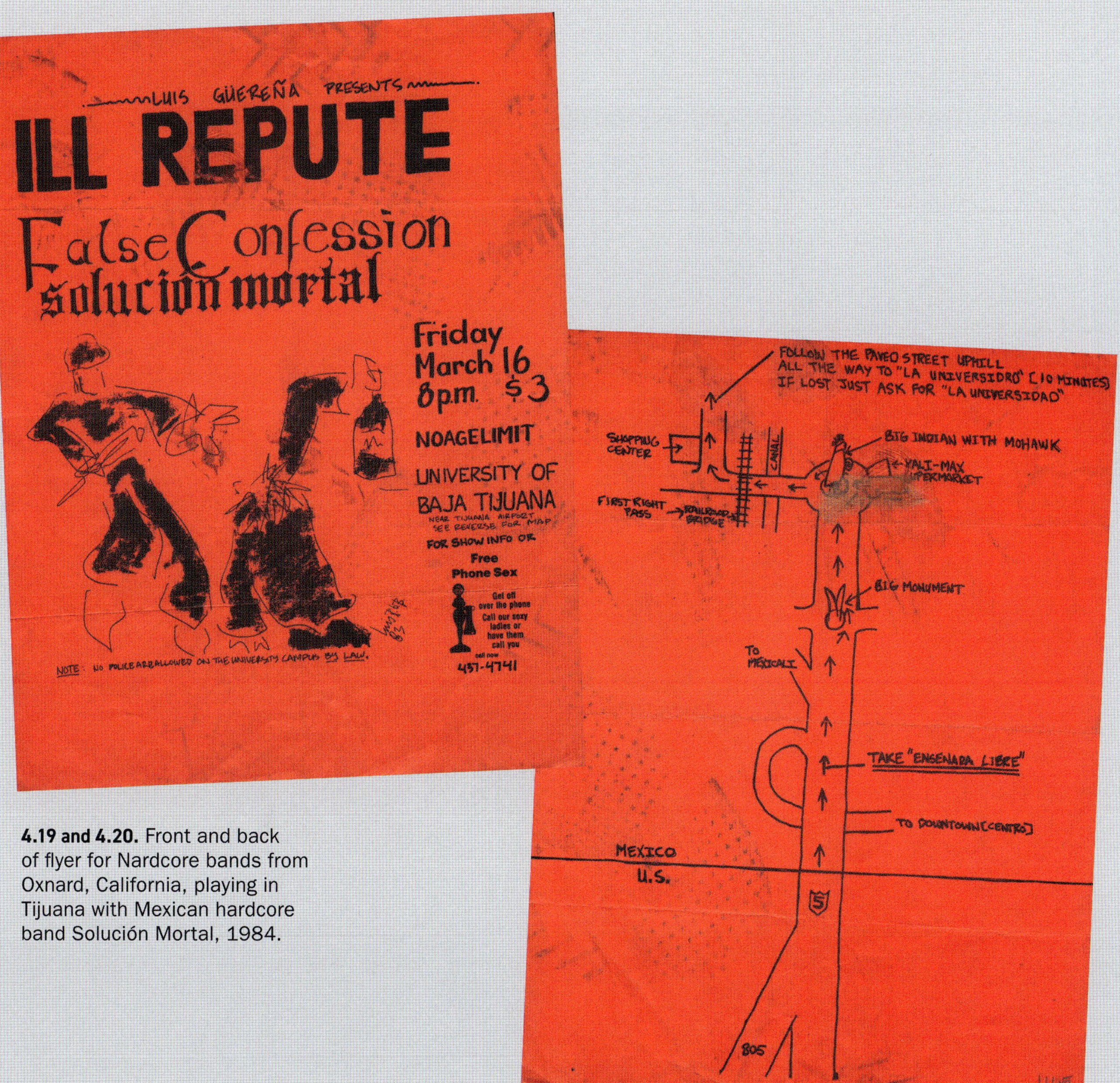

4.19 and 4.20. Front and back of flyer for Nardcore bands from Oxnard, California, playing in Tijuana with Mexican hardcore band Solución Mortal, 1984.

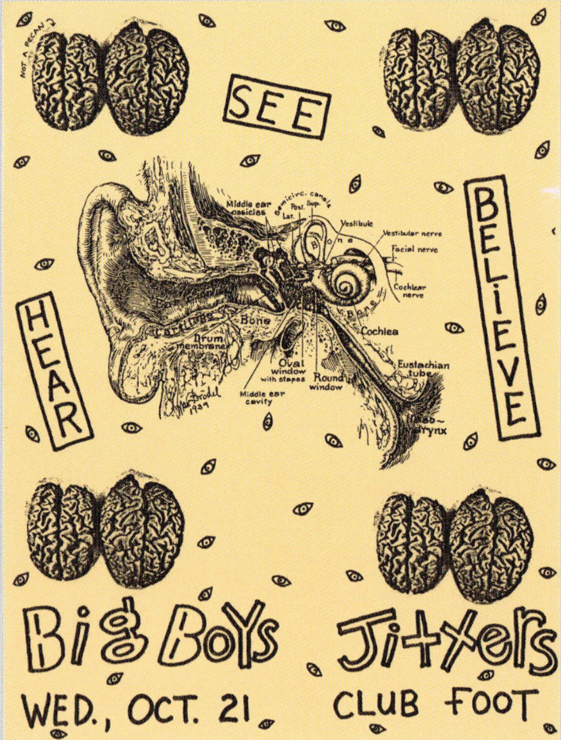

4.21. Flyer for Big Boys at Club Foot, Austin, Texas, 1981.

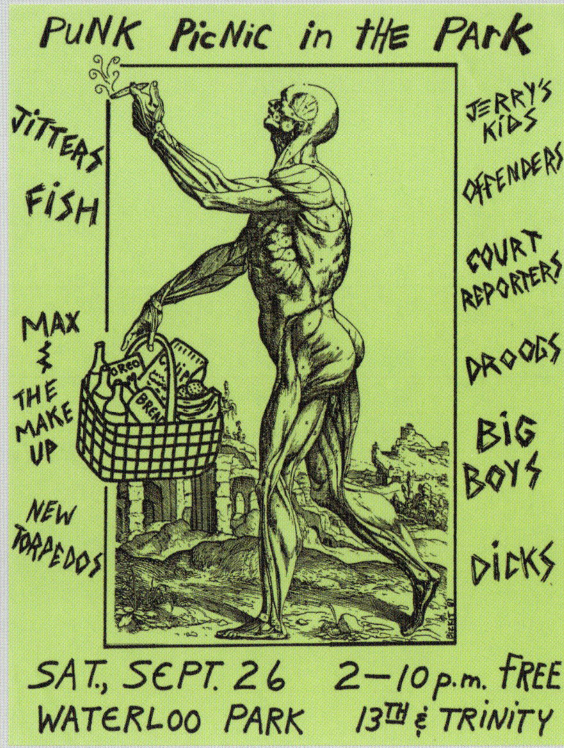

4.22. Flyer for Punk Picnic in the Park festival, Austin, September 1981.

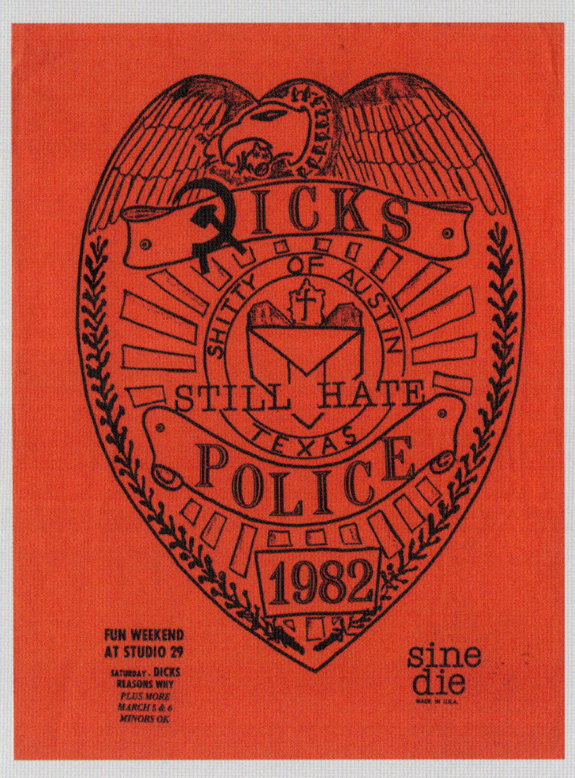

4.23. Flyer for the Dicks at Studio 29, Austin, 1982.

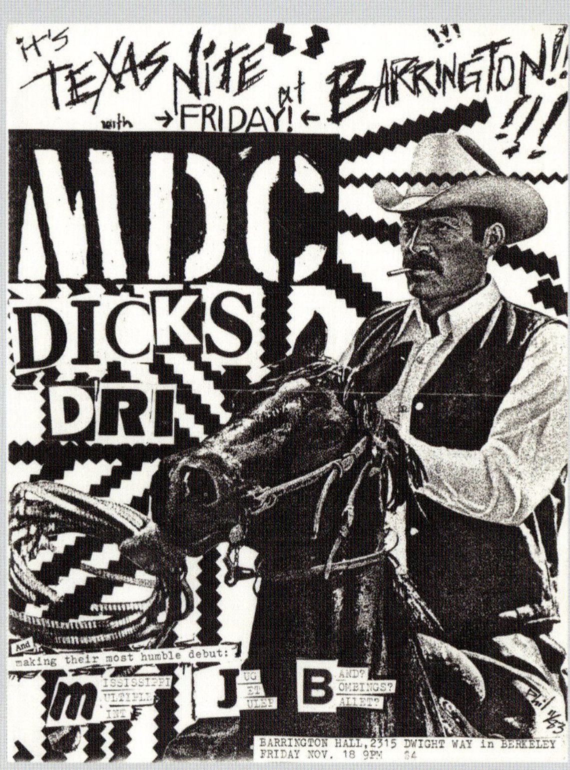

4.24. Flyer for Texas Nite at Barrington Hall, Berkeley, November 1983.

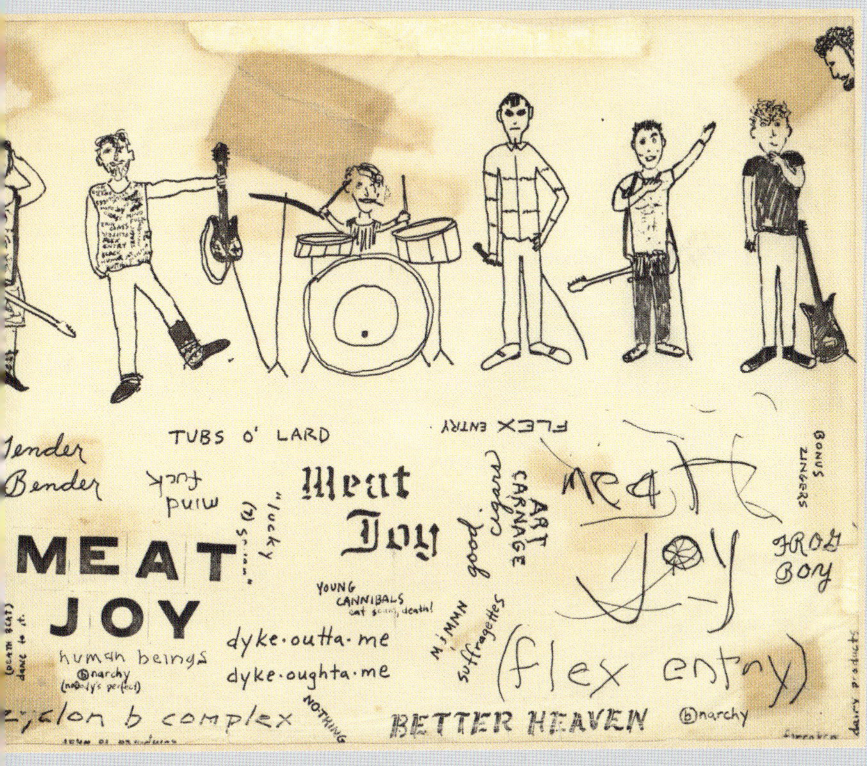

4.25. Flyer for Meat Joy, Austin, 1982.

We had no band photos early on, no proof, so I drew this in part to document something I was thrilled to be a part of. If we were to break up the next day, I'd have this. I recall it was also a survey of band names we'd considered. This was a group ballot of sorts—we were leaning toward Meat Joy—to aid in our final decision.
—John (Perkins) Hawkes of Meat Joy

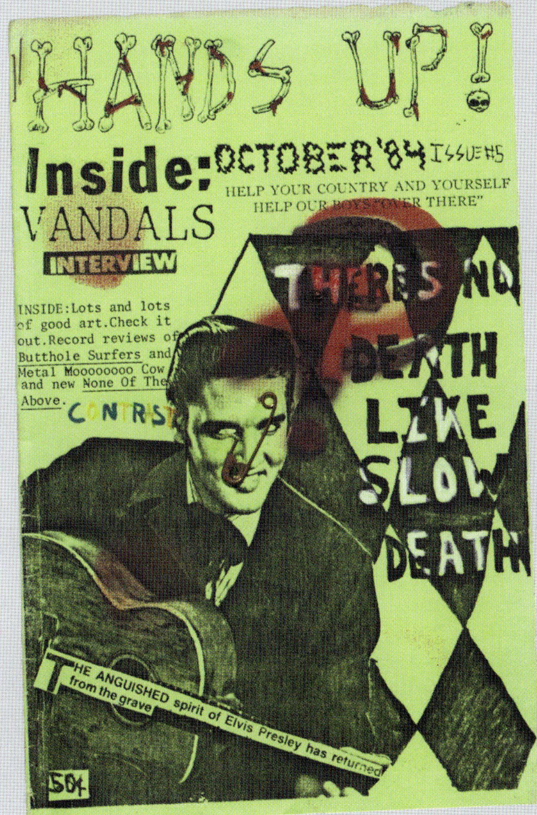

Our beautiful community aesthetic wasn't that you just went to Kinkos and you're done. It's like Kinkos is merely the first step in the process to personalize and make it cool.
—Gretchen Phillips

4.26. (*Left*) *Hands Up!* zine from Austin, October 1984. Hand-colored, with safety pin.

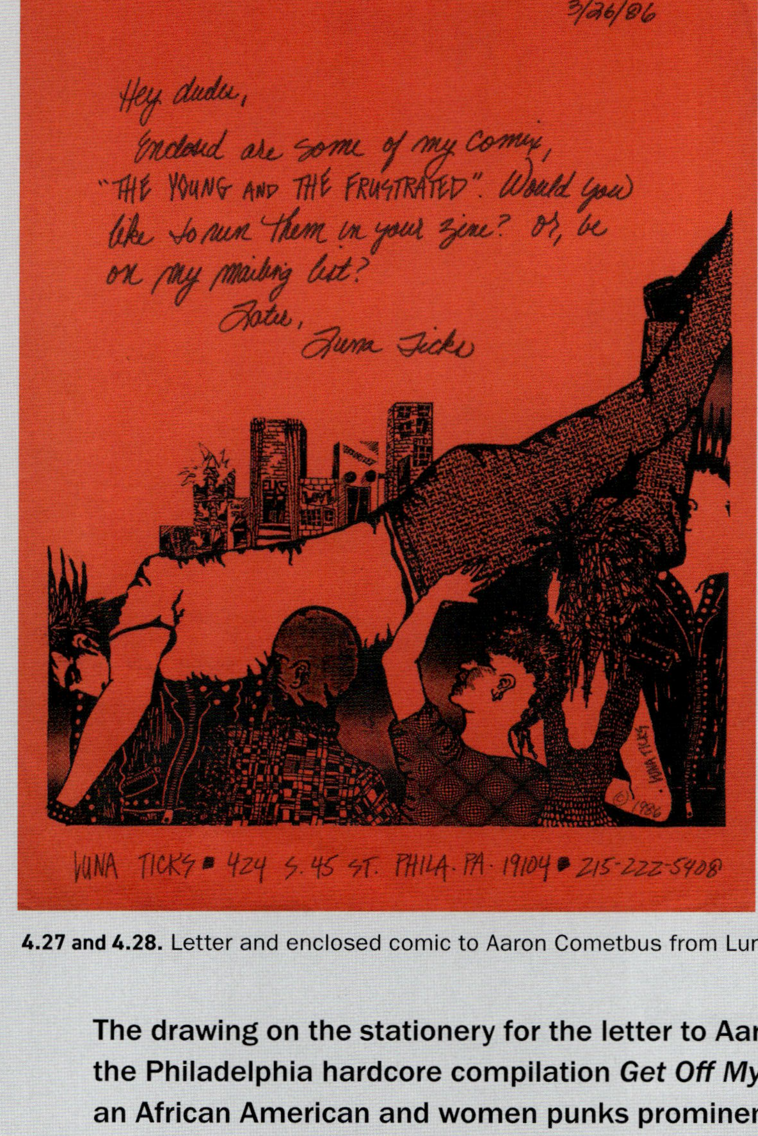

3/26/86

Hey dude,

Enclosed are some of my comix, "THE YOUNG AND THE FRUSTRATED". Would you like to run them in your zine? Or, be on my mailing list?

Later,

Luna Ticks

LUNA TICKS ■ 424 S. 45 ST. PHILA. PA. 19104 ■ 215-222-5408

4.27 and 4.28. Letter and enclosed comic to Aaron Cometbus from Luna Ticks, Philadelphia, March 1986.

The drawing on the stationery for the letter to Aaron Cometbus is part of an album cover I did for the Philadelphia hardcore compilation *Get Off My Back.* I also named the LP. The drawing portrays an African American and women punks prominently, which I think is quite unique for a hardcore LP. The comic enclosed with the letter is the first page of *Brain: A Tender Tale of Two Sisters.* It was later printed in the comic book *Weirdo*, issue #20. —Elizabeth Fiend (aka Luna Ticks), slide guitar player in the psychedelic hardcore band *More Fiends*

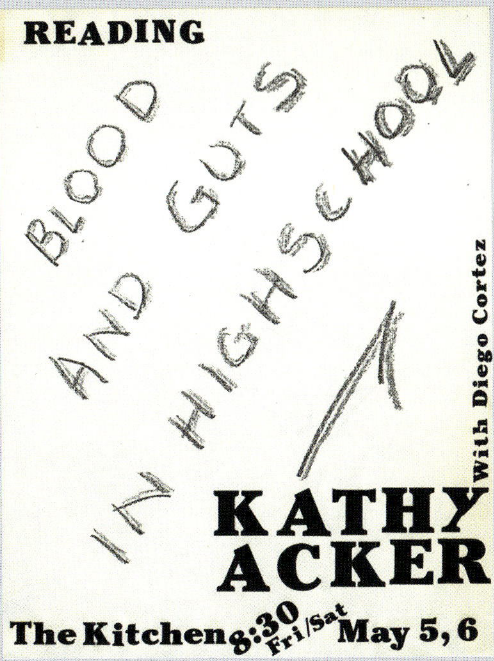

4.29. Flyer for Kathy Acker reading from her book *Blood and Guts in High School*, at the Kitchen, New York, May 1978.

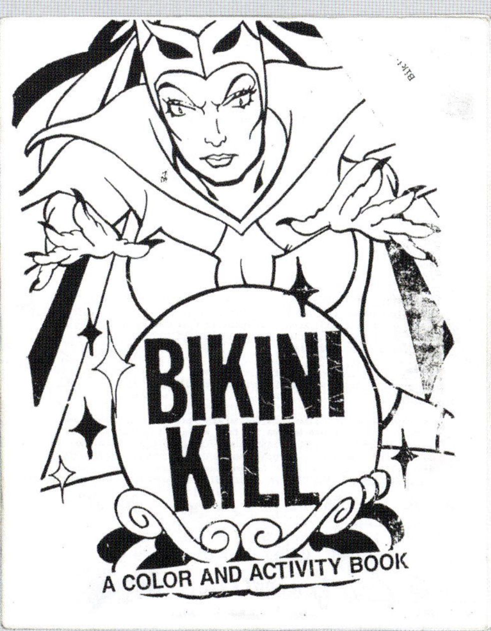

4.30. *Bikini Kill* zine produced by the band and given out at shows, January 1990.

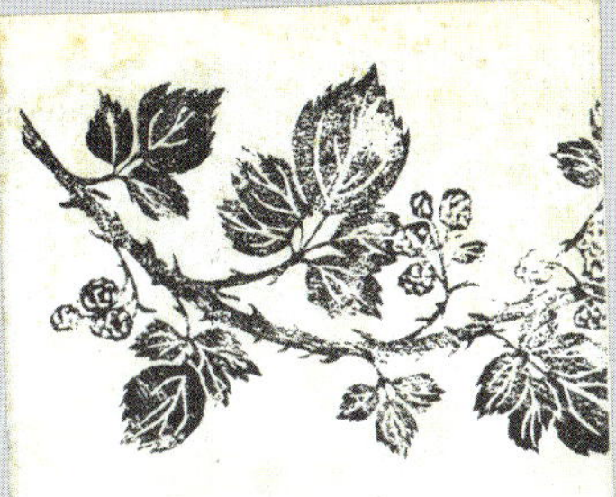

The International Pop Underground Convention, Olympia, Washington
August 20-25

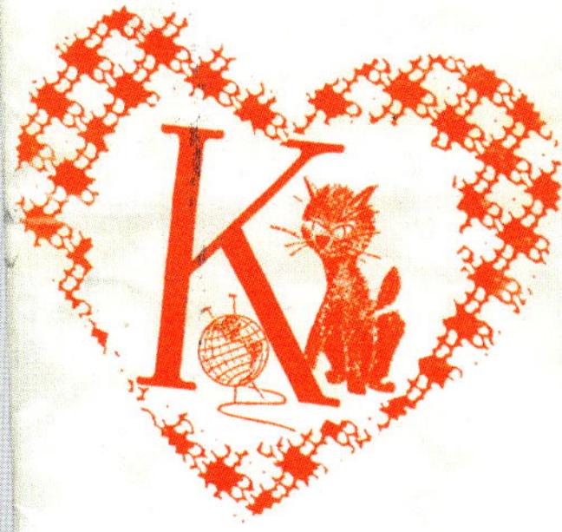

Program Schedule

4.31 and 4.32. Program cover and page 6 of schedule for the International Pop Underground Convention, Olympia, Washington, August 1991.

Capitol Theater, 9:00 PM
Shadows and Substance
This is a show featuring ten to fifteen minute performances by artists who work outside of the rock'n'roll medium. The **Olympia Chamber Orchestra**, lead by conductor Timothy Brock, will debut a new work by local musicians and composers Connie Bunyer and Jeff Bartone entitled *Mrs. Warhola*. **Terry Lee Hale** is a sometimes folk singer in a cowboy hat who releases cassettes of his songs. **Heather Perkins** hails from Eugene, Ore., where she has been forging her own cassette economy. **Infamous Menagerie** are three women from Seattle who annoyed city councilman Gil Carbone when they played Capitol Lake Park in 1989. **Rich Jensen and Steve Peters** will make up some songs sometime before they are supposed to perform them. **Steve Fisk, Mark Hosler** and **Bob Basanich** are a trio of double income types with no kids.
$5.00

Thursday August 22

Smithfield Cafe, 2:00 PM
Someone Said...
This will be an afternoon of poetry and spoken stuff organized by **Slim Moon**, whose Kill Rock Stars records label is releasing a series of wordcore 7" 45s. Reading will be **Slim Moon**; **Jean Smith**, a Vancouver poet who also performs in the band Mecca Normal; **Billy Childish**, of Chatham, England, currently editing a new series of novels by North Kent writers; **Kathleen Hanna**, the author of two books and several tirades; **Stacy Lavine** and **Peter Tolliver**, two Seattle writers who will share the next wordcore 7" on Kill Rock Stars.
donation requested

North Shore Surf Club, 5:00 PM
Solomon Grundy
Mecca Normal
Bikini Kill
Dumbhead
$4.00

Capitol Theater, 9:00 PM
Scrawl
Pastels
BEAT HAPPENING
Nation of Ulysses
$5.00

Disco Dance Till Dawn

Friday August 23

Alexander Berkman Collective, 10:00 AM
Jad Fair
Kicking Giant
Bratmobile
$4.00

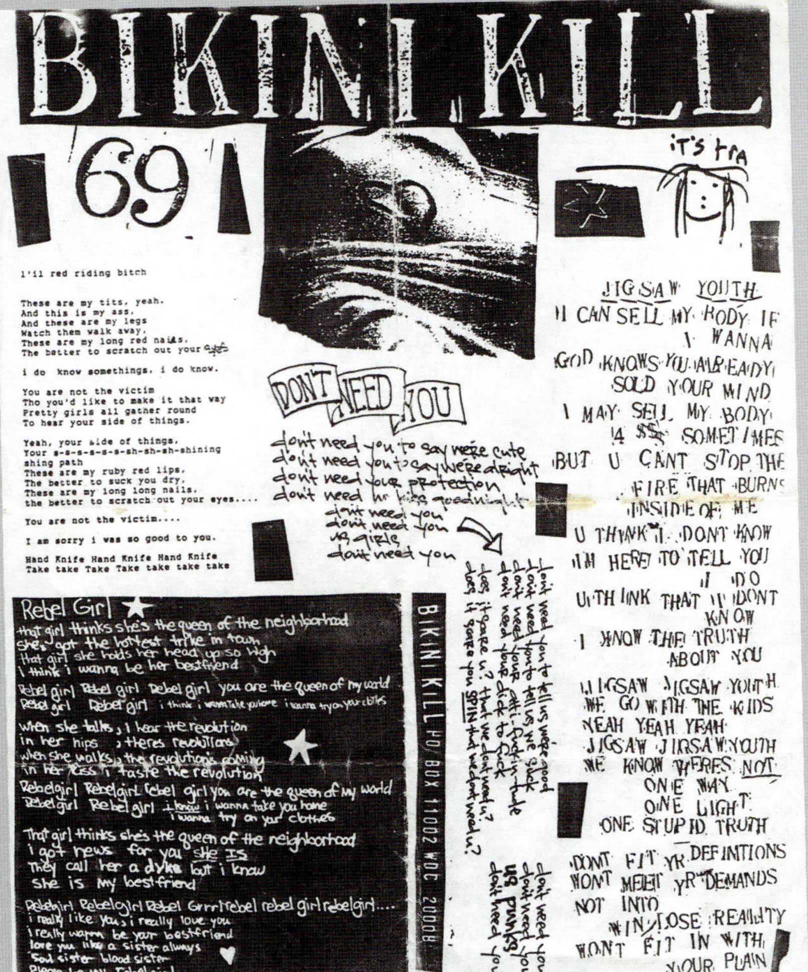

4.33 and 4.34. Bikini Kill lyric sheets handed out at shows.

1. Do you get shit from people either because you are a predominantly female band or because of your feminist slant?

1. For girls to pick up guitars and scream their heads off (or even just sing quiet-like for that matter) and to start bands in a totally oppressive, fucked up, male dominated culture is to seize power...we recognise this as a political act. When we 'get shit from people' (mostly always it's from guys) it is usually because these people are assholes. Bikini Kill's articulation of the pre-existing mainstream ideologies that perpetuate girl oppression etc. implicitly sets forth our (feminist) girl power stance, thus making confrontations with assholes seem more politically direct. However, to me, it is always an act of political terrorism when girls are given shit--on stage or walking down the street, the message is the same: don't stray from the path of silence or the big bad woolf is gonna eat you up (see Bikini Kill's "LIL RED" for more) Similarly, when girls start bands they are directly intervening in the reality prescribed by male hegemony regardless of whether or not they choose to align themselves with "feminism", per se.

2. Which is more important to you, music or lyrics?

2. Both. When we play live we try to make sure the vocals are loud enough to be heard in the mix and sometimes Kathleen passes out lyric sheets. Obviously, a lot of Bikini Kill's political content comes through in the lyrics but we have problems with making clear cut distinctions between form and content and therefore recognise Bikini Kill's total aesthetic as something which comes together when we play: music, lyrics, [illegible], lipstick, etc.

3. How do you see yourselves fitting in with the whole Riot Grrl thing?

3. Riot Grrrl is a grassroots girl power movement that is happening right now in various locations throughout the U.S.-mostly on the East and West coasts... It isn't centralized or readily definable ~~[illegible]~~ but so far seems to mostly have taken the form of group meetings and fanzines that provide girls with the inspiration necessary to start taking direct action... I see this type of thing as essential if anything's ever gonna start happening for real in terms of revolutionary social change--like if abortion for real becomes illegal girls are gonna need this kind of network resource as a [illegible] of survival. The first riot grrl meetings and fanzines happened last summer when Bikini Kill and Bratmobile were here in D.C. visiting friends and wanted to meet up with other girls in this area who would be in on the girl revolution tip. Since this time, the impetus has spread and riot grrrls have been showing up at Bikini Kill shows all over. Bikini Kill's direct connections to Riot Grrrl DC are pretty minimal, except for Kathleen, our singer, who is working with them on various projects-- Hopefully BK will continue to be involved in helping to incite this kind of participatory interactions between girls, revolution girl [illegible] to be just as common for girls to be in bands as for guys and this riot grrl scene phenomenon seems pretty cool in terms of girls encouraging other girls to start their own thing--yeah, creativity rules ok, like riot grrrlstyle now, you know....

4. How does the scene in D.C. compare to the scene in Olympia?

4. It's hard for me to say really because there's really alot going on in both places and what I know about here is really particular to who I hang out with...in general, taking my limited involvement in the "dc scene" into account, Olympia seems more desparate and out of control--like every show is cathartic on some level because the small town reality is so pervasive and the kids there really live for punk rock. Shows here have so far seemed really anti-climactic to me, although there are some really great bands in dc right now. Maybe it's just because DC Space closed down right before we moved here but there doesn't really seem to be much happening as far as shows go--we don't like going to shows in churches (or playing in churches for that matter) because we have problems with the architectural ambiance implicit in places of worship for organised religion--it just seems wrong to have punk rock shows in such an inherantly repressed atmosphere, so I think I might feel differently if there was somewhere else to have shows. Right now in Olympia bands like Unwound and KARP and WITCHY POO AND Heaven's to Betsy are starting the new Kill Rock Stars generation and so it's pretty much like New York in 76-77 as far as punk rock soul inegrity goes...also the kids I know in Olympia are closer to age 19-23 while the kids I know here are more like 23-30, but agin this is all particular to who I know and DC is a lot bigger than Olympia and so my experience of DC is really insular while in Olympia I pretty much know everybody, also there has been records coming out of DC on a major scale for like over ten years while although there has been a strong scene in Olympia since like at least 1981, things are just now starting to get noticed in the other world--zeno-types etc. so there is a really young energy-and the girls rule Olympia hands down but while dc has and has had a strong high female input aspect, simply the fact that all the "big" bands from DC are almost always all guy bands seems to set a very different tone ...but really creative things are happening in both places and I think the two scenes are connecteding for a reason: now, more than ever is the time to forge the underground idea, cuz in the face of corporate co-optation, us true punks gotta stick together, you know, and both towns have and have had and will most likely continue to have more of an anti-industry focus and seem to be more into community than the individualistic thing of getting signed, I mean, it's now not a simple thing, some of my best friends are in bands that are on major labels and I respect their choice, but its not the sound of the revolution...also both scenes seem to have intense kinds of inter-politics, socially, which to me seems indicative of really strong, passionate and intense feelings about punk rock and stuff in general, and I don't get the same feeling from other places--its genuinely insane in both places, which is cool...

The following is a mail interveiw done by BK drummer (and sometime vocalist, bass player) Tobi Vail. Because touring can be hectic, etc...... and some of us are shy/not always willing to engage in potentially abusive interactions with people at our shows, we have compiled this to answer some questions you may have. And also....We don't have any zines left (1+2) so please don't send us any money or requests for these. ♥♥

5. What do you think of the coverage you've received in places like Sassy?

5. we have mixed feelings about Sassy magazine in particular, and as for [illegible] general--I assume that by saying "places like Sassy" you mean the more mainstream press we've been getting-Spin, Option, Rolling Stone mentioning us etc.--we think these magazines pretty much suck. Um...when magazines are so in with the power structure of [illegible] corporations and focusing mainly on major label bands they just aren't gonna get Bikini Kill--cus we're all about destroying their very existence, I mean really, that is pretty much the whole point of everything--we have found that when we have talked to the mainstream press we have either been misunderstood and thus subsequently misrepresented or else we've been deliberatly slammed. We have found that when we have declined interviews, our wishes were not respected and we were written about anyway. In both cases, what was written about was fucked up and sexist, although women were writing the articles. These experiences not only were frustrating but hurt our feelings and ended up being way too time consuming in terms of explaining our ideas to kids who read these dumb articles. As a result, Bikini Kill is less willing to do interviews in general, and only talk to mainstream publications, if at all very hesitantly and not without reason. [illegible] we wrote a song called Thurston ♥'s the Who in reaction to these experiences-which was the last song we played live at our show with L-7 and Fugazi here in DC. I think we are gonna release it on our first single which will come out on the Kill Rock Stars label, sometime this summer--also we have been writing about this for the Bikini Kill fanzine #3.
As for Sassy magazine in particular, the women who work there seem pretty cool and precisely because they have a wide audience of teenage girls all accross the US we are more willing to talk to them than we are to other "big" magazines-but we didn't really liked what they wrote about us, cus they printed gossip-y type stuff we didn't tell them and seemed fairly condescending, which is something we are quite familiar with and do not appreciate. Basically, these things have given us more of a reason to continue to make our own fanzine, where we are in complete control of how our ideas get represented--something which is very important for girls living in a culture where the media is integral to male hegemony.

6. Can we be expecting any new recordings from Bikini Kill in the near future?

We have a record coming out. It,ll be 6 songs on 12". If you want one send six dollars to Kill Rock Stars 120 NE State #418 Olympia WA 98501

8107 5-18

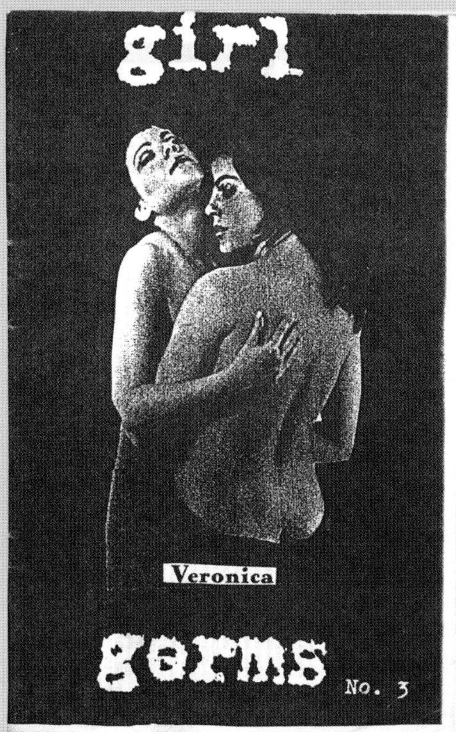

4.35. *Girl Germs* no. 3, zine created by Allison Wolfe and Molly Neuman, Eugene, Oregon, circa 1992.

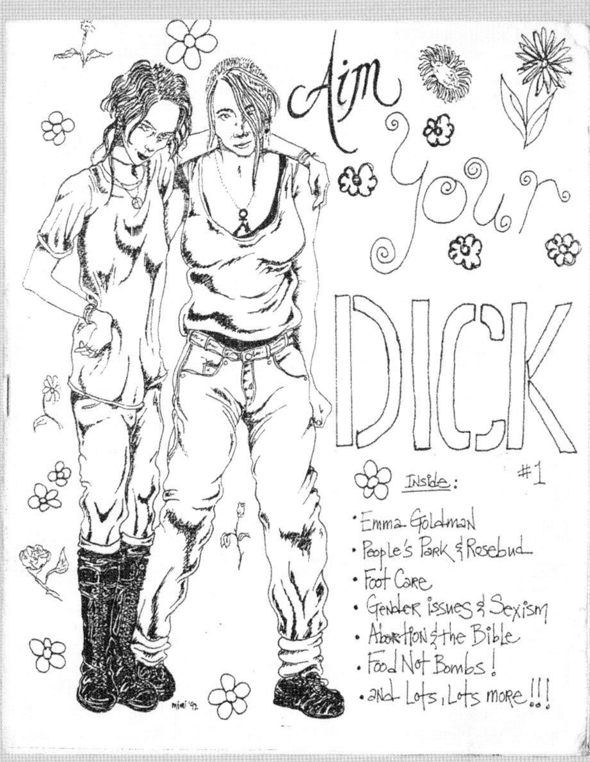

4.36. *Aim Your Dick* zine created by Mimi Nguyen and Marike, Berkeley, 1992.

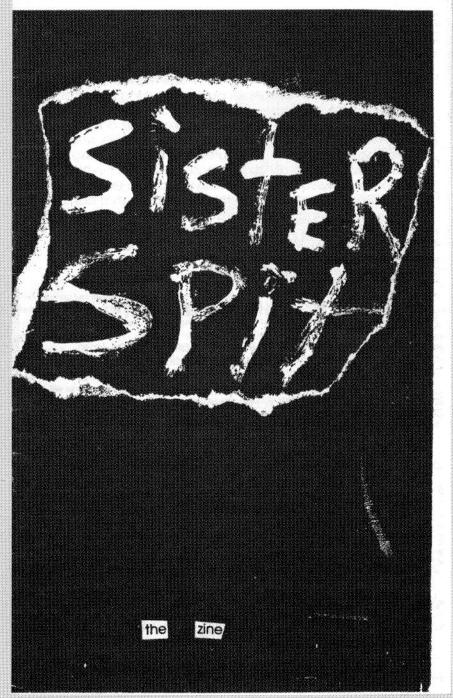

Hey and welcome to the Sister Spit Zine! Whoopee! What you have here in your hands is a collection of some of the chicks who have featured at Sister Spit,

San Francisco's only all-girl open mic performance night. There are too many to track down under the very short notice we had for putting this thing together, so unfortunatly some really great girls are missing, as are performers whose art can't be xeroxed - the dancers, musicians, castrators and pig decapitators. Also, since we had to restrict this to features, the many amazing girls who hop onto the open mic each week aren't in here - hopefully in issue #2, if everything works out. I want to tell all the girls everywhere that this is something that can and should be happening in your city. It's easy, find a bar, a cafe, someone's apartment, anywhere, print up some flyers and there you are. Its fucking rad to be in a room full of intensly creative girls showing off for each other!

We want your spit!

Be our penpals! Send us your rants and writings, love letters, evil breakup stories, lace panties, and abduction stories, and we'll read them at Sister Spit, put them in the next zine, write you back, send you a prize, I don't know, something magical will happen, trust me. Send your sick shit to:

Sister Spit
251 14th Street
San Francisco CA 94103

OR: 5 BALMY
SAN FRANCISCO CA 94110

Don't forget-
poetry is cool,
girls are generally more talented than boys,
you can do whatever the hell you want.

Have fun!
Love,
you hosts
Sini & Michelle
xxxooo

← COCO CLUB • 8TH ST. AT MISSION • SAN FRANCISCO

4.37 and 4.38. Cover and page 1 of *Sister Spit* zine, San Francisco, 1994.

Dear Aaron — thanks for the zine. Here's mine. It was interesting to read about yr experience(s) in Europe cuz we were just at a lot of the same places as you were but it was really different cuz we were playing like everynight and had barely any hang out time at all (In Paris we had 45 minutes out of the van so we, literally, RAN to Gertrude Stein's apartment, took a picture & RAN back to the van - it sorta sucked) anyways, yr zine made me think about a lot and kept me amused three strait nights in a row [you write a lot my fucking god] But there was one thing I was thinking, if I was a girl who went out w/you I'd be freaked out it would end up in yr zine - I'm sure you've thought about this before its just weird cuz I had a boyfriend who wrote this big thing from his perspective about OUR relationship and I was really hurt by it, by the fact he made my life, our thing public without asking me first. I mean it's just something to think about also because there's obviously already a male/female power imbalance situation and well it's just kinda complicated in certain ways... →

4.39 and 4.40. Kathleen Hanna letter to Aaron Cometbus, dated February 16, 1996.

Obviously I'm into what yr doing ie yr writing or I wouldn't bother trying to say something. BUT I assume you want honest feedback so that's what I'm trying to do. Anyways I hope yr having fun doing whatever OH YEAH which McDonald's in Hamburg did you go to? Cuz there's 2, a normal one and a Fifties one! (I figured if you went to the 50's one you woulda said so) But I'm telling you I went to McDonald's in Hamburg (it's a long story) but it was all decorated like America in the 50's — James Dean, Elvis, Marilyn Monroe, an old jukebox + a real shiny 50's motorbike. WEIRD. also did you notice what the hookers over there wore? Ski suits. Not kidding. Oh well → Hopefully we'll run into each other someday and we can swap stories or something if either of us feels up to it. XOX kathleen

PS they are filming a Disney movie here tomorrow.

PPS Obviously this is the personal letter please no zine submission

PPPS. I'm glad you use handwriting in yr Cometbus.

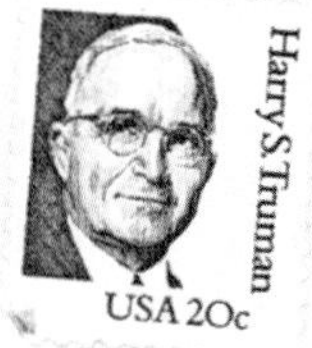

If you haven't already heard...Riot Grrrl NYC is having a girl convention the weekend of August 16-18 and we want you to be there! It's taking place at Coney Island High (directions to come). We have tons of bands lined up, including Cold Cold Hearts, God Is My Co-Pilot, Yum Yum Tree and Vitapup. There will be spoken word performances, art, and workshops dealing with a whole range of topics, from queer identity to women in media to violence/sexual violence and of course much more. And it will be lots more fun if you come...we need you all to bring stuff to sell or trade, boogie at our dance party and meet each other. So what are you waiting for? If you preregister, the cost for the weekend is $15; if you pay when you get here, it will be $20. We do have housing available and we can arrange to meet you at the bus/train/airport. Return the other half of this card along with a SASE and please for yr own safety, DO NOT SEND CASH!

return to: Riot Grrrl NYC / Attn: Cheryl / PO Box 1320/ Stuyvesant Station / New York, NY 10009

name________
address________
phone________
email________
do you need housing?
yes___ no___
can you provide housing?
yes___ no___
can you give a ride to NY?
yes___ no___
do you need a ride to NY?
yes___ no___
would you like to do:
spoken word___ band___
workshop___ sell stuff___
amount of $ enclosed____

CHECK OR M.O. PAYABLE TO LISA WILDMAN. PLEASE NO CASH!

Call our hotline for the most up-to-date info or to leave a message: 212-388-7138

4.41 and 4.42. Front and back of 1991 Riot Grrrl NYC convention invitation.

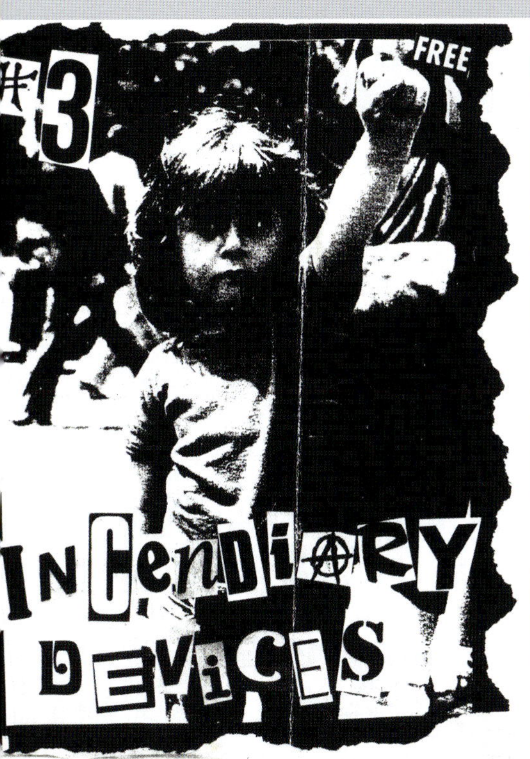

4.43. *Incendiary Devices* zine from Olympia, Washington, 1991–1993.

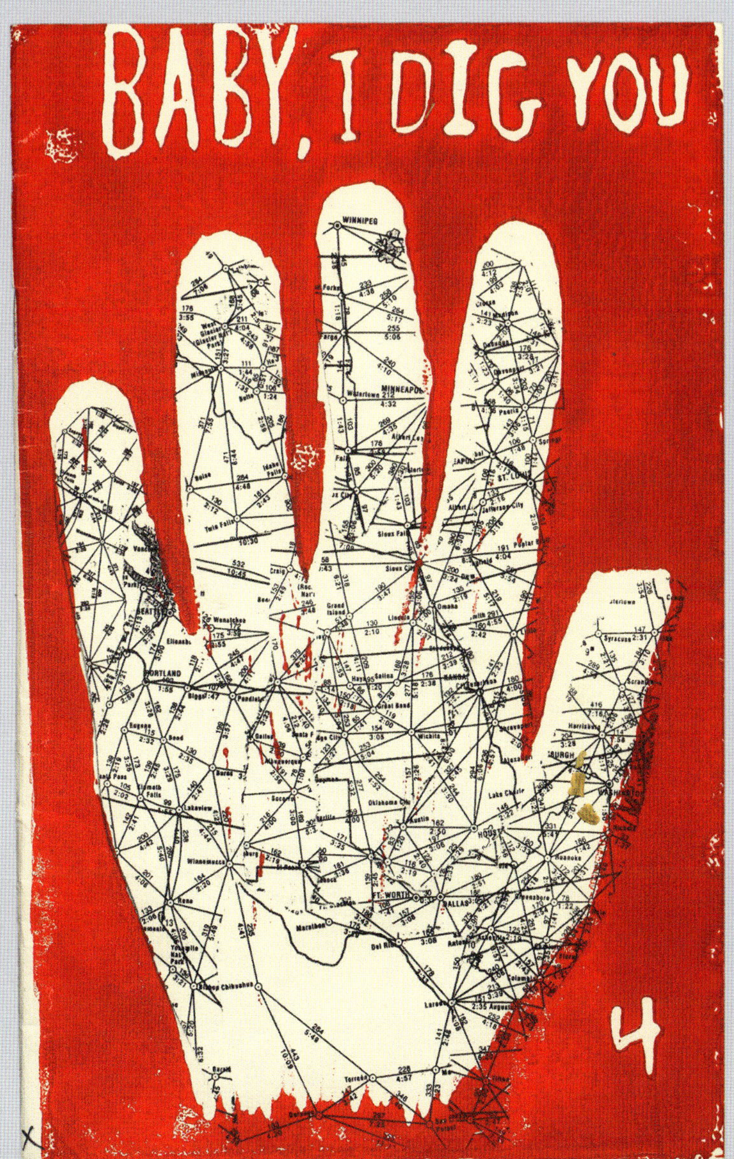

4.44. *Baby, I Dig You* zine created by Sara Lorimer, Olympia, Washington, 1994–1996.

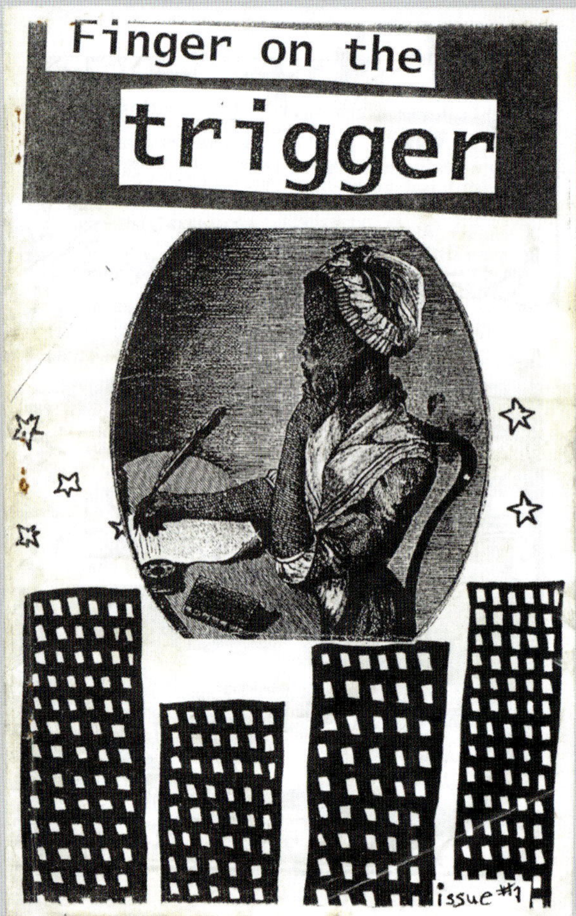

4.45, 4.46, 4.47, 4.48, 4.49. (*Above and right*) *Finger on the Trigger*, created by Adee R. (aka Adee Licious), 2001–2003.

I started making zines in high school, around 1999. My first zine was just music reviews and interviews of punk bands. *Finger on the Trigger* came about when I moved to Pensacola, Florida. There were so many white men writing about their lives and travel stories, through zines. And though I did not make mine to counter theirs, I did want to storytell through my experience as a Black queer woman. Sharing my emotions, train-hopping stories, fiction writing, and book reviews even. I also wanted to connect with other Black punks around the states, so I ended up having a few pen pals through the zine as well. It was twenty years ago, so seems a bit embarrassing to me now, but at the time it was really therapeutic/cathartic. —Adee Roberson

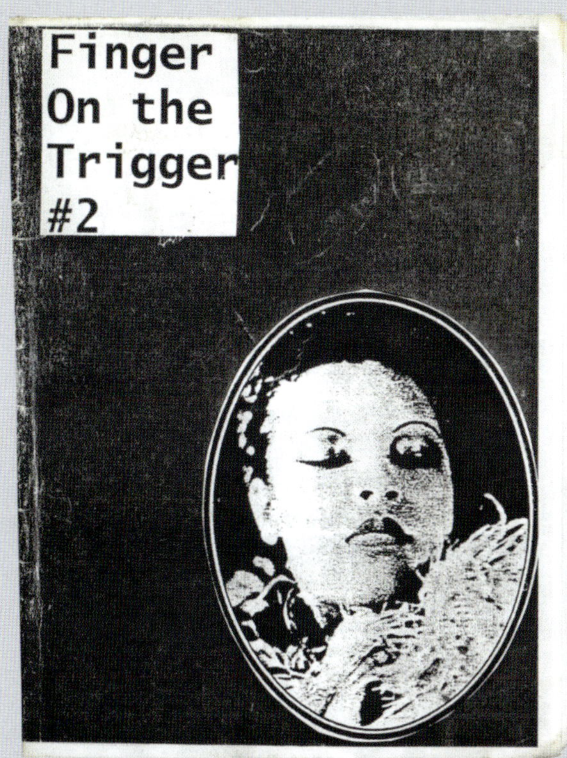
Finger
On the
Trigger
#2

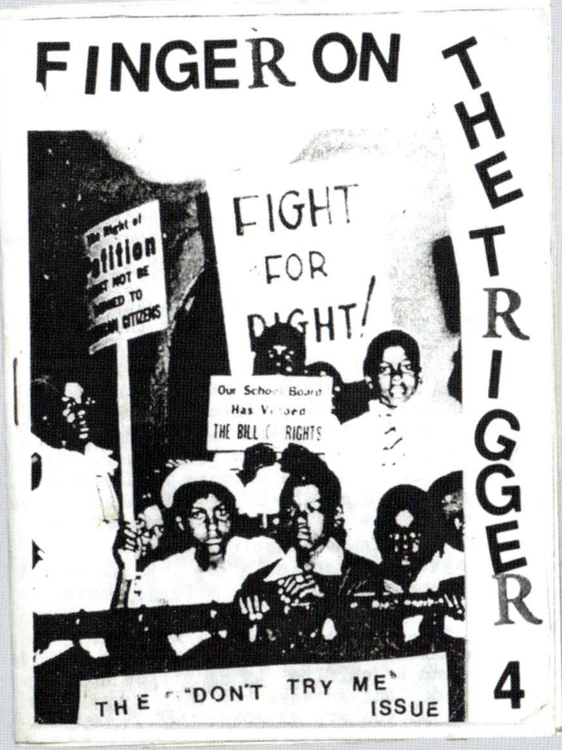
FINGER ON THE TRIGGER
FIGHT FOR RIGHT!
Our School Board Has Vetoed THE BILL
THE "DON'T TRY ME" ISSUE
4

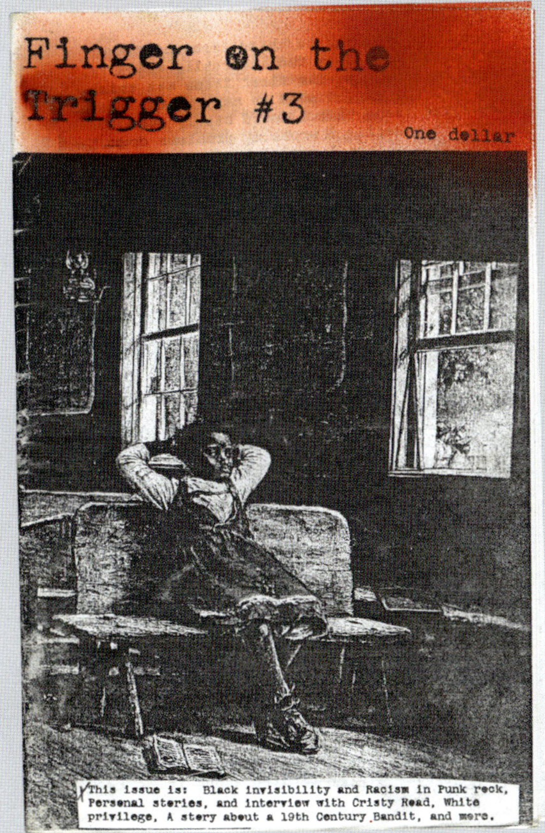
Finger on the Trigger #3
One dollar
This issue is: Black invisibility and Racism in Punk rock, Personal stories, and interview with Cristy Road, White privilege, A story about a 19th Century Bandit, and more.

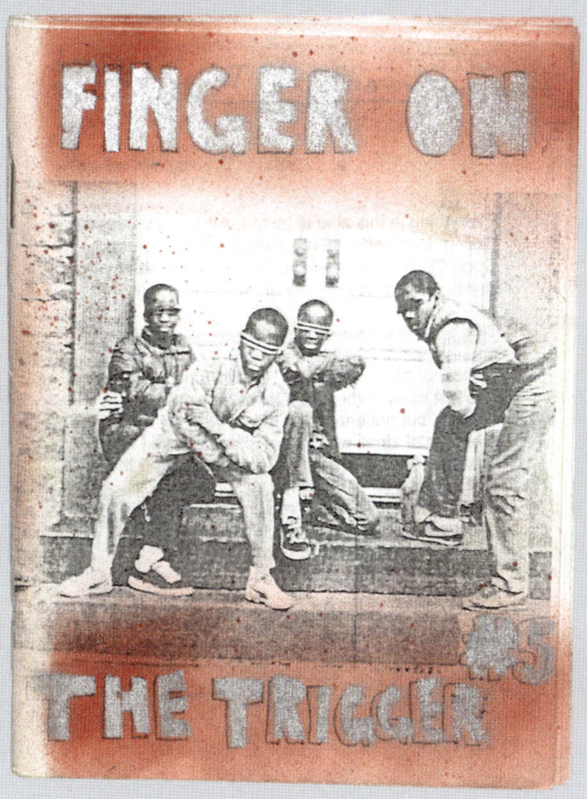
FINGER ON
THE TRIGGER
#5

The High Desert is a graphic novel about my first year finding punk, living in a small desert town in Southern California. I was one of two Black punks in the scene there. The town had a serious Nazi problem. This was my introduction to punk rock. If not for the Do It Yourself movement and the politics preached by punks outside of my hometown, punk may have been a phase. DIY made me who I am today. The ethics and morals intrinsic to certain parts of the scene raised me. For that I will always be indebted to the scene. My way to give back to my community is by telling stories that both challenge and celebrate who we are and what we do for one another. *The High Desert* is a love letter to the misfits, weirdos, and one-of-a-kind intellects cultivated within punk rock. —James Spooner

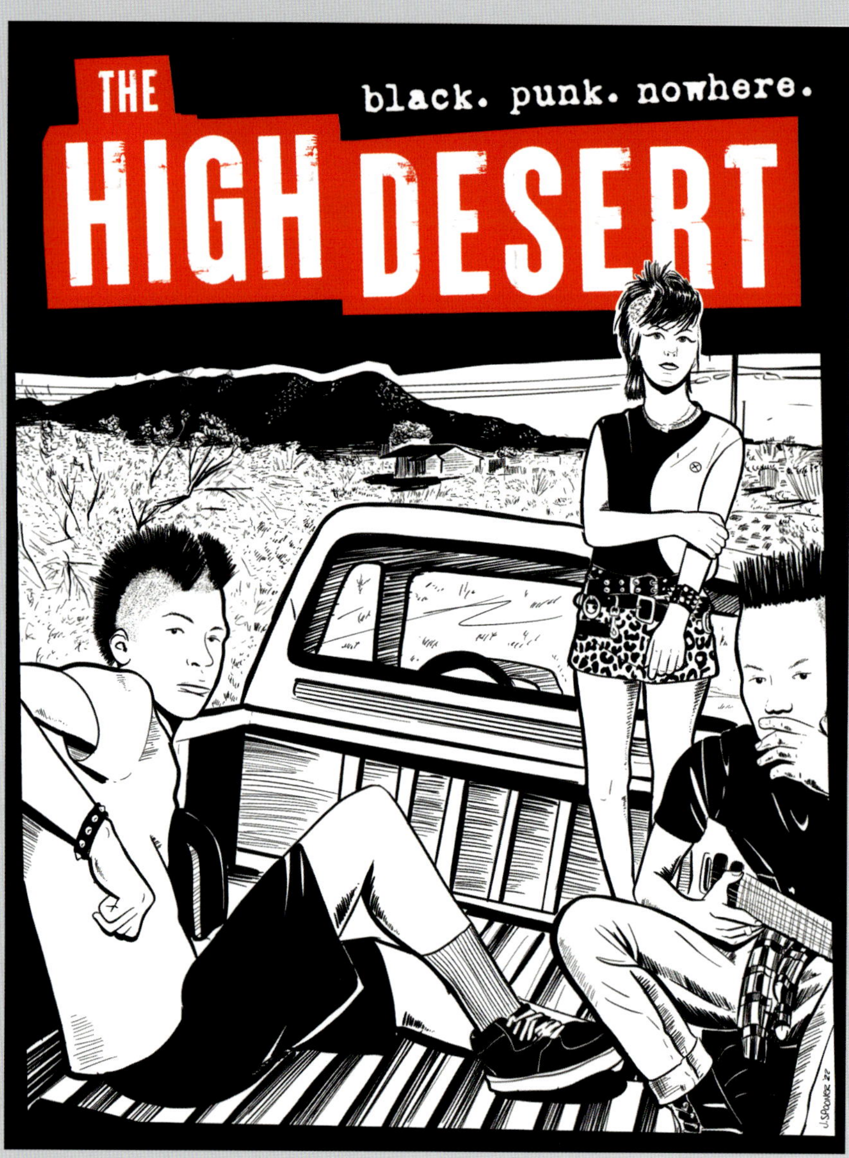

4.50. Promotional poster for the 2022 graphic memoir by James Spooner, director of *Afro-Punk* (2003) and cofounder of the Afropunk Festival.

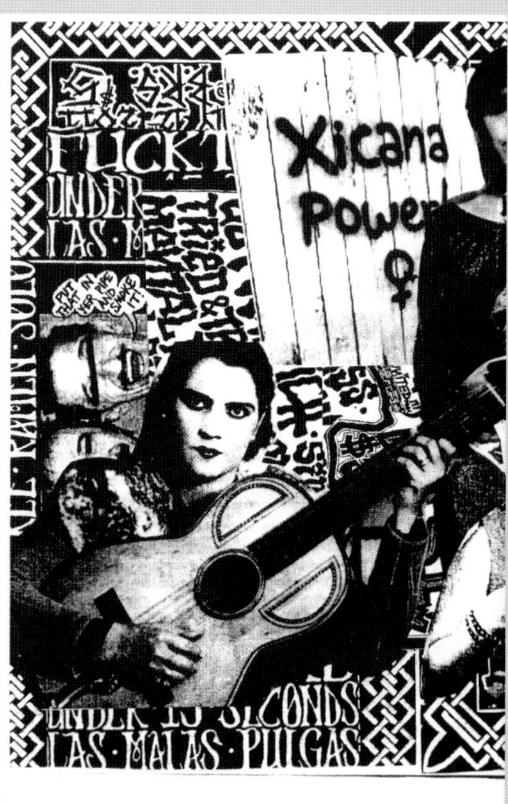

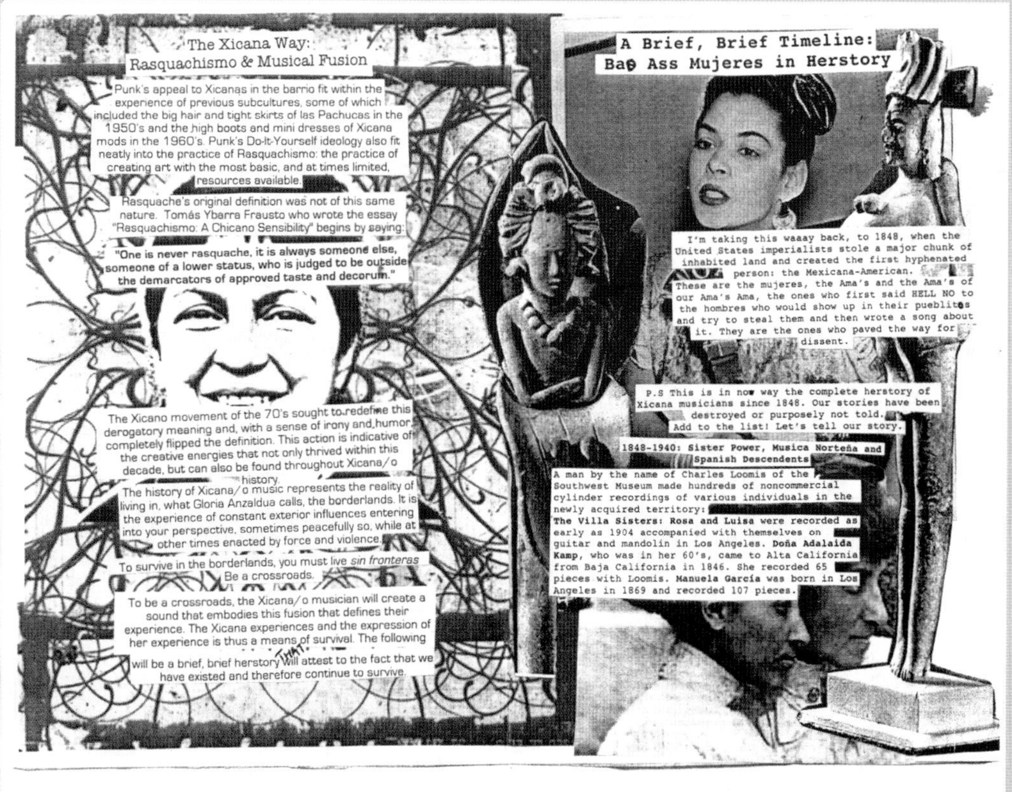

The Xicana Way:
Rasquachismo & Musical Fusion

Punk's appeal to Xicanas in the barrio fit within the experience of previous subcultures, some of which included the big hair and tight skirts of las Pachucas in the 1950's and the high boots and mini dresses of Xicana mods in the 1960's. Punk's Do-It-Yourself ideology also fit neatly into the practice of Rasquachismo: the practice of creating art with the most basic, and at times limited, resources available.

Rasquache's original definition was not of this same nature. Tomás Ybarra Frausto who wrote the essay "Rasquachismo: A Chicano Sensibility" begins by saying:

"One is never rasquache, it is always someone else, someone of a lower status, who is judged to be outside the demarcators of approved taste and decorum."

The Xicano movement of the 70's sought to redefine this derogatory meaning and, with a sense of irony and humor, completely flipped the definition. This action is indicative of the creative energies that not only thrived within this decade, but can also be found throughout Xicana/o history.

The history of Xicana/o music represents the reality of living in, what Gloria Anzaldua calls, the borderlands. It is the experience of constant exterior influences entering into your perspective, sometimes peacefully so, while at other times enacted by force and violence.

To survive in the borderlands, you must live *sin fronteras*
Be a crossroads.

To be a crossroads, the Xicana/o musician will create a sound that embodies this fusion that defines their experience. The Xicana experiences and the expression of her experience is thus a means of survival. The following will be a brief, brief herstory THAT will attest to the fact that we have existed and therefore continue to survive.

A Brief, Brief Timeline:
Bad Ass Mujeres in Herstory

I'm taking this waaay back, to 1848, when the United States imperialists stole a major chunk of inhabited land and created the first hyphenated person: the Mexicana-American. These are the mujeres, the Ama's and the Ama's of our Ama's Ama, the ones who first said HELL NO to the hombres who would show up in their pueblitos and try to steal them and then wrote a song about it. They are the ones who paved the way for dissent.

P.S This is in no way the complete herstory of Xicana musicians since 1848. Our stories have been destroyed or purposely not told. Add to the list! Let's tell our story.

1848-1940: Sister Power, Musica Norteña and Spanish Descendents

A man by the name of Charles Loomis of the Southwest Museum made hundreds of noncommercial cylinder recordings of various individuals in the newly acquired territory: **The Villa Sisters: Rosa and Luisa** were recorded as early as 1904 accompanied with themselves on guitar and mandolin in Los Angeles. **Doña Adalaida Kamp**, who was in her 60's, came to Alta California from Baja California in 1846. She recorded 65 pieces with Loomis. **Manuela García** was born in Los Angeles in 1869 and recorded 107 pieces.

4.51 and 4.52. Cover and first two pages of *Xicanistas and Punkeristas Say It Loud!*, circa 2013.

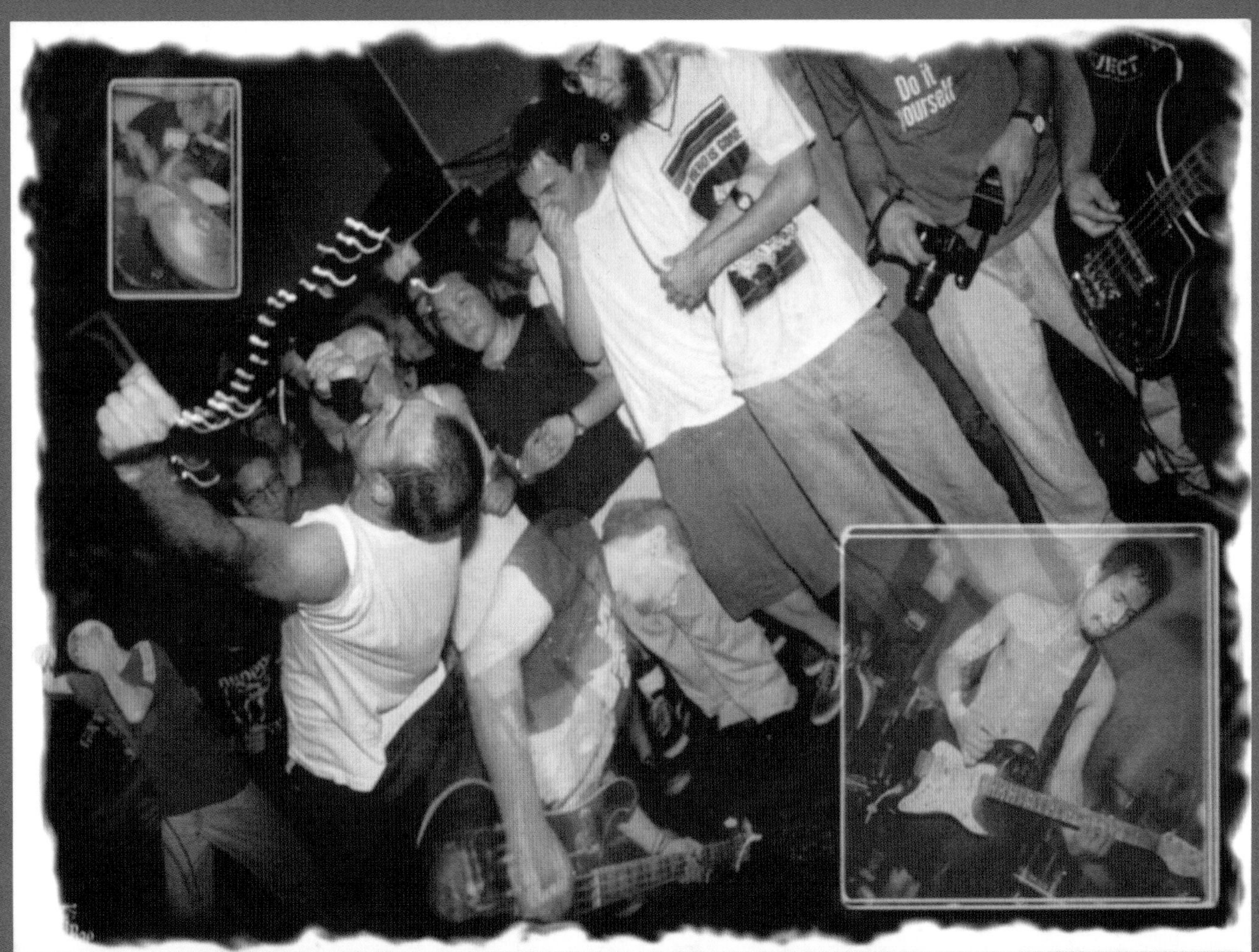

4.53. Los Crudos postcard, circa 1997. Photo: Kim Bae.

CH. 18

"You got to make it happen or it ain't going to happen"

AN INTERVIEW WITH MARTÍN SORRONDEGUY

Forming in the early 1990s, Chicago's Los Crudos and their singer **Martín Sorrondeguy** disrupted the entrenched image of hardcore punk as an overwhelmingly white and straight scene. In 1998, he formed the queercore band Limp Wrist, marking another significant challenge to associations between hardcore and machismo, as well as to homophobic stereotypes of gay men as essentially effeminate. In this interview, conducted on July 1 and 15, 2021, Martín discusses his early musical influences and the local music scenes in Chicago in the 1980s and '90s; the importance of community to his formation of Los Crudos; touring the US, South America, and Japan as a Spanish-only hardcore activist punk band; and Limp Wrist's playful queer commentary on hardcore culture.

JUDITH: The first thing I wanted to ask stems from the end of your documentary *Beyond the Screams: A U.S. Latino Hardcore Punk Documentary* (1999). You make this beautiful comment that for you being punk didn't mean breaking away from the family, but meant working within the community and the family in a different way. Can you say more about the ways in which that positions punk in a really different relationship to the family than normally understood?

MARTÍN: Yeah. I've always felt that punk was viewed as this rebellious subculture, where it always came with being anti-parent. I understood the root of that. But I felt that we—especially the punks in the community here—we all still lived in the community. We didn't leave home or leave the city. We stayed where we were. It places punk and your ideologies and philosophy in a unique position where you think, "Well, I'm not running away from anyone here. I'm not necessarily angry with mom and dad." There may be some of that, and I think it's individually based, but I felt welcomed in the community. We weren't outcasts. We were accepted by a lot of the arts community and the artists and the muralists. There was already an existing vibrant community of people who were creative types, and we were more than pleased to work with them. Some of our families definitely rejected what we were doing because it countered a lot of the tradition. It countered the Catholicism, which a lot of the Latino punks were rooted in. So I'm not going to lie and say that wasn't something. But I wasn't really young. I had already gone through a lot of that conflict with my parents.

We wanted to be a part of the existing community rather than just hide away from it or challenge it per se. We were critical of what was happening in the community, but we also wanted to do something positive about it. We weren't just like "Screw this, fuck that." So, I think it was important for the really young punks coming up, seeing what we were doing and thinking, "You don't have to go away anywhere." We're all a part of this community. Let's work together, let's do something! And it was a beautiful intersection of us coming together. We were crossing roads and paths, and we were bringing people in, and we were showing the younger punks, "Hey, there's a lot of possibility here." We saw the results of that, and it was wonderful. That's why I felt that our punk was a little different than some of my peers in other parts of the city, or peers who had moved or left their towns to be in the big city. I just felt like our situation was a little different.

JUDITH: So when you say "here," are you talking about the Pilsen neighborhood in Chicago, or the larger Latine community?

MARTÍN: The funny thing is when I say "here," I really am referring to the South Side of Chicago—Pilsen, Little Village, and Back of the Yards. But, Judith, I say "here," and then when I would travel and, let's say, go to San Antonio, it was *here*. That was the era. It's interesting. We could go to LA, we could be in New Mexico and Arizona. We were finding that a lot of the punks had similarities. So "here" felt like we were all a part of it.

JUDITH: Thinking through the thrust of your interest in becoming a punk, it sounds like it grew more from a sensibility of yourself within a Latine community, rather than in a punk community. Did you feel that you were coming from a Chicago punk scene when you put your band together?

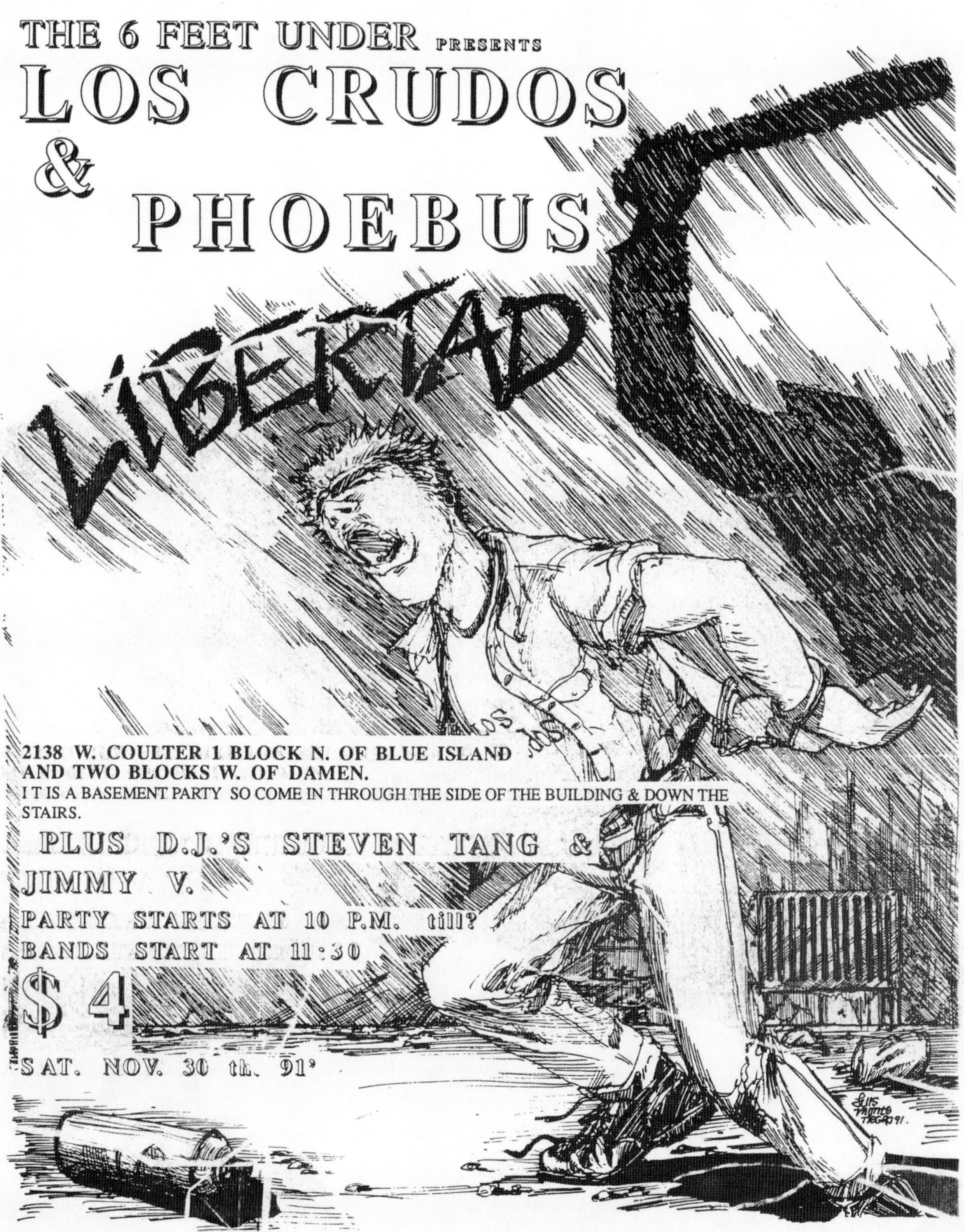

4.54. Flyer for Los Crudos first show, Chicago, 1991. Drawing: Luis Montenegro.

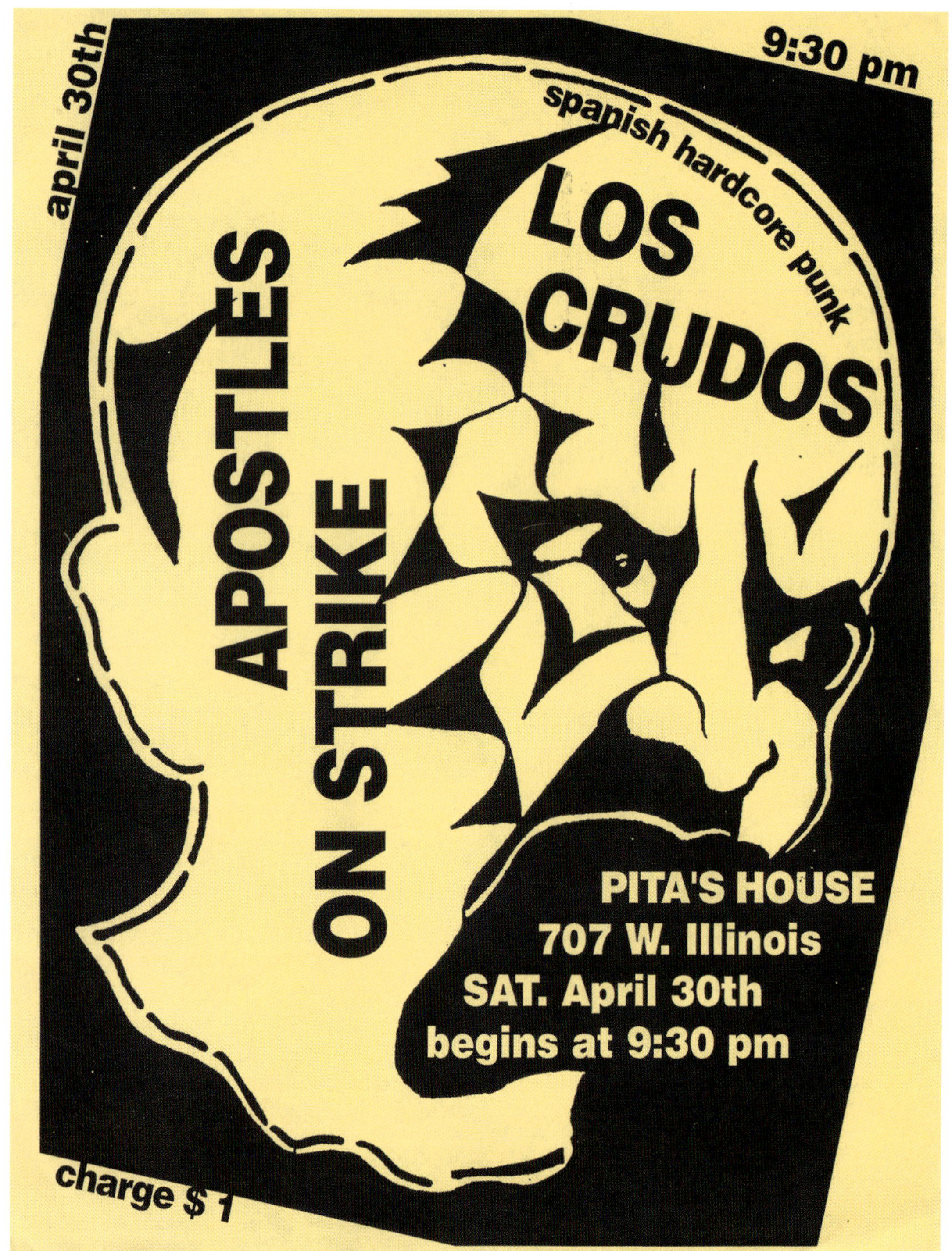

4.55. Flyer for Los Crudos show, 1994.

This is a great one. This was over on the campus in Champaign-Urbana [at the University of Illinois]. Pita is a really good old friend of mine who grew up in the same neighborhood. She happened to take classes there. The university didn't invite us, it really came through her. We played at her home, and we played on campus, at some sort of event. —Martín Sorrondeguy

This is a friend of mine. We call him Cryptas. He did a fanzine in Mexico City and helped book our tour. They had somebody there do the graphics on that. On the back is some interview questions sent to us. —Martín Sorrondeguy

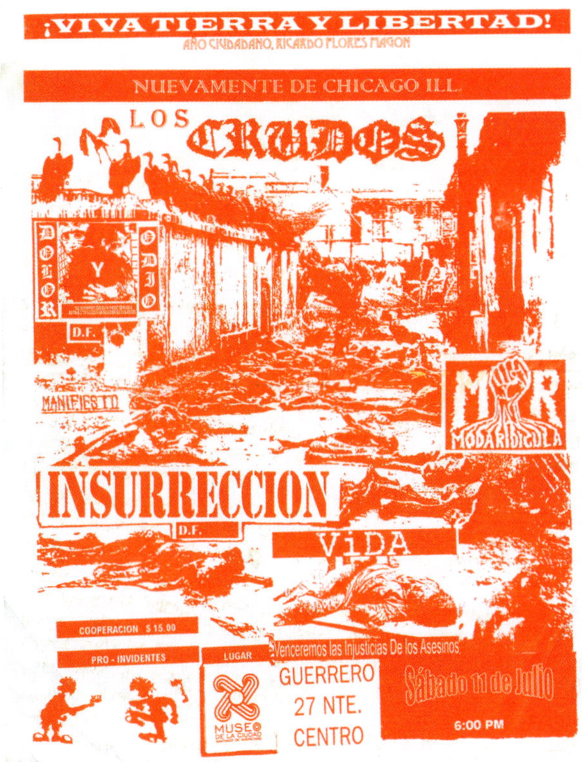

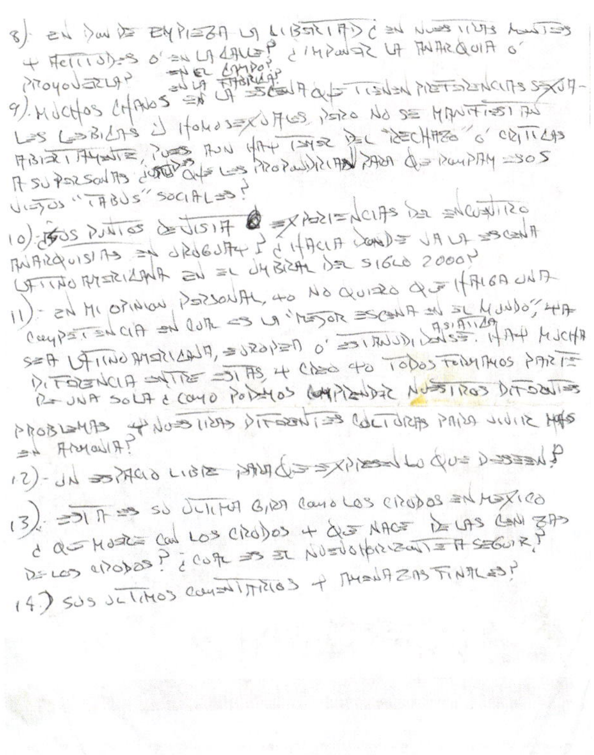
8). EN DONDE EMPIEZA LA LIBERTAD ¿EN NUESTRAS MENTES Y ACTITUDES O EN LA CALLE? ¿IMPONER LA ANARQUIA O PROVOCARLA? EN EL CAMPO? EN LA FABRICA?

9). MUCHOS CHAVOS EN LA ESCENA QUE TIENEN PREFERENCIAS SEXUALES LESBICAS Y HOMOSEXUALES, PERO NO SE MANIFIESTAN ABIERTAMENTE, PUES AUN HAY TEMOR DEL "RECHAZO" O CRITICAS A SU PERSONA ¿QUE LES PROPONDRIAN PARA QUE ROMPAN ESOS VIEJOS "TABUS" SOCIALES?

10). ¿SUS PUNTOS DE VISTA Y EXPERIENCIAS DEL ENCUENTRO ANARQUISTA EN URUGUAY? ¿HACIA DONDE VA LA ESCENA LATINOAMERICANA EN EL UMBRAL DEL SIGLO 2000?

11). EN MI OPINION PERSONAL, YO NO QUIERO QUE HAIGA UNA COMPETENCIA EN CUAL ES LA "MEJOR ESCENA EN EL MUNDO", YA SEA LATINOAMERICANA, EUROPEA O ESTADUNIDENSE, ASIATICA. HAY MUCHA DIFERENCIA ENTRE ESTAS, Y CREO YO TODOS FORMAMOS PARTE DE UNA SOLA ¿COMO PODEMOS COMPRENDER NUESTROS DIFERENTES PROBLEMAS Y NUESTRAS DIFERENTES CULTURAS PARA VIVIR MAS EN ARMONIA?

12). UN ESPACIO LIBRE PARA QUE EXPRESEN LO QUE DESEEN.

13). ESTA ES SU ULTIMA GIRA COMO LOS CRUDOS EN MEXICO ¿QUE MUERE CON LOS CRUDOS Y QUE NACE DE LAS CENIZAS DE LOS CRUDOS? ¿CUAL ES EL NUEVO HORIZONTE A SEGUIR?

14.) SUS ULTIMOS COMENTARIOS Y AMENAZAS FINALES?

4.56 and 4.57. Front and back of flyer for *Los Crudos* show, Mexico City, 1994.

MARTÍN: It's interesting because there was definitely a shift that happened. When I first entered into punk, I went into the general punk scene, which was predominantly on the North Side. There were shows at the Cubby Bear, at the Cabaret Metro, at Club Dreamers, and I would go to all of it. That was the point that I felt like I was away from *here*, from my neighborhood or my community, because I was immersing myself in what was just punk. I think there were so many shifts that began to happen from the mid-to-late 1980s. A lot of things were changing sonically. Ideas were changing within punk.

There was a new energy happening in punk that was pushing the old punk view and mentality—whole new systems of ideas. There were women speaking up about things. There were people of color speaking up about things, there were queer people speaking up about things. We had homocore in Chicago. A lot was going on, and it was exciting that things pivoted. It wasn't just a singular punk voice, under this umbrella of what people thought punk was. It was branching out more.

JUDITH: I am thinking about my own days when I would run from the suburbs into the city and go to Wax Trax Records, and that was where I found my people.

MARTÍN: I loved it because I did too.

It's some rant against Youth of Today. I have a different flyer for the same show, and it doesn't have that rant. One has Jimi Hendrix on it. It's the same show, same space, but somebody definitely felt like they had to address something, so they did it on a flyer. —Martín Sorrondeguy

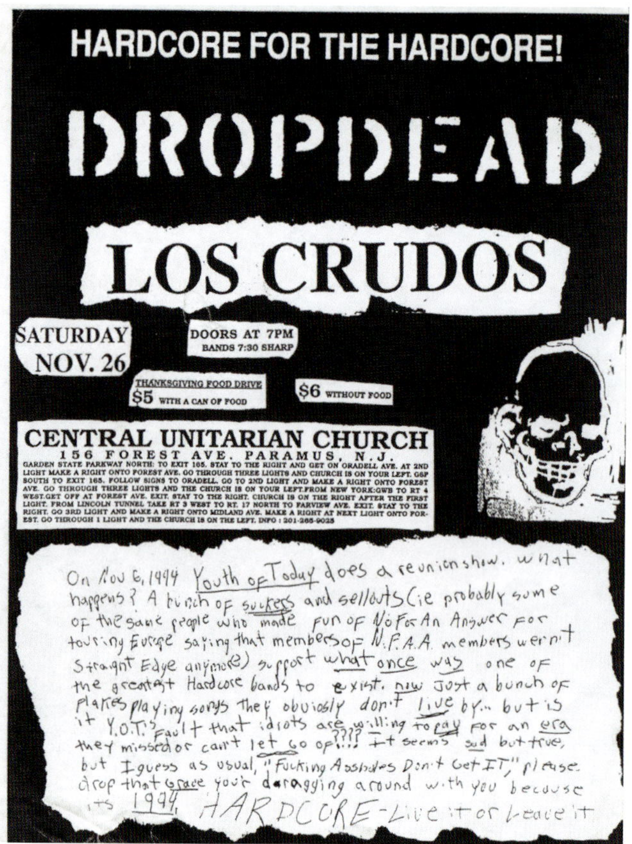

4.58. Annotated flyer for Los Crudos show, Paramus, New Jersey, November 1994.

JUDITH: We might've been flipping through the records side by side.

MARTÍN: Yes! I loved going upstairs to the fanzines and the clothes and the hair dye, and then going downstairs for music. It was amazing. I had that experience as well, but even Wax Trax changed at some point. The focus for me with the band changed too: I no longer aspired to play the clubs. I loved Naked Raygun, but that wasn't my aim or my goal to play with Naked Raygun (4.5). I saw them a ton of times, but my ideas were different. I wanted to play these weird, cool shows. The whole punk world was doing that: there were shows happening in so many nontraditionally rock and roll spots. You'd hear about shows happening at cultural centers, art centers, laundromats, basements, backyards, anywhere. I remember we played a laundromat in the Little Village—just anything that was off and different was exciting.

JUDITH: There's a great video on YouTube of you playing "Ilegal ¿Y Qué?" on Daley Plaza. What do you remember about that show, in the middle of the business district?

MARTÍN: The downtown show was a unique one because someone in the scene got a permit. When they invited Los Crudos, we were like, "Wow, Daley Plaza, OK, let's wear suits!" We borrowed or bought thrift store suits, and I had this old briefcase—I don't know where I got it. We thought we were going to play into this role of downtown. That was a wonderful show. We had people from the community follow us out there, friends of ours, punks came from all over. It confused the police at first, because when I got there, I started talking to these punks, and the police started getting closer to us because they got scared. They thought that the punks were harassing me.

JUDITH: Did you get the business folks to turn their heads and stop to listen?

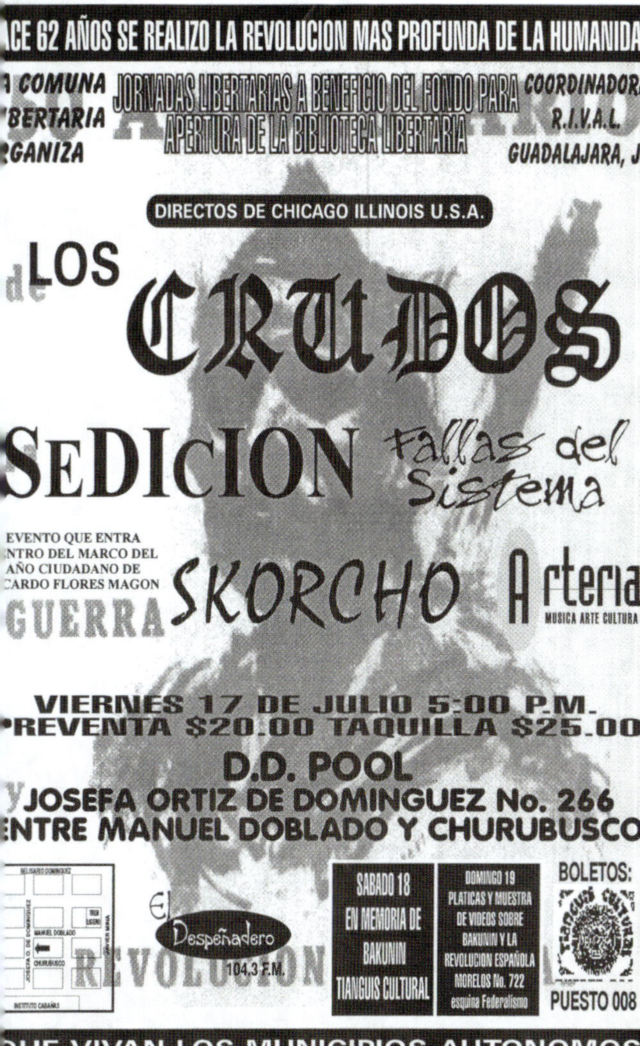

4.59. Flyer for Los Crudos show, Guadalajara, Jalisco, Mexico, July 1994.

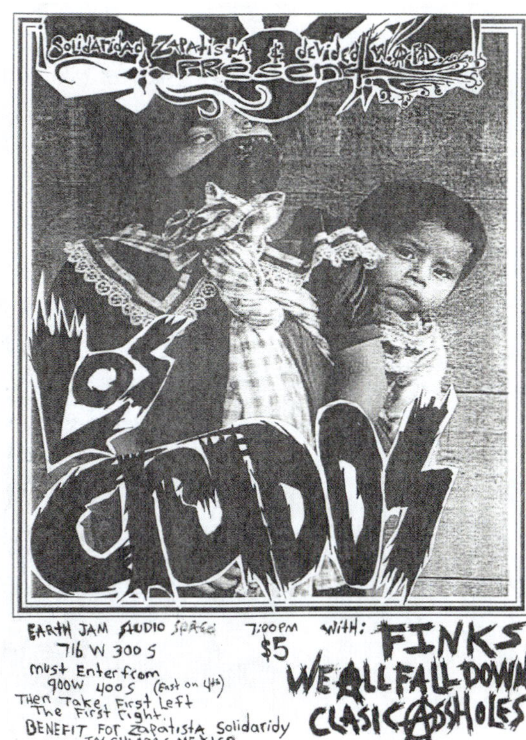

4.60. Flyer for Los Crudos show at Earth Jam Studio Space [Salt Lake City?], circa 1997.

(*Above*) That was a great show. It was a very rainy night. It was like an art cultural center. There wasn't a roof on a part of it, so rain was just coming in while we played, but it was beautiful. I have video of it, and people are just dancing and water's just splashing up.
—Martín Sorrondeguy

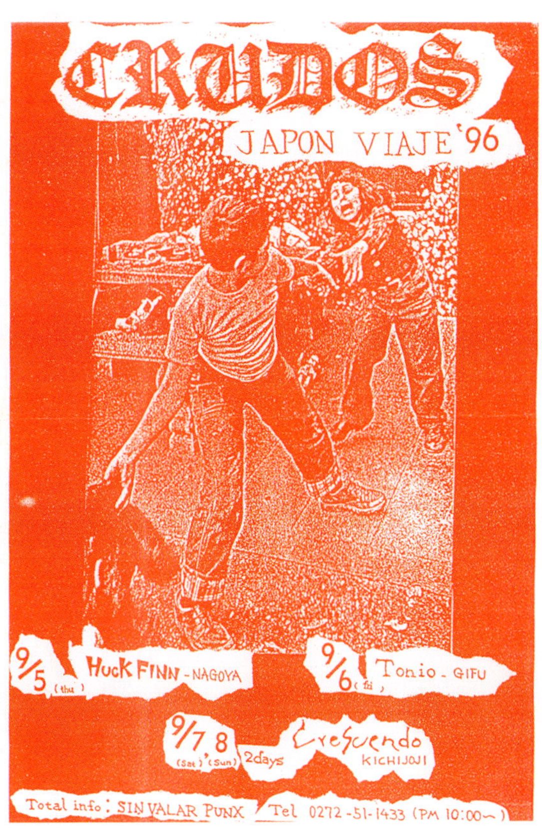

4.61. Flyer from Los Crudos Japan tour, 1996.

MARTÍN: I think a lot of people were walking by and turning their head. "What is going on? What is this?" Some people started dancing.

JUDITH: So, backtracking a little bit, I'm wondering if you could talk about your early punk heroes. Who were you listening to? And how did you focus in on hardcore as the sound?

MARTÍN: I first heard of punk through my cousins. They lived in New York. I was, I want to say eleven years old. We visited them in 1979. They lived in Jackson Heights, Queens, and they had Ramones ticket stubs on the wall mirror from shows they had seen. They had a couple of records, Ramones, Sex Pistols. I liked Kiss at the time. I remember getting exposed to them and being like, "Wow, this is really different, like wild." There was something about it that drew me in. And as the years went on, it was difficult to find that. I didn't live on the North Side of Chicago; you wouldn't see it regularly. It would randomly come into my life in some weird way, and I'd be like, "Oh, there's that thing, that punk thing." It wasn't until the 1980s that I was coming out of a scene. I was an early b-boy. I used to be a break dancer. That was common in the community, something that a lot of young people did. You know, Chicago punks—a lot of us, we grew up on house music, especially the ones that are on the South Side of town.

We were all about house music or at least soul and all that. But when I was leaving the b-boy thing, and it was kind of coming to an end, I recall telling somebody, "I'm going punk." And

I laid out the artwork on that one, so that's Carlos Damián Rodriguez, the singer of Fun People from Argentina. We put this show together at the Fireside Bowl (*below*), and the show on the left is at an art space in the neighborhood. —Martín Sorrondeguy

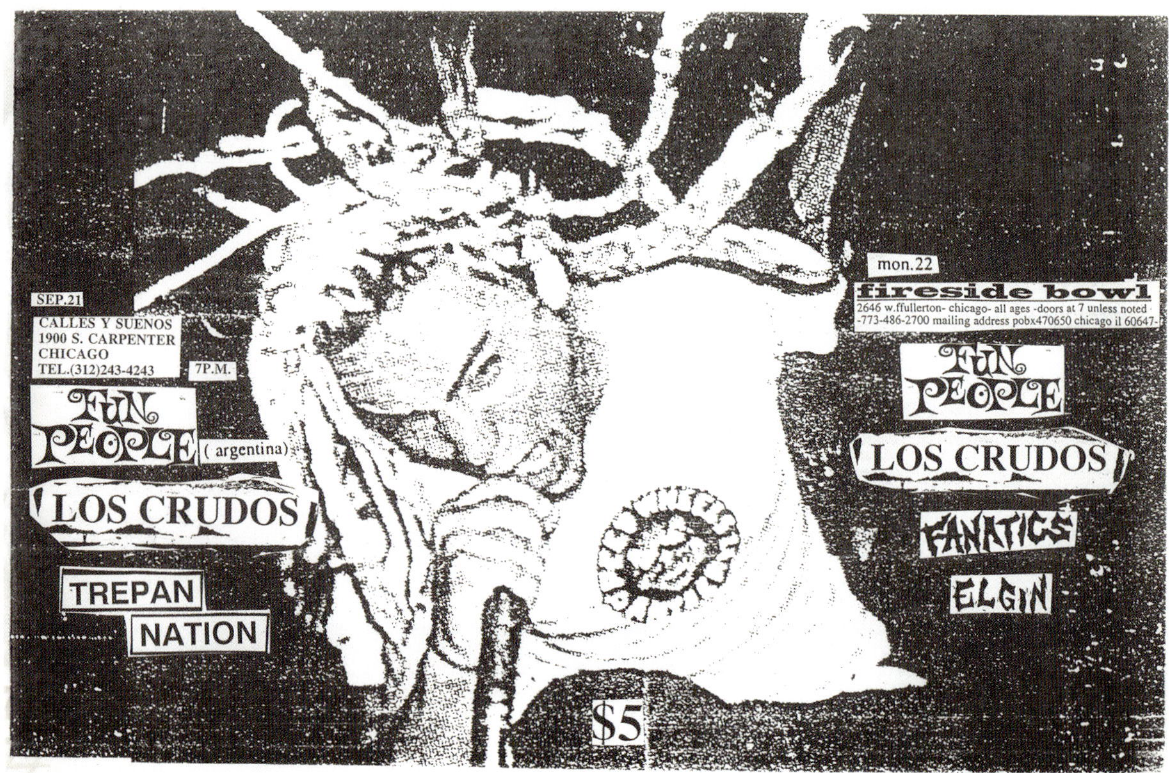

4.62. Flyer for shows at Calles y Sueños and Fireside Bowl, Chicago, September 1997. Design: Martín Sorrondeguy.

they were like "What? What do you mean you're going punk?" I'm like, "No, I am!" I was determined to search this out and find it. At that time, too, I was starved for anything different. In the city of Chicago, MTV didn't show up. So you relied on *Night Flight* or some weird cable TV channel 60 programming bringing video programs from LA. Prior to that, you weren't going to get it. So I watched everything imaginable. That was our reality. We didn't have a Rodney [Bingenheimer] on KROQ in Illinois. At one point, too, if you were lucky, you connected into the college radio station. I think it was WNUR [broadcast from Northwestern University] who did a radio show called *Fast 'n' Loud*. I lived on the South Side, so I would hit record on my tape deck, and I would extend my arms up against the wall as high as I could, and my body to the wire to the wall allowed for it to come through. I would stand there as long as I could to record that hour-long show, then go back and just jam to these great songs that I loved.

I was still in high school, and I had an old friend who lived near me. He started getting into punk. My younger sister and I, we both started getting into it. We would see other kids from some of the other high schools, and if we saw you and you looked remotely different, alternative, we would run up to you and we'd ask, "Are you into punk?" And they'd be like, "yes" or "no"—mostly it was "yes." And we'd say, "We need to hang out! We're going to be friends." We started accumulating this little mass of kids who all lived on the South Side of Chicago. We eventually started hearing about Wax Trax. I started picking up flyers, started going to shows in these groups, and it was almost a protection for us when you looked really different. You put yourself at risk. Looking punk, people related that to gay. I was on a bus and got attacked with one of my punk friends when we were younger. My dad initially thought that me getting into punk was me trying to say that I'm gay. It was a challenging time because that wasn't what I was saying at that point in my life.

JUDITH: This is so fascinating because it's exactly the experience I had out in the suburbs of Chicago. I went to a Devo show at the Aragon Ballroom in 1981. In my high school culture, everyone wore concert T-shirts the day after the concerts if they went. Other students wore Iron Maiden, Rush, Styx, and REO Speedwagon T-shirts. I wore my Devo T-shirt, and the students called me queer in the hallway. I felt the same thing as you. I wasn't quite at that realization yet, but it started pushing me in that direction. I wonder if that's a Midwest thing in a sense, how punk read as queer at that time.

MARTÍN: Yeah, well, without even trying it pushed you there. So I recall when I wasn't even out of the closet and I started working at a record store up north, and this is like 1990, '91, and I remember this trucker drove by calling me faggot and stuff. I was this target. I could get queer bashed or attacked, and it didn't matter if I was or if I wasn't, because in their eyes, I was. How are you going to have a conversation with somebody when they're coming at you with violence? So it didn't matter. I think looking different or doing things that were off the path, it already placed you in a certain space.

So I think you're right, Judith. I think this could be something that a lot of us can relate to. When we were younger, we would travel in packs, and we were terrifying to people because we weren't an easy target. It was almost always when there were just two of us, we would get so much harassment. But when you had especially all these young brown faces with leather jackets, and twenty of us getting on the train, the train would go silent. But we weren't there to scare people. We just wanted to go see music and do our thing.

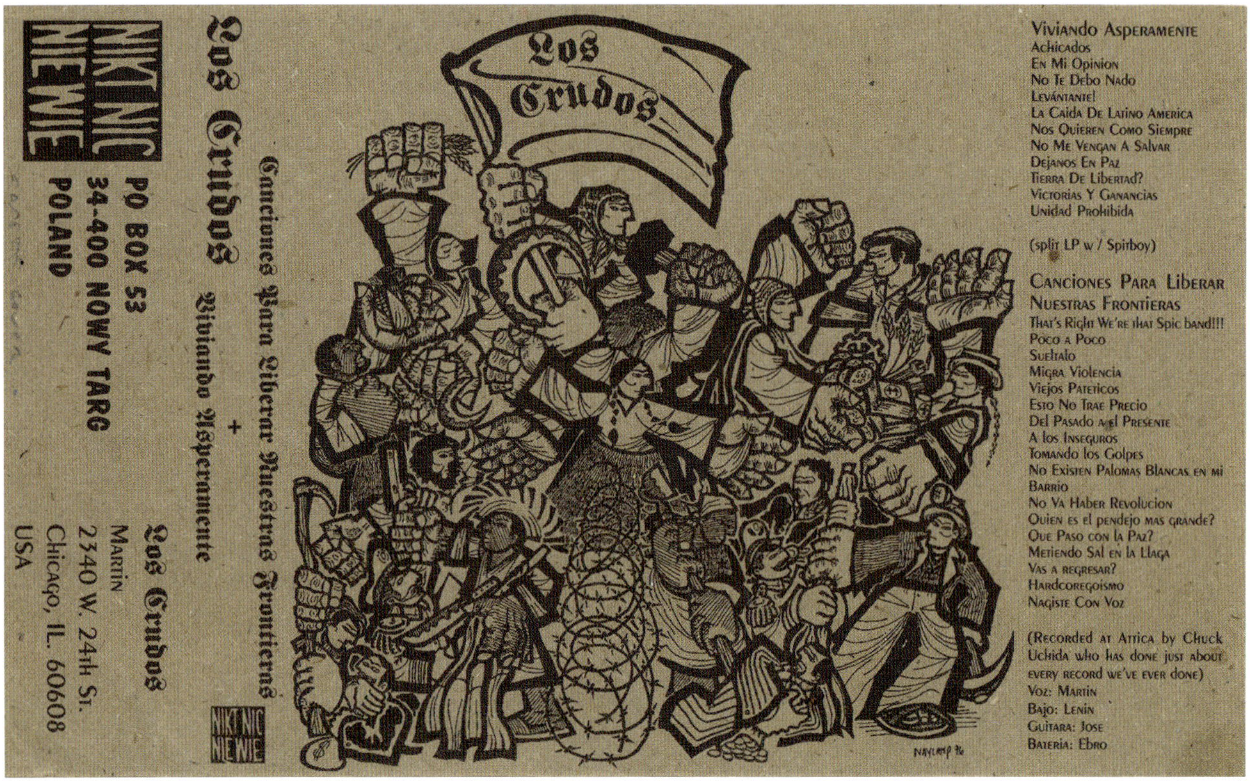

Los Crudos

Viviando Asperamente
Achicados
En Mi Opinion
No Te Debo Nado
Levántante!
La Caida De Latino America
Nos Quieren Como Siempre
No Me Vengan A Salvar
Dejanos En Paz
Tierra De Libertad?
Victorias Y Ganancias
Unidad Prohibida

(split LP w / Spitboy)

Canciones Para Liberar Nuestras Frontieras
That's Right We're that Spic band!!!
Poco a Poco
Sueltalo
Migra Violencia
Viejos Pateticos
Esto No Trae Precio
Del Pasado a el Presente
A los Insequros
Tomando los Golpes
No Existen Palomas Blancas en mi Barrio
No Va Haber Revolucion
Quien es el pendejo mas grande?
Que Paso con la Paz?
Metiendo Sal en la Llaga
Vas a regresar?
Hardcoregoismo
Nagiste Con Voz

(Recorded at Attica by Chuck Uchida who has done just about every record we've ever done)
Voz: Martin
Bajo: Lenin
Guitara: Jose
Bateria: Ebro

Los Crudos
Canciones Para Liberar Nuestras Frontieras
+
Viviando Asperamente

Los Crudos
Martin
2340 W. 24th St.
Chicago, IL. 60608
USA

NIKT NIC NIE WIE
PO BOX 53
34-400 NOWY TARG
POLAND

4.63. Cassette J-card from a release in Poland. Artwork: David Naylamp, 1996.

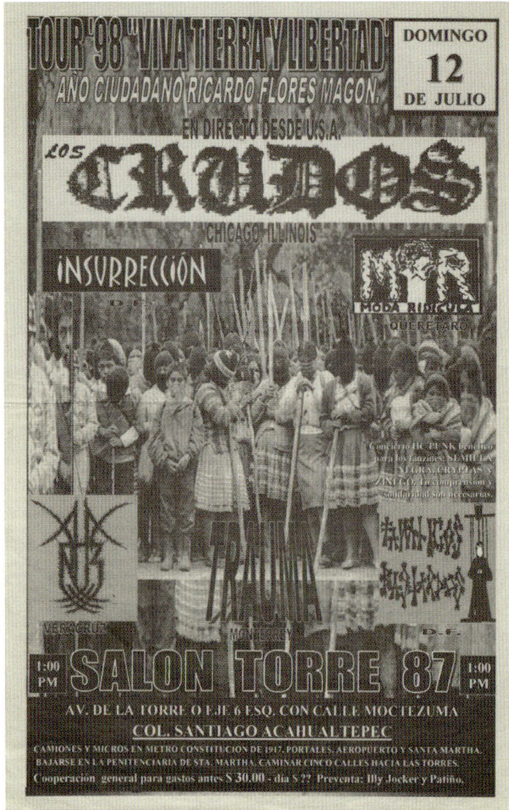

4.64. Flyer for show at Salon Torre 87, Mexico City, 1998.

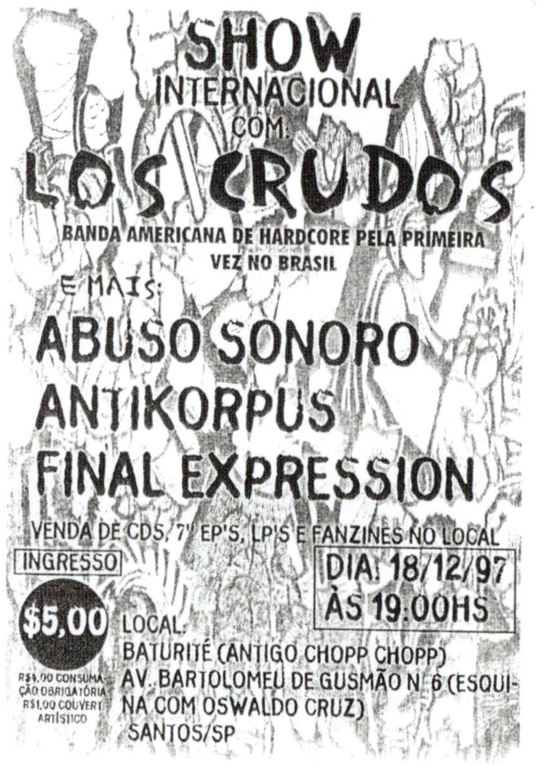

4.65. Flyer for Los Crudos South American tour show at Baturité, Santos, Brazil, December 1997.

JUDITH: Thinking about hardcore: when you finally do get into a hardcore band, that world of the more flamboyant punk with the dyed hair and the different haircuts and clothing and badges—that's quite different from what the hardcore scene ends up looking like. I'm thinking about the hardcore masculinist fashion of it. In some way, a lot less of a signal as queer, if not outright heterosexualized masculinity. So how did that become the vehicle for you, especially when you were starting to think about the Latine politics that you wanted to express through punk. How did you carve that space for yourself, and how did you get there?

MARTÍN: That's a good question. You've caught me on the visuals. There was something about the look. I always loved punk women because they looked so tough. As a young male who wasn't even in tune yet to who I was sexually or anything like a sexual identity, I was drawn to the women. I was like, "Oh my God, I want to hang out with these girls because they look so tough!" The boots and the shaved head. I'll never forget: it was actually at Wax Trax, it was a rainy night, and two women who came out had these massive combat boots on. One of them was completely bald. The other had a mohawk with hair dyes still stuck on her head. I thought, "Who would mess with those girls?" I remember thinking, "I love that!" The guys, it was OK to have a shaved head and boots. That was common. But to see women like that was like, "Oh, those are some tough girls" [*laughs*]. I think later on with the carving out, I just came to a point in punk when it stopped giving me what I wanted. . . . An age when I realized I have to *make* it. I think just prior to Los Crudos happening, there was this moment when it felt like you have to tell the story. What is your story? Where are you in all of this? Do you just go along with everybody else and kind of blend in, or do you begin to voice who it is you are in this?

That's the beginnings of what Crudos was going to come out of. As I went on, I realized that, yes, this is exactly what needs to happen; you need to tell this story. You asked what was I listening to earlier, and it went from the real early Chicago stuff, Naked Raygun, the Effigies, all the Chicago bands, Articles of Faith (4.4). I liked all these bands, and then it was Bhopal Stiffs. There was a lot. I was absorbing so much, but then I was looking at bands from overseas, and I was drawn in the mid- to late-1980s to a lot of the peace punk stuff like Crass and Conflict, the Instigators; all the Crass record bands. We were super drawn to their politics. We're like, "What is the squatting stuff?" They were singing about animal rights. They were singing about all these things. We were so politicized, and we were looking at the bands in Chicago and going, "Why do these bands feel so different than that?" I thought there were interesting things happening depending on where you were grabbing your punk from. So as time went on, I was exploring more and more—"Oh, who's this band? The single is two dollars, and this person's wearing a Dead Kennedys shirt. I'm going to buy it. I don't know who they are, but I'm going to check it out." Because there was no reference, no internet, no nothing.

A lot of it was by chance, or an old punk, which was very common, would hand you a tape and turn you on to things. You're like, "Oh wow, what is this? This band's amazing." Or, "I love this song," or "I never heard that style." There was so much happening, not just in Chicago, but in other cities. So, *Maximumrocknroll* was a massive publication for punk. It was the underground news. They'd do scene reports, different bands, different cities. At one point, I would write somebody a letter, or I would order a record or a tape—this system of writing to people, pen palling. I went into Columbia College in Chicago. I worked in the photography department; I would give out equipment. It's funny because at first they weren't going to hire me; they were all Deadheads, Grateful Dead freaks. They were honest and told me, "We were really afraid of you." But when I worked I would play punk music, and I remember so many times somebody would just peek their head in and go, "Who's playing this?" and "Oh my God, I'm an old New York punk." Or "I'm an old DC punk." Or "I'm a punk from here," and I would build these relationships, talking to people. There was this wonderful connected, I don't know, these dots that were just connecting with people everywhere. Again, the *Maximumrocknroll* thing—you were learning about DIY, it went beyond just being a fan of music, but it was—do *everything* yourself. That's when it started feeding me: "Yeah, you have to do it. You have to make it, you have to sing about it. You have to write about it." I started realizing my experience being where I'm from in Chicago, being Latino, being whatever it was like, this is really unique. Nobody's written a song about this that I know of, or there's very few songs about this, coming from this Chicago angle. So I learned that you got to make it happen or it ain't going to happen. And that was where I just dove in.

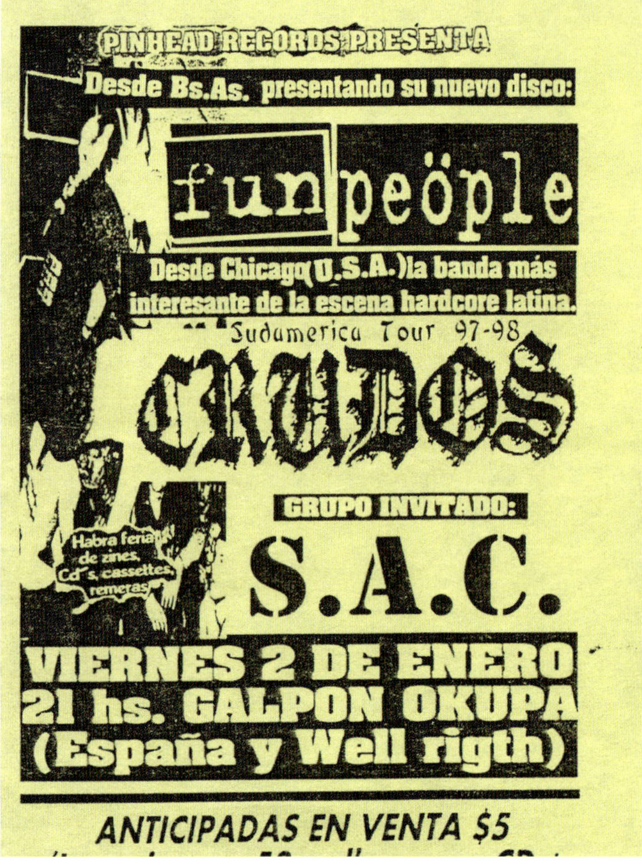

4.66. Flyer from Los Crudos South American tour at Galpón Okupa, Rosario, Argentina, January 1998.

JUDITH: When you were casting about for a sound, who were your models? You so clearly went in one direction. Punk is great because you can be on the pop side or the goth side or the hardcore side, and you found that hardcore was the voice for you. What was it about that sound that was what was giving you the food for your creativity?

MARTÍN: There was something about the rapid fire, one, two, three, four, one-minute long songs, going right at what you wanted to say. Of course, American hardcore: I saw the Bad Brains. It was in 1986. They were amazing. Adolescents, Bad Brains. I never caught Minor Threat. I saw the first Fugazi show, but I already loved Minor Threat. There were so many early US hardcore bands where their sound was just—there was no time wasted. It was like an assault. You just went crazy and you let it all out. It was energy, you know? There were a lot of great bands, a lot of great records, from the very late seventies, early eighties, that I still love today. It could be the Circle Jerks' *Group Sex*. It could be the Bad Brains' *Rock for Light*. It could be the Minor Threat EPs. It could be the Fix from Lansing, Michigan. There's so many bands, so many scenes. A lot of the early LA stuff was great. The Germs were great, the Bags. With the hardcore stuff it's definitely a lot of energy. When I'd go to the shows, I would see the explosiveness of the audience and the reaction. There was something that drew me to that. My little body would be tossed around [*laughs*]. It's this unreal, inexplicable burst of energy.

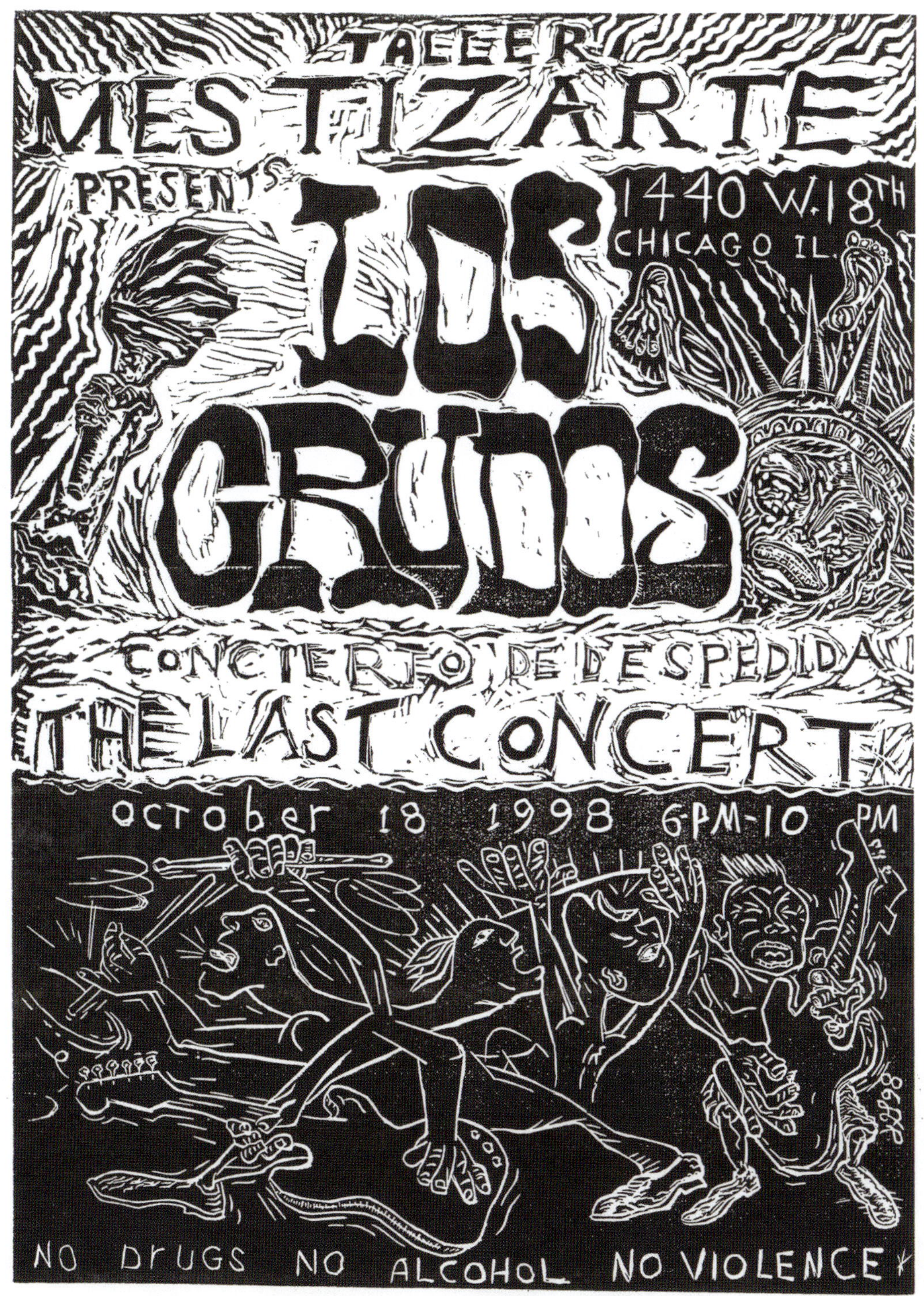

4.67. Flyer for Los Crudos last concert, Chicago, October 1998. Artist: José Guerrero.

It's originally a woodcut from this wonderful print shop in Pilsen called El Taller Mestizarte, and we played our last show there in '98 when we stopped for a while. That was a really great show. It was a fundraiser for them. —Martín Sorrondeguy

It felt like you could get hurt. It felt dangerous, but it felt wild. I don't know. It's so hard to express. The first time, I was afraid to go in the pit, and some pits were much more aggressive than others, depending on the band. I think there was an early DRI show I went to; it was out of control. I was like, "Oh my God, I just saw a guy limp away holding his leg. I think he really got hurt" [*laughs*].

I loved a lot of the old hardcore punk stuff. The first more DIY show I want to say was a Naked Raygun show, and wow! I just felt like it was raining bodies. I remember people stage diving at the Metro. It was nonstop. In the late eighties, you wouldn't see it anymore. Everything changed. The sound was changing, people were starting to explore other genres and mixes, and that's great, but I wanted to get back to a root. That's what we did with Los Crudos. Most of the bands weren't playing that style, so we stood out. Even though ten years earlier, or, eight years earlier, that was *the* sound, things shifted. We kind of went back to where we felt we really connected with that sound.

JUDITH: That makes a lot of sense, and it's interesting to me, especially because of the indie rock sound, what was going on in Wicker Park, and all those bands coming in around 1992 and '93, as a Chicago sound.

MARTÍN: They were great! I mean we played with a lot of bands from that era as well, and I think there were bands that were just like, "Oh yeah, wow, you're doing this thing that some people might've done earlier." So the Wicker Park thing, you had bands like Scissor Girls and the Flying Luttenbachers. A lot of bands were experimental, but supercool. But, yeah, we would play shows with bands like that. That was the beauty of it. We played with folk singers. We performed this important show in Pilsen with this drag queen. It was called the "Cabaret Rojo," and it was part of this cultural arts space Calles y Sueños, and so we did everything. We loved it.

JUDITH: So you were in Los Crudos, you were singing in Spanish, which was part of the determination you made. Can you say more about what that meant to you, and also what it might've meant for you to see non-Latine people in your audience, either singing back to you in Spanish or even singing the "We're that Spic Band" refrain. How did that feel to you on the other side of it as the performer?

MARTÍN: I think when I realized that this transcended certain—I don't want to call them barriers—it just transcended something, this invisible line. I was honored that there were non-Latino people singing along with me. There's some power there, that you are making the effort to communicate and put this energy out there with me. I remember when Crudos played in Japan, and the audience, I mean, they were singing along! They were enunciating as best as they could, and I was floored. I think punk for a lot of us felt international, it felt global. It felt like it didn't matter where you were from. That is the beauty of art is that it can move somebody, and it doesn't have to be necessarily in your language. We experienced a lot of that, and I think even in the US, if I was connecting with some young kid in the suburbs who maybe his parents were so afraid to raise them in the city or whatever their circumstances were and that kid is connecting with me and singing along with me—that is power! I was always moved by that. Music and heart, when it does that, it's a force to be reckoned with. I saw that definitely happened in Los Crudos because when we'd go on these tours, we would play in places that were so far from our world.

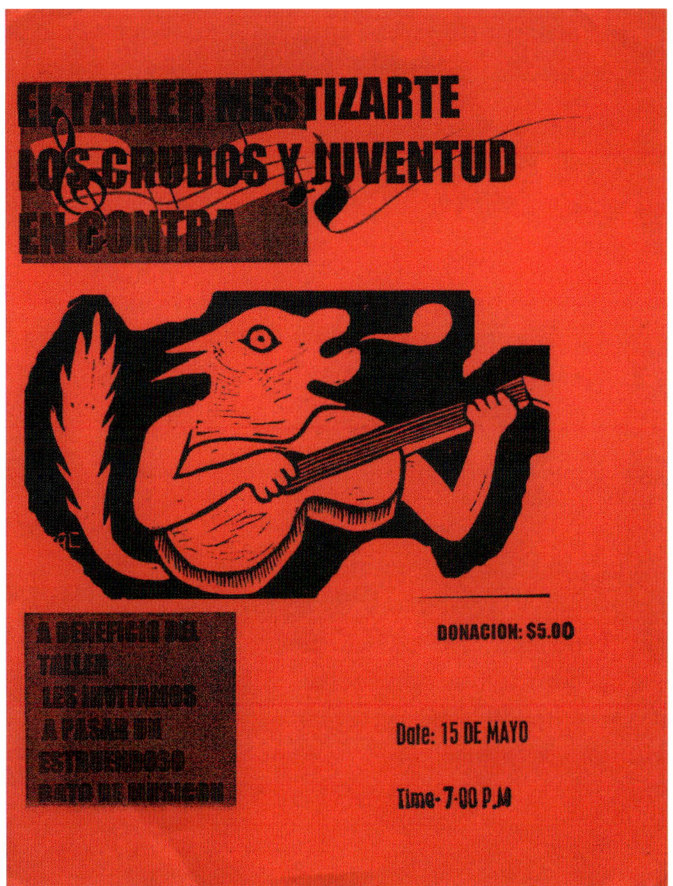

4.68. Flyer for Los Crudos show at El Taller Mestizarte, Chicago, circa 1995.

JUDITH: Talk about audience reactions in Japan versus South America and Mexico, where they related more directly to the lyrics about the problems of being from Latin America in the US or border issues or other types of oppression, and economics. How did you feel the difference in energy? Was it big, or was it more subtle?

MARTÍN: It's big. Let's say if I was playing in some US town and somebody got emotional about it, we would talk afterward. But then, when you crossed the border and you went to Mexico, Chile, Argentina, any of these countries, and we played, and you're talking another kind of energy. They know exactly what you're talking about. I think the first time we played in Mexico, we came back, and then somebody interviewed us and asked what was that like compared to the US, and we said, "The US is tame." That's all we can say is "tame" in comparison. Because with Crudos, when you look at those lyrics and you place them in Latin America, it goes right to the core of something, and when you're talking about military dictatorships or whatever, and you're singing this in Argentina, and they lived that. . . . That's where that song "Asesinos" came from. I was born in Uruguay, and my family had left Uruguay, and this is at the time of the *golpe* [military coup in 1973]. You realize: this isn't my song, this is *our* song. So, yeah, it just takes on another life, and the energy definitely shifts. I can't describe it besides saying it's at the core of who a lot of the people were who attend these shows, it's at their parents' core. It sounds really weak to say it hits home, but it does in this different way.

It definitely can also cause you trouble, depending where you're at. The last time we played Chile, a full-on riot broke out, and water tanks rolled in, the city street got destroyed, and they were looking for the band. We had to cancel everything from that point on in Chile. We were hiding out, and it was terrible. I remember being in the cab going to the airport to go to Argentina, and the cab driver says, "Oh, you're the band they're looking for," because it came out on the news. I was watching the news the morning after the show, and I'm watching us and they're saying, "Chilean punk band Los Crudos." They didn't know that we weren't Chilean. They were piecing things together, and the news would go out throughout the day, and then they finally, toward the end of the day, said, "a Chicago punk band Los Crudos" caused this riot. This is the thing, young people in other parts of the world are very angry about stuff, and they express their anger in ways that maybe US teens don't. Something happened. It went out of control.

We were being blamed for this riot, and it's like, "No, we didn't start a riot. You started the riot. We played a show, and how your youth are responding to what we're doing is something you created, not what we created." But I was scared. I was like, we got to get the hell out of here.

JUDITH: What a story! It's, to use a cliché, one of those "power of music" stories. There's revolutionary energy that gets stirred up. Your shows were so clearly involved in making those communal moments and that synergy, that's a testament to the power of it, but yeah, scary!

MARTÍN: Yeah [*laughs*]. I called home. I was like, "Something big just happened, and we may get arrested." I had family members sending me the US consulate's number. We literally were hiding out in a hotel in Santiago for close to two days until we had to leave. So it was a little intense.

JUDITH: I want to ask about your creative process. How do you put together a song? Do you bring lyrics to the band? Or do songs spring out of the moment?

MARTÍN: It could be I have an idea, or there's something that inspires me to want to write. I may have some feeling I want to write. It could be a lyrical idea first, or sometimes it could be a musical idea, like a sound or riff that I have in my head and I go, "Oh, let's play this, and I'm going to put some lyrics to it afterwards." With Los Crudos, at one point we did a record with Spitboy, it was a split LP. I remember with that record we had lost our drummer, and I became the drummer. So we wrote all these songs based on sound. It wasn't until we went into the studio to record it that I found myself writing half the lyrics on the spot. So it's been a little bit of everything, I think.

JUDITH: Let's turn to Limp Wrist. You had a last show in Chicago with Los Crudos in 1998, and you were already starting Limp Wrist at that time. How did that transition work?

MARTÍN: I had come out during Los Crudos, so in the last Los Crudos record, there were two songs in particular that I wrote that definitely dealt with my queerness. I made these wonderful connections during the time of Los Crudos, and I remember reaching out to certain friends who we knew were gay. We were like, "Hey, you're gay, I'm gay. Cool!" I thought they were cool people, and I thought, wouldn't it be great to do a band that really just went full on. Los Crudos was a wonderful project. I'm still connected to Crudos in so many ways, but it was also a very heavy project. I just felt so weighed down. It felt like a massive responsibility, and it was tough to carry that for a while. I felt that my punk needed to be a little more fun for a bit. While Crudos was going on, I had this life that was outside of punk that was going to house clubs, going to gay clubs and bars, and kind of having this other life at the same time. I was enjoying that, and it created this beautiful balance. The rapid-fire political, aggressive Crudos, but then . . . I needed my time to unwind, just tap into another part of myself.

I thought, "Wow, wouldn't it be wonderful if there was a band that could be political but fun, and it could have a lot more humor injected into it. That's what became Limp Wrist. It was almost my dream band because I didn't want to stop playing music and stop writing songs. I wanted to keep on with that, but I wanted to channel more energy into this other part of me and put that out there as well. So Limp Wrist was the perfect vehicle for that. It became a lot more fun, but also it was jolting for people, like, "Oh, how could you have been in Crudos and then do this?" But it was happening all the time in my world. I just wasn't expressing it with music.

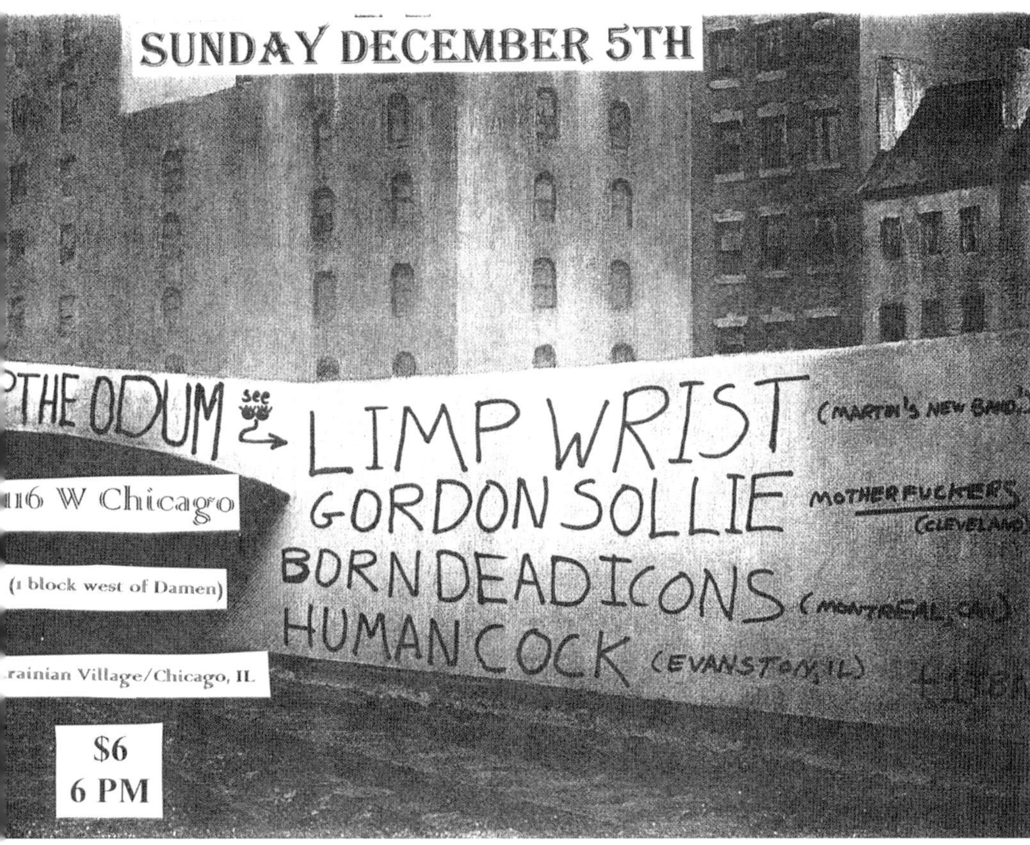

4.69. Flyer for Limp Wrist's first show at ODUM, Chicago, December 1999.

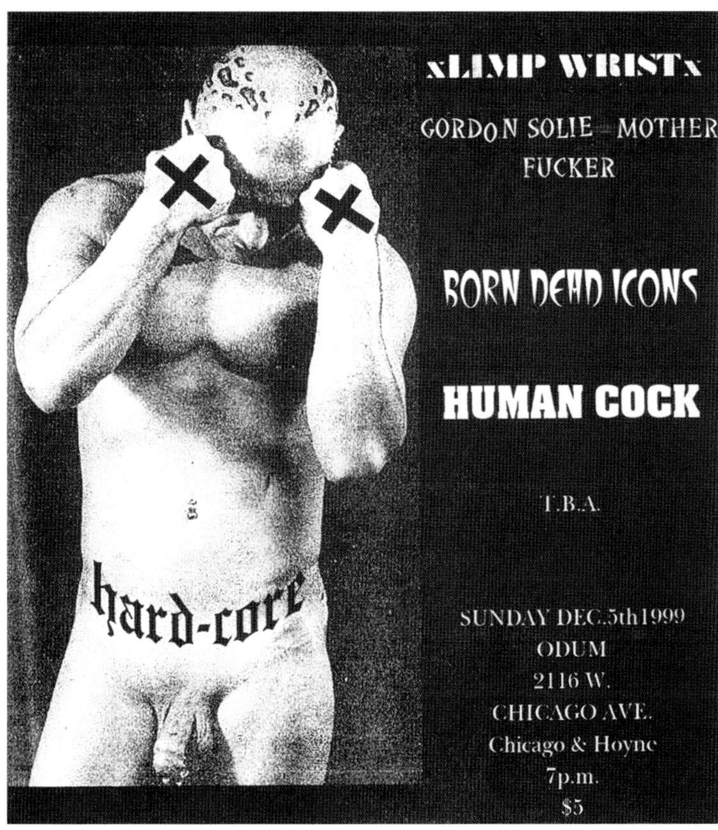

4.70. Flyer for Limp Wrist's first show at ODUM, Chicago, December 1999.

JUDITH: This is what intersectionality looks like, right?

MARTÍN: Yes, exactly! We were all familiar with intersectionality a long time ago. We're going, "Hey, there's a lot to us. We're not this singular thing."

JUDITH: I want to ask about the song "The Ode" because it offers this beautiful history of queer punk, and the name checking is great. You mention Jayne County, who is also in this book.

MARTÍN: Yay!

JUDITH: So I'm wondering about that sense of history. Do you feel that's an important aspect of your project in both Los Crudos, but also in Limp Wrist? Do punks need to know their history?

MARTÍN: Yeah. Yeah, we do. That was an interesting time because I think people weren't connecting the dots enough, like queer and punk are synonymous. It was important for me and for other people, maybe, who followed what I was doing previously with Crudos to realize this is not that different. This is connected, and there's a real rich history in this.

I think with time people forget the roots. So a lot of the "hardcore scene," and I say that in quotes, cause it can get pretty hard, and it can get super masculine—I don't want us to be cheap and say "bro," but it *is* very bro. It tends to get lumped into, "Oh, it's super hetero. It's super jock, it's super white, it's super suburban." As a punk, I felt it was my job to challenge that. So for me, connecting it to the history of the people who came before us was critical. Now you're hearing so much coming out about these histories. There are massive efforts, studies being done on the history of punk. But for a long time

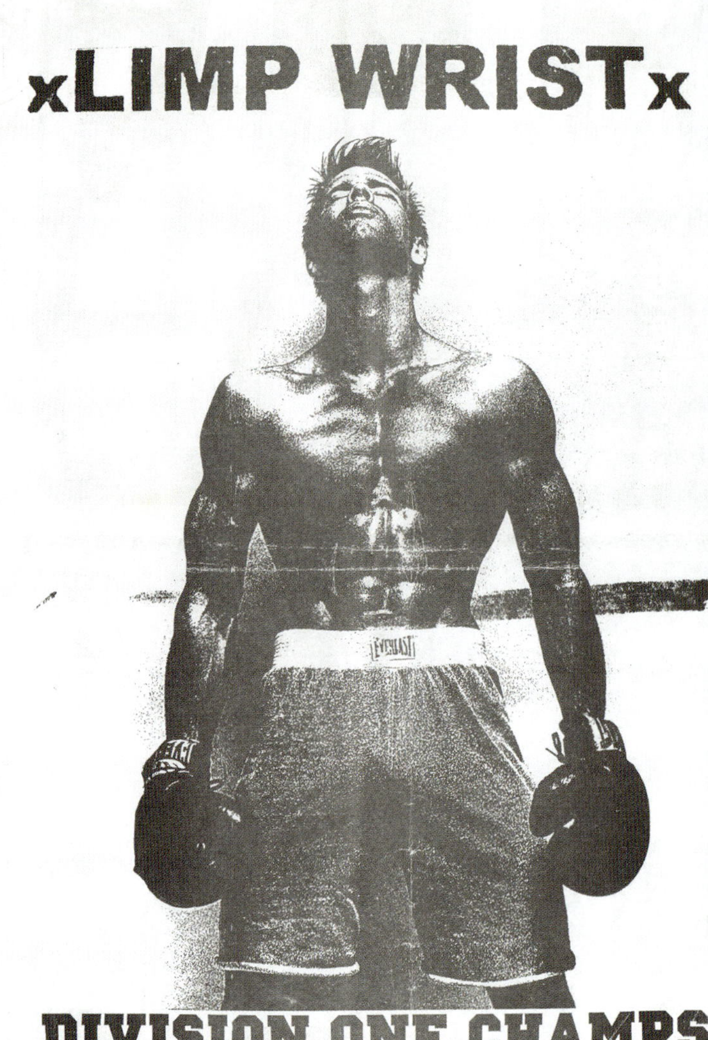

4.71. Front of lyric sheet for Limp Wrist, 1999. Design: Martín Sorrondeguy.

I was making fun of the alpha male straight edge scene for sure. Some straight edge band of the time might have used that Division One Champs on their record. I was kind of poking at it. —Martín Sorrondeguy

Editors' note: the straight edge hardcore band Floorpunch released an EP called Division One Champs in 1996.

I remember the band in a Kinko's late at night in Philly laying these out. This was a lyric sheet for our first show ever in 1999. I would just hand these out. The first band that I recall getting a lyric sheet at a show ever from was Fugazi, and I still have them. I have two different lyrics sheets from two different shows in the eighties: their first show ever and the second one in Chicago. I thought it was brilliant. It was saying, "This is important to us. The lyrics are important." So we did a similar thing, really just wanting people to laugh with us, but also to see where we were coming from in terms of making fun of the hyper-masculine hardcore scene, straight edge scenes. That's what we did with the artwork. It's this super queered-out image. We threw the Judge shirt logo on it. Judge is a New York hardcore band. A lot of tough guys love that band. I'm sure it probably upset some people, but it's OK. If it's not upsetting somebody that's not punk.

—Martín Sorrondeguy

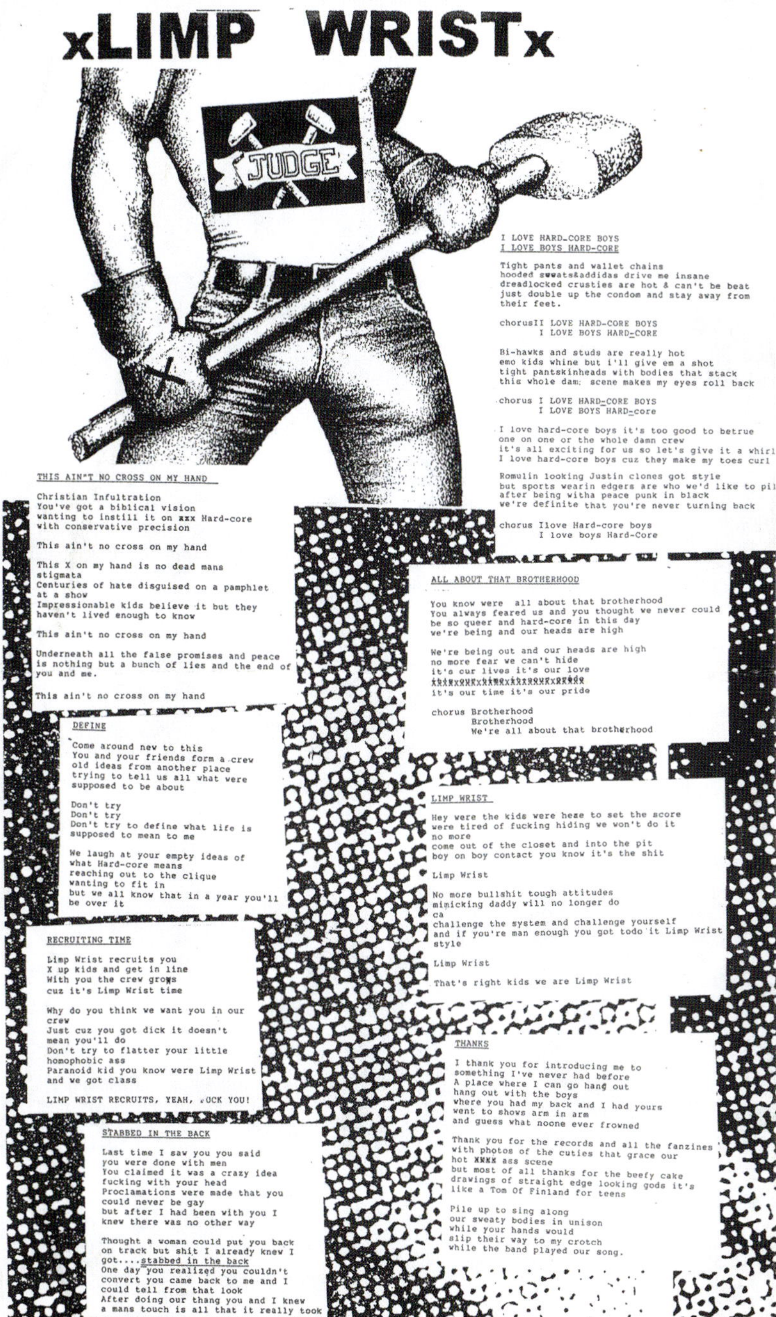

xLIMP WRISTx

I LOVE HARD-CORE BOYS
I LOVE BOYS HARD-CORE

Tight pants and wallet chains
hooded sweats&addidas drive me insane
dreadlocked crusties are hot & can't be beat
just double up the condom and stay away from
their feet.

chorusI I LOVE HARD-CORE BOYS
I LOVE BOYS HARD-CORE

Bi-hawks and studs are really hot
emo kids whine but i'll give em a shot
tight pantskinheads with bodies that stack
this whole dam: scene makes my eyes roll back

chorus I LOVE HARD-CORE BOYS
I LOVE BOYS HARD-core

I love hard-core boys it's too good to betrue
one on one or the whole damn crew
it's all exciting for us so let's give it a whirl
I love hard-core boys cuz they make my toes curl

Romulin looking Justin clones got style
but sports wearin edgers are who we'd like to pil
after being witha peace punk in black
we're definite that you're never turning back

chorus Ilove Hard-core boys
I love boys Hard-Core

THIS AIN"T NO CROSS ON MY HAND

Christian Infultration
You've got a biblical vision
wanting to instill it on xxx Hard-core
with conservative precision

This ain't no cross on my hand

This X on my hand is no dead mans
stigmata
Centuries of hate disguised on a pamphlet
at a show
Impressionable kids believe it but they
haven't lived enough to know

This ain't no cross on my hand

Underneath all the false promises and peace
is nothing but a bunch of lies and the end of
you and me.

This ain't no cross on my hand

ALL ABOUT THAT BROTHERHOOD

You know were all about that brotherhood
You always feared us and you thought we never could
be so queer and hard-core in this day
we're being and our heads are high

We're being out and our heads are high
no more fear we can't hide
it's cur lives it's our love
XXXXXXXXXXXXXXXXXXXXXXX
it's our time it's our pride

chorus Brotherhood
Brotherhood
We're all about that brotherhood

DEFINE

Come around new to this
You and your friends form a crew
old ideas from another place
trying to tell us all what were
supposed to be about

Don't try
Don't try
Don't try to define what life is
supposed to mean to me

We laugh at your empty ideas of
what Hard-core means
reaching out to the clique
wanting to fit in
but we all know that in a year you'll
be over it

LIMP WRIST

Hey were the kids were here to set the score
were tired of fucking hiding we won't do it
no more
come out of the closet and into the pit
boy on boy contact you know it's the shit

Limp Wrist

No more bullshit tough attitudes
mimicking daddy will no longer do
ca
challenge the system and challenge yourself
and if you're man enough you got todo it Limp Wrist
style

Limp Wrist

That's right kids we are Limp Wrist

RECRUITING TIME

Limp Wrist recruits you
X up kids and get in line
With you the crew grows
cuz it's Limp Wrist time

Why do you think we want you in our
crew
Just cuz you got dick it doesn't
mean you'll do
Don't try to flatter your little
homophobic ass
Paranoid kid you know were Limp Wrist
and we got class

LIMP WRIST RECRUITS, YEAH, FUCK YOU!

THANKS

I thank you for introducing me to
something I've never had before
A place where I can go hang out
hang out with the boys
where you had my back and I had yours
went to shows arm in arm
and guess what noone ever frowned

Thank you for the records and all the fanzines
with photos of the cuties that grace our
hot XXXX ass scene
but most of all thanks for the beefy cake
drawings of straight edge looking gods it's
like a Tom Of Finland for teens

Pile up to sing along
our sweaty bodies in unison
while your hands would
slip their way to my crotch
while the band played our song.

STABBED IN THE BACK

Last time I saw you you said
you were done with men
You claimed it was a crazy idea
fucking with your head
Proclamations were made that you
could never be gay
but after I had been with you I
knew there was no other way

Thought a woman could put you back
on track but shit I already knew I
got....stabbed in the back
One day you realized you couldn't
convert you came back to me and I
could tell from that look
After doing our thang you and I knew
a mans touch is all that it really took

4.72. Limp Wrist lyric sheet, circa 1999.

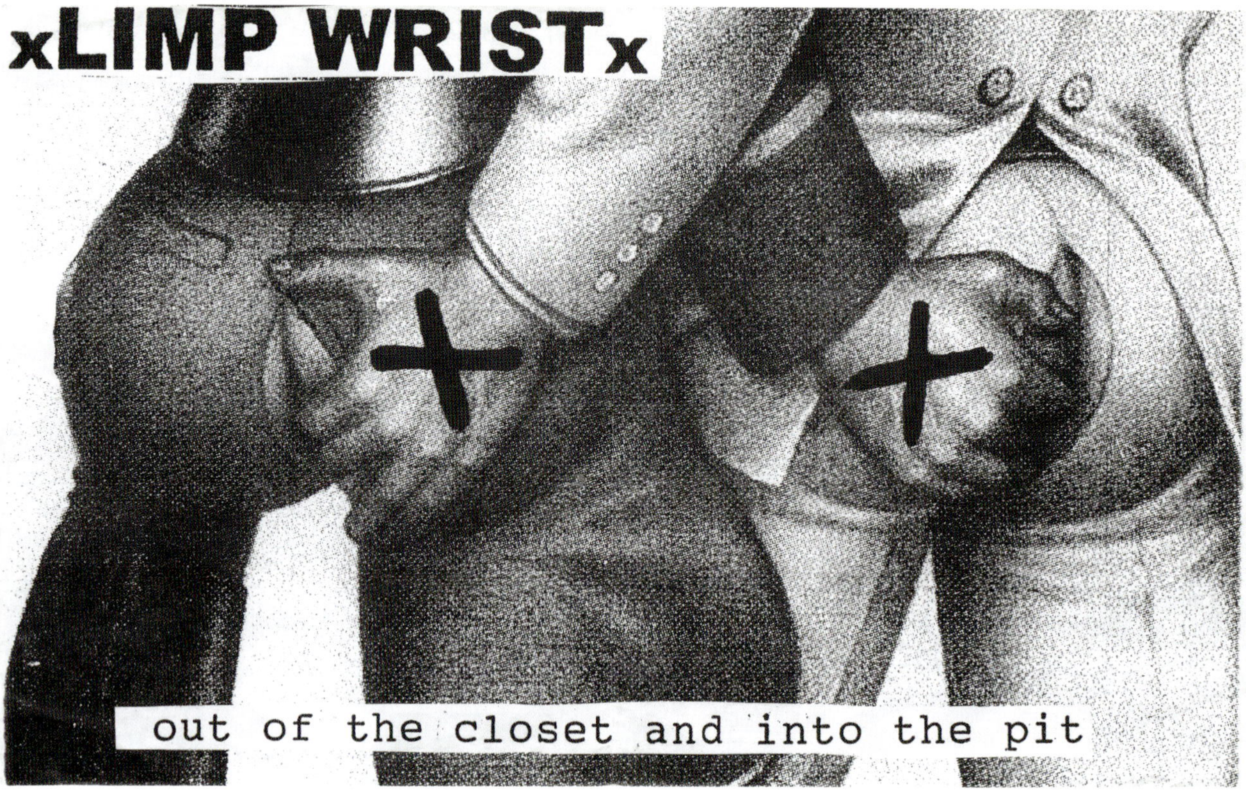

4.73. Flyer for Limp Wrist. Design: Martín Sorrondeguy.

4.74. Flyer for Limp Wrist show at ODUM, Chicago, 2001.

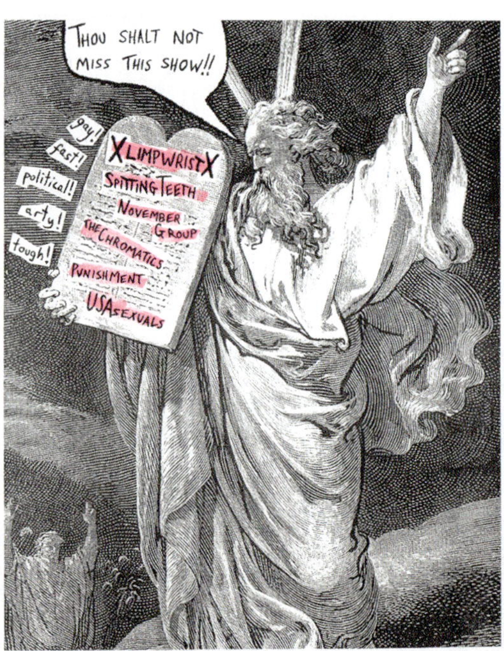

4.75. Flyer for Limp Wrist show at the Paradox, Seattle, 2001.

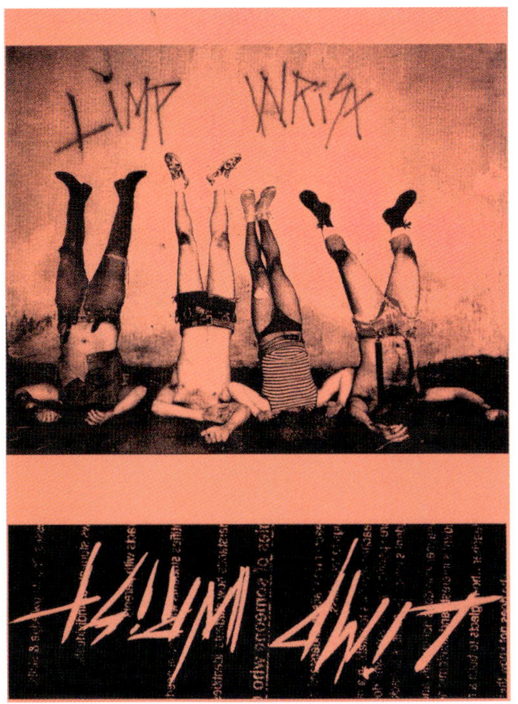

4.76. Cassette J-card. Photo: Karoline Collins.

there wasn't this information out there. So we were the storytellers. I think "The Ode" was telling the story. Trans punks like Jayne County. . . . I'm doing a shout-out to the queers who came before us, you know? Limp Wrist didn't invent queer punk, and we knew that. But maybe a lot of young kids don't know about that. So that song was kind of like a banner. Like, "Yay! Here's some names. Some people to look into."

JUDITH: Yeah, go do your homework.

MARTÍN: Yes. For sure. People will say punk is a white person thing, or punk is a straight, a hetero thing. I'm always one of the first to say, "No, it's not!" There's so much evidence that will prove that theory wrong. But people, they like to hang on to their story about that.

JUDITH: One of the brilliant things about Limp Wrist is how you call out the homoeroticism that's embedded in hardcore shows anyway.

MARTÍN: Hello! I know, but that was part of the humor, right? We were poking fun at, especially the straight edge world. The straight edge world was super guy—not gay, but *guy*. You can play with that, right? But it was poking at it. "Yeah, you're all over each other. You guys are piling on each other. There's so much physical contact." So we made fun of that. I mean, we thought it was great, but also funny. It was worthy to use as material for some of our songs, for sure.

JUDITH: Were you also speaking to or critiquing, to some extent, parts of the gay culture? I'm just thinking about the rise of bear subculture.

MARTÍN: Oh yeah. Yeah.

JUDITH: And against the Castro clone look.

MARTÍN: Mm-hmm [*affirmative*]. Yeah, we definitely were critical. We used to say we were too queer for the punks and too punk for the queers. We were always in this weird space because we were also very critical of mainstream gay culture. People say heteronormative, we say homonormative, because there is a homonormative thing that happens. Even with the bear stuff—I love parts of the bear culture, but I'm also very critical. Within queerness, you found its faults, and you were like, "OK, so there's things to be addressed on all sides. Nothing is pure or perfect." Right? Even under the LGBTQI umbrella, there's issues and problems. It could be racial, it could be misogynistic. So we're going for everybody. Nobody escaped. But with that too, you have to be critical of yourself. We were also criticizing and putting a lot of things under the microscope and examining it. And we did that with the more mainstream elements of gay culture and punk as well.

JUDITH: Did you have a large gay following in the Limp Wrist era?

MARTÍN: You know what, it's hard to say. A lot of the homocore stuff and the queercore stuff that came before us, a lot of it sonically—I loved a lot of it—but sonically it was more pop and alternative. In terms of rapid-fire hardcore punk, there wasn't a ton of that. So we definitely were getting a following from everywhere. What we found is some kid who was at the show maybe in 1999 or 2000 would come up to me in 2015 and say, "I'm out now, but when I first saw you, I remember just being like, 'Oh my God, what is this?'"

I think it's always hard to gauge. I remember it was in the Crudos era, I started to see in Chicago, this little crew who would follow us. They were rough trans kids who followed us through Limp Wrist. I think that's a good question to ask other queer people, how they viewed Limp Wrist, but we definitely had kids who connected to the band.

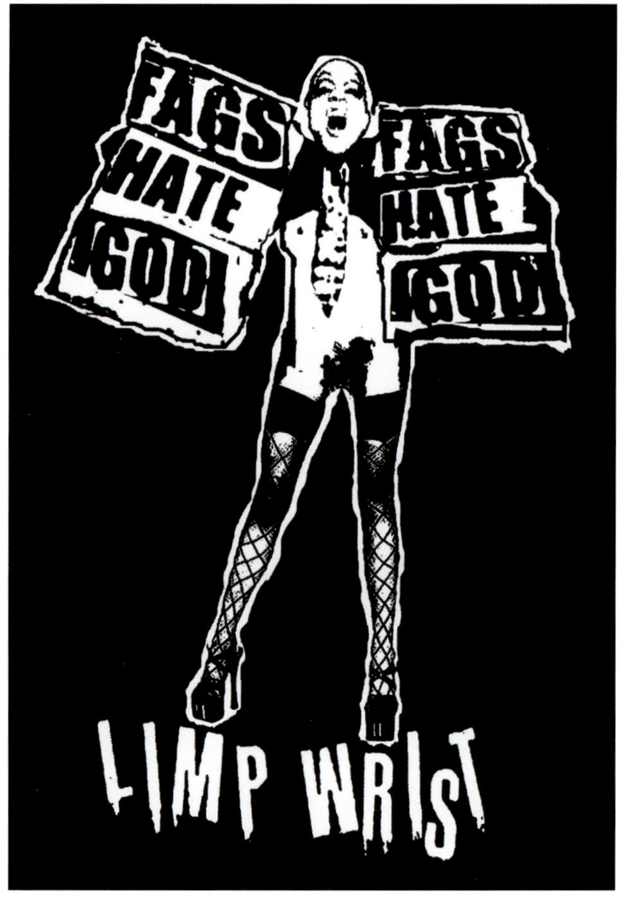

4.77. Flyer and T-shirt design by Martín Sorrondeguy.

JUDITH: You have that song "Crusin' at the Show," which is a story of a guy who wanders into your show and is getting cruised, but doesn't realize it's a queercore show.

MARTÍN: I mean, hey, we were always honest! [*laughs*] We're like: there's guys at these shows who are hot, we're not gonna lie. Again, that was a playful era for Limp Wrist, that first record. We wrote a lot of the songs in Philadelphia at some twenty-four-hour diner in the gay neighborhood. I forget the name of it. We would be out there two in the morning, three in the morning having coffee late at night, and just writing lyrics. We were definitely picking at the scene and going for it. Yeah.

JUDITH: It's interesting you brought up Philadelphia because it brings me to the question of regionalism and scene locations. So Limp Wrist didn't really have a particular location, did it?

MARTÍN: No. I was in Chicago, two members were living in Philadelphia, and another one was in upstate New York. So we were spread out. I was taking Greyhound buses to go to band practice in Philadelphia. A majority of the members lived up on the East Coast, and I was so determined to do this project that I was traveling and going on the buses up to Philly to work on material.

JUDITH: I think a lot of people consider Limp Wrist more of a San Francisco band, or Bay Area band, but it really isn't.

MARTÍN: No, it's not. What happened was one of the members from Philly and I, we migrated to the West Coast at one point. Then we had two people living in San Francisco, and

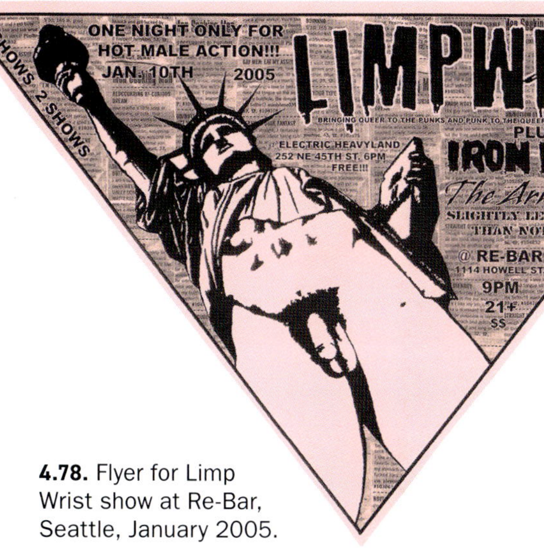

4.78. Flyer for Limp Wrist show at Re-Bar, Seattle, January 2005.

a lot of what was happening would be on either the West Coast or East Coast. We were active in the later years in California, particularly. I also lived in Southern California and would book shows, so there was a lot happening down there. That's probably why people associated us with California.

JUDITH: I like the fact that there's no particular location for this band.

MARTÍN: Yeah. A lot of punk bands get superlocal, like, "Oh, we're from this city," and you hear that all the time. Limp Wrist is, "We have no home."

JUDITH: I want to ask about the constellation of queerness, Spanish, Latine identity, and the Catholic Church. As you mentioned before, there are tensions there. Did you ever feel, yourself, a sense of tension between the two parts of your identity as, perhaps, complicated by the Catholicism in the Latin community? Or was that something that drove you to be a little bit more rebellious?

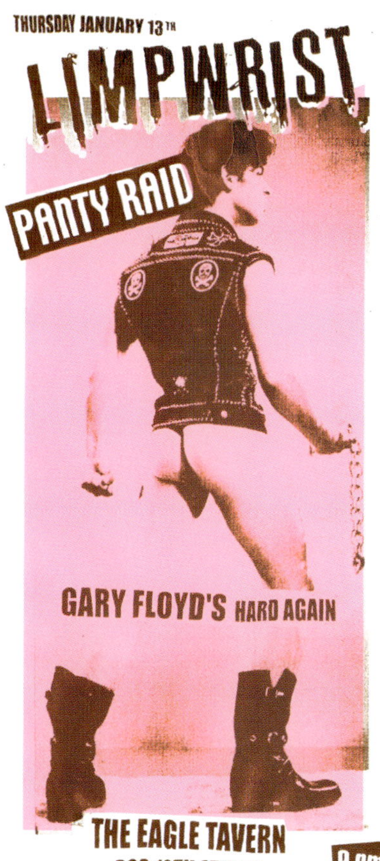

4.79. Flyer for Limp Wrist show at the Eagle Tavern, San Francisco, January 2005.

MARTÍN: Absolutely, Judith. I had already worked on so much of that earlier on in my life, because there was a point even before Crudos when I was battling myself and all these things that I was raised in, and the church was a huge one. I remember doing art projects around this, and trying to undo so much that had been done. I had already gone through this struggle, and I recall even having a push-and-pull with my mom about it early on. So when I was ready for Limp Wrist, I was *ready* for Limp Wrist. This T-shirt we made? It is so out there that I could see it causing problems for people.

JUDITH: The "Fags Hate God" T-shirt?

MARTÍN: Yeah. It's wild because I put that shirt together. It was a play on "God hates fags." OK, you know what? I'm not going to be like, "Oh, this is not true. God loves us all." No, no—"Fags hate God!" [*laughs*] We were all about taking a stand and being like, "No, no, we're going to put something out there that's just going to smack right up against those people who are on this whole 'God hates fags' thing" (4.77).

JUDITH: So you weren't worried about alienating some part of your former audience? Or you didn't think that was going to happen?

MARTÍN: You know what? It's OK if it happens. We all tap in and tap out when we can, or when we feel comfortable or uncomfortable. As a punk, it's not my job to make everyone comfortable. In the beginning, Crudos made a lot of punks uncomfortable in Chicago. I had old friends who were like, "Why are you singing in Spanish? Why are you doing that?" They felt alienated because they didn't understand the lyrics, but I was saying, "You got to understand there's something else going on here." There were people who felt alienated then. So when Limp Wrist came about . . . yeah, punk should make people a little uneasy. That's what punk is about. There's no reason for punk to exist if not making somebody stop or pause and think about something.

JUDITH: Since you've worked in the schools as an educator, and thinking about the relationship of your punk identity to your educator identity, how do you see those in concert or in tension with each other? Also, what do you think an educator like me should be teaching about punk?

MARTÍN: I don't teach punk, but as a punk, I think understanding the dynamics. You have these key figures in punk, but there's so much around it that is happening and supporting it. Key figures can't survive without the whole. So much emphasis gets put on musicians and certain vocalists or lyricists. But the reality is, the fanzine

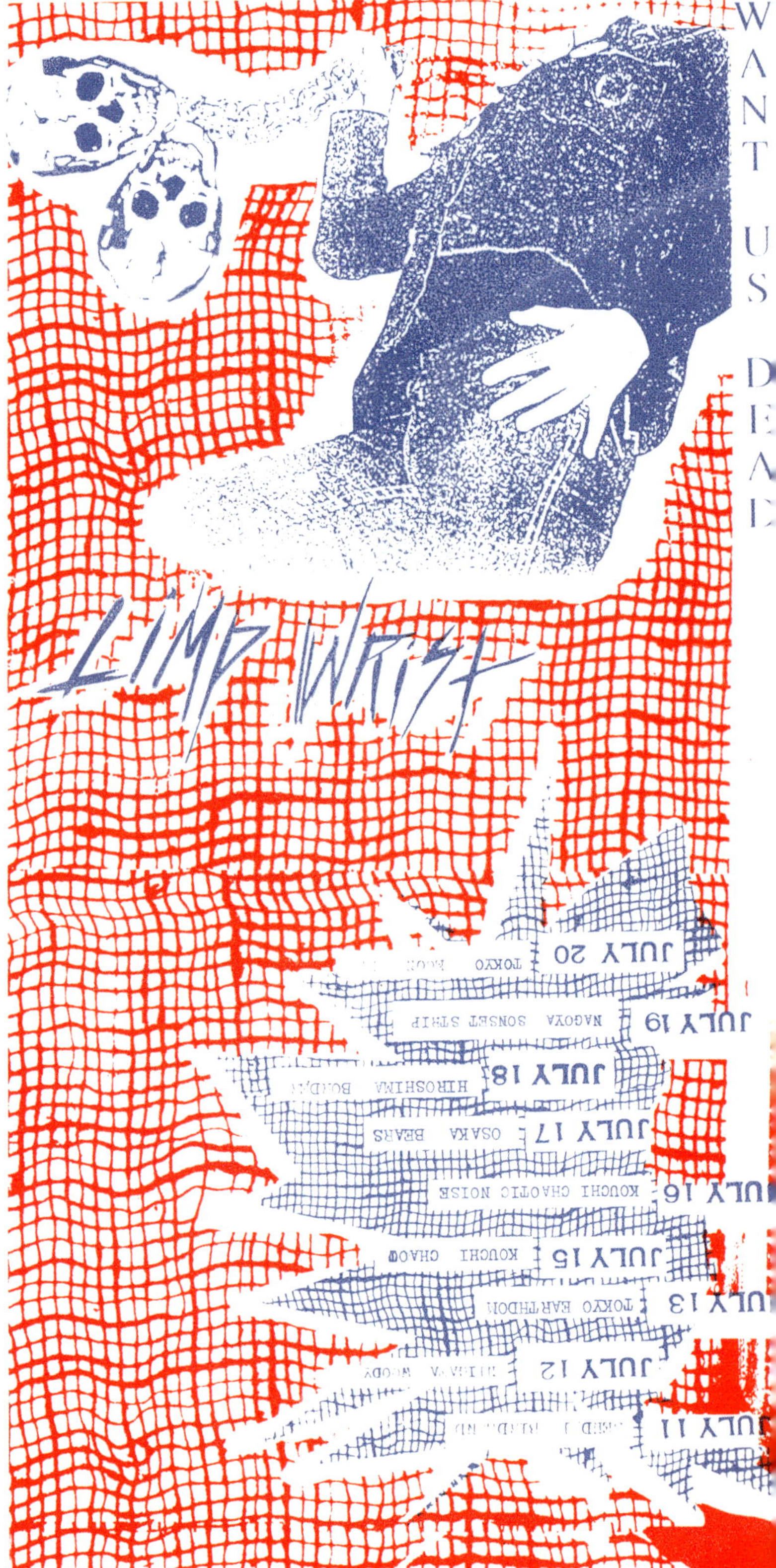

4.80. Flyer for Limp Wrist Japan tour, July 2008. Design: Martín Sorrondeguy.

writers and all the people who are all participating in their own unique way, that to me is important because it speaks to the collaborativeness of punk. One can't exist without the other.

I also feel that it would be great to look at its impacts on greater society. We can see things that are being talked about in mainstream culture right now that were never touched twenty years, thirty years ago, but punk was talking about them. I think back to, I want to say it's issue number six of *Maximumrocknroll* with the Dicks on the cover. It says "commie faggot band." It's 1983, and we're talking: visibility where? And this is on the cover of this magazine. I don't think any of the old gay papers would be that bold. So I think it's punk's place in arts and culture to push and challenge things.

For me as an educator, I just think punk provided me—not just provided me—I *found* these tools that I needed to learn how to use and adapt them to whatever came my way in life. So, I use a lot of the same tools when I work with students. I think there's so much that punk has offered to the world, but because it's punk, you ain't getting shit of recognition. I laugh about this because in San Antonio I had won a first-time filmmaker award when I made *Beyond the Screams*, and I went on stage and they handed me this award at the San Antonio cultural art space. And I said, "Hey, thank you. We're not used to winning anything." All I know is, for me at least, punk has always been about giving, giving, giving, and that's kind of how I still view it.

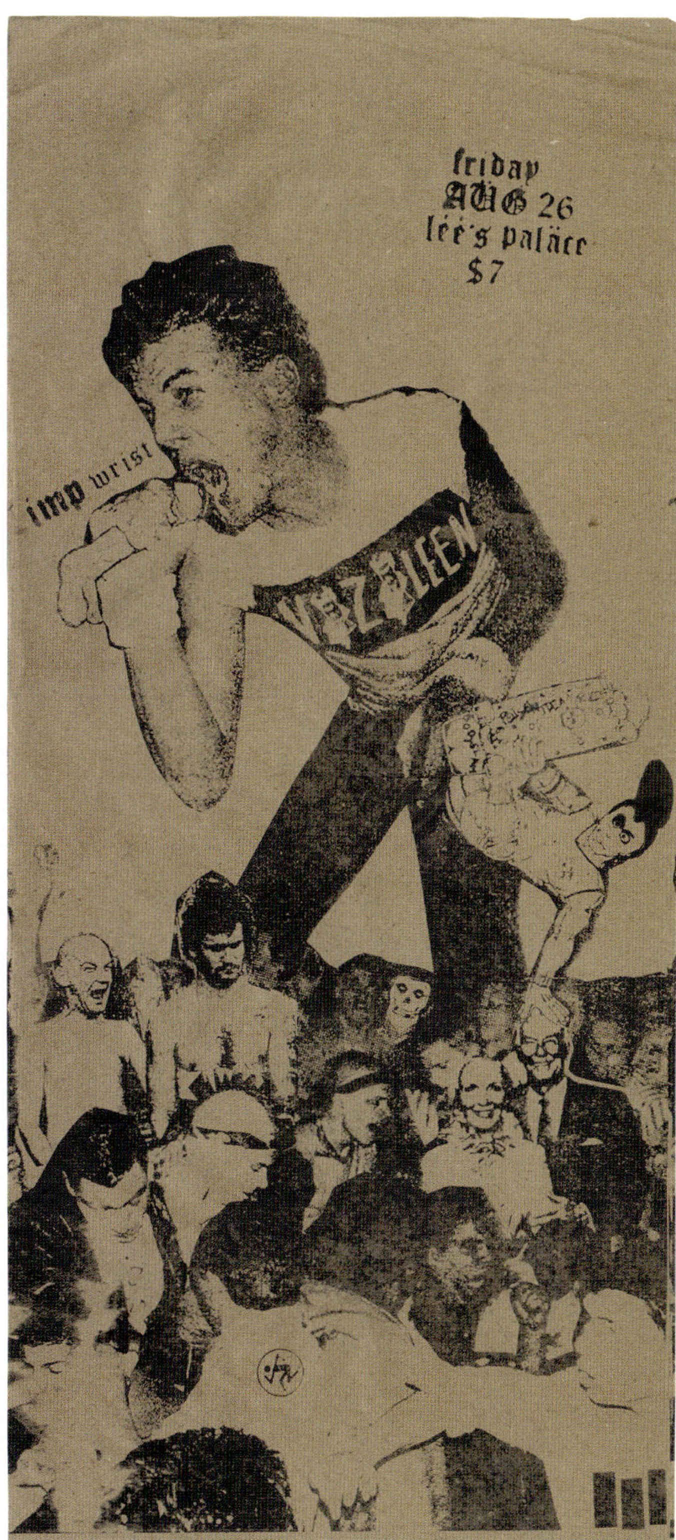

4.81. Flyer for Los Crudos show at Lee's Palace, Toronto, August 2005. Commissioned by Will Munro, designed and printed by Michael Comeau, courtesy the Estate of Will Munro and Paul Petro Contemporary Art, Toronto.

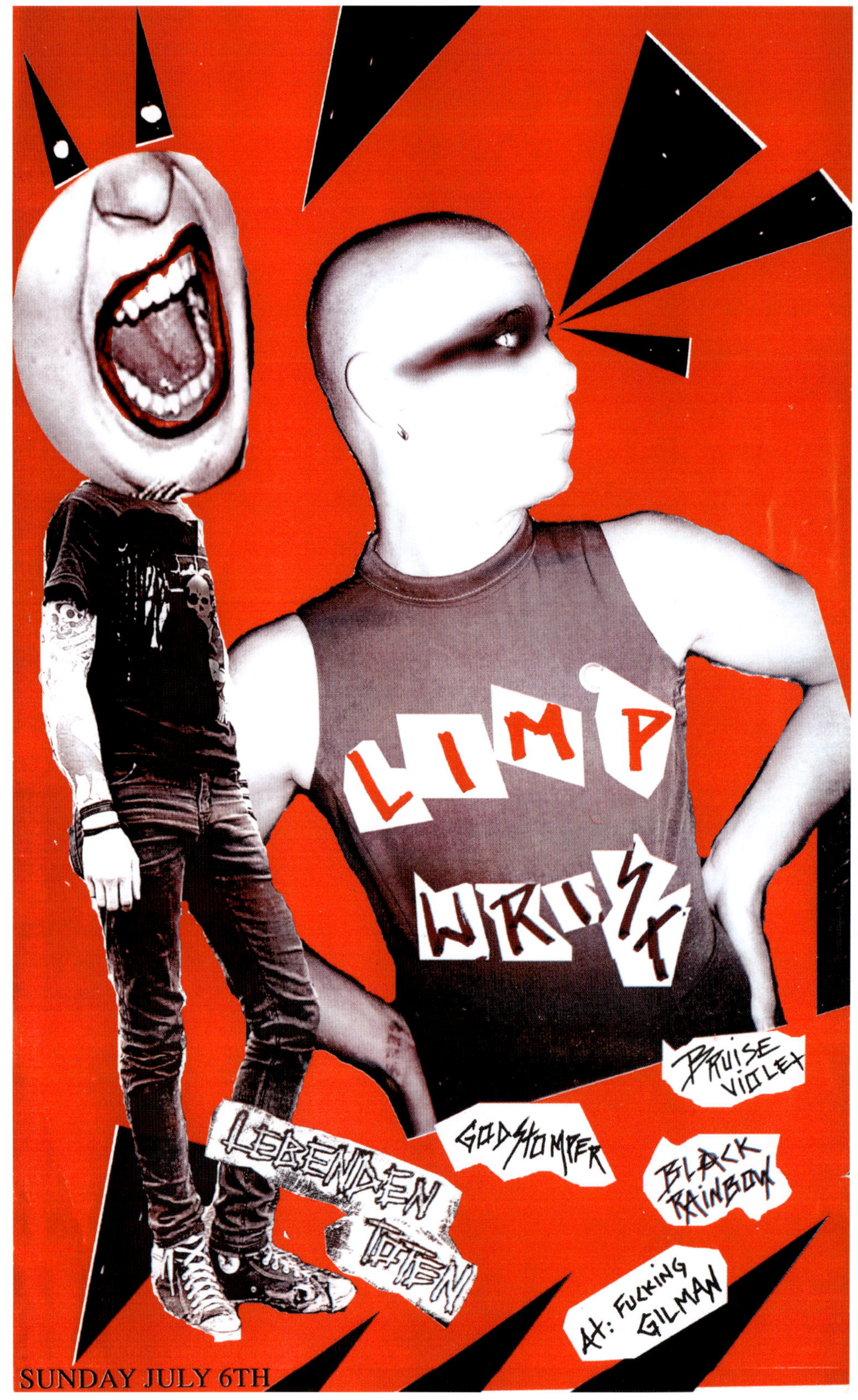

4.82. Flyer for Limp Wrist show at Gilman, Berkeley, July 2008. Design: Martín Sorrondeguy.

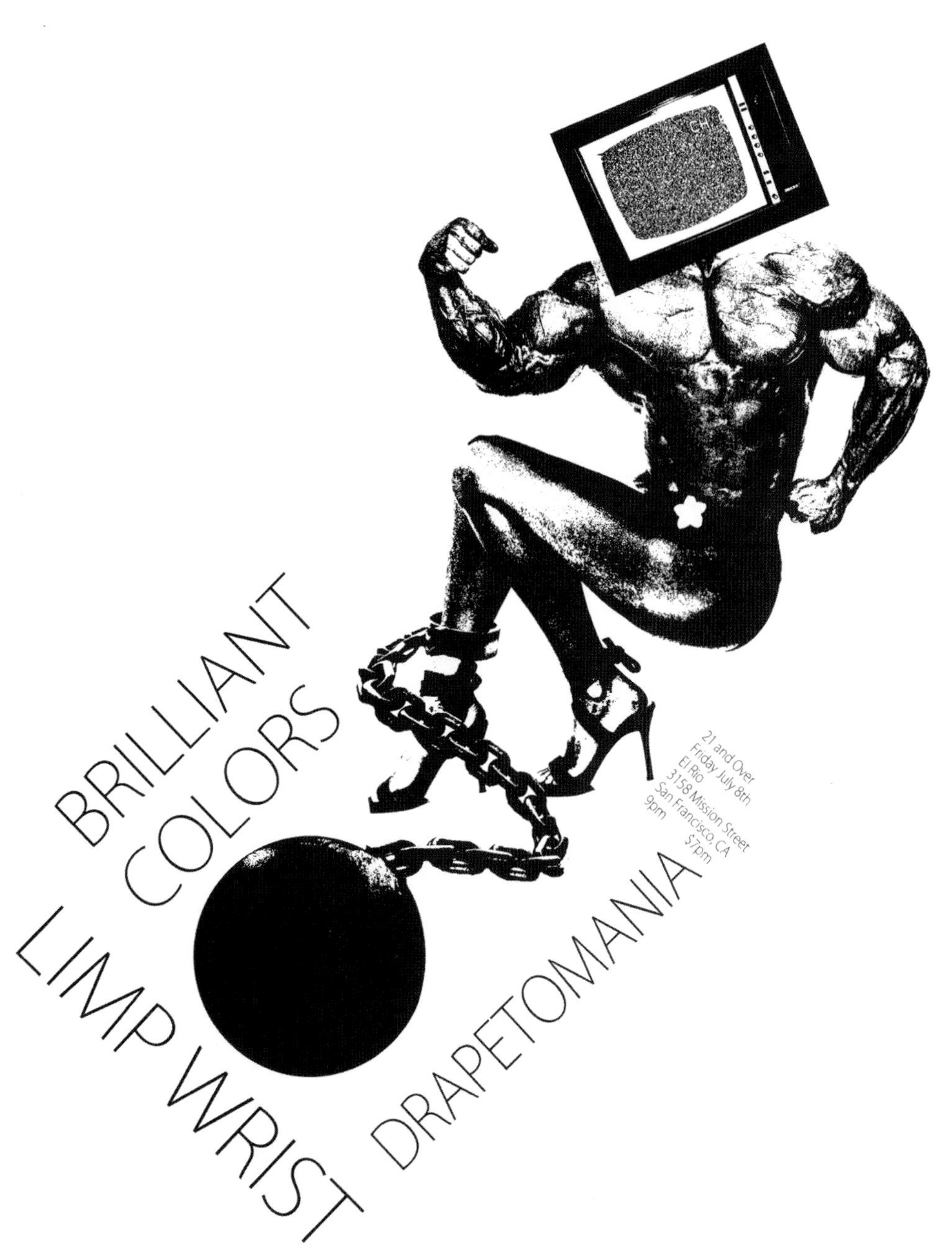

4.83. Flyer for Limp Wrist show at El Rio, San Francisco, circa 2011. Design: Martín Sorrondeguy.

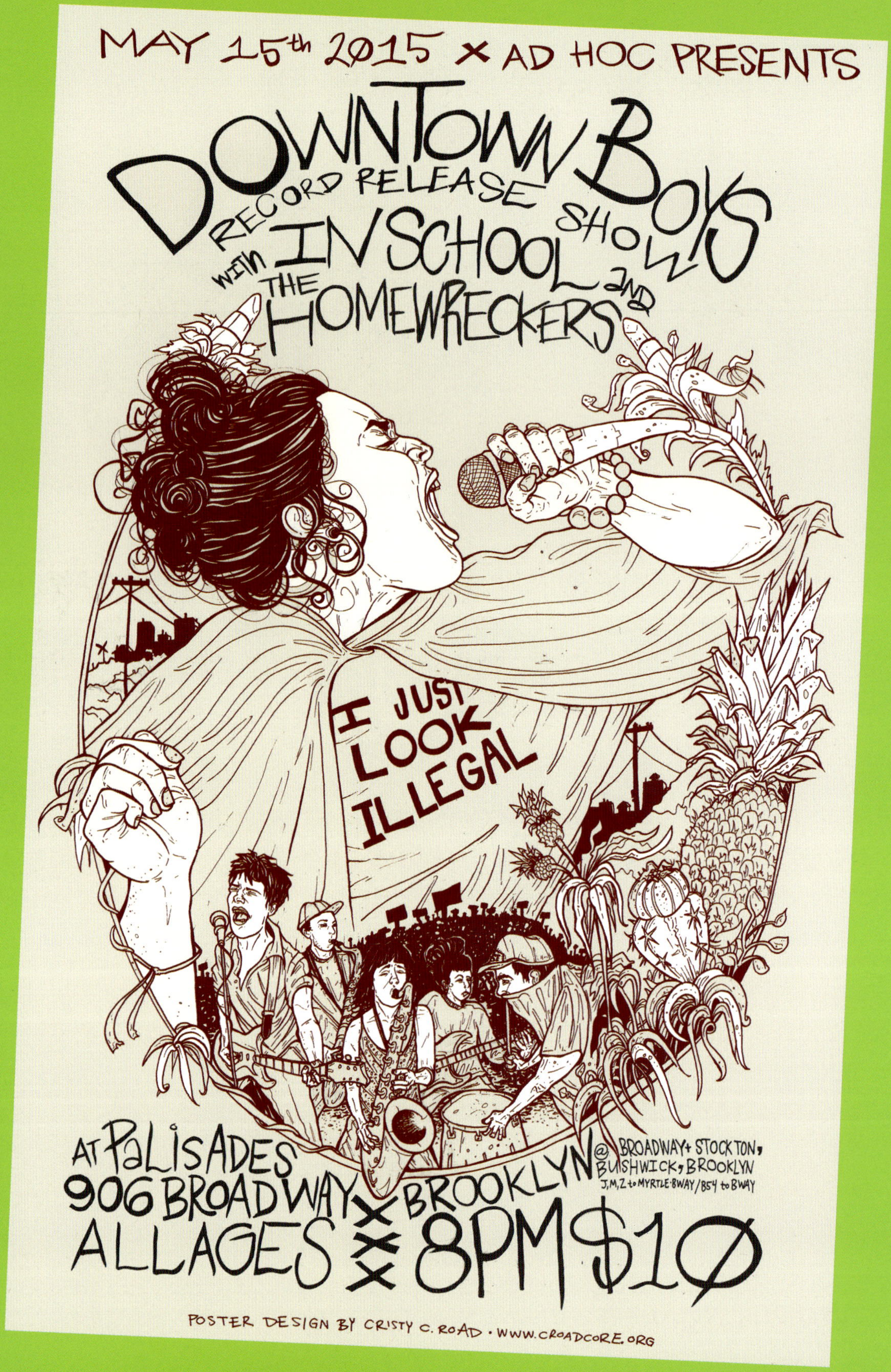

MAY 15th 2015 × AD HOC PRESENTS

DOWNTOWN BOYS

RECORD RELEASE SHOW

with IN SCHOOL and THE HOMEWRECKERS

I JUST LOOK ILLEGAL

AT PALISADES

906 BROADWAY × BROOKLYN

@ BROADWAY + STOCKTON, BUSHWICK, BROOKLYN

J, M, Z to MYRTLE-BWAY / B54 to BWAY

ALL AGES ××× 8PM $10

POSTER DESIGN BY CRISTY C. ROAD • WWW.CROADCORE.ORG

Punk and the Means of Production

CH. 19

NO DREAM OR NIGHTMARE DEFERRED

VICTORIA RUIZ

DEFINITIONS: Have you ever filled out a job application, paperwork for some type of social service benefit, or basically any type of form that ties you to something else? Likely, I'd guess, yes. And we always add our name. Our title, often from birth, from the womb or from a chosen identity. With PUNK, your definition of it, knowledge of it, and expression of it, is just like adding your name to it. It is impossible to take part in punk without your own ideas, even if punk is a complete questioning of what punk means.

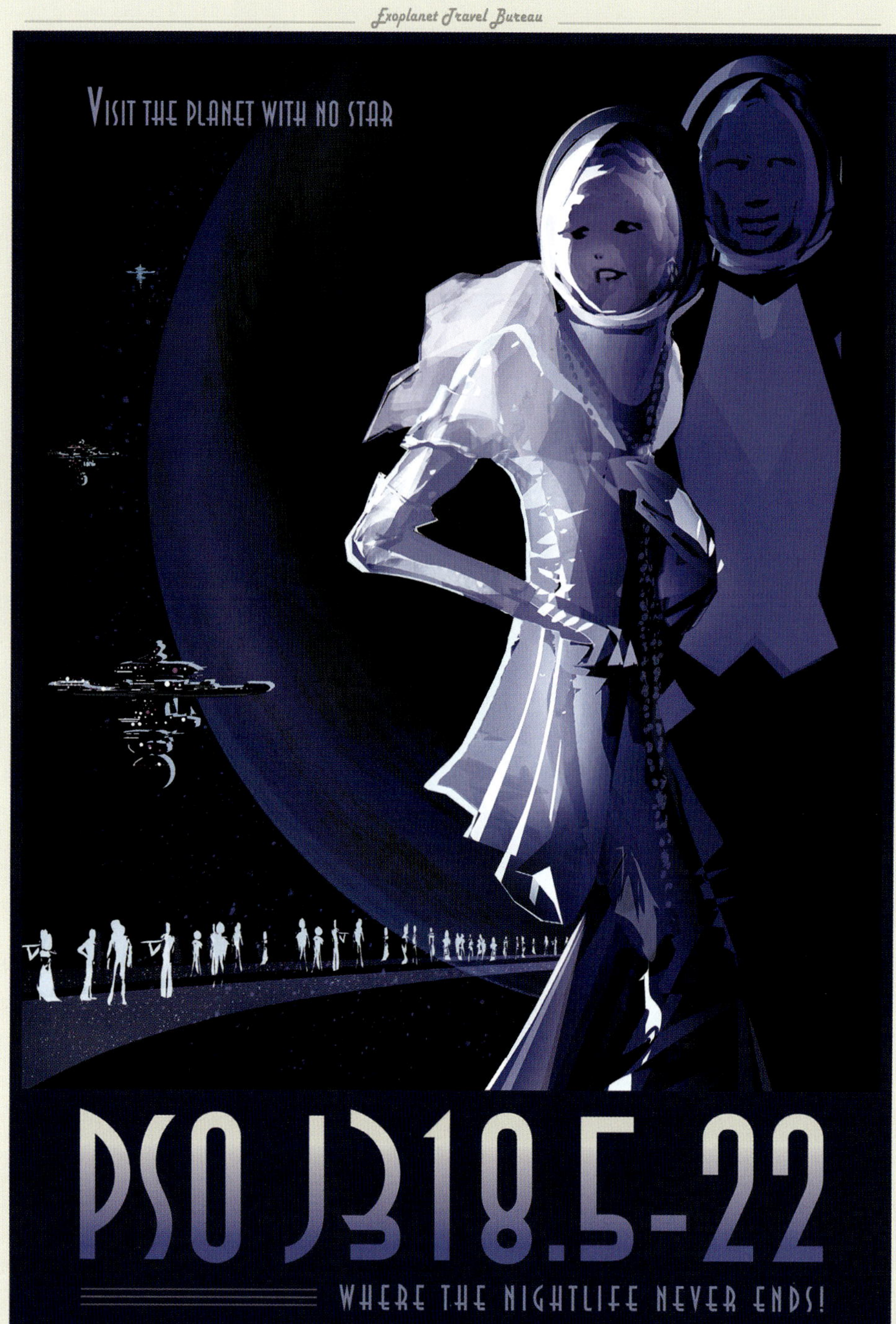

4.84. NASA Jet Propulsion Laboratory at the California Institute of Technology, Visions of the Future Poster, 2020.

LIKE A PLANET OUT OF ORBIT

Maybe you can relate.

There are masses of matter in space that aren't stars—so they aren't big balls of gas that give light. They also aren't space rocks like asteroids or comets. They are simply rogue. Sometimes they have fallen out, ejected, failed out of an orbit, and sometimes they simply did not make it into one. Nevertheless, they are in space, and since they are not a moon and have no star to guide them, so to speak, they are always "dark." NASA designed a poster (4.84) for a rogue planet named PSO J318.5-22. It reads fondly, "where the night never ends." Beautiful, these rogue planets, also referred to as interstellar, nomads, free-floating, unbound, orphan, wandering, starless, or sunless planets. They have never been gravitationally bound.

These starless planets can be enormous. In fact, the Milky Way, the galaxy home to punk, has rogue planets the size of Jupiter. The scientist David J. Stevenson theorized that while these planets do not produce any heat, their thick atmosphere keeps them from being cold. They won't freeze—they manage warmth without sun.

In many ways punk embodies an unbound, orphan, free-floating planet. What some may see as having failed out of an orbit, others may see as being rogue enough to reject authoritarian gravity and use the darkness of the night to make a space that will never go numb or frozen. A common, yet maybe not tired, question that comes up for many punk musicians is how we define punk. Perhaps it would benefit us to move beyond the bounds of the gravity of music, government, nationalism, and consumerism to think of how to describe a mass that often feels like it is floating on its own. It may not get the recognition of a planet, but its thick atmosphere results in a stamina to take on capitalist attempts at culture and give us a night that never ends.

What is punk? A rogue planet.

PURPOSE

Probes into the multitudes of why we must reject authority fuse to form the punk cell's nucleus. Just how much do we recognize and reject the power structures that make us want to assimilate and conform to Eurocentric business-man maledom? Perhaps the reason that we look toward punk isn't to see an open door, but to believe that there is an open portal for all the feelings of loss, anxiety, anger, and longing that we experience—and that we know is like being a host for the parasite of patriarchy. What helps us to see an open door, to ignite a desire, to figure out a path to it better than each other?

Perhaps the most antiauthority way to practice punk is to recognize that there is no perfect narrative of history and that history is created by imperfect people and institutions. So this imperfect path we find ourselves shaping by our own means and production extends into an infinite galaxy.

POWER AND PURPOSE

Alice Bag, a Chicana musician based in Los Angeles, has continued to chisel away at the portal of punk for decades now. She never ceases to write music and play shows, and authors many things including books, lyrics, and memoirs. In an interview, she shared, "I don't lament what has come after me in punk. Things are cyclical. It does bother me that people have been led to believe that punk is music created for and by white males. . . . Punk's diverse roots are bound to come to the surface. I will shout it from the rooftops!"[1] And it's overwhelming that so much of how we are often forced to define punk is in contrast or contradiction to everything that punk isn't.

It's like a soup of double negatives.

Punk isn't listening to what everyone wants you to be.

Punk isn't funded by the same shit that is on the radio or playing stadiums. Punk isn't suits.

Punk isn't given permission by permits and leases.

So—what the fuck is it then?

WELL, IT'S NOT CREATED OR DRIVEN BY WHITE MEN. THIS MUCH MUST BE TRUE.

So, then, why are we left shouting this both from capitalism's rooftops and from underground basement stages? Maybe this hole that keeps digging itself in punk is a reflection of the same power imbalances that we knock on the door of punk with a desire to reject and even change.

People of color, nonbinary people, femmes, Black musicians, migrant musicians—they all made the game not by inventing rules but simply by playing the game. And every time the belief that punk is created by white males is perpetuated either by a statement or by asking us nonwhite nonmales, "How does it feel to be in a white space like punk?" an erasure takes place. Poly Styrene passed away in 2011, but even after her death, she continues to influence and inspire. Bikini Kill's Kathleen Hanna wrote a powerful tribute on her personal website when Poly died: "Poly lit the way for me as a female singer who wanted to sing about ideas. She taught me, by example, that fame was less the goal than something to back away from when it started to invade your core."[2] Poly Styrene, a female musician born to a Somali dockworker and an Irish secretary. Styrene, who started making music at age eighteen—a smattering of reggae singles under the name Mari Elliott. The same person, who, a year later, saw the Sex Pistols perform in London and, inspired, put out an ad looking for bandmates for her own punk outfit, X-Ray Spex. She, in turn, inspired Kathleen Hanna, who is often lauded as the (anti)royalty of American punk. How we think and memorialize this history can lose track of the roots of this tree from which grows the fruit everyone sees and picks. Also, once we start drawing the primordial constellation's lines, connections like Somali dockworker to Styrene playing reggae to the Sex Pistols to X-Ray Spex to Kathleen Hanna and riot grrrl become so complex that our power analysis of punk must be deep and delicate.

The idea of "first" in anything should be taken with a grain of salt, because *whyyyy* would we give into hierarchies like this? Notably, there has been somewhat of a much welcome consensus that the "first" punk band can be traced to Los Saicos in Peru. A *Consequence of Sound* article worded it best by including who *wasn't* the first punk in the history of punk bands. "Peru's own Los Saicos, and not Sex Pistols, The Ramones, New York Dolls, The Stooges, The Dictators, or even Death, was the first punk band in the history of punk bands."[3] How and why does the history of "who punk is for," or "who is in punk" get so warped? How? Likely because Eurocentric and Western tellings of history warp reality. And we shouldn't be surprised by the telling of punk's history, because after all, it is being shot through the same colonial-minded prism. Unless we speak up about it and clear the air of it. This is what punk as a medium should do best, right? Disentangle and tear apart oppressive and authoritarian power structures by any means possible.

This can make the feeling of constantly being asked about the "punk is a white space" myth seem like an opportunity for the glass to be half full. Being a singer in a band is a dream and a half. Getting to sing in front of other people forges a feeling of what I imagine getting to go into space must inspire. So, this is no diss. Being asked what it feels like to be a brown person, person of color, Latinx, or Latina person in punk can feel like a basic yet daunting question. Because it feels so wrong or rooted in a history of misinformation. So, I need to remind myself it is because so many narratives are rooted in a history of misinformation. The hope is that one day, instead of explaining how it feels to be the "exception," we are asked what it feels like when whiteness has fueled a narrative of nonwhite men as the exception instead of as the foundation.

To give an idea, these are some answers from me and the band about race and punk [Editors' note: At the time of these excerpts the Downtown Boys included Joey La Neve DeFrancesco (guitar) Mary Regalado (bass), Norlan Olivo (drums), and Joe DeGeorge (saxophone and keyboards)]:

From *FADER* magazine: A similar ideology fuels their performances, which aim to make punk spaces more accessible for people of color. "I don't care if [non-Spanish-speaking] people are receptive to having our songs in Spanish—it's not for them," Regalado said. "There have been instances where Latinos will come to the shows and stand in the front because they hear Spanish. Remember that little kid in Portland?" Ruiz nodded, fiddling with a stuffed turtle she'd plucked from a nearby shelf. "His dad brought him to the very front of the stage on his shoulders," she said. "We put him on the stage and he started dancing." DeFrancesco laughs, blowing on his fingernails, which he'd just painted dark purple. "His dad just, like, handed him to Victoria," he said. "There was a lot of trust in that moment."[4]

From *AdHoc* magazine: [Question:] What kind of extra labor—emotional, intellectual, or physical—do you feel is expected from you as a female musician of color?

Ruiz: I think that there are a lot of expectations that are put on me that men don't receive, and that white women don't receive. I think that there's this huge demand for me to be this frontperson, but also to be in the back, pushing this band along. Because I'm a woman, because I'm brown, there are a lot of expectations that I get from the audience, from journalists, from my own bandmates. I think there's this idea that, because I have this position in the band, I somehow have access to more resources or more information than other people do. These types of expectations are something that I don't see white people getting in the same way. Oftentimes, when you see white people say some of the things I do, they get praised, they get put on a pedestal. They don't get asked to then be the free therapist or the free social worker or the free psychic worker for the scene.[5]

From the *Austin Chronicle*: So bellows Victoria Ruiz on "Monstro," a rallying cry off Downtown Boys' 2015 debut, *Full Communism*. Rooted in both activism and the DIY scene of Providence, R.I., the five piece is definitive of punk in 2016, pushing for accessibility in predominantly white spaces.

"We don't believe in a monolithic model of being a political punk band, and we're not trying to find a monolithic fan base," states Ruiz.[6]

From *AfroPunk* magazine: [Question:] You're in these spaces that view themselves as radical or at the very least progressive, but are in reality pretty traditionally straight white male macho spaces. Have you had situations where like tall boys come up to you and be like "oh I didn't realize I was being a macho asshole"?

Victoria: It's definitely been mixed. We've had people come up to us and be like "oh my god that song ["Tall Boys"] describes someone that I know" or "it describes the way that people treat me." And people are really supportive of it. But we actually don't play it anymore because we've had literal tall boys come up to us and be like "why are you hating? Why do you gotta judge tall men?" And took it really literally. And it's kind of ridiculous because it's not about actual height, it's about how you're using your dominant power and privilege. I remember when Pitchfork was reviewing the album, they asked us the night before "how tall is Victoria" because I think they wanted to comment on that song, so I wrote back and said "I'm 10 feet tall" just to not even go there, because it's not about that. So it's definitely a mix of people being really down and other people being threatened, because they know that we're talking about power and it makes them feel uncomfortable.[7]

There could be a plethora of reasons for why punk loses its meaning. Maybe we need to press the genre for this reality of our narrative. Often punk doubles down on aesthetics, and this shouldn't be confused with an actual answer to our purpose or our definition. Just like wanted posters for band members, audience members get an invitation. So, how do those invitations remind the masses at the top of our lungs that in fact this space was meant to confront white male-run hierarchies and inaccessibility to culture, not create a dogma of what "against authority" must look like? Punk inhibits erasure at its core. Anytime we give in to erasure, we are undermining the whole space. As a Latina who comes from a population targeted and often eaten alive by neoliberalism, consumption, and capitalism—it's sacred to hold back the beast of White American Culture from my mind and memory. You can't throw a planet into any galaxy's orbit. The cosmos is too intentional and intricate to be erased by our incomplete understanding of it. Punk at its core operates like the cosmos.

WHO IS WANTED?

My own entry into music happened when I moved to Providence, Rhode Island: home to wonderful outfits, from folk rock Deer Tick to punk noise brilliance like Black Pus. It's like a

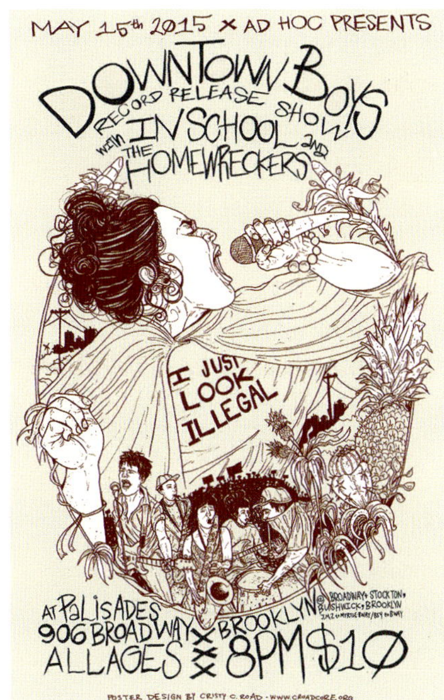

4.85. Flyer for Downtown Boys Record Release show, 2015, featuring seminal hardcore group *In School* and the artist Cristy C. Road's former band the Homewreckers.

This flyer encapsulates a regional scene that ushered anti-racism into the forefront of modern punk ideology. Cristy C. Road is a Cuban American artist and musician who began playing in punk bands and self-publishing *Green'zine* in 1997. She has evolved into a graphic novelist, tackling mental health, sexuality, cultural identity, and surviving through the lens of punk. Road currently fronts the melodic punk band Choked Up. She continues to create art for punk, social movements, and beyond. She can be found at croadcore.org.

welcoming beehive for artists, musicians, and kids who didn't mind walking just about a mile to get anywhere in the city. A landscape made of buzzing warehouses turned into show spaces, walls with wheat paste, and posters crowding any open cafe bulletin board or light pole.

Without even an ounce of musical skill or experience, I knew that picking up a guitar might not be my most accessible door. So I took to learning screen printing and made posters for my new favorite band: Downtown Boys!

The band was led by a group of new friends including one I met working at a hotel: Joey La Neve DeFrancesco. Joey would kick me a guest-spot ticket at shows and money for paint and paper to rip images and fonts that I would collage into a poster, and we would go around town and hang them up in between shifts.

Sure enough, the band names, the words, the names of the venues, the images, the colors—all of it kind of collages into a portal.

When thinking about a wanted poster, whether you're "wanted to join a band" or you're "wanted to get to the gig," the physical poster and where you see it means something. What can get read between the lines can also be *who* is wanted. Maybe that tells us something about the junk science behind punk being such a white space. Are we just judging a book by its cover? Turning to a glimpse of the material history of our planet that doesn't give in to the gravity of a galaxy and refuses to be a rock, the Cornell University punk archive gleaned and then made public two incredible portals to history. Their digital collection offers 2,091 images of punk flyers, from Johan Kugelberg, who worked for Matador Records and Def Jam Records, and Aaron Cometbus's own Punk and Underground Press Collection. Years of flyers that communicated musician classifieds, shows, benefits, and other integral earthly delights are brought together for the world to see.

Of course, this is a cross section of who knows how many telephone lines to the home that we call punk. But words are important, and after traveling to venues from basements to black box bars to backyards, I can't see that the words that we glean from the posters are *atypical.* Without generalizing or making assumptions, if we apply the same apparatus of questioning and reason to our aesthetic, maybe there's a reason why we might associate our identity with certain social spaces, genders, and frameworks of the US American experience.

Think of how language is used to pigeonhole so many of us. The number of times people have decided to say "hola," or "gracias" to me, as a Latina/Latine person, is immeasurable. The number of times my ethnicity gets aesthetically stuffed into boxes of that Rage Against the Machine block letter font that is also seen on Che Guevara T-shirts and posters is pretty wild. Words and the way we express them mean something, they push a button in our mind that makes us associate them with other reference points in our cultural constellation.

I pulled the words from a cross section of the posters. I'm not trying to think for you here, but another of the rings around the world of punk is that we write the history. We don't use halls of fame or record sales numbers or even one type of medium. Fortunately, archives like those that make up the Cornell poster and flyer digital collection are here not only for us to read the history, but to think about how we want to write the future of it.

This list I've compiled—of venues, band names, and language from wanted posters—is for those of us familiar with the jargon, but even more for those that see these words and use them to define all of us in the space. Hopefully, through this essay and this entire text, we can show that, in fact, words don't suffice.

Venues:

Camel Barn Museum
Cesar's
Electric Church
Nexus
Icky's Teahouse
Cathay de Grande

Band names:

Separate Ways
Green Day
Bumbuldum
Blatz
Sluglords
Shadow
Image
Eugene Chadbourne
Blind Illusion
Mordred
Special Forces
Fang
Hell's Kitchen
Joy Dog
Art Faggots
Camper Van Beethoven
Operation Ivy
As Is
The McGuires
Didjits
Attitude
Forethought
Freesinger
No Dogs
Capitol of Punishment
Corrupted Morals
Crimpshrine
Assassins of God
Well Hung Monks
Dig to China
Brewtality, Inc
Dickies
Jawbreaker
Asexuals
Verbal Assault
Unskilled Labor
Violent Coercion
Corrosion of Conformity
No Rockstars
No Labels
Tales of Terror
Sleeping Dogs
Meat Puppets
Black Flag
No Sisters
Le Tigre
Tami Hart
Los Microwaves
White Trash
Bleed

Musicians wanted posters:[8]

(1) We need a Vocalist!!!
diverse
creative
dedicated
call Jon, Idon, Ron,
or Todd

(2) Wanted: Musicians Bass & Guitar for Noisy Psyco [sic] Fast Rock Band
under 20 years of age
and no education required
[call] Dan

(3) Wanted! Drummer
fast
dynamic
hard hitting

(4) Girl Drummer Wanted for the Ramonas
nothing fancy
fast
strong
reliable

(5) The Startles are Looking for Girl Musicians
drummers & guitarists
age 18 on up
call Jane or Wendy

(6) Drummer & Singer Needed
preferred ages 15–22
call Richard or Tom

(7) Drummer Wanted—this could be you!
[call] Sergie, Ryan, Aaron

Band influences:

Chrome
Big Black
Rudimentary Peni
Early Sabbath
the Buzzcocks
the Ramones
the Jam
999
Gen. X
Descendents
ACDC
Hüsker Dü
Chili Peppers
Clown Alley
Bad Brains
the Stones
Johnny Thunders
Aerosmith

Without guiding the reading too much, is it worth questioning whether a "wanted musician" poster that doesn't indicate "girl" or "female" just defaults to "boy" or "man"? If you were to think of words associated with a flyer, without defining the genres of music, what would those words indicate about who you think the genre is "for" or "by"? We tread on a slippery slope where a framework of culture built on confronting and opposing normative US consumerist values can easily re-create those values or the assumptions that the same power structure we oppose projects onto us. But how we are defined by people who don't care to actually know what punk is about maybe shouldn't take too much space in our mind. The issue for me as someone who wouldn't necessarily fit the description on many of these posters is that I don't want assumptions about the genre to close doors to people who might not feel welcome, while they might love the space, and we might love them! There is no set conclusion here. More a desire to interrogate the idea that white people created punk and therefore people like myself should be asked about how it feels not to be white. Would you care about the answer if you found out that punk isn't actually a white history?

The show poster spectrum for just my one small band casts a story of what people think of us and our music, or whether they even take us into consideration at all. One artist who designs for a lot of punk artists and has archived her work is Cristy Road. The poster she created for our album release show spoke volumes about how she interpreted who we are as a band and who I am as a singer (4.85). Beyond identity politics, I think Cristy communicated that all we want is to be enough sometimes, to have a voice, to recognize that, collectively, we are the night that never ends.

Needless to say, there have been posters that exaggerate my facial or body features, I think to drive home that I do not present as a white man. Before, I would feel some type of way about the design choices of posters for our gigs because I read so much into the expectations of our punk band. For those who are unfamiliar with us, we have songs that address race, borders, capitalism. Frequently shouted lines include, "she's brown, she's smart," "I'm enough, I want more," "A wall is just a wall and nothing more at all," and "somos chulas, no somos pendejas." We sing charged songs. I wouldn't have it any other way. In retrospect, the role of the show poster and the artist's invite to a future night memorializes a night before it's happened, and relates context with the music. What a beautiful tool that punk engages. When we think about accessibility and our writing history, punk's propaganda often intensifies and communicates our purpose.

WHOSE IS IT?

Also, in *Violence Girl: East LA Rage to Hollywood Stage; A Chicana Punk Story*, Alice proclaims, "I took big, hungry bites out of life, and I'm still not full." Yeah, right, why be full? Patriarchy, consumerism, and any pull-yourself-up-by-your bootstraps ideas of success have these imaginary finish lines that are based on anything except being hungry for everything but alienation. And the discontents of what we shorthand as punk somehow allow even those of us who are often told not to take a bite to take it in from a water hose. As a brown kid of a single mom and raised by a house of single women in the Eastside of what would become the heart of the Silicon Valley, even I somehow carved a space in this geography where nights filled with moshing or standing in the back watching people go off fill you with something bigger than yourself.

But part of the culture is the incredible method of communication. Before the chorus and verse, we have zines, magazines, posters, and scribbles on paper saying what we WANT! We want you to come to the gig. We want you to read our beautifully bizarre lines of poetry on black-and-white xerox copies. We want you to take a magnifying glass to our record insert where we pour our hearts out in size six font or with photos that show who we think we are. I WANT TO BE WANTED, TOO. I WANT TO WANT YOU, TOO. This want becomes the hunger for the show to never end.

GEOGRAPHY

Another prime example of punk aside from rogue planets and Alice Bag is a special person: my grandma. She grew up in a family of thirteen siblings. She was a tomboy and domestic worker from the time she was able to carry a young sibling in her arms. As a Mexican American farmworker, she was the first to go on tour. She would travel from what she calls "camp to camp," to work different fields. Never learning to read or write, she took to music. This is very

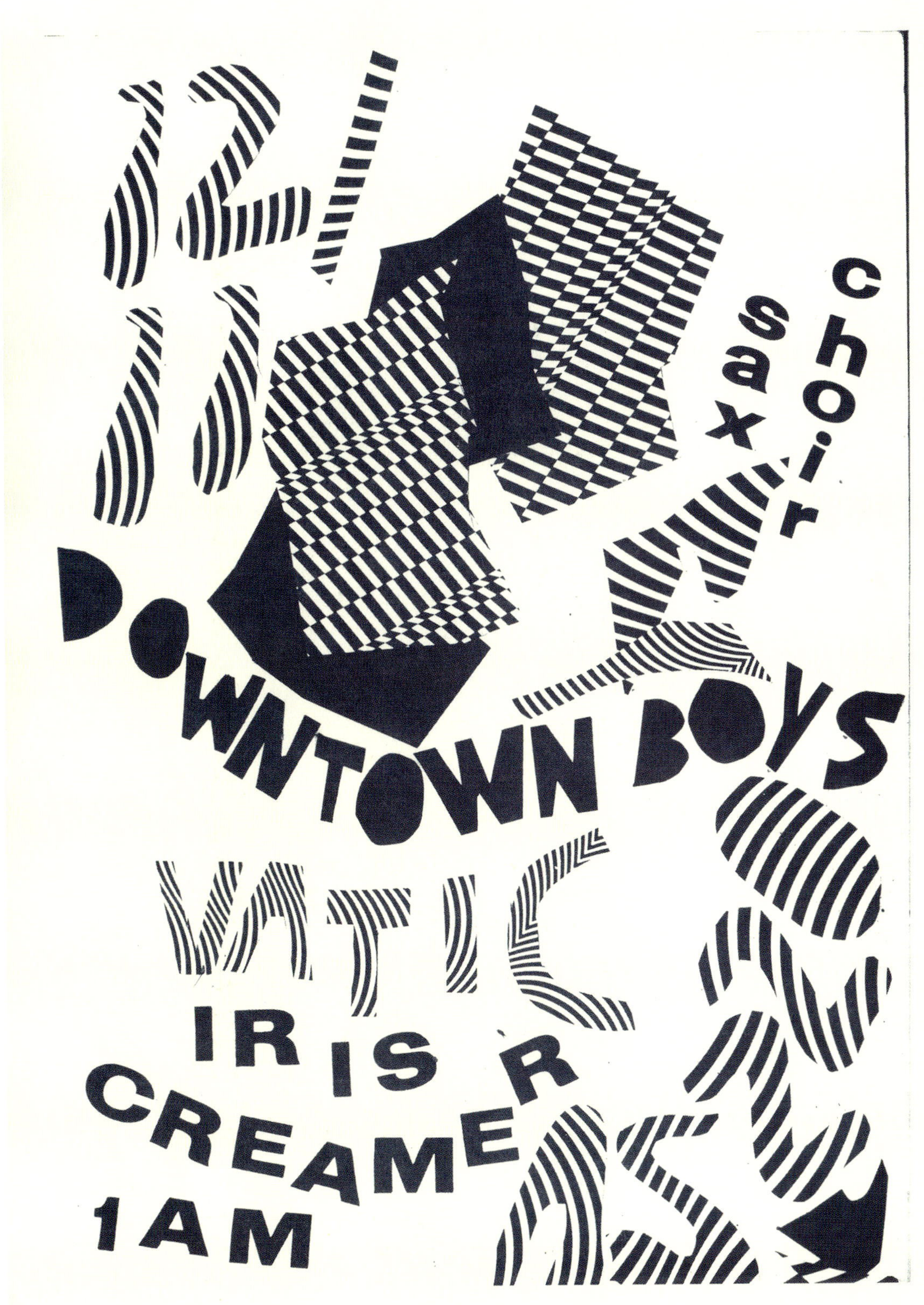

4.86. Flyer for Downtown Boys show, Providence, Rhode Island, circa 2016.

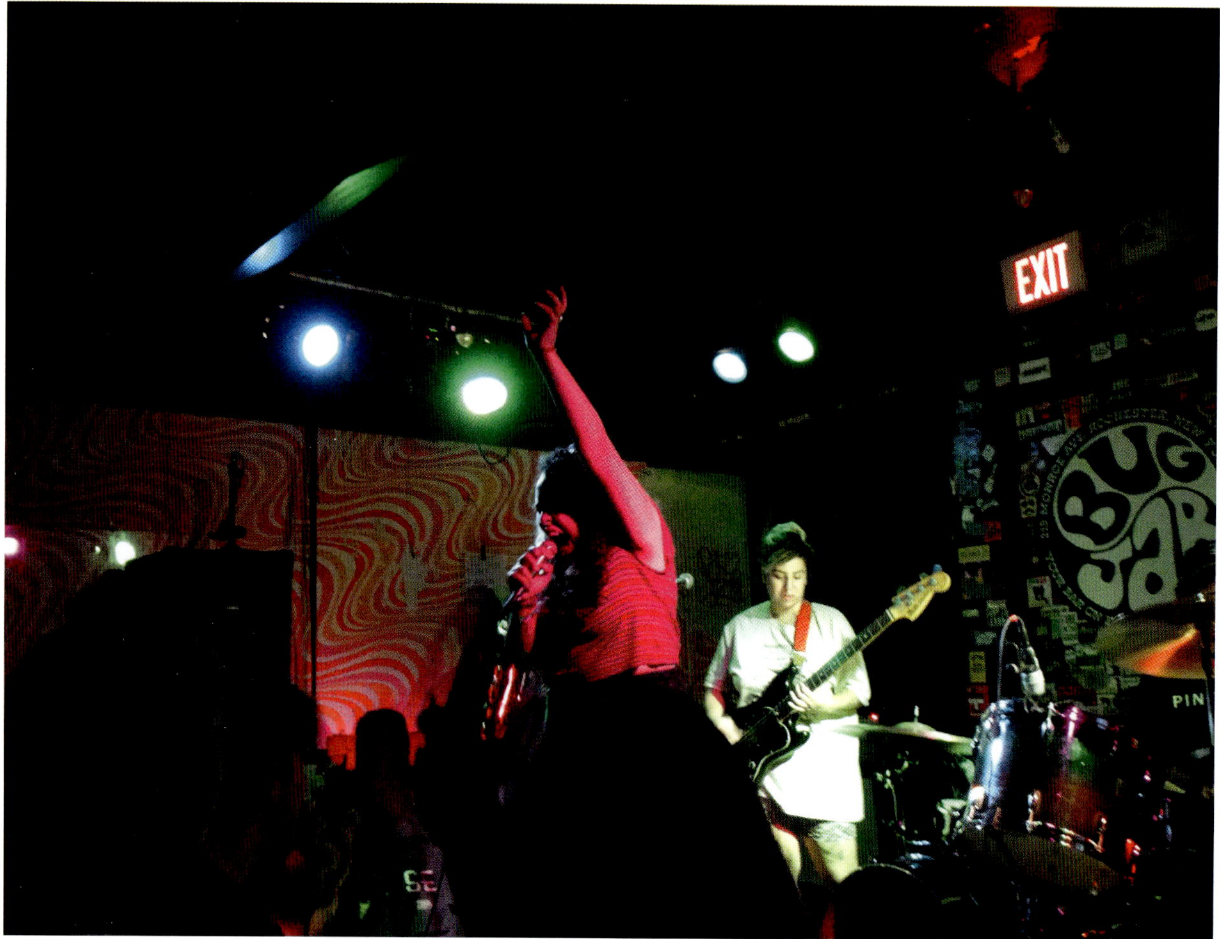

4.87. Downtown Boys at the Bug Jar, Rochester, New York, August 2017. Photo: Judith Peraino.

uncommon in the US, I think, but she speaks both Spanish and English completely fluently. However, English is her second language, and she learned it without ever writing or reading a word in Spanish.

Very very similar to how so many of us pick up a mike or an instrument, or paper to make a zine or a poster, when we have no idea how to "formally" use these objects. But we pick them up, and we never look back.

My grandma was always obsessed with the physical objects of music. Music was this way to take in ideas and words that others might get to do by reading. It's not quite a text, it's not quite just a sound—it's a braid of waves that gives us a tool of both hegemony and revolution. I have over a hundred mix tapes that my grandma has made for me in English and Spanish. She uses stickers to decorate, and she even writes liner notes by having someone else write the words on a sheet of paper. Then, in pencil, she draws the letters as if they are objects on the tape insert. Finally, she goes over it with a colored marker of her choice. She dates each one. I have one tape from 1998 that has a commercial from a Spanish radio station in San José, California, from 1964. The tape itself is a time portal. There would be no way for me to learn of these gorgeous mariachi and norteño ballads if not for this tape. There is no internet search that would ever enter my mind to find these tapes, and I have never met another person who could teach me this. This is the power of punk.

OUR ROGUE STAR, OUR FAILED PLANET

So, maybe punk can't do everything, but it feels like it can do *anything*, and that is what makes even a limited word become unlimited in directions that its boundaries don't reach. Like a rogue star: no orbit, more than a rock, and unlimited in its night.

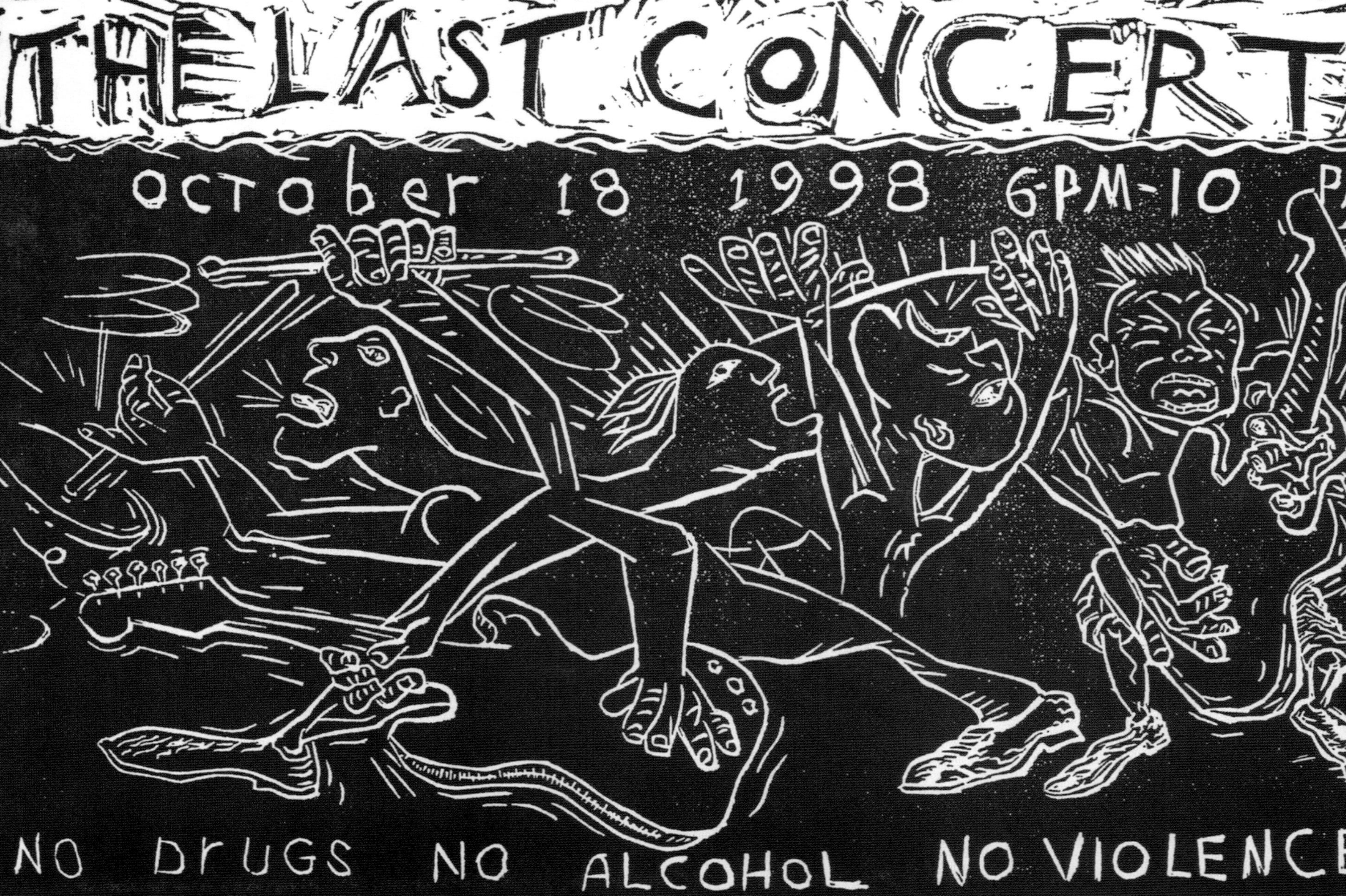

CONCIERTO DE DESPEDIDA
THE LAST CONCERT
october 18 1998 6PM-10 PM
NO drugs NO ALCOHOL NO VIOLENCE

APPENDIX: GUIDE TO THE COLLECTIONS FEATURED IN THIS BOOK AND IMAGE INFORMATION

THE CORNELL COLLECTIONS, IN COLLECTION NUMBER ORDER:

7568: Michael Scherker Research Files, 1989

7738: Larry Blagg Gay Club Matchbook Covers and Ephemera, 1969–1989

7790: Los Crudos Collection, 1991–1998

7839: Gretchen Phillips Papers, 1977–2017

7848: Limp Wrist Collection, 1998–2011

7897: Cockettes Publicity Collection, 1969–1976

8054: Geoffrey Weiss Punk Collection, 1970–2000

8060: Johan Kugelberg Punk Collection, 1974–1986

8061: Jon Savage Punk Music Collection, 1970–1989

8062: Janet Hamill Archive, 1967–2010

8105: Velvet Underground Collection, 964–2015

8107: Aaron Cometbus Punk and Underground Press Collection, ca. 1977–2013

8117: Diego Cortez Mudd Club Collection, ca. 1977–1979

8120: Diego Cortez No Wave Collection, 1972–1981

8125: Riot Grrrl Zine and Music Collection, ca. 1989–1997

8126: Screamers Collection, 1963–1981

8129: West Coast Punk and New Wave Club Flyers, ca. 1979–1982 (Suzanne Onodera)

8135: Michael Whittaker SST Records Collection

8138: Tracy Dodgson Punk and New Wave Collection, 1970–2007

COLLECTIONS AND PERMISSIONS INFORMATION FOR IMAGES:

0.1. #8107, box 10, folder 24
0.2. #8107, box 10, folder 28
0.3. #8060, box 24, folder 1
0.4. #8124, box 1, folder 1. Published by permission of Suzanne Onodera.
0.5. Reproduced from *We're Desperate: The Punk Photography of Jim Jocoy*. Published by permission of Jim Jocoy.
0.6. #8107, box 10, folder 7. Published by permission of Suzanne Onodera.
0.7. #8124, map case 1. Published by permission of Suzanne Onodera.
0.8. #7848, box 1, folder 3. Published by permission of Martín Sorrondeguy.
0.9. #8107, box 10, folder 35. Published by permission of Raymond Pettibon.
0.10. #8107, box 10, folder 9
0.11–0.12. #8107, box 17, folder 23
0.13–0.14. #8017, box 10, folder 24
0.15. #8107, box 5, folder 12
0.16. #8107, map case, folder 1. Published by permission of Atrocity.
0.17. #8061, SR1633
0.19. #8107, box 10, folder 14
0.20. Richard Nagler personal collection, published by permission.

1.1. #8120, box 1, folder 17. Published by permission of Bobby Grossman.
1.2. #8105, box 16, portfolio 1
1.3. #8105, box 1, folder 3
1.4. #8105, map case, folder 1
1.5. #8105, box 3, folder 8. Published by permission of Adam Ritchie.
1.6. #8105, box 13, portfolio 2. Published by permission of Adam Ritchie.
1.7. # 8105, box 1, folder 8. Published by permission of Adam Ritchie.
1.8–1.9. #8105, box 3, folder 8
1.10. # 8062, box 8, folder 13
1.11. #8054, box 20, folder 15
1.12. #8054, box 21, folder 9
1.13–1.14. #7568, box 1, folder 12
1.15. #8060, box 28, folder 13. Published by permission of Bob Gruen.
1.16. Cornell Rare and Manuscript Collections, Rare Books ML3534 .C58 1974
1.17. Personal collection of Bob Gruen, published by permission.
1.18. #8060, box 9, folder 26. Published by permission of Chris Stein.
1.19. #8060, box 27, folder 1. Published by permission of Chris Stein.
1.20. #8054, box 22, folder 10
1.21. #8126, box 3, folder 11
1.22. #8117, box 1, folder 1
1.23. #8060, box 27, folder 3
1.24. #8060, box 25, folder 28
1.25–1.29. #8060, box 28, folder 1
1.30. #8120, box 1, folder 2
1.31. #8060, box 28, folder 21. Published by permission of Roberta Bayley.
1.32. #8117, box 1, folder 3
1.33. #8060, box 13, folder 8. Cover of *New York Rocker* #3 reproduced by permission of Andy Schwartz (publisher and editor) and Lisa Jane Persky.
1.34. Personal collection of Lisa Jane Persky, published by permission.
1.35–1.36. #8054, box 22, folder 6
1.37. #8120, box 1, folder 23
1.38. #8060, box 28, folder 20. Published by permission of Roberta Bayley.
1.39. #8060, box 25, folder 43
1.40. #8060, box 30, folder 6
1.41. #7738, box 1, folder 3
1.42. #8060, box 13, folder 9. Reproduced by permission

of Andy Schwartz (publisher and editor).

1.43. #8060, box 28, folder 15
1.44. #8060, box 25, folder 30
1.45–1.46. #8060, box 25
1.47. #8120, box 1, folder 22
1.48–1.49. #8126, box 1, folder 5
1.50. #8060, box 25, folder 38
1.51. #8060, box 27, folder 3
1.53. #8120, box 1, folder 19
1.54. #8054, box 21, folder 9
1.55–1.56. #8060, box 29, folder 6
1.57. #860, box 25, folder 28. Revised layout provided by John Holmstrom, published by permission.
1.58. #7738, box 1, folder 3
1.59 and 1.60. Personal collection of Judith Peraino, courtesy of Lisa Jane Persky.
1.61–162. #8060, box 29, folder 6
1.63. Personal collection of GODLIS, published by permission.
1.64. Personal collection of James Chance. Published by permission of Sylvia Reed.
1.65. #8120, box 1, folder 16
1.66–1.67. Personal collection of James Chance. Published by permission of Anya Phillips Estate / James Chance.
1.68. Personal collection of Allan Tannenbaum, published by permission.
1.69. #8117, box 1, folder 1
1.70–1.71. #8120, box 1, folder 17
1.72. #8060, box 25, folder 29. Published by permission of Chris Stein.
1.73. #8120, box 1, folder 16. courtesy of Diego Cortez Estate / Katherine Hudson.
1.74. Personal collection of James Chance. Published by permission of Anya Phillips Estate / James Chance.
1.75–1.76. #8120, box 1, folder 1. courtesy of Diego Cortez Estate / Katherine Hudson.

2.1. #8126, box 4, folder 3
2.2–2.3. #8126, box 3, folder 11
2.4–2.6. Personal collection of Fayette Hauser, published by permission.
2.7–2.9. #7897, portfolio 1. Published by permission of Fayette Hauser.
2.10. #8126, map case
2.11. #8126, box 3, folder 12. Published by permission of Fayette Hauser.
2.12. Photo published by permission of Fayette Hauser.
2.13–2.16. #8126, box 7. Published by permission of Tomata du Plenty Estate / Fayette Hauser.
2.17. #8060, box 25, folder 7
2.18. #8054, box 21, folder 16. Published by permission of Bomp! Records.
2.19. #8060, box 9, folder 24
2.20. #8054, box 20, folder 19
2.21. #8060, box 27, folder 3
2.22. #2054, box 20, folder 15
2.23. #8060, box 9, folder 16
2.24. #8060, box 28, folder 21
2.25–2.26. #8126, box 3, folder 7
2.27. #8126, box 3, folder 11
2.28. #8126, box 2, folder 4. Published by permission of Fayette Hauser.
2.29. #8126, box 2, folder 4. Published by permission of Jenny Lens.
2.30–2.31. #8060, box 16, folder 10
2.32. #8126, box 6, folder 7. Published by permission of Tommy Gear.
2.33. #8126, box 6, folder 6. Published by permission of Tommy Gear.
2.34. #8126, box 2, folder 5
2.35. #8126, box 1, folder 5. Published by permission of Tommy Gear.
2.36. #8126, box 6

2.37. #8126, box 1, folder 5. Published by permission of Tommy Gear.
2.38. #8126, box 1, folder 2
2.39. #8126, box 1, folder 3
2.40. #8126, box 1, folder 3
2.41. #8126, box 1, folder 3
2.42. Personal collection of Fayette Hauser. Published by permission of Fayette Hauser.
2.43–2.44. #8126, box 1, folder 5. Published by permission of Tommy Gear.
2.45. #8126, box 3, folder 12. Published by permission of Tommy Gear.
2.46. #8126, box 3, folder 12. Published by permission of Gary Panter.
2.47. #8126, box 1, folder 16. Published by permission of Tommy Gear.
2.48. #8126, box 2, folder 5
2.49. #8126box 2, folder 5
2.50–2.52. #8126, box 6, folder 6. Published by permission of Gary Panter.
2.53. #8126, box 4, folder 2
2.54. #8126, box 1, folder 5. Published by permission of Tommy Gear.
2.55. #8126, box 4, folder 6. Published by permission of Salomon Emquies.
2.56. #8126, box 1, folder 5. Published by permission of Tommy Gear.
2.57. #8126, box 1, folder 5. Published by permission of Tommy Gear.
2.58. #8126, box 2, folder 4. Published by permission of Eric Blum.
2.59. #8126, box 4, folder 6. Published by permission of Tommy Gear.
2.60–2.61. #8126, box 1, folder 5. Published by permission of Tommy Gear.
2.62–2.63. #8126, box 6, folder 7. Published by permission of Gary Panter.
2.64. #8126, box 1, folder 7. Published by permission of Tommy Gear.
2.65. #8126, box 2, folder 8. Published by permission of Tommy Gear.
2.66. Lisa Jane Persky personal archive. Published by permission of Lisa Jane Persky.
2.67–2.70. #8126, box 1, folder 4. Published by permission of Bianca Daalder-van Iersel.
2.71. #8126, box 2, folder 7. Published by permission of Tommy Gear.
2.72. #8126, box 1, folder 3. Published by permission of Tommy Gear.
2.73. #8126, box 3, folder 8. Published by permission of Tommy Gear.
2.74–2.75. #8126, box 3, folder 9. Published by permission of Bianca Daalder-van Iersel.
2.76. #8126, box 4, folder 6. Published by permission of Tommy Gear.
2.77. #8126, box6, folder 7. Published by permission of Tommy Gear.
2.78. #8126, box 7, folder 2. Published by permission of Gary Panter.
2.79. #8060, box 9, folder 24
2.80. #8060, box 9, folder 23
2.81. #8060, box 9, folder 18
2.82. #8060, box 9, folder 24
2.83. #8107, box 10, folder 28. Published by permission of Raymond Pettibon.
2.84–2.85. #8135, box 1, folder 3
2.86. #8135, box 1, folder 4. Published by permission of Edward Colver.
2.87–2.88. #8135, box 1, folder 9. Published by permission of M. Leslie Wimmer.
2.89. #8060, box 8, folder 4
2.90. #8060, box 9, folder 25

3.1–3.2. #8060, box 16, folder 6
3.3. #8138, box 2, folder 2
3.4. #8129, box 1, folder 3
3.5. #8138, box 2, folder 1
3.6. #8129, box 1, folder 1
3.7. #8107, box 10, folder 33
3.8. #8129, box 2, folder 6
3.9. #8107, box 5, folder 43
3.10. #8107, box 6, folder 1. Published by permission of Aaron Cometbus.
3.11. #8107, box 5, folder 13. Published by permission of Aaron Cometbus.

3.12–3.13. #8107, box 5, folder 6
3.14. #8107, box 2, folder 9
3.15. #8124, box 1, folder 1
3.16. #8107, box 10, folder 1
3.17. #8107, box 5, folder 40
3.18. #8107, box 5, folder 24. Published by permission of Aaron Cometbus.
3.19. #8107, box 5, folder 24
3.20. #8107, box 5, folder 38. Published by permission of Aaron Cometbus.
3.21. #8107, box 10, folder 14
3.22. #8107, box 10, folder 4
3.23. #8107, box 9, folder 18
3.24. #8107, box 5, folder 37. Published by permission of Aaron Cometbus.
3.25–3.26. #8107, box 5, folder 38. Published by permission of Aaron Cometbus.
3.27. #8107, box 10, folder 15
3.28–3.29. #8107, box 5, folder 12
3.30. #8107, box 5, folder 12. Published by permission of Aaron Cometbus.
3.31–3.32. #8107, box 5, folder 12. Published by permission of Aaron Cometbus.
3.33. #8107, box 5, folder 12. Published by permission of Atrocity.
3.34. #8107, box 5, folder 23
3.35. #8107, box 10, folder 35
3.36. #8107, box 1, folder 11
3.37. #8107, box 10, folder 36
3.38. #8107, box 2, folder 30
3.39–3.44. #8107, box 5, folder 38. Published by permission of Aaron Cometbus.
3.45. #8107, box 5, folder 31
3.46. #8107, box 5, folder 31. Published by permission of Aaron Cometbus.
3.47–3.48. #8107, box 5, folder 3. Published by permission of Aaron Cometbus.
3.49. #8107, box 5, folder 3
3.50. #8107, box 10, folder 40
3.51–3.58. #8107, box 5, folder 3
3.59. #8107, box 10, folder 9
3.60. #8107, box 10, folder 28
3.61–3.63. #8107, box 10, folder 11
3.64–3.67. #8107, box 5, folder 38. Published by permission of Aaron Cometbus.
3.68–3.69. #8107, box 17. Published by permission of Aaron Cometbus.
3.70–3.72. #8107, box 5, folder 19. Published by permission of Aaron Cometbus.
3.73. #8107, box 5, folder 32. Published by permission of Dave Mello.
3.74. #8107, box 10, folder 38
3.75–3.77. #8107, box 5, folder. Published by permission of Jesse Michaels.
3.78. #8107, box 17, folder 12. Published by permission of Jesse Michaels.
3.79–3.80. #8107, box 5, folder 26. Published by permission of Aaron Cometbus.
3.81–3.83. #8107, box 5, folder 26
3.84. #8107, box 5, folder 34. Published by permission of Aaron Cometbus.
3.85. #8107, box 5, folder 26, box 9, folder 17
3.86. #8107, box 2, folder 15
3.87. #8107, box 1, folder 2
3.88. #8107, box 1, folder 14
3.89. #8107, box 5, folder 32
3.90. #8107, box 17, folder 15
3.91. #8107, box 10, folder 41
3.92. #8107, box 12, folder 13
3.93. #7790, box 1
3.94. #8107, box 10, folder 13
3.95–3.96. #8107, box 5, folder 42
3.97–3.104. #8107, box 17, folder 19
3.105–3.106. #8107, box 10, folder 66
3.107–3.108. #8107, box 5, folder 42. Published by permission of Karoline Collins.
3.109–3.110. #8107, box 5, folder 42
3.111–3.112. #8107, box 10, folder 42. Published by permission of Aaron Cometbus.
3.113–3.114. #8107, box 15
3.115. #8107, box 19, folder 1. Published by permission of Mitzi Waltz.
3.116. #8107, box 10, folder 47
3.117. #8107, box 7, folder 24
3.118–3.119. #8107, box 10, folder 61. Published by permission of Aaron Cometbus.
3.120–3.121. #8107, box 17, folder 9
3.122. #8107, box 4, folder 82
3.123–3.125. #8107, box 9, folder 16
3.126. #8107, box 5, folder 30
3.127. #8107, box 5, folder 30
3.128–3.133. Personal collection of Anna Joy Springer, published by permission.

3.134. #8107, box 5, folder 42.
3.135. Personal collection of Anna Joy Springer, published by permission.
3.136. #8107, box 10, folder 10
3.137. #8107, box 4, folder 17
3.138. #8107, box 5, folder 37. Published by permission of Aaron Cometbus.
3.139. #8107, box 10, folder 8
3.140. #8107, box 10, folder 20
3.141. #8107, box 5, folder 38. Published by permission of Aaron Cometbus.
3.142. #8107, box 5, folder 38. Published by permission of Aaron Cometbus.
3.143. #8107, box 10, folder 9
3.144–3.145. #8107, box 5, folder 36

4.1–4.2. #8060, box 28, folder 15
4.3. #8060, box 30, folder 1
4.4. #8107, box 10, folder 30
4.5. #8107, box 10, folder 8
4.6. #8107, box 4, folder 28
4.7. #8107, box 4, folder 16
4.8–4.9. #8107, box 10, folder 30
4.10. #8107, box 3, folder 54
4.11. #8107, box 4, folder 12
4.12. #8107, box 3, folder 36
4.13. #8107, box 10, folder 30
4.14. #8107, box 2, folder 43
4.15–4.17. #8107, box 17, folder 21
4.18. #8107, box 10, folder 31
4.19–4.20. #8107, box 10, folder 31
4.21. #8060, box 9, folder 16
4.22. #8060, box 9, folder 22
4.23. #8060, box 9, folder 18
4.24. #8107, box 10, folder 2
4.25. #7839, box 6, folder 7. Published by permission of John Hawkes and Gretchen Phillips.
4.26. #7839, box 4, folder 7
4.27–4.28. #8107, box 17, folder 07. Published by permission of Elizabeth Fiend.
4.29. #8117, box 1, folder 4
4.30. #8125, box 1, folder 21. Published by permission of Kathleen Hanna.
4.31–4.32. #8107, box 5, folder 43
4.33–4.34. #8107, box 5, folder 30. Published by permission of Kathleen Hanna.
4.35. #8107, box 12, folder 79
4.36. #8107, box 1, folder 3
4.37–4.38. #8107, box 2, folder 12
4.39–4.40. #8107, box 21, folder 1. Published by permission of Kathleen Hanna.
4.41–4.42. #8125, box 8, folder 8
4.43. #8107, box 3, folder 41
4.44. #8107, box 2, folder 50
4.45–4.49. #8107, box 3, folder 10. Published by permission of Adee Roberson.
4.50. Personal collection of Judith Peraino. Image provided by James Spooner, published by permission.
4.51–4.52. #8125, box 8, folder 4
4.53–4.68. #7790, box 1
4.53. Published by permission of Kim Bae.
4.62. Published by permission of Martín Sorrondeguy.
4.63. Published by permission of David Naylamp.
4.69–4.70. #7848, box 1, folder 2. Flyers designed by Martín Sorrondeguy, published by permission.
4.71–4.83. #7848, box 1, folder 3
4.84. Poster available at https://www.jpl.nasa.gov/galleries/visions-of-the-future#grid-127451-14.
4.85. Image provided by Cristy C. Road, published by permission.
4.86. Personal collection of Judith Peraino.
4.87. Personal collection of Judith Peraino, published by permission.

NOTES

PREFACE

1. See Foucault, *The Archaeology of Knowledge*. Earlier philosophers, like the German-Jewish writer Walter Benjamin, were especially attuned to the limits and hopeful possibilities of archives.
2. Osborne, "Ordinariness of the Archive."
3. Our thinking about punk's relationship to the archive draws on the work of Daphne Brooks (*Liner Notes for the Revolution*), Ann Cvetkovich (*Archive of Feelings*), Saidiya Hartman ("Venus in Two Acts"), Ann Stoler (*Along the Archival Grain*), among others.
4. Cvetkovich, *Archive of Feelings*, 7.

INTRODUCTION

1. Scordelis, "Interview with Mike Watt."
2. See Beeber, *Heebie-Jeebies at CBGB's*.
3. See Nguyen, "It's (Not) a White World"; Duncombe and Tremblay, *White Riot*.
4. *Maximumrocknroll* no. 18, October 1984; see also Reveron, "In 1984 Maximum Rock N Roll Covered the Summer of Hate!"
5. See Beeber, *Heebie Jeebies at CBGB's*.
6. Sarah Borruso explains that "the piece of paper that was torn from the lower right of the set list was originally a drawing of a heart, because the song's title was 'This Is Not Love.' That might help explain why the very last line appears: 'This is art!' which was written in context to the song title above." Email correspondence with Judith Peraino, January 16, 2024.
7. Biafra and Mullen interviews in Letts, *Punk: Attitude*, 2005.

1. BEING DIFFERENT IN NEW YORK

1. Quoted in Savage, *England's Dreaming*, 133.
2. Quote from Krim, "Shock Treatment for Psychiatrists."
3. For example, Ferris, "David Bowie in America," 41; Garvin, "Transformer's About to Blow," 10.
4. See Harry and Simmons, *Face It*, 105.
5. Hell, *I Dreamed I Was a Very Clean Tramp*, 101.
6. Kristian Hoffman quoted in Loud, *Lance Out Loud*, 21.
7. Quoted in Yardley, "Arturo Vega, Shepherd for the Ramones, Dies at 65."
8. Persky, "Are the Ramones or Is the Ramone?," 29.

3. "PUNK WAS ME ONSTAGE WRECKING"

1. In the 1920s, Dorothy Parker along with other New York writers, critics, and actors met for lunch each day at the Algonquin Hotel, eventually publicizing their witty banter in newspaper columns. The group was variously nicknamed "the Vicious Circle" and "the Round Table."
2. Sewall-Ruskin, *High on Rebellion*.
3. County, *Man Enough to Be a Woman*, 131.

5. DOING THE FUTURE YOURSELF

1. Powers, *Some New Kind of Kick*, 41 (Kindle).

2. Quoted in Doe and DeSavia, *Under the Big Black Sun*, 96.
3. Spitz and Mullen, *We Got the Neutron Bomb*, 75.
4. "*Slash* Presents . . . The Future!," *Slash* vol. 1, no. 1 (May 1977): 9.
5. Bugatti refers to the brand name of Italian-designed racing and sports cars of the 1920s and '30s.
6. Collection 8126, box 3, folder 4, "Tomasino—Questionaire" [*sic*], 1; and "Tomata's Questionaire" [*sic*], 3.
7. "A Better World Begins with . . . ," *Slash* vol. 1, no. 13 (one year anniversary special issue): 15–18, quote at 16.
8. Bob Taylor, "Camarillo State Mental Hospital, 3-23-1978," *Slash* vol., 1, no. 10 (May 1978): 24.
9. "The Screamers' Tomata du Plenty" (interview with Jack Rabid on May 3, 2000), *byNWR*, https://www.bynwr.com/articles/the-screamers-tomata-du-plenty. Accessed December 21, 2021.
10. MacLeod, *Kids of the Black Hole*, 94.
11. Quoted in Doe and DeSavia, *Under the Big Black Sun*, 109.
12. Quoted in Russo, *We Were Going to Change the World*, 42.
13. Quoted in Russo, 33 and 34.

14. MAPS FOR THE GROUNDLESS

1. Box 15, TR-15977–15993, Cometbus Punk and Underground Press, ca. 1977–218, collection 8107, Cornell University Library Division of Rare and Manuscript Collections.
2. Box 10, TR-15955, Riot Grrrl Zine and Music, ca. 1989–1997, collection 8125, Cornell University Library Division of Rare and Manuscript Collections.
3. Nguyen, "Making Waves," 355–59.
4. See Gretchen Phillips Papers, 1977–2017, collection 7839, Cornell University Library Division of Rare and Manuscript Collections.

16. BE A CROSSROADS!

1. Azerrad, *Our Band Could Be Your Life*, 24.
2. McPheeters, "For the Faithful."
3. Azerrad, *Our Band Could Be Your Life*, 320.
4. Gretchen Phillips, Zoom interview with Judith Peraino, November 8, 2023.
5. Quoted in Blashill, *Texas Is the Reason*, 141.
6. See Marcus, *Girls to the Front* (Kindle ed.), 34.
7. Ruiz, "Downtown Boys Are Here to Make You Uncomfortable."

19. PUNK AND THE MEANS OF PRODUCTION

1. Alice Bag, interview with Vitoria Ruiz, *Media*, October 7, 2016.
2. Hanna, "Poly Styrene."
3. Young, "Fact: Los Saicos Was the First Punk Band Ever."
4. Mejia, "Meet Downtown Boys."
5. Bieser, "Downtown Boys' Victoria Ruiz Bites Back."
6. Webster, "Wednesday SXSW Interview."
7. Sound Check, "Interview: Downtown Boys Get Real."
8. The musicians wanted posters quoted here from the following bands respectively (1) members of Christ on Parade, Crimpshrine, and Econochrist, (2) Anarchistical Follies, (3) the Breakouts, (4) Ramonas, (5) the Startles, (6) Unskilled Labor, (7) Samiam. They can all be found in the Aaron Cometbus Punk and Underground Press Collection, #8107, box 10, folder 39, or accessed through Cornell's digital collection: https://digital.library.cornell.edu/collections/punkflyers.

BIBLIOGRAPHY

Alvarado, Jimmy. "A History of East LA Punk." *Razorcake*, no. 3, 2001.

Alvarado, Jimmy. "Teenage Alcoholics: Punk Rock in East Los Angeles; Updated and Revised 2017." *Razorcake*, December 7, 2017. https://razorcake.org/teenage-alcoholics-punk-rock-east-los-angeles-jimmy-alvarado/.

Anderson, Sini, dir. *The Punk Singer: A Film about Kathleen Hanna*. Sundance Selects, 2013.

Azerrad, Michael. *Our Band Could Be Your Life: Scenes From the American Indie Underground, 1981–1991*. Boston: Back Bay Books, 2002.

Bag, Alice. *Violence Girl: East L.A. Rage to Hollywood Stage, a Chicana Punk Story*. Port Townsend, WA: Feral House, 2011.

Bangs, Lester. *Psychotic Reactions and Carburetor Dung: The Work of a Legendary Rock Critic; Rock 'n' Roll as Literature and Literature as Rock 'n' Roll*. New York: Anchor Books, 1988.

Beeber, Steven Lee. *The Heebie-Jeebies at CBGB's: A Secret History of Jewish Punk*. Chicago: Chicago Review, 2006.

Belsito, Peter, and Bob Davis. *Hardcore California: A History of Punk and New Wave*. San Francisco: Last Gasp of San Francisco, 1983.

Bessman, Jim. *Ramones: An American Band*. New York: St. Martin's, 1993.

Bieser, Ben. "Downtown Boys' Victoria Ruiz Bites Back." *AdHoc*, November 14, 2017. https://adhoc.fm/post/downtown-boys-victoria-ruiz-bites-back/.

Blashill, Pat. *Texas Is the Reason: The Mavericks of Lone Star Punk*. New York: Bazillion Points, 2020.

Boulware, Jack, and Silke Tudor. *Gimme Something Better: The Profound, Progressive, and Occasionally Pointless History of Bay Area Punk from Dead Kennedys to Green Day*. New York: Penguin Books, 2009.

Brooks, Daphne A. *Liner Notes for the Revolution: The Intellectual Life of Black Feminist Sound*. Cambridge, MA: Belknap Press of Harvard University Press, 2021.

Case, Kate. "I Was There . . . " Originally recorded for the 2004 audiozine *Long Ago and Right Now*. Archived at https://www.foundsf.org/index.php?title=Epicenter_Zone.

Chang, Jeff. *Can't Stop Won't Stop: A History of the Hip-Hop Generation*. New York: Picador, 2005.

Chantry, Art. *Instant Litter: Concert Posters from Seattle Punk Culture*. Seattle: Real Comet, 1985.

Cooper, Leonie. "The Unsung—Texacala Jones Is the Trashy Queen of Cowpunk." *Forty-Five*, May 17, 2021. https://thefortyfive.com/opinion/texacala-jones-queen-of-cowpunk/ Cortina, Lene. "Mary Monday." PunkGirlDiaries, August 5, 2021. https://punkgirldiaries.com/mary-monday/.

County, Jayne. *Man Enough to Be a Woman*. New York: Serpent's Tail, 1985.

Cvetkovich, Ann. *An Archive of Feelings: Trauma, Sexuality, and Lesbian Public Cultures*. Durham, NC: Duke University Press, 2003.

Deleuze, Gilles. "On Philosophy." In *Negotiations, 1972–1990*, 135–55. New York: Columbia University Press, 1997.

Doe, John, and Tom DeSavia. *More Fun in the New World: The Unmaking and Legacy of L.A. Punk*. Boston: Da Capo, 2019.

Doe, John, and Tom DeSavia. *Under the Big Black Sun: A Personal History of L.A. Punk*. Boston: Da Capo, 2016.

Duncombe, Stephen, and Maxwell Tremblay, eds. *White Riot: Punk Rock and the Politics of Race*. New York: Verso, 2011.

Edge, Brian, ed. *924 Gilman: The Story So Far . . .* . San Francisco: Maximum Rock N Roll, 2004.

Ensminger, David A. *Left of the Dial: Conversations with Punk Icons*. Oakland, CA: PM, 2013.

Ensminger, David A. *The Politics of Punk: Protest and Revolt from the Streets*. Lanham, MD: Rowman & Littlefield, 2016.

Ensminger, David A. *Visual Vitriol: The Street Art and Subcultures of the Punk and Hardcore Generation*. Jackson: University of Mississippi Press, 2011.

Ferris, Timothy. "David Bowie in America" (interview with David Bowie). *Rolling Stone*, November 9, 1972.

Fields, Danny. *My Ramones*. London: Real Art, 2018.

Foley, Michael Stewart. *33⅓: Fresh Fruit for Rotting Vegetables*. London: Bloomsbury Academic, 2015.

Foucault, Michel. *The Archaeology of Knowledge and the Discourse on Language*. New York: Pantheon Books, 1972.

Galil, Leor. "Chicago Punk Was Born Queer." *Chicago Reader*, June 23, 2020. https://chicagoreader.com/music/chicago-punk-was-born-queer/.

Garvin, Jerry. "The Transformer's About to Blow" (interview with Lou Reed). *Rock*, August 1973.

Ginoli, Jon. *Deflowered: My Life in Pansy Division*. New York: Simon & Schuster, 2009.

Gonzales, Michelle Cruz. *The Spitboy Rule: Tales of a Xicana in a Female Punk Band*. Oakland, CA: PM, 2016.

Gottlieb, Joanne, and Gayle Wald. "Smells Like Teen Spirit: Riot Grrrls, Revolution and Women in Independent Rock." In *Microphone Fiends: Youth Music and Youth Culture*, edited by A. Ross and T. Rose, 250–57. New York: Routledge, 1994.

Graffin, Greg, and Steve Olson. *Anarchy Evolution: Faith, Science, and Bad Religion in a World without God*. New York: Harper Perennial, 2011.

Graham, Dan. *Rock/Music Writings*. New York: Primary Information, 2009.

Greene, Shane. *Punk and Revolution: Seven More Interpretations of Peruvian Reality*. Durham, NC: Duke University Press, 2016.

Hanna, Kathleen. "Poly Styrene." April 26, 2011. http://www.kathleenhanna.com/poly-styrene/.

Harry, Debbie, and Sylvie Simmons. *Face It*. New York: Dey Street Books, 2019.

Hartman, Saidiya. "Venus in Two Acts." *Small Axe* 26 (June 2008): 1–14.

Hebdige, Dick. *Subculture: The Meaning of Style*. London: Routledge, 1979.

Hell, Richard. *I Dreamed I Was a Very Clean Tramp: An Autobiography*. New York: Ecco, 2013.

Henry, Tricia. "Fanzines." In *Break All Rules: Punk Rock and the Making of a Style*, 93–112. Ann Arbor, MI: Umi Research, 1989.

Hermes, Will. *Love Goes to Buildings on Fire: Five Years in New York That Changed Music Forever*. New York: Faber & Faber, 2012.

Holmstrom, John, and Bridget Hurd, eds. *The Best of PUNK Magazine*. New York: HarperCollins, 2012.

Iqbal, Nosheen. "Fashion . . . or Fascist? The Long Tussle over That Fred Perry Logo." *Guardian*, October 4, 2020. https://www.theguardian.com/fashion/2020/oct/04/fashion-or-fascist-the-long-tussle-over-that-fred-perry-logo.

Jones, J. R. "Chicago's Wax Trax! Records Portrayed as a Romance Etched in Vinyl in New Documentary." June 4, 2018. https://chicagoreader.com/film/chicagos-wax-trax-records-portrayed-as-a-romance-etched-in-vinyl-in-new-documentary/.

Juno, Andrea, ed. "Tribe 8." In *Angry Women in Rock*, 48–67. New York: powerHouse Books, 1996.

Kozak, Roman. *This Ain't No Disco: The Story of CBGB*. Boston: Faber & Faber, 1988.

Krim, Seymour. "Shock Treatment for Psychiatrists." *New York Herald Tribune*, January 14, 1966.

Kugelberg, Johan. *The Velvet Underground: New York Art*. New York: Rizzoli, 2009.

Kugelberg, Johan, and Jon Savage, eds. *Punk: An Aesthetic*. New York: Rizzoli, 2012.

Larson, Jen B. *Hit Girls: Women of Punk in the USA, 1975–1983*. Port Townsend, WA: Feral House, 2023.

Lawrence, Tim. *Love Saves the Day*. Durham, NC: Duke University Press, 2003.

Letts, Don, dir. *Culture Clash: Dread Meets Punk Rockers*. SAF, 2006.

Letts, Don, dir. *Punk: Attitude*. Freemantlemedia 3DD Metropolis, 2005.

Losurdo, Joe, and Christina Tillman, dirs. *You Weren't There: A History of Chicago Punk, 1977–1984*. Regressive Films, 2009.

Loud, Pat. *Lance Out Loud*. New York: Glitterati Incorporated, 2012.

Macari, Rachel. "There's More Than Meets the Eye to the Bangles and You Should Know Why." Medium, November 18, 2018. https://rachel-macari.medium.com/theres-more-than-meets-the-eye-to-the-bangles-9bfdb968ec2e MacLeod, Dewar. *Kids of the Black Hole: Punk Rock in Postsuburban California*. Tulsa: University of Oklahoma Press, 2010.

Marcus, Greil. *Lipstick Traces: A Secret History of the 20th Century*. Cambridge, MA: Harvard University Press, 1989.

Marcus, Sara. *Girls to the Front: The True Story of the Riot Grrrl Revolution*. New York: Harper Perennial, 2010.

"Mary Monday." Hozac Records. https://hozacrecords.com/bands/mary-monday-the-bitches/.

Mayer, Jane. "A Palm Beach Proud Boy at the Putsch." *New Yorker*, January 9, 2021. https://www.newyorker.com/magazine/2021/01/18/a-palm-beach-proud-boy-at-the-putsch.

McLeod, Kembrew. *Downtown Pop Underground: New York City and the Literary Punks, Renegade Artists, DIY Filmmakers, Mad Playwrights, and Rock 'n' Roll Glitter Queens Who Revolutionized Culture*. New York: Abrams, 2018.

McMurry, Jacob. *Taking Punk to the Masses: From Nowhere to Nevermind*. Seattle: Fantagraphics, 2011.

McNeil, Legs, and Gillian McCain, eds. *Please Kill Me: The Uncensored Oral History of Punk*. New York: Grove, 1996.

McPheeters, Sam. "For the Faithful." *Chicago Reader*, October 7, 2010. https://chicagoreader.com/music/for-the-faithful/.

Meat Joy. *The True Story of Meat Joy*. Austin, TX: Flesh and Blood Books, 2023.

Mejia, Paula. "Meet Downtown Boys, Bilingual Punks Who Are Never Not Real." *Fader*, October 4, 2016. https://www.thefader.com/2016/10/04/downtown-boys-interview-gen-f Nevarez, Leonard. "In Exile: The Rootless Cosmopolitanism of Jeffrey Lee Pierce and the Gun Club." *musical Urbanism* (blog), June 23, 2015. https://pages.vassar.edu/musicalurbanism/2015/06/23/in-exile-the-rootless-cosmopolitanism-of-jeffrey-lee-pierce-and-the-gun-club/.

Nguyen, Mimi Thi. "It's (Not) a White World: Looking for Race in Punk." *Punk Planet* 8 (November/December 1998): 256–68.

Nguyen, Mimi Thi. "Making Waves: Other Punk Feminisms." *Women and Performance* 22, no. 2–3: 355–59.

Osborne, Thomas. "The Ordinariness of the Archive." *History of the Human Sciences* 12, no. 2 (1999): 51–64.

Persky, Lisa Jane. "Are the Ramones or Is the Ramone?" *New York Rocker*, September 1976, 28–29.

Pinkus, Karen. "Self-Representation in Futurism and Punk." *South Central Review* 13, no. 2/3 (1996): 180–93.

Powers, Kid Congo, with Chris Campion. *Some New Kind of Kick: A Memoir*. New York: Hachette Books, 2022.

Rabid, Jack, and Greg Sahagian. "The Screamers Tomata du Plenty Interview." *byNWR*, May 3, 2000. https://bynwr.com/posts/the-screamers-tomata-du-plenty.

Rapport, Evan. *Damaged: Musicality and Race in Early American Punk*. Jackson: University of Mississippi Press, 2020.

Rathe, Adam, ed. "Queer to the Core: An Oral History." *Out*, April 12, 2012. https://www.out.com/entertainment/music/2012/04/12/history-queer-core-gay-punk-GB-JONES.

Raymer, Miles. "Chicago Punk, Vol. 1." *Chicago Reader*, November 22, 2007. https://chicagoreader.com/music/chicago-punk-vol-1/.

RazorcakeGorsky. "Eastside Punks, Episode 2: The Brat." YouTube, 2020. https://www.youtube.com/watch?v=97Y7sBVWkl0.

Redford, Corbett, dir. *Turn It Around: The Story of East Bay Punk*. Abramorama, 2017.

Reveron, Sean. "In 1984 Maximum Rock N Roll Covered the Summer of Hate! How Skinheads Invaded the Bay Area Scene." *CVLT Nation*, May 4, 2020. https://cvltnation.com/in-1984-maximum-rock-n-roll-covered-the-summer-of-hate-how-skinheads-invaded-the-bay-area-scene/.

Rodríguez-Ulloa, Olga, Rodrigo Quijano, and Shane Greene. *Punk: Las Américas Edition*. Chicago: University of Chicago Press, 2021.

Ruiz, Matthew Ismael. "Downtown Boys Are Here to Make You Uncomfortable—and You Should Let Them." *Remezcla*, August 11, 2017. https://remezcla.com/features/music/downtown-boys-cost-of-living-album-interview/.

Ruiz, Victoria. "Alice Bag." Interview in *The Media*, October 7, 2016. http://www.fvckthemedia.com/issue72/frontpage.

Ruland, Jim. *Corporate Rock Sucks: The Rise and Fall of SST Records*. New York: Hachette, 2022.

Russo, Stacy, ed. *We Were Going to Change the World: Interviews with Women from the 1970s and 1980s Southern California Punk Rock Scene*. Los Angeles: Santa Monica, 2017.

Savage, Jon. *England's Dreaming, Revised Edition: Anarchy, Sex Pistols, Punk Rock, and Beyond*. London: St. Martin's Griffin, 2002.

Savage, Jon. *The England's Dreaming Tapes*. Minneapolis: University of Minnesota Press, 2010.

Scordelis, Alex. "Interview with Mike Watt." *Believer*, September 1, 2017. https://www.thebeliever.net/an-interview-with-mike-watt/.

Sewall-Ruskin, Yvonne. *High on Rebellion: Inside the Underground at Max's Kansas City*. New York: Thunder's Mouth, 1998.

Sinker, Daniel, ed. *We Owe You Nothing. Punk Planet: The Collected Interviews*. New York: Akashic, 2001.

Slash (magazine). "A Better World Begins With You." Vol. 1, No. 13 (One Year Anniversary Issue), August 1978.

Smith, Patti. *Just Kids*. New York: Ecco, 2010.

Sorrondeguy, Martín, dir. *Beyond the Screams / Más allá de los gritos: A Hardcore Punk Documentary*. 1999.

Sound Check. "Interview: Downtown Boys Get Real about Intersectionality and Punk Rock." Afropunk, August 5, 2016. https://afropunk.com/2016/08/interview-downtown-boys-get-real-about-intersectionality-and-punk-rock-soundcheck/.

Spitz, Marc, and Brendan Mullen. *We Got the Neutron Bomb: The Untold Story of L.A. Punk*. New York: Three Rivers, 2001.

Spooner, James, dir. *Afro-Punk*. James Spooner, 2003.

Stein, Chris. *Chris Stein / Negative: Me, Blondie, and the Advent of Punk*. New York: Rizzoli, 2014.

Stoever, Jennifer. "Splicing the Sonic Color-Line: Tony Schwartz Remixes Postwar *Nueva York*." *Social Text* 28, no. 1 (Spring 2010): 59–85.

Stoler, Ann. *Along the Archival Grain: Epistemic Anxieties and Colonial Common Sense*. Princeton, NJ: Princeton University Press, 2009.

Taylor, Bob. "Camarillo State Mental Hospital, 3-23-1978." *Slash* 1, no. 10. http://www.synthpunk.org/screamers/3-23-78slash.html.

Threadgould, Michelle. "Theresa Kereakes' Intimate Portraits Capture Punk's Latino Roots in 1970s LA." *Remezcla*, March 5, 2016. https://remezcla.com/features/music/theresa-kereakes-profile/.

Torres Rotondo, Carlos. *Se acabó el show: 1985, El estallido del rock subterráneo*. Lima: Mutante, 2014.

Vollmann, William T. *The Rainbow Stories*. New York: Atheneum, 1989.

Waksman, Steve. *This Ain't the Summer of Love: Conflict and Crossover in Heavy Metal and Punk*. Berkeley: University of California Press, 2009.

Warfield, Liam, Walter Crasshole, and Yony Leyser. *Queercore: How to Punk a Revolution; An Oral History*. Introduction by Anna Joy Springer and Lynn Breedlove. Oakland, CA: PM, 2021.

Waterman, Bryan. *33⅓: Marquee Moon*. New York: Bloomsbury, 2011.

Webster, Libby. "Wednesday SXSW Interview: Downtown Boys." *Austin Chronicle*, March 18, 2016. https://www.austinchronicle.com/music/2016-03-18/wednesday-sxsw-interview-downtown-boys/.

White, Dennis R. "Tomata du Plenty." *Jive Time Records*, January 30, 2018. https://jivetimerecords.com/northwest/tomata-du-plenty/.

Yardley, William. "Arturo Vega, Shepherd for the Ramones, Dies at 65." *New York Times*, June 11, 2013. https://www.nytimes.com/2013/06/12/arts/music/arturo-vega-spokesman-and-designer-for-the-ramones-dies-at-65.html.

Young, Alex. "Fact: Los Saicos Was the First Punk Band Ever." *Consequence,* August 18, 2013. https://consequence.net/2013/08/fact-los-saicos-was-the-first-punk-band-ever/.

ESSAY CONTRIBUTORS

Biographical information for the people interviewed in this book can be found at the beginning of their respective interviews.

Aaron Cometbus is a dedicated fan and staple of the underground, an author as well as publisher, distributor, and booster of other people's good works. He holds no degrees or honors, but his junk-strewn teenage room has been preserved in a vault at an Ivy League college back east. Every item described or shown in this book—and on Cornell's Digital Collection online—is just the tip of a very punk iceberg, all fully accessible to the public and ready to be held in your hands. So come check it out, you freaks.

Tommy Gear cofounded the Screamers with Tomatâ du Plenty in Los Angeles, circa 1976.

Ian MacKaye is a musician, producer, archivist, activist, and abberationist. He has played in many bands, including the Teen Idles, Minor Threat, Embrace, Fugazi, the Evens, and Coriky. MacKaye is a cofounder and co-owner of Dischord Records, an independent record label that has been documenting the underground music scene in Washington, DC, since 1980. In addition to hundreds of interviews he has given to zines, magazines, and newspapers over the years, he has appeared in documentaries, books, and podcasts about the history of punk, among other topics.

Tom McEnaney is the author of *Acoustic Properties: Radio, Narrative, and the New Neighborhood of the Americas* (2017) and many articles about sound technology, music, and Latin American literature. He is an associate professor of Comparative Literature and Spanish and Portuguese at UC Berkeley, where he is also the current director of the Berkeley Center for New Media. He has played in punk bands since he was thirteen, but you haven't heard of any of them.

Judith A. Peraino grew up in the Chicago area, going to punk clubs and hanging out at Wax Trax Records in the early 1980s. She is now professor of Music and Sound Studies at Cornell University and writes on queer cultures and rock, punk, and pop music. She has given talks at the Rock and Roll Hall of Fame in Cleveland, the SXSW festival in Austin, and the Museum of Pop Culture in Seattle, and continues to teach the course on punk music and culture that she and Tom first taught together in 2014.

Victoria Maria Ruiz is a Chicana artist born in the Bay Area. She now resides in New York City as an artist, activist, and advocate. She is the lead singer of Downtown Boys and Malportado Kids, with music released on Sub Pop Records, Sister Polygon Records, Don Giovanni, and Dead Labour Records. She has recorded and produced music with her bandmate Joey La Neve DeFrancesco, Greg Norman of Electric Audio, and Guy Picciotto of Fugazi. Her words are featured in interviews with *Remezcla*, *Rolling Stone*, the *New York Times*, and elsewhere. Her writing has appeared in *Talkhouse*, *Fvck the Media*, *Remezcla*, and other outlets. Her family came to California as farmworkers, a different tech worker. She holds degrees from Columbia University and the University of California Law San Francisco.

Anna Joy Springer is the author of *The Vicious Red Relic, Love* (Jaded Ibis, 2011), an illustrated fabulist memoir with soundscape by Rachel Carns and Tara Jane O'neil called "Your Metaforest Guidebook," as well as *The Birdwisher: A Murder Mystery for Very Old Young Adults* (Birds of Lace, 2009). Her writing appears in zines, journals, anthologies, and recordings. Anna Joy is an associate professor of Literature at UC San Diego, where her research interests include visual literatures, multimodal narrative, spiritual absurdism, and the universality of bird symbols. Her current graphic narrative project is a sprawling hand-painted rebus called *Why We Defy Augury*. Anna Joy has been in the bands Blatz, the Gr'ups, and Cypher in the Snow and toured the US with the writers of Sister Spit.

INDEX

C

E

F

G

O

P

Q

Z